The Complete Poetical Works of Percy Bysshe Shelley Volume I

The Complete Poetical Works of Percy Bysshe Shelley Volume I

Percy Bysshe Shelley

MINT EDITIONS

The Complete Poetical Works of Percy Bysshe Shelley Volume I was first published in 1800.

This edition published by Mint Editions 2021.

ISBN 9781513277745 | E-ISBN 9781513278155

Published by Mint Editions®

minteditionbooks.com

Publishing Director: Jennifer Newens
Design & Production: Rachel Lopez Metzger
Project Manager: Micaela Clark
Typesetting: Westchester Publishing Services

Contents

Two Letters from Mrs. Mary Shelley	11
The Daemon of the World	
Part 1	23
Part 2	32
Alastor: Or, the Spirit of Solitude	
Preface	45
Alastor: Or, the Spirit of Solitude	47
Note on Alastor, by Mrs. Shelley	67
The Revolt of Islam	
A Poem in Twelve Cantos	71
Author's Preface	72
Dedication	80
To Mary — —	81
Canto 1	86
Canto 2	106
Canto 3	123
Canto 4	135

Canto 5	147
Canto 6	170
Canto 7	189
Canto 8	203
Canto 9	213
Canto 10	225
Canto 11	241
Canto 12	250
Note on the "Revolt of Islam", by Mrs. Shelley	264

Prince Athanase

Part 1	271
Part 2	276

Rosalind and Helen

Advertisement	285
Rosalind, Helen, and her Child	286
Note by Mrs. Shelley	322

Julian and Maddalo

Preface	325
Note by Mrs. Shelley	344

PROMETHEUS UNBOUND

PREFACE	347
DRAMATIS PERSONAE	351
ACT 1	352
ACT 2	375
ACT 3	395
ACT 4	410
NOTE ON "PROMETHEUS UNBOUND", BY MRS. SHELLEY	429

THE CENCI

DEDICATION, TO LEIGH HUNT, ESQ.	439
THE CENCI: PREFACE	440
THE CENCI: A TRAGEDY IN FIVE ACTS	445
ACT 1	446
ACT 2	459
ACT 3	470
ACT 4	485
ACT 5	502
NOTE ON THE CENCI, BY MRS. SHELLEY	521

THE MASK OF ANARCHY

NOTE ON THE MASK OF ANARCHY, BY MRS. SHELLEY 546

PETER BELL THE THIRD

DEDICATION 551

PROLOGUE 553

PART 1 555

PART 2 559

PART 3 563

PART 4 568

PART 5 573

PART 6 577

PART 7 586

NOTE ON PETER BELL THE THIRD, BY MRS. SHELLEY 591

LETTER TO MARIA GISBORNE

LEGHORN, JULY 1, 1820 595

THE WITCH OF ATLAS

TO MARY 607

THE WITCH OF ATLAS 609

NOTE ON THE WITCH OF ATLAS, BY MRS. SHELLEY 632

OEDIPUS TYRANNUS OR SWELLFOOT THE TYRANT

ADVERTISEMENT 637

DRAMATIS PERSONAE 638

ACT 1 639

ACT 2 652

NOTE ON OEDIPUS TYRANNUS, BY MRS. SHELLEY 663

EPIPSYCHIDION

ADVERTISEMENT 667

EPIPSYCHIDION 668

FRAGMENTS CONNECTED WITH EPIPSYCHIDION 685

ADONAIS

PREFACE 695

ADONAIS 697

CANCELLED PASSAGES OF ADONAIS 716

HELLAS

TO HIS EXCELLENCY 721

PREFACE 722

PROLOGUE TO HELLAS 725

Hellas	731
Notes	762
Note on Hellas, by Mrs. Shelley	765
Fragments of an Unfinished Drama	768
Charles the First	776
The Triumph of Life	801

Two Letters from Mrs. Mary Shelley

In nobil sangue vita umile e queta,
Ed in alto intelletto un puro core
Frutto senile in sul giovenil fibre,
E in aspetto pensoso anima lieta.

—Petrarca

It had been my wish, on presenting the public with the Posthumous Poems of Mr. Shelley, to have accompanied them by a biographical notice; as it appeared to me that at this moment a narration of the events of my husband's life would come more gracefully from other hands than mine, I applied to Mr. Leigh Hunt. The distinguished friendship that Mr. Shelley felt for him, and the enthusiastic affection with which Mr. Leigh Hunt clings to his friend's memory, seemed to point him out as the person best calculated for such an undertaking. His absence from this country, which prevented our mutual explanation, has unfortunately rendered my scheme abortive. I do not doubt but that on some other occasion he will pay this tribute to his lost friend, and sincerely regret that the volume which I edit has not been honoured by its insertion.

The comparative solitude in which Mr. Shelley lived was the occasion that he was personally known to few; and his fearless enthusiasm in the cause which he considered the most sacred upon earth, the improvement of the moral and physical state of mankind, was the chief reason why he, like other illustrious reformers, was pursued by hatred and calumny. No man was ever more devoted than he to the endeavour of making those around him happy; no man ever possessed friends more unfeignedly attached to him. The ungrateful world did not feel his loss, and the gap it made seemed to close as quickly over his memory as the murderous sea above his living frame. Hereafter men will lament that his transcendent powers of intellect were extinguished before they had bestowed on them their choicest treasures. To his friends his loss is irremediable: the wise, the brave, the gentle, is gone for ever! He is to them as a bright vision, whose radiant track, left behind in the memory, is worth all the realities that society can afford. Before the critics contradict me, let them appeal to any one who had ever known him. To see him was to love him: and his presence, like Ithuriel's spear, was alone sufficient to disclose the falsehood of the tale which his enemies whispered in the ear of the ignorant world.

His life was spent in the contemplation of Nature, in arduous study, or in acts of kindness and affection. He was an elegant scholar and a profound metaphysician; without possessing much scientific knowledge, he was unrivalled in the justness and extent of his observations on natural objects; he knew every plant by its name, and was familiar with the history and habits of every production of the earth; he could interpret without a fault each appearance in the sky; and the varied phenomena of heaven and earth filled him with deep emotion. He made his study and reading-room of the shadowed copse, the stream, the lake, and the waterfall. Ill health and continual pain preyed upon his powers; and the solitude in which we lived, particularly on our first arrival in Italy, although congenial to his feelings, must frequently have weighed upon his spirits; those beautiful and affecting "Lines written in Dejection near Naples" were composed at such an interval; but, when in health, his spirits were buoyant and youthful to an extraordinary degree.

Such was his love for Nature that every page of his poetry is associated, in the minds of his friends, with the loveliest scenes of the countries which he inhabited. In early life he visited the most beautiful parts of this country and Ireland. Afterwards the Alps of Switzerland became his inspirers. "Prometheus Unbound" was written among the deserted and flower-grown ruins of Rome; and, when he made his home under the Pisan hills, their roofless recesses harboured him as he composed the "Witch of Atlas", "Adonais", and "Hellas". In the wild but beautiful Bay of Spezzia, the winds and waves which he loved became his playmates. His days were chiefly spent on the water; the management of his boat, its alterations and improvements, were his principal occupation. At night, when the unclouded moon shone on the calm sea, he often went alone in his little shallop to the rocky caves that bordered it, and, sitting beneath their shelter, wrote the "Triumph of Life", the last of his productions. The beauty but strangeness of this lonely place, the refined pleasure which he felt in the companionship of a few selected friends, our entire sequestration from the rest of the world, all contributed to render this period of his life one of continued enjoyment. I am convinced that the two months we passed there were the happiest which he had ever known: his health even rapidly improved, and he was never better than when I last saw him, full of spirits and joy, embark for Leghorn, that he might there welcome Leigh Hunt to Italy. I was to have accompanied him; but illness confined me to my room, and thus put the seal on my misfortune. His vessel bore out of sight with a favourable wind, and I remained awaiting his return by the breakers of that sea which was about to engulf him.

He spent a week at Pisa, employed in kind offices toward his friend, and enjoying with keen delight the renewal of their intercourse. He then embarked with Mr. Williams, the chosen and beloved sharer of his pleasures and of his fate, to return to us. We waited for them in vain; the sea by its restless moaning seemed to desire to inform us of what we would not learn:—but a veil may well be drawn over such misery. The real anguish of those moments transcended all the fictions that the most glowing imagination ever portrayed; our seclusion, the savage nature of the inhabitants of the surrounding villages, and our immediate vicinity to the troubled sea, combined to imbue with strange horror our days of uncertainty. The truth was at last known,—a truth that made our loved and lovely Italy appear a tomb, its sky a pall. Every heart echoed the deep lament, and my only consolation was in the praise and earnest love that each voice bestowed and each countenance demonstrated for him we had lost,—not, I fondly hope, for ever; his unearthly and elevated nature is a pledge of the continuation of his being, although in an altered form. Rome received his ashes; they are deposited beneath its weed-grown wall, and 'the world's sole monument' is enriched by his remains.

I must add a few words concerning the contents of this volume. "Julian and Maddalo", the "Witch of Atlas", and most of the "Translations", were written some years ago; and, with the exception of the "Cyclops", and the Scenes from the "Magico Prodigioso", may be considered as having received the author's ultimate corrections. The "Triumph of Life" was his last work, and was left in so unfinished a state that I arranged it in its present form with great difficulty. All his poems which were scattered in periodical works are collected in this volume, and I have added a reprint of "Alastor, or the Spirit of Solitude": the difficulty with which a copy can be obtained is the cause of its republication. Many of the Miscellaneous Poems, written on the spur of the occasion, and never retouched, I found among his manuscript books, and have carefully copied. I have subjoined, whenever I have been able, the date of their composition.

I do not know whether the critics will reprehend the insertion of some of the most imperfect among them; but I frankly own that I have been more actuated by the fear lest any monument of his genius should escape me than the wish of presenting nothing but what was complete to the fastidious reader. I feel secure that the lovers of Shelley's poetry (who know how, more than any poet of the present day, every line and word he wrote is instinct with peculiar beauty) will pardon and thank me: I consecrate this volume to them.

The size of this collection has prevented the insertion of any prose pieces. They will hereafter appear in a separate publication.

Mary W. Shelley
London, June 1, 1824

Obstacles have long existed to my presenting the public with a perfect edition of Shelley's Poems. These being at last happily removed, I hasten to fulfil an important duty,—that of giving the productions of a sublime genius to the world, with all the correctness possible, and of, at the same time, detailing the history of those productions, as they sprang, living and warm, from his heart and brain. I abstain from any remark on the occurrences of his private life, except inasmuch as the passions which they engendered inspired his poetry. This is not the time to relate the truth; and I should reject any colouring of the truth. No account of these events has ever been given at all approaching reality in their details, either as regards himself or others; nor shall I further allude to them than to remark that the errors of action committed by a man as noble and generous as Shelley, may, as far as he only is concerned, be fearlessly avowed by those who loved him, in the firm conviction that, were they judged impartially, his character would stand in fairer and brighter light than that of any contemporary. Whatever faults he had ought to find extenuation among his fellows, since they prove him to be human; without them, the exalted nature of his soul would have raised him into something divine.

The qualities that struck any one newly introduced to Shelley were,— First, a gentle and cordial goodness that animated his intercourse with warm affection and helpful sympathy. The other, the eagerness and ardour with which he was attached to the cause of human happiness and improvement; and the fervent eloquence with which he discussed such subjects. His conversation was marked by its happy abundance, and the beautiful language in which he clothed his poetic ideas and philosophical notions. To defecate life of its misery and its evil was the ruling passion of his soul; he dedicated to it every power of his mind, every pulsation of his heart. He looked on political freedom as the direct agent to effect the happiness of mankind; and thus any new-sprung hope of liberty inspired a joy and an exultation more intense and wild than he could have felt for any personal advantage. Those who have never experienced the workings of passion on general and unselfish subjects cannot understand this; and it must be difficult of comprehension to the younger generation rising around, since they cannot remember the scorn and hatred with which the partisans of reform were regarded some few years ago, nor the persecutions to which they were exposed. He had been from youth the victim of the state of feeling inspired by the reaction of the French Revolution; and believing firmly in the justice and excellence of his views, it cannot be wondered that a nature as sensitive, as impetuous, and as generous as his, should put its whole force into the attempt to alleviate for others the evils of those systems from which he had himself suffered. Many advantages attended his birth; he spurned them all when balanced with what he considered his duties. He was generous to imprudence, devoted to heroism.

These characteristics breathe throughout his poetry. The struggle for human weal; the resolution firm to martyrdom; the impetuous pursuit, the glad triumph in good; the determination not to despair;—such were the features that marked those of his works which he regarded with most complacency, as sustained by a lofty subject and useful aim.

In addition to these, his poems may be divided into two classes,— the purely imaginative, and those which sprang from the emotions of his heart. Among the former may be classed the "Witch of Atlas", "Adonais", and his latest composition, left imperfect, the "Triumph of Life". In the first of these particularly he gave the reins to his fancy, and luxuriated in every idea as it rose; in all there is that sense of mystery which formed an essential portion of his perception of life—a clinging to the subtler inner spirit, rather than to the outward form—a curious and metaphysical anatomy of human passion and perception.

The second class is, of course, the more popular, as appealing at once to emotions common to us all; some of these rest on the passion of love; others on grief and despondency; others on the sentiments inspired by natural objects. Shelley's conception of love was exalted, absorbing, allied to all that is purest and noblest in our nature, and warmed by earnest passion; such it appears when he gave it a voice in verse. Yet he was usually averse to expressing these feelings, except when highly idealized; and many of his more beautiful effusions he had cast aside unfinished, and they were never seen by me till after I had lost him. Others, as for instance "Rosalind and Helen" and "Lines written among the Euganean Hills", I found among his papers by chance; and with some difficulty urged him to complete them. There are others, such as the "Ode to the Skylark and The Cloud", which, in the opinion of many critics, bear a purer poetical stamp than any other of his productions. They were written as his mind prompted: listening to the carolling of the bird, aloft in the azure sky of Italy; or marking the cloud as it sped across the heavens, while he floated in his boat on the Thames.

No poet was ever warmed by a more genuine and unforced inspiration. His extreme sensibility gave the intensity of passion to his intellectual pursuits; and rendered his mind keenly alive to every perception of outward objects, as well as to his internal sensations. Such a gift is, among the sad vicissitudes of human life, the disappointments we meet, and the galling sense of our own mistakes and errors, fraught with pain; to escape from such, he delivered up his soul to poetry, and felt happy when he sheltered himself, from the influence of human sympathies, in the wildest regions of fancy. His imagination has been termed too brilliant, his thoughts too subtle. He loved to idealize reality; and this is a taste shared by few. We are willing to have our passing whims exalted into passions, for this gratifies our vanity; but few of us understand or sympathize with the endeavour to ally the love of abstract beauty, and adoration of abstract good, the to agathon kai to kalon of the Socratic philosophers, with our sympathies with our kind. In this, Shelley resembled Plato; both taking more delight in the abstract and the ideal than in the special and tangible. This did not result from imitation; for it was not till Shelley resided in Italy that he made Plato his study. He then translated his "Symposium" and his "Ion"; and the English language boasts of no more brilliant composition than Plato's Praise of Love translated by Shelley. To return to his own poetry. The luxury of imagination, which sought nothing beyond itself (as a child burdens itself with spring flowers, thinking of no use beyond the enjoyment of gathering them), often showed itself in his verses: they will be only appreciated by minds which have resemblance to his own; and the mystic subtlety of many of his thoughts will share the same fate. The metaphysical strain that characterizes much of what he has written was, indeed, the portion of his works to which, apart from those whose scope was to awaken mankind to aspirations for what he considered the true and good, he was himself particularly attached. There is much, however, that speaks to the many. When he would consent to dismiss these huntings after the obscure (which, entwined with his nature as they were, he did with difficulty), no poet ever expressed in sweeter, more heart-reaching, or more passionate verse, the gentler or more forcible emotions of the soul.

A wise friend once wrote to Shelley: 'You are still very young, and in certain essential respects you do not yet sufficiently perceive that you are so.' It is seldom that the young know what youth is, till they have got beyond its period; and time was not given him to attain this knowledge. It must be remembered that there is the stamp of such inexperience on all he wrote; he had not completed his nine-and-twentieth year when he died. The calm of middle life did not add the seal of the virtues which adorn maturity to those generated by the vehement spirit of youth. Through life also he was a martyr to ill-health, and constant pain wound up his nerves to a pitch of susceptibility that rendered his views of life different from those of a man in the enjoyment of healthy sensations. Perfectly gentle and forbearing in manner, he suffered a good deal of internal irritability, or rather excitement, and his fortitude to bear was almost always on the stretch; and thus, during a short life, he had gone through more experience of sensation than many whose existence is protracted. 'If I die to-morrow,' he said, on the eve of his unanticipated death, 'I have lived to be older than my father.' The weight of thought and feeling burdened him heavily; you read his sufferings in his attenuated frame, while you perceived the mastery he held over them in his animated countenance and brilliant eyes.

He died, and the world showed no outward sign. But his influence over mankind, though slow in growth, is fast augmenting; and, in the ameliorations that have taken place in the political state of his country, we may trace in part the operation of his arduous struggles. His spirit gathers peace in its new state from the sense that, though late, his exertions were not made in vain, and in the progress of the liberty he so fondly loved.

He died, and his place, among those who knew him intimately, has never been filled up. He walked beside them like a spirit of good to comfort and benefit—to enlighten the darkness of life with irradiations of genius, to cheer it with his sympathy and love. Any one, once attached to Shelley, must feel all other affections, however true and fond, as wasted on barren soil in comparison. It is our best consolation to know that such a pure-minded and exalted being was once among us, and now exists where we hope one day to join him;—although the intolerant, in their blindness, poured down anathemas, the Spirit of Good, who can judge the heart, never rejected him.

In the notes appended to the poems I have endeavoured to narrate the origin and history of each. The loss of nearly all letters and papers which refer to his early life renders the execution more imperfect than it would otherwise have been. I have, however, the liveliest recollection of all that was done and said during the period of my knowing him. Every impression is as clear as if stamped yesterday, and I have no apprehension of any mistake in my statements as far as they go. In other respects I am indeed incompetent: but I feel the importance of the task, and regard it as my most sacred duty. I endeavour to fulfil it in a manner he would himself approve; and hope, in this publication, to lay the first stone of a monument due to Shelley's genius, his sufferings, and his virtues:—

> *Se al seguir son tarda,*
> *Forse avverra che 'l bel nome gentile*
> *Consacrero con questa stanca penna.*

Mary W. Shelley, 1839

THE DAEMON OF THE WORLD

A Fragment

Part 1

(Sections 1 and 2 of "Queen Mab" rehandled, and published by Shelley in the "Alastor" volume, 1816. See "Bibliographical List", and the Editor's Introductory Note to "Queen Mab".)

Nec tantum prodere vati,
Quantum scire licet. Venit aetas omnis in unam
Congeriem, miserumque premunt tot saecula pectus.
LUCAN, Phars. v. 176.

How wonderful is Death,
Death and his brother Sleep!
One pale as yonder wan and horned moon,
With lips of lurid blue,
The other glowing like the vital morn,
When throned on ocean's wave
It breathes over the world:
Yet both so passing strange and wonderful!

Hath then the iron-sceptred Skeleton,
Whose reign is in the tainted sepulchres,
To the hell dogs that couch beneath his throne
Cast that fair prey? Must that divinest form,
Which love and admiration cannot view
Without a beating heart, whose azure veins
Steal like dark streams along a field of snow,
Whose outline is as fair as marble clothed
In light of some sublimest mind, decay?
Nor putrefaction's breath
Leave aught of this pure spectacle
But loathsomeness and ruin?—
Spare aught but a dark theme,
On which the lightest heart might moralize?
Or is it but that downy-winged slumbers
Have charmed their nurse coy Silence near her lids
To watch their own repose?
Will they, when morning's beam

Flows through those wells of light,
Seek far from noise and day some western cave,
Where woods and streams with soft and pausing winds
A lulling murmur weave?—
Ianthe doth not sleep
The dreamless sleep of death:
Nor in her moonlight chamber silently
Doth Henry hear her regular pulses throb,
Or mark her delicate cheek
With interchange of hues mock the broad moon,
Outwatching weary night,
Without assured reward.
Her dewy eyes are closed;
On their translucent lids, whose texture fine
Scarce hides the dark blue orbs that burn below
With unapparent fire,
The baby Sleep is pillowed:
Her golden tresses shade
The bosom's stainless pride,
Twining like tendrils of the parasite
Around a marble column.

Hark! whence that rushing sound?
'Tis like a wondrous strain that sweeps
Around a lonely ruin
When west winds sigh and evening waves respond
In whispers from the shore:
'Tis wilder than the unmeasured notes
Which from the unseen lyres of dells and groves
The genii of the breezes sweep.
Floating on waves of music and of light,
The chariot of the Daemon of the World
Descends in silent power:
Its shape reposed within: slight as some cloud
That catches but the palest tinge of day
When evening yields to night,
Bright as that fibrous woof when stars indue
Its transitory robe.
Four shapeless shadows bright and beautiful

Draw that strange car of glory, reins of light
Check their unearthly speed; they stop and fold
Their wings of braided air:
The Daemon leaning from the ethereal car
Gazed on the slumbering maid.
Human eye hath ne'er beheld
A shape so wild, so bright, so beautiful,
As that which o'er the maiden's charmed sleep
Waving a starry wand,
Hung like a mist of light.
Such sounds as breathed around like odorous winds
Of wakening spring arose,
Filling the chamber and the moonlight sky.
Maiden, the world's supremest spirit
Beneath the shadow of her wings
Folds all thy memory doth inherit
From ruin of divinest things,
Feelings that lure thee to betray,
And light of thoughts that pass away.
For thou hast earned a mighty boon,
The truths which wisest poets see
Dimly, thy mind may make its own,
Rewarding its own majesty,
Entranced in some diviner mood
Of self-oblivious solitude.

Custom, and Faith, and Power thou spurnest;
From hate and awe thy heart is free;
Ardent and pure as day thou burnest,
For dark and cold mortality
A living light, to cheer it long,
The watch-fires of the world among.

Therefore from nature's inner shrine,
Where gods and fiends in worship bend,
Majestic spirit, be it thine
The flame to seize, the veil to rend,
Where the vast snake Eternity
In charmed sleep doth ever lie.

All that inspires thy voice of love,
Or speaks in thy unclosing eyes,
Or through thy frame doth burn or move,
Or think or feel, awake, arise!
Spirit, leave for mine and me
Earth's unsubstantial mimicry!

It ceased, and from the mute and moveless frame
A radiant spirit arose,
All beautiful in naked purity.
Robed in its human hues it did ascend,
Disparting as it went the silver clouds,
It moved towards the car, and took its seat
Beside the Daemon shape.

Obedient to the sweep of aery song,
The mighty ministers
Unfurled their prismy wings.
The magic car moved on;
The night was fair, innumerable stars
Studded heaven's dark blue vault;
The eastern wave grew pale
With the first smile of morn.
The magic car moved on.
From the swift sweep of wings
The atmosphere in flaming sparkles flew;
And where the burning wheels
Eddied above the mountain's loftiest peak
Was traced a line of lightning.
Now far above a rock the utmost verge
Of the wide earth it flew,
The rival of the Andes, whose dark brow
Frowned o'er the silver sea.
Far, far below the chariot's stormy path,
Calm as a slumbering babe,
Tremendous ocean lay.
Its broad and silent mirror gave to view
The pale and waning stars,
The chariot's fiery track,

And the grey light of morn
Tingeing those fleecy clouds
That cradled in their folds the infant dawn.
The chariot seemed to fly
Through the abyss of an immense concave,
Radiant with million constellations, tinged
With shades of infinite colour,
And semicircled with a belt
Flashing incessant meteors.

As they approached their goal,
The winged shadows seemed to gather speed.
The sea no longer was distinguished; earth
Appeared a vast and shadowy sphere, suspended
In the black concave of heaven
With the sun's cloudless orb,
Whose rays of rapid light
Parted around the chariot's swifter course,
And fell like ocean's feathery spray
Dashed from the boiling surge
Before a vessel's prow.

The magic car moved on.
Earth's distant orb appeared
The smallest light that twinkles in the heavens,
Whilst round the chariot's way
Innumerable systems widely rolled,
And countless spheres diffused
An ever varying glory.
It was a sight of wonder! Some were horned,
And like the moon's argentine crescent hung
In the dark dome of heaven; some did shed
A clear mild beam like Hesperus, while the sea
Yet glows with fading sunlight; others dashed
Athwart the night with trains of bickering fire,
Like sphered worlds to death and ruin driven;
Some shone like stars, and as the chariot passed
Bedimmed all other light.

Spirit of Nature! here
In this interminable wilderness
Of worlds, at whose involved immensity
Even soaring fancy staggers,
Here is thy fitting temple.
Yet not the lightest leaf
That quivers to the passing breeze
Is less instinct with thee,—
Yet not the meanest worm.
That lurks in graves and fattens on the dead,
Less shares thy eternal breath.
Spirit of Nature! thou
Imperishable as this glorious scene,
Here is thy fitting temple.

If solitude hath ever led thy steps
To the shore of the immeasurable sea,
And thou hast lingered there
Until the sun's broad orb
Seemed resting on the fiery line of ocean,
Thou must have marked the braided webs of gold
That without motion hang
Over the sinking sphere:
Thou must have marked the billowy mountain clouds,
Edged with intolerable radiancy,
Towering like rocks of jet
Above the burning deep:
And yet there is a moment
When the sun's highest point
Peers like a star o'er ocean's western edge,
When those far clouds of feathery purple gleam
Like fairy lands girt by some heavenly sea:
Then has thy rapt imagination soared
Where in the midst of all existing things
The temple of the mightiest Daemon stands.

Yet not the golden islands
That gleam amid yon flood of purple light,
Nor the feathery curtains

That canopy the sun's resplendent couch,
Nor the burnished ocean waves
Paving that gorgeous dome,
So fair, so wonderful a sight
As the eternal temple could afford.
The elements of all that human thought
Can frame of lovely or sublime, did join
To rear the fabric of the fane, nor aught
Of earth may image forth its majesty.
Yet likest evening's vault that faery hall,
As heaven low resting on the wave it spread
Its floors of flashing light,
Its vast and azure dome;
And on the verge of that obscure abyss
Where crystal battlements o'erhang the gulf
Of the dark world, ten thousand spheres diffuse
Their lustre through its adamantine gates.

The magic car no longer moved;
The Daemon and the Spirit
Entered the eternal gates.
Those clouds of aery gold
That slept in glittering billows
Beneath the azure canopy,
With the ethereal footsteps trembled not;
While slight and odorous mists
Floated to strains of thrilling melody
Through the vast columns and the pearly shrines.

The Daemon and the Spirit
Approached the overhanging battlement,
Below lay stretched the boundless universe!
There, far as the remotest line
That limits swift imagination's flight.
Unending orbs mingled in mazy motion,
Immutably fulfilling
Eternal Nature's law.
Above, below, around,
The circling systems formed

A wilderness of harmony.
Each with undeviating aim
In eloquent silence through the depths of space
Pursued its wondrous way.—

Awhile the Spirit paused in ecstasy.
Yet soon she saw, as the vast spheres swept by,
Strange things within their belted orbs appear.
Like animated frenzies, dimly moved
Shadows, and skeletons, and fiendly shapes,
Thronging round human graves, and o'er the dead
Sculpturing records for each memory
In verse, such as malignant gods pronounce,
Blasting the hopes of men, when heaven and hell
Confounded burst in ruin o'er the world:
And they did build vast trophies, instruments
Of murder, human bones, barbaric gold,
Skins torn from living men, and towers of skulls
With sightless holes gazing on blinder heaven,
Mitres, and crowns, and brazen chariots stained
With blood, and scrolls of mystic wickedness,
The sanguine codes of venerable crime.
The likeness of a throned king came by.
When these had passed, bearing upon his brow
A threefold crown; his countenance was calm.
His eye severe and cold; but his right hand
Was charged with bloody coin, and he did gnaw
By fits, with secret smiles, a human heart
Concealed beneath his robe; and motley shapes,
A multitudinous throng, around him knelt.
With bosoms bare, and bowed heads, and false looks
Of true submission, as the sphere rolled by.
Brooking no eye to witness their foul shame,
Which human hearts must feel, while human tongues
Tremble to speak, they did rage horribly,
Breathing in self-contempt fierce blasphemies
Against the Daemon of the World, and high
Hurling their armed hands where the pure Spirit,
Serene and inaccessibly secure,

Stood on an isolated pinnacle.
The flood of ages combating below,
The depth of the unbounded universe
Above, and all around
Necessity's unchanging harmony.

Part 2

(Sections 8 and 9 of "Queen Mab" rehandled by Shelley. First printed in 1876 by Mr. H. Buxton Forman, C.B., by whose kind permission it is here reproduced. See Editor's Introductory Note to "Queen Mab".)

O happy Earth! reality of Heaven!
To which those restless powers that ceaselessly
Throng through the human universe aspire;
Thou consummation of all mortal hope!
Thou glorious prize of blindly-working will!
Whose rays, diffused throughout all space and time,
Verge to one point and blend for ever there:
Of purest spirits thou pure dwelling-place!
Where care and sorrow, impotence and crime,
Languor, disease, and ignorance dare not come:
O happy Earth, reality of Heaven!

Genius has seen thee in her passionate dreams,
And dim forebodings of thy loveliness,
Haunting the human heart, have there entwined
Those rooted hopes, that the proud Power of Evil
Shall not for ever on this fairest world
Shake pestilence and war, or that his slaves
With blasphemy for prayer, and human blood
For sacrifice, before his shrine for ever
In adoration bend, or Erebus
With all its banded fiends shall not uprise
To overwhelm in envy and revenge
The dauntless and the good, who dare to hurl
Defiance at his throne, girt tho' it be
With Death's omnipotence. Thou hast beheld
His empire, o'er the present and the past;
It was a desolate sight—now gaze on mine,
Futurity. Thou hoary giant Time,
Render thou up thy half-devoured babes,—
And from the cradles of eternity,
Where millions lie lulled to their portioned sleep

By the deep murmuring stream of passing things,
Tear thou that gloomy shroud.—Spirit, behold
Thy glorious destiny!

The Spirit saw
The vast frame of the renovated world
Smile in the lap of Chaos, and the sense
Of hope thro' her fine texture did suffuse
Such varying glow, as summer evening casts
On undulating clouds and deepening lakes.
Like the vague sighings of a wind at even,
That wakes the wavelets of the slumbering sea
And dies on the creation of its breath,
And sinks and rises, fails and swells by fits,
Was the sweet stream of thought that with wild motion
Flowed o'er the Spirit's human sympathies.
The mighty tide of thought had paused awhile,
Which from the Daemon now like Ocean's stream
Again began to pour.—

To me is given
The wonders of the human world to keep-
Space, matter, time and mind—let the sight
Renew and strengthen all thy failing hope.
All things are recreated, and the flame
Of consentaneous love inspires all life:
The fertile bosom of the earth gives suck
To myriads, who still grow beneath her care,
Rewarding her with their pure perfectness:
The balmy breathings of the wind inhale
Her virtues, and diffuse them all abroad:
Health floats amid the gentle atmosphere,
Glows in the fruits, and mantles on the stream;
No storms deform the beaming brow of heaven,
Nor scatter in the freshness of its pride
The foliage of the undecaying trees;
But fruits are ever ripe, flowers ever fair,
And Autumn proudly bears her matron grace,
Kindling a flush on the fair cheek of Spring,

Whose virgin bloom beneath the ruddy fruit
Reflects its tint and blushes into love.

The habitable earth is full of bliss;
Those wastes of frozen billows that were hurled
By everlasting snow-storms round the poles,
Where matter dared not vegetate nor live,
But ceaseless frost round the vast solitude
Bound its broad zone of stillness, are unloosed;
And fragrant zephyrs there from spicy isles
Ruffle the placid ocean-deep, that rolls
Its broad, bright surges to the sloping sand,
Whose roar is wakened into echoings sweet
To murmur through the heaven-breathing groves
And melodise with man's blest nature there.

The vast tract of the parched and sandy waste
Now teems with countless rills and shady woods,
Corn-fields and pastures and white cottages;
And where the startled wilderness did hear
A savage conqueror stained in kindred blood,
Hymmng his victory, or the milder snake
Crushing the bones of some frail antelope
Within his brazen folds—the dewy lawn,
Offering sweet incense to the sunrise, smiles
To see a babe before his mother's door,
Share with the green and golden basilisk
That comes to lick his feet, his morning's meal.

Those trackless deeps, where many a weary sail
Has seen, above the illimitable plain,
Morning on night and night on morning rise,
Whilst still no land to greet the wanderer spread
Its shadowy mountains on the sunbright sea,
Where the loud roarings of the tempest-waves
So long have mingled with the gusty wind
In melancholy loneliness, and swept
The desert of those ocean solitudes,
But vocal to the sea-bird's harrowing shriek,

The bellowing monster, and the rushing storm,
Now to the sweet and many-mingling sounds
Of kindliest human impulses respond:
Those lonely realms bright garden-isles begem,
With lightsome clouds and shining seas between,
And fertile valleys resonant with bliss,
Whilst green woods overcanopy the wave,
Which like a toil-worn labourer leaps to shore,
To meet the kisses of the flowerets there.

Man chief perceives the change, his being notes
The gradual renovation, and defines
Each movement of its progress on his mind.
Man, where the gloom of the long polar night
Lowered o'er the snow-clad rocks and frozen soil,
Where scarce the hardiest herb that braves the frost
Basked in the moonlight's ineffectual glow,
Shrank with the plants, and darkened with the night;
Nor where the tropics bound the realms of day
With a broad belt of mingling cloud and flame,
Where blue mists through the unmoving atmosphere
Scattered the seeds of pestilence, and fed
Unnatural vegetation, where the land
Teemed with all earthquake, tempest and disease,
Was man a nobler being; slavery
Had crushed him to his country's blood-stained dust.

Even where the milder zone afforded man
A seeming shelter, yet contagion there,
Blighting his being with unnumbered ills,
Spread like a quenchless fire; nor truth availed
Till late to arrest its progress, or create
That peace which first in bloodless victory waved
Her snowy standard o'er this favoured clime:
There man was long the train-bearer of slaves,
The mimic of surrounding misery,
The jackal of ambition's lion-rage,
The bloodhound of religion's hungry zeal.

Here now the human being stands adorning
This loveliest earth with taintless body and mind;
Blest from his birth with all bland impulses,
Which gently in his noble bosom wake
All kindly passions and all pure desires.
Him, still from hope to hope the bliss pursuing,
Which from the exhaustless lore of human weal
Dawns on the virtuous mind, the thoughts that rise
In time-destroying infiniteness gift
With self-enshrined eternity, that mocks
The unprevailing hoariness of age,
And man, once fleeting o'er the transient scene
Swift as an unremembered vision, stands
Immortal upon earth: no longer now
He slays the beast that sports around his dwelling
And horribly devours its mangled flesh,
Or drinks its vital blood, which like a stream
Of poison thro' his fevered veins did flow
Feeding a plague that secretly consumed
His feeble frame, and kindling in his mind
Hatred, despair, and fear and vain belief,
The germs of misery, death, disease and crime.
No longer now the winged habitants,
That in the woods their sweet lives sing away,
Flee from the form of man; but gather round,
And prune their sunny feathers on the hands
Which little children stretch in friendly sport
Towards these dreadless partners of their play.
All things are void of terror: man has lost
His desolating privilege, and stands
An equal amidst equals: happiness
And science dawn though late upon the earth;
Peace cheers the mind, health renovates the frame;
Disease and pleasure cease to mingle here,
Reason and passion cease to combat there;
Whilst mind unfettered o'er the earth extends
Its all-subduing energies, and wields
The sceptre of a vast dominion there.

Mild is the slow necessity of death:
The tranquil spirit fails beneath its grasp,
Without a groan, almost without a fear,
Resigned in peace to the necessity,
Calm as a voyager to some distant land,
And full of wonder, full of hope as he.
The deadly germs of languor and disease
Waste in the human frame, and Nature gifts
With choicest boons her human worshippers.
How vigorous now the athletic form of age!
How clear its open and unwrinkled brow!
Where neither avarice, cunning, pride, or care,
Had stamped the seal of grey deformity
On all the mingling lineaments of time.
How lovely the intrepid front of youth!
How sweet the smiles of taintless infancy.

Within the massy prison's mouldering courts,
Fearless and free the ruddy children play,
Weaving gay chaplets for their innocent brows
With the green ivy and the red wall-flower,
That mock the dungeon's unavailing gloom;
The ponderous chains, and gratings of strong iron,
There rust amid the accumulated ruins
Now mingling slowly with their native earth:
There the broad beam of day, which feebly once
Lighted the cheek of lean captivity
With a pale and sickly glare, now freely shines
On the pure smiles of infant playfulness:
No more the shuddering voice of hoarse despair
Peals through the echoing vaults, but soothing notes
Of ivy-fingered winds and gladsome birds
And merriment are resonant around.

The fanes of Fear and Falsehood hear no more
The voice that once waked multitudes to war
Thundering thro' all their aisles: but now respond
To the death dirge of the melancholy wind:
It were a sight of awfulness to see

The works of faith and slavery, so vast,
So sumptuous, yet withal so perishing!
Even as the corpse that rests beneath their wall.
A thousand mourners deck the pomp of death
To-day, the breathing marble glows above
To decorate its memory, and tongues
Are busy of its life: to-morrow, worms
In silence and in darkness seize their prey.
These ruins soon leave not a wreck behind:
Their elements, wide-scattered o'er the globe,
To happier shapes are moulded, and become
Ministrant to all blissful impulses:
Thus human things are perfected, and earth,
Even as a child beneath its mother's love,
Is strengthened in all excellence, and grows
Fairer and nobler with each passing year.

Now Time his dusky pennons o'er the scene
Closes in steadfast darkness, and the past
Fades from our charmed sight. My task is done:
Thy lore is learned. Earth's wonders are thine own,
With all the fear and all the hope they bring.
My spells are past: the present now recurs.
Ah me! a pathless wilderness remains
Yet unsubdued by man's reclaiming hand.

Yet, human Spirit, bravely hold thy course,
Let virtue teach thee firmly to pursue
The gradual paths of an aspiring change:
For birth and life and death, and that strange state
Before the naked powers that thro' the world
Wander like winds have found a human home,
All tend to perfect happiness, and urge
The restless wheels of being on their way,
Whose flashing spokes, instinct with infinite life,
Bicker and burn to gain their destined goal:
For birth but wakes the universal mind
Whose mighty streams might else in silence flow
Thro' the vast world, to individual sense

Of outward shows, whose unexperienced shape
New modes of passion to its frame may lend;
Life is its state of action, and the store
Of all events is aggregated there
That variegate the eternal universe;
Death is a gate of dreariness and gloom,
That leads to azure isles and beaming skies
And happy regions of eternal hope.
Therefore, O Spirit! fearlessly bear on:
Though storms may break the primrose on its stalk,
Though frosts may blight the freshness of its bloom,
Yet spring's awakening breath will woo the earth,
To feed with kindliest dews its favourite flower,
That blooms in mossy banks and darksome glens,
Lighting the green wood with its sunny smile.

Fear not then, Spirit, death's disrobing hand,
So welcome when the tyrant is awake,
So welcome when the bigot's hell-torch flares;
'Tis but the voyage of a darksome hour,
The transient gulf-dream of a startling sleep.
For what thou art shall perish utterly,
But what is thine may never cease to be;
Death is no foe to virtue: earth has seen
Love's brightest roses on the scaffold bloom,
Mingling with freedom's fadeless laurels there,
And presaging the truth of visioned bliss.
Are there not hopes within thee, which this scene
Of linked and gradual being has confirmed?
Hopes that not vainly thou, and living fires
Of mind as radiant and as pure as thou,
Have shone upon the paths of men—return,
Surpassing Spirit, to that world, where thou
Art destined an eternal war to wage
With tyranny and falsehood, and uproot
The germs of misery from the human heart.
Thine is the hand whose piety would soothe
The thorny pillow of unhappy crime,
Whose impotence an easy pardon gains,

Watching its wanderings as a friend's disease:
Thine is the brow whose mildness would defy
Its fiercest rage, and brave its sternest will,
When fenced by power and master of the world.
Thou art sincere and good; of resolute mind,
Free from heart-withering custom's cold control,
Of passion lofty, pure and unsubdued.
Earth's pride and meanness could not vanquish thee,
And therefore art thou worthy of the boon
Which thou hast now received: virtue shall keep
Thy footsteps in the path that thou hast trod,
And many days of beaming hope shall bless
Thy spotless life of sweet and sacred love.
Go, happy one, and give that bosom joy
Whose sleepless spirit waits to catch
Light, life and rapture from thy smile.

The Daemon called its winged ministers.
Speechless with bliss the Spirit mounts the car,
That rolled beside the crystal battlement,
Bending her beamy eyes in thankfulness.
The burning wheels inflame
The steep descent of Heaven's untrodden way.
Fast and far the chariot flew:
The mighty globes that rolled
Around the gate of the Eternal Fane
Lessened by slow degrees, and soon appeared
Such tiny twinklers as the planet orbs
That ministering on the solar power
With borrowed light pursued their narrower way.
Earth floated then below:
The chariot paused a moment;
The Spirit then descended:
And from the earth departing
The shadows with swift wings
Speeded like thought upon the light of Heaven.

The Body and the Soul united then,
A gentle start convulsed Ianthe's frame:

Her veiny eyelids quietly unclosed;
Moveless awhile the dark blue orbs remained:
She looked around in wonder and beheld
Henry, who kneeled in silence by her couch,
Watching her sleep with looks of speechless love,
And the bright beaming stars
That through the casement shone.

ALASTOR: OR, THE SPIRIT OF SOLITUDE

(Composed at Bishopsgate Heath, near Windsor Park, 1815 (autumn); published, as the title-piece of a slender volume containing other poems (see "Biographical List", by Baldwin, Cradock and Joy, London, 1816 (March). Reprinted—the first edition being sold out—amongst the "Posthumous Poems", 1824. Sources of the text are (1) the editio princeps, 1816; (2) "Posthumous Poems", 1824; (3) "Poetical Works", 1839, editions 1st and 2nd. For (2) and (3) Mrs. Shelley is responsible.)

Preface

The poem entitled "Alastor" may be considered as allegorical of one of the most interesting situations of the human mind. It represents a youth of uncorrupted feelings and adventurous genius led forth by an imagination inflamed and purified through familiarity with all that is excellent and majestic, to the contemplation of the universe. He drinks deep of the fountains of knowledge, and is still insatiate. The magnificence and beauty of the external world sinks profoundly into the frame of his conceptions, and affords to their modifications at variety not to be exhausted. so long as it is possible for his desires to point towards objects thus infinite and unmeasured, he is joyous, and tranquil, and self-possessed. But the period arrives when these objects cease to suffice. His mind is at length suddenly awakened and thirsts for intercourse with an intelligence similar to itself. He images to himself the Being whom he loves. Conversant with speculations of the sublimest and most perfect natures, the vision in which he embodies his own imaginations unites all of wonderful, or wise, or beautiful, which the poet, the philosopher, or the lover could depicture. The intellectual faculties, the imagination, the functions of sense, have their respective requisitions on the sympathy of corresponding powers in other human beings. The Poet is represented as uniting these requisitions, and attaching them to a single image. He seeks in vain for a prototype of his conception. Blasted by his disappointment, he descends to an untimely grave.

The picture is not barren of instruction to actual men. The Poet's self-centred seclusion was avenged by the furies of an irresistible passion pursuing him to speedy ruin. But that Power which strikes the luminaries of the world with sudden darkness and extinction, by awakening them to too exquisite a perception of its influences, dooms to a slow and poisonous decay those manner spirits that dare to abjure its dominion. Their destiny is more abject and inglorious as their delinquency is more contemptible and pernicious. They who, deluded by no generous error, instigated by no sacred thirst of doubtful knowledge, duped by no illustrious superstition, loving nothing on this earth, and cherishing no hopes beyond, yet keep aloof from sympathies with their kind, rejoicing neither in human joy nor mourning with human grief; these, and such as they, have their apportioned curse. They languish, because none feel with them their common nature. They are morally dead. They are neither friends, nor lovers, nor fathers, nor citizens of the world, nor benefactors of their country. Among those who attempt to exist without human sympathy, the pure and tender-hearted perish through the intensity and passion of their search after its communities, when the vacancy of their spirit suddenly makes itself felt. All else, selfish, blind, and torpid, are those unforeseeing multitudes who constitute, together with their own, the lasting misery and loneliness of the world. Those who love not their fellow-beings live unfruitful lives, and prepare for their old age a miserable grave.

> *'The good die first,*
> *And those whose hearts are dry as summer dust,*
> *Burn to the socket!'*

December 14, 1815

Alastor: Or, the Spirit of Solitude

Earth, Ocean, Air, beloved brotherhood!
If our great Mother has imbued my soul
With aught of natural piety to feel
Your love, and recompense the boon with mine;
If dewy morn, and odorous noon, and even,
With sunset and its gorgeous ministers,
And solemn midnight's tingling silentness;
If autumn's hollow sighs in the sere wood,
And winter robing with pure snow and crowns
Of starry ice the grey grass and bare boughs;
If spring's voluptuous pantings when she breathes
Her first sweet kisses, have been dear to me;
If no bright bird, insect, or gentle beast
I consciously have injured, but still loved
And cherished these my kindred; then forgive
This boast, beloved brethren, and withdraw
No portion of your wonted favour now!

Mother of this unfathomable world!
Favour my solemn song, for I have loved
Thee ever, and thee only; I have watched
Thy shadow, and the darkness of thy steps,
And my heart ever gazes on the depth
Of thy deep mysteries. I have made my bed
In charnels and on coffins, where black death
Keeps record of the trophies won from thee,
Hoping to still these obstinate questionings
Of thee and thine, by forcing some lone ghost,
Thy messenger, to render up the tale
Of what we are. In lone and silent hours,
When night makes a weird sound of its own stillness,
Like an inspired and desperate alchymist
Staking his very life on some dark hope,
Have I mixed awful talk and asking looks
With my most innocent love, until strange tears,
Uniting with those breathless kisses, made

Such magic as compels the charmed night
To render up thy charge: . . . and, though ne'er yet
Thou hast unveiled thy inmost sanctuary,
Enough from incommunicable dream,
And twilight phantasms, and deep noon-day thought,
Has shone within me, that serenely now
And moveless, as a long-forgotten lyre
Suspended in the solitary dome
Of some mysterious and deserted fane,
I wait thy breath, Great Parent, that my strain
May modulate with murmurs of the air,
And motions of the forests and the sea,
And voice of living beings, and woven hymns
Of night and day, and the deep heart of man.

There was a Poet whose untimely tomb
No human hands with pious reverence reared,
But the charmed eddies of autumnal winds
Built o'er his mouldering bones a pyramid
Of mouldering leaves in the waste wilderness:—
A lovely youth,—no mourning maiden decked
With weeping flowers, or votive cypress wreath,
The lone couch of his everlasting sleep:—
Gentle, and brave, and generous,—no lorn bard
Breathed o'er his dark fate one melodious sigh:
He lived, he died, he sung in solitude.
Strangers have wept to hear his passionate notes,
And virgins, as unknown he passed, have pined
And wasted for fond love of his wild eyes.
The fire of those soft orbs has ceased to burn,
And Silence, too enamoured of that voice,
Locks its mute music in her rugged cell.

By solemn vision, and bright silver dream
His infancy was nurtured. Every sight
And sound from the vast earth and ambient air,
Sent to his heart its choicest impulses.
The fountains of divine philosophy
Fled not his thirsting lips, and all of great,

Or good, or lovely, which the sacred past
In truth or fable consecrates, he felt
And knew. When early youth had passed, he left
His cold fireside and alienated home
To seek strange truths in undiscovered lands.
Many a wide waste and tangled wilderness
Has lured his fearless steps; and he has bought
With his sweet voice and eyes, from savage men,
His rest and food. Nature's most secret steps
He like her shadow has pursued, where'er
The red volcano overcanopies
Its fields of snow and pinnacles of ice
With burning smoke, or where bitumen lakes
On black bare pointed islets ever beat
With sluggish surge, or where the secret caves,
Rugged and dark, winding among the springs
Of fire and poison, inaccessible
To avarice or pride, their starry domes
Of diamond and of gold expand above
Numberless and immeasurable halls,
Frequent with crystal column, and clear shrines
Of pearl, and thrones radiant with chrysolite.
Nor had that scene of ampler majesty
Than gems or gold, the varying roof of heaven
And the green earth lost in his heart its claims
To love and wonder; he would linger long
In lonesome vales, making the wild his home,
Until the doves and squirrels would partake
From his innocuous hand his bloodless food,
Lured by the gentle meaning of his looks,
And the wild antelope, that starts whene'er
The dry leaf rustles in the brake, suspend
Her timid steps, to gaze upon a form
More graceful than her own.
His wandering step,
Obedient to high thoughts, has visited
The awful ruins of the days of old:
Athens, and Tyre, and Balbec, and the waste
Where stood Jerusalem, the fallen towers

Of Babylon, the eternal pyramids,
Memphis and Thebes, and whatsoe'er of strange,
Sculptured on alabaster obelisk,
Or jasper tomb, or mutilated sphynx,
Dark Aethiopia in her desert hills
Conceals. Among the ruined temples there,
Stupendous columns, and wild images
Of more than man, where marble daemons watch
The Zodiac's brazen mystery, and dead men
Hang their mute thoughts on the mute walls around,
He lingered, poring on memorials
Of the world's youth: through the long burning day
Gazed on those speechless shapes; nor, when the moon
Filled the mysterious halls with floating shades
Suspended he that task, but ever gazed
And gazed, till meaning on his vacant mind
Flashed like strong inspiration, and he saw
The thrilling secrets of the birth of time.

Meanwhile an Arab maiden brought his food,
Her daily portion, from her father's tent,
And spread her matting for his couch, and stole
From duties and repose to tend his steps,
Enamoured, yet not daring for deep awe
To speak her love:—and watched his nightly sleep,
Sleepless herself, to gaze upon his lips
Parted in slumber, whence the regular breath
Of innocent dreams arose; then, when red morn
Made paler the pale moon, to her cold home
Wildered, and wan, and panting, she returned.

The Poet, wandering on, through Arabie,
And Persia, and the wild Carmanian waste,
And o'er the aerial mountains which pour down
Indus and Oxus from their icy caves,
In joy and exultation held his way;
Till in the vale of Cashmire, far within
Its loneliest dell, where odorous plants entwine
Beneath the hollow rocks a natural bower,

Beside a sparkling rivulet he stretched
His languid limbs. A vision on his sleep
There came, a dream of hopes that never yet
Had flushed his cheek. He dreamed a veiled maid
Sate near him, talking in low solemn tones.
Her voice was like the voice of his own soul
Heard in the calm of thought; its music long,
Like woven sounds of streams and breezes, held
His inmost sense suspended in its web
Of many-coloured woof and shifting hues.
Knowledge and truth and virtue were her theme,
And lofty hopes of divine liberty,
Thoughts the most dear to him, and poesy,
Herself a poet. Soon the solemn mood
Of her pure mind kindled through all her frame
A permeating fire; wild numbers then
She raised, with voice stifled in tremulous sobs
Subdued by its own pathos; her fair hands
Were bare alone, sweeping from some strange harp
Strange symphony, and in their branching veins
The eloquent blood told an ineffable tale.
The beating of her heart was heard to fill
The pauses of her music, and her breath
Tumultuously accorded with those fits
Of intermitted song. Sudden she rose,
As if her heart impatiently endured
Its bursting burthen: at the sound he turned,
And saw by the warm light of their own life
Her glowing limbs beneath the sinuous veil
Of woven wind, her outspread arms now bare,
Her dark locks floating in the breath of night,
Her beamy bending eyes, her parted lips
Outstretched, and pale, and quivering eagerly.
His strong heart sunk and sickened with excess
Of love. He reared his shuddering limbs and quelled
His gasping breath, and spread his arms to meet
Her panting bosom: . . . she drew back a while,
Then, yielding to the irresistible joy,
With frantic gesture and short breathless cry

Folded his frame in her dissolving arms.
Now blackness veiled his dizzy eyes, and night
Involved and swallowed up the vision; sleep,
Like a dark flood suspended in its course,
Rolled back its impulse on his vacant brain.

Roused by the shock he started from his trance—
The cold white light of morning, the blue moon
Low in the west, the clear and garish hills,
The distinct valley and the vacant woods,
Spread round him where he stood. Whither have fled
The hues of heaven that canopied his bower
Of yesternight? The sounds that soothed his sleep,
The mystery and the majesty of Earth,
The joy, the exultation? His wan eyes
Gaze on the empty scene as vacantly
As ocean's moon looks on the moon in heaven.
The spirit of sweet human love has sent
A vision to the sleep of him who spurned
Her choicest gifts. He eagerly pursues
Beyond the realms of dream that fleeting shade;
He overleaps the bounds. Alas! Alas!
Were limbs, and breath, and being intertwined
Thus treacherously? Lost, lost, for ever lost
In the wide pathless desert of dim sleep,
That beautiful shape! Does the dark gate of death
Conduct to thy mysterious paradise,
O Sleep? Does the bright arch of rainbow clouds
And pendent mountains seen in the calm lake,
Lead only to a black and watery depth,
While death's blue vault, with loathliest vapours hung,
Where every shade which the foul grave exhales
Hides its dead eye from the detested day,
Conducts, O Sleep, to thy delightful realms?
This doubt with sudden tide flowed on his heart;
The insatiate hope which it awakened, stung
His brain even like despair.
While daylight held
The sky, the Poet kept mute conference

With his still soul. At night the passion came,
Like the fierce fiend of a distempered dream,
And shook him from his rest, and led him forth
Into the darkness.—As an eagle, grasped
In folds of the green serpent, feels her breast
Burn with the poison, and precipitates
Through night and day, tempest, and calm, and cloud,
Frantic with dizzying anguish, her blind flight
O'er the wide aery wilderness: thus driven
By the bright shadow of that lovely dream,
Beneath the cold glare of the desolate night,
Through tangled swamps and deep precipitous dells,
Startling with careless step the moonlight snake,
He fled. Red morning dawned upon his flight,
Shedding the mockery of its vital hues
Upon his cheek of death. He wandered on
Till vast Aornos seen from Petra's steep
Hung o'er the low horizon like a cloud;
Through Balk, and where the desolated tombs
Of Parthian kings scatter to every wind
Their wasting dust, wildly he wandered on,
Day after day a weary waste of hours,
Bearing within his life the brooding care
That ever fed on its decaying flame.
And now his limbs were lean; his scattered hair,
Sered by the autumn of strange suffering
Sung dirges in the wind; his listless hand
Hung like dead bone within its withered skin;
Life, and the lustre that consumed it, shone
As in a furnace burning secretly
From his dark eyes alone. The cottagers,
Who ministered with human charity
His human wants, beheld with wondering awe
Their fleeting visitant. The mountaineer,
Encountering on some dizzy precipice
That spectral form, deemed that the Spirit of wind
With lightning eyes, and eager breath, and feet
Disturbing not the drifted snow, had paused
In its career: the infant would conceal

His troubled visage in his mother's robe
In terror at the glare of those wild eyes,
To remember their strange light in many a dream
Of after-times; but youthful maidens, taught
By nature, would interpret half the woe
That wasted him, would call him with false names
Brother and friend, would press his pallid hand
At parting, and watch, dim through tears, the path
Of his departure from their father's door.

At length upon the lone Chorasmian shore
He paused, a wide and melancholy waste
Of putrid marshes. A strong impulse urged
His steps to the sea-shore. A swan was there,
Beside a sluggish stream among the reeds.
It rose as he approached, and, with strong wings
Scaling the upward sky, bent its bright course
High over the immeasurable main.
His eyes pursued its flight:—'Thou hast a home,
Beautiful bird; thou voyagest to thine home,
Where thy sweet mate will twine her downy neck
With thine, and welcome thy return with eyes
Bright in the lustre of their own fond joy.
And what am I that I should linger here,
With voice far sweeter than thy dying notes,
Spirit more vast than thine, frame more attuned
To beauty, wasting these surpassing powers
In the deaf air, to the blind earth, and heaven
That echoes not my thoughts?' A gloomy smile
Of desperate hope wrinkled his quivering lips.
For sleep, he knew, kept most relentlessly
Its precious charge, and silent death exposed,
Faithless perhaps as sleep, a shadowy lure,
With doubtful smile mocking its own strange charms.

Startled by his own thoughts he looked around.
There was no fair fiend near him, not a sight
Or sound of awe but in his own deep mind.
A little shallop floating near the shore

Caught the impatient wandering of his gaze.
It had been long abandoned, for its sides
Gaped wide with many a rift, and its frail joints
Swayed with the undulations of the tide.
A restless impulse urged him to embark
And meet lone Death on the drear ocean's waste;
For well he knew that mighty Shadow loves
The slimy caverns of the populous deep.

The day was fair and sunny; sea and sky
Drank its inspiring radiance, and the wind
Swept strongly from the shore, blackening the waves.
Following his eager soul, the wanderer
Leaped in the boat, he spread his cloak aloft
On the bare mast, and took his lonely seat,
And felt the boat speed o'er the tranquil sea
Like a torn cloud before the hurricane.

As one that in a silver vision floats
Obedient to the sweep of odorous winds
Upon resplendent clouds, so rapidly
Along the dark and ruffled waters fled
The straining boat.—A whirlwind swept it on,
With fierce gusts and precipitating force,
Through the white ridges of the chafed sea.
The waves arose. Higher and higher still
Their fierce necks writhed beneath the tempest's scourge
Like serpents struggling in a vulture's grasp.
Calm and rejoicing in the fearful war
Of wave ruining on wave, and blast on blast
Descending, and black flood on whirlpool driven
With dark obliterating course, he sate:
As if their genii were the ministers
Appointed to conduct him to the light
Of those beloved eyes, the Poet sate,
Holding the steady helm. Evening came on,
The beams of sunset hung their rainbow hues
High 'mid the shifting domes of sheeted spray
That canopied his path o'er the waste deep;

Twilight, ascending slowly from the east,
Entwined in duskier wreaths her braided locks
O'er the fair front and radiant eyes of day;
Night followed, clad with stars. On every side
More horribly the multitudinous streams
Of ocean's mountainous waste to mutual war
Rushed in dark tumult thundering, as to mock
The calm and spangled sky. The little boat
Still fled before the storm; still fled, like foam
Down the steep cataract of a wintry river;
Now pausing on the edge of the riven wave;
Now leaving far behind the bursting mass
That fell, convulsing ocean: safely fled—
As if that frail and wasted human form,
Had been an elemental god.

At midnight
The moon arose; and lo! the ethereal cliffs
Of Caucasus, whose icy summits shone
Among the stars like sunlight, and around
Whose caverned base the whirlpools and the waves
Bursting and eddying irresistibly
Rage and resound forever.—Who shall save?—
The boat fled on,—the boiling torrent drove,—
The crags closed round with black and jagged arms,
The shattered mountain overhung the sea,
And faster still, beyond all human speed,
Suspended on the sweep of the smooth wave,
The little boat was driven. A cavern there
Yawned, and amid its slant and winding depths
Ingulfed the rushing sea. The boat fled on
With unrelaxing speed.—'Vision and Love!'
The Poet cried aloud, 'I have beheld
The path of thy departure. Sleep and death
Shall not divide us long.'

The boat pursued
The windings of the cavern. Daylight shone
At length upon that gloomy river's flow;

Now, where the fiercest war among the waves
Is calm, on the unfathomable stream
The boat moved slowly. Where the mountain, riven,
Exposed those black depths to the azure sky,
Ere yet the flood's enormous volume fell
Even to the base of Caucasus, with sound
That shook the everlasting rocks, the mass
Filled with one whirlpool all that ample chasm:
Stair above stair the eddying waters rose,
Circling immeasurably fast, and laved
With alternating dash the gnarled roots
Of mighty trees, that stretched their giant arms
In darkness over it. I' the midst was left,
Reflecting, yet distorting every cloud,
A pool of treacherous and tremendous calm.
Seized by the sway of the ascending stream,
With dizzy swiftness, round, and round, and round,
Ridge after ridge the straining boat arose,
Till on the verge of the extremest curve,
Where, through an opening of the rocky bank,
The waters overflow, and a smooth spot
Of glassy quiet mid those battling tides
Is left, the boat paused shuddering.—Shall it sink
Down the abyss? Shall the reverting stress
Of that resistless gulf embosom it?
Now shall it fall?—A wandering stream of wind,
Breathed from the west, has caught the expanded sail,
And, lo! with gentle motion, between banks
Of mossy slope, and on a placid stream,
Beneath a woven grove it sails, and, hark!
The ghastly torrent mingles its far roar,
With the breeze murmuring in the musical woods.
Where the embowering trees recede, and leave
A little space of green expanse, the cove
Is closed by meeting banks, whose yellow flowers
For ever gaze on their own drooping eyes,
Reflected in the crystal calm. The wave
Of the boat's motion marred their pensive task,
Which naught but vagrant bird, or wanton wind,

Or falling spear-grass, or their own decay
Had e'er disturbed before. The Poet longed
To deck with their bright hues his withered hair,
But on his heart its solitude returned,
And he forbore. Not the strong impulse hid
In those flushed cheeks, bent eyes, and shadowy frame
Had yet performed its ministry: it hung
Upon his life, as lightning in a cloud
Gleams, hovering ere it vanish, ere the floods
Of night close over it.
The noonday sun
Now shone upon the forest, one vast mass
Of mingling shade, whose brown magnificence
A narrow vale embosoms. There, huge caves,
Scooped in the dark base of their aery rocks,
Mocking its moans, respond and roar for ever.
The meeting boughs and implicated leaves
Wove twilight o'er the Poet's path, as led
By love, or dream, or god, or mightier Death,
He sought in Nature's dearest haunt some bank,
Her cradle, and his sepulchre. More dark
And dark the shades accumulate. The oak,
Expanding its immense and knotty arms,
Embraces the light beech. The pyramids
Of the tall cedar overarching frame
Most solemn domes within, and far below,
Like clouds suspended in an emerald sky,
The ash and the acacia floating hang
Tremulous and pale. Like restless serpents, clothed
In rainbow and in fire, the parasites,
Starred with ten thousand blossoms, flow around
The grey trunks, and, as gamesome infants' eyes,
With gentle meanings, and most innocent wiles,
Fold their beams round the hearts of those that love,
These twine their tendrils with the wedded boughs
Uniting their close union; the woven leaves
Make net-work of the dark blue light of day,
And the night's noontide clearness, mutable
As shapes in the weird clouds. Soft mossy lawns

Beneath these canopies extend their swells,
Fragrant with perfumed herbs, and eyed with blooms
Minute yet beautiful. One darkest glen
Sends from its woods of musk-rose, twined with jasmine,
A soul-dissolving odour to invite
To some more lovely mystery. Through the dell,
Silence and Twilight here, twin-sisters, keep
Their noonday watch, and sail among the shades,
Like vaporous shapes half-seen; beyond, a well,
Dark, gleaming, and of most translucent wave,
Images all the woven boughs above,
And each depending leaf, and every speck
Of azure sky, darting between their chasms;
Nor aught else in the liquid mirror laves
Its portraiture, but some inconstant star
Between one foliaged lattice twinkling fair,
Or painted bird, sleeping beneath the moon,
Or gorgeous insect floating motionless,
Unconscious of the day, ere yet his wings
Have spread their glories to the gaze of noon.

Hither the Poet came. His eyes beheld
Their own wan light through the reflected lines
Of his thin hair, distinct in the dark depth
Of that still fountain; as the human heart,
Gazing in dreams over the gloomy grave,
Sees its own treacherous likeness there. He heard
The motion of the leaves, the grass that sprung
Startled and glanced and trembled even to feel
An unaccustomed presence, and the sound
Of the sweet brook that from the secret springs
Of that dark fountain rose. A Spirit seemed
To stand beside him—clothed in no bright robes
Of shadowy silver or enshrining light,
Borrowed from aught the visible world affords
Of grace, or majesty, or mystery;—
But, undulating woods, and silent well,
And leaping rivulet, and evening gloom
Now deepening the dark shades, for speech assuming,

Held commune with him, as if he and it
Were all that was,—only... when his regard
Was raised by intense pensiveness, ... two eyes,
Two starry eyes, hung in the gloom of thought,
And seemed with their serene and azure smiles
To beckon him.

Obedient to the light
That shone within his soul, he went, pursuing
The windings of the dell.—The rivulet,
Wanton and wild, through many a green ravine
Beneath the forest flowed. Sometimes it fell
Among the moss with hollow harmony
Dark and profound. Now on the polished stones
It danced; like childhood laughing as it went:
Then, through the plain in tranquil wanderings crept,
Reflecting every herb and drooping bud
That overhung its quietness.—'O stream!
Whose source is inaccessibly profound,
Whither do thy mysterious waters tend?
Thou imagest my life. Thy darksome stillness,
Thy dazzling waves, thy loud and hollow gulfs,
Thy searchless fountain, and invisible course
Have each their type in me; and the wide sky,
And measureless ocean may declare as soon
What oozy cavern or what wandering cloud
Contains thy waters, as the universe
Tell where these living thoughts reside, when stretched
Upon thy flowers my bloodless limbs shall waste
I' the passing wind!'

Beside the grassy shore
Of the small stream he went; he did impress
On the green moss his tremulous step, that caught
Strong shuddering from his burning limbs. As one
Roused by some joyous madness from the couch
Of fever, he did move; yet, not like him,
Forgetful of the grave, where, when the flame
Of his frail exultation shall be spent,

He must descend. With rapid steps he went
Beneath the shade of trees, beside the flow
Of the wild babbling rivulet; and now
The forest's solemn canopies were changed
For the uniform and lightsome evening sky.
Grey rocks did peep from the spare moss, and stemmed
The struggling brook; tall spires of windlestrae
Threw their thin shadows down the rugged slope,
And nought but gnarled roots of ancient pines
Branchless and blasted, clenched with grasping roots
The unwilling soil. A gradual change was here,
Yet ghastly. For, as fast years flow away,
The smooth brow gathers, and the hair grows thin
And white, and where irradiate dewy eyes
Had shone, gleam stony orbs:—so from his steps
Bright flowers departed, and the beautiful shade
Of the green groves, with all their odorous winds
And musical motions. Calm, he still pursued
The stream, that with a larger volume now
Rolled through the labyrinthine dell; and there
Fretted a path through its descending curves
With its wintry speed. On every side now rose
Rocks, which, in unimaginable forms,
Lifted their black and barren pinnacles
In the light of evening, and its precipice
Obscuring the ravine, disclosed above,
Mid toppling stones, black gulfs and yawning caves,
Whose windings gave ten thousand various tongues
To the loud stream. Lo! where the pass expands
Its stony jaws, the abrupt mountain breaks,
And seems, with its accumulated crags,
To overhang the world: for wide expand
Beneath the wan stars and descending moon
Islanded seas, blue mountains, mighty streams,
Dim tracts and vast, robed in the lustrous gloom
Of leaden-coloured even, and fiery hills
Mingling their flames with twilight, on the verge
Of the remote horizon. The near scene,
In naked and severe simplicity,

Made contrast with the universe. A pine,
Rock-rooted, stretched athwart the vacancy
Its swinging boughs, to each inconstant blast
Yielding one only response, at each pause
In most familiar cadence, with the howl
The thunder and the hiss of homeless streams
Mingling its solemn song, whilst the broad river
Foaming and hurrying o'er its rugged path,
Fell into that immeasurable void
Scattering its waters to the passing winds.

Yet the grey precipice and solemn pine
And torrent were not all;—one silent nook
Was there. Even on the edge of that vast mountain,
Upheld by knotty roots and fallen rocks,
It overlooked in its serenity
The dark earth, and the bending vault of stars.
It was a tranquil spot, that seemed to smile
Even in the lap of horror. Ivy clasped
The fissured stones with its entwining arms,
And did embower with leaves for ever green,
And berries dark, the smooth and even space
Of its inviolated floor, and here
The children of the autumnal whirlwind bore,
In wanton sport, those bright leaves, whose decay,
Red, yellow, or ethereally pale,
Rivals the pride of summer. 'Tis the haunt
Of every gentle wind, whose breath can teach
The wilds to love tranquillity. One step,
One human step alone, has ever broken
The stillness of its solitude:—one voice
Alone inspired its echoes;—even that voice
Which hither came, floating among the winds,
And led the loveliest among human forms
To make their wild haunts the depository
Of all the grace and beauty that endued
Its motions, render up its majesty,
Scatter its music on the unfeeling storm,
And to the damp leaves and blue cavern mould,

Nurses of rainbow flowers and branching moss,
Commit the colours of that varying cheek,
That snowy breast, those dark and drooping eyes.

The dim and horned moon hung low, and poured
A sea of lustre on the horizon's verge
That overflowed its mountains. Yellow mist
Filled the unbounded atmosphere, and drank
Wan moonlight even to fulness; not a star
Shone, not a sound was heard; the very winds,
Danger's grim playmates, on that precipice
Slept, clasped in his embrace.—O, storm of death!
Whose sightless speed divides this sullen night:
And thou, colossal Skeleton, that, still
Guiding its irresistible career
In thy devastating omnipotence,
Art king of this frail world, from the red field
Of slaughter, from the reeking hospital,
The patriot's sacred couch, the snowy bed
Of innocence, the scaffold and the throne,
A mighty voice invokes thee. Ruin calls
His brother Death. A rare and regal prey
He hath prepared, prowling around the world;
Glutted with which thou mayst repose, and men
Go to their graves like flowers or creeping worms,
Nor ever more offer at thy dark shrine
The unheeded tribute of a broken heart.

When on the threshold of the green recess
The wanderer's footsteps fell, he knew that death
Was on him. Yet a little, ere it fled,
Did he resign his high and holy soul
To images of the majestic past,
That paused within his passive being now,
Like winds that bear sweet music, when they breathe
Through some dim latticed chamber. He did place
His pale lean hand upon the rugged trunk
Of the old pine. Upon an ivied stone
Reclined his languid head, his limbs did rest,

Diffused and motionless, on the smooth brink
Of that obscurest chasm;—and thus he lay,
Surrendering to their final impulses
The hovering powers of life. Hope and despair,
The torturers, slept; no mortal pain or fear
Marred his repose; the influxes of sense,
And his own being unalloyed by pain,
Yet feebler and more feeble, calmly fed
The stream of thought, till he lay breathing there
At peace, and faintly smiling:—his last sight
Was the great moon, which o'er the western line
Of the wide world her mighty horn suspended,
With whose dun beams inwoven darkness seemed
To mingle. Now upon the jagged hills
It rests; and still as the divided frame
Of the vast meteor sunk, the Poet's blood,
That ever beat in mystic sympathy
With nature's ebb and flow, grew feebler still:
And when two lessening points of light alone
Gleamed through the darkness, the alternate gasp
Of his faint respiration scarce did stir
The stagnate night:—till the minutest ray
Was quenched, the pulse yet lingered in his heart.
It paused—it fluttered. But when heaven remained
Utterly black, the murky shades involved
An image, silent, cold, and motionless,
As their own voiceless earth and vacant air.
Even as a vapour fed with golden beams
That ministered on sunlight, ere the west
Eclipses it, was now that wondrous frame—
No sense, no motion, no divinity—
A fragile lute, on whose harmonious strings
The breath of heaven did wander—a bright stream
Once fed with many-voiced waves—a dream
Of youth, which night and time have quenched for ever,
Still, dark, and dry, and unremembered now.

Oh, for Medea's wondrous alchemy,
Which wheresoe'er it fell made the earth gleam

With bright flowers, and the wintry boughs exhale
From vernal blooms fresh fragrance! O, that God,
Profuse of poisons, would concede the chalice
Which but one living man has drained, who now,
Vessel of deathless wrath, a slave that feels
No proud exemption in the blighting curse
He bears, over the world wanders for ever,
Lone as incarnate death! O, that the dream
Of dark magician in his visioned cave,
Raking the cinders of a crucible
For life and power, even when his feeble hand
Shakes in its last decay, were the true law
Of this so lovely world! But thou art fled,
Like some frail exhalation; which the dawn
Robes in its golden beams,—ah! thou hast fled!
The brave, the gentle and the beautiful,
The child of grace and genius. Heartless things
Are done and said i' the world, and many worms
And beasts and men live on, and mighty Earth
From sea and mountain, city and wilderness,
In vesper low or joyous orison,
Lifts still its solemn voice:—but thou art fled—
Thou canst no longer know or love the shapes
Of this phantasmal scene, who have to thee
Been purest ministers, who are, alas!
Now thou art not. Upon those pallid lips
So sweet even in their silence, on those eyes
That image sleep in death, upon that form
Yet safe from the worm's outrage, let no tear
Be shed—not even in thought. Nor, when those hues
Are gone, and those divinest lineaments,
Worn by the senseless wind, shall live alone
In the frail pauses of this simple strain,
Let not high verse, mourning the memory
Of that which is no more, or painting's woe
Or sculpture, speak in feeble imagery
Their own cold powers. Art and eloquence,
And all the shows o' the world are frail and vain
To weep a loss that turns their lights to shade.

It is a woe "too deep for tears," when all
Is reft at once, when some surpassing Spirit,
Whose light adorned the world around it, leaves
Those who remain behind, not sobs or groans,
The passionate tumult of a clinging hope;
But pale despair and cold tranquillity,
Nature's vast frame, the web of human things,
Birth and the grave, that are not as they were.

Note on Alastor, by Mrs. Shelley

"Alastor" is written in a very different tone from "Queen Mab". In the latter, Shelley poured out all the cherished speculations of his youth—all the irrepressible emotions of sympathy, censure, and hope, to which the present suffering, and what he considers the proper destiny of his fellow-creatures, gave birth. "Alastor", on the contrary, contains an individual interest only. A very few years, with their attendant events, had checked the ardour of Shelley's hopes, though he still thought them well-grounded, and that to advance their fulfilment was the noblest task man could achieve.

This is neither the time nor place to speak of the misfortunes that chequered his life. It will be sufficient to say that, in all he did, he at the time of doing it believed himself justified to his own conscience; while the various ills of poverty and loss of friends brought home to him the sad realities of life. Physical suffering had also considerable influence in causing him to turn his eyes inward; inclining him rather to brood over the thoughts and emotions of his own soul than to glance abroad, and to make, as in "Queen Mab", the whole universe the object and subject of his song. In the Spring of 1815, an eminent physician pronounced that he was dying rapidly of a consumption; abscesses were formed on his lungs, and he suffered acute spasms. Suddenly a complete change took place; and though through life he was a martyr to pain and debility, every symptom of pulmonary disease vanished. His nerves, which nature had formed sensitive to an unexampled degree, were rendered still more susceptible by the state of his health.

As soon as the peace of 1814 had opened the Continent, he went abroad. He visited some of the more magnificent scenes of Switzerland, and returned to England from Lucerne, by the Reuss and the Rhine. This river-navigation enchanted him. In his favourite poem of "Thalaba", his imagination had been excited by a description of such a voyage. In the summer of 1815, after a tour along the southern coast of Devonshire and a visit to Clifton, he rented a house on Bishopgate Heath, on the borders of Windsor Forest, where he enjoyed several months of comparative health and tranquil happiness. The later summer months were warm and dry. Accompanied by a few friends, he visited the source of the Thames, making a voyage in a wherry from Windsor to Crichlade. His beautiful stanzas in the churchyard of Lechlade were written on that occasion. "Alastor" was composed on his return. He spent his days under the oak-shades of Windsor Great Park; and the magnificent woodland was a fitting study to inspire the various descriptions of forest scenery we find in the poem.

None of Shelley's poems is more characteristic than this. The solemn spirit that reigns throughout, the worship of the majesty of nature, the broodings of a poet's heart in solitude—the mingling of the exulting joy which the various aspects of the visible universe inspires with the sad and struggling pangs which human passion imparts—give a touching interest to the whole. The death which he had often contemplated during the last months as certain and near he here represented in such colours as had, in his lonely musings, soothed his soul to peace. The versification sustains the solemn spirit which breathes throughout: it is peculiarly melodious. The poem ought rather to be considered didactic than narrative: it was the outpouring of his own emotions, embodied in the purest form he could conceive, painted in the ideal hues which his brilliant imagination inspired, and softened by the recent anticipation of death.

THE REVOLT OF ISLAM

A Poem in Twelve Cantos

Osais de Broton ethnos aglaiais aptomestha
perainei pros eschaton
ploon nausi d oute pezos ion an eurois
es Uperboreon agona thaumatan odon.

—Pind. Pyth. x.

(Composed in the neighbourhood of Bisham Wood, near Great Marlow, Bucks, 1817 (April–September 23); printed, with title (dated 1818), "Laon and Cythna; or, The Revolution of the Golden City: A Vision of the Nineteenth Century", October, November, 1817, but suppressed, pending revision, by the publishers, C & J. Ollier. (A few copies had got out, but these were recalled, and some recovered.) Published, with a fresh title-page and twenty-seven cancel-leaves, as "The Revolt of Islam", January 10, 1818. Sources of the text are (1) "Laon and Cythna", 1818; (2) "The Revolt of Islam", 1818; (3) "Poetical Works", 1839, editions 1st and 2nd—both edited by Mrs. Shelley. A copy, with several pages missing, of the "Preface", the Dedication", and "Canto 1" of "Laon and Cythna" is amongst the Shelley manuscripts at the Bodleian. For a full collation of this manuscript see Mr. C.D. Locock's "Examination of the Shelley Manuscripts at the Bodleian Library". Oxford: Clarendon Press, 1903. Two manuscript fragments from the Hunt papers are also extant: one (twenty-four lines) in the possession of Mr. W.M. Rossetti, another (9 23 9 to 29 6) in that of Mr. H. Buxton Forman, C.B. See "The Shelley Library", pages 83–86, for an account of the copy of "Laon" upon which Shelley worked in revising for publication.)

Author's Preface

The Poem which I now present to the world is an attempt from which I scarcely dare to expect success, and in which a writer of established fame might fail without disgrace. It is an experiment on the temper of the public mind, as to how far a thirst for a happier condition of moral and political society survives, among the enlightened and refined, the tempests which have shaken the age in which we live. I have sought to enlist the harmony of metrical language, the ethereal combinations of the fancy, the rapid and subtle transitions of human passion, all those elements which essentially compose a Poem, in the cause of a liberal and comprehensive morality; and in the view of kindling within the bosoms of my readers a virtuous enthusiasm for those doctrines of liberty and justice, that faith and hope in something good, which neither violence nor misrepresentation nor prejudice can ever totally extinguish among mankind.

For this purpose I have chosen a story of human passion in its most universal character, diversified with moving and romantic adventures, and appealing, in contempt of all artificial opinions or institutions, to the common sympathies of every human breast. I have made no attempt to recommend the motives which I would substitute for those at present governing mankind, by methodical and systematic argument. I would only awaken the feelings, so that the reader should see the beauty of true virtue, and be incited to those inquiries which have led to my moral and political creed, and that of some of the sublimest intellects in the world. The Poem therefore (with the exception of the first canto, which is purely introductory) is narrative, not didactic. It is a succession of pictures illustrating the growth and progress of individual mind aspiring after excellence, and devoted to the love of mankind; its influence in refining and making pure the most daring and uncommon impulses of the imagination, the understanding, and the senses; its impatience at 'all the oppressions which are done under the sun;' its tendency to awaken public hope, and to enlighten and improve mankind; the rapid effects of the application of that tendency; the awakening of an immense nation from their slavery and degradation to a true sense of moral dignity and freedom; the bloodless dethronement of their oppressors, and the unveiling of the religious frauds by which they had been deluded into submission; the tranquillity of successful patriotism, and the universal toleration and benevolence of true philanthropy; the treachery and barbarity of hired soldiers; vice not the object of punishment and hatred, but kindness and pity; the faithlessness of tyrants; the confederacy of the Rulers of the World and the restoration of the expelled Dynasty by foreign arms; the massacre and extermination of the Patriots, and the victory of established power; the consequences of legitimate despotism,—civil war, famine, plague, superstition, and an utter extinction of the domestic affections; the judicial murder of the advocates of Liberty; the temporary triumph of oppression, that secure earnest of its final and inevitable fall; the transient nature of ignorance and error and the eternity of genius and virtue. Such is the series of delineations of which the Poem consists. And, if the lofty passions with which it has been my scope to distinguish this story shall not excite in the reader a generous impulse, an ardent thirst for excellence, an interest profound and strong such as belongs to no meaner desires, let not the failure be imputed to a natural unfitness for human sympathy in these sublime and animating themes. It is the business of the Poet to communicate to others the pleasure and the enthusiasm arising out of those images and feelings in the vivid presence of which within his own mind consists at once his inspiration and his reward.

The panic which, like an epidemic transport, seized upon all classes of men during the excesses consequent upon the French Revolution, is gradually giving place to sanity. It has ceased to be believed that whole generations of mankind ought to consign themselves to a hopeless inheritance of ignorance and misery, because a nation of men who had been dupes and slaves for centuries were incapable of conducting themselves with the wisdom and tranquillity of freemen so soon as some of their fetters were partially loosened. That their conduct could not have been marked by any other characters than ferocity and thoughtlessness is the historical fact from which liberty derives all its recommendations, and falsehood the worst features of its deformity. There is a reflux in the tide of human things which bears the shipwrecked hopes of men into a secure haven after the storms are past. Methinks, those who now live have survived an age of despair.

The French Revolution may be considered as one of those manifestations of a general state of feeling among civilised mankind produced by a defect of correspondence between the knowledge existing in society and the improvement or gradual abolition of political institutions. The year 1788 may be assumed as the epoch of one of the most important crises produced by this feeling. The sympathies connected with that event extended to every bosom. The most generous and amiable natures were those which participated the most extensively in these sympathies. But such a degree of unmingled good was expected as it was impossible to realise. If the Revolution had been in every respect prosperous, then misrule and superstition would lose half their claims to our abhorrence, as fetters which the captive can unlock with the slightest motion of his fingers, and which do not eat with poisonous rust into the soul. The revulsion occasioned by the atrocities of the demagogues, and the re-establishment of successive tyrannies in France, was terrible, and felt in the remotest corner of the civilised world. Could they listen to the plea of reason who had groaned under the calamities of a social state according to the provisions of which one man riots in luxury whilst another famishes for want of bread? Can he who the day before was a trampled slave suddenly become liberal-minded, forbearing, and independent? This is the consequence of the habits of a state of society to be produced by resolute perseverance and indefatigable hope, and long-suffering and long-believing courage, and the systematic efforts of generations of men of intellect and virtue. Such is the lesson which experience teaches now. But, on the first reverses of hope in the progress of French liberty, the sanguine eagerness for good overleaped the solution of these questions, and for a time extinguished itself in the unexpectedness of their result. Thus, many of the most ardent and tender-hearted of the worshippers of public good have been morally ruined by what a partial glimpse of the events they deplored appeared to show as the melancholy desolation of all their cherished hopes. Hence gloom and misanthropy have become the characteristics of the age in which we live, the solace of a disappointment that unconsciously finds relief only in the wilful exaggeration of its own despair. This influence has tainted the literature of the age with the hopelessness of the minds from which it flows. Metaphysics (I ought to except sir W. Drummond's "Academical Questions"; a volume of very acute and powerful metaphysical criticism.), and inquiries into moral and political science, have become little else than vain attempts to revive exploded superstitions, or sophisms like those of Mr. Malthus (It is remarkable, as a symptom of the revival of public hope, that Mr. Malthus has assigned, in the later editions of his work, an indefinite dominion to moral restraint over the principle of population. This concession answers all the inferences from his doctrine unfavourable to human improvement, and reduces the "Essay on Population" to a commentary illustrative of the unanswerableness of "Political Justice".), calculated to lull the oppressors of mankind into a security of everlasting triumph. Our works of fiction and poetry have been overshadowed by the same infectious gloom. But mankind appear to me to be emerging from their trance. I am aware, methinks, of a slow, gradual, silent change. In that belief I have composed the following Poem.

I do not presume to enter into competition with our greatest contemporary Poets. Yet I am unwilling to tread in the footsteps of any who have preceded me. I have sought to avoid the imitation of any style of language or versification peculiar to the original minds of which it is the character; designing that, even if what I have produced be worthless, it should still be properly my own. Nor have I permitted any system relating to mere words to divert the attention of the reader, from whatever interest I may have succeeded in creating, to my own ingenuity in contriving to disgust them according to the rules of criticism. I have simply clothed my thoughts in what appeared to me the most obvious and appropriate language. A person familiar with nature, and with the most celebrated productions of the human mind, can scarcely err in following the instinct, with respect to selection of language, produced by that familiarity. There is an education peculiarly fitted for a Poet, without which genius and sensibility can hardly fill the circle of their capacities. No education, indeed, can entitle to this appellation a dull and unobservant mind, or one, though neither dull nor unobservant, in which the channels of communication between thought and expression have been obstructed or closed. How far it is my fortune to belong to either of the latter classes I cannot know. I aspire to be something better. The circumstances of my accidental education have been favourable to this ambition. I have been familiar from boyhood with mountains and lakes and the sea, and the solitude of forests: Danger, which sports upon the brink of precipices, has been my playmate. I have trodden the glaciers of the Alps, and lived under the eye of Mont Blanc. I have been a wanderer among distant fields. I have sailed down mighty rivers, and seen the sun rise and set, and the stars come forth, whilst I have sailed night and day down a rapid stream among mountains. I have seen populous cities, and have watched the passions which rise and spread, and sink and change, amongst assembled multitudes of men. I have seen the theatre of the more visible ravages of tyranny and war, cities and villages reduced to scattered groups of black and roofless houses, and the naked inhabitants sitting famished upon their desolated thresholds. I have conversed with living men of genius. The poetry of ancient Greece and Rome, and modern Italy, and our own country, has been to me, like external nature, a passion and an enjoyment. Such are the sources from which the materials for the imagery of my Poem have been drawn. I have considered Poetry in its most comprehensive sense; and have read the Poets and the Historians and the Metaphysicians (In this sense there may be such a thing as perfectibility in works of fiction, notwithstanding the concession often made by the advocates of human improvement, that perfectibility is a term applicable only to science.) whose writings have been accessible to me, and have looked upon the beautiful and majestic scenery of the earth, as common sources of those elements which it is the province of the Poet to embody and combine. Yet the experience and the feelings to which I refer do not in themselves constitute men Poets, but only prepares them to be the auditors of those who are. How far I shall be found to possess that more essential attribute of Poetry, the power of awakening in others sensations like those which animate my own bosom, is that which, to speak sincerely, I know not; and which, with an acquiescent and contented spirit, I expect to be taught by the effect which I shall produce upon those whom I now address.

I have avoided, as I have said before, the imitation of any contemporary style. But there must be a resemblance, which does not depend upon their own will, between all the writers of any particular age. They cannot escape from subjection to a common influence which arises out of an infinite combination of circumstances belonging to the times in which they live; though each is in a degree the author of the very influence by which his being is thus pervaded. Thus, the tragic poets of the age of Pericles; the Italian revivers of ancient learning; those mighty intellects of our own country that succeeded the Reformation, the translators of the Bible, Shakespeare, Spenser, the Dramatists of the reign of Elizabeth, and Lord Bacon (Milton stands alone in the age which he illumined.); the colder spirits of the interval that succeeded;—all resemble each other, and differ from every other in their several classes. In this view of things, Ford can no more be called the imitator of Shakespeare than Shakespeare the imitator of Ford. There were perhaps few other points of resemblance between these two men than that which the universal and inevitable influence of their age produced. And this is an influence which neither the meanest scribbler nor the sublimest genius of any era can escape; and which I have not attempted to escape.

I have adopted the stanza of Spenser (a measure inexpressibly beautiful), not because I consider it a finer model of poetical harmony than the blank verse of Shakespeare and Milton, but because in the latter there is no shelter for mediocrity; you must either succeed or fail. This perhaps an aspiring spirit should desire. But I was enticed also by the brilliancy and magnificence of sound which a mind that has been nourished upon musical thoughts can produce by a just and harmonious arrangement of the pauses of this measure. Yet there will be found some instances where I have completely failed in this attempt, and one, which I here request the reader to consider as an erratum, where there is left, most inadvertently, an alexandrine in the middle of a stanza.

But in this, as in every other respect, I have written fearlessly. It is the misfortune of this age that its Writers, too thoughtless of immortality, are exquisitely sensible to temporary praise or blame. They write with the fear of Reviews before their eyes. This system of criticism sprang up in that torpid interval when Poetry was not. Poetry, and the art which professes to regulate and limit its powers, cannot subsist together. Longinus could not have been the contemporary of Homer, nor Boileau of Horace. Yet this species of criticism never presumed to assert an understanding of its own; it has always, unlike true science, followed, not preceded, the opinion of mankind, and would even now bribe with worthless adulation some of our greatest Poets to impose gratuitous fetters on their own imaginations, and become unconscious accomplices in the daily murder of all genius either not so aspiring or not so fortunate as their own. I have sought therefore to write, as I believe that Homer, Shakespeare, and Milton wrote, with an utter disregard of anonymous censure. I am certain that calumny and misrepresentation, though it may move me to compassion, cannot disturb my peace. I shall understand the expressive silence of those sagacious enemies who dare not trust themselves to speak. I shall endeavour to extract, from the midst of insult and contempt and maledictions, those admonitions which may tend to correct whatever imperfections such censurers may discover in this my first serious appeal to the Public. If certain Critics were as clear-sighted as they are malignant, how great would be the benefit to be derived from their virulent writings! As it is, I fear I shall be malicious enough to be amused with their paltry tricks and lame invectives. Should the Public judge that my composition is worthless, I shall indeed bow before the tribunal from which Milton received his crown of immortality, and shall seek to gather, if I live, strength from that defeat, which may nerve me to some new enterprise of thought which may not be worthless. I cannot conceive that Lucretius, when he meditated that poem whose doctrines are yet the basis of our metaphysical knowledge, and whose eloquence has been the wonder of mankind, wrote in awe of such censure as the hired sophists of the impure and superstitious noblemen of Rome might affix to what he should produce. It was at the period when Greece was led captive and Asia made tributary to the Republic, fast verging itself to slavery and ruin, that a multitude of Syrian captives, bigoted to the worship of their obscene Ashtaroth, and the unworthy successors of Socrates and Zeno, found there a precarious subsistence by administering, under the name of freedmen, to the vices and vanities of the great. These wretched men were skilled to plead, with a superficial but plausible set of sophisms, in favour of that contempt for virtue which is the portion of slaves, and that faith in portents, the most fatal substitute for benevolence in the imaginations of men, which, arising from the enslaved communities of the East, then first began to overwhelm the western nations in its stream. Were these the kind of men whose disapprobation the wise and lofty-minded Lucretius should have regarded with a salutary awe? The latest and perhaps the meanest of those who follow in his footsteps would disdain to hold life on such conditions.

The Poem now presented to the Public occupied little more than six months in the composition. That period has been devoted to the task with unremitting ardour and enthusiasm. I have exercised a watchful and earnest criticism on my work as it grew under my hands. I would willingly have sent it forth to the world with that perfection which long labour and revision is said to bestow. But I found that, if I should gain something in exactness by this method, I might lose much of the newness and energy of imagery and language as it flowed fresh from my mind. And, although the mere composition occupied no more than six months, the thoughts thus arranged were slowly gathered in as many years.

I trust that the reader will carefully distinguish between those opinions which have a dramatic propriety in reference to the characters which they are designed to elucidate, and such as are properly my own. The erroneous and degrading idea which men have conceived of a Supreme Being, for instance, is spoken against, but not the Supreme Being itself. The belief which some superstitious persons whom I have brought upon the stage entertain of the Deity, as injurious to the character of his benevolence, is widely different from my own. In recommending also a great and important change in the spirit which animates the social institutions of mankind, I have avoided all flattery to those violent and malignant passions of our nature which are ever on the watch to mingle with and to alloy the most beneficial innovations. There is no quarter given to Revenge, or Envy, or Prejudice. Love is celebrated everywhere as the sole law which should govern the moral world.

Dedication

There is no danger to a man that knows
What life and death is: there's not any law
Exceeds his knowledge; neither is it lawful
That he should stoop to any other law.

—Chapman

To Mary — —

1

So now my summer-task is ended, Mary,
And I return to thee, mine own heart's home;
As to his Queen some victor Knight of Faery,
Earning bright spoils for her enchanted dome;
Nor thou disdain, that ere my fame become
A star among the stars of mortal night,
If it indeed may cleave its natal gloom,
Its doubtful promise thus I would unite
With thy beloved name, thou Child of love and light.

2

The toil which stole from thee so many an hour,
Is ended,—and the fruit is at thy feet!
No longer where the woods to frame a bower
With interlaced branches mix and meet,
Or where with sound like many voices sweet,
Waterfalls leap among wild islands green,
Which framed for my lone boat a lone retreat
Of moss-grown trees and weeds, shall I be seen;
But beside thee, where still my heart has ever been.

3

Thoughts of great deeds were mine, dear Friend, when first
The clouds which wrap this world from youth did pass.
I do remember well the hour which burst
My spirit's sleep. A fresh May-dawn it was,
When I walked forth upon the glittering grass,
And wept, I knew not why; until there rose
From the near schoolroom, voices that, alas!
Were but one echo from a world of woes—
The harsh and grating strife of tyrants and of foes.

4

And then I clasped my hands and looked around—
—But none was near to mock my streaming eyes,
Which poured their warm drops on the sunny ground—
So without shame I spake:—'I will be wise,
And just, and free, and mild, if in me lies
Such power, for I grow weary to behold
The selfish and the strong still tyrannise
Without reproach or check.' I then controlled
My tears, my heart grew calm, and I was meek and bold.

5

And from that hour did I with earnest thought
Heap knowledge from forbidden mines of lore;
Yet nothing that my tyrants knew or taught
I cared to learn, but from that secret store
Wrought linked armour for my soul, before
It might walk forth to war among mankind;
Thus power and hope were strengthened more and more
Within me, till there came upon my mind
A sense of loneliness, a thirst with which I pined.

6

Alas, that love should be a blight and snare
To those who seek all sympathies in one!—
Such once I sought in vain; then black despair,
The shadow of a starless night, was thrown
Over the world in which I moved alone:—
Yet never found I one not false to me,
Hard hearts, and cold, like weights of icy stone
Which crushed and withered mine, that could not be
Aught but a lifeless clod, until revived by thee.

7

Thou Friend, whose presence on my wintry heart
Fell, like bright Spring upon some herbless plain;
How beautiful and calm and free thou wert
In thy young wisdom, when the mortal chain
Of Custom thou didst burst and rend in twain,
And walked as free as light the clouds among,
Which many an envious slave then breathed in vain
From his dim dungeon, and my spirit sprung
To meet thee from the woes which had begirt it long!

8

No more alone through the world's wilderness,
Although I trod the paths of high intent,
I journeyed now: no more companionless,
Where solitude is like despair, I went.—
There is the wisdom of a stern content
When Poverty can blight the just and good,
When Infamy dares mock the innocent,
And cherished friends turn with the multitude
To trample: this was ours, and we unshaken stood!

9

Now has descended a serener hour,
And with inconstant fortune, friends return;
Though suffering leaves the knowledge and the power
Which says:—Let scorn be not repaid with scorn.
And from thy side two gentle babes are born
To fill our home with smiles, and thus are we
Most fortunate beneath life's beaming morn;
And these delights, and thou, have been to me
The parents of the Song I consecrate to thee.

10

Is it that now my inexperienced fingers
But strike the prelude of a loftier strain?
Or, must the lyre on which my spirit lingers
Soon pause in silence, ne'er to sound again,
Though it might shake the Anarch Custom's reign,
And charm the minds of men to Truth's own sway
Holier than was Amphion's? I would fain
Reply in hope—but I am worn away,
And Death and Love are yet contending for their prey.

11

And what art thou? I know, but dare not speak:
Time may interpret to his silent years.
Yet in the paleness of thy thoughtful cheek,
And in the light thine ample forehead wears,
And in thy sweetest smiles, and in thy tears,
And in thy gentle speech, a prophecy
Is whispered, to subdue my fondest fears:
And through thine eyes, even in thy soul I see
A lamp of vestal fire burning internally.

12

They say that thou wert lovely from thy birth,
Of glorious parents thou aspiring Child.
I wonder not—for One then left this earth
Whose life was like a setting planet mild,
Which clothed thee in the radiance undefiled
Of its departing glory; still her fame
Shines on thee, through the tempests dark and wild
Which shake these latter days; and thou canst claim
The shelter, from thy Sire, of an immortal name.

13

One voice came forth from many a mighty spirit,
Which was the echo of three thousand years;
And the tumultuous world stood mute to hear it,
As some lone man who in a desert hears
The music of his home:—unwonted fears
Fell on the pale oppressors of our race,
And Faith, and Custom, and low-thoughted cares,
Like thunder-stricken dragons, for a space
Left the torn human heart, their food and dwelling-place.

14

Truth's deathless voice pauses among mankind!
If there must be no response to my cry—
If men must rise and stamp with fury blind
On his pure name who loves them,—thou and I,
Sweet friend! can look from our tranquillity
Like lamps into the world's tempestuous night,—
Two tranquil stars, while clouds are passing by
Which wrap them from the foundering seaman's sight,
That burn from year to year with unextinguished light.

Canto 1

1

When the last hope of trampled France had failed
Like a brief dream of unremaining glory,
From visions of despair I rose, and scaled
The peak of an aerial promontory,
Whose caverned base with the vexed surge was hoary;
And saw the golden dawn break forth, and waken
Each cloud, and every wave:—but transitory
The calm; for sudden, the firm earth was shaken,
As if by the last wreck its frame were overtaken.

2

So as I stood, one blast of muttering thunder
Burst in far peals along the waveless deep,
When, gathering fast, around, above, and under,
Long trains of tremulous mist began to creep,
Until their complicating lines did steep
The orient sun in shadow:—not a sound
Was heard; one horrible repose did keep
The forests and the floods, and all around
Darkness more dread than night was poured upon the ground.

3

Hark! 'tis the rushing of a wind that sweeps
Earth and the ocean. See! the lightnings yawn
Deluging Heaven with fire, and the lashed deeps
Glitter and boil beneath: it rages on,
One mighty stream, whirlwind and waves upthrown,
Lightning, and hail, and darkness eddying by.
There is a pause—the sea-birds, that were gone
Into their caves to shriek, come forth, to spy
What calm has fall'n on earth, what light is in the sky.

4

For, where the irresistible storm had cloven
That fearful darkness, the blue sky was seen
Fretted with many a fair cloud interwoven
Most delicately, and the ocean green,
Beneath that opening spot of blue serene,
Quivered like burning emerald; calm was spread
On all below; but far on high, between
Earth and the upper air, the vast clouds fled,
Countless and swift as leaves on autumn's tempest shed.

5

For ever, as the war became more fierce
Between the whirlwinds and the rack on high,
That spot grew more serene; blue light did pierce
The woof of those white clouds, which seem to lie
Far, deep, and motionless; while through the sky
The pallid semicircle of the moon
Passed on, in slow and moving majesty;
Its upper horn arrayed in mists, which soon
But slowly fled, like dew beneath the beams of noon.

6

I could not choose but gaze; a fascination
Dwelt in that moon, and sky, and clouds, which drew
My fancy thither, and in expectation
Of what I knew not, I remained:—the hue
Of the white moon, amid that heaven so blue,
Suddenly stained with shadow did appear;
A speck, a cloud, a shape, approaching grew,
Like a great ship in the sun's sinking sphere
Beheld afar at sea, and swift it came anear.

7

Even like a bark, which from a chasm of mountains,
Dark, vast and overhanging, on a river
Which there collects the strength of all its fountains,
Comes forth, whilst with the speed its frame doth quiver,
Sails, oars and stream, tending to one endeavour;
So, from that chasm of light a winged Form
On all the winds of heaven approaching ever
Floated, dilating as it came; the storm
Pursued it with fierce blasts, and lightnings swift and warm.

8

A course precipitous, of dizzy speed,
Suspending thought and breath; a monstrous sight!
For in the air do I behold indeed
An Eagle and a Serpent wreathed in fight:—
And now, relaxing its impetuous flight,
Before the aerial rock on which I stood,
The Eagle, hovering, wheeled to left and right,
And hung with lingering wings over the flood,
And startled with its yells the wide air's solitude.

9

A shaft of light upon its wings descended,
And every golden feather gleamed therein—
Feather and scale, inextricably blended.
The Serpent's mailed and many-coloured skin
Shone through the plumes its coils were twined within
By many a swoln and knotted fold, and high
And far, the neck, receding lithe and thin,
Sustained a crested head, which warily
Shifted and glanced before the Eagle's steadfast eye.

10

Around, around, in ceaseless circles wheeling
With clang of wings and scream, the Eagle sailed
Incessantly—sometimes on high concealing
Its lessening orbs, sometimes as if it failed,
Drooped through the air; and still it shrieked and wailed,
And casting back its eager head, with beak
And talon unremittingly assailed
The wreathed Serpent, who did ever seek
Upon his enemy's heart a mortal wound to wreak.

11

What life, what power, was kindled and arose
Within the sphere of that appalling fray!
For, from the encounter of those wondrous foes,
A vapour like the sea's suspended spray
Hung gathered; in the void air, far away,
Floated the shattered plumes; bright scales did leap,
Where'er the Eagle's talons made their way,
Like sparks into the darkness;—as they sweep,
Blood stains the snowy foam of the tumultuous deep.

12

Swift chances in that combat—many a check,
And many a change, a dark and wild turmoil;
Sometimes the Snake around his enemy's neck
Locked in stiff rings his adamantine coil,
Until the Eagle, faint with pain and toil,
Remitted his strong flight, and near the sea
Languidly fluttered, hopeless so to foil
His adversary, who then reared on high
His red and burning crest, radiant with victory.

13

Then on the white edge of the bursting surge,
Where they had sunk together, would the Snake
Relax his suffocating grasp, and scourge
The wind with his wild writhings; for to break
That chain of torment, the vast bird would shake
The strength of his unconquerable wings
As in despair, and with his sinewy neck,
Dissolve in sudden shock those linked rings—
Then soar, as swift as smoke from a volcano springs.

14

Wile baffled wile, and strength encountered strength,
Thus long, but unprevailing:—the event
Of that portentous fight appeared at length:
Until the lamp of day was almost spent
It had endured, when lifeless, stark, and rent,
Hung high that mighty Serpent, and at last
Fell to the sea, while o'er the continent
With clang of wings and scream the Eagle passed,
Heavily borne away on the exhausted blast.

15

And with it fled the tempest, so that ocean
And earth and sky shone through the atmosphere—
Only, 'twas strange to see the red commotion
Of waves like mountains o'er the sinking sphere
Of sunset sweep, and their fierce roar to hear
Amid the calm: down the steep path I wound
To the sea-shore—the evening was most clear
And beautiful, and there the sea I found
Calm as a cradled child in dreamless slumber bound.

16

There was a Woman, beautiful as morning,
Sitting beneath the rocks, upon the sand
Of the waste sea—fair as one flower adorning
An icy wilderness; each delicate hand
Lay crossed upon her bosom, and the band
Of her dark hair had fall'n, and so she sate
Looking upon the waves; on the bare strand
Upon the sea-mark a small boat did wait,
Fair as herself, like Love by Hope left desolate.

17

It seemed that this fair Shape had looked upon
That unimaginable fight, and now
That her sweet eyes were weary of the sun,
As brightly it illustrated her woe;
For in the tears which silently to flow
Paused not, its lustre hung: she watching aye
The foam-wreaths which the faint tide wove below
Upon the spangled sands, groaned heavily,
And after every groan looked up over the sea.

18

And when she saw the wounded Serpent make
His path between the waves, her lips grew pale,
Parted, and quivered; the tears ceased to break
From her immovable eyes; no voice of wail
Escaped her; but she rose, and on the gale
Loosening her star-bright robe and shadowy hair
Poured forth her voice; the caverns of the vale
That opened to the ocean, caught it there,
And filled with silver sounds the overflowing air.

19

She spake in language whose strange melody
Might not belong to earth. I heard alone,
What made its music more melodious be,
The pity and the love of every tone;
But to the Snake those accents sweet were known
His native tongue and hers; nor did he beat
The hoar spray idly then, but winding on
Through the green shadows of the waves that meet
Near to the shore, did pause beside her snowy feet.

20

Then on the sands the Woman sate again,
And wept and clasped her hands, and all between,
Renewed the unintelligible strain
Of her melodious voice and eloquent mien;
And she unveiled her bosom, and the green
And glancing shadows of the sea did play
O'er its marmoreal depth:—one moment seen,
For ere the next, the Serpent did obey
Her voice, and, coiled in rest in her embrace it lay.

21

Then she arose, and smiled on me with eyes
Serene yet sorrowing, like that planet fair,
While yet the daylight lingereth in the skies
Which cleaves with arrowy beams the dark-red air,
And said: 'To grieve is wise, but the despair
Was weak and vain which led thee here from sleep:
This shalt thou know, and more, if thou dost dare
With me and with this Serpent, o'er the deep,
A voyage divine and strange, companionship to keep.'

22

Her voice was like the wildest, saddest tone,
Yet sweet, of some loved voice heard long ago.
I wept. 'Shall this fair woman all alone,
Over the sea with that fierce Serpent go?
His head is on her heart, and who can know
How soon he may devour his feeble prey?'—
Such were my thoughts, when the tide gan to flow;
And that strange boat like the moon's shade did sway
Amid reflected stars that in the waters lay:—

23

A boat of rare device, which had no sail
But its own curved prow of thin moonstone,
Wrought like a web of texture fine and frail,
To catch those gentlest winds which are not known
To breathe, but by the steady speed alone
With which it cleaves the sparkling sea; and now
We are embarked—the mountains hang and frown
Over the starry deep that gleams below,
A vast and dim expanse, as o'er the waves we go.

24

And as we sailed, a strange and awful tale
That Woman told, like such mysterious dream
As makes the slumberer's cheek with wonder pale!
'Twas midnight, and around, a shoreless stream,
Wide ocean rolled, when that majestic theme
Shrined in her heart found utterance, and she bent
Her looks on mine; those eyes a kindling beam
Of love divine into my spirit sent,
And ere her lips could move, made the air eloquent.

25

'Speak not to me, but hear! Much shalt thou learn,
Much must remain unthought, and more untold,
In the dark Future's ever-flowing urn:
Know then, that from the depth of ages old
Two Powers o'er mortal things dominion hold,
Ruling the world with a divided lot,
Immortal, all-pervading, manifold,
Twin Genii, equal Gods—when life and thought
Sprang forth, they burst the womb of inessential Nought.

26

'The earliest dweller of the world, alone,
Stood on the verge of chaos. Lo! afar
O'er the wide wild abyss two meteors shone,
Sprung from the depth of its tempestuous jar:
A blood-red Comet and the Morning Star
Mingling their beams in combat—as he stood,
All thoughts within his mind waged mutual war,
In dreadful sympathy—when to the flood
That fair Star fell, he turned and shed his brother's blood.

27

'Thus evil triumphed, and the Spirit of evil,
One Power of many shapes which none may know,
One Shape of many names; the Fiend did revel
In victory, reigning o'er a world of woe,
For the new race of man went to and fro,
Famished and homeless, loathed and loathing, wild,
And hating good—for his immortal foe,
He changed from starry shape, beauteous and mild,
To a dire Snake, with man and beast unreconciled.

28

'The darkness lingering o'er the dawn of things,
Was Evil's breath and life; this made him strong
To soar aloft with overshadowing wings;
And the great Spirit of Good did creep among
The nations of mankind, and every tongue
Cursed and blasphemed him as he passed; for none
Knew good from evil, though their names were hung
In mockery o'er the fane where many a groan,
As King, and Lord, and God, the conquering Fiend did own,—

29

'The Fiend, whose name was Legion: Death, Decay,
Earthquake and Blight, and Want, and Madness pale,
Winged and wan diseases, an array
Numerous as leaves that strew the autumnal gale;
Poison, a snake in flowers, beneath the veil
Of food and mirth, hiding his mortal head;
And, without whom all these might nought avail,
Fear, Hatred, Faith, and Tyranny, who spread
Those subtle nets which snare the living and the dead.

30

'His spirit is their power, and they his slaves
In air, and light, and thought, and language, dwell;
And keep their state from palaces to graves,
In all resorts of men—invisible,
But when, in ebon mirror, Nightmare fell
To tyrant or impostor bids them rise,
Black winged demon forms—whom, from the hell,
His reign and dwelling beneath nether skies,
He loosens to their dark and blasting ministries.

31

'In the world's youth his empire was as firm
As its foundations. . . Soon the Spirit of Good,
Though in the likeness of a loathsome worm,
Sprang from the billows of the formless flood,
Which shrank and fled; and with that Fiend of blood
Renewed the doubtful war. . . Thrones then first shook,
And earth's immense and trampled multitude
In hope on their own powers began to look,
And Fear, the demon pale, his sanguine shrine forsook.

32

'Then Greece arose, and to its bards and sages,
In dream, the golden-pinioned Genii came,
Even where they slept amid the night of ages,
Steeping their hearts in the divinest flame
Which thy breath kindled, Power of holiest name!
And oft in cycles since, when darkness gave
New weapons to thy foe, their sunlike fame
Upon the combat shone—a light to save,
Like Paradise spread forth beyond the shadowy grave.

33

'Such is this conflict—when mankind doth strive
With its oppressors in a strife of blood,
Or when free thoughts, like lightnings, are alive,
And in each bosom of the multitude
Justice and truth with Custom's hydra brood
Wage silent war; when Priests and Kings dissemble
In smiles or frowns their fierce disquietude,
When round pure hearts a host of hopes assemble,
The Snake and Eagle meet—the world's foundations tremble!

34

'Thou hast beheld that fight—when to thy home
Thou dost return, steep not its hearth in tears;
Though thou may'st hear that earth is now become
The tyrant's garbage, which to his compeers,
The vile reward of their dishonoured years,
He will dividing give.—The victor Fiend,
Omnipotent of yore, now quails, and fears
His triumph dearly won, which soon will lend
An impulse swift and sure to his approaching end.

35

'List, stranger, list, mine is an human form,
Like that thou wearest—touch me—shrink not now!
My hand thou feel'st is not a ghost's, but warm
With human blood.—'Twas many years ago,
Since first my thirsting soul aspired to know
The secrets of this wondrous world, when deep
My heart was pierced with sympathy, for woe
Which could not be mine own, and thought did keep,
In dream, unnatural watch beside an infant's sleep.

36

'Woe could not be mine own, since far from men
I dwelt, a free and happy orphan child,
By the sea-shore, in a deep mountain glen;
And near the waves, and through the forests wild,
I roamed, to storm and darkness reconciled:
For I was calm while tempest shook the sky:
But when the breathless heavens in beauty smiled,
I wept, sweet tears, yet too tumultuously
For peace, and clasped my hands aloft in ecstasy.

37

'These were forebodings of my fate—before
A woman's heart beat in my virgin breast,
It had been nurtured in divinest lore:
A dying poet gave me books, and blessed
With wild but holy talk the sweet unrest
In which I watched him as he died away—
A youth with hoary hair—a fleeting guest
Of our lone mountains: and this lore did sway
My spirit like a storm, contending there alway.

38

'Thus the dark tale which history doth unfold
I knew, but not, methinks, as others know,
For they weep not; and Wisdom had unrolled
The clouds which hide the gulf of mortal woe,—
To few can she that warning vision show—
For I loved all things with intense devotion;
So that when Hope's deep source in fullest flow,
Like earthquake did uplift the stagnant ocean
Of human thoughts—mine shook beneath the wide emotion.

39

'When first the living blood through all these veins
Kindled a thought in sense, great France sprang forth,
And seized, as if to break, the ponderous chains
Which bind in woe the nations of the earth.
I saw, and started from my cottage-hearth;
And to the clouds and waves in tameless gladness
Shrieked, till they caught immeasurable mirth—
And laughed in light and music: soon, sweet madness
Was poured upon my heart, a soft and thrilling sadness.

40

'Deep slumber fell on me:—my dreams were fire—
Soft and delightful thoughts did rest and hover
Like shadows o'er my brain; and strange desire,
The tempest of a passion, raging over
My tranquil soul, its depths with light did cover,
Which passed; and calm, and darkness, sweeter far,
Came—then I loved; but not a human lover!
For when I rose from sleep, the Morning Star
Shone through the woodbine-wreaths which round my casement were.

41

'Twas like an eye which seemed to smile on me.
I watched, till by the sun made pale, it sank
Under the billows of the heaving sea;
But from its beams deep love my spirit drank,
And to my brain the boundless world now shrank
Into one thought—one image—yes, for ever!
Even like the dayspring, poured on vapours dank,
The beams of that one Star did shoot and quiver
Through my benighted mind—and were extinguished never.

42

'The day passed thus: at night, methought, in dream
A shape of speechless beauty did appear:
It stood like light on a careering stream
Of golden clouds which shook the atmosphere;
A winged youth, his radiant brow did wear
The Morning Star: a wild dissolving bliss
Over my frame he breathed, approaching near,
And bent his eyes of kindling tenderness
Near mine, and on my lips impressed a lingering kiss,—

43

'And said: "A Spirit loves thee, mortal maiden,
How wilt thou prove thy worth?" Then joy and sleep
Together fled; my soul was deeply laden,
And to the shore I went to muse and weep;
But as I moved, over my heart did creep
A joy less soft, but more profound and strong
Than my sweet dream; and it forbade to keep
The path of the sea-shore: that Spirit's tongue
Seemed whispering in my heart, and bore my steps along.

44

'How, to that vast and peopled city led,
Which was a field of holy warfare then,
I walked among the dying and the dead,
And shared in fearless deeds with evil men,
Calm as an angel in the dragon's den—
How I braved death for liberty and truth,
And spurned at peace, and power, and fame—and when
Those hopes had lost the glory of their youth,
How sadly I returned—might move the hearer's ruth:

45

'Warm tears throng fast! the tale may not be said—
Know then, that when this grief had been subdued,
I was not left, like others, cold and dead;
The Spirit whom I loved, in solitude
Sustained his child: the tempest-shaken wood,
The waves, the fountains, and the hush of night—
These were his voice, and well I understood
His smile divine, when the calm sea was bright
With silent stars, and Heaven was breathless with delight.

46

'In lonely glens, amid the roar of rivers,
When the dim nights were moonless, have I known
Joys which no tongue can tell; my pale lip quivers
When thought revisits them:—know thou alone,
That after many wondrous years were flown,
I was awakened by a shriek of woe;
And over me a mystic robe was thrown,
By viewless hands, and a bright Star did glow
Before my steps—the Snake then met his mortal foe.'

47

'Thou fearest not then the Serpent on thy heart?'
'Fear it!' she said, with brief and passionate cry,
And spake no more: that silence made me start—
I looked, and we were sailing pleasantly,
Swift as a cloud between the sea and sky;
Beneath the rising moon seen far away,
Mountains of ice, like sapphire, piled on high,
Hemming the horizon round, in silence lay
On the still waters—these we did approach alway.

48

And swift and swifter grew the vessel's motion,
So that a dizzy trance fell on my brain—
Wild music woke me; we had passed the ocean
Which girds the pole, Nature's remotest reign—
And we glode fast o'er a pellucid plain
Of waters, azure with the noontide day.
Ethereal mountains shone around—a Fane
Stood in the midst, girt by green isles which lay
On the blue sunny deep, resplendent far away.

49

It was a Temple, such as mortal hand
Has never built, nor ecstasy, nor dream
Reared in the cities of enchanted land:
'Twas likest Heaven, ere yet day's purple stream
Ebbs o'er the western forest, while the gleam
Of the unrisen moon among the clouds
Is gathering—when with many a golden beam
The thronging constellations rush in crowds,
Paving with fire the sky and the marmoreal floods.

50

Like what may be conceived of this vast dome,
When from the depths which thought can seldom pierce
Genius beholds it rise, his native home,
Girt by the deserts of the Universe;
Yet, nor in painting's light, or mightier verse,
Or sculpture's marble language, can invest
That shape to mortal sense—such glooms immerse
That incommunicable sight, and rest
Upon the labouring brain and overburdened breast.

51

Winding among the lawny islands fair,
Whose blosmy forests starred the shadowy deep,
The wingless boat paused where an ivory stair
Its fretwork in the crystal sea did steep,
Encircling that vast Fane's aerial heap:
We disembarked, and through a portal wide
We passed—whose roof of moonstone carved, did keep
A glimmering o'er the forms on every side,
Sculptures like life and thought, immovable, deep-eyed.

52

We came to a vast hall, whose glorious roof
Was diamond, which had drunk the lightning's sheen
In darkness, and now poured it through the woof
Of spell-inwoven clouds hung there to screen
Its blinding splendour—through such veil was seen
That work of subtlest power, divine and rare;
Orb above orb, with starry shapes between,
And horned moons, and meteors strange and fair,
On night-black columns poised—one hollow hemisphere!

53

Ten thousand columns in that quivering light
Distinct—between whose shafts wound far away
The long and labyrinthine aisles—more bright
With their own radiance than the Heaven of Day;
And on the jasper walls around, there lay
Paintings, the poesy of mightiest thought,
Which did the Spirit's history display;
A tale of passionate change, divinely taught,
Which, in their winged dance, unconscious Genii wrought.

54

Beneath, there sate on many a sapphire throne,
The Great, who had departed from mankind,
A mighty Senate;—some, whose white hair shone
Like mountain snow, mild, beautiful, and blind;
Some, female forms, whose gestures beamed with mind;
And ardent youths, and children bright and fair;
And some had lyres whose strings were intertwined
With pale and clinging flames, which ever there
Waked faint yet thrilling sounds that pierced the crystal air.

55

One seat was vacant in the midst, a throne,
Reared on a pyramid like sculptured flame,
Distinct with circling steps which rested on
Their own deep fire—soon as the Woman came
Into that hall, she shrieked the Spirit's name
And fell; and vanished slowly from the sight.
Darkness arose from her dissolving frame,
Which gathering, filled that dome of woven light,
Blotting its sphered stars with supernatural night.

56

Then first, two glittering lights were seen to glide
In circles on the amethystine floor,
Small serpent eyes trailing from side to side,
Like meteors on a river's grassy shore,
They round each other rolled, dilating more
And more—then rose, commingling into one,
One clear and mighty planet hanging o'er
A cloud of deepest shadow, which was thrown
Athwart the glowing steps and the crystalline throne.

57

The cloud which rested on that cone of flame
Was cloven; beneath the planet sate a Form,
Fairer than tongue can speak or thought may frame,
The radiance of whose limbs rose-like and warm
Flowed forth, and did with softest light inform
The shadowy dome, the sculptures, and the state
Of those assembled shapes—with clinging charm
Sinking upon their hearts and mine. He sate
Majestic, yet most mild—calm, yet compassionate.

58

Wonder and joy a passing faintness threw
Over my brow—a hand supported me,
Whose touch was magic strength; an eye of blue
Looked into mine, like moonlight, soothingly;
And a voice said:—'Thou must a listener be
This day—two mighty Spirits now return,
Like birds of calm, from the world's raging sea,
They pour fresh light from Hope's immortal urn;
A tale of human power—despair not—list and learn!

59

I looked, and lo! one stood forth eloquently.
His eyes were dark and deep, and the clear brow
Which shadowed them was like the morning sky,
The cloudless Heaven of Spring, when in their flow
Through the bright air, the soft winds as they blow
Wake the green world—his gestures did obey
The oracular mind that made his features glow,
And where his curved lips half-open lay,
Passion's divinest stream had made impetuous way.

60

Beneath the darkness of his outspread hair
He stood thus beautiful; but there was One
Who sate beside him like his shadow there,
And held his hand—far lovelier; she was known
To be thus fair, by the few lines alone
Which through her floating locks and gathered cloak,
Glances of soul-dissolving glory, shone:—
None else beheld her eyes—in him they woke
Memories which found a tongue as thus he silence broke.

Canto 2

1

The starlight smile of children, the sweet looks
Of women, the fair breast from which I fed,
The murmur of the unreposing brooks,
And the green light which, shifting overhead,
Some tangled bower of vines around me shed,
The shells on the sea-sand, and the wild flowers,
The lamp-light through the rafters cheerly spread,
And on the twining flax—in life's young hours
These sights and sounds did nurse my spirit's folded powers.

2

In Argolis, beside the echoing sea,
Such impulses within my mortal frame
Arose, and they were dear to memory,
Like tokens of the dead:—but others came
Soon, in another shape: the wondrous fame
Of the past world, the vital words and deeds
Of minds whom neither time nor change can tame,
Traditions dark and old, whence evil creeds
Start forth, and whose dim shade a stream of poison feeds.

3

I heard, as all have heard, the various story
Of human life, and wept unwilling tears.
Feeble historians of its shame and glory,
False disputants on all its hopes and fears,
Victims who worshipped ruin, chroniclers
Of daily scorn, and slaves who loathed their state
Yet, flattering power, had given its ministers
A throne of judgement in the grave:—'twas fate,
That among such as these my youth should seek its mate.

4

The land in which I lived, by a fell bane
Was withered up. Tyrants dwelt side by side,
And stabled in our homes,—until the chain
Stifled the captive's cry, and to abide
That blasting curse men had no shame—all vied
In evil, slave and despot; fear with lust
Strange fellowship through mutual hate had tied,
Like two dark serpents tangled in the dust,
Which on the paths of men their mingling poison thrust.

5

Earth, our bright home, its mountains and its waters,
And the ethereal shapes which are suspended
Over its green expanse, and those fair daughters,
The clouds, of Sun and Ocean, who have blended
The colours of the air since first extended
It cradled the young world, none wandered forth
To see or feel; a darkness had descended
On every heart; the light which shows its worth,
Must among gentle thoughts and fearless take its birth.

6

This vital world, this home of happy spirits,
Was as a dungeon to my blasted kind;
All that despair from murdered hope inherits
They sought, and in their helpless misery blind,
A deeper prison and heavier chains did find,
And stronger tyrants:—a dark gulf before,
The realm of a stern Ruler, yawned; behind,
Terror and Time conflicting drove, and bore
On their tempestuous flood the shrieking wretch from shore.

7

Out of that Ocean's wrecks had Guilt and Woe
Framed a dark dwelling for their homeless thought,
And, starting at the ghosts which to and fro
Glide o'er its dim and gloomy strand, had brought
The worship thence which they each other taught.
Well might men loathe their life, well might they turn
Even to the ills again from which they sought
Such refuge after death!—well might they learn
To gaze on this fair world with hopeless unconcern!

8

For they all pined in bondage; body and soul,
Tyrant and slave, victim and torturer, bent
Before one Power, to which supreme control
Over their will by their own weakness lent,
Made all its many names omnipotent;
All symbols of things evil, all divine;
And hymns of blood or mockery, which rent
The air from all its fanes, did intertwine
Imposture's impious toils round each discordant shrine.

9

I heard, as all have heard, life's various story,
And in no careless heart transcribed the tale;
But, from the sneers of men who had grown hoary
In shame and scorn, from groans of crowds made pale
By famine, from a mother's desolate wail
O'er her polluted child, from innocent blood
Poured on the earth, and brows anxious and pale
With the heart's warfare, did I gather food
To feed my many thoughts—a tameless multitude!

10

I wandered through the wrecks of days departed
Far by the desolated shore, when even
O'er the still sea and jagged islets darted
The light of moonrise; in the northern Heaven,
Among the clouds near the horizon driven,
The mountains lay beneath one planet pale;
Around me, broken tombs and columns riven
Looked vast in twilight, and the sorrowing gale
Waked in those ruins gray its everlasting wail!

11

I knew not who had framed these wonders then,
Nor had I heard the story of their deeds;
But dwellings of a race of mightier men,
And monuments of less ungentle creeds
Tell their own tale to him who wisely heeds
The language which they speak; and now, to me
The moonlight making pale the blooming weeds,
The bright stars shining in the breathless sea,
Interpreted those scrolls of mortal mystery.

12

Such man has been, and such may yet become!
Ay, wiser, greater, gentler even than they
Who on the fragments of yon shattered dome
Have stamped the sign of power—I felt the sway
Of the vast stream of ages bear away
My floating thoughts—my heart beat loud and fast—
Even as a storm let loose beneath the ray
Of the still moon, my spirit onward passed
Beneath truth's steady beams upon its tumult cast.

13

It shall be thus no more! too long, too long,
Sons of the glorious dead, have ye lain bound
In darkness and in ruin!—Hope is strong,
Justice and Truth their winged child have found—
Awake! arise! until the mighty sound
Of your career shall scatter in its gust
The thrones of the oppressor, and the ground
Hide the last altar's unregarded dust,
Whose Idol has so long betrayed your impious trust!

14

It must be so—I will arise and waken
The multitude, and like a sulphurous hill,
Which on a sudden from its snows has shaken
The swoon of ages, it shall burst and fill
The world with cleansing fire; it must, it will—
It may not be restrained!—and who shall stand
Amid the rocking earthquake steadfast still,
But Laon? on high Freedom's desert land
A tower whose marble walls the leagued storms withstand!

15

One summer night, in commune with the hope
Thus deeply fed, amid those ruins gray
I watched, beneath the dark sky's starry cope;
And ever from that hour upon me lay
The burden of this hope, and night or day,
In vision or in dream, clove to my breast:
Among mankind, or when gone far away
To the lone shores and mountains, 'twas a guest
Which followed where I fled, and watched when I did rest.

16

These hopes found words through which my spirit sought
To weave a bondage of such sympathy,
As might create some response to the thought
Which ruled me now—and as the vapours lie
Bright in the outspread morning's radiancy,
So were these thoughts invested with the light
Of language: and all bosoms made reply
On which its lustre streamed, whene'er it might
Through darkness wide and deep those tranced spirits smite.

17

Yes, many an eye with dizzy tears was dim,
And oft I thought to clasp my own heart's brother,
When I could feel the listener's senses swim,
And hear his breath its own swift gaspings smother
Even as my words evoked them—and another,
And yet another, I did fondly deem,
Felt that we all were sons of one great mother;
And the cold truth such sad reverse did seem
As to awake in grief from some delightful dream.

18

Yes, oft beside the ruined labyrinth
Which skirts the hoary caves of the green deep,
Did Laon and his friend, on one gray plinth,
Round whose worn base the wild waves hiss and leap,
Resting at eve, a lofty converse keep:
And that this friend was false, may now be said
Calmly—that he like other men could weep
Tears which are lies, and could betray and spread
Snares for that guileless heart which for his own had bled.

19

Then, had no great aim recompensed my sorrow,
I must have sought dark respite from its stress
In dreamless rest, in sleep that sees no morrow—
For to tread life's dismaying wilderness
Without one smile to cheer, one voice to bless,
Amid the snares and scoffs of human kind,
Is hard—but I betrayed it not, nor less
With love that scorned return sought to unbind
The interwoven clouds which make its wisdom blind.

20

With deathless minds which leave where they have passed
A path of light, my soul communion knew;
Till from that glorious intercourse, at last,
As from a mine of magic store, I drew
Words which were weapons;—round my heart there grew
The adamantine armour of their power;
And from my fancy wings of golden hue
Sprang forth—yet not alone from wisdom's tower,
A minister of truth, these plumes young Laon bore.

21

An orphan with my parents lived, whose eyes
Were lodestars of delight, which drew me home
When I might wander forth; nor did I prize
Aught human thing beneath Heaven's mighty dome
Beyond this child; so when sad hours were come,
And baffled hope like ice still clung to me,
Since kin were cold, and friends had now become
Heartless and false, I turned from all, to be,
Cythna, the only source of tears and smiles to thee.

22

What wert thou then? A child most infantine,
Yet wandering far beyond that innocent age
In all but its sweet looks and mien divine;
Even then, methought, with the world's tyrant rage
A patient warfare thy young heart did wage,
When those soft eyes of scarcely conscious thought
Some tale, or thine own fancies, would engage
To overflow with tears, or converse fraught
With passion, o'er their depths its fleeting light had wrought.

23

She moved upon this earth a shape of brightness,
A power, that from its objects scarcely drew
One impulse of her being—in her lightness
Most like some radiant cloud of morning dew,
Which wanders through the waste air's pathless blue,
To nourish some far desert; she did seem
Beside me, gathering beauty as she grew,
Like the bright shade of some immortal dream
Which walks, when tempest sleeps, the wave of life's dark stream.

24

As mine own shadow was this child to me,
A second self, far dearer and more fair;
Which clothed in undissolving radiancy
All those steep paths which languor and despair
Of human things, had made so dark and bare,
But which I trod alone—nor, till bereft
Of friends, and overcome by lonely care,
Knew I what solace for that loss was left,
Though by a bitter wound my trusting heart was cleft.

25

Once she was dear, now she was all I had
To love in human life—this playmate sweet,
This child of twelve years old—so she was made
My sole associate, and her willing feet
Wandered with mine where earth and ocean meet,
Beyond the aereal mountains whose vast cells
The unreposing billows ever beat,
Through forests wild and old, and lawny dells
Where boughs of incense droop over the emerald wells.

26

And warm and light I felt her clasping hand
When twined in mine; she followed where I went,
Through the lone paths of our immortal land.
It had no waste but some memorial lent
Which strung me to my toil—some monument
Vital with mind; then Cythna by my side,
Until the bright and beaming day were spent,
Would rest, with looks entreating to abide,
Too earnest and too sweet ever to be denied.

27

And soon I could not have refused her—thus
For ever, day and night, we two were ne'er
Parted, but when brief sleep divided us:
And when the pauses of the lulling air
Of noon beside the sea had made a lair
For her soothed senses, in my arms she slept,
And I kept watch over her slumbers there,
While, as the shifting visions over her swept,
Amid her innocent rest by turns she smiled and wept.

28

And, in the murmur of her dreams was heard
Sometimes the name of Laon:—suddenly
She would arise, and, like the secret bird
Whom sunset wakens, fill the shore and sky
With her sweet accents, a wild melody!
Hymns which my soul had woven to Freedom, strong
The source of passion, whence they rose, to be;
Triumphant strains, which, like a spirit's tongue,
To the enchanted waves that child of glory sung—

29

Her white arms lifted through the shadowy stream
Of her loose hair. Oh, excellently great
Seemed to me then my purpose, the vast theme
Of those impassioned songs, when Cythna sate
Amid the calm which rapture doth create
After its tumult, her heart vibrating,
Her spirit o'er the Ocean's floating state
From her deep eyes far wandering, on the wing
Of visions that were mine, beyond its utmost spring!

30

For, before Cythna loved it, had my song
Peopled with thoughts the boundless universe,
A mighty congregation, which were strong
Where'er they trod the darkness to disperse
The cloud of that unutterable curse
Which clings upon mankind:—all things became
Slaves to my holy and heroic verse,
Earth, sea and sky, the planets, life and fame
And fate, or whate'er else binds the world's wondrous frame.

31

And this beloved child thus felt the sway
Of my conceptions, gathering like a cloud
The very wind on which it rolls away:
Hers too were all my thoughts, ere yet, endowed
With music and with light, their fountains flowed
In poesy; and her still and earnest face,
Pallid with feelings which intensely glowed
Within, was turned on mine with speechless grace,
Watching the hopes which there her heart had learned to trace.

32

In me, communion with this purest being
Kindled intenser zeal, and made me wise
In knowledge, which, in hers mine own mind seeing,
Left in the human world few mysteries:
How without fear of evil or disguise
Was Cythna!—what a spirit strong and mild,
Which death, or pain or peril could despise,
Yet melt in tenderness! what genius wild
Yet mighty, was enclosed within one simple child!

33

New lore was this—old age with its gray hair,
And wrinkled legends of unworthy things,
And icy sneers, is nought: it cannot dare
To burst the chains which life for ever flings
On the entangled soul's aspiring wings,
So is it cold and cruel, and is made
The careless slave of that dark power which brings
Evil, like blight, on man, who, still betrayed,
Laughs o'er the grave in which his living hopes are laid.

34

Nor are the strong and the severe to keep
The empire of the world: thus Cythna taught
Even in the visions of her eloquent sleep,
Unconscious of the power through which she wrought
The woof of such intelligible thought,
As from the tranquil strength which cradled lay
In her smile-peopled rest, my spirit sought
Why the deceiver and the slave has sway
O'er heralds so divine of truth's arising day.

35

Within that fairest form, the female mind,
Untainted by the poison clouds which rest
On the dark world, a sacred home did find:
But else, from the wide earth's maternal breast,
Victorious Evil, which had dispossessed
All native power, had those fair children torn,
And made them slaves to soothe his vile unrest,
And minister to lust its joys forlorn,
Till they had learned to breathe the atmosphere of scorn.

36

This misery was but coldly felt, till she
Became my only friend, who had endued
My purpose with a wider sympathy;
Thus, Cythna mourned with me the servitude
In which the half of humankind were mewed
Victims of lust and hate, the slaves of slaves,
She mourned that grace and power were thrown as food
To the hyena lust, who, among graves,
Over his loathed meal, laughing in agony, raves.

37

And I, still gazing on that glorious child,
Even as these thoughts flushed o'er her:—'Cythna sweet,
Well with the world art thou unreconciled;
Never will peace and human nature meet
Till free and equal man and woman greet
Domestic peace; and ere this power can make
In human hearts its calm and holy seat,
This slavery must be broken'—as I spake,
From Cythna's eyes a light of exultation brake.

38

She replied earnestly:—'It shall be mine,
This task,—mine, Laon!—thou hast much to gain;
Nor wilt thou at poor Cythna's pride repine,
If she should lead a happy female train
To meet thee over the rejoicing plain,
When myriads at thy call shall throng around
The Golden City.'—Then the child did strain
My arm upon her tremulous heart, and wound
Her own about my neck, till some reply she found.

39

I smiled, and spake not.—'Wherefore dost thou smile
At what I say? Laon, I am not weak,
And, though my cheek might become pale the while,
With thee, if thou desirest, will I seek
Through their array of banded slaves to wreak
Ruin upon the tyrants. I had thought
It was more hard to turn my unpractised cheek
To scorn and shame, and this beloved spot
And thee, O dearest friend, to leave and murmur not.

40

'Whence came I what I am? Thou, Laon, knowest
How a young child should thus undaunted be;
Methinks, it is a power which thou bestowest,
Through which I seek, by most resembling thee,
So to become most good and great and free;
Yet far beyond this Ocean's utmost roar,
In towers and huts are many like to me,
Who, could they see thine eyes, or feel such lore
As I have learnt from them, like me would fear no more.

41

'Think'st thou that I shall speak unskilfully,
And none will heed me? I remember now,
How once, a slave in tortures doomed to die,
Was saved, because in accents sweet and low
He sung a song his Judge loved long ago,
As he was led to death.—All shall relent
Who hear me—tears, as mine have flowed, shall flow,
Hearts beat as mine now beats, with such intent
As renovates the world; a will omnipotent!

42

'Yes, I will tread Pride's golden palaces,
Through Penury's roofless huts and squalid cells
Will I descend, where'er in abjectness
Woman with some vile slave her tyrant dwells,
There with the music of thine own sweet spells
Will disenchant the captives, and will pour
For the despairing, from the crystal wells
Of thy deep spirit, reason's mighty lore,
And power shall then abound, and hope arise once more.

43

'Can man be free if woman be a slave?
Chain one who lives, and breathes this boundless air,
To the corruption of a closed grave!
Can they whose mates are beasts, condemned to bear
Scorn, heavier far than toil or anguish, dare
To trample their oppressors? in their home
Among their babes, thou knowest a curse would wear
The shape of woman—hoary Crime would come
Behind, and Fraud rebuild religion's tottering dome.

44

'I am a child:—I would not yet depart.
When I go forth alone, bearing the lamp
Aloft which thou hast kindled in my heart,
Millions of slaves from many a dungeon damp
Shall leap in joy, as the benumbing cramp
Of ages leaves their limbs—no ill may harm
Thy Cythna ever—truth its radiant stamp
Has fixed, as an invulnerable charm,
Upon her children's brow, dark Falsehood to disarm.

45

'Wait yet awhile for the appointed day—
Thou wilt depart, and I with tears shall stand
Watching thy dim sail skirt the ocean gray;
Amid the dwellers of this lonely land
I shall remain alone—and thy command
Shall then dissolve the world's unquiet trance,
And, multitudinous as the desert sand
Borne on the storm, its millions shall advance,
Thronging round thee, the light of their deliverance.

46

'Then, like the forests of some pathless mountain,
Which from remotest glens two warring winds
Involve in fire which not the loosened fountain
Of broadest floods might quench, shall all the kinds
Of evil, catch from our uniting minds
The spark which must consume them;—Cythna then
Will have cast off the impotence that binds
Her childhood now, and through the paths of men
Will pass, as the charmed bird that haunts the serpent's den.

47

'We part!—O Laon, I must dare nor tremble,
To meet those looks no more!—Oh, heavy stroke!
Sweet brother of my soul! can I dissemble
The agony of this thought?'—As thus she spoke
The gathered sobs her quivering accents broke,
And in my arms she hid her beating breast.
I remained still for tears—sudden she woke
As one awakes from sleep, and wildly pressed
My bosom, her whole frame impetuously possessed.

48

'We part to meet again—but yon blue waste,
Yon desert wide and deep, holds no recess,
Within whose happy silence, thus embraced
We might survive all ills in one caress:
Nor doth the grave—I fear 'tis passionless—
Nor yon cold vacant Heaven:—we meet again
Within the minds of men, whose lips shall bless
Our memory, and whose hopes its light retain
When these dissevered bones are trodden in the plain.'

49

I could not speak, though she had ceased, for now
The fountains of her feeling, swift and deep,
Seemed to suspend the tumult of their flow;
So we arose, and by the starlight steep
Went homeward—neither did we speak nor weep,
But, pale, were calm with passion—thus subdued
Like evening shades that o'er the mountains creep,
We moved towards our home; where, in this mood,
Each from the other sought refuge in solitude.

Canto 3

1

What thoughts had sway o'er Cythna's lonely slumber
That night, I know not; but my own did seem
As if they might ten thousand years outnumber
Of waking life, the visions of a dream
Which hid in one dim gulf the troubled stream
Of mind; a boundless chaos wild and vast,
Whose limits yet were never memory's theme:
And I lay struggling as its whirlwinds passed,
Sometimes for rapture sick, sometimes for pain aghast.

2

Two hours, whose mighty circle did embrace
More time than might make gray the infant world,
Rolled thus, a weary and tumultuous space:
When the third came, like mist on breezes curled,
From my dim sleep a shadow was unfurled:
Methought, upon the threshold of a cave
I sate with Cythna; drooping briony, pearled
With dew from the wild streamlet's shattered wave,
Hung, where we sate to taste the joys which Nature gave.

3

We lived a day as we were wont to live,
But Nature had a robe of glory on,
And the bright air o'er every shape did weave
Intenser hues, so that the herbless stone,
The leafless bough among the leaves alone,
Had being clearer than its own could be,
And Cythna's pure and radiant self was shown,
In this strange vision, so divine to me,
That if I loved before, now love was agony.

4

Morn fled, noon came, evening, then night descended,
And we prolonged calm talk beneath the sphere
Of the calm moon—when suddenly was blended
With our repose a nameless sense of fear;
And from the cave behind I seemed to hear
Sounds gathering upwards!—accents incomplete,
And stifled shrieks,—and now, more near and near,
A tumult and a rush of thronging feet
The cavern's secret depths beneath the earth did beat.

5

The scene was changed, and away, away, away!
Through the air and over the sea we sped,
And Cythna in my sheltering bosom lay,
And the winds bore me—through the darkness spread
Around, the gaping earth then vomited
Legions of foul and ghastly shapes, which hung
Upon my flight; and ever, as we fled,
They plucked at Cythna—soon to me then clung
A sense of actual things those monstrous dreams among.

6

And I lay struggling in the impotence
Of sleep, while outward life had burst its bound,
Though, still deluded, strove the tortured sense
To its dire wanderings to adapt the sound
Which in the light of morn was poured around
Our dwelling; breathless, pale and unaware
I rose, and all the cottage crowded found
With armed men, whose glittering swords were bare,
And whose degraded limbs the tyrant's garb did wear.

7

And, ere with rapid lips and gathered brow
I could demand the cause—a feeble shriek—
It was a feeble shriek, faint, far and low,
Arrested me—my mien grew calm and meek,
And grasping a small knife, I went to seek
That voice among the crowd—'twas Cythna's cry!
Beneath most calm resolve did agony wreak
Its whirlwind rage:—so I passed quietly
Till I beheld, where bound, that dearest child did lie.

8

I started to behold her, for delight
And exultation, and a joyance free,
Solemn, serene and lofty, filled the light
Of the calm smile with which she looked on me:
So that I feared some brainless ecstasy,
Wrought from that bitter woe, had wildered her—
'Farewell! farewell!' she said, as I drew nigh;
'At first my peace was marred by this strange stir,
Now I am calm as truth—its chosen minister.

9

'Look not so, Laon—say farewell in hope,
These bloody men are but the slaves who bear
Their mistress to her task—it was my scope
The slavery where they drag me now, to share,
And among captives willing chains to wear
Awhile—the rest thou knowest—return, dear friend!
Let our first triumph trample the despair
Which would ensnare us now, for in the end,
In victory or in death our hopes and fears must blend.'

10

These words had fallen on my unheeding ear,
Whilst I had watched the motions of the crew
With seeming-careless glance; not many were
Around her, for their comrades just withdrew
To guard some other victim—so I drew
My knife, and with one impulse, suddenly
All unaware three of their number slew,
And grasped a fourth by the throat, and with loud cry
My countrymen invoked to death or liberty!

11

What followed then, I know not—for a stroke
On my raised arm and naked head, came down,
Filling my eyes with blood.—When I awoke,
I felt that they had bound me in my swoon,
And up a rock which overhangs the town,
By the steep path were bearing me; below,
The plain was filled with slaughter,—overthrown
The vineyards and the harvests, and the glow
Of blazing roofs shone far o'er the white Ocean's flow.

12

Upon that rock a mighty column stood,
Whose capital seemed sculptured in the sky,
Which to the wanderers o'er the solitude
Of distant seas, from ages long gone by,
Had made a landmark; o'er its height to fly
Scarcely the cloud, the vulture, or the blast,
Has power—and when the shades of evening lie
On Earth and Ocean, its carved summits cast
The sunken daylight far through the aerial waste.

13

They bore me to a cavern in the hill
Beneath that column, and unbound me there;
And one did strip me stark; and one did fill
A vessel from the putrid pool; one bare
A lighted torch, and four with friendless care
Guided my steps the cavern-paths along,
Then up a steep and dark and narrow stair
We wound, until the torch's fiery tongue
Amid the gushing day beamless and pallid hung.

14

They raised me to the platform of the pile,
That column's dizzy height:—the grate of brass
Through which they thrust me, open stood the while,
As to its ponderous and suspended mass,
With chains which eat into the flesh, alas!
With brazen links, my naked limbs they bound:
The grate, as they departed to repass,
With horrid clangour fell, and the far sound
Of their retiring steps in the dense gloom was drowned.

15

The noon was calm and bright:—around that column
The overhanging sky and circling sea
Spread forth in silentness profound and solemn
The darkness of brief frenzy cast on me,
So that I knew not my own misery:
The islands and the mountains in the day
Like clouds reposed afar; and I could see
The town among the woods below that lay,
And the dark rocks which bound the bright and glassy bay.

16

It was so calm, that scarce the feathery weed
Sown by some eagle on the topmost stone
Swayed in the air:—so bright, that noon did breed
No shadow in the sky beside mine own—
Mine, and the shadow of my chain alone.
Below, the smoke of roofs involved in flame
Rested like night, all else was clearly shown
In that broad glare; yet sound to me none came,
But of the living blood that ran within my frame.

17

The peace of madness fled, and ah, too soon!
A ship was lying on the sunny main,
Its sails were flagging in the breathless noon—
Its shadow lay beyond—that sight again
Waked, with its presence, in my tranced brain
The stings of a known sorrow, keen and cold:
I knew that ship bore Cythna o'er the plain
Of waters, to her blighting slavery sold,
And watched it with such thoughts as must remain untold.

18

I watched until the shades of evening wrapped
Earth like an exhalation—then the bark
Moved, for that calm was by the sunset snapped.
It moved a speck upon the Ocean dark:
Soon the wan stars came forth, and I could mark
Its path no more!—I sought to close mine eyes,
But like the balls, their lids were stiff and stark;
I would have risen, but ere that I could rise,
My parched skin was split with piercing agonies.

19

I gnawed my brazen chain, and sought to sever
Its adamantine links, that I might die:
O Liberty! forgive the base endeavour,
Forgive me, if, reserved for victory,
The Champion of thy faith e'er sought to fly.—
That starry night, with its clear silence, sent
Tameless resolve which laughed at misery
Into my soul—linked remembrance lent
To that such power, to me such a severe content.

20

To breathe, to be, to hope, or to despair
And die, I questioned not; nor, though the Sun
Its shafts of agony kindling through the air
Moved over me, nor though in evening dun,
Or when the stars their visible courses run,
Or morning, the wide universe was spread
In dreary calmness round me, did I shun
Its presence, nor seek refuge with the dead
From one faint hope whose flower a dropping poison shed.

21

Two days thus passed—I neither raved nor died—
Thirst raged within me, like a scorpion's nest
Built in mine entrails; I had spurned aside
The water-vessel, while despair possessed
My thoughts, and now no drop remained! The uprest
Of the third sun brought hunger—but the crust
Which had been left, was to my craving breast
Fuel, not food. I chewed the bitter dust,
And bit my bloodless arm, and licked the brazen rust.

22

My brain began to fail when the fourth morn
Burst o'er the golden isles—a fearful sleep,
Which through the caverns dreary and forlorn
Of the riven soul, sent its foul dreams to sweep
With whirlwind swiftness—a fall far and deep,—
A gulf, a void, a sense of senselessness—
These things dwelt in me, even as shadows keep
Their watch in some dim charnel's loneliness,
A shoreless sea, a sky sunless and planetless!

23

The forms which peopled this terrific trance
I well remember—like a choir of devils,
Around me they involved a giddy dance;
Legions seemed gathering from the misty levels
Of Ocean, to supply those ceaseless revels,
Foul, ceaseless shadows:—thought could not divide
The actual world from these entangling evils,
Which so bemocked themselves, that I descried
All shapes like mine own self, hideously multiplied.

24

The sense of day and night, of false and true,
Was dead within me. Yet two visions burst
That darkness—one, as since that hour I knew,
Was not a phantom of the realms accursed,
Where then my spirit dwelt—but of the first
I know not yet, was it a dream or no.
But both, though not distincter, were immersed
In hues which, when through memory's waste they flow,
Make their divided streams more bright and rapid now.

25

Methought that grate was lifted, and the seven
Who brought me thither four stiff corpses bare,
And from the frieze to the four winds of Heaven
Hung them on high by the entangled hair;
Swarthy were three—the fourth was very fair;
As they retired, the golden moon upsprung,
And eagerly, out in the giddy air,
Leaning that I might eat, I stretched and clung
Over the shapeless depth in which those corpses hung.

26

A woman's shape, now lank and cold and blue,
The dwelling of the many-coloured worm,
Hung there; the white and hollow cheek I drew
To my dry lips—what radiance did inform
Those horny eyes? whose was that withered form?
Alas, alas! it seemed that Cythna's ghost
Laughed in those looks, and that the flesh was warm
Within my teeth!—a whirlwind keen as frost
Then in its sinking gulfs my sickening spirit tossed.

27

Then seemed it that a tameless hurricane
Arose, and bore me in its dark career
Beyond the sun, beyond the stars that wane
On the verge of formless space—it languished there,
And dying, left a silence lone and drear,
More horrible than famine:—in the deep
The shape of an old man did then appear,
Stately and beautiful; that dreadful sleep
His heavenly smiles dispersed, and I could wake and weep.

28

And, when the blinding tears had fallen, I saw
That column, and those corpses, and the moon,
And felt the poisonous tooth of hunger gnaw
My vitals, I rejoiced, as if the boon
Of senseless death would be accorded soon;—
When from that stony gloom a voice arose,
Solemn and sweet as when low winds attune
The midnight pines; the grate did then unclose,
And on that reverend form the moonlight did repose.

29

He struck my chains, and gently spake and smiled;
As they were loosened by that Hermit old,
Mine eyes were of their madness half beguiled,
To answer those kind looks; he did enfold
His giant arms around me, to uphold
My wretched frame; my scorched limbs he wound
In linen moist and balmy, and as cold
As dew to drooping leaves;—the chain, with sound
Like earthquake, through the chasm of that steep stair did bound,

30

As, lifting me, it fell!—What next I heard,
Were billows leaping on the harbour-bar,
And the shrill sea-wind, whose breath idly stirred
My hair;—I looked abroad, and saw a star
Shining beside a sail, and distant far
That mountain and its column, the known mark
Of those who in the wide deep wandering are,
So that I feared some Spirit, fell and dark,
In trance had lain me thus within a fiendish bark.

31

For now indeed, over the salt sea-billow
I sailed: yet dared not look upon the shape
Of him who ruled the helm, although the pillow
For my light head was hollowed in his lap,
And my bare limbs his mantle did enwrap,
Fearing it was a fiend: at last, he bent
O'er me his aged face; as if to snap
Those dreadful thoughts the gentle grandsire bent,
And to my inmost soul his soothing looks he sent.

32

A soft and healing potion to my lips
At intervals he raised—now looked on high,
To mark if yet the starry giant dips
His zone in the dim sea—now cheeringly,
Though he said little, did he speak to me.
'It is a friend beside thee—take good cheer,
Poor victim, thou art now at liberty!'
I joyed as those a human tone to hear,
Who in cells deep and lone have languished many a year.

33

A dim and feeble joy, whose glimpses oft
Were quenched in a relapse of wildering dreams;
Yet still methought we sailed, until aloft
The stars of night grew pallid, and the beams
Of morn descended on the ocean-streams,
And still that aged man, so grand and mild,
Tended me, even as some sick mother seems
To hang in hope over a dying child,
Till in the azure East darkness again was piled.

34

And then the night-wind steaming from the shore,
Sent odours dying sweet across the sea,
And the swift boat the little waves which bore,
Were cut by its keen keel, though slantingly;
Soon I could hear the leaves sigh, and could see
The myrtle-blossoms starring the dim grove,
As past the pebbly beach the boat did flee
On sidelong wing, into a silent cove,
Where ebon pines a shade under the starlight wove.

Canto 4

1

The old man took the oars, and soon the bark
Smote on the beach beside a tower of stone;
It was a crumbling heap, whose portal dark
With blooming ivy-trails was overgrown;
Upon whose floor the spangling sands were strown,
And rarest sea-shells, which the eternal flood,
Slave to the mother of the months, had thrown
Within the walls of that gray tower, which stood
A changeling of man's art nursed amid Nature's brood.

2

When the old man his boat had anchored,
He wound me in his arms with tender care,
And very few, but kindly words he said,
And bore me through the tower adown a stair,
Whose smooth descent some ceaseless step to wear
For many a year had fallen.—We came at last
To a small chamber, which with mosses rare
Was tapestried, where me his soft hands placed
Upon a couch of grass and oak-leaves interlaced.

3

The moon was darting through the lattices
Its yellow light, warm as the beams of day—
So warm, that to admit the dewy breeze,
The old man opened them; the moonlight lay
Upon a lake whose waters wove their play
Even to the threshold of that lonely home:
Within was seen in the dim wavering ray
The antique sculptured roof, and many a tome
Whose lore had made that sage all that he had become.

4

The rock-built barrier of the sea was past,—
And I was on the margin of a lake,
A lonely lake, amid the forests vast
And snowy mountains:—did my spirit wake
From sleep as many-coloured as the snake
That girds eternity? in life and truth,
Might not my heart its cravings ever slake?
Was Cythna then a dream, and all my youth,
And all its hopes and fears, and all its joy and ruth?

5

Thus madness came again,—a milder madness,
Which darkened nought but time's unquiet flow
With supernatural shades of clinging sadness;
That gentle Hermit, in my helpless woe,
By my sick couch was busy to and fro,
Like a strong spirit ministrant of good:
When I was healed, he led me forth to show
The wonders of his sylvan solitude,
And we together sate by that isle-fretted flood.

6

He knew his soothing words to weave with skill
From all my madness told; like mine own heart,
Of Cythna would he question me, until
That thrilling name had ceased to make me start,
From his familiar lips—it was not art,
Of wisdom and of justice when he spoke—
When mid soft looks of pity, there would dart
A glance as keen as is the lightning's stroke
When it doth rive the knots of some ancestral oak.

7

Thus slowly from my brain the darkness rolled,
My thoughts their due array did re-assume
Through the enchantments of that Hermit old;
Then I bethought me of the glorious doom
Of those who sternly struggle to relume
The lamp of Hope o'er man's bewildered lot,
And, sitting by the waters, in the gloom
Of eve, to that friend's heart I told my thought—
That heart which had grown old, but had corrupted not.

8

That hoary man had spent his livelong age
In converse with the dead, who leave the stamp
Of ever-burning thoughts on many a page,
When they are gone into the senseless damp
Of graves;—his spirit thus became a lamp
Of splendour, like to those on which it fed;
Through peopled haunts, the City and the Camp,
Deep thirst for knowledge had his footsteps led,
And all the ways of men among mankind he read.

9

But custom maketh blind and obdurate
The loftiest hearts;—he had beheld the woe
In which mankind was bound, but deemed that fate
Which made them abject, would preserve them so;
And in such faith, some steadfast joy to know,
He sought this cell: but when fame went abroad
That one in Argolis did undergo
Torture for liberty, and that the crowd
High truths from gifted lips had heard and understood;

10

And that the multitude was gathering wide,—
His spirit leaped within his aged frame;
In lonely peace he could no more abide,
But to the land on which the victor's flame
Had fed, my native land, the Hermit came:
Each heart was there a shield, and every tongue
Was as a sword of truth—young Laon's name
Rallied their secret hopes, though tyrants sung
Hymns of triumphant joy our scattered tribes among.

11

He came to the lone column on the rock,
And with his sweet and mighty eloquence
The hearts of those who watched it did unlock,
And made them melt in tears of penitence.
They gave him entrance free to bear me thence.
'Since this,' the old man said, 'seven years are spent,
While slowly truth on thy benighted sense
Has crept; the hope which wildered it has lent
Meanwhile, to me the power of a sublime intent.

12

'Yes, from the records of my youthful state,
And from the lore of bards and sages old,
From whatsoe'er my wakened thoughts create
Out of the hopes of thine aspirings bold,
Have I collected language to unfold
Truth to my countrymen; from shore to shore
Doctrines of human power my words have told,
They have been heard, and men aspire to more
Than they have ever gained or ever lost of yore.

13

'In secret chambers parents read, and weep,
My writings to their babes, no longer blind;
And young men gather when their tyrants sleep,
And vows of faith each to the other bind;
And marriageable maidens, who have pined
With love, till life seemed melting through their look,
A warmer zeal, a nobler hope, now find;
And every bosom thus is rapt and shook,
Like autumn's myriad leaves in one swoln mountain-brook.

14

'The tyrants of the Golden City tremble
At voices which are heard about the streets;
The ministers of fraud can scarce dissemble
The lies of their own heart, but when one meets
Another at the shrine, he inly weets,
Though he says nothing, that the truth is known;
Murderers are pale upon the judgement-seats,
And gold grows vile even to the wealthy crone,
And laughter fills the Fane, and curses shake the Throne.

15

'Kind thoughts, and mighty hopes, and gentle deeds
Abound, for fearless love, and the pure law
Of mild equality and peace, succeeds
To faiths which long have held the world in awe,
Bloody and false, and cold:—as whirlpools draw
All wrecks of Ocean to their chasm, the sway
Of thy strong genius, Laon, which foresaw
This hope, compels all spirits to obey,
Which round thy secret strength now throng in wide array.

16

'For I have been thy passive instrument'—
(As thus the old man spake, his countenance
Gleamed on me like a spirit's)—'thou hast lent
To me, to all, the power to advance
Towards this unforeseen deliverance
From our ancestral chains—ay, thou didst rear
That lamp of hope on high, which time nor chance
Nor change may not extinguish, and my share
Of good, was o'er the world its gathered beams to bear.

17

'But I, alas! am both unknown and old,
And though the woof of wisdom I know well
To dye in hues of language, I am cold
In seeming, and the hopes which inly dwell,
My manners note that I did long repel;
But Laon's name to the tumultuous throng
Were like the star whose beams the waves compel
And tempests, and his soul-subduing tongue
Were as a lance to quell the mailed crest of wrong.

18

'Perchance blood need not flow, if thou at length
Wouldst rise, perchance the very slaves would spare
Their brethren and themselves; great is the strength
Of words—for lately did a maiden fair,
Who from her childhood has been taught to bear
The Tyrant's heaviest yoke, arise, and make
Her sex the law of truth and freedom hear,
And with these quiet words—"for thine own sake
I prithee spare me;"—did with ruth so take.

19

'All hearts, that even the torturer who had bound
Her meek calm frame, ere it was yet impaled,
Loosened her, weeping then; nor could be found
One human hand to harm her—unassailed
Therefore she walks through the great City, veiled
In virtue's adamantine eloquence,
'Gainst scorn, and death and pain thus trebly mailed,
And blending, in the smiles of that defence,
The Serpent and the Dove, Wisdom and Innocence.

20

'The wild-eyed women throng around her path:
From their luxurious dungeons, from the dust
Of meaner thralls, from the oppressor's wrath,
Or the caresses of his sated lust
They congregate:—in her they put their trust;
The tyrants send their armed slaves to quell
Her power;—they, even like a thunder-gust
Caught by some forest, bend beneath the spell
Of that young maiden's speech, and to their chiefs rebel.

21

'Thus she doth equal laws and justice teach
To woman, outraged and polluted long;
Gathering the sweetest fruit in human reach
For those fair hands now free, while armed wrong
Trembles before her look, though it be strong;
Thousands thus dwell beside her, virgins bright,
And matrons with their babes, a stately throng!
Lovers renew the vows which they did plight
In early faith, and hearts long parted now unite.

22

'And homeless orphans find a home near her,
And those poor victims of the proud, no less,
Fair wrecks, on whom the smiling world with stir,
Thrusts the redemption of its wickedness:—
In squalid huts, and in its palaces
Sits Lust alone, while o'er the land is borne
Her voice, whose awful sweetness doth repress
All evil, and her foes relenting turn,
And cast the vote of love in hope's abandoned urn.

23

'So in the populous City, a young maiden
Has baffled Havoc of the prey which he
Marks as his own, whene'er with chains o'erladen
Men make them arms to hurl down tyranny,—
False arbiter between the bound and free;
And o'er the land, in hamlets and in towns
The multitudes collect tumultuously,
And throng in arms; but tyranny disowns
Their claim, and gathers strength around its trembling thrones.

24

'Blood soon, although unwillingly, to shed
The free cannot forbear—the Queen of Slaves,
The hoodwinked Angel of the blind and dead,
Custom, with iron mace points to the graves
Where her own standard desolately waves
Over the dust of Prophets and of Kings.
Many yet stand in her array—"she paves
Her path with human hearts," and o'er it flings
The wildering gloom of her immeasurable wings.

25

'There is a plain beneath the City's wall,
Bounded by misty mountains, wide and vast,
Millions there lift at Freedom's thrilling call
Ten thousand standards wide, they load the blast
Which bears one sound of many voices past,
And startles on his throne their sceptred foe:
He sits amid his idle pomp aghast,
And that his power hath passed away, doth know—
Why pause the victor swords to seal his overthrow?

26

'The tyrant's guards resistance yet maintain:
Fearless, and fierce, and hard as beasts of blood,
They stand a speck amid the peopled plain;
Carnage and ruin have been made their food
From infancy—ill has become their good,
And for its hateful sake their will has wove
The chains which eat their hearts. The multitude
Surrounding them, with words of human love,
Seek from their own decay their stubborn minds to move.

27

'Over the land is felt a sudden pause,
As night and day those ruthless bands around,
The watch of love is kept:—a trance which awes
The thoughts of men with hope; as when the sound
Of whirlwind, whose fierce blasts the waves and clouds confound,
Dies suddenly, the mariner in fear
Feels silence sink upon his heart—thus bound,
The conquerors pause, and oh! may freemen ne'er
Clasp the relentless knees of Dread, the murderer!

28

'If blood be shed, 'tis but a change and choice
Of bonds,—from slavery to cowardice
A wretched fall!—Uplift thy charmed voice!
Pour on those evil men the love that lies
Hovering within those spirit-soothing eyes—
Arise, my friend, farewell!'—As thus he spake,
From the green earth lightly I did arise,
As one out of dim dreams that doth awake,
And looked upon the depth of that reposing lake.

29

I saw my countenance reflected there;—
And then my youth fell on me like a wind
Descending on still waters—my thin hair
Was prematurely gray, my face was lined
With channels, such as suffering leaves behind,
Not age; my brow was pale, but in my cheek
And lips a flush of gnawing fire did find
Their food and dwelling; though mine eyes might speak
A subtle mind and strong within a frame thus weak.

30

And though their lustre now was spent and faded,
Yet in my hollow looks and withered mien
The likeness of a shape for which was braided
The brightest woof of genius, still was seen—
One who, methought, had gone from the world's scene,
And left it vacant—'twas her lover's face—
It might resemble her—it once had been
The mirror of her thoughts, and still the grace
Which her mind's shadow cast, left there a lingering trace.

31

What then was I? She slumbered with the dead.
Glory and joy and peace, had come and gone.
Doth the cloud perish, when the beams are fled
Which steeped its skirts in gold? or, dark and lone,
Doth it not through the paths of night unknown,
On outspread wings of its own wind upborne
Pour rain upon the earth? The stars are shown,
When the cold moon sharpens her silver horn
Under the sea, and make the wide night not forlorn.

32

Strengthened in heart, yet sad, that aged man
I left, with interchange of looks and tears,
And lingering speech, and to the Camp began
My war. O'er many a mountain-chain which rears
Its hundred crests aloft, my spirit bears
My frame; o'er many a dale and many a moor,
And gaily now meseems serene earth wears
The blosmy spring's star-bright investiture,
A vision which aught sad from sadness might allure.

33

My powers revived within me, and I went,
As one whom winds waft o'er the bending grass,
Through many a vale of that broad continent.
At night when I reposed, fair dreams did pass
Before my pillow;—my own Cythna was,
Not like a child of death, among them ever;
When I arose from rest, a woful mass
That gentlest sleep seemed from my life to sever,
As if the light of youth were not withdrawn for ever.

34

Aye as I went, that maiden who had reared
The torch of Truth afar, of whose high deeds
The Hermit in his pilgrimage had heard,
Haunted my thoughts.—Ah, Hope its sickness feeds
With whatsoe'er it finds, or flowers or weeds!
Could she be Cythna?—Was that corpse a shade
Such as self-torturing thought from madness breeds?
Why was this hope not torture? Yet it made
A light around my steps which would not ever fade.

Canto 5

1

Over the utmost hill at length I sped,
A snowy steep:—the moon was hanging low
Over the Asian mountains, and outspread
The plain, the City, and the Camp below,
Skirted the midnight Ocean's glimmering flow;
The City's moonlit spires and myriad lamps,
Like stars in a sublunar sky did glow,
And fires blazed far amid the scattered camps,
Like springs of flame, which burst where'er swift Earthquake stamps.

2

All slept but those in watchful arms who stood,
And those who sate tending the beacon's light,
And the few sounds from that vast multitude
Made silence more profound.—Oh, what a might
Of human thought was cradled in that night!
How many hearts impenetrably veiled
Beat underneath its shade, what secret fight
Evil and good, in woven passions mailed,
Waged through that silent throng—a war that never failed!

3

And now the Power of Good held victory.
So, through the labyrinth of many a tent,
Among the silent millions who did lie
In innocent sleep, exultingly I went;
The moon had left Heaven desert now, but lent
From eastern morn the first faint lustre showed
An armed youth—over his spear he bent
His downward face.—'A friend!' I cried aloud,
And quickly common hopes made freemen understood.

4

I sate beside him while the morning beam
Crept slowly over Heaven, and talked with him
Of those immortal hopes, a glorious theme!
Which led us forth, until the stars grew dim:
And all the while, methought, his voice did swim
As if it drowned in remembrance were
Of thoughts which make the moist eyes overbrim:
At last, when daylight 'gan to fill the air,
He looked on me, and cried in wonder—'Thou art here!'

5

Then, suddenly, I knew it was the youth
In whom its earliest hopes my spirit found;
But envious tongues had stained his spotless truth,
And thoughtless pride his love in silence bound,
And shame and sorrow mine in toils had wound,
Whilst he was innocent, and I deluded;
The truth now came upon me, on the ground
Tears of repenting joy, which fast intruded,
Fell fast, and o'er its peace our mingling spirits brooded.

6

Thus, while with rapid lips and earnest eyes
We talked, a sound of sweeping conflict spread
As from the earth did suddenly arise;
From every tent roused by that clamour dread,
Our bands outsprung and seized their arms—we sped
Towards the sound: our tribes were gathering far.
Those sanguine slaves amid ten thousand dead
Stabbed in their sleep, trampled in treacherous war
The gentle hearts whose power their lives had sought to spare.

7

Like rabid snakes, that sting some gentle child
Who brings them food, when winter false and fair
Allures them forth with its cold smiles, so wild
They rage among the camp;—they overbear
The patriot hosts—confusion, then despair,
Descends like night—when 'Laon!' one did cry;
Like a bright ghost from Heaven that shout did scare
The slaves, and widening through the vaulted sky,
Seemed sent from Earth to Heaven in sign of victory.

8

In sudden panic those false murderers fled,
Like insect tribes before the northern gale:
But swifter still, our hosts encompassed
Their shattered ranks, and in a craggy vale,
Where even their fierce despair might nought avail,
Hemmed them around!—and then revenge and fear
Made the high virtue of the patriots fail:
One pointed on his foe the mortal spear—
I rushed before its point, and cried 'Forbear, forbear!'

9

The spear transfixed my arm that was uplifted
In swift expostulation, and the blood
Gushed round its point: I smiled, and—'Oh! thou gifted
With eloquence which shall not be withstood,
Flow thus!' I cried in joy, 'thou vital flood,
Until my heart be dry, ere thus the cause
For which thou wert aught worthy be subdued—
Ah, ye are pale,—ye weep,—your passions pause,—
'Tis well! ye feel the truth of love's benignant laws.

10

'Soldiers, our brethren and our friends are slain.
Ye murdered them, I think, as they did sleep!
Alas, what have ye done? the slightest pain
Which ye might suffer, there were eyes to weep,
But ye have quenched them—there were smiles to steep
Your hearts in balm, but they are lost in woe;
And those whom love did set his watch to keep
Around your tents, truth's freedom to bestow,
Ye stabbed as they did sleep—but they forgive ye now.

11

'Oh wherefore should ill ever flow from ill,
And pain still keener pain for ever breed?
We all are brethren—even the slaves who kill
For hire, are men; and to avenge misdeed
On the misdoer, doth but Misery feed
With her own broken heart! O Earth, O Heaven!
And thou, dread Nature, which to every deed
And all that lives, or is, to be hath given,
Even as to thee have these done ill, and are forgiven!

12

'Join then your hands and hearts, and let the past
Be as a grave which gives not up its dead
To evil thoughts.'—A film then overcast
My sense with dimness, for the wound, which bled
Freshly, swift shadows o'er mine eyes had shed.
When I awoke, I lay mid friends and foes,
And earnest countenances on me shed
The light of questioning looks, whilst one did close
My wound with balmiest herbs, and soothed me to repose;

13

And one whose spear had pierced me, leaned beside
With quivering lips and humid eyes;—and all
Seemed like some brothers on a journey wide
Gone forth, whom now strange meeting did befall
In a strange land, round one whom they might call
Their friend, their chief, their father, for assay
Of peril, which had saved them from the thrall
Of death, now suffering. Thus the vast array
Of those fraternal bands were reconciled that day.

14

Lifting the thunder of their acclamation,
Towards the City then the multitude,
And I among them, went in joy—a nation
Made free by love;—a mighty brotherhood
Linked by a jealous interchange of good;
A glorious pageant, more magnificent
Than kingly slaves arrayed in gold and blood,
When they return from carnage, and are sent
In triumph bright beneath the populous battlement.

15

Afar, the city-walls were thronged on high,
And myriads on each giddy turret clung,
And to each spire far lessening in the sky
Bright pennons on the idle winds were hung;
As we approached, a shout of joyance sprung
At once from all the crowd, as if the vast
And peopled Earth its boundless skies among
The sudden clamour of delight had cast,
When from before its face some general wreck had passed.

16

Our armies through the City's hundred gates
Were poured, like brooks which to the rocky lair
Of some deep lake, whose silence them awaits,
Throng from the mountains when the storms are there
And, as we passed through the calm sunny air
A thousand flower-inwoven crowns were shed,
The token flowers of truth and freedom fair,
And fairest hands bound them on many a head,
Those angels of love's heaven that over all was spread.

17

I trod as one tranced in some rapturous vision:
Those bloody bands so lately reconciled,
Were, ever as they went, by the contrition
Of anger turned to love, from ill beguiled,
And every one on them more gently smiled,
Because they had done evil:—the sweet awe
Of such mild looks made their own hearts grow mild,
And did with soft attraction ever draw
Their spirits to the love of freedom's equal law.

18

And they, and all, in one loud symphony
My name with Liberty commingling, lifted,
'The friend and the preserver of the free!
The parent of this joy!' and fair eyes gifted
With feelings, caught from one who had uplifted
The light of a great spirit, round me shone;
And all the shapes of this grand scenery shifted
Like restless clouds before the steadfast sun,—
Where was that Maid? I asked, but it was known of none.

19

Laone was the name her love had chosen,
For she was nameless, and her birth none knew:
Where was Laone now?—The words were frozen
Within my lips with fear; but to subdue
Such dreadful hope, to my great task was due,
And when at length one brought reply, that she
To-morrow would appear, I then withdrew
To judge what need for that great throng might be,
For now the stars came thick over the twilight sea.

20

Yet need was none for rest or food to care,
Even though that multitude was passing great,
Since each one for the other did prepare
All kindly succour—Therefore to the gate
Of the Imperial House, now desolate,
I passed, and there was found aghast, alone,
The fallen Tyrant!—Silently he sate
Upon the footstool of his golden throne,
Which, starred with sunny gems, in its own lustre shone.

21

Alone, but for one child, who led before him
A graceful dance: the only living thing
Of all the crowd, which thither to adore him
Flocked yesterday, who solace sought to bring
In his abandonment!—She knew the King
Had praised her dance of yore, and now she wove
Its circles, aye weeping and murmuring
Mid her sad task of unregarded love,
That to no smiles it might his speechless sadness move.

22

She fled to him, and wildly clasped his feet
When human steps were heard:—he moved nor spoke,
Nor changed his hue, nor raised his looks to meet
The gaze of strangers—our loud entrance woke
The echoes of the hall, which circling broke
The calm of its recesses,—like a tomb
Its sculptured walls vacantly to the stroke
Of footfalls answered, and the twilight's gloom
Lay like a charnel's mist within the radiant dome.

23

The little child stood up when we came nigh;
Her lips and cheeks seemed very pale and wan,
But on her forehead, and within her eye
Lay beauty, which makes hearts that feed thereon
Sick with excess of sweetness; on the throne
She leaned;—the King, with gathered brow, and lips
Wreathed by long scorn, did inly sneer and frown
With hue like that when some great painter dips
His pencil in the gloom of earthquake and eclipse.

24

She stood beside him like a rainbow braided
Within some storm, when scarce its shadows vast
From the blue paths of the swift sun have faded;
A sweet and solemn smile, like Cythna's, cast
One moment's light, which made my heart beat fast,
O'er that child's parted lips—a gleam of bliss,
A shade of vanished days,—as the tears passed
Which wrapped it, even as with a father's kiss
I pressed those softest eyes in trembling tenderness.

25

The sceptred wretch then from that solitude
I drew, and, of his change compassionate,
With words of sadness soothed his rugged mood.
But he, while pride and fear held deep debate,
With sullen guile of ill-dissembled hate
Glared on me as a toothless snake might glare:
Pity, not scorn I felt, though desolate
The desolator now, and unaware
The curses which he mocked had caught him by the hair.

26

I led him forth from that which now might seem
A gorgeous grave: through portals sculptured deep
With imagery beautiful as dream
We went, and left the shades which tend on sleep
Over its unregarded gold to keep
Their silent watch.—The child trod faintingly,
And as she went, the tears which she did weep
Glanced in the starlight; wildered seemed she,
And, when I spake, for sobs she could not answer me.

27

At last the tyrant cried, 'She hungers, slave!
Stab her, or give her bread!'—It was a tone
Such as sick fancies in a new-made grave
Might hear. I trembled, for the truth was known;
He with this child had thus been left alone,
And neither had gone forth for food,—but he
In mingled pride and awe cowered near his throne,
And she a nursling of captivity
Knew nought beyond those walls, nor what such change might be.

28

And he was troubled at a charm withdrawn
Thus suddenly; that sceptres ruled no more—
That even from gold the dreadful strength was gone,
Which once made all things subject to its power—
Such wonder seized him, as if hour by hour
The past had come again; and the swift fall
Of one so great and terrible of yore,
To desolateness, in the hearts of all
Like wonder stirred, who saw such awful change befall.

29

A mighty crowd, such as the wide land pours
Once in a thousand years, now gathered round
The fallen tyrant;—like the rush of showers
Of hail in spring, pattering along the ground,
Their many footsteps fell, else came no sound
From the wide multitude: that lonely man
Then knew the burden of his change, and found,
Concealing in the dust his visage wan,
Refuge from the keen looks which through his bosom ran.

30

And he was faint withal: I sate beside him
Upon the earth, and took that child so fair
From his weak arms, that ill might none betide him
Or her;—when food was brought to them, her share
To his averted lips the child did bear,
But, when she saw he had enough, she ate
And wept the while;—the lonely man's despair
Hunger then overcame, and of his state
Forgetful, on the dust as in a trance he sate.

31

Slowly the silence of the multitudes
Passed, as when far is heard in some lone dell
The gathering of a wind among the woods—
'And he is fallen!' they cry, 'he who did dwell
Like famine or the plague, or aught more fell
Among our homes, is fallen! the murderer
Who slaked his thirsting soul as from a well
Of blood and tears with ruin! he is here!
Sunk in a gulf of scorn from which none may him rear!'

32

Then was heard—'He who judged let him be brought
To judgement! blood for blood cries from the soil
On which his crimes have deep pollution wrought!
Shall Othman only unavenged despoil?
Shall they who by the stress of grinding toil
Wrest from the unwilling earth his luxuries,
Perish for crime, while his foul blood may boil,
Or creep within his veins at will?—Arise!
And to high justice make her chosen sacrifice!'

33

'What do ye seek? what fear ye,' then I cried,
Suddenly starting forth, 'that ye should shed
The blood of Othman?—if your hearts are tried
In the true love of freedom, cease to dread
This one poor lonely man—beneath Heaven spread
In purest light above us all, through earth—
Maternal earth, who doth her sweet smiles shed
For all, let him go free; until the worth
Of human nature win from these a second birth.

34

'What call ye "justice"? Is there one who ne'er
In secret thought has wished another's ill?—
Are ye all pure? Let those stand forth who hear
And tremble not. Shall they insult and kill,
If such they be? their mild eyes can they fill
With the false anger of the hypocrite?
Alas, such were not pure!—the chastened will
Of virtue sees that justice is the light
Of love, and not revenge, and terror and despite.'

35

The murmur of the people, slowly dying,
Paused as I spake, then those who near me were,
Cast gentle looks where the lone man was lying
Shrouding his head, which now that infant fair
Clasped on her lap in silence;—through the air
Sobs were then heard, and many kissed my feet
In pity's madness, and to the despair
Of him whom late they cursed, a solace sweet
His very victims brought—soft looks and speeches meet.

36

Then to a home for his repose assigned,
Accompanied by the still throng, he went
In silence, where, to soothe his rankling mind,
Some likeness of his ancient state was lent;
And if his heart could have been innocent
As those who pardoned him, he might have ended
His days in peace; but his straight lips were bent,
Men said, into a smile which guile portended,
A sight with which that child like hope with fear was blended.

37

'Twas midnight now, the eve of that great day
Whereon the many nations at whose call
The chains of earth like mist melted away,
Decreed to hold a sacred Festival,
A rite to attest the equality of all
Who live. So to their homes, to dream or wake
All went. The sleepless silence did recall
Laone to my thoughts, with hopes that make
The flood recede from which their thirst they seek to slake.

38

The dawn flowed forth, and from its purple fountains
I drank those hopes which make the spirit quail,
As to the plain between the misty mountains
And the great City, with a countenance pale,
I went:—it was a sight which might avail
To make men weep exulting tears, for whom
Now first from human power the reverend veil
Was torn, to see Earth from her general womb
Pour forth her swarming sons to a fraternal doom:

39

To see, far glancing in the misty morning,
The signs of that innumerable host;
To hear one sound of many made, the warning
Of Earth to Heaven from its free children tossed,
While the eternal hills, and the sea lost
In wavering light, and, starring the blue sky
The city's myriad spires of gold, almost
With human joy made mute society—
Its witnesses with men who must hereafter be.

40

To see, like some vast island from the Ocean,
The Altar of the Federation rear
Its pile i' the midst; a work, which the devotion
Of millions in one night created there,
Sudden as when the moonrise makes appear
Strange clouds in the east; a marble pyramid
Distinct with steps: that mighty shape did wear
The light of genius; its still shadow hid
Far ships: to know its height the morning mists forbid!

41

To hear the restless multitudes for ever
Around the base of that great Altar flow,
As on some mountain-islet burst and shiver
Atlantic waves; and solemnly and slow
As the wind bore that tumult to and fro,
To feel the dreamlike music, which did swim
Like beams through floating clouds on waves below
Falling in pauses, from that Altar dim,
As silver-sounding tongues breathed an aerial hymn.

42

To hear, to see, to live, was on that morn
Lethean joy! so that all those assembled
Cast off their memories of the past outworn;
Two only bosoms with their own life trembled,
And mine was one,—and we had both dissembled;
So with a beating heart I went, and one,
Who having much, covets yet more, resembled;
A lost and dear possession, which not won,
He walks in lonely gloom beneath the noonday sun.

43

To the great Pyramid I came: its stair
With female choirs was thronged: the loveliest
Among the free, grouped with its sculptures rare;
As I approached, the morning's golden mist,
Which now the wonder-stricken breezes kissed
With their cold lips, fled, and the summit shone
Like Athos seen from Samothracia, dressed
In earliest light, by vintagers, and one
Sate there, a female Shape upon an ivory throne:

44

A Form most like the imagined habitant
Of silver exhalations sprung from dawn,
By winds which feed on sunrise woven, to enchant
The faiths of men: all mortal eyes were drawn,
As famished mariners through strange seas gone
Gaze on a burning watch-tower, by the light
Of those divinest lineaments—alone
With thoughts which none could share, from that fair sight
I turned in sickness, for a veil shrouded her countenance bright.

45

And neither did I hear the acclamations,
Which from brief silence bursting, filled the air
With her strange name and mine, from all the nations
Which we, they said, in strength had gathered there
From the sleep of bondage; nor the vision fair
Of that bright pageantry beheld,—but blind
And silent, as a breathing corpse did fare,
Leaning upon my friend, till like a wind
To fevered cheeks, a voice flowed o'er my troubled mind.

46

Like music of some minstrel heavenly gifted,
To one whom fiends enthral, this voice to me;
Scarce did I wish her veil to be uplifted,
I was so calm and joyous.—I could see
The platform where we stood, the statues three
Which kept their marble watch on that high shrine,
The multitudes, the mountains, and the sea;
As when eclipse hath passed, things sudden shine
To men's astonished eyes most clear and crystalline.

47

At first Laone spoke most tremulously:
But soon her voice the calmness which it shed
Gathered, and—'Thou art whom I sought to see,
And thou art our first votary here,' she said:
'I had a dear friend once, but he is dead!—
And of all those on the wide earth who breathe,
Thou dost resemble him alone—I spread
This veil between us two that thou beneath
Shouldst image one who may have been long lost in death.

48

'For this wilt thou not henceforth pardon me?
Yes, but those joys which silence well requite
Forbid reply;—why men have chosen me
To be the Priestess of this holiest rite
I scarcely know, but that the floods of light
Which flow over the world, have borne me hither
To meet thee, long most dear; and now unite
Thine hand with mine, and may all comfort wither
From both the hearts whose pulse in joy now beat together,

49

'If our own will as others' law we bind,
If the foul worship trampled here we fear;
If as ourselves we cease to love our kind!'—
She paused, and pointed upwards—sculptured there
Three shapes around her ivory throne appear;
One was a Giant, like a child asleep
On a loose rock, whose grasp crushed, as it were
In dream, sceptres and crowns; and one did keep
Its watchful eyes in doubt whether to smile or weep;

50

A Woman sitting on the sculptured disk
Of the broad earth, and feeding from one breast
A human babe and a young basilisk;
Her looks were sweet as Heaven's when loveliest
In Autumn eves. The third Image was dressed
In white wings swift as clouds in winter skies;
Beneath his feet, 'mongst ghastliest forms, repressed
Lay Faith, an obscene worm, who sought to rise,
While calmly on the Sun he turned his diamond eyes.

51

Beside that Image then I sate, while she
Stood, mid the throngs which ever ebbed and flowed,
Like light amid the shadows of the sea
Cast from one cloudless star, and on the crowd
That touch which none who feels forgets, bestowed;
And whilst the sun returned the steadfast gaze
Of the great Image, as o'er Heaven it glode,
That rite had place; it ceased when sunset's blaze
Burned o'er the isles. All stood in joy and deep amaze—
—When in the silence of all spirits there
Laone's voice was felt, and through the air
Her thrilling gestures spoke, most eloquently fair:—

51.1

'Calm art thou as yon sunset! swift and strong
As new-fledged Eagles, beautiful and young,
That float among the blinding beams of morning;
And underneath thy feet writhe Faith, and Folly,
Custom, and Hell, and mortal Melancholy—
Hark! the Earth starts to hear the mighty warning
Of thy voice sublime and holy;
Its free spirits here assembled
See thee, feel thee, know thee now,—
To thy voice their hearts have trembled
Like ten thousand clouds which flow
With one wide wind as it flies!—
Wisdom! thy irresistible children rise
To hail thee, and the elements they chain
And their own will, to swell the glory of thy train.

51.2

'O Spirit vast and deep as Night and Heaven!
Mother and soul of all to which is given
The light of life, the loveliness of being,
Lo! thou dost re-ascend the human heart,
Thy throne of power, almighty as thou wert
In dreams of Poets old grown pale by seeing
The shade of thee;—now, millions start
To feel thy lightnings through them burning:
Nature, or God, or Love, or Pleasure,
Or Sympathy the sad tears turning
To mutual smiles, a drainless treasure,
Descends amidst us;—Scorn and Hate,
Revenge and Selfishness are desolate—
A hundred nations swear that there shall be
Pity and Peace and Love, among the good and free!

51.3

'Eldest of things, divine Equality!
Wisdom and Love are but the slaves of thee,
The Angels of thy sway, who pour around thee
Treasures from all the cells of human thought,
And from the Stars, and from the Ocean brought,
And the last living heart whose beatings bound thee:
The powerful and the wise had sought
Thy coming, thou in light descending
O'er the wide land which is thine own
Like the Spring whose breath is blending
All blasts of fragrance into one,
Comest upon the paths of men!—
Earth bares her general bosom to thy ken,
And all her children here in glory meet
To feed upon thy smiles, and clasp thy sacred feet.

51.4

'My brethren, we are free! the plains and mountains,
The gray sea-shore, the forests and the fountains,
Are haunts of happiest dwellers;—man and woman,
Their common bondage burst, may freely borrow
From lawless love a solace for their sorrow;
For oft we still must weep, since we are human.
A stormy night's serenest morrow,
Whose showers are pity's gentle tears,
Whose clouds are smiles of those that die
Like infants without hopes or fears,
And whose beams are joys that lie
In blended hearts, now holds dominion;
The dawn of mind, which upwards on a pinion
Borne, swift as sunrise, far illumines space,
And clasps this barren world in its own bright embrace!

51.5

'My brethren, we are free! The fruits are glowing
Beneath the stars, and the night-winds are flowing
O'er the ripe corn, the birds and beasts are dreaming—
Never again may blood of bird or beast
Stain with its venomous stream a human feast,
To the pure skies in accusation steaming;
Avenging poisons shall have ceased
To feed disease and fear and madness,
The dwellers of the earth and air
Shall throng around our steps in gladness,
Seeking their food or refuge there.
Our toil from thought all glorious forms shall cull,
To make this Earth, our home, more beautiful,
And Science, and her sister Poesy,
Shall clothe in light the fields and cities of the free!

51.6

'Victory, Victory to the prostrate nations!
Bear witness Night, and ye mute Constellations
Who gaze on us from your crystalline cars!
Thoughts have gone forth whose powers can sleep no more!
Victory! Victory! Earth's remotest shore,
Regions which groan beneath the Antarctic stars,
The green lands cradled in the roar
Of western waves, and wildernesses
Peopled and vast, which skirt the oceans
Where morning dyes her golden tresses,
Shall soon partake our high emotions:
Kings shall turn pale! Almighty Fear,
The Fiend-God, when our charmed name he hear,
Shall fade like shadow from his thousand fanes,
While Truth with Joy enthroned o'er his lost empire reigns!'

52

Ere she had ceased, the mists of night entwining
Their dim woof, floated o'er the infinite throng;
She, like a spirit through the darkness shining,
In tones whose sweetness silence did prolong,
As if to lingering winds they did belong,
Poured forth her inmost soul: a passionate speech
With wild and thrilling pauses woven among,
Which whoso heard was mute, for it could teach
To rapture like her own all listening hearts to reach.

53

Her voice was as a mountain stream which sweeps
The withered leaves of Autumn to the lake,
And in some deep and narrow bay then sleeps
In the shadow of the shores; as dead leaves wake,
Under the wave, in flowers and herbs which make
Those green depths beautiful when skies are blue,
The multitude so moveless did partake
Such living change, and kindling murmurs flew
As o'er that speechless calm delight and wonder grew.

54

Over the plain the throngs were scattered then
In groups around the fires, which from the sea
Even to the gorge of the first mountain-glen
Blazed wide and far: the banquet of the free
Was spread beneath many a dark cypress-tree,
Beneath whose spires, which swayed in the red flame,
Reclining, as they ate, of Liberty,
And Hope, and Justice, and Laone's name,
Earth's children did a woof of happy converse frame.

55

Their feast was such as Earth, the general mother,
Pours from her fairest bosom, when she smiles
In the embrace of Autumn;—to each other
As when some parent fondly reconciles
Her warring children, she their wrath beguiles
With her own sustenance, they relenting weep:
Such was this Festival, which from their isles
And continents, and winds, and oceans deep,
All shapes might throng to share, that fly, or walk or creep,—

56

Might share in peace and innocence, for gore
Or poison none this festal did pollute,
But, piled on high, an overflowing store
Of pomegranates and citrons, fairest fruit,
Melons, and dates, and figs, and many a root
Sweet and sustaining, and bright grapes ere yet
Accursed fire their mild juice could transmute
Into a mortal bane, and brown corn set
In baskets; with pure streams their thirsting lips they wet.

57

Laone had descended from the shrine,
And every deepest look and holiest mind
Fed on her form, though now those tones divine
Were silent as she passed; she did unwind
Her veil, as with the crowds of her own kind
She mixed; some impulse made my heart refrain
From seeking her that night, so I reclined
Amidst a group, where on the utmost plain
A festal watchfire burned beside the dusky main.

58

And joyous was our feast; pathetic talk,
And wit, and harmony of choral strains,
While far Orion o'er the waves did walk
That flow among the isles, held us in chains
Of sweet captivity which none disdains
Who feels; but when his zone grew dim in mist
Which clothes the Ocean's bosom, o'er the plains
The multitudes went homeward, to their rest,
Which that delightful day with its own shadow blessed.

Canto 6

1

Beside the dimness of the glimmering sea,
Weaving swift language from impassioned themes,
With that dear friend I lingered, who to me
So late had been restored, beneath the gleams
Of the silver stars; and ever in soft dreams
Of future love and peace sweet converse lapped
Our willing fancies, till the pallid beams
Of the last watchfire fell, and darkness wrapped
The waves, and each bright chain of floating fire was snapped;

2

And till we came even to the City's wall
And the great gate; then, none knew whence or why,
Disquiet on the multitudes did fall:
And first, one pale and breathless passed us by,
And stared and spoke not;—then with piercing cry
A troop of wild-eyed women, by the shrieks
Of their own terror driven,—tumultuously
Hither and thither hurrying with pale cheeks,
Each one from fear unknown a sudden refuge seeks—

3

Then, rallying cries of treason and of danger
Resounded: and—'They come! to arms! to arms!
The Tyrant is amongst us, and the stranger
Comes to enslave us in his name! to arms!'
In vain: for Panic, the pale fiend who charms
Strength to forswear her right, those millions swept
Like waves before the tempest—these alarms
Came to me, as to know their cause I lept
On the gate's turret, and in rage and grief and scorn I wept!

4

For to the North I saw the town on fire,
And its red light made morning pallid now,
Which burst over wide Asia;—louder, higher,
The yells of victory and the screams of woe
I heard approach, and saw the throng below
Stream through the gates like foam-wrought waterfalls
Fed from a thousand storms—the fearful glow
Of bombs flares overhead—at intervals
The red artillery's bolt mangling among them falls.

5

And now the horsemen come—and all was done
Swifter than I have spoken—I beheld
Their red swords flash in the unrisen sun.
I rushed among the rout, to have repelled
That miserable flight—one moment quelled
By voice and looks and eloquent despair,
As if reproach from their own hearts withheld
Their steps, they stood; but soon came pouring there
New multitudes, and did those rallied bands o'erbear.

6

I strove, as, drifted on some cataract
By irresistible streams, some wretch might strive
Who hears its fatal roar:—the files compact
Whelmed me, and from the gate availed to drive
With quickening impulse, as each bolt did rive
Their ranks with bloodier chasm:—into the plain
Disgorged at length the dead and the alive
In one dread mass, were parted, and the stain
Of blood, from mortal steel fell o'er the fields like rain.

7

For now the despot's bloodhounds with their prey
Unarmed and unaware, were gorging deep
Their gluttony of death; the loose array
Of horsemen o'er the wide fields murdering sweep,
And with loud laughter for their tyrant reap
A harvest sown with other hopes; the while,
Far overhead, ships from Propontis keep
A killing rain of fire:—when the waves smile
As sudden earthquakes light many a volcano-isle,

8

Thus sudden, unexpected feast was spread
For the carrion-fowls of Heaven.—I saw the sight—
I moved—I lived—as o'er the heaps of dead,
Whose stony eyes glared in the morning light
I trod;—to me there came no thought of flight,
But with loud cries of scorn, which whoso heard
That dreaded death, felt in his veins the might
Of virtuous shame return, the crowd I stirred,
And desperation's hope in many hearts recurred.

9

A band of brothers gathering round me, made,
Although unarmed, a steadfast front, and still
Retreating, with stern looks beneath the shade
Of gathered eyebrows, did the victors fill
With doubt even in success; deliberate will
Inspired our growing troop; not overthrown
It gained the shelter of a grassy hill,
And ever still our comrades were hewn down,
And their defenceless limbs beneath our footsteps strown.

10

Immovably we stood—in joy I found,
Beside me then, firm as a giant pine
Among the mountain-vapours driven around,
The old man whom I loved—his eyes divine
With a mild look of courage answered mine,
And my young friend was near, and ardently
His hand grasped mine a moment—now the line
Of war extended, to our rallying cry
As myriads flocked in love and brotherhood to die.

11

For ever while the sun was climbing Heaven
The horseman hewed our unarmed myriads down
Safely, though when by thirst of carnage driven
Too near, those slaves were swiftly overthrown
By hundreds leaping on them:—flesh and bone
Soon made our ghastly ramparts; then the shaft
Of the artillery from the sea was thrown
More fast and fiery, and the conquerors laughed
In pride to hear the wind our screams of torment waft.

12

For on one side alone the hill gave shelter,
So vast that phalanx of unconquered men,
And there the living in the blood did welter
Of the dead and dying, which in that green glen,
Like stifled torrents, made a plashy fen
Under the feet—thus was the butchery waged
While the sun clomb Heaven's eastern steep—but when
It 'gan to sink—a fiercer combat raged,
For in more doubtful strife the armies were engaged.

13

Within a cave upon the hill were found
A bundle of rude pikes, the instrument
Of those who war but on their native ground
For natural rights: a shout of joyance sent
Even from our hearts the wide air pierced and rent,
As those few arms the bravest and the best
Seized, and each sixth, thus armed, did now present
A line which covered and sustained the rest,
A confident phalanx, which the foes on every side invest.

14

That onset turned the foes to flight almost;
But soon they saw their present strength, and knew
That coming night would to our resolute host
Bring victory; so dismounting, close they drew
Their glittering files, and then the combat grew
Unequal but most horrible;—and ever
Our myriads, whom the swift bolt overthrew,
Or the red sword, failed like a mountain river
Which rushes forth in foam to sink in sands for ever.

15

Sorrow and shame, to see with their own kind
Our human brethren mix, like beasts of blood,
To mutual ruin armed by one behind
Who sits and scoffs!—That friend so mild and good,
Who like its shadow near my youth had stood,
Was stabbed!—my old preserver's hoary hair
With the flesh clinging to its roots, was strewed
Under my feet!—I lost all sense or care,
And like the rest I grew desperate and unaware.

16

The battle became ghastlier—in the midst
I paused, and saw, how ugly and how fell
O Hate! thou art, even when thy life thou shedd'st
For love. The ground in many a little dell
Was broken, up and down whose steeps befell
Alternate victory and defeat, and there
The combatants with rage most horrible
Strove, and their eyes started with cracking stare,
And impotent their tongues they lolled into the air,

17

Flaccid and foamy, like a mad dog's hanging;
Want, and Moon-madness, and the pest's swift Bane
When its shafts smite—while yet its bow is twanging—
Have each their mark and sign—some ghastly stain;
And this was thine, O War! of hate and pain
Thou loathed slave! I saw all shapes of death
And ministered to many, o'er the plain
While carnage in the sunbeam's warmth did seethe,
Till twilight o'er the east wove her serenest wreath.

18

The few who yet survived, resolute and firm
Around me fought. At the decline of day
Winding above the mountain's snowy term
New banners shone; they quivered in the ray
Of the sun's unseen orb—ere night the array
Of fresh troops hemmed us in—of those brave bands
I soon survived alone—and now I lay
Vanquished and faint, the grasp of bloody hands
I felt, and saw on high the glare of falling brands,

19

When on my foes a sudden terror came,
And they fled, scattering—lo! with reinless speed
A black Tartarian horse of giant frame
Comes trampling over the dead, the living bleed
Beneath the hoofs of that tremendous steed,
On which, like to an Angel, robed in white,
Sate one waving a sword;—the hosts recede
And fly, as through their ranks with awful might,
Sweeps in the shadow of eve that Phantom swift and bright;

20

And its path made a solitude.—I rose
And marked its coming: it relaxed its course
As it approached me, and the wind that flows
Through night, bore accents to mine ear whose force
Might create smiles in death—the Tartar horse
Paused, and I saw the shape its might which swayed,
And heard her musical pants, like the sweet source
Of waters in the desert, as she said,
'Mount with me, Laon, now'—I rapidly obeyed.

21

Then: 'Away! away!' she cried, and stretched her sword
As 'twere a scourge over the courser's head,
And lightly shook the reins.—We spake no word,
But like the vapour of the tempest fled
Over the plain; her dark hair was dispread
Like the pine's locks upon the lingering blast;
Over mine eyes its shadowy strings it spread
Fitfully, and the hills and streams fled fast,
As o'er their glimmering forms the steed's broad shadow passed.

22

And his hoofs ground the rocks to fire and dust,
His strong sides made the torrents rise in spray,
And turbulence, as of a whirlwind's gust
Surrounded us;—and still away! away!
Through the desert night we sped, while she alway
Gazed on a mountain which we neared, whose crest,
Crowned with a marble ruin, in the ray
Of the obscure stars gleamed;—its rugged breast
The steed strained up, and then his impulse did arrest.

23

A rocky hill which overhung the Ocean:—
From that lone ruin, when the steed that panted
Paused, might be heard the murmur of the motion
Of waters, as in spots for ever haunted
By the choicest winds of Heaven, which are enchanted
To music, by the wand of Solitude,
That wizard wild, and the far tents implanted
Upon the plain, be seen by those who stood
Thence marking the dark shore of Ocean's curved flood.

24

One moment these were heard and seen—another
Passed; and the two who stood beneath that night,
Each only heard, or saw, or felt the other;
As from the lofty steed she did alight,
Cythna, (for, from the eyes whose deepest light
Of love and sadness made my lips feel pale
With influence strange of mournfullest delight,
My own sweet Cythna looked), with joy did quail,
And felt her strength in tears of human weakness fail.

25

And for a space in my embrace she rested,
Her head on my unquiet heart reposing,
While my faint arms her languid frame invested;
At length she looked on me, and half unclosing
Her tremulous lips, said, 'Friend, thy bands were losing
The battle, as I stood before the King
In bonds.—I burst them then, and swiftly choosing
The time, did seize a Tartar's sword, and spring
Upon his horse, and swift, as on the whirlwind's wing,

26

'Have thou and I been borne beyond pursuer,
And we are here.'—Then, turning to the steed,
She pressed the white moon on his front with pure
And rose-like lips, and many a fragrant weed
From the green ruin plucked, that he might feed;—
But I to a stone seat that Maiden led,
And, kissing her fair eyes, said, 'Thou hast need
Of rest,' and I heaped up the courser's bed
In a green mossy nook, with mountain flowers dispread.

27

Within that ruin, where a shattered portal
Looks to the eastern stars, abandoned now
By man, to be the home of things immortal,
Memories, like awful ghosts which come and go,
And must inherit all he builds below,
When he is gone, a hall stood; o'er whose roof
Fair clinging weeds with ivy pale did grow,
Clasping its gray rents with a verdurous woof,
A hanging dome of leaves, a canopy moon-proof.

28

The autumnal winds, as if spell-bound, had made
A natural couch of leaves in that recess,
Which seasons none disturbed, but, in the shade
Of flowering parasites, did Spring love to dress
With their sweet blooms the wintry loneliness
Of those dead leaves, shedding their stars, whene'er
The wandering wind her nurslings might caress;
Whose intertwining fingers ever there
Made music wild and soft that filled the listening air.

29

We know not where we go, or what sweet dream
May pilot us through caverns strange and fair
Of far and pathless passion, while the stream
Of life, our bark doth on its whirlpools bear,
Spreading swift wings as sails to the dim air;
Nor should we seek to know, so the devotion
Of love and gentle thoughts be heard still there
Louder and louder from the utmost Ocean
Of universal life, attuning its commotion.

30

To the pure all things are pure! Oblivion wrapped
Our spirits, and the fearful overthrow
Of public hope was from our being snapped,
Though linked years had bound it there; for now
A power, a thirst, a knowledge, which below
All thoughts, like light beyond the atmosphere,
Clothing its clouds with grace, doth ever flow,
Came on us, as we sate in silence there,
Beneath the golden stars of the clear azure air;—

31

In silence which doth follow talk that causes
The baffled heart to speak with sighs and tears,
When wildering passion swalloweth up the pauses
Of inexpressive speech:—the youthful years
Which we together passed, their hopes and fears,
The blood itself which ran within our frames,
That likeness of the features which endears
The thoughts expressed by them, our very names,
And all the winged hours which speechless memory claims,

32

Had found a voice—and ere that voice did pass,
The night grew damp and dim, and, through a rent
Of the ruin where we sate, from the morass
A wandering Meteor by some wild wind sent,
Hung high in the green dome, to which it lent
A faint and pallid lustre; while the song
Of blasts, in which its blue hair quivering bent,
Strewed strangest sounds the moving leaves among;
A wondrous light, the sound as of a spirit's tongue.

33

The Meteor showed the leaves on which we sate,
And Cythna's glowing arms, and the thick ties
Of her soft hair, which bent with gathered weight
My neck near hers; her dark and deepening eyes,
Which, as twin phantoms of one star that lies
O'er a dim well, move, though the star reposes,
Swam in our mute and liquid ecstasies,
Her marble brow, and eager lips, like roses,
With their own fragrance pale, which Spring but half uncloses.

34

The Meteor to its far morass returned:
The beating of our veins one interval
Made still; and then I felt the blood that burned
Within her frame, mingle with mine, and fall
Around my heart like fire; and over all
A mist was spread, the sickness of a deep
And speechless swoon of joy, as might befall
Two disunited spirits when they leap
In union from this earth's obscure and fading sleep.

35

Was it one moment that confounded thus
All thought, all sense, all feeling, into one
Unutterable power, which shielded us
Even from our own cold looks, when we had gone
Into a wide and wild oblivion
Of tumult and of tenderness? or now
Had ages, such as make the moon and sun,
The seasons, and mankind their changes know,
Left fear and time unfelt by us alone below?

36

I know not. What are kisses whose fire clasps
The failing heart in languishment, or limb
Twined within limb? or the quick dying gasps
Of the life meeting, when the faint eyes swim
Through tears of a wide mist boundless and dim,
In one caress? What is the strong control
Which leads the heart that dizzy steep to climb,
Where far over the world those vapours roll
Which blend two restless frames in one reposing soul?

37

It is the shadow which doth float unseen,
But not unfelt, o'er blind mortality,
Whose divine darkness fled not from that green
And lone recess, where lapped in peace did lie
Our linked frames, till, from the changing sky
That night and still another day had fled;
And then I saw and felt. The moon was high,
And clouds, as of a coming storm, were spread
Under its orb,—loud winds were gathering overhead.

38

Cythna's sweet lips seemed lurid in the moon,
Her fairest limbs with the night wind were chill,
And her dark tresses were all loosely strewn
O'er her pale bosom:—all within was still,
And the sweet peace of joy did almost fill
The depth of her unfathomable look;—
And we sate calmly, though that rocky hill,
The waves contending in its caverns strook,
For they foreknew the storm, and the gray ruin shook.

39

There we unheeding sate, in the communion
Of interchanged vows, which, with a rite
Of faith most sweet and sacred, stamped our union.—
Few were the living hearts which could unite
Like ours, or celebrate a bridal night
With such close sympathies, for they had sprung
From linked youth, and from the gentle might
Of earliest love, delayed and cherished long,
Which common hopes and fears made, like a tempest, strong.

40

And such is Nature's law divine, that those
Who grow together cannot choose but love,
If faith or custom do not interpose,
Or common slavery mar what else might move
All gentlest thoughts; as in the sacred grove
Which shades the springs of Ethiopian Nile,
That living tree which, if the arrowy dove
Strike with her shadow, shrinks in fear awhile,
But its own kindred leaves clasps while the sunbeams smile;

41

And clings to them, when darkness may dissever
The close caresses of all duller plants
Which bloom on the wide earth—thus we for ever
Were linked, for love had nursed us in the haunts
Where knowledge, from its secret source enchants
Young hearts with the fresh music of its springing,
Ere yet its gathered flood feeds human wants,
As the great Nile feeds Egypt; ever flinging
Light on the woven boughs which o'er its waves are swinging.

42

The tones of Cythna's voice like echoes were
Of those far murmuring streams; they rose and fell,
Mixed with mine own in the tempestuous air,—
And so we sate, until our talk befell
Of the late ruin, swift and horrible,
And how those seeds of hope might yet be sown,
Whose fruit is evil's mortal poison: well,
For us, this ruin made a watch-tower lone,
But Cythna's eyes looked faint, and now two days were gone

43

Since she had food:—therefore I did awaken
The Tartar steed, who, from his ebon mane
Soon as the clinging slumbers he had shaken,
Bent his thin head to seek the brazen rein,
Following me obediently; with pain
Of heart, so deep and dread, that one caress,
When lips and heart refuse to part again
Till they have told their fill, could scarce express
The anguish of her mute and fearful tenderness,

44

Cythna beheld me part, as I bestrode
That willing steed—the tempest and the night,
Which gave my path its safety as I rode
Down the ravine of rocks, did soon unite
The darkness and the tumult of their might
Borne on all winds.—Far through the streaming rain
Floating at intervals the garments white
Of Cythna gleamed, and her voice once again
Came to me on the gust, and soon I reached the plain.

45

I dreaded not the tempest, nor did he
Who bore me, but his eyeballs wide and red
Turned on the lightning's cleft exultingly;
And when the earth beneath his tameless tread,
Shook with the sullen thunder, he would spread
His nostrils to the blast, and joyously
Mock the fierce peal with neighings;—thus we sped
O'er the lit plain, and soon I could descry
Where Death and Fire had gorged the spoil of victory.

46

There was a desolate village in a wood
Whose bloom-inwoven leaves now scattering fed
The hungry storm; it was a place of blood,
A heap of heartless walls;—the flames were dead
Within those dwellings now,—the life had fled
From all those corpses now,—but the wide sky
Flooded with lightning was ribbed overhead
By the black rafters, and around did lie
Women, and babes, and men, slaughtered confusedly.

47

Beside the fountain in the market-place
Dismounting, I beheld those corpses stare
With horny eyes upon each other's face,
And on the earth and on the vacant air,
And upon me, close to the waters where
I stooped to slake my thirst;—I shrank to taste,
For the salt bitterness of blood was there;
But tied the steed beside, and sought in haste
If any yet survived amid that ghastly waste.

48

No living thing was there beside one woman,
Whom I found wandering in the streets, and she
Was withered from a likeness of aught human
Into a fiend, by some strange misery:
Soon as she heard my steps she leaped on me,
And glued her burning lips to mine, and laughed
With a loud, long, and frantic laugh of glee,
And cried, 'Now, Mortal, thou hast deeply quaffed
The Plague's blue kisses—soon millions shall pledge the draught!

49

'My name is Pestilence—this bosom dry,
Once fed two babes—a sister and a brother—
When I came home, one in the blood did lie
Of three death-wounds—the flames had ate the other!
Since then I have no longer been a mother,
But I am Pestilence;—hither and thither
I flit about, that I may slay and smother:—
All lips which I have kissed must surely wither,
But Death's—if thou art he, we'll go to work together!

50

'What seek'st thou here? The moonlight comes in flashes,—
The dew is rising dankly from the dell—
'Twill moisten her! and thou shalt see the gashes
In my sweet boy, now full of worms—but tell
First what thou seek'st.'—'I seek for food.'—''Tis well,
Thou shalt have food. Famine, my paramour,
Waits for us at the feast—cruel and fell
Is Famine, but he drives not from his door
Those whom these lips have kissed, alone. No more, no more!'

51

As thus she spake, she grasped me with the strength
Of madness, and by many a ruined hearth
She led, and over many a corpse:—at length
We came to a lone hut where on the earth
Which made its floor, she in her ghastly mirth,
Gathering from all those homes now desolate,
Had piled three heaps of loaves, making a dearth
Among the dead—round which she set in state
A ring of cold, stiff babes; silent and stark they sate.

52

She leaped upon a pile, and lifted high
Her mad looks to the lightning, and cried: 'Eat!
Share the great feast—to-morrow we must die!'
And then she spurned the loaves with her pale feet,
Towards her bloodless guests;—that sight to meet,
Mine eyes and my heart ached, and but that she
Who loved me, did with absent looks defeat
Despair, I might have raved in sympathy;
But now I took the food that woman offered me;

53

And vainly having with her madness striven
If I might win her to return with me,
Departed. In the eastern beams of Heaven
The lightning now grew pallid—rapidly,
As by the shore of the tempestuous sea
The dark steed bore me; and the mountain gray
Soon echoed to his hoofs, and I could see
Cythna among the rocks, where she alway
Had sate with anxious eyes fixed on the lingering day.

54

And joy was ours to meet: she was most pale,
Famished, and wet and weary, so I cast
My arms around her, lest her steps should fail
As to our home we went, and thus embraced,
Her full heart seemed a deeper joy to taste
Than e'er the prosperous know; the steed behind
Trod peacefully along the mountain waste;
We reached our home ere morning could unbind
Night's latest veil, and on our bridal-couch reclined.

55

Her chilled heart having cherished in my bosom,
And sweetest kisses past, we two did share
Our peaceful meal:—as an autumnal blossom
Which spreads its shrunk leaves in the sunny air,
After cold showers, like rainbows woven there,
Thus in her lips and cheeks the vital spirit
Mantled, and in her eyes, an atmosphere
Of health, and hope; and sorrow languished near it,
And fear, and all that dark despondence doth inherit.

Canto 7

1

So we sate joyous as the morning ray
Which fed upon the wrecks of night and storm
Now lingering on the winds; light airs did play
Among the dewy weeds, the sun was warm,
And we sate linked in the inwoven charm
Of converse and caresses sweet and deep,
Speechless caresses, talk that might disarm
Time, though he wield the darts of death and sleep,
And those thrice mortal barbs in his own poison steep.

2

I told her of my sufferings and my madness,
And how, awakened from that dreamy mood
By Liberty's uprise, the strength of gladness
Came to my spirit in my solitude;
And all that now I was—while tears pursued
Each other down her fair and listening cheek
Fast as the thoughts which fed them, like a flood
From sunbright dales; and when I ceased to speak,
Her accents soft and sweet the pausing air did wake.

3

She told me a strange tale of strange endurance,
Like broken memories of many a heart
Woven into one; to which no firm assurance,
So wild were they, could her own faith impart.
She said that not a tear did dare to start
From the swoln brain, and that her thoughts were firm
When from all mortal hope she did depart,
Borne by those slaves across the Ocean's term,
And that she reached the port without one fear infirm.

4

One was she among many there, the thralls
Of the cold Tyrant's cruel lust; and they
Laughed mournfully in those polluted halls;
But she was calm and sad, musing alway
On loftiest enterprise, till on a day
The Tyrant heard her singing to her lute
A wild, and sad, and spirit-thrilling lay,
Like winds that die in wastes—one moment mute
The evil thoughts it made, which did his breast pollute.

5

Even when he saw her wondrous loveliness,
One moment to great Nature's sacred power
He bent, and was no longer passionless;
But when he bade her to his secret bower
Be borne, a loveless victim, and she tore
Her locks in agony, and her words of flame
And mightier looks availed not; then he bore
Again his load of slavery, and became
A king, a heartless beast, a pageant and a name.

6

She told me what a loathsome agony
Is that when selfishness mocks love's delight,
Foul as in dream's most fearful imagery,
To dally with the mowing dead—that night
All torture, fear, or horror made seem light
Which the soul dreams or knows, and when the day
Shone on her awful frenzy, from the sight
Where like a Spirit in fleshly chains she lay
Struggling, aghast and pale the Tyrant fled away.

7

Her madness was a beam of light, a power
Which dawned through the rent soul; and words it gave,
Gestures and looks, such as in whirlwinds bore
Which might not be withstood—whence none could save—
All who approached their sphere,—like some calm wave
Vexed into whirlpools by the chasms beneath;
And sympathy made each attendant slave
Fearless and free, and they began to breathe
Deep curses, like the voice of flames far underneath.

8

The King felt pale upon his noonday throne:
At night two slaves he to her chamber sent,—
One was a green and wrinkled eunuch, grown
From human shape into an instrument
Of all things ill—distorted, bowed and bent.
The other was a wretch from infancy
Made dumb by poison; who nought knew or meant
But to obey: from the fire isles came he,
A diver lean and strong, of Oman's coral sea.

9

They bore her to a bark, and the swift stroke
Of silent rowers clove the blue moonlight seas,
Until upon their path the morning broke;
They anchored then, where, be there calm or breeze,
The gloomiest of the drear Symplegades
Shakes with the sleepless surge;—the Ethiop there
Wound his long arms around her, and with knees
Like iron clasped her feet, and plunged with her
Among the closing waves out of the boundless air.

10

'Swift as an eagle stooping from the plain
Of morning light, into some shadowy wood,
He plunged through the green silence of the main,
Through many a cavern which the eternal flood
Had scooped, as dark lairs for its monster brood;
And among mighty shapes which fled in wonder,
And among mightier shadows which pursued
His heels, he wound: until the dark rocks under
He touched a golden chain—a sound arose like thunder.

11

'A stunning clang of massive bolts redoubling
Beneath the deep—a burst of waters driven
As from the roots of the sea, raging and bubbling:
And in that roof of crags a space was riven
Through which there shone the emerald beams of heaven,
Shot through the lines of many waves inwoven,
Like sunlight through acacia woods at even,
Through which, his way the diver having cloven,
Passed like a spark sent up out of a burning oven.

12

'And then,' she said, 'he laid me in a cave
Above the waters, by that chasm of sea,
A fountain round and vast, in which the wave
Imprisoned, boiled and leaped perpetually,
Down which, one moment resting, he did flee,
Winning the adverse depth; that spacious cell
Like an hupaithric temple wide and high,
Whose aery dome is inaccessible,
Was pierced with one round cleft through which the sunbeams fell.

13

'Below, the fountain's brink was richly paven
With the deep's wealth, coral, and pearl, and sand
Like spangling gold, and purple shells engraven
With mystic legends by no mortal hand,
Left there, when thronging to the moon's command,
The gathering waves rent the Hesperian gate
Of mountains, and on such bright floor did stand
Columns, and shapes like statues, and the state
Of kingless thrones, which Earth did in her heart create.

14

'The fiend of madness which had made its prey
Of my poor heart, was lulled to sleep awhile:
There was an interval of many a day,
And a sea-eagle brought me food the while,
Whose nest was built in that untrodden isle,
And who, to be the gaoler had been taught
Of that strange dungeon; as a friend whose smile
Like light and rest at morn and even is sought
That wild bird was to me, till madness misery brought.

15

'The misery of a madness slow and creeping,
Which made the earth seem fire, the sea seem air,
And the white clouds of noon which oft were sleeping,
In the blue heaven so beautiful and fair,
Like hosts of ghastly shadows hovering there;
And the sea-eagle looked a fiend, who bore
Thy mangled limbs for food!—Thus all things were
Transformed into the agony which I wore
Even as a poisoned robe around my bosom's core.

16

'Again I knew the day and night fast fleeing,
The eagle, and the fountain, and the air;
Another frenzy came—there seemed a being
Within me—a strange load my heart did bear,
As if some living thing had made its lair
Even in the fountains of my life:—a long
And wondrous vision wrought from my despair,
Then grew, like sweet reality among
Dim visionary woes, an unreposing throng.

17

'Methought I was about to be a mother—
Month after month went by, and still I dreamed
That we should soon be all to one another,
I and my child; and still new pulses seemed
To beat beside my heart, and still I deemed
There was a babe within—and, when the rain
Of winter through the rifted cavern streamed,
Methought, after a lapse of lingering pain,
I saw that lovely shape, which near my heart had lain.

18

'It was a babe, beautiful from its birth,—
It was like thee, dear love, its eyes were thine,
Its brow, its lips, and so upon the earth
It laid its fingers, as now rest on mine
Thine own, beloved!—'twas a dream divine;
Even to remember how it fled, how swift,
How utterly, might make the heart repine,—
Though 'twas a dream.'—Then Cythna did uplift
Her looks on mine, as if some doubt she sought to shift:

19

A doubt which would not flee, a tenderness
Of questioning grief, a source of thronging tears;
Which having passed, as one whom sobs oppress
She spoke: 'Yes, in the wilderness of years
Her memory, aye, like a green home appears;
She sucked her fill even at this breast, sweet love,
For many months. I had no mortal fears;
Methought I felt her lips and breath approve,—
It was a human thing which to my bosom clove.

20

'I watched the dawn of her first smiles; and soon
When zenith stars were trembling on the wave,
Or when the beams of the invisible moon,
Or sun, from many a prism within the cave
Their gem-born shadows to the water gave,
Her looks would hunt them, and with outspread hand,
From the swift lights which might that fountain pave,
She would mark one, and laugh, when that command
Slighting, it lingered there, and could not understand.

21

'Methought her looks began to talk with me;
And no articulate sounds, but something sweet
Her lips would frame,—so sweet it could not be,
That it was meaningless; her touch would meet
Mine, and our pulses calmly flow and beat
In response while we slept; and on a day
When I was happiest in that strange retreat,
With heaps of golden shells we two did play,—
Both infants, weaving wings for time's perpetual way.

22

'Ere night, methought, her waning eyes were grown
Weary with joy, and tired with our delight,
We, on the earth, like sister twins lay down
On one fair mother's bosom:—from that night
She fled,—like those illusions clear and bright,
Which dwell in lakes, when the red moon on high
Pause ere it wakens tempest;—and her flight,
Though 'twas the death of brainless fantasy,
Yet smote my lonesome heart more than all misery.

23

'It seemed that in the dreary night the diver
Who brought me thither, came again, and bore
My child away. I saw the waters quiver,
When he so swiftly sunk, as once before:
Then morning came—it shone even as of yore,
But I was changed—the very life was gone
Out of my heart—I wasted more and more,
Day after day, and sitting there alone,
Vexed the inconstant waves with my perpetual moan.

24

'I was no longer mad, and yet methought
My breasts were swoln and changed:—in every vein
The blood stood still one moment, while that thought
Was passing—with a gush of sickening pain
It ebbed even to its withered springs again:
When my wan eyes in stern resolve I turned
From that most strange delusion, which would fain
Have waked the dream for which my spirit yearned
With more than human love,—then left it unreturned.

25

'So now my reason was restored to me
I struggled with that dream, which, like a beast
Most fierce and beauteous, in my memory
Had made its lair, and on my heart did feast;
But all that cave and all its shapes, possessed
By thoughts which could not fade, renewed each one
Some smile, some look, some gesture which had blessed
Me heretofore: I, sitting there alone,
Vexed the inconstant waves with my perpetual moan.

26

'Time passed, I know not whether months or years;
For day, nor night, nor change of seasons made
Its note, but thoughts and unavailing tears:
And I became at last even as a shade,
A smoke, a cloud on which the winds have preyed,
Till it be thin as air; until, one even,
A Nautilus upon the fountain played,
Spreading his azure sail where breath of Heaven
Descended not, among the waves and whirlpools driven.

27

'And, when the Eagle came, that lovely thing,
Oaring with rosy feet its silver boat,
Fled near me as for shelter; on slow wing,
The Eagle, hovering o'er his prey did float;
But when he saw that I with fear did note
His purpose, proffering my own food to him,
The eager plumes subsided on his throat—
He came where that bright child of sea did swim,
And o'er it cast in peace his shadow broad and dim.

28

'This wakened me, it gave me human strength;
And hope, I know not whence or wherefore, rose,
But I resumed my ancient powers at length;
My spirit felt again like one of those
Like thine, whose fate it is to make the woes
Of humankind their prey—what was this cave?
Its deep foundation no firm purpose knows
Immutable, resistless, strong to save,
Like mind while yet it mocks the all-devouring grave.

29

'And where was Laon? might my heart be dead,
While that far dearer heart could move and be?
Or whilst over the earth the pall was spread,
Which I had sworn to rend? I might be free,
Could I but win that friendly bird to me,
To bring me ropes; and long in vain I sought
By intercourse of mutual imagery
Of objects, if such aid he could be taught;
But fruit, and flowers, and boughs, yet never ropes he brought.

30

'We live in our own world, and mine was made
From glorious fantasies of hope departed:
Aye we are darkened with their floating shade,
Or cast a lustre on them—time imparted
Such power to me—I became fearless-hearted,
My eye and voice grew firm, calm was my mind,
And piercing, like the morn, now it has darted
Its lustre on all hidden things, behind
Yon dim and fading clouds which load the weary wind.

31

'My mind became the book through which I grew
Wise in all human wisdom, and its cave,
Which like a mine I rifled through and through,
To me the keeping of its secrets gave—
One mind, the type of all, the moveless wave
Whose calm reflects all moving things that are,
Necessity, and love, and life, the grave,
And sympathy, fountains of hope and fear,
Justice, and truth, and time, and the world's natural sphere.

32

'And on the sand would I make signs to range
These woofs, as they were woven, of my thought;
Clear, elemental shapes, whose smallest change
A subtler language within language wrought:
The key of truths which once were dimly taught
In old Crotona;—and sweet melodies
Of love, in that lorn solitude I caught
From mine own voice in dream, when thy dear eyes
Shone through my sleep, and did that utterance harmonize.

33

'Thy songs were winds whereon I fled at will,
As in a winged chariot, o'er the plain
Of crystal youth; and thou wert there to fill
My heart with joy, and there we sate again
On the gray margin of the glimmering main,
Happy as then but wiser far, for we
Smiled on the flowery grave in which were lain
Fear, Faith and Slavery; and mankind was free,
Equal, and pure, and wise, in Wisdom's prophecy.

34

'For to my will my fancies were as slaves
To do their sweet and subtile ministries;
And oft from that bright fountain's shadowy waves
They would make human throngs gather and rise
To combat with my overflowing eyes,
And voice made deep with passion—thus I grew
Familiar with the shock and the surprise
And war of earthly minds, from which I drew
The power which has been mine to frame their thoughts anew.

35

'And thus my prison was the populous earth—
Where I saw—even as misery dreams of morn
Before the east has given its glory birth—
Religion's pomp made desolate by the scorn
Of Wisdom's faintest smile, and thrones uptorn,
And dwellings of mild people interspersed
With undivided fields of ripening corn,
And love made free,—a hope which we have nursed
Even with our blood and tears,—until its glory burst.

36

'All is not lost! There is some recompense
For hope whose fountain can be thus profound,
Even throned Evil's splendid impotence,
Girt by its hell of power, the secret sound
Of hymns to truth and freedom—the dread bound
Of life and death passed fearlessly and well,
Dungeons wherein the high resolve is found,
Racks which degraded woman's greatness tell,
And what may else be good and irresistible.

37

'Such are the thoughts which, like the fires that flare
In storm-encompassed isles, we cherish yet
In this dark ruin—such were mine even there;
As in its sleep some odorous violet,
While yet its leaves with nightly dews are wet,
Breathes in prophetic dreams of day's uprise,
Or as, ere Scythian frost in fear has met
Spring's messengers descending from the skies,
The buds foreknow their life—this hope must ever rise.

38

'So years had passed, when sudden earthquake rent
The depth of ocean, and the cavern cracked
With sound, as if the world's wide continent
Had fallen in universal ruin wracked:
And through the cleft streamed in one cataract
The stifling waters—when I woke, the flood
Whose banded waves that crystal cave had sacked
Was ebbing round me, and my bright abode
Before me yawned—a chasm desert, and bare, and broad.

39

'Above me was the sky, beneath the sea:
I stood upon a point of shattered stone,
And heard loose rocks rushing tumultuously
With splash and shock into the deep—anon
All ceased, and there was silence wide and lone.
I felt that I was free! The Ocean-spray
Quivered beneath my feet, the broad Heaven shone
Around, and in my hair the winds did play
Lingering as they pursued their unimpeded way.

40

'My spirit moved upon the sea like wind
Which round some thymy cape will lag and hover,
Though it can wake the still cloud, and unbind
The strength of tempest: day was almost over,
When through the fading light I could discover
A ship approaching—its white sails were fed
With the north wind—its moving shade did cover
The twilight deep; the mariners in dread
Cast anchor when they saw new rocks around them spread.

41

'And when they saw one sitting on a crag,
They sent a boat to me;—the Sailors rowed
In awe through many a new and fearful jag
Of overhanging rock, through which there flowed
The foam of streams that cannot make abode.
They came and questioned me, but when they heard
My voice, they became silent, and they stood
And moved as men in whom new love had stirred
Deep thoughts: so to the ship we passed without a word.

Canto 8

1

'I sate beside the Steersman then, and gazing
Upon the west, cried, "Spread the sails! Behold!
The sinking moon is like a watch-tower blazing
Over the mountains yet;—the City of Gold
Yon Cape alone does from the sight withhold;
The stream is fleet—the north breathes steadily
Beneath the stars; they tremble with the cold!
Ye cannot rest upon the dreary sea!—
Haste, haste to the warm home of happier destiny!"

2

'The Mariners obeyed—the Captain stood
Aloof, and, whispering to the Pilot, said,
"Alas, alas! I fear we are pursued
By wicked ghosts; a Phantom of the Dead,
The night before we sailed, came to my bed
In dream, like that!" The Pilot then replied,
"It cannot be—she is a human Maid—
Her low voice makes you weep—she is some bride,
Or daughter of high birth—she can be nought beside."

3

'We passed the islets, borne by wind and stream,
And as we sailed, the Mariners came near
And thronged around to listen;—in the gleam
Of the pale moon I stood, as one whom fear
May not attaint, and my calm voice did rear;
"Ye are all human—yon broad moon gives light
To millions who the selfsame likeness wear,
Even while I speak—beneath this very night,
Their thoughts flow on like ours, in sadness or delight.

4

'"What dream ye? Your own hands have built an home,
Even for yourselves on a beloved shore:
For some, fond eyes are pining till they come,
How they will greet him when his toils are o'er,
And laughing babes rush from the well-known door!
Is this your care? ye toil for your own good—
Ye feel and think—has some immortal power
Such purposes? or in a human mood,
Dream ye some Power thus builds for man in solitude?

5

'"What is that Power? Ye mock yourselves, and give
A human heart to what ye cannot know:
As if the cause of life could think and live!
'Twere as if man's own works should feel, and show
The hopes, and fears, and thoughts from which they flow,
And he be like to them! Lo! Plague is free
To waste, Blight, Poison, Earthquake, Hail, and Snow,
Disease, and Want, and worse Necessity
Of hate and ill, and Pride, and Fear, and Tyranny!

6

'"What is that Power? Some moon-struck sophist stood
Watching the shade from his own soul upthrown
Fill Heaven and darken Earth, and in such mood
The Form he saw and worshipped was his own,
His likeness in the world's vast mirror shown;
And 'twere an innocent dream, but that a faith
Nursed by fear's dew of poison, grows thereon,
And that men say, that Power has chosen Death
On all who scorn its laws, to wreak immortal wrath.

7

'"Men say that they themselves have heard and seen,
Or known from others who have known such things,
A Shade, a Form, which Earth and Heaven between
Wields an invisible rod—that Priests and Kings,
Custom, domestic sway, ay, all that brings
Man's freeborn soul beneath the oppressor's heel,
Are his strong ministers, and that the stings
Of death will make the wise his vengeance feel,
Though truth and virtue arm their hearts with tenfold steel.

8

'"And it is said, this Power will punish wrong;
Yes, add despair to crime, and pain to pain!
And deepest hell, and deathless snakes among,
Will bind the wretch on whom is fixed a stain,
Which, like a plague, a burden, and a bane,
Clung to him while he lived; for love and hate,
Virtue and vice, they say are difference vain—
The will of strength is right—this human state
Tyrants, that they may rule, with lies thus desolate.

9

'"Alas, what strength? Opinion is more frail
Than yon dim cloud now fading on the moon
Even while we gaze, though it awhile avail
To hide the orb of truth—and every throne
Of Earth or Heaven, though shadow, rests thereon,
One shape of many names:—for this ye plough
The barren waves of ocean, hence each one
Is slave or tyrant; all betray and bow,
Command, or kill, or fear, or wreak, or suffer woe.

10

"'Its names are each a sign which maketh holy
All power—ay, the ghost, the dream, the shade
Of power—lust, falsehood, hate, and pride, and folly;
The pattern whence all fraud and wrong is made,
A law to which mankind has been betrayed;
And human love, is as the name well known
Of a dear mother, whom the murderer laid
In bloody grave, and into darkness thrown,
Gathered her wildered babes around him as his own.

11

"'O Love, who to the hearts of wandering men
Art as the calm to Ocean's weary waves!
Justice, or Truth, or Joy! those only can
From slavery and religion's labyrinth caves
Guide us, as one clear star the seaman saves.
To give to all an equal share of good,
To track the steps of Freedom, though through graves
She pass, to suffer all in patient mood,
To weep for crime, though stained with thy friend's dearest blood,—

12

"'To feel the peace of self-contentment's lot,
To own all sympathies, and outrage none,
And in the inmost bowers of sense and thought,
Until life's sunny day is quite gone down,
To sit and smile with Joy, or, not alone,
To kiss salt tears from the worn cheek of Woe;
To live, as if to love and live were one,—
This is not faith or law, nor those who bow
To thrones on Heaven or Earth, such destiny may know.

13

"'But children near their parents tremble now,
Because they must obey—one rules another,
And as one Power rules both high and low,
So man is made the captive of his brother,
And Hate is throned on high with Fear her mother,
Above the Highest—and those fountain-cells,
Whence love yet flowed when faith had choked all other,
Are darkened—Woman as the bond-slave dwells
Of man, a slave; and life is poisoned in its wells.

14

"'Man seeks for gold in mines, that he may weave
A lasting chain for his own slavery;—
In fear and restless care that he may live
He toils for others, who must ever be
The joyless thralls of like captivity;
He murders, for his chiefs delight in ruin;
He builds the altar, that its idol's fee
May be his very blood; he is pursuing—
O, blind and willing wretch!—his own obscure undoing.

15

"'Woman!—she is his slave, she has become
A thing I weep to speak—the child of scorn,
The outcast of a desolated home;
Falsehood, and fear, and toil, like waves have worn
Channels upon her cheek, which smiles adorn,
As calm decks the false Ocean:—well ye know
What Woman is, for none of Woman born
Can choose but drain the bitter dregs of woe,
Which ever from the oppressed to the oppressors flow.

16

'"This need not be; ye might arise, and will
That gold should lose its power, and thrones their glory;
That love, which none may bind, be free to fill
The world, like light; and evil faith, grown hoary
With crime, be quenched and die.—Yon promontory
Even now eclipses the descending moon!—
Dungeons and palaces are transitory—
High temples fade like vapour—Man alone
Remains, whose will has power when all beside is gone.

17

'"Let all be free and equal!—From your hearts
I feel an echo; through my inmost frame
Like sweetest sound, seeking its mate, it darts—
Whence come ye, friends? Alas, I cannot name
All that I read of sorrow, toil, and shame,
On your worn faces; as in legends old
Which make immortal the disastrous fame
Of conquerors and impostors false and bold,
The discord of your hearts, I in your looks behold.

18

'"Whence come ye, friends? from pouring human blood
Forth on the earth? Or bring ye steel and gold,
That Kings may dupe and slay the multitude?
Or from the famished poor, pale, weak and cold,
Bear ye the earnings of their toil? Unfold!
Speak! Are your hands in slaughter's sanguine hue
Stained freshly? have your hearts in guile grown old?
Know yourselves thus! ye shall be pure as dew,
And I will be a friend and sister unto you.

19

'"Disguise it not—we have one human heart—
All mortal thoughts confess a common home:
Blush not for what may to thyself impart
Stains of inevitable crime: the doom
Is this, which has, or may, or must become
Thine, and all humankind's. Ye are the spoil
Which Time thus marks for the devouring tomb—
Thou and thy thoughts and they, and all the toil
Wherewith ye twine the rings of life's perpetual coil.

20

'"Disguise it not—ye blush for what ye hate,
And Enmity is sister unto Shame;
Look on your mind—it is the book of fate—
Ah! it is dark with many a blazoned name
Of misery—all are mirrors of the same;
But the dark fiend who with his iron pen
Dipped in scorn's fiery poison, makes his fame
Enduring there, would o'er the heads of men
Pass harmless, if they scorned to make their hearts his den.

21

'"Yes, it is Hate, that shapeless fiendly thing
Of many names, all evil, some divine,
Whom self-contempt arms with a mortal sting;
Which, when the heart its snaky folds entwine
Is wasted quite, and when it doth repine
To gorge such bitter prey, on all beside
It turns with ninefold rage, as with its twine
When Amphisbaena some fair bird has tied,
Soon o'er the putrid mass he threats on every side.

22

'"Reproach not thine own soul, but know thyself,
Nor hate another's crime, nor loathe thine own.
It is the dark idolatry of self,
Which, when our thoughts and actions once are gone,
Demands that man should weep, and bleed, and groan;
Oh, vacant expiation! Be at rest.—
The past is Death's, the future is thine own;
And love and joy can make the foulest breast
A paradise of flowers, where peace might build her nest.

23

'"Speak thou! whence come ye?"—A Youth made reply:
"Wearily, wearily o'er the boundless deep
We sail;—thou readest well the misery
Told in these faded eyes, but much doth sleep
Within, which there the poor heart loves to keep,
Or dare not write on the dishonoured brow;
Even from our childhood have we learned to steep
The bread of slavery in the tears of woe,
And never dreamed of hope or refuge until now.

24

'"Yes—I must speak—my secret should have perished
Even with the heart it wasted, as a brand
Fades in the dying flame whose life it cherished,
But that no human bosom can withstand
Thee, wondrous Lady, and the mild command
Of thy keen eyes:—yes, we are wretched slaves,
Who from their wonted loves and native land
Are reft, and bear o'er the dividing waves
The unregarded prey of calm and happy graves.

25

'"We drag afar from pastoral vales the fairest
Among the daughters of those mountains lone,
We drag them there, where all things best and rarest
Are stained and trampled:—years have come and gone
Since, like the ship which bears me, I have known
No thought;—but now the eyes of one dear Maid
On mine with light of mutual love have shone—
She is my life,—I am but as the shade
Of her,—a smoke sent up from ashes, soon to fade.

26

'"For she must perish in the Tyrant's hall—
Alas, alas!"—He ceased, and by the sail
Sate cowering—but his sobs were heard by all,
And still before the ocean and the gale
The ship fled fast till the stars 'gan to fail;
And, round me gathered with mute countenance,
The Seamen gazed, the Pilot, worn and pale
With toil, the Captain with gray locks, whose glance
Met mine in restless awe—they stood as in a trance.

27

'"Recede not! pause not now! Thou art grown old,
But Hope will make thee young, for Hope and Youth
Are children of one mother, even Love—behold!
The eternal stars gaze on us!—is the truth
Within your soul? care for your own, or ruth
For others' sufferings? do ye thirst to bear
A heart which not the serpent Custom's tooth
May violate?—Be free! and even here,
Swear to be firm till death!" They cried, "We swear! We swear!"

28

'The very darkness shook, as with a blast
Of subterranean thunder, at the cry;
The hollow shore its thousand echoes cast
Into the night, as if the sea and sky,
And earth, rejoiced with new-born liberty,
For in that name they swore! Bolts were undrawn,
And on the deck, with unaccustomed eye
The captives gazing stood, and every one
Shrank as the inconstant torch upon her countenance shone.

29

'They were earth's purest children, young and fair,
With eyes the shrines of unawakened thought,
And brows as bright as Spring or Morning, ere
Dark time had there its evil legend wrought
In characters of cloud which wither not.—
The change was like a dream to them; but soon
They knew the glory of their altered lot,
In the bright wisdom of youth's breathless noon,
Sweet talk, and smiles, and sighs, all bosoms did attune.

30

'But one was mute; her cheeks and lips most fair,
Changing their hue like lilies newly blown,
Beneath a bright acacia's shadowy hair,
Waved by the wind amid the sunny noon,
Showed that her soul was quivering; and full soon
That Youth arose, and breathlessly did look
On her and me, as for some speechless boon:
I smiled, and both their hands in mine I took,
And felt a soft delight from what their spirits shook.

Canto 9

1

'That night we anchored in a woody bay,
And sleep no more around us dared to hover
Than, when all doubt and fear has passed away,
It shades the couch of some unresting lover,
Whose heart is now at rest: thus night passed over
In mutual joy:—around, a forest grew
Of poplars and dark oaks, whose shade did cover
The waning stars pranked in the waters blue,
And trembled in the wind which from the morning flew.

2

'The joyous Mariners, and each free Maiden
Now brought from the deep forest many a bough,
With woodland spoil most innocently laden;
Soon wreaths of budding foliage seemed to flow
Over the mast and sails, the stern and prow
Were canopied with blooming boughs,—the while
On the slant sun's path o'er the waves we go
Rejoicing, like the dwellers of an isle
Doomed to pursue those waves that cannot cease to smile.

3

'The many ships spotting the dark blue deep
With snowy sails, fled fast as ours came nigh,
In fear and wonder; and on every steep
Thousands did gaze, they heard the startling cry,
Like Earth's own voice lifted unconquerably
To all her children, the unbounded mirth,
The glorious joy of thy name—Liberty!
They heard!—As o'er the mountains of the earth
From peak to peak leap on the beams of Morning's birth:

4

'So from that cry over the boundless hills
Sudden was caught one universal sound,
Like a volcano's voice, whose thunder fills
Remotest skies,—such glorious madness found
A path through human hearts with stream which drowned
Its struggling fears and cares, dark Custom's brood;
They knew not whence it came, but felt around
A wide contagion poured—they called aloud
On Liberty—that name lived on the sunny flood.

5

'We reached the port.—Alas! from many spirits
The wisdom which had waked that cry, was fled,
Like the brief glory which dark Heaven inherits
From the false dawn, which fades ere it is spread,
Upon the night's devouring darkness shed:
Yet soon bright day will burst—even like a chasm
Of fire, to burn the shrouds outworn and dead,
Which wrap the world; a wide enthusiasm,
To cleanse the fevered world as with an earthquake's spasm!

6

'I walked through the great City then, but free
From shame or fear; those toil-worn Mariners
And happy Maidens did encompass me;
And like a subterranean wind that stirs
Some forest among caves, the hopes and fears
From every human soul, a murmur strange
Made as I passed; and many wept, with tears
Of joy and awe, and winged thoughts did range,
And half-extinguished words, which prophesied of change.

7

'For, with strong speech I tore the veil that hid
Nature, and Truth, and Liberty, and Love,—
As one who from some mountain's pyramid
Points to the unrisen sun!—the shades approve
His truth, and flee from every stream and grove.
Thus, gentle thoughts did many a bosom fill,—
Wisdom, the mail of tried affections wove
For many a heart, and tameless scorn of ill,
Thrice steeped in molten steel the unconquerable will.

8

'Some said I was a maniac wild and lost;
Some, that I scarce had risen from the grave,
The Prophet's virgin bride, a heavenly ghost:—
Some said, I was a fiend from my weird cave,
Who had stolen human shape, and o'er the wave,
The forest, and the mountain, came;—some said
I was the child of God, sent down to save
Woman from bonds and death, and on my head
The burden of their sins would frightfully be laid.

9

'But soon my human words found sympathy
In human hearts: the purest and the best,
As friend with friend, made common cause with me,
And they were few, but resolute;—the rest,
Ere yet success the enterprise had blessed,
Leagued with me in their hearts;—their meals, their slumber,
Their hourly occupations, were possessed
By hopes which I had armed to overnumber
Those hosts of meaner cares, which life's strong wings encumber.

10

'But chiefly women, whom my voice did waken
From their cold, careless, willing slavery,
Sought me: one truth their dreary prison has shaken,—
They looked around, and lo! they became free!
Their many tyrants sitting desolately
In slave-deserted halls, could none restrain;
For wrath's red fire had withered in the eye,
Whose lightning once was death,—nor fear, nor gain
Could tempt one captive now to lock another's chain.

11

'Those who were sent to bind me, wept, and felt
Their minds outsoar the bonds which clasped them round,
Even as a waxen shape may waste and melt
In the white furnace; and a visioned swound,
A pause of hope and awe the City bound,
Which, like the silence of a tempest's birth,
When in its awful shadow it has wound
The sun, the wind, the ocean, and the earth,
Hung terrible, ere yet the lightnings have leaped forth.

12

'Like clouds inwoven in the silent sky,
By winds from distant regions meeting there,
In the high name of truth and liberty,
Around the City millions gathered were,
By hopes which sprang from many a hidden lair,—
Words which the lore of truth in hues of flame
Arrayed, thine own wild songs which in the air
Like homeless odours floated, and the name
Of thee, and many a tongue which thou hadst dipped in flame.

13

'The Tyrant knew his power was gone, but Fear,
The nurse of Vengeance, bade him wait the event—
That perfidy and custom, gold and prayer,
And whatsoe'er, when force is impotent,
To fraud the sceptre of the world has lent,
Might, as he judged, confirm his failing sway.
Therefore throughout the streets, the Priests he sent
To curse the rebels.—To their gods did they
For Earthquake, Plague, and Want, kneel in the public way.

14

'And grave and hoary men were bribed to tell
From seats where law is made the slave of wrong,
How glorious Athens in her splendour fell,
Because her sons were free,—and that among
Mankind, the many to the few belong,
By Heaven, and Nature, and Necessity.
They said, that age was truth, and that the young
Marred with wild hopes the peace of slavery,
With which old times and men had quelled the vain and free.

15

'And with the falsehood of their poisonous lips
They breathed on the enduring memory
Of sages and of bards a brief eclipse;
There was one teacher, who necessity
Had armed with strength and wrong against mankind,
His slave and his avenger aye to be;
That we were weak and sinful, frail and blind,
And that the will of one was peace, and we
Should seek for nought on earth but toil and misery—

16

'"For thus we might avoid the hell hereafter."
So spake the hypocrites, who cursed and lied;
Alas, their sway was past, and tears and laughter
Clung to their hoary hair, withering the pride
Which in their hollow hearts dared still abide;
And yet obscener slaves with smoother brow,
And sneers on their strait lips, thin, blue and wide,
Said that the rule of men was over now,
And hence, the subject world to woman's will must bow;

17

'And gold was scattered through the streets, and wine
Flowed at a hundred feasts within the wall.
In vain! the steady towers in Heaven did shine
As they were wont, nor at the priestly call
Left Plague her banquet in the Ethiop's hall,
Nor Famine from the rich man's portal came,
Where at her ease she ever preys on all
Who throng to kneel for food: nor fear nor shame,
Nor faith, nor discord, dimmed hope's newly kindled flame.

18

'For gold was as a god whose faith began
To fade, so that its worshippers were few,
And Faith itself, which in the heart of man
Gives shape, voice, name, to spectral Terror, knew
Its downfall, as the altars lonelier grew,
Till the Priests stood alone within the fane;
The shafts of falsehood unpolluting flew,
And the cold sneers of calumny were vain,
The union of the free with discord's brand to stain.

19

'The rest thou knowest.—Lo! we two are here—
We have survived a ruin wide and deep—
Strange thoughts are mine.—I cannot grieve or fear,
Sitting with thee upon this lonely steep
I smile, though human love should make me weep.
We have survived a joy that knows no sorrow,
And I do feel a mighty calmness creep
Over my heart, which can no longer borrow
Its hues from chance or change, dark children of to-morrow.

20

'We know not what will come—yet, Laon, dearest,
Cythna shall be the prophetess of Love,
Her lips shall rob thee of the grace thou wearest,
To hide thy heart, and clothe the shapes which rove
Within the homeless Future's wintry grove;
For I now, sitting thus beside thee, seem
Even with thy breath and blood to live and move,
And violence and wrong are as a dream
Which rolls from steadfast truth, an unreturning stream.

21

'The blasts of Autumn drive the winged seeds
Over the earth,—next come the snows, and rain,
And frosts, and storms, which dreary Winter leads
Out of his Scythian cave, a savage train;
Behold! Spring sweeps over the world again,
Shedding soft dews from her ethereal wings;
Flowers on the mountains, fruits over the plain,
And music on the waves and woods she flings,
And love on all that lives, and calm on lifeless things.

22

'O Spring, of hope, and love, and youth, and gladness
Wind-winged emblem! brightest, best and fairest!
Whence comest thou, when, with dark Winter's sadness
The tears that fade in sunny smiles thou sharest?
Sister of joy, thou art the child who wearest
Thy mother's dying smile, tender and sweet;
Thy mother Autumn, for whose grave thou bearest
Fresh flowers, and beams like flowers, with gentle feet,
Disturbing not the leaves which are her winding-sheet.

23

'Virtue, and Hope, and Love, like light and Heaven,
Surround the world.—We are their chosen slaves.
Has not the whirlwind of our spirit driven
Truth's deathless germs to thought's remotest caves?
Lo, Winter comes!—the grief of many graves,
The frost of death, the tempest of the sword,
The flood of tyranny, whose sanguine waves
Stagnate like ice at Faith the enchanter's word,
And bind all human hearts in its repose abhorred.

24

'The seeds are sleeping in the soil: meanwhile
The Tyrant peoples dungeons with his prey,
Pale victims on the guarded scaffold smile
Because they cannot speak; and, day by day,
The moon of wasting Science wanes away
Among her stars, and in that darkness vast
The sons of earth to their foul idols pray,
And gray Priests triumph, and like blight or blast
A shade of selfish care o'er human looks is cast.

25

'This is the winter of the world;—and here
We die, even as the winds of Autumn fade,
Expiring in the frore and foggy air.
Behold! Spring comes, though we must pass, who made
The promise of its birth,—even as the shade
Which from our death, as from a mountain, flings
The future, a broad sunrise; thus arrayed
As with the plumes of overshadowing wings,
From its dark gulf of chains, Earth like an eagle springs.

26

'O dearest love! we shall be dead and cold
Before this morn may on the world arise;
Wouldst thou the glory of its dawn behold?
Alas! gaze not on me, but turn thine eyes
On thine own heart—it is a paradise
Which everlasting Spring has made its own,
And while drear Winter fills the naked skies,
Sweet streams of sunny thought, and flowers fresh-blown,
Are there, and weave their sounds and odours into one.

27

'In their own hearts the earnest of the hope
Which made them great, the good will ever find;
And though some envious shade may interlope
Between the effect and it, One comes behind,
Who aye the future to the past will bind—
Necessity, whose sightless strength for ever
Evil with evil, good with good must wind
In bands of union, which no power may sever:
They must bring forth their kind, and be divided never!

28

'The good and mighty of departed ages
Are in their graves, the innocent and free,
Heroes, and Poets, and prevailing Sages,
Who leave the vesture of their majesty
To adorn and clothe this naked world;—and we
Are like to them—such perish, but they leave
All hope, or love, or truth, or liberty,
Whose forms their mighty spirits could conceive,
To be a rule and law to ages that survive.

29

'So be the turf heaped over our remains
Even in our happy youth, and that strange lot,
Whate'er it be, when in these mingling veins
The blood is still, be ours; let sense and thought
Pass from our being, or be numbered not
Among the things that are; let those who come
Behind, for whom our steadfast will has bought
A calm inheritance, a glorious doom,
Insult with careless tread, our undivided tomb.

30

'Our many thoughts and deeds, our life and love,
Our happiness, and all that we have been,
Immortally must live, and burn and move,
When we shall be no more;—the world has seen
A type of peace; and—as some most serene
And lovely spot to a poor maniac's eye,
After long years, some sweet and moving scene
Of youthful hope, returning suddenly,
Quells his long madness—thus man shall remember thee.

31

'And Calumny meanwhile shall feed on us,
As worms devour the dead, and near the throne
And at the altar, most accepted thus
Shall sneers and curses be;—what we have done
None shall dare vouch, though it be truly known;
That record shall remain, when they must pass
Who built their pride on its oblivion;
And fame, in human hope which sculptured was,
Survive the perished scrolls of unenduring brass.

32

'The while we two, beloved, must depart,
And Sense and Reason, those enchanters fair,
Whose wand of power is hope, would bid the heart
That gazed beyond the wormy grave despair:
These eyes, these lips, this blood, seems darkly there
To fade in hideous ruin; no calm sleep
Peopling with golden dreams the stagnant air,
Seems our obscure and rotting eyes to steep
In joy;—but senseless death—a ruin dark and deep!

33

'These are blind fancies—reason cannot know
What sense can neither feel, nor thought conceive;
There is delusion in the world—and woe,
And fear, and pain—we know not whence we live,
Or why, or how, or what mute Power may give
Their being to each plant, and star, and beast,
Or even these thoughts.—Come near me! I do weave
A chain I cannot break—I am possessed
With thoughts too swift and strong for one lone human breast.

34

'Yes, yes—thy kiss is sweet, thy lips are warm—
O! willingly, beloved, would these eyes,
Might they no more drink being from thy form,
Even as to sleep whence we again arise,
Close their faint orbs in death: I fear nor prize
Aught that can now betide, unshared by thee—
Yes, Love when Wisdom fails makes Cythna wise:
Darkness and death, if death be true, must be
Dearer than life and hope, if unenjoyed with thee.

35

'Alas, our thoughts flow on with stream, whose waters
Return not to their fountain—Earth and Heaven,
The Ocean and the Sun, the Clouds their daughters,
Winter, and Spring, and Morn, and Noon, and Even,
All that we are or know, is darkly driven
Towards one gulf.—Lo! what a change is come
Since I first spake—but time shall be forgiven,
Though it change all but thee!'—She ceased—night's gloom
Meanwhile had fallen on earth from the sky's sunless dome.

36

Though she had ceased, her countenance uplifted
To Heaven, still spake, with solemn glory bright;
Her dark deep eyes, her lips, whose motions gifted
The air they breathed with love, her locks undight.
'Fair star of life and love,' I cried, 'my soul's delight,
Why lookest thou on the crystalline skies?
O, that my spirit were yon Heaven of night,
Which gazes on thee with its thousand eyes!'
She turned to me and smiled—that smile was Paradise!

Canto 10

1

Was there a human spirit in the steed,
That thus with his proud voice, ere night was gone,
He broke our linked rest? or do indeed
All living things a common nature own,
And thought erect an universal throne,
Where many shapes one tribute ever bear?
And Earth, their mutual mother, does she groan
To see her sons contend? and makes she bare
Her breast, that all in peace its drainless stores may share?

2

I have heard friendly sounds from many a tongue
Which was not human—the lone nightingale
Has answered me with her most soothing song,
Out of her ivy bower, when I sate pale
With grief, and sighed beneath; from many a dale
The antelopes who flocked for food have spoken
With happy sounds, and motions, that avail
Like man's own speech; and such was now the token
Of waning night, whose calm by that proud neigh was broken.

3

Each night, that mighty steed bore me abroad,
And I returned with food to our retreat,
And dark intelligence; the blood which flowed
Over the fields, had stained the courser's feet;
Soon the dust drinks that bitter dew,—then meet
The vulture, and the wild dog, and the snake,
The wolf, and the hyaena gray, and eat
The dead in horrid truce: their throngs did make
Behind the steed, a chasm like waves in a ship's wake.

4

For, from the utmost realms of earth came pouring
The banded slaves whom every despot sent
At that throned traitor's summons; like the roaring
Of fire, whose floods the wild deer circumvent
In the scorched pastures of the South; so bent
The armies of the leagued Kings around
Their files of steel and flame;—the continent
Trembled, as with a zone of ruin bound,
Beneath their feet, the sea shook with their Navies' sound.

5

From every nation of the earth they came,
The multitude of moving heartless things,
Whom slaves call men: obediently they came,
Like sheep whom from the fold the shepherd brings
To the stall, red with blood; their many kings
Led them, thus erring, from their native land;
Tartar and Frank, and millions whom the wings
Of Indian breezes lull, and many a band
The Arctic Anarch sent, and Idumea's sand,

6

Fertile in prodigies and lies;—so there
Strange natures made a brotherhood of ill.
The desert savage ceased to grasp in fear
His Asian shield and bow, when, at the will
Of Europe's subtler son, the bolt would kill
Some shepherd sitting on a rock secure;
But smiles of wondering joy his face would fill,
And savage sympathy: those slaves impure,
Each one the other thus from ill to ill did lure.

7

For traitorously did that foul Tyrant robe
His countenance in lies,—even at the hour
When he was snatched from death, then o'er the globe,
With secret signs from many a mountain-tower,
With smoke by day, and fire by night, the power
Of Kings and Priests, those dark conspirators,
He called:—they knew his cause their own, and swore
Like wolves and serpents to their mutual wars
Strange truce, with many a rite which Earth and Heaven abhors.

8

Myriads had come—millions were on their way;
The Tyrant passed, surrounded by the steel
Of hired assassins, through the public way,
Choked with his country's dead:—his footsteps reel
On the fresh blood—he smiles. 'Ay, now I feel
I am a King in truth!' he said, and took
His royal seat, and bade the torturing wheel
Be brought, and fire, and pincers, and the hook,
And scorpions, that his soul on its revenge might look.

9

'But first, go slay the rebels—why return
The victor bands?' he said, 'millions yet live,
Of whom the weakest with one word might turn
The scales of victory yet;—let none survive
But those within the walls—each fifth shall give
The expiation for his brethren here.—
Go forth, and waste and kill!'—'O king, forgive
My speech,' a soldier answered—'but we fear
The spirits of the night, and morn is drawing near;

10

'For we were slaying still without remorse,
And now that dreadful chief beneath my hand
Defenceless lay, when on a hell-black horse,
An Angel bright as day, waving a brand
Which flashed among the stars, passed.'—'Dost thou stand
Parleying with me, thou wretch?' the king replied;
'Slaves, bind him to the wheel; and of this band,
Whoso will drag that woman to his side
That scared him thus, may burn his dearest foe beside;

11

'And gold and glory shall be his.—Go forth!'
They rushed into the plain.—Loud was the roar
Of their career: the horsemen shook the earth;
The wheeled artillery's speed the pavement tore;
The infantry, file after file, did pour
Their clouds on the utmost hills. Five days they slew
Among the wasted fields; the sixth saw gore
Stream through the city; on the seventh, the dew
Of slaughter became stiff, and there was peace anew:

12

Peace in the desert fields and villages,
Between the glutted beasts and mangled dead!
Peace in the silent streets! save when the cries
Of victims to their fiery judgement led,
Made pale their voiceless lips who seemed to dread
Even in their dearest kindred, lest some tongue
Be faithless to the fear yet unbetrayed;
Peace in the Tyrant's palace, where the throng
Waste the triumphal hours in festival and song!

13

Day after day the burning sun rolled on
Over the death-polluted land—it came
Out of the east like fire, and fiercely shone
A lamp of Autumn, ripening with its flame
The few lone ears of corn;—the sky became
Stagnate with heat, so that each cloud and blast
Languished and died,—the thirsting air did claim
All moisture, and a rotting vapour passed
From the unburied dead, invisible and fast.

14

First Want, then Plague came on the beasts; their food
Failed, and they drew the breath of its decay.
Millions on millions, whom the scent of blood
Had lured, or who, from regions far away,
Had tracked the hosts in festival array,
From their dark deserts; gaunt and wasting now,
Stalked like fell shades among their perished prey;
In their green eyes a strange disease did glow,
They sank in hideous spasm, or pains severe and slow.

15

The fish were poisoned in the streams; the birds
In the green woods perished; the insect race
Was withered up; the scattered flocks and herds
Who had survived the wild beasts' hungry chase
Died moaning, each upon the other's face
In helpless agony gazing; round the City
All night, the lean hyaenas their sad case
Like starving infants wailed; a woeful ditty!
And many a mother wept, pierced with unnatural pity.

16

Amid the aereal minarets on high,
The Ethiopian vultures fluttering fell
From their long line of brethren in the sky,
Startling the concourse of mankind.—Too well
These signs the coming mischief did foretell:—
Strange panic first, a deep and sickening dread
Within each heart, like ice, did sink and dwell,
A voiceless thought of evil, which did spread
With the quick glance of eyes, like withering lightnings shed.

17

Day after day, when the year wanes, the frosts
Strip its green crown of leaves, till all is bare;
So on those strange and congregated hosts
Came Famine, a swift shadow, and the air
Groaned with the burden of a new despair;
Famine, than whom Misrule no deadlier daughter
Feeds from her thousand breasts, though sleeping there
With lidless eyes, lie Faith, and Plague, and Slaughter,
A ghastly brood; conceived of Lethe's sullen water.

18

There was no food, the corn was trampled down,
The flocks and herds had perished; on the shore
The dead and putrid fish were ever thrown;
The deeps were foodless, and the winds no more
Creaked with the weight of birds, but, as before
Those winged things sprang forth, were void of shade;
The vines and orchards, Autumn's golden store,
Were burned;—so that the meanest food was weighed
With gold, and Avarice died before the god it made.

19

There was no corn—in the wide market-place
All loathliest things, even human flesh, was sold;
They weighed it in small scales—and many a face
Was fixed in eager horror then: his gold
The miser brought; the tender maid, grown bold
Through hunger, bared her scorned charms in vain;
The mother brought her eldest born, controlled
By instinct blind as love, but turned again
And bade her infant suck, and died in silent pain.

20

Then fell blue Plague upon the race of man.
'O, for the sheathed steel, so late which gave
Oblivion to the dead, when the streets ran
With brothers' blood! O, that the earthquake's grave
Would gape, or Ocean lift its stifling wave!'
Vain cries—throughout the streets thousands pursued
Each by his fiery torture howl and rave,
Or sit in frenzy's unimagined mood,
Upon fresh heaps of dead; a ghastly multitude.

21

It was not hunger now, but thirst. Each well
Was choked with rotting corpses, and became
A cauldron of green mist made visible
At sunrise. Thither still the myriads came,
Seeking to quench the agony of the flame,
Which raged like poison through their bursting veins;
Naked they were from torture, without shame,
Spotted with nameless scars and lurid blains,
Childhood, and youth, and age, writhing in savage pains.

22

It was not thirst, but madness! Many saw
Their own lean image everywhere, it went
A ghastlier self beside them, till the awe
Of that dread sight to self-destruction sent
Those shrieking victims; some, ere life was spent,
Sought, with a horrid sympathy, to shed
Contagion on the sound; and others rent
Their matted hair, and cried aloud, 'We tread
On fire! the avenging Power his hell on earth has spread!'

23

Sometimes the living by the dead were hid.
Near the great fountain in the public square,
Where corpses made a crumbling pyramid
Under the sun, was heard one stifled prayer
For life, in the hot silence of the air;
And strange 'twas, amid that hideous heap to see
Some shrouded in their long and golden hair,
As if not dead, but slumbering quietly
Like forms which sculptors carve, then love to agony.

24

Famine had spared the palace of the king:—
He rioted in festival the while,
He and his guards and priests; but Plague did fling
One shadow upon all. Famine can smile
On him who brings it food, and pass, with guile
Of thankful falsehood, like a courtier gray,
The house-dog of the throne; but many a mile
Comes Plague, a winged wolf, who loathes alway
The garbage and the scum that strangers make her prey.

25

So, near the throne, amid the gorgeous feast,
Sheathed in resplendent arms, or loosely dight
To luxury, ere the mockery yet had ceased
That lingered on his lips, the warrior's might
Was loosened, and a new and ghastlier night
In dreams of frenzy lapped his eyes; he fell
Headlong, or with stiff eyeballs sate upright
Among the guests, or raving mad did tell
Strange truths; a dying seer of dark oppression's hell.

26

The Princes and the Priests were pale with terror;
That monstrous faith wherewith they ruled mankind,
Fell, like a shaft loosed by the bowman's error,
On their own hearts: they sought and they could find
No refuge—'twas the blind who led the blind!
So, through the desolate streets to the high fane,
The many-tongued and endless armies wind
In sad procession: each among the train
To his own Idol lifts his supplications vain.

27

'O God!' they cried, 'we know our secret pride
Has scorned thee, and thy worship, and thy name;
Secure in human power we have defied
Thy fearful might; we bend in fear and shame
Before thy presence; with the dust we claim
Kindred; be merciful, O King of Heaven!
Most justly have we suffered for thy fame
Made dim, but be at length our sins forgiven,
Ere to despair and death thy worshippers be driven.

28

'O King of Glory! thou alone hast power!
Who can resist thy will? who can restrain
Thy wrath, when on the guilty thou dost shower
The shafts of thy revenge, a blistering rain?
Greatest and best, be merciful again!
Have we not stabbed thine enemies, and made
The Earth an altar, and the Heavens a fane,
Where thou wert worshipped with their blood, and laid
Those hearts in dust which would thy searchless works have weighed?

29

'Well didst thou loosen on this impious City
Thine angels of revenge: recall them now;
Thy worshippers, abased, here kneel for pity,
And bind their souls by an immortal vow:
We swear by thee! and to our oath do thou
Give sanction, from thine hell of fiends and flame,
That we will kill with fire and torments slow,
The last of those who mocked thy holy name,
And scorned the sacred laws thy prophets did proclaim.'

30

Thus they with trembling limbs and pallid lips
Worshipped their own hearts' image, dim and vast,
Scared by the shade wherewith they would eclipse
The light of other minds;—troubled they passed
From the great Temple;—fiercely still and fast
The arrows of the plague among them fell,
And they on one another gazed aghast,
And through the hosts contention wild befell,
As each of his own god the wondrous works did tell.

31

And Oromaze, Joshua, and Mahomet,
Moses, and Buddh, Zerdusht, and Brahm, and Foh,
A tumult of strange names, which never met
Before, as watchwords of a single woe,
Arose; each raging votary 'gan to throw
Aloft his armed hands, and each did howl
'Our God alone is God!'—and slaughter now
Would have gone forth, when from beneath a cowl
A voice came forth, which pierced like ice through every soul.

32

'Twas an Iberian Priest from whom it came,
A zealous man, who led the legioned West,
With words which faith and pride had steeped in flame,
To quell the unbelievers; a dire guest
Even to his friends was he, for in his breast
Did hate and guile lie watchful, intertwined,
Twin serpents in one deep and winding nest;
He loathed all faith beside his own, and pined
To wreak his fear of Heaven in vengeance on mankind.

33

But more he loathed and hated the clear light
Of wisdom and free thought, and more did fear,
Lest, kindled once, its beams might pierce the night,
Even where his Idol stood; for, far and near
Did many a heart in Europe leap to hear
That faith and tyranny were trampled down;
Many a pale victim, doomed for truth to share
The murderer's cell, or see, with helpless groan,
The priests his children drag for slaves to serve their own.

34

He dared not kill the infidels with fire
Or steel, in Europe; the slow agonies
Of legal torture mocked his keen desire:
So he made truce with those who did despise
The expiation, and the sacrifice,
That, though detested, Islam's kindred creed
Might crush for him those deadlier enemies;
For fear of God did in his bosom breed
A jealous hate of man, an unreposing need.

35

'Peace! Peace!' he cried, 'when we are dead, the Day
Of Judgement comes, and all shall surely know
Whose God is God, each fearfully shall pay
The errors of his faith in endless woe!
But there is sent a mortal vengeance now
On earth, because an impious race had spurned
Him whom we all adore,—a subtle foe,
By whom for ye this dread reward was earned,
And kingly thrones, which rest on faith, nigh overturned.

36

'Think ye, because ye weep, and kneel, and pray,
That God will lull the pestilence? It rose
Even from beneath his throne, where, many a day,
His mercy soothed it to a dark repose:
It walks upon the earth to judge his foes;
And what are thou and I, that he should deign
To curb his ghastly minister, or close
The gates of death, ere they receive the twain
Who shook with mortal spells his undefended reign?

37

'Ay, there is famine in the gulf of hell,
Its giant worms of fire for ever yawn.—
Their lurid eyes are on us! those who fell
By the swift shafts of pestilence ere dawn,
Are in their jaws! they hunger for the spawn
Of Satan, their own brethren, who were sent
To make our souls their spoil. See! see! they fawn
Like dogs, and they will sleep with luxury spent,
When those detested hearts their iron fangs have rent!

38

'Our God may then lull Pestilence to sleep:—
Pile high the pyre of expiation now,
A forest's spoil of boughs, and on the heap
Pour venomous gums, which sullenly and slow,
When touched by flame, shall burn, and melt, and flow,
A stream of clinging fire,—and fix on high
A net of iron, and spread forth below
A couch of snakes, and scorpions, and the fry
Of centipedes and worms, earth's hellish progeny!

39

'Let Laon and Laone on that pyre,
Linked tight with burning brass, perish!—then pray
That, with this sacrifice, the withering ire
Of Heaven may be appeased.' He ceased, and they
A space stood silent, as far, far away
The echoes of his voice among them died;
And he knelt down upon the dust, alway
Muttering the curses of his speechless pride,
Whilst shame, and fear, and awe, the armies did divide.

40

His voice was like a blast that burst the portal
Of fabled hell; and as he spake, each one
Saw gape beneath the chasms of fire immortal,
And Heaven above seemed cloven, where, on a throne
Girt round with storms and shadows, sate alone
Their King and Judge—fear killed in every breast
All natural pity then, a fear unknown
Before, and with an inward fire possessed,
They raged like homeless beasts whom burning woods invest.

41

'Twas morn.—At noon the public crier went forth,
Proclaiming through the living and the dead,
'The Monarch saith, that his great Empire's worth
Is set on Laon and Laone's head:
He who but one yet living here can lead,
Or who the life from both their hearts can wring,
Shall be the kingdom's heir—a glorious meed!
But he who both alive can hither bring,
The Princess shall espouse, and reign an equal King.'

42

Ere night the pyre was piled, the net of iron
Was spread above, the fearful couch below;
It overtopped the towers that did environ
That spacious square; for Fear is never slow
To build the thrones of Hate, her mate and foe;
So, she scourged forth the maniac multitude
To rear this pyramid—tottering and slow,
Plague-stricken, foodless, like lean herds pursued
By gadflies, they have piled the heath, and gums, and wood.

43

Night came, a starless and a moonless gloom.
Until the dawn, those hosts of many a nation
Stood round that pile, as near one lover's tomb
Two gentle sisters mourn their desolation;
And in the silence of that expectation,
Was heard on high the reptiles' hiss and crawl—
It was so deep—save when the devastation
Of the swift pest, with fearful interval,
Marking its path with shrieks, among the crowd would fall.

44

Morn came,—among those sleepless multitudes,
Madness, and Fear, and Plague, and Famine still
Heaped corpse on corpse, as in autumnal woods
The frosts of many a wind with dead leaves fill
Earth's cold and sullen brooks; in silence, still
The pale survivors stood; ere noon, the fear
Of Hell became a panic, which did kill
Like hunger or disease, with whispers drear,
As 'Hush! hark! Come they yet?—Just Heaven! thine hour is near!'

45

And Priests rushed through their ranks, some counterfeiting
The rage they did inspire, some mad indeed
With their own lies; they said their god was waiting
To see his enemies writhe, and burn, and bleed,—
And that, till then, the snakes of Hell had need
Of human souls:—three hundred furnaces
Soon blazed through the wide City, where, with speed,
Men brought their infidel kindred to appease
God's wrath, and, while they burned, knelt round on quivering knees.

46

The noontide sun was darkened with that smoke,
The winds of eve dispersed those ashes gray.
The madness which these rites had lulled, awoke
Again at sunset.—Who shall dare to say
The deeds which night and fear brought forth, or weigh
In balance just the good and evil there?
He might man's deep and searchless heart display,
And cast a light on those dim labyrinths, where
Hope, near imagined chasms, is struggling with despair.

47

'Tis said, a mother dragged three children then,
To those fierce flames which roast the eyes in the head,
And laughed, and died; and that unholy men,
Feasting like fiends upon the infidel dead,
Looked from their meal, and saw an Angel tread
The visible floor of Heaven, and it was she!
And, on that night, one without doubt or dread
Came to the fire, and said, 'Stop, I am he!
Kill me!'—They burned them both with hellish mockery.

48

And, one by one, that night, young maidens came,
Beauteous and calm, like shapes of living stone
Clothed in the light of dreams, and by the flame
Which shrank as overgorged, they laid them down,
And sung a low sweet song, of which alone
One word was heard, and that was Liberty;
And that some kissed their marble feet, with moan
Like love, and died; and then that they did die
With happy smiles, which sunk in white tranquillity.

Canto 11

1

She saw me not—she heard me not—alone
Upon the mountain's dizzy brink she stood;
She spake not, breathed not, moved not—there was thrown
Over her look, the shadow of a mood
Which only clothes the heart in solitude,
A thought of voiceless depth;—she stood alone,
Above, the Heavens were spread;—below, the flood
Was murmuring in its caves;—the wind had blown
Her hair apart, through which her eyes and forehead shone.

2

A cloud was hanging o'er the western mountains;
Before its blue and moveless depth were flying
Gray mists poured forth from the unresting fountains
Of darkness in the North:—the day was dying:—
Sudden, the sun shone forth, its beams were lying
Like boiling gold on Ocean, strange to see,
And on the shattered vapours, which defying
The power of light in vain, tossed restlessly
In the red Heaven, like wrecks in a tempestuous sea.

3

It was a stream of living beams, whose bank
On either side by the cloud's cleft was made;
And where its chasms that flood of glory drank,
Its waves gushed forth like fire, and as if swayed
By some mute tempest, rolled on HER; the shade
Of her bright image floated on the river
Of liquid light, which then did end and fade—
Her radiant shape upon its verge did shiver;
Aloft, her flowing hair like strings of flame did quiver.

4

I stood beside her, but she saw me not—
She looked upon the sea, and skies, and earth;
Rapture, and love, and admiration wrought
A passion deeper far than tears, or mirth,
Or speech, or gesture, or whate'er has birth
From common joy; which with the speechless feeling
That led her there united, and shot forth
From her far eyes a light of deep revealing,
All but her dearest self from my regard concealing.

5

Her lips were parted, and the measured breath
Was now heard there;—her dark and intricate eyes
Orb within orb, deeper than sleep or death,
Absorbed the glories of the burning skies,
Which, mingling with her heart's deep ecstasies,
Burst from her looks and gestures;—and a light
Of liquid tenderness, like love, did rise
From her whole frame, an atmosphere which quite
Arrayed her in its beams, tremulous and soft and bright.

6

She would have clasped me to her glowing frame;
Those warm and odorous lips might soon have shed
On mine the fragrance and the invisible flame
Which now the cold winds stole;—she would have laid
Upon my languid heart her dearest head;
I might have heard her voice, tender and sweet;
Her eyes, mingling with mine, might soon have fed
My soul with their own joy.—One moment yet
I gazed—we parted then, never again to meet!

7

Never but once to meet on Earth again!
She heard me as I fled—her eager tone
Sunk on my heart, and almost wove a chain
Around my will to link it with her own,
So that my stern resolve was almost gone.
'I cannot reach thee! whither dost thou fly?
My steps are faint—Come back, thou dearest one—
Return, ah me! return!'—The wind passed by
On which those accents died, faint, far, and lingeringly.

8

Woe! Woe! that moonless midnight!—Want and Pest
Were horrible, but one more fell doth rear,
As in a hydra's swarming lair, its crest
Eminent among those victims—even the Fear
Of Hell: each girt by the hot atmosphere
Of his blind agony, like a scorpion stung
By his own rage upon his burning bier
Of circling coals of fire; but still there clung
One hope, like a keen sword on starting threads uphung:

9

Not death—death was no more refuge or rest;
Not life—it was despair to be!—not sleep,
For fiends and chasms of fire had dispossessed
All natural dreams: to wake was not to weep,
But to gaze mad and pallid, at the leap
To which the Future, like a snaky scourge,
Or like some tyrant's eye, which aye doth keep
Its withering beam upon his slaves, did urge
Their steps; they heard the roar of Hell's sulphureous surge.

10

Each of that multitude, alone, and lost
To sense of outward things, one hope yet knew;
As on a foam-girt crag some seaman tossed
Stares at the rising tide, or like the crew
Whilst now the ship is splitting through and through;
Each, if the tramp of a far steed was heard,
Started from sick despair, or if there flew
One murmur on the wind, or if some word
Which none can gather yet, the distant crowd has stirred.

11

Why became cheeks, wan with the kiss of death,
Paler from hope? they had sustained despair.
Why watched those myriads with suspended breath
Sleepless a second night? they are not here,
The victims, and hour by hour, a vision drear,
Warm corpses fall upon the clay-cold dead;
And even in death their lips are wreathed with fear.—
The crowd is mute and moveless—overhead
Silent Arcturus shines—'Ha! hear'st thou not the tread

12

'Of rushing feet? laughter? the shout, the scream,
Of triumph not to be contained? See! hark!
They come, they come! give way!' Alas, ye deem
Falsely—'tis but a crowd of maniacs stark
Driven, like a troop of spectres, through the dark,
From the choked well, whence a bright death-fire sprung,
A lurid earth-star, which dropped many a spark
From its blue train, and spreading widely, clung
To their wild hair, like mist the topmost pines among.

13

And many, from the crowd collected there,
Joined that strange dance in fearful sympathies;
There was the silence of a long despair,
When the last echo of those terrible cries
Came from a distant street, like agonies
Stifled afar.—Before the Tyrant's throne
All night his aged Senate sate, their eyes
In stony expectation fixed; when one
Sudden before them stood, a Stranger and alone.

14

Dark Priests and haughty Warriors gazed on him
With baffled wonder, for a hermit's vest
Concealed his face; but when he spake, his tone,
Ere yet the matter did their thoughts arrest,—
Earnest, benignant, calm, as from a breast
Void of all hate or terror—made them start;
For as with gentle accents he addressed
His speech to them, on each unwilling heart
Unusual awe did fall—a spirit-quelling dart.

15

'Ye Princes of the Earth, ye sit aghast
Amid the ruin which yourselves have made,
Yes, Desolation heard your trumpet's blast,
And sprang from sleep!—dark Terror has obeyed
Your bidding—O, that I whom ye have made
Your foe, could set my dearest enemy free
From pain and fear! but evil casts a shade,
Which cannot pass so soon, and Hate must be
The nurse and parent still of an ill progeny.

16

'Ye turn to Heaven for aid in your distress;
Alas, that ye, the mighty and the wise,
Who, if ye dared, might not aspire to less
Than ye conceive of power, should fear the lies
Which thou, and thou, didst frame for mysteries
To blind your slaves:—consider your own thought,
An empty and a cruel sacrifice
Ye now prepare, for a vain idol wrought
Out of the fears and hate which vain desires have brought.

17

'Ye seek for happiness—alas, the day!
Ye find it not in luxury nor in gold,
Nor in the fame, nor in the envied sway
For which, O willing slaves to Custom old,
Severe taskmistress! ye your hearts have sold.
Ye seek for peace, and when ye die, to dream
No evil dreams: all mortal things are cold
And senseless then; if aught survive, I deem
It must be love and joy, for they immortal seem.

18

'Fear not the future, weep not for the past.
Oh, could I win your ears to dare be now
Glorious, and great, and calm! that ye would cast
Into the dust those symbols of your woe,
Purple, and gold, and steel! that ye would go
Proclaiming to the nations whence ye came,
That Want, and Plague, and Fear, from slavery flow;
And that mankind is free, and that the shame
Of royalty and faith is lost in freedom's fame!

19

'If thus, 'tis well—if not, I come to say
That Laon—' while the Stranger spoke, among
The Council sudden tumult and affray
Arose, for many of those warriors young,
Had on his eloquent accents fed and hung
Like bees on mountain-flowers; they knew the truth,
And from their thrones in vindication sprung;
The men of faith and law then without ruth
Drew forth their secret steel, and stabbed each ardent youth.

20

They stabbed them in the back and sneered—a slave
Who stood behind the throne, those corpses drew
Each to its bloody, dark, and secret grave;
And one more daring raised his steel anew
To pierce the Stranger. 'What hast thou to do
With me, poor wretch?'—Calm, solemn and severe,
That voice unstrung his sinews, and he threw
His dagger on the ground, and pale with fear,
Sate silently—his voice then did the Stranger rear.

21

'It doth avail not that I weep for ye—
Ye cannot change, since ye are old and gray,
And ye have chosen your lot—your fame must be
A book of blood, whence in a milder day
Men shall learn truth, when ye are wrapped in clay:
Now ye shall triumph. I am Laon's friend,
And him to your revenge will I betray,
So ye concede one easy boon. Attend!
For now I speak of things which ye can apprehend.

22

'There is a People mighty in its youth,
A land beyond the Oceans of the West,
Where, though with rudest rites, Freedom and Truth
Are worshipped; from a glorious Mother's breast,
Who, since high Athens fell, among the rest
Sate like the Queen of Nations, but in woe,
By inbred monsters outraged and oppressed,
Turns to her chainless child for succour now,
It draws the milk of Power in Wisdom's fullest flow.

23

'That land is like an Eagle, whose young gaze
Feeds on the noontide beam, whose golden plume
Floats moveless on the storm, and in the blaze
Of sunrise gleams when Earth is wrapped in gloom;
An epitaph of glory for the tomb
Of murdered Europe may thy fame be made,
Great People! as the sands shalt thou become;
Thy growth is swift as morn, when night must fade;
The multitudinous Earth shall sleep beneath thy shade.

24

'Yes, in the desert there is built a home
For Freedom. Genius is made strong to rear
The monuments of man beneath the dome
Of a new Heaven; myriads assemble there,
Whom the proud lords of man, in rage or fear,
Drive from their wasted homes: the boon I pray
Is this—that Cythna shall be convoyed there—
Nay, start not at the name—America!
And then to you this night Laon will I betray.

25

'With me do what ye will. I am your foe!'
The light of such a joy as makes the stare
Of hungry snakes like living emeralds glow,
Shone in a hundred human eyes—'Where, where
Is Laon? Haste! fly! drag him swiftly here!
We grant thy boon.'—'I put no trust in ye,
Swear by the Power ye dread.'—'We swear, we swear!'
The Stranger threw his vest back suddenly,
And smiled in gentle pride, and said, 'Lo! I am he!'

Canto 12

1

The transport of a fierce and monstrous gladness
Spread through the multitudinous streets, fast flying
Upon the winds of fear; from his dull madness
The starveling waked, and died in joy; the dying,
Among the corpses in stark agony lying,
Just heard the happy tidings, and in hope
Closed their faint eyes; from house to house replying
With loud acclaim, the living shook Heaven's cope,
And filled the startled Earth with echoes: morn did ope

2

Its pale eyes then; and lo! the long array
Of guards in golden arms, and Priests beside,
Singing their bloody hymns, whose garbs betray
The blackness of the faith it seems to hide;
And see, the Tyrant's gem-wrought chariot glide
Among the gloomy cowls and glittering spears—
A Shape of light is sitting by his side,
A child most beautiful. I' the midst appears
Laon,—exempt alone from mortal hopes and fears.

3

His head and feet are bare, his hands are bound
Behind with heavy chains, yet none do wreak
Their scoffs on him, though myriads throng around;
There are no sneers upon his lip which speak
That scorn or hate has made him bold; his cheek
Resolve has not turned pale,—his eyes are mild
And calm, and, like the morn about to break,
Smile on mankind—his heart seems reconciled
To all things and itself, like a reposing child.

4

Tumult was in the soul of all beside,
Ill joy, or doubt, or fear; but those who saw
Their tranquil victim pass, felt wonder glide
Into their brain, and became calm with awe.—
See, the slow pageant near the pile doth draw.
A thousand torches in the spacious square,
Borne by the ready slaves of ruthless law,
Await the signal round: the morning fair
Is changed to a dim night by that unnatural glare.

5

And see! beneath a sun-bright canopy,
Upon a platform level with the pile,
The anxious Tyrant sit, enthroned on high,
Girt by the chieftains of the host; all smile
In expectation, but one child: the while
I, Laon, led by mutes, ascend my bier
Of fire, and look around: each distant isle
Is dark in the bright dawn; towers far and near,
Pierce like reposing flames the tremulous atmosphere.

6

There was such silence through the host, as when
An earthquake trampling on some populous town,
Has crushed ten thousand with one tread, and men
Expect the second; all were mute but one,
That fairest child, who, bold with love, alone
Stood up before the King, without avail,
Pleading for Laon's life—her stifled groan
Was heard—she trembled like one aspen pale
Among the gloomy pines of a Norwegian vale.

7

What were his thoughts linked in the morning sun,
Among those reptiles, stingless with delay,
Even like a tyrant's wrath?—The signal-gun
Roared—hark, again! In that dread pause he lay
As in a quiet dream—the slaves obey—
A thousand torches drop,—and hark, the last
Bursts on that awful silence; far away,
Millions, with hearts that beat both loud and fast,
Watch for the springing flame expectant and aghast.

8

They fly—the torches fall—a cry of fear
Has startled the triumphant!—they recede!
For, ere the cannon's roar has died, they hear
The tramp of hoofs like earthquake, and a steed
Dark and gigantic, with the tempest's speed,
Bursts through their ranks: a woman sits thereon,
Fairer, it seems, than aught that earth can breed,
Calm, radiant, like the phantom of the dawn,
A spirit from the caves of daylight wandering gone.

9

All thought it was God's Angel come to sweep
The lingering guilty to their fiery grave;
The Tyrant from his throne in dread did leap,—
Her innocence his child from fear did save;
Scared by the faith they feigned, each priestly slave
Knelt for his mercy whom they served with blood,
And, like the refluence of a mighty wave
Sucked into the loud sea, the multitude
With crushing panic, fled in terror's altered mood.

10

They pause, they blush, they gaze,—a gathering shout
Bursts like one sound from the ten thousand streams
Of a tempestuous sea:—that sudden rout
One checked, who, never in his mildest dreams
Felt awe from grace or loveliness, the seams
Of his rent heart so hard and cold a creed
Had seared with blistering ice—but he misdeems
That he is wise, whose wounds do only bleed
Inly for self,—thus thought the Iberian Priest indeed,

11

And others, too, thought he was wise to see,
In pain, and fear, and hate, something divine;
In love and beauty, no divinity.—
Now with a bitter smile, whose light did shine
Like a fiend's hope upon his lips and eyne,
He said, and the persuasion of that sneer
Rallied his trembling comrades—'Is it mine
To stand alone, when kings and soldiers fear
A woman? Heaven has sent its other victim here.'

12

'Were it not impious,' said the King, 'to break
Our holy oath?'—'Impious to keep it, say!'
Shrieked the exulting Priest:—'Slaves, to the stake
Bind her, and on my head the burden lay
Of her just torments:—at the Judgement Day
Will I stand up before the golden throne
Of Heaven, and cry, "To Thee did I betray
An infidel; but for me she would have known
Another moment's joy! the glory be thine own."'

13

They trembled, but replied not, nor obeyed,
Pausing in breathless silence. Cythna sprung
From her gigantic steed, who, like a shade
Chased by the winds, those vacant streets among
Fled tameless, as the brazen rein she flung
Upon his neck, and kissed his mooned brow.
A piteous sight, that one so fair and young,
The clasp of such a fearful death should woo
With smiles of tender joy as beamed from Cythna now.

14

The warm tears burst in spite of faith and fear
From many a tremulous eye, but like soft dews
Which feed Spring's earliest buds, hung gathered there,
Frozen by doubt,—alas! they could not choose
But weep; for when her faint limbs did refuse
To climb the pyre, upon the mutes she smiled;
And with her eloquent gestures, and the hues
Of her quick lips, even as a weary child
Wins sleep from some fond nurse with its caresses mild,

15

She won them, though unwilling, her to bind
Near me, among the snakes. When there had fled
One soft reproach that was most thrilling kind,
She smiled on me, and nothing then we said,
But each upon the other's countenance fed
Looks of insatiate love; the mighty veil
Which doth divide the living and the dead
Was almost rent, the world grew dim and pale,—
All light in Heaven or Earth beside our love did fail.—

16

Yet—yet—one brief relapse, like the last beam
Of dying flames, the stainless air around
Hung silent and serene—a blood-red gleam
Burst upwards, hurling fiercely from the ground
The globed smoke,—I heard the mighty sound
Of its uprise, like a tempestuous ocean;
And through its chasms I saw, as in a swound,
The tyrant's child fall without life or motion
Before his throne, subdued by some unseen emotion.—

17

And is this death?—The pyre has disappeared,
The Pestilence, the Tyrant, and the throng;
The flames grow silent—slowly there is heard
The music of a breath-suspending song,
Which, like the kiss of love when life is young,
Steeps the faint eyes in darkness sweet and deep;
With ever-changing notes it floats along,
Till on my passive soul there seemed to creep
A melody, like waves on wrinkled sands that leap.

18

The warm touch of a soft and tremulous hand
Wakened me then; lo! Cythna sate reclined
Beside me, on the waved and golden sand
Of a clear pool, upon a bank o'ertwined
With strange and star-bright flowers, which to the wind
Breathed divine odour; high above, was spread
The emerald heaven of trees of unknown kind,
Whose moonlike blooms and bright fruit overhead
A shadow, which was light, upon the waters shed.

19

And round about sloped many a lawny mountain
With incense-bearing forests and vast caves
Of marble radiance, to that mighty fountain;
And where the flood its own bright margin laves,
Their echoes talk with its eternal waves,
Which, from the depths whose jagged caverns breed
Their unreposing strife, it lifts and heaves,—
Till through a chasm of hills they roll, and feed
A river deep, which flies with smooth but arrowy speed.

20

As we sate gazing in a trance of wonder,
A boat approached, borne by the musical air
Along the waves which sung and sparkled under
Its rapid keel—a winged shape sate there,
A child with silver-shining wings, so fair,
That as her bark did through the waters glide,
The shadow of the lingering waves did wear
Light, as from starry beams; from side to side,
While veering to the wind her plumes the bark did guide.

21

The boat was one curved shell of hollow pearl,
Almost translucent with the light divine
Of her within; the prow and stern did curl
Horned on high, like the young moon supine,
When o'er dim twilight mountains dark with pine,
It floats upon the sunset's sea of beams,
Whose golden waves in many a purple line
Fade fast, till borne on sunlight's ebbing streams,
Dilating, on earth's verge the sunken meteor gleams.

22

Its keel has struck the sands beside our feet;—
Then Cythna turned to me, and from her eyes
Which swam with unshed tears, a look more sweet
Than happy love, a wild and glad surprise,
Glanced as she spake: 'Ay, this is Paradise
And not a dream, and we are all united!
Lo, that is mine own child, who in the guise
Of madness came, like day to one benighted
In lonesome woods: my heart is now too well requited!'

23

And then she wept aloud, and in her arms
Clasped that bright Shape, less marvellously fair
Than her own human hues and living charms;
Which, as she leaned in passion's silence there,
Breathed warmth on the cold bosom of the air,
Which seemed to blush and tremble with delight;
The glossy darkness of her streaming hair
Fell o'er that snowy child, and wrapped from sight
The fond and long embrace which did their hearts unite.

24

Then the bright child, the plumed Seraph came,
And fixed its blue and beaming eyes on mine,
And said, 'I was disturbed by tremulous shame
When once we met, yet knew that I was thine
From the same hour in which thy lips divine
Kindled a clinging dream within my brain,
Which ever waked when I might sleep, to twine
Thine image with HER memory dear—again
We meet; exempted now from mortal fear or pain.

25

'When the consuming flames had wrapped ye round,
The hope which I had cherished went away;
I fell in agony on the senseless ground,
And hid mine eyes in dust, and far astray
My mind was gone, when bright, like dawning day,
The Spectre of the Plague before me flew,
And breathed upon my lips, and seemed to say,
"They wait for thee, beloved!"—then I knew
The death-mark on my breast, and became calm anew.

26

'It was the calm of love—for I was dying.
I saw the black and half-extinguished pyre
In its own gray and shrunken ashes lying;
The pitchy smoke of the departed fire
Still hung in many a hollow dome and spire
Above the towers, like night,—beneath whose shade
Awed by the ending of their own desire
The armies stood; a vacancy was made
In expectation's depth, and so they stood dismayed.

27

'The frightful silence of that altered mood,
The tortures of the dying clove alone,
Till one uprose among the multitude,
And said—"The flood of time is rolling on;
We stand upon its brink, whilst They are gone
To glide in peace down death's mysterious stream.
Have ye done well? They moulder, flesh and bone,
Who might have made this life's envenomed dream
A sweeter draught than ye will ever taste, I deem.

28

'"These perish as the good and great of yore
Have perished, and their murderers will repent,—
Yes, vain and barren tears shall flow before
Yon smoke has faded from the firmament
Even for this cause, that ye who must lament
The death of those that made this world so fair,
Cannot recall them now; but there is lent
To man the wisdom of a high despair,
When such can die, and he live on and linger here.

29

'"Ay, ye may fear not now the Pestilence,
From fabled hell as by a charm withdrawn;
All power and faith must pass, since calmly hence
In pain and fire have unbelievers gone;
And ye must sadly turn away, and moan
In secret, to his home each one returning;
And to long ages shall this hour be known;
And slowly shall its memory, ever burning,
Fill this dark night of things with an eternal morning.

30

'"For me that world is grown too void and cold,
Since Hope pursues immortal Destiny
With steps thus slow—therefore shall ye behold
How those who love, yet fear not, dare to die;
Tell to your children this!" Then suddenly
He sheathed a dagger in his heart and fell;
My brain grew dark in death, and yet to me
There came a murmur from the crowd, to tell
Of deep and mighty change which suddenly befell.

31

'Then suddenly I stood, a winged Thought,
Before the immortal Senate, and the seat
Of that star-shining spirit, whence is wrought
The strength of its dominion, good and great,
The better Genius of this world's estate.
His realm around one mighty Fane is spread,
Elysian islands bright and fortunate,
Calm dwellings of the free and happy dead,
Where I am sent to lead!' These winged words she said,

32

And with the silence of her eloquent smile,
Bade us embark in her divine canoe;
Then at the helm we took our seat, the while
Above her head those plumes of dazzling hue
Into the winds' invisible stream she threw,
Sitting beside the prow: like gossamer
On the swift breath of morn, the vessel flew
O'er the bright whirlpools of that fountain fair,
Whose shores receded fast, while we seemed lingering there;

33

Till down that mighty stream, dark, calm, and fleet,
Between a chasm of cedarn mountains riven,
Chased by the thronging winds whose viewless feet
As swift as twinkling beams, had, under Heaven,
From woods and waves wild sounds and odours driven,
The boat fled visibly—three nights and days,
Borne like a cloud through morn, and noon, and even,
We sailed along the winding watery ways
Of the vast stream, a long and labyrinthine maze.

34

A scene of joy and wonder to behold
That river's shapes and shadows changing ever,
Where the broad sunrise filled with deepening gold
Its whirlpools, where all hues did spread and quiver;
And where melodious falls did burst and shiver
Among rocks clad with flowers, the foam and spray
Sparkled like stars upon the sunny river,
Or when the moonlight poured a holier day,
One vast and glittering lake around green islands lay.

35

Morn, noon, and even, that boat of pearl outran
The streams which bore it, like the arrowy cloud
Of tempest, or the speedier thought of man,
Which flieth forth and cannot make abode;
Sometimes through forests, deep like night, we glode,
Between the walls of mighty mountains crowned
With Cyclopean piles, whose turrets proud,
The homes of the departed, dimly frowned
O'er the bright waves which girt their dark foundations round.

36

Sometimes between the wide and flowering meadows,
Mile after mile we sailed, and 'twas delight
To see far off the sunbeams chase the shadows
Over the grass; sometimes beneath the night
Of wide and vaulted caves, whose roofs were bright
With starry gems, we fled, whilst from their deep
And dark-green chasms, shades beautiful and white,
Amid sweet sounds across our path would sweep,
Like swift and lovely dreams that walk the waves of sleep.

37

And ever as we sailed, our minds were full
Of love and wisdom, which would overflow
In converse wild, and sweet, and wonderful,
And in quick smiles whose light would come and go
Like music o'er wide waves, and in the flow
Of sudden tears, and in the mute caress—
For a deep shade was cleft, and we did know,
That virtue, though obscured on Earth, not less
Survives all mortal change in lasting loveliness.

38

Three days and nights we sailed, as thought and feeling
Number delightful hours—for through the sky
The sphered lamps of day and night, revealing
New changes and new glories, rolled on high,
Sun, Moon and moonlike lamps, the progeny
Of a diviner Heaven, serene and fair:
On the fourth day, wild as a windwrought sea
The stream became, and fast and faster bare
The spirit-winged boat, steadily speeding there.

39

Steady and swift, where the waves rolled like mountains
Within the vast ravine, whose rifts did pour
Tumultuous floods from their ten thousand fountains,
The thunder of whose earth-uplifting roar
Made the air sweep in whirlwinds from the shore,
Calm as a shade, the boat of that fair child
Securely fled, that rapid stress before,
Amid the topmost spray, and sunbows wild,
Wreathed in the silver mist: in joy and pride we smiled.

40

The torrent of that wide and raging river
Is passed, and our aereal speed suspended.
We look behind; a golden mist did quiver
When its wild surges with the lake were blended,—
Our bark hung there, as on a line suspended
Between two heavens,—that windless waveless lake
Which four great cataracts from four vales, attended
By mists, aye feed; from rocks and clouds they break,
And of that azure sea a silent refuge make.

41

Motionless resting on the lake awhile,
I saw its marge of snow-bright mountains rear
Their peaks aloft, I saw each radiant isle,
And in the midst, afar, even like a sphere
Hung in one hollow sky, did there appear
The Temple of the Spirit; on the sound
Which issued thence, drawn nearer and more near,
Like the swift moon this glorious earth around,
The charmed boat approached, and there its haven found.

Note on the "Revolt of Islam",
by Mrs. Shelley

Shelley possessed two remarkable qualities of intellect—a brilliant imagination, and a logical exactness of reason. His inclinations led him (he fancied) almost alike to poetry and metaphysical discussions. I say 'he fancied,' because I believe the former to have been paramount, and that it would have gained the mastery even had he struggled against it. However, he said that he deliberated at one time whether he should dedicate himself to poetry or metaphysics; and, resolving on the former, he educated himself for it, discarding in a great measure his philosophical pursuits, and engaging himself in the study of the poets of Greece, Italy, and England. To these may be added a constant perusal of portions of the old Testament—the Psalms, the Book of Job, the Prophet Isaiah, and others, the sublime poetry of which filled him with delight.

As a poet, his intellect and compositions were powerfully influenced by exterior circumstances, and especially by his place of abode. He was very fond of travelling, and ill-health increased this restlessness. The sufferings occasioned by a cold English winter made him pine, especially when our colder spring arrived, for a more genial climate. In 1816 he again visited Switzerland, and rented a house on the banks of the Lake of Geneva; and many a day, in cloud or sunshine, was passed alone in his boat—sailing as the wind listed, or weltering on the calm waters. The majestic aspect of Nature ministered such thoughts as he afterwards enwove in verse. His lines on the Bridge of the Arve, and his "Hymn to Intellectual Beauty", were written at this time. Perhaps during this summer his genius was checked by association with another poet whose nature was utterly dissimilar to his own, yet who, in the poem he wrote at that time, gave tokens that he shared for a period the more abstract and etherealised inspiration of Shelley. The saddest events awaited his return to England; but such was his fear to wound the feelings of others that he never expressed the anguish he felt, and seldom gave vent to the indignation roused by the persecutions he underwent; while the course of deep unexpressed passion, and the sense of injury, engendered the desire to embody themselves in forms defecated of all the weakness and evil which cling to real life.

He chose therefore for his hero a youth nourished in dreams of liberty, some of whose actions are in direct opposition to the opinions of the world; but who is animated throughout by an ardent love of virtue, and a resolution to confer the boons of political and intellectual freedom on his fellow-creatures. He created for this youth a woman such as he delighted to imagine—full of enthusiasm for the same objects; and they both, with will unvanquished, and the deepest sense of the justice of their cause, met adversity and death. There exists in this poem a memorial of a friend of his youth. The character of the old man who liberates Laon from his tower prison, and tends on him in sickness, is founded on that of Doctor Lind, who, when Shelley was at Eton, had often stood by to befriend and support him, and whose name he never mentioned without love and veneration.

During the year 1817 we were established at Marlow in Buckinghamshire. Shelley's choice of abode was fixed chiefly by this town being at no great distance from London, and its neighbourhood to the Thames. The poem was written in his boat, as it floated under the beech groves of Bisham, or during wanderings in the neighbouring country, which is distinguished for peculiar beauty. The chalk hills break into cliffs that overhang the Thames, or form valleys clothed with beech; the wilder portion of the country is rendered beautiful by exuberant vegetation; and the cultivated part is peculiarly fertile. With all this wealth of Nature which, either in the form of gentlemen's parks or soil dedicated to agriculture, flourishes around, Marlow was inhabited (I hope it is altered now) by a very poor population. The women are lacemakers, and lose their health by sedentary labour, for which they were very ill paid. The Poor-laws ground to the dust not only the paupers, but those who had risen just above that state, and were obliged to pay poor-rates. The changes produced by peace following a long war, and a bad harvest, brought with them the most heart-rending evils to the poor. Shelley afforded what alleviation he could. In the winter, while bringing out his poem, he had a severe attack of ophthalmia, caught while visiting the poor cottages. I mention these things,—for this minute and active sympathy with his fellow-creatures gives a thousandfold interest to his speculations, and stamps with reality his pleadings for the human race.

The poem, bold in its opinions and uncompromising in their expression, met with many censurers, not only among those who allow of no virtue but such as supports the cause they espouse, but even among those whose opinions were similar to his own. I extract a portion of a letter written in answer to one of these friends. It best details the impulses of Shelley's mind, and his motives: it was written with entire unreserve; and is therefore a precious monument of his own opinion of his powers, of the purity of his designs, and the ardour with which he clung, in adversity and through the valley of the shadow of death, to views from which he believed the permanent happiness of mankind must eventually spring.

'Marlowe, December 11, 1817

'I have read and considered all that you say about my general powers, and the particular instance of the poem in which I have attempted to develop them. Nothing can be more satisfactory to me than the interest which your admonitions express. But I think you are mistaken in some points with regard to the peculiar nature of my powers, whatever be their amount. I listened with deference and self-suspicion to your censures of "The Revolt of Islam"; but the productions of mine which you commend hold a very low place in my own esteem; and this reassures me, in some degree at least. The poem was produced by a series of thoughts which filled my mind with unbounded and sustained enthusiasm. I felt the precariousness of my life, and I engaged in this task, resolved to leave some record of myself. Much of what the volume contains was written with the same feeling—as real, though not so prophetic—as the communications of a dying man. I never presumed indeed to consider it anything approaching to faultless; but, when I consider contemporary productions of the same apparent pretensions, I own I was filled with confidence. I felt that it was in many respects a genuine picture of my own mind. I felt that the sentiments were true, not assumed. And in this have I long believed that my power consists; in sympathy, and that part of the imagination which relates to sentiment and contemplation. I am formed, if for anything not in common with the herd of mankind, to apprehend minute and remote distinctions of feeling, whether relative to external nature or the living beings which surround us, and to communicate the conceptions which result from considering either the moral or the material universe as a whole. Of course, I believe these faculties, which perhaps comprehend all that is sublime in man, to exist very imperfectly in my own mind. But, when you advert to my Chancery-paper, a cold, forced, unimpassioned, insignificant piece of cramped and cautious argument, and to the little scrap about "Mandeville", which expressed my feelings indeed, but cost scarcely two minutes' thought to express, as specimens of my powers more favourable than that which grew as it were from "the agony and bloody sweat" of intellectual travail; surely I must feel that, in some manner, either I am mistaken in believing that I have any talent at all, or you in the selection of the specimens of it. Yet, after all, I cannot but be conscious, in much of what I write, of an absence of that tranquillity which is the attribute and accompaniment of power. This feeling alone would make your most kind and wise admonitions, on the subject of the economy of intellectual force, valuable to me. And, if I live, or if I see any trust in coming years, doubt not but that I shall do something, whatever it may be, which a serious and earnest estimate of my powers will suggest to me, and which will be in every respect accommodated to their utmost limits.

(Shelley to Godwin.)

PRINCE ATHANASE

A Fragment

(The idea Shelley had formed of Prince Athanase was a good deal modelled on "Alastor". In the first sketch of the poem, he named it "Pandemos and Urania". Athanase seeks through the world the One whom he may love. He meets, in the ship in which he is embarked, a lady who appears to him to embody his ideal of love and beauty. But she proves to be Pandemos, or the earthly and unworthy Venus; who, after disappointing his cherished dreams and hopes, deserts him. Athanase, crushed by sorrow, pines and dies. 'On his deathbed, the lady who can really reply to his soul comes and kisses his lips' ("The Deathbed of Athanase"). The poet describes her (in the words of the final fragment, page 164). This slender note is all we have to aid our imagination in shaping out the form of the poem, such as its author imagined. (Mrs. Shelley's Note.))

(Written at Marlow in 1817, towards the close of the year; first published in "Posthumous Poems", 1824. Part 1 is dated by Mrs. Shelley, 'December, 1817,' the remainder, 'Marlow, 1817.' The verses were probably rehandled in Italy during the following year. Sources of the text are (1) "Posthumous Poems", 1824; (2) "Poetical Works" 1839, editions 1st and 2nd; (3) a much-tortured draft amongst the Bodleian manuscripts, collated by Mr. C.D. Locock. For (1) and (2) Mrs. Shelley is responsible. Our text (enlarged by about thirty lines fro the Bodleian manuscript) follows for the most part the "Poetical Works", 1839; verbal exceptions are pointed out in the footnotes. See also the Editor's Notes at the end of this volume, and Mr. Locock's "Examination of Shelley Manuscripts in the Bodleian Library", Oxford: Clarendon Press, 1903.)

Part 1

There was a youth, who, as with toil and travel,
Had grown quite weak and gray before his time;
Nor any could the restless griefs unravel

Which burned within him, withering up his prime
And goading him, like fiends, from land to land.
Not his the load of any secret crime,

For nought of ill his heart could understand,
But pity and wild sorrow for the same;—
Not his the thirst for glory or command,

Baffled with blast of hope-consuming shame;
Nor evil joys which fire the vulgar breast,
And quench in speedy smoke its feeble flame,

Had left within his soul their dark unrest:
Nor what religion fables of the grave
Feared he,—Philosophy's accepted guest.

For none than he a purer heart could have,
Or that loved good more for itself alone;
Of nought in heaven or earth was he the slave.

What sorrow, strange, and shadowy, and unknown,
Sent him, a hopeless wanderer, through mankind?—
If with a human sadness he did groan,

He had a gentle yet aspiring mind;
Just, innocent, with varied learning fed;
And such a glorious consolation find

In others' joy, when all their own is dead:
He loved, and laboured for his kind in grief,
And yet, unlike all others, it is said

That from such toil he never found relief.
Although a child of fortune and of power,
Of an ancestral name the orphan chief,

His soul had wedded Wisdom, and her dower
Is love and justice, clothed in which he sate
Apart from men, as in a lonely tower,

Pitying the tumult of their dark estate.—
Yet even in youth did he not e'er abuse
The strength of wealth or thought, to consecrate

Those false opinions which the harsh rich use
To blind the world they famish for their pride;
Nor did he hold from any man his dues,

But, like a steward in honest dealings tried,
With those who toiled and wept, the poor and wise,
His riches and his cares he did divide.

Fearless he was, and scorning all disguise,
What he dared do or think, though men might start,
He spoke with mild yet unaverted eyes;

Liberal he was of soul, and frank of heart,
And to his many friends—all loved him well—
Whate'er he knew or felt he would impart,

If words he found those inmost thoughts to tell;
If not, he smiled or wept; and his weak foes
He neither spurned nor hated—though with fell

And mortal hate their thousand voices rose,
They passed like aimless arrows from his ear—
Nor did his heart or mind its portal close

To those, or them, or any, whom life's sphere
May comprehend within its wide array.
What sadness made that vernal spirit sere?—

He knew not. Though his life, day after day,
Was failing like an unreplenished stream,
Though in his eyes a cloud and burthen lay,

Through which his soul, like Vesper's serene beam
Piercing the chasms of ever rising clouds,
Shone, softly burning; though his lips did seem

Like reeds which quiver in impetuous floods;
And through his sleep, and o'er each waking hour,
Thoughts after thoughts, unresting multitudes,

Were driven within him by some secret power,
Which bade them blaze, and live, and roll afar,
Like lights and sounds, from haunted tower to tower

O'er castled mountains borne, when tempest's war
Is levied by the night-contending winds,
And the pale dalesmen watch with eager ear;—

Though such were in his spirit, as the fiends
Which wake and feed an everliving woe,—
What was this grief, which ne'er in other minds

A mirror found,—he knew not—none could know;
But on whoe'er might question him he turned
The light of his frank eyes, as if to show

He knew not of the grief within that burned,
But asked forbearance with a mournful look;
Or spoke in words from which none ever learned

The cause of his disquietude; or shook
With spasms of silent passion; or turned pale:
So that his friends soon rarely undertook

To stir his secret pain without avail;—
For all who knew and loved him then perceived
That there was drawn an adamantine veil

Between his heart and mind,—both unrelieved
Wrought in his brain and bosom separate strife.
Some said that he was mad, others believed

That memories of an antenatal life
Made this, where now he dwelt, a penal hell;
And others said that such mysterious grief

From God's displeasure, like a darkness, fell
On souls like his, which owned no higher law
Than love; love calm, steadfast, invincible

By mortal fear or supernatural awe;
And others,—"Tis the shadow of a dream
Which the veiled eye of Memory never saw,

'But through the soul's abyss, like some dark stream
Through shattered mines and caverns underground,
Rolls, shaking its foundations; and no beam

'Of joy may rise, but it is quenched and drowned
In the dim whirlpools of this dream obscure;
Soon its exhausted waters will have found

'A lair of rest beneath thy spirit pure,
O Athanase!—in one so good and great,
Evil or tumult cannot long endure.

So spake they: idly of another's state
Babbling vain words and fond philosophy;
This was their consolation; such debate

Men held with one another; nor did he,
Like one who labours with a human woe,
Decline this talk: as if its theme might be

Another, not himself, he to and fro
Questioned and canvassed it with subtlest wit;
And none but those who loved him best could know

That which he knew not, how it galled and bit
His weary mind, this converse vain and cold;
For like an eyeless nightmare grief did sit

Upon his being; a snake which fold by fold
Pressed out the life of life, a clinging fiend
Which clenched him if he stirred with deadlier hold;—
And so his grief remained—let it remain—untold.

Part 2

Fragment 1

Prince Athanase had one beloved friend,
An old, old man, with hair of silver white,
And lips where heavenly smiles would hang and blend

With his wise words; and eyes whose arrowy light
Shone like the reflex of a thousand minds.
He was the last whom superstition's blight

Had spared in Greece—the blight that cramps and blinds,—
And in his olive bower at Oenoe
Had sate from earliest youth. Like one who finds

A fertile island in the barren sea,
One mariner who has survived his mates
Many a drear month in a great ship—so he

With soul-sustaining songs, and sweet debates
Of ancient lore, there fed his lonely being:—
'The mind becomes that which it contemplates,'—

And thus Zonoras, by for ever seeing
Their bright creations, grew like wisest men;
And when he heard the crash of nations fleeing

A bloodier power than ruled thy ruins then,
O sacred Hellas! many weary years
He wandered, till the path of Laian's glen

Was grass-grown—and the unremembered tears
Were dry in Laian for their honoured chief,
Who fell in Byzant, pierced by Moslem spears:—

And as the lady looked with faithful grief
From her high lattice o'er the rugged path,
Where she once saw that horseman toil, with brief

And blighting hope, who with the news of death
Struck body and soul as with a mortal blight,
She saw between the chestnuts, far beneath,

An old man toiling up, a weary wight;
And soon within her hospitable hall
She saw his white hairs glittering in the light

Of the wood fire, and round his shoulders fall;
And his wan visage and his withered mien,
Yet calm and gentle and majestical.

And Athanase, her child, who must have been
Then three years old, sate opposite and gazed
In patient silence.

Fragment 2

Such was Zonoras; and as daylight finds
One amaranth glittering on the path of frost,
When autumn nights have nipped all weaker kinds,

Thus through his age, dark, cold, and tempest-tossed,
Shone truth upon Zonoras; and he filled
From fountains pure, nigh overgrown and lost,

The spirit of Prince Athanase, a child,
With soul-sustaining songs of ancient lore
And philosophic wisdom, clear and mild.

And sweet and subtle talk they evermore,
The pupil and the master, shared; until,
Sharing that undiminishable store,

The youth, as shadows on a grassy hill
Outrun the winds that chase them, soon outran
His teacher, and did teach with native skill

Strange truths and new to that experienced man;
Still they were friends, as few have ever been
Who mark the extremes of life's discordant span.

So in the caverns of the forest green,
Or on the rocks of echoing ocean hoar,
Zonoras and Prince Athanase were seen

By summer woodmen; and when winter's roar
Sounded o'er earth and sea its blast of war,
The Balearic fisher, driven from shore,

Hanging upon the peaked wave afar,
Then saw their lamp from Laian's turret gleam,
Piercing the stormy darkness, like a star

Which pours beyond the sea one steadfast beam,
Whilst all the constellations of the sky
Seemed reeling through the storm. . . They did but seem—

For, lo! the wintry clouds are all gone by,
And bright Arcturus through yon pines is glowing,
And far o'er southern waves, immovably

Belted Orion hangs—warm light is flowing
From the young moon into the sunset's chasm.—
'O, summer eve! with power divine, bestowing

'On thine own bird the sweet enthusiasm
Which overflows in notes of liquid gladness,
Filling the sky like light! How many a spasm

'Of fevered brains, oppressed with grief and madness,
Were lulled by thee, delightful nightingale,—
And these soft waves, murmuring a gentle sadness,—

'And the far sighings of yon piny dale
Made vocal by some wind we feel not here.—
I bear alone what nothing may avail

'To lighten—a strange load!'—No human ear
Heard this lament; but o'er the visage wan
Of Athanase, a ruffling atmosphere

Of dark emotion, a swift shadow, ran,
Like wind upon some forest-bosomed lake,
Glassy and dark.—And that divine old man

Beheld his mystic friend's whole being shake,
Even where its inmost depths were gloomiest—
And with a calm and measured voice he spake,

And, with a soft and equal pressure, pressed
That cold lean hand:—'Dost thou remember yet
When the curved moon then lingering in the west

'Paused, in yon waves her mighty horns to wet,
How in those beams we walked, half resting on the sea?
'Tis just one year—sure thou dost not forget—

'Then Plato's words of light in thee and me
Lingered like moonlight in the moonless east,
For we had just then read—thy memory

'Is faithful now—the story of the feast;
And Agathon and Diotima seemed
From death and dark forgetfulness released. . .'

Fragment 3

And when the old man saw that on the green
Leaves of his opening. . . a blight had lighted
He said: 'My friend, one grief alone can wean

A gentle mind from all that once delighted:—
Thou lovest, and thy secret heart is laden
With feelings which should not be unrequited.'

And Athanase. . . then smiled, as one o'erladen
With iron chains might smile to talk (?) of bands
Twined round her lover's neck by some blithe maiden,
And said. . .

Fragment 4

'Twas at the season when the Earth upsprings
From slumber, as a sphered angel's child,
Shadowing its eyes with green and golden wings,

Stands up before its mother bright and mild,
Of whose soft voice the air expectant seems—
So stood before the sun, which shone and smiled

To see it rise thus joyous from its dreams,
The fresh and radiant Earth. The hoary grove
Waxed green—and flowers burst forth like starry beams;—

The grass in the warm sun did start and move,
And sea-buds burst under the waves serene:—
How many a one, though none be near to love,

Loves then the shade of his own soul, half seen
In any mirror—or the spring's young minions,
The winged leaves amid the copses green;—

How many a spirit then puts on the pinions
Of fancy, and outstrips the lagging blast,
And his own steps—and over wide dominions

Sweeps in his dream-drawn chariot, far and fast,
More fleet than storms—the wide world shrinks below,
When winter and despondency are past.

Fragment 5

'Twas at this season that Prince Athanase
Passed the white Alps—those eagle-baffling mountains
Slept in their shrouds of snow;—beside the ways

The waterfalls were voiceless—for their fountains
Were changed to mines of sunless crystal now,
Or by the curdling winds—like brazen wings

Which clanged along the mountain's marble brow—
Warped into adamantine fretwork, hung
And filled with frozen light the chasms below.

Vexed by the blast, the great pines groaned and swung
Under their load of (snow)—
. . .
. . .
Such as the eagle sees, when he dives down
From the gray deserts of wide air, (beheld)
(Prince) Athanase; and o'er his mien (?) was thrown

The shadow of that scene, field after field,
Purple and dim and wide. . .

Fragment 6

Thou art the wine whose drunkenness is all
We can desire, O Love! and happy souls,
Ere from thy vine the leaves of autumn fall,

Catch thee, and feed from their o'erflowing bowls
Thousands who thirst for thine ambrosial dew;—
Thou art the radiance which where ocean rolls

Investeth it; and when the heavens are blue
Thou fillest them; and when the earth is fair
The shadow of thy moving wings imbue

Its deserts and its mountains, till they wear
Beauty like some light robe;—thou ever soarest
Among the towers of men, and as soft air

In spring, which moves the unawakened forest,
Clothing with leaves its branches bare and bleak,
Thou floatest among men; and aye implorest

That which from thee they should implore:—the weak
Alone kneel to thee, offering up the hearts
The strong have broken—yet where shall any seek

A garment whom thou clothest not? the darts
Of the keen winter storm, barbed with frost,
Which, from the everlasting snow that parts

The Alps from Heaven, pierce some traveller lost
In the wide waved interminable snow
Ungarmented, . . .

Another Fragment (A)

Yes, often when the eyes are cold and dry,
And the lips calm, the Spirit weeps within
Tears bitterer than the blood of agony

Trembling in drops on the discoloured skin
Of those who love their kind and therefore perish
In ghastly torture—a sweet medicine

Of peace and sleep are tears, and quietly
Them soothe from whose uplifted eyes they fall
But. . .

Another Fragment (B)

Her hair was brown, her sphered eyes were brown,
And in their dark and liquid moisture swam,
Like the dim orb of the eclipsed moon;

Yet when the spirit flashed beneath, there came
The light from them, as when tears of delight
Double the western planet's serene flame.

ROSALIND AND HELEN

A Modern Eclogue

(Begun at Marlow, 1817 (summer); already in the press, March, 1818; finished at the Baths of Lucca, August, 1818; published with other poems, as the title-piece of a slender volume, by C. & J. Ollier, London, 1819 (spring). See "Biographical List". Sources of the text are (1) editio princeps, 1819; (2) "Poetical Works", edition Mrs. Shelley, 1839, editions 1st and 2nd. A fragment of the text is amongst the Boscombe manuscripts. The poem is reprinted here from the editio princeps; verbal alterations are recorded in the footnotes, punctual in the Editor's Notes at the end of Volume 3.)

Advertisement

The story of "Rosalind and Helen" is, undoubtedly, not an attempt in the highest style of poetry. It is in no degree calculated to excite profound meditation; and if, by interesting the affections and amusing the imagination, it awakens a certain ideal melancholy favourable to the reception of more important impressions, it will produce in the reader all that the writer experienced in the composition. I resigned myself, as I wrote, to the impulses of the feelings which moulded the conception of the story; and this impulse determined the pauses of a measure, which only pretends to be regular inasmuch as it corresponds with, and expresses, the irregularity of the imaginations which inspired it.

I do not know which of the few scattered poems I left in England will be selected by my bookseller to add to this collection. One ("Lines written among the Euganean Hills".—Editor.), which I sent from Italy, was written after a day's excursion among those lovely mountains which surround what was once the retreat, and where is now the sepulchre, of Petrarch. If any one is inclined to condemn the insertion of the introductory lines, which image forth the sudden relief of a state of deep despondency by the radiant visions disclosed by the sudden burst of an Italian sunrise in autumn on the highest peak of those delightful mountains, I can only offer as my excuse, that they were not erased at the request of a dear friend, with whom added years of intercourse only add to my apprehension of its value, and who would have had more right than any one to complain, that she has not been able to extinguish in me the very power of delineating sadness.

Naples, December 20, 1818

Rosalind, Helen, and her Child

Scene. *The Shore of the Lake of Como.*
Helen: Come hither, my sweet Rosalind.
  'Tis long since thou and I have met;
  And yet methinks it were unkind
  Those moments to forget.
  Come, sit by me. I see thee stand
  By this lone lake, in this far land,
  Thy loose hair in the light wind flying,
  Thy sweet voice to each tone of even
  United, and thine eyes replying
  To the hues of yon fair heaven.
  Come, gentle friend: wilt sit by me?
  And be as thou wert wont to be
  Ere we were disunited?
  None doth behold us now; the power
  That led us forth at this lone hour
  Will be but ill requited
  If thou depart in scorn: oh! come,
  And talk of our abandoned home.
  Remember, this is Italy,
  And we are exiles. Talk with me
  Of that our land, whose wilds and floods,
  Barren and dark although they be,
  Were dearer than these chestnut woods:
  Those heathy paths, that inland stream,
  And the blue mountains, shapes which seem
  Like wrecks of childhood's sunny dream:
  Which that we have abandoned now,
  Weighs on the heart like that remorse
  Which altered friendship leaves. I seek
  No more our youthful intercourse.
  That cannot be! Rosalind, speak.
  Speak to me. Leave me not.—When morn did come,
  When evening fell upon our common home,
  When for one hour we parted,—do not frown:
  I would not chide thee, though thy faith is broken:

But turn to me. Oh! by this cherished token,
Of woven hair, which thou wilt not disown,
Turn, as 'twere but the memory of me,
And not my scorned self who prayed to thee.
ROSALIND: Is it a dream, or do I see
And hear frail Helen? I would flee
Thy tainting touch; but former years
Arise, and bring forbidden tears;
And my o'erburthened memory
Seeks yet its lost repose in thee.
I share thy crime. I cannot choose
But weep for thee: mine own strange grief
But seldom stoops to such relief:
Nor ever did I love thee less,
Though mourning o'er thy wickedness
Even with a sister's woe. I knew
What to the evil world is due,
And therefore sternly did refuse
To link me with the infamy
Of one so lost as Helen. Now
Bewildered by my dire despair,
Wondering I blush, and weep that thou
Should'st love me still,—thou only!—There,
Let us sit on that gray stone
Till our mournful talk be done.
HELEN: Alas! not there; I cannot bear
The murmur of this lake to hear.
A sound from there, Rosalind dear,
Which never yet I heard elsewhere
But in our native land, recurs,
Even here where now we meet. It stirs
Too much of suffocating sorrow!
In the dell of yon dark chestnutwood
Is a stone seat, a solitude
Less like our own. The ghost of Peace
Will not desert this spot. To-morrow,
If thy kind feelings should not cease,
We may sit here.

ROSALIND: Thou lead, my sweet,
   And I will follow.
HENRY: 'Tis Fenici's seat
   Where you are going? This is not the way,
   Mamma; it leads behind those trees that grow
   Close to the little river.
HELEN: Yes: I know;
   I was bewildered. Kiss me and be gay,
   Dear boy: why do you sob?
HENRY: I do not know:
   But it might break any one's heart to see
   You and the lady cry so bitterly.
HELEN: It is a gentle child, my friend. Go home,
   Henry, and play with Lilla till I come.
   We only cried with joy to see each other;
   We are quite merry now: Good-night.

The boy
Lifted a sudden look upon his mother,
And in the gleam of forced and hollow joy
Which lightened o'er her face, laughed with the glee
Of light and unsuspecting infancy,
And whispered in her ear, 'Bring home with you
That sweet strange lady-friend.' Then off he flew,
But stopped, and beckoned with a meaning smile,
Where the road turned. Pale Rosalind the while,
Hiding her face, stood weeping silently.

In silence then they took the way
Beneath the forest's solitude.
It was a vast and antique wood,
Thro' which they took their way;
And the gray shades of evening
O'er that green wilderness did fling
Still deeper solitude.
Pursuing still the path that wound
The vast and knotted trees around
Through which slow shades were wandering,
To a deep lawny dell they came,

To a stone seat beside a spring,
O'er which the columned wood did frame
A roofless temple, like the fane
Where, ere new creeds could faith obtain,
Man's early race once knelt beneath
The overhanging deity.
O'er this fair fountain hung the sky,
Now spangled with rare stars. The snake,
The pale snake, that with eager breath
Creeps here his noontide thirst to slake,
Is beaming with many a mingled hue,
Shed from yon dome's eternal blue,
When he floats on that dark and lucid flood
In the light of his own loveliness;
And the birds that in the fountain dip
Their plumes, with fearless fellowship
Above and round him wheel and hover.
The fitful wind is heard to stir
One solitary leaf on high;
The chirping of the grasshopper
Fills every pause. There is emotion
In all that dwells at noontide here;
Then, through the intricate wild wood,
A maze of life and light and motion
Is woven. But there is stillness now:
Gloom, and the trance of Nature now:
The snake is in his cave asleep;
The birds are on the branches dreaming:
Only the shadows creep:
Only the glow-worm is gleaming:
Only the owls and the nightingales
Wake in this dell when daylight fails,
And gray shades gather in the woods:
And the owls have all fled far away
In a merrier glen to hoot and play,
For the moon is veiled and sleeping now.
The accustomed nightingale still broods
On her accustomed bough,

But she is mute; for her false mate
Has fled and left her desolate.

This silent spot tradition old
Had peopled with the spectral dead.
For the roots of the speaker's hair felt cold
And stiff, as with tremulous lips he told
That a hellish shape at midnight led
The ghost of a youth with hoary hair,
And sate on the seat beside him there,
Till a naked child came wandering by,
When the fiend would change to a lady fair!
A fearful tale! The truth was worse:
For here a sister and a brother
Had solemnized a monstrous curse,
Meeting in this fair solitude:
For beneath yon very sky,
Had they resigned to one another
Body and soul. The multitude:
Tracking them to the secret wood,
Tore limb from limb their innocent child,
And stabbed and trampled on its mother;
But the youth, for God's most holy grace,
A priest saved to burn in the market-place.

Duly at evening Helen came
To this lone silent spot,
From the wrecks of a tale of wilder sorrow
So much of sympathy to borrow
As soothed her own dark lot.
Duly each evening from her home,
With her fair child would Helen come
To sit upon that antique seat,
While the hues of day were pale;
And the bright boy beside her feet
Now lay, lifting at intervals
His broad blue eyes on her;
Now, where some sudden impulse calls
Following. He was a gentle boy

And in all gentle sorts took joy;
Oft in a dry leaf for a boat,
With a small feather for a sail,
His fancy on that spring would float,
If some invisible breeze might stir
Its marble calm: and Helen smiled
Through tears of awe on the gay child,
To think that a boy as fair as he,
In years which never more may be,
By that same fount, in that same wood,
The like sweet fancies had pursued;
And that a mother, lost like her,
Had mournfully sate watching him.
Then all the scene was wont to swim
Through the mist of a burning tear.

For many months had Helen known
This scene; and now she thither turned
Her footsteps, not alone.
The friend whose falsehood she had mourned,
Sate with her on that seat of stone.
Silent they sate; for evening,
And the power its glimpses bring
Had, with one awful shadow, quelled
The passion of their grief. They sate
With linked hands, for unrepelled
Had Helen taken Rosalind's.
Like the autumn wind, when it unbinds
The tangled locks of the nightshade's hair,
Which is twined in the sultry summer air
Round the walls of an outworn sepulchre,
Did the voice of Helen, sad and sweet,
And the sound of her heart that ever beat,
As with sighs and words she breathed on her,
Unbind the knots of her friend's despair,
Till her thoughts were free to float and flow;
And from her labouring bosom now,
Like the bursting of a prisoned flame,
The voice of a long pent sorrow came.

ROSALIND: I saw the dark earth fall upon
 The coffin; and I saw the stone
 Laid over him whom this cold breast
 Had pillowed to his nightly rest!
 Thou knowest not, thou canst not know
 My agony. Oh! I could not weep:
 The sources whence such blessings flow
 Were not to be approached by me!
 But I could smile, and I could sleep,
 Though with a self-accusing heart.
 In morning's light, in evening's gloom,
 I watched,—and would not thence depart—
 My husband's unlamented tomb.
 My children knew their sire was gone,
 But when I told them,—'He is dead,'—
 They laughed aloud in frantic glee,
 They clapped their hands and leaped about,
 Answering each other's ecstasy
 With many a prank and merry shout.
 But I sate silent and alone,
 Wrapped in the mock of mourning weed.

 They laughed, for he was dead: but I
 Sate with a hard and tearless eye,
 And with a heart which would deny
 The secret joy it could not quell,
 Low muttering o'er his loathed name;
 Till from that self-contention came
 Remorse where sin was none; a hell
 Which in pure spirits should not dwell.

 I'll tell thee truth. He was a man
 Hard, selfish, loving only gold,
 Yet full of guile; his pale eyes ran
 With tears, which each some falsehood told,
 And oft his smooth and bridled tongue
 Would give the lie to his flushing cheek;
 He was a coward to the strong:
 He was a tyrant to the weak,

On whom his vengeance he would wreak:
For scorn, whose arrows search the heart,
From many a stranger's eye would dart,
And on his memory cling, and follow
His soul to its home so cold and hollow.
He was a tyrant to the weak,
And we were such, alas the day!
Oft, when my little ones at play,
Were in youth's natural lightness gay,
Or if they listened to some tale
Of travellers, or of fairy land,—
When the light from the wood-fire's dying brand
Flashed on their faces,—if they heard
Or thought they heard upon the stair
His footstep, the suspended word
Died on my lips: we all grew pale:
The babe at my bosom was hushed with fear
If it thought it heard its father near;
And my two wild boys would near my knee
Cling, cowed and cowering fearfully.

I'll tell thee truth: I loved another.
His name in my ear was ever ringing,
His form to my brain was ever clinging:
Yet if some stranger breathed that name,
My lips turned white, and my heart beat fast:
My nights were once haunted by dreams of flame,
My days were dim in the shadow cast
By the memory of the same!
Day and night, day and night,
He was my breath and life and light,
For three short years, which soon were passed.
On the fourth, my gentle mother
Led me to the shrine, to be
His sworn bride eternally.
And now we stood on the altar stair,
When my father came from a distant land,
And with a loud and fearful cry
Rushed between us suddenly.

I saw the stream of his thin gray hair,
I saw his lean and lifted hand,
And heard his words,—and live! Oh God!
Wherefore do I live?—'Hold, hold!'
He cried, 'I tell thee 'tis her brother!
Thy mother, boy, beneath the sod
Of yon churchyard rests in her shroud so cold:
I am now weak, and pale, and old:
We were once dear to one another,
I and that corpse! Thou art our child!'
Then with a laugh both long and wild
The youth upon the pavement fell:
They found him dead! All looked on me,
The spasms of my despair to see:
But I was calm. I went away:
I was clammy-cold like clay!
I did not weep: I did not speak:
But day by day, week after week,
I walked about like a corpse alive!
Alas! sweet friend, you must believe
This heart is stone: it did not break.
My father lived a little while,
But all might see that he was dying,
He smiled with such a woeful smile!
When he was in the churchyard lying
Among the worms, we grew quite poor,
So that no one would give us bread:
My mother looked at me, and said
Faint words of cheer, which only meant
That she could die and be content;
So I went forth from the same church door
To another husband's bed.
And this was he who died at last,
When weeks and months and years had passed,
Through which I firmly did fulfil
My duties, a devoted wife,
With the stern step of vanquished will,
Walking beneath the night of life,
Whose hours extinguished, like slow rain

Falling for ever, pain by pain,
The very hope of death's dear rest;
Which, since the heart within my breast
Of natural life was dispossessed,
Its strange sustainer there had been.

When flowers were dead, and grass was green
Upon my mother's grave,—that mother
Whom to outlive, and cheer, and make
My wan eyes glitter for her sake,
Was my vowed task, the single care
Which once gave life to my despair,—
When she was a thing that did not stir
And the crawling worms were cradling her
To a sleep more deep and so more sweet
Than a baby's rocked on its nurse's knee,
I lived: a living pulse then beat
Beneath my heart that awakened me.
What was this pulse so warm and free?
Alas! I knew it could not be
My own dull blood: 'twas like a thought
Of liquid love, that spread and wrought
Under my bosom and in my brain,
And crept with the blood through every vein;
And hour by hour, day after day,
The wonder could not charm away,
But laid in sleep, my wakeful pain,
Until I knew it was a child,
And then I wept. For long, long years
These frozen eyes had shed no tears:
But now—'twas the season fair and mild
When April has wept itself to May:
I sate through the sweet sunny day
By my window bowered round with leaves,
And down my cheeks the quick tears fell
Like twinkling rain-drops from the eaves,
When warm spring showers are passing o'er.
O Helen, none can ever tell
The joy it was to weep once more!

I wept to think how hard it were
To kill my babe, and take from it
The sense of light, and the warm air,
And my own fond and tender care,
And love and smiles; ere I knew yet
That these for it might, as for me,
Be the masks of a grinning mockery.
And haply, I would dream, 'twere sweet
To feed it from my faded breast,
Or mark my own heart's restless beat
Rock it to its untroubled rest,
And watch the growing soul beneath
Dawn in faint smiles; and hear its breath,
Half interrupted by calm sighs,
And search the depth of its fair eyes
For long departed memories!
And so I lived till that sweet load
Was lightened. Darkly forward flowed
The stream of years, and on it bore
Two shapes of gladness to my sight;
Two other babes, delightful more
In my lost soul's abandoned night,
Than their own country ships may be
Sailing towards wrecked mariners,
Who cling to the rock of a wintry sea.
For each, as it came, brought soothing tears;
And a loosening warmth, as each one lay
Sucking the sullen milk away
About my frozen heart, did play,
And weaned it, oh how painfully—
As they themselves were weaned each one
From that sweet food,—even from the thirst
Of death, and nothingness, and rest,
Strange inmate of a living breast!
Which all that I had undergone
Of grief and shame, since she, who first
The gates of that dark refuge closed,
Came to my sight, and almost burst
The seal of that Lethean spring;

But these fair shadows interposed:
For all delights are shadows now!
And from my brain to my dull brow
The heavy tears gather and flow:
I cannot speak: Oh, let me weep!

The tears which fell from her wan eyes
Glimmered among the moonlight dew:
Her deep hard sobs and heavy sighs
Their echoes in the darkness threw.
When she grew calm, she thus did keep
The tenor of her tale:
He died:
I know not how: he was not old,
If age be numbered by its years:
But he was bowed and bent with fears,
Pale with the quenchless thirst of gold,
Which, like fierce fever, left him weak;
And his strait lip and bloated cheek
Were warped in spasms by hollow sneers;
And selfish cares with barren plough,
Not age, had lined his narrow brow,
And foul and cruel thoughts, which feed
Upon the withering life within,
Like vipers on some poisonous weed.
Whether his ill were death or sin
None knew, until he died indeed,
And then men owned they were the same.

Seven days within my chamber lay
That corse, and my babes made holiday:
At last, I told them what is death:
The eldest, with a kind of shame,
Came to my knees with silent breath,
And sate awe-stricken at my feet;
And soon the others left their play,
And sate there too. It is unmeet
To shed on the brief flower of youth
The withering knowledge of the grave;

From me remorse then wrung that truth.
I could not bear the joy which gave
Too just a response to mine own.
In vain. I dared not feign a groan,
And in their artless looks I saw,
Between the mists of fear and awe,
That my own thought was theirs, and they
Expressed it not in words, but said,
Each in its heart, how every day
Will pass in happy work and play,
Now he is dead and gone away.

After the funeral all our kin
Assembled, and the will was read.
My friend, I tell thee, even the dead
Have strength, their putrid shrouds within,
To blast and torture. Those who live
Still fear the living, but a corse
Is merciless, and power doth give
To such pale tyrants half the spoil
He rends from those who groan and toil,
Because they blush not with remorse
Among their crawling worms. Behold,
I have no child! my tale grows old
With grief, and staggers: let it reach
The limits of my feeble speech,
And languidly at length recline
On the brink of its own grave and mine.

Thou knowest what a thing is Poverty
Among the fallen on evil days:
'Tis Crime, and Fear, and Infamy,
And houseless Want in frozen ways
Wandering ungarmented, and Pain,
And, worse than all, that inward stain
Foul Self-contempt, which drowns in sneers
Youth's starlight smile, and makes its tears
First like hot gall, then dry for ever!
And well thou knowest a mother never

Could doom her children to this ill,
And well he knew the same. The will
Imported, that if e'er again
I sought my children to behold,
Or in my birthplace did remain
Beyond three days, whose hours were told,
They should inherit nought: and he,
To whom next came their patrimony,
A sallow lawyer, cruel and cold,
Aye watched me, as the will was read,
With eyes askance, which sought to see
The secrets of my agony;
And with close lips and anxious brow
Stood canvassing still to and fro
The chance of my resolve, and all
The dead man's caution just did call;
For in that killing lie 'twas said—
'She is adulterous, and doth hold
In secret that the Christian creed
Is false, and therefore is much need
That I should have a care to save
My children from eternal fire.'
Friend, he was sheltered by the grave,
And therefore dared to be a liar!
In truth, the Indian on the pyre
Of her dead husband, half consumed,
As well might there be false, as I
To those abhorred embraces doomed,
Far worse than fire's brief agony
As to the Christian creed, if true
Or false, I never questioned it:
I took it as the vulgar do:
Nor my vexed soul had leisure yet
To doubt the things men say, or deem
That they are other than they seem.

All present who those crimes did hear,
In feigned or actual scorn and fear,
Men, women, children, slunk away,

Whispering with self-contented pride,
Which half suspects its own base lie.
I spoke to none, nor did abide,
But silently I went my way,
Nor noticed I where joyously
Sate my two younger babes at play,
In the court-yard through which I passed;
But went with footsteps firm and fast
Till I came to the brink of the ocean green,
And there, a woman with gray hairs,
Who had my mother's servant been,
Kneeling, with many tears and prayers,
Made me accept a purse of gold,
Half of the earnings she had kept
To refuge her when weak and old.

With woe, which never sleeps or slept,
I wander now. 'Tis a vain thought—
But on yon alp, whose snowy head
'Mid the azure air is islanded,
(We see it o'er the flood of cloud,
Which sunrise from its eastern caves
Drives, wrinkling into golden waves,
Hung with its precipices proud,
From that gray stone where first we met)
There now—who knows the dead feel nought?—
Should be my grave; for he who yet
Is my soul's soul, once said: "Twere sweet
'Mid stars and lightnings to abide,
And winds and lulling snows, that beat
With their soft flakes the mountain wide,
Where weary meteor lamps repose,
And languid storms their pinions close:
And all things strong and bright and pure,
And ever during, aye endure:
Who knows, if one were buried there,
But these things might our spirits make,
Amid the all-surrounding air,
Their own eternity partake?'

Then 'twas a wild and playful saying
At which I laughed, or seemed to laugh:
They were his words: now heed my praying,
And let them be my epitaph.
Thy memory for a term may be
My monument. Wilt remember me?
I know thou wilt, and canst forgive
Whilst in this erring world to live
My soul disdained not, that I thought
Its lying forms were worthy aught
And much less thee.

HELEN: O speak not so,
But come to me and pour thy woe
Into this heart, full though it be,
Ay, overflowing with its own:
I thought that grief had severed me
From all beside who weep and groan;
Its likeness upon earth to be,
Its express image; but thou art
More wretched. Sweet! we will not part
Henceforth, if death be not division;
If so, the dead feel no contrition.
But wilt thou hear since last we parted
All that has left me broken hearted?

ROSALIND: Yes, speak. The faintest stars are scarcely shorn
Of their thin beams by that delusive morn
Which sinks again in darkness, like the light
Of early love, soon lost in total night.

HELEN: Alas! Italian winds are mild,
But my bosom is cold—wintry cold—
When the warm air weaves, among the fresh leaves,
Soft music, my poor brain is wild,
And I am weak like a nursling child,
Though my soul with grief is gray and old.

ROSALIND: Weep not at thine own words, though they must make
Me weep. What is thy tale?

HELEN: I fear 'twill shake
Thy gentle heart with tears. Thou well
Rememberest when we met no more,

And, though I dwelt with Lionel,
That friendless caution pierced me sore
With grief; a wound my spirit bore
Indignantly, but when he died,
With him lay dead both hope and pride.
Alas! all hope is buried now.
But then men dreamed the aged earth
Was labouring in that mighty birth,
Which many a poet and a sage
Has aye foreseen—the happy age
When truth and love shall dwell below
Among the works and ways of men;
Which on this world not power but will
Even now is wanting to fulfil.

Among mankind what thence befell
Of strife, how vain, is known too well;
When Liberty's dear paean fell
'Mid murderous howls. To Lionel,
Though of great wealth and lineage high,
Yet through those dungeon walls there came
Thy thrilling light, O Liberty!
And as the meteor's midnight flame
Startles the dreamer, sun-like truth
Flashed on his visionary youth,
And filled him, not with love, but faith,
And hope, and courage mute in death;
For love and life in him were twins,
Born at one birth: in every other
First life then love its course begins,
Though they be children of one mother;
And so through this dark world they fleet
Divided, till in death they meet;
But he loved all things ever. Then
He passed amid the strife of men,
And stood at the throne of armed power
Pleading for a world of woe:
Secure as one on a rock-built tower
O'er the wrecks which the surge trails to and fro,

'Mid the passions wild of human kind
He stood, like a spirit calming them;
For, it was said, his words could bind
Like music the lulled crowd, and stem
That torrent of unquiet dream
Which mortals truth and reason deem,
But is revenge and fear and pride.
Joyous he was; and hope and peace
On all who heard him did abide,
Raining like dew from his sweet talk,
As where the evening star may walk
Along the brink of the gloomy seas,
Liquid mists of splendour quiver.
His very gestures touched to tears
The unpersuaded tyrant, never
So moved before: his presence stung
The torturers with their victim's pain,
And none knew how; and through their ears
The subtle witchcraft of his tongue
Unlocked the hearts of those who keep
Gold, the world's bond of slavery.
Men wondered, and some sneered to see
One sow what he could never reap:
For he is rich, they said, and young,
And might drink from the depths of luxury.
If he seeks Fame, Fame never crowned
The champion of a trampled creed:
If he seeks Power, Power is enthroned
'Mid ancient rights and wrongs, to feed
Which hungry wolves with praise and spoil,
Those who would sit near Power must toil;
And such, there sitting, all may see.
What seeks he? All that others seek
He casts away, like a vile weed
Which the sea casts unreturningly.
That poor and hungry men should break
The laws which wreak them toil and scorn,
We understand; but Lionel
We know, is rich and nobly born.

So wondered they: yet all men loved
Young Lionel, though few approved;
All but the priests, whose hatred fell
Like the unseen blight of a smiling day,
The withering honey dew, which clings
Under the bright green buds of May,
Whilst they unfold their emerald wings:
For he made verses wild and queer
On the strange creeds priests hold so dear,
Because they bring them land and gold.
Of devils and saints and all such gear,
He made tales which whoso heard or read
Would laugh till he were almost dead.
So this grew a proverb: 'Don't get old
Till Lionel's "Banquet in Hell" you hear,
And then you will laugh yourself young again.'
So the priests hated him, and he
Repaid their hate with cheerful glee.

Ah, smiles and joyance quickly died,
For public hope grew pale and dim
In an altered time and tide,
And in its wasting withered him,
As a summer flower that blows too soon
Droops in the smile of the waning moon,
When it scatters through an April night
The frozen dews of wrinkling blight.
None now hoped more. Gray Power was seated
Safely on her ancestral throne;
And Faith, the Python, undefeated,
Even to its blood-stained steps dragged on
Her foul and wounded train, and men
Were trampled and deceived again,
And words and shows again could bind
The wailing tribes of human kind
In scorn and famine. Fire and blood
Raged round the raging multitude,
To fields remote by tyrants sent
To be the scorned instrument

With which they drag from mines of gore
The chains their slaves yet ever wore:
And in the streets men met each other,
And by old altars and in halls,
And smiled again at festivals.
But each man found in his heart's brother
Cold cheer; for all, though half deceived,
The outworn creeds again believed,
And the same round anew began,
Which the weary world yet ever ran.

Many then wept, not tears, but gall
Within their hearts, like drops which fall
Wasting the fountain-stone away.
And in that dark and evil day
Did all desires and thoughts, that claim
Men's care—ambition, friendship, fame,
Love, hope, though hope was now despair—
Indue the colours of this change,
As from the all-surrounding air
The earth takes hues obscure and strange,
When storm and earthquake linger there.

And so, my friend, it then befell
To many, most to Lionel,
Whose hope was like the life of youth
Within him, and when dead, became
A spirit of unresting flame,
Which goaded him in his distress
Over the world's vast wilderness.
Three years he left his native land,
And on the fourth, when he returned,
None knew him: he was stricken deep
With some disease of mind, and turned
Into aught unlike Lionel.
On him, on whom, did he pause in sleep,
Serenest smiles were wont to keep,
And, did he wake, a winged band
Of bright persuasions, which had fed

On his sweet lips and liquid eyes,
Kept their swift pinions half outspread
To do on men his least command;
On him, whom once 'twas paradise
Even to behold, now misery lay:
In his own heart 'twas merciless,
To all things else none may express
Its innocence and tenderness.

'Twas said that he had refuge sought
In love from his unquiet thought
In distant lands, and been deceived
By some strange show; for there were found,
Blotted with tears as those relieved
By their own words are wont to do,
These mournful verses on the ground,
By all who read them blotted too.

'How am I changed! my hopes were once like fire:
I loved, and I believed that life was love.
How am I lost! on wings of swift desire
Among Heaven's winds my spirit once did move.
I slept, and silver dreams did aye inspire
My liquid sleep: I woke, and did approve
All nature to my heart, and thought to make
A paradise of earth for one sweet sake.

'I love, but I believe in love no more.
I feel desire, but hope not. O, from sleep
Most vainly must my weary brain implore
Its long lost flattery now: I wake to weep,
And sit through the long day gnawing the core
Of my bitter heart, and, like a miser, keep,
Since none in what I feel take pain or pleasure,
To my own soul its self-consuming treasure.'

He dwelt beside me near the sea;
And oft in evening did we meet,
When the waves, beneath the starlight, flee

O'er the yellow sands with silver feet,
And talked: our talk was sad and sweet,
Till slowly from his mien there passed
The desolation which it spoke;
And smiles,—as when the lightning's blast
Has parched some heaven-delighting oak,
The next spring shows leaves pale and rare,
But like flowers delicate and fair,
On its rent boughs,—again arrayed
His countenance in tender light:
His words grew subtile fire, which made
The air his hearers breathed delight:
His motions, like the winds, were free,
Which bend the bright grass gracefully,
Then fade away in circlets faint:
And winged Hope, on which upborne
His soul seemed hovering in his eyes,
Like some bright spirit newly born
Floating amid the sunny skies,
Sprang forth from his rent heart anew.
Yet o'er his talk, and looks, and mien,
Tempering their loveliness too keen,
Past woe its shadow backward threw,
Till like an exhalation, spread
From flowers half drunk with evening dew,
They did become infectious: sweet
And subtle mists of sense and thought:
Which wrapped us soon, when we might meet,
Almost from our own looks and aught
The wild world holds. And so, his mind
Was healed, while mine grew sick with fear:
For ever now his health declined,
Like some frail bark which cannot bear
The impulse of an altered wind,
Though prosperous: and my heart grew full
'Mid its new joy of a new care:
For his cheek became, not pale, but fair,
As rose-o'ershadowed lilies are;
And soon his deep and sunny hair,

In this alone less beautiful,
Like grass in tombs grew wild and rare.
The blood in his translucent veins
Beat, not like animal life, but love
Seemed now its sullen springs to move,
When life had failed, and all its pains:
And sudden sleep would seize him oft
Like death, so calm, but that a tear,
His pointed eyelashes between,
Would gather in the light serene
Of smiles, whose lustre bright and soft
Beneath lay undulating there.
His breath was like inconstant flame,
As eagerly it went and came;
And I hung o'er him in his sleep,
Till, like an image in the lake
Which rains disturb, my tears would break
The shadow of that slumber deep:
Then he would bid me not to weep,
And say, with flattery false, yet sweet,
That death and he could never meet,
If I would never part with him.
And so we loved, and did unite
All that in us was yet divided:
For when he said, that many a rite,
By men to bind but once provided,
Could not be shared by him and me,
Or they would kill him in their glee,
I shuddered, and then laughing said—
'We will have rites our faith to bind,
But our church shall be the starry night,
Our altar the grassy earth outspread,
And our priest the muttering wind.'

'Twas sunset as I spoke: one star
Had scarce burst forth, when from afar
The ministers of misrule sent,
Seized upon Lionel, and bore
His chained limbs to a dreary tower,

In the midst of a city vast and wide.
For he, they said, from his mind had bent
Against their gods keen blasphemy,
For which, though his soul must roasted be
In hell's red lakes immortally,
Yet even on earth must he abide
The vengeance of their slaves: a trial,
I think, men call it. What avail
Are prayers and tears, which chase denial
From the fierce savage, nursed in hate?
What the knit soul that pleading and pale
Makes wan the quivering cheek, which late
It painted with its own delight?
We were divided. As I could,
I stilled the tingling of my blood,
And followed him in their despite,
As a widow follows, pale and wild,
The murderers and corse of her only child;
And when we came to the prison door
And I prayed to share his dungeon floor
With prayers which rarely have been spurned,
And when men drove me forth and I
Stared with blank frenzy on the sky,
A farewell look of love he turned,
Half calming me; then gazed awhile,
As if thro' that black and massy pile,
And thro' the crowd around him there,
And thro' the dense and murky air,
And the thronged streets, he did espy
What poets know and prophesy;
And said, with voice that made them shiver
And clung like music in my brain,
And which the mute walls spoke again
Prolonging it with deepened strain:
'Fear not the tyrants shall rule for ever,
Or the priests of the bloody faith;
They stand on the brink of that mighty river,
Whose waves they have tainted with death:
It is fed from the depths of a thousand dells,

Around them it foams, and rages, and swells,
And their swords and their sceptres I floating see,
Like wrecks in the surge of eternity.'

I dwelt beside the prison gate;
And the strange crowd that out and in
Passed, some, no doubt, with mine own fate,
Might have fretted me with its ceaseless din,
But the fever of care was louder within.
Soon, but too late, in penitence
Or fear, his foes released him thence:
I saw his thin and languid form,
As leaning on the jailor's arm,
Whose hardened eyes grew moist the while,
To meet his mute and faded smile,
And hear his words of kind farewell,
He tottered forth from his damp cell.
Many had never wept before,
From whom fast tears then gushed and fell:
Many will relent no more,
Who sobbed like infants then; aye, all
Who thronged the prison's stony hall,
The rulers or the slaves of law,
Felt with a new surprise and awe
That they were human, till strong shame
Made them again become the same.
The prison blood-hounds, huge and grim,
From human looks the infection caught,
And fondly crouched and fawned on him;
And men have heard the prisoners say,
Who in their rotting dungeons lay,
That from that hour, throughout one day,
The fierce despair and hate which kept
Their trampled bosoms almost slept:
Where, like twin vultures, they hung feeding
On each heart's wound, wide torn and bleeding,—
Because their jailors' rule, they thought,
Grew merciful, like a parent's sway.

I know not how, but we were free:
And Lionel sate alone with me,
As the carriage drove thro' the streets apace;
And we looked upon each other's face;
And the blood in our fingers intertwined
Ran like the thoughts of a single mind,
As the swift emotions went and came
Thro' the veins of each united frame.
So thro' the long long streets we passed
Of the million-peopled City vast;
Which is that desert, where each one
Seeks his mate yet is alone,
Beloved and sought and mourned of none;
Until the clear blue sky was seen,
And the grassy meadows bright and green,
And then I sunk in his embrace,
Enclosing there a mighty space
Of love: and so we travelled on
By woods, and fields of yellow flowers,
And towns, and villages, and towers,
Day after day of happy hours.
It was the azure time of June,
When the skies are deep in the stainless noon,
And the warm and fitful breezes shake
The fresh green leaves of the hedgerow briar,
And there were odours then to make
The very breath we did respire
A liquid element, whereon
Our spirits, like delighted things
That walk the air on subtle wings,
Floated and mingled far away,
'Mid the warm winds of the sunny day.
And when the evening star came forth
Above the curve of the new bent moon,
And light and sound ebbed from the earth,
Like the tide of the full and the weary sea
To the depths of its own tranquillity,
Our natures to its own repose

Did the earth's breathless sleep attune:
Like flowers, which on each other close
Their languid leaves when daylight's gone,
We lay, till new emotions came,
Which seemed to make each mortal frame
One soul of interwoven flame,
A life in life, a second birth
In worlds diviner far than earth,
Which, like two strains of harmony
That mingle in the silent sky
Then slowly disunite, passed by
And left the tenderness of tears,
A soft oblivion of all fears,
A sweet sleep: so we travelled on
Till we came to the home of Lionel,
Among the mountains wild and lone,
Beside the hoary western sea,
Which near the verge of the echoing shore
The massy forest shadowed o'er.

The ancient steward, with hair all hoar,
As we alighted, wept to see
His master changed so fearfully;
And the old man's sobs did waken me
From my dream of unremaining gladness;
The truth flashed o'er me like quick madness
When I looked, and saw that there was death
On Lionel: yet day by day
He lived, till fear grew hope and faith,
And in my soul I dared to say,
Nothing so bright can pass away:
Death is dark, and foul, and dull,
But he is—O how beautiful!
Yet day by day he grew more weak,
And his sweet voice, when he might speak,
Which ne'er was loud, became more low;
And the light which flashed through his waxen cheek
Grew faint, as the rose-like hues which flow

From sunset o'er the Alpine snow:
And death seemed not like death in him,
For the spirit of life o'er every limb
Lingered, a mist of sense and thought.
When the summer wind faint odours brought
From mountain flowers, even as it passed
His cheek would change, as the noonday sea
Which the dying breeze sweeps fitfully.
If but a cloud the sky o'ercast,
You might see his colour come and go,
And the softest strain of music made
Sweet smiles, yet sad, arise and fade
Amid the dew of his tender eyes;
And the breath, with intermitting flow,
Made his pale lips quiver and part.
You might hear the beatings of his heart,
Quick, but not strong; and with my tresses
When oft he playfully would bind
In the bowers of mossy lonelinesses
His neck, and win me so to mingle
In the sweet depth of woven caresses,
And our faint limbs were intertwined,
Alas! the unquiet life did tingle
From mine own heart through every vein,
Like a captive in dreams of liberty,
Who beats the walls of his stony cell.
But his, it seemed already free,
Like the shadow of fire surrounding me!
On my faint eyes and limbs did dwell
That spirit as it passed, till soon,
As a frail cloud wandering o'er the moon,
Beneath its light invisible,
Is seen when it folds its gray wings again
To alight on midnight's dusky plain,
I lived and saw, and the gathering soul
Passed from beneath that strong control,
And I fell on a life which was sick with fear
Of all the woe that now I bear.

Amid a bloomless myrtle wood,
On a green and sea-girt promontory,
Not far from where we dwelt, there stood
In record of a sweet sad story,
An altar and a temple bright
Circled by steps, and o'er the gate
Was sculptured, 'To Fidelity;'
And in the shrine an image sate,
All veiled: but there was seen the light
Of smiles which faintly could express
A mingled pain and tenderness
Through that ethereal drapery.
The left hand held the head, the right—
Beyond the veil, beneath the skin,
You might see the nerves quivering within—
Was forcing the point of a barbed dart
Into its side-convulsing heart.
An unskilled hand, yet one informed
With genius, had the marble warmed
With that pathetic life. This tale
It told: A dog had from the sea,
When the tide was raging fearfully,
Dragged Lionel's mother, weak and pale,
Then died beside her on the sand,
And she that temple thence had planned;
But it was Lionel's own hand
Had wrought the image. Each new moon
That lady did, in this lone fane,
The rites of a religion sweet,
Whose god was in her heart and brain:
The seasons' loveliest flowers were strewn
On the marble floor beneath her feet,
And she brought crowns of sea-buds white
Whose odour is so sweet and faint,
And weeds, like branching chrysolite,
Woven in devices fine and quaint.
And tears from her brown eyes did stain
The altar: need but look upon
That dying statue fair and wan,

If tears should cease, to weep again:
And rare Arabian odours came,
Through the myrtle copses steaming thence
From the hissing frankincense,
Whose smoke, wool-white as ocean foam,
Hung in dense flocks beneath the dome—
That ivory dome, whose azure night
With golden stars, like heaven, was bright—
O'er the split cedar's pointed flame;
And the lady's harp would kindle there
The melody of an old air,
Softer than sleep; the villagers
Mixed their religion up with hers,
And, as they listened round, shed tears.

One eve he led me to this fane:
Daylight on its last purple cloud
Was lingering gray, and soon her strain
The nightingale began; now loud,
Climbing in circles the windless sky,
Now dying music; suddenly
'Tis scattered in a thousand notes,
And now to the hushed ear it floats
Like field smells known in infancy,
Then failing, soothes the air again.
We sate within that temple lone,
Pavilioned round with Parian stone:
His mother's harp stood near, and oft
I had awakened music soft
Amid its wires: the nightingale
Was pausing in her heaven-taught tale:
'Now drain the cup,' said Lionel,
'Which the poet-bird has crowned so well
With the wine of her bright and liquid song!
Heardst thou not sweet words among
That heaven-resounding minstrelsy?
Heard'st thou not that those who die
Awake in a world of ecstasy?
That love, when limbs are interwoven,

And sleep, when the night of life is cloven,
And thought, to the world's dim boundaries clinging,
And music, when one beloved is singing,
Is death? Let us drain right joyously
The cup which the sweet bird fills for me.'
He paused, and to my lips he bent
His own: like spirit his words went
Through all my limbs with the speed of fire;
And his keen eyes, glittering through mine,
Filled me with the flame divine,
Which in their orbs was burning far,
Like the light of an unmeasured star,
In the sky of midnight dark and deep:
Yes, 'twas his soul that did inspire
Sounds, which my skill could ne'er awaken;
And first, I felt my fingers sweep
The harp, and a long quivering cry
Burst from my lips in symphony:
The dusk and solid air was shaken,
As swift and swifter the notes came
From my touch, that wandered like quick flame,
And from my bosom, labouring
With some unutterable thing:
The awful sound of my own voice made
My faint lips tremble; in some mood
Of wordless thought Lionel stood
So pale, that even beside his cheek
The snowy column from its shade
Caught whiteness: yet his countenance,
Raised upward, burned with radiance
Of spirit-piercing joy, whose light,
Like the moon struggling through the night
Of whirlwind-rifted clouds, did break
With beams that might not be confined.
I paused, but soon his gestures kindled
New power, as by the moving wind
The waves are lifted, and my song
To low soft notes now changed and dwindled,
And from the twinkling wires among,

My languid fingers drew and flung
Circles of life-dissolving sound,
Yet faint; in aery rings they bound
My Lionel, who, as every strain
Grew fainter but more sweet, his mien
Sunk with the sound relaxedly;
And slowly now he turned to me,
As slowly faded from his face
That awful joy: with looks serene
He was soon drawn to my embrace,
And my wild song then died away
In murmurs: words I dare not say
We mixed, and on his lips mine fed
Till they methought felt still and cold:
'What is it with thee, love?' I said:
No word, no look, no motion! yes,
There was a change, but spare to guess,
Nor let that moment's hope be told.
I looked, and knew that he was dead,
And fell, as the eagle on the plain
Falls when life deserts her brain,
And the mortal lightning is veiled again.
O that I were now dead! but such
(Did they not, love, demand too much,
Those dying murmurs?) he forbade.
O that I once again were mad!
And yet, dear Rosalind, not so,
For I would live to share thy woe.
Sweet boy! did I forget thee too?
Alas, we know not what we do
When we speak words.
No memory more
Is in my mind of that sea shore.
Madness came on me, and a troop
Of misty shapes did seem to sit
Beside me, on a vessel's poop,
And the clear north wind was driving it.
Then I heard strange tongues, and saw strange flowers,
And the stars methought grew unlike ours,

And the azure sky and the stormless sea
Made me believe that I had died,
And waked in a world, which was to me
Drear hell, though heaven to all beside:
Then a dead sleep fell on my mind,
Whilst animal life many long years
Had rescued from a chasm of tears;
And when I woke, I wept to find
That the same lady, bright and wise,
With silver locks and quick brown eyes,
The mother of my Lionel,
Had tended me in my distress,
And died some months before. Nor less
Wonder, but far more peace and joy,
Brought in that hour my lovely boy;
For through that trance my soul had well
The impress of thy being kept;
And if I waked, or if I slept,
No doubt, though memory faithless be,
Thy image ever dwelt on me;
And thus, O Lionel, like thee
Is our sweet child. 'Tis sure most strange
I knew not of so great a change,
As that which gave him birth, who now
Is all the solace of my woe.

That Lionel great wealth had left
By will to me, and that of all
The ready lies of law bereft
My child and me, might well befall.
But let me think not of the scorn,
Which from the meanest I have borne,
When, for my child's beloved sake,
I mixed with slaves, to vindicate
The very laws themselves do make:
Let me not say scorn is my fate,
Lest I be proud, suffering the same
With those who live in deathless fame.

She ceased.—'Lo, where red morning thro' the woods
Is burning o'er the dew;' said Rosalind.
And with these words they rose, and towards the flood
Of the blue lake, beneath the leaves now wind
With equal steps and fingers intertwined:
Thence to a lonely dwelling, where the shore
Is shadowed with steep rocks, and cypresses
Cleave with their dark green cones the silent skies,
And with their shadows the clear depths below,
And where a little terrace from its bowers,
Of blooming myrtle and faint lemon-flowers,
Scatters its sense-dissolving fragrance o'er
The liquid marble of the windless lake;
And where the aged forest's limbs look hoar,
Under the leaves which their green garments make,
They come: 'Tis Helen's home, and clean and white,
Like one which tyrants spare on our own land
In some such solitude, its casements bright
Shone through their vine-leaves in the morning sun,
And even within 'twas scarce like Italy.
And when she saw how all things there were planned,
As in an English home, dim memory
Disturbed poor Rosalind: she stood as one
Whose mind is where his body cannot be,
Till Helen led her where her child yet slept,
And said, 'Observe, that brow was Lionel's,
Those lips were his, and so he ever kept
One arm in sleep, pillowing his head with it.
You cannot see his eyes—they are two wells
Of liquid love: let us not wake him yet.'
But Rosalind could bear no more, and wept
A shower of burning tears, which fell upon
His face, and so his opening lashes shone
With tears unlike his own, as he did leap
In sudden wonder from his innocent sleep.

So Rosalind and Helen lived together
Thenceforth, changed in all else, yet friends again,

Such as they were, when o'er the mountain heather
They wandered in their youth, through sun and rain.
And after many years, for human things
Change even like the ocean and the wind,
Her daughter was restored to Rosalind,
And in their circle thence some visitings
Of joy 'mid their new calm would intervene:
A lovely child she was, of looks serene,
And motions which o'er things indifferent shed
The grace and gentleness from whence they came.
And Helen's boy grew with her, and they fed
From the same flowers of thought, until each mind
Like springs which mingle in one flood became,
And in their union soon their parents saw
The shadow of the peace denied to them.
And Rosalind, for when the living stem
Is cankered in its heart, the tree must fall,
Died ere her time; and with deep grief and awe
The pale survivors followed her remains
Beyond the region of dissolving rains,
Up the cold mountain she was wont to call
Her tomb; and on Chiavenna's precipice
They raised a pyramid of lasting ice,
Whose polished sides, ere day had yet begun,
Caught the first glow of the unrisen sun,
The last, when it had sunk; and thro' the night
The charioteers of Arctos wheeled round
Its glittering point, as seen from Helen's home,
Whose sad inhabitants each year would come,
With willing steps climbing that rugged height,
And hang long locks of hair, and garlands bound
With amaranth flowers, which, in the clime's despite,
Filled the frore air with unaccustomed light:
Such flowers, as in the wintry memory bloom
Of one friend left, adorned that frozen tomb.

Helen, whose spirit was of softer mould,
Whose sufferings too were less, Death slowlier led
Into the peace of his dominion cold:

She died among her kindred, being old.
And know, that if love die not in the dead
As in the living, none of mortal kind
Are blest, as now Helen and Rosalind.

Note by Mrs. Shelley

"Rosalind and Helen" was begun at Marlow, and thrown aside—till I found it; and, at my request, it was completed. Shelley had no care for any of his poems that did not emanate from the depths of his mind, and develop some high or abstruse truth. When he does touch on human life and the human heart, no pictures can be more faithful, more delicate, more subtle, or more pathetic. He never mentioned Love but he shed a grace borrowed from his own nature, that scarcely any other poet has bestowed on that passion. When he spoke of it as the law of life, which inasmuch as we rebel against we err and injure ourselves and others, he promulgated that which he considered an irrefragable truth. In his eyes it was the essence of our being, and all woe and pain arose from the war made against it by selfishness, or insensibility, or mistake. By reverting in his mind to this first principle, he discovered the source of many emotions, and could disclose the secrets of all hearts, and his delineations of passion and emotion touch the finest chords of our nature.

"Rosalind and Helen" was finished during the summer of 1818, while we were at the Baths of Lucca.

JULIAN AND MADDALO

A Conversation

(Composed at Este after Shelley's first visit to Venice, 1818 (Autumn); first published in the "Posthumous Poems", London, 1824 (edition Mrs. Shelley). Shelley's original intention had been to print the poem in Leigh Hunt's "Examiner"; but he changed his mind and, on August 15, 1819, sent the manuscript to Hunt to be published anonymously by Ollier. This manuscript, found by Mr. Townshend Mayer, and by him placed in the hands of Mr. H. Buxton Forman, C.B., is described at length in Mr. Forman's Library Edition of the poems (volume 3 page 107). The date, 'May, 1819,' affixed to "Julian and Maddalo" in the "Posthumous Poems", 1824, indicates the time when the text was finally revised by Shelley. Sources of the text are (1) "Posthumous Poems", 1824; (2) the Hunt manuscript; (3) a fair draft of the poem amongst the Boscombe manuscripts; (4) "Poetical Works", 1839, 1st and 2nd editions (Mrs. Shelley). Our text is that of the Hunt manuscript, as printed in Forman's Library Edition of the Poems, 1876, volume 3, pages 103–30; variants of 1824 are indicated in the footnotes; questions of punctuation are dealt with in the notes at the end of the volume.)

Preface

The meadows with fresh streams, the bees with thyme,
The goats with the green leaves of budding Spring,
Are saturated not—nor Love with tears.

—Virgil's "Gallus"

Count Maddalo is a Venetian nobleman of ancient family and of great fortune, who, without mixing much in the society of his countrymen, resides chiefly at his magnificent palace in that city. He is a person of the most consummate genius, and capable, if he would direct his energies to such an end, of becoming the redeemer of his degraded country. But it is his weakness to be proud: he derives, from a comparison of his own extraordinary mind with the dwarfish intellects that surround him, an intense apprehension of the nothingness of human life. His passions and his powers are incomparably greater than those of other men; and, instead of the latter having been employed in curbing the former, they have mutually lent each other strength. His ambition preys upon itself, for want of objects which it can consider worthy of exertion. I say that Maddalo is proud, because I can find no other word to express the concentred and impatient feelings which consume him; but it is on his own hopes and affections only that he seems to trample, for in social life no human being can be more gentle, patient and unassuming than Maddalo. He is cheerful, frank and witty. His more serious conversation is a sort of intoxication; men are held by it as by a spell. He has travelled much; and there is an inexpressible charm in his relation of his adventures in different countries.

Julian is an Englishman of good family, passionately attached to those philosophical notions which assert the power of man over his own mind, and the immense improvements of which, by the extinction of certain moral superstitions, human society may be yet susceptible. Without concealing the evil in the world he is for ever speculating how good may be made superior. He is a complete infidel, and a scoffer at all things reputed holy; and Maddalo takes a wicked pleasure in drawing out his taunts against religion. What Maddalo thinks on these matters is not exactly known. Julian, in spite of his heterodox opinions, is conjectured by his friends to possess some good qualities. How far this is possible the pious reader will determine. Julian is rather serious.

Of the Maniac I can give no information. He seems, by his own account, to have been disappointed in love. He was evidently a very cultivated and amiable person when in his right senses. His story, told at length, might be like many other stories of the same kind: the unconnected exclamations of his agony will perhaps be found a sufficient comment for the text of every heart.

I rode one evening with Count Maddalo
Upon the bank of land which breaks the flow
Of Adria towards Venice: a bare strand
Of hillocks, heaped from ever-shifting sand,
Matted with thistles and amphibious weeds,
Such as from earth's embrace the salt ooze breeds,
Is this; an uninhabited sea-side,
Which the lone fisher, when his nets are dried,
Abandons; and no other object breaks
The waste, but one dwarf tree and some few stakes
Broken and unrepaired, and the tide makes
A narrow space of level sand thereon,
Where 'twas our wont to ride while day went down.
This ride was my delight. I love all waste
And solitary places; where we taste
The pleasure of believing what we see
Is boundless, as we wish our souls to be:
And such was this wide ocean, and this shore
More barren than its billows; and yet more
Than all, with a remembered friend I love
To ride as then I rode;—for the winds drove
The living spray along the sunny air
Into our faces; the blue heavens were bare,
Stripped to their depths by the awakening north;
And, from the waves, sound like delight broke forth
Harmonising with solitude, and sent
Into our hearts aereal merriment.
So, as we rode, we talked; and the swift thought,
Winging itself with laughter, lingered not,
But flew from brain to brain,—such glee was ours,

Charged with light memories of remembered hours,
None slow enough for sadness: till we came
Homeward, which always makes the spirit tame.
This day had been cheerful but cold, and now
The sun was sinking, and the wind also.
Our talk grew somewhat serious, as may be
Talk interrupted with such raillery
As mocks itself, because it cannot scorn
The thoughts it would extinguish: —'twas forlorn,
Yet pleasing, such as once, so poets tell,
The devils held within the dales of Hell
Concerning God, freewill and destiny:
Of all that earth has been or yet may be,
All that vain men imagine or believe,
Or hope can paint or suffering may achieve,
We descanted; and I (for ever still
Is it not wise to make the best of ill?)
Argued against despondency, but pride
Made my companion take the darker side.
The sense that he was greater than his kind
Had struck, methinks, his eagle spirit blind
By gazing on its own exceeding light.
Meanwhile the sun paused ere it should alight,
Over the horizon of the mountains;—Oh,
How beautiful is sunset, when the glow
Of Heaven descends upon a land like thee,
Thou Paradise of exiles, Italy!
Thy mountains, seas and vineyards, and the towers
Of cities they encircle!—it was ours
To stand on thee, beholding it: and then,
Just where we had dismounted, the Count's men
Were waiting for us with the gondola.—
As those who pause on some delightful way
Though bent on pleasant pilgrimage, we stood
Looking upon the evening, and the flood
Which lay between the city and the shore,
Paved with the image of the sky. . . the hoar
And aery Alps towards the North appeared
Through mist, an heaven-sustaining bulwark reared

Between the East and West; and half the sky
Was roofed with clouds of rich emblazonry
Dark purple at the zenith, which still grew
Down the steep West into a wondrous hue
Brighter than burning gold, even to the rent
Where the swift sun yet paused in his descent
Among the many-folded hills: they were
Those famous Euganean hills, which bear,
As seen from Lido thro' the harbour piles,
The likeness of a clump of peaked isles—
And then—as if the Earth and Sea had been
Dissolved into one lake of fire, were seen
Those mountains towering as from waves of flame
Around the vaporous sun, from which there came
The inmost purple spirit of light, and made
Their very peaks transparent. 'Ere it fade,'
Said my companion, 'I will show you soon
A better station'—so, o'er the lagune
We glided; and from that funereal bark
I leaned, and saw the city, and could mark
How from their many isles, in evening's gleam,
Its temples and its palaces did seem
Like fabrics of enchantment piled to Heaven.
I was about to speak, when—'We are even
Now at the point I meant,' said Maddalo,
And bade the gondolieri cease to row.
'Look, Julian, on the west, and listen well
If you hear not a deep and heavy bell.'
I looked, and saw between us and the sun
A building on an island; such a one
As age to age might add, for uses vile,
A windowless, deformed and dreary pile;
And on the top an open tower, where hung
A bell, which in the radiance swayed and swung;
We could just hear its hoarse and iron tongue:
The broad sun sunk behind it, and it tolled
In strong and black relief.—'What we behold
Shall be the madhouse and its belfry tower,'
Said Maddalo, 'and ever at this hour

Those who may cross the water, hear that bell
Which calls the maniacs, each one from his cell,
To vespers.'—'As much skill as need to pray
In thanks or hope for their dark lot have they
To their stern maker,' I replied. 'O ho!
You talk as in years past,' said Maddalo.
"'Tis strange men change not. You were ever still
Among Christ's flock a perilous infidel,
A wolf for the meek lambs—if you can't swim
Beware of Providence.' I looked on him,
But the gay smile had faded in his eye.
'And such,'—he cried, 'is our mortality,
And this must be the emblem and the sign
Of what should be eternal and divine!—
And like that black and dreary bell, the soul,
Hung in a heaven-illumined tower, must toll
Our thoughts and our desires to meet below
Round the rent heart and pray—as madmen do
For what? they know not,—till the night of death
As sunset that strange vision, severeth
Our memory from itself, and us from all
We sought and yet were baffled.' I recall
The sense of what he said, although I mar
The force of his expressions. The broad star
Of day meanwhile had sunk behind the hill,
And the black bell became invisible,
And the red tower looked gray, and all between
The churches, ships and palaces were seen
Huddled in gloom;—into the purple sea
The orange hues of heaven sunk silently.
We hardly spoke, and soon the gondola
Conveyed me to my lodging by the way.
The following morn was rainy, cold, and dim:
Ere Maddalo arose, I called on him,
And whilst I waited with his child I played;
A lovelier toy sweet Nature never made;
A serious, subtle, wild, yet gentle being,
Graceful without design and unforeseeing,
With eyes—Oh speak not of her eyes!—which seem

Twin mirrors of Italian Heaven, yet gleam
With such deep meaning, as we never see
But in the human countenance: with me
She was a special favourite: I had nursed
Her fine and feeble limbs when she came first
To this bleak world; and she yet seemed to know
On second sight her ancient playfellow,
Less changed than she was by six months or so;
For after her first shyness was worn out
We sate there, rolling billiard balls about,
When the Count entered. Salutations past—
'The word you spoke last night might well have cast
A darkness on my spirit—if man be
The passive thing you say, I should not see
Much harm in the religions and old saws
(Tho' I may never own such leaden laws)
Which break a teachless nature to the yoke:
Mine is another faith.'—thus much I spoke
And noting he replied not, added: 'See
This lovely child, blithe, innocent and free;
She spends a happy time with little care,
While we to such sick thoughts subjected are
As came on you last night. It is our will
That thus enchains us to permitted ill—
We might be otherwise—we might be all
We dream of happy, high, majestical.
Where is the love, beauty, and truth we seek,
But in our mind? and if we were not weak
Should we be less in deed than in desire?'
'Ay, if we were not weak—and we aspire
How vainly to be strong!' said Maddalo:
'You talk Utopia.' 'It remains to know,'
I then rejoined, 'and those who try may find
How strong the chains are which our spirit bind;
Brittle perchance as straw. . . We are assured
Much may be conquered, much may be endured,
Of what degrades and crushes us. We know
That we have power over ourselves to do
And suffer—what, we know not till we try;

But something nobler than to live and die—
So taught those kings of old philosophy
Who reigned, before Religion made men blind;
And those who suffer with their suffering kind
Yet feel their faith, religion.' 'My dear friend,'
Said Maddalo, 'my judgement will not bend
To your opinion, though I think you might
Make such a system refutation-tight
As far as words go. I knew one like you
Who to this city came some months ago,
With whom I argued in this sort, and he
Is now gone mad,—and so he answered me,—
Poor fellow! but if you would like to go,
We'll visit him, and his wild talk will show
How vain are such aspiring theories.'
'I hope to prove the induction otherwise,
And that a want of that true theory, still,
Which seeks a "soul of goodness" in things ill
Or in himself or others, has thus bowed
His being—there are some by nature proud,
Who patient in all else demand but this—
To love and be beloved with gentleness;
And being scorned, what wonder if they die
Some living death? this is not destiny
But man's own wilful ill.'
As thus I spoke
Servants announced the gondola, and we
Through the fast-falling rain and high-wrought sea
Sailed to the island where the madhouse stands.
We disembarked. The clap of tortured hands,
Fierce yells and howlings and lamentings keen,
And laughter where complaint had merrier been,
Moans, shrieks, and curses, and blaspheming prayers
Accosted us. We climbed the oozy stairs
Into an old courtyard. I heard on high,
Then, fragments of most touching melody,
But looking up saw not the singer there—
Through the black bars in the tempestuous air
I saw, like weeds on a wrecked palace growing,

Long tangled locks flung wildly forth, and flowing,
Of those who on a sudden were beguiled
Into strange silence, and looked forth and smiled
Hearing sweet sounds. Then I: 'Methinks there were
A cure of these with patience and kind care,
If music can thus move... but what is he
Whom we seek here?' 'Of his sad history
I know but this,' said Maddalo: 'he came
To Venice a dejected man, and fame
Said he was wealthy, or he had been so;
Some thought the loss of fortune wrought him woe;
But he was ever talking in such sort
As you do—far more sadly—he seemed hurt,
Even as a man with his peculiar wrong,
To hear but of the oppression of the strong,
Or those absurd deceits (I think with you
In some respects, you know) which carry through
The excellent impostors of this earth
When they outface detection—he had worth,
Poor fellow! but a humorist in his way'—
'Alas, what drove him mad?' 'I cannot say:
A lady came with him from France, and when
She left him and returned, he wandered then
About yon lonely isles of desert sand
Till he grew wild—he had no cash or land
Remaining,—the police had brought him here—
Some fancy took him and he would not bear
Removal; so I fitted up for him
Those rooms beside the sea, to please his whim,
And sent him busts and books and urns for flowers,
Which had adorned his life in happier hours,
And instruments of music—you may guess
A stranger could do little more or less
For one so gentle and unfortunate:
And those are his sweet strains which charm the weight
From madmen's chains, and make this Hell appear
A heaven of sacred silence, hushed to hear.'—
'Nay, this was kind of you—he had no claim,
As the world says'—'None—but the very same

Which I on all mankind were I as he
Fallen to such deep reverse;—his melody
Is interrupted—now we hear the din
Of madmen, shriek on shriek, again begin;
Let us now visit him; after this strain
He ever communes with himself again,
And sees nor hears not any.' Having said
These words, we called the keeper, and he led
To an apartment opening on the sea—
There the poor wretch was sitting mournfully
Near a piano, his pale fingers twined
One with the other, and the ooze and wind
Rushed through an open casement, and did sway
His hair, and starred it with the brackish spray;
His head was leaning on a music book,
And he was muttering, and his lean limbs shook;
His lips were pressed against a folded leaf
In hue too beautiful for health, and grief
Smiled in their motions as they lay apart—
As one who wrought from his own fervid heart
The eloquence of passion, soon he raised
His sad meek face and eyes lustrous and glazed
And spoke—sometimes as one who wrote, and thought
His words might move some heart that heeded not,
If sent to distant lands: and then as one
Reproaching deeds never to be undone
With wondering self-compassion; then his speech
Was lost in grief, and then his words came each
Unmodulated, cold, expressionless,—
But that from one jarred accent you might guess
It was despair made them so uniform:
And all the while the loud and gusty storm
Hissed through the window, and we stood behind
Stealing his accents from the envious wind
Unseen. I yet remember what he said
Distinctly: such impression his words made.

'Month after month,' he cried, 'to bear this load
And as a jade urged by the whip and goad

To drag life on, which like a heavy chain
Lengthens behind with many a link of pain!—
And not to speak my grief—O, not to dare
To give a human voice to my despair,
But live, and move, and, wretched thing! smile on
As if I never went aside to groan,
And wear this mask of falsehood even to those
Who are most dear—not for my own repose—
Alas! no scorn or pain or hate could be
So heavy as that falsehood is to me—
But that I cannot bear more altered faces
Than needs must be, more changed and cold embraces,
More misery, disappointment, and mistrust
To own me for their father. . . Would the dust
Were covered in upon my body now!
That the life ceased to toil within my brow!
And then these thoughts would at the least be fled;
Let us not fear such pain can vex the dead.

'What Power delights to torture us? I know
That to myself I do not wholly owe
What now I suffer, though in part I may.
Alas! none strewed sweet flowers upon the way
Where wandering heedlessly, I met pale Pain
My shadow, which will leave me not again—
If I have erred, there was no joy in error,
But pain and insult and unrest and terror;
I have not as some do, bought penitence
With pleasure, and a dark yet sweet offence,
For then,—if love and tenderness and truth
Had overlived hope's momentary youth,
My creed should have redeemed me from repenting;
But loathed scorn and outrage unrelenting
Met love excited by far other seeming
Until the end was gained. . . as one from dreaming
Of sweetest peace, I woke, and found my state
Such as it is.—
'O Thou, my spirit's mate
Who, for thou art compassionate and wise,

Wouldst pity me from thy most gentle eyes
If this sad writing thou shouldst ever see—
My secret groans must be unheard by thee,
Thou wouldst weep tears bitter as blood to know
Thy lost friend's incommunicable woe.

'Ye few by whom my nature has been weighed
In friendship, let me not that name degrade
By placing on your hearts the secret load
Which crushes mine to dust. There is one road
To peace and that is truth, which follow ye!
Love sometimes leads astray to misery.
Yet think not though subdued—and I may well
Say that I am subdued—that the full Hell
Within me would infect the untainted breast
Of sacred nature with its own unrest;
As some perverted beings think to find
In scorn or hate a medicine for the mind
Which scorn or hate have wounded—O how vain!
The dagger heals not but may rend again. . .
Believe that I am ever still the same
In creed as in resolve, and what may tame
My heart, must leave the understanding free,
Or all would sink in this keen agony—
Nor dream that I will join the vulgar cry;
Or with my silence sanction tyranny;
Or seek a moment's shelter from my pain
In any madness which the world calls gain,
Ambition or revenge or thoughts as stern
As those which make me what I am; or turn
To avarice or misanthropy or lust. . .
Heap on me soon, O grave, thy welcome dust!
Till then the dungeon may demand its prey,
And Poverty and Shame may meet and say—
Halting beside me on the public way—
"That love-devoted youth is ours—let's sit
Beside him—he may live some six months yet."
Or the red scaffold, as our country bends,
May ask some willing victim; or ye friends

May fall under some sorrow which this heart
Or hand may share or vanquish or avert;
I am prepared—in truth, with no proud joy—
To do or suffer aught, as when a boy
I did devote to justice and to love
My nature, worthless now! . . .
'I must remove
A veil from my pent mind. 'Tis torn aside!
O, pallid as Death's dedicated bride,
Thou mockery which art sitting by my side,
Am I not wan like thee? at the grave's call
I haste, invited to thy wedding-ball
To greet the ghastly paramour, for whom
Thou hast deserted me. . . and made the tomb
Thy bridal bed. . . But I beside your feet
Will lie and watch ye from my winding-sheet—
Thus. . . wide awake tho' dead. . . yet stay, O stay!
Go not so soon—I know not what I say—
Hear but my reasons. . . I am mad, I fear,
My fancy is o'erwrought. . . thou art not here. . .
Pale art thou, 'tis most true. . . but thou art gone,
Thy work is finished. . . I am left alone!—
. . .
'Nay, was it I who wooed thee to this breast
Which, like a serpent, thou envenomest
As in repayment of the warmth it lent?
Didst thou not seek me for thine own content?
Did not thy love awaken mine? I thought
That thou wert she who said, "You kiss me not
Ever, I fear you do not love me now"—
In truth I loved even to my overthrow
Her, who would fain forget these words: but they
Cling to her mind, and cannot pass away.
. . .
'You say that I am proud—that when I speak
My lip is tortured with the wrongs which break
The spirit it expresses. . . Never one
Humbled himself before, as I have done!
Even the instinctive worm on which we tread

Turns, though it wound not—then with prostrate head
Sinks in the dusk and writhes like me—and dies?
No: wears a living death of agonies!
As the slow shadows of the pointed grass
Mark the eternal periods, his pangs pass,
Slow, ever-moving,—making moments be
As mine seem—each an immortality!

. . .

'That you had never seen me—never heard
My voice, and more than all had ne'er endured
The deep pollution of my loathed embrace—
That your eyes ne'er had lied love in my face—
That, like some maniac monk, I had torn out
The nerves of manhood by their bleeding root
With mine own quivering fingers, so that ne'er
Our hearts had for a moment mingled there
To disunite in horror—these were not
With thee, like some suppressed and hideous thought
Which flits athwart our musings, but can find
No rest within a pure and gentle mind. . .
Thou sealedst them with many a bare broad word,
And searedst my memory o'er them,—for I heard
And can forget not. . . they were ministered
One after one, those curses. Mix them up
Like self-destroying poisons in one cup,
And they will make one blessing which thou ne'er
Didst imprecate for, on me,—death.

. . .

'It were
A cruel punishment for one most cruel,
If such can love, to make that love the fuel
Of the mind's hell; hate, scorn, remorse, despair:
But ME—whose heart a stranger's tear might wear
As water-drops the sandy fountain-stone,
Who loved and pitied all things, and could moan
For woes which others hear not, and could see
The absent with the glance of phantasy,
And with the poor and trampled sit and weep,
Following the captive to his dungeon deep;

Me—who am as a nerve o'er which do creep
The else unfelt oppressions of this earth,
And was to thee the flame upon thy hearth,
When all beside was cold—that thou on me
Shouldst rain these plagues of blistering agony—
Such curses are from lips once eloquent
With love's too partial praise—let none relent
Who intend deeds too dreadful for a name
Henceforth, if an example for the same
They seek. . . for thou on me lookedst so, and so—
And didst speak thus. . . and thus. . . I live to show
How much men bear and die not!

. . .

'Thou wilt tell
With the grimace of hate, how horrible
It was to meet my love when thine grew less;
Thou wilt admire how I could e'er address
Such features to love's work. . . this taunt, though true,
(For indeed Nature nor in form nor hue
Bestowed on me her choicest workmanship)
Shall not be thy defence. . . for since thy lip
Met mine first, years long past, since thine eye kindled
With soft fire under mine, I have not dwindled
Nor changed in mind or body, or in aught
But as love changes what it loveth not
After long years and many trials.

'How vain
Are words! I thought never to speak again,
Not even in secret,—not to mine own heart—
But from my lips the unwilling accents start,
And from my pen the words flow as I write,
Dazzling my eyes with scalding tears. . . my sight
Is dim to see that charactered in vain
On this unfeeling leaf which burns the brain
And eats into it. . . blotting all things fair
And wise and good which time had written there.

'Those who inflict must suffer, for they see
The work of their own hearts, and this must be
Our chastisement or recompense—O child!
I would that thine were like to be more mild
For both our wretched sakes... for thine the most
Who feelest already all that thou hast lost
Without the power to wish it thine again;
And as slow years pass, a funereal train
Each with the ghost of some lost hope or friend
Following it like its shadow, wilt thou bend
No thought on my dead memory?

. . .

'Alas, love!
Fear me not... against thee I would not move
A finger in despite. Do I not live
That thou mayst have less bitter cause to grieve?
I give thee tears for scorn and love for hate;
And that thy lot may be less desolate
Than his on whom thou tramplest, I refrain
From that sweet sleep which medicines all pain.
Then, when thou speakest of me, never say
"He could forgive not." Here I cast away
All human passions, all revenge, all pride;
I think, speak, act no ill; I do but hide
Under these words, like embers, every spark
Of that which has consumed me—quick and dark
The grave is yawning... as its roof shall cover
My limbs with dust and worms under and over
So let Oblivion hide this grief... the air
Closes upon my accents, as despair
Upon my heart—let death upon despair!'

He ceased, and overcome leant back awhile,
Then rising, with a melancholy smile
Went to a sofa, and lay down, and slept
A heavy sleep, and in his dreams he wept
And muttered some familiar name, and we
Wept without shame in his society.
I think I never was impressed so much;

The man who were not, must have lacked a touch
Of human nature. . . then we lingered not,
Although our argument was quite forgot,
But calling the attendants, went to dine
At Maddalo's; yet neither cheer nor wine
Could give us spirits, for we talked of him
And nothing else, till daylight made stars dim;
And we agreed his was some dreadful ill
Wrought on him boldly, yet unspeakable,
By a dear friend; some deadly change in love
Of one vowed deeply which he dreamed not of;
For whose sake he, it seemed, had fixed a blot
Of falsehood on his mind which flourished not
But in the light of all-beholding truth;
And having stamped this canker on his youth
She had abandoned him—and how much more
Might be his woe, we guessed not—he had store
Of friends and fortune once, as we could guess
From his nice habits and his gentleness;
These were now lost. . . it were a grief indeed
If he had changed one unsustaining reed
For all that such a man might else adorn.
The colours of his mind seemed yet unworn;
For the wild language of his grief was high,
Such as in measure were called poetry;
And I remember one remark which then
Maddalo made. He said: 'Most wretched men
Are cradled into poetry by wrong,
They learn in suffering what they teach in song.'

If I had been an unconnected man,
I, from this moment, should have formed some plan
Never to leave sweet Venice,—for to me
It was delight to ride by the lone sea;
And then, the town is silent—one may write
Or read in gondolas by day or night,
Having the little brazen lamp alight,
Unseen, uninterrupted; books are there,
Pictures, and casts from all those statues fair

Which were twin-born with poetry, and all
We seek in towns, with little to recall
Regrets for the green country. I might sit
In Maddalo's great palace, and his wit
And subtle talk would cheer the winter night
And make me know myself, and the firelight
Would flash upon our faces, till the day
Might dawn and make me wonder at my stay:
But I had friends in London too: the chief
Attraction here, was that I sought relief
From the deep tenderness that maniac wrought
Within me—'twas perhaps an idle thought—
But I imagined that if day by day
I watched him, and but seldom went away,
And studied all the beatings of his heart
With zeal, as men study some stubborn art
For their own good, and could by patience find
An entrance to the caverns of his mind,
I might reclaim him from this dark estate:
In friendships I had been most fortunate—
Yet never saw I one whom I would call
More willingly my friend; and this was all
Accomplished not; such dreams of baseless good
Oft come and go in crowds or solitude
And leave no trace—but what I now designed
Made for long years impression on my mind.
The following morning, urged by my affairs,
I left bright Venice.
After many years
And many changes I returned; the name
Of Venice, and its aspect, was the same;
But Maddalo was travelling far away
Among the mountains of Armenia.
His dog was dead. His child had now become
A woman; such as it has been my doom
To meet with few,—a wonder of this earth,
Where there is little of transcendent worth,
Like one of Shakespeare's women: kindly she,
And, with a manner beyond courtesy,

Received her father's friend; and when I asked
Of the lorn maniac, she her memory tasked,
And told as she had heard the mournful tale:
'That the poor sufferer's health began to fail
Two years from my departure, but that then
The lady who had left him, came again.
Her mien had been imperious, but she now
Looked meek—perhaps remorse had brought her low.
Her coming made him better, and they stayed
Together at my father's—for I played,
As I remember, with the lady's shawl—
I might be six years old—but after all
She left him.' . . . 'Why, her heart must have been tough:
How did it end?' 'And was not this enough?
They met—they parted.'—'Child, is there no more?'
'Something within that interval which bore
The stamp of WHY they parted, How they met:
Yet if thine aged eyes disdain to wet
Those wrinkled cheeks with youth's remembered tears,
Ask me no more, but let the silent years
Be closed and cered over their memory
As yon mute marble where their corpses lie.'
I urged and questioned still, she told me how
All happened—but the cold world shall not know.

Cancelled Fragments of Julian and Maddalo

'What think you the dead are?' 'Why, dust and clay,
What should they be?' ''Tis the last hour of day.
Look on the west, how beautiful it is
Vaulted with radiant vapours! The deep bliss
Of that unutterable light has made
The edges of that cloud. . . fade
Into a hue, like some harmonious thought,
Wasting itself on that which it had wrought,
Till it dies. . . and. . . between
The light hues of the tender, pure, serene,
And infinite tranquillity of heaven.
Ay, beautiful! but when not. . .'

. . .
'Perhaps the only comfort which remains
Is the unheeded clanking of my chains,
The which I make, and call it melody.'

Note by Mrs. Shelley

From the Baths of Lucca, in 1818, Shelley visited Venice; and, circumstances rendering it eligible that we should remain a few weeks in the neighbourhood of that city, he accepted the offer of Lord Byron, who lent him the use of a villa he rented near Este; and he sent for his family from Lucca to join him.

I Capuccini was a villa built on the site of a Capuchin convent, demolished when the French suppressed religious houses; it was situated on the very overhanging brow of a low hill at the foot of a range of higher ones. The house was cheerful and pleasant; a vine-trellised walk, a pergola, as it is called in Italian, led from the hall-door to a summer-house at the end of the garden, which Shelley made his study, and in which he began the "Prometheus"; and here also, as he mentions in a letter, he wrote "Julian and Maddalo". A slight ravine, with a road in its depth, divided the garden from the hill, on which stood the ruins of the ancient castle of Este, whose dark massive wall gave forth an echo, and from whose ruined crevices owls and bats flitted forth at night, as the crescent moon sunk behind the black and heavy battlements. We looked from the garden over the wide plain of Lombardy, bounded to the west by the far Apennines, while to the east the horizon was lost in misty distance. After the picturesque but limited view of mountain, ravine, and chestnut-wood, at the Baths of Lucca, there was something infinitely gratifying to the eye in the wide range of prospect commanded by our new abode.

Our first misfortune, of the kind from which we soon suffered even more severely, happened here. Our little girl, an infant in whose small features I fancied that I traced great resemblance to her father, showed symptoms of suffering from the heat of the climate. Teething increased her illness and danger. We were at Este, and when we became alarmed, hastened to Venice for the best advice. When we arrived at Fusina, we found that we had forgotten our passport, and the soldiers on duty attempted to prevent our crossing the laguna; but they could not resist Shelley's impetuosity at such a moment. We had scarcely arrived at Venice before life fled from the little sufferer, and we returned to Este to weep her loss.

After a few weeks spent in this retreat, which was interspersed by visits to Venice, we proceeded southward.

PROMETHEUS UNBOUND

A Lyrical Drama in Four Acts

AUDISNE HAEC AMPHIARAE, SUB TERRAM ABDITE?

(Composed at Este, September, October, 1818 (Act 1); at Rome, March-April 6, 1819 (Acts 2, 3); at Florence, close of 1819 (Act 4). Published by C. and J. Ollier, London, summer of 1820. Sources of the text are (1) edition of 1820; (2) text in "Poetical Works", 1839, prepared with the aid of a list of errata in (1) written out by Shelley; (3) a fair draft in Shelley's autograph, now in the Bodleian. This has been carefully collated by Mr. C.D. Locock, who prints the result in his "Examination of the Shelley Manuscripts in the Bodleian Library", Oxford (Clarendon Press), 1903. Our text is that of 1820, modified by edition 1839, and by the Bodleian fair copy. In the following notes B = the Bodleian manuscript; 1820 = the editio princeps, printed by Marchant for C. and J. Ollier, London; and 1839 = the text as edited by Mrs. Shelley in the "Poetical Works", 1st and 2nd editions, 1839. The reader should consult the notes on the Play at the end of the volume.)

Preface

The Greek tragic writers, in selecting as their subject any portion of their national history or mythology, employed in their treatment of it a certain arbitrary discretion. They by no means conceived themselves bound to adhere to the common interpretation or to imitate in story as in title their rivals and predecessors. Such a system would have amounted to a resignation of those claims to preference over their competitors which incited the composition. The Agamemnonian story was exhibited on the Athenian theatre with as many variations as dramas.

I have presumed to employ a similar license. The "Prometheus Unbound" of Aeschylus supposed the reconciliation of Jupiter with his victim as the price of the disclosure of the danger threatened to his empire by the consummation of his marriage with Thetis. Thetis, according to this view of the subject, was given in marriage to Peleus, and Prometheus, by the permission of Jupiter, delivered from his captivity by Hercules. Had I framed my story on this model, I should have done no more than have attempted to restore the lost drama of Aeschylus; an ambition which, if my preference to this mode of treating the subject had incited me to cherish, the recollection of the high comparison such an attempt would challenge might well abate. But, in truth, I was averse from a catastrophe so feeble as that of reconciling the Champion with the Oppressor of mankind. The moral interest of the fable, which is so powerfully sustained by the sufferings and endurance of Prometheus, would be annihilated if we could conceive of him as unsaying his high language and quailing before his successful and perfidious adversary. The only imaginary being resembling in any degree Prometheus, is Satan; and Prometheus is, in my judgement, a more poetical character than Satan, because, in addition to courage, and majesty, and firm and patient opposition to omnipotent force, he is susceptible of being described as exempt from the taints of ambition, envy, revenge, and a desire for personal aggrandisement, which, in the Hero of "Paradise Lost", interfere with the interest. The character of Satan engenders in the mind a pernicious casuistry which leads us to weigh his faults with his wrongs, and to excuse the former because the latter exceed all measure. In the minds of those who consider that magnificent fiction with a religious feeling it engenders something worse. But Prometheus is, as it were, the type of the highest perfection of moral and intellectual nature, impelled by the purest and the truest motives to the best and noblest ends.

This Poem was chiefly written upon the mountainous ruins of the Baths of Caracalla, among the flowery glades, and thickets of odoriferous blossoming trees, which are extended in ever winding labyrinths upon its immense platforms and dizzy arches suspended in the air. The bright blue sky of Rome, and the effect of the vigorous awakening spring in that divinest climate, and the new life with which it drenches the spirits even to intoxication, were the inspiration of this drama.

The imagery which I have employed will be found, in many instances, to have been drawn from the operations of the human mind, or from those external actions by which they are expressed. This is unusual in modern poetry, although Dante and Shakespeare are full of instances of the same kind: Dante indeed more than any other poet, and with greater success. But the Greek poets, as writers to whom no resource of awakening the sympathy of their contemporaries was unknown, were in the habitual use of this power; and it is the study of their works (since a higher merit would probably be denied me) to which I am willing that my readers should impute this singularity.

One word is due in candour to the degree in which the study of contemporary writings may have tinged my composition, for such has been a topic of censure with regard to poems far more popular, and indeed more deservedly popular, than mine. It is impossible that any one who inhabits the same age with such writers as those who stand in the foremost ranks of our own, can conscientiously assure himself that his language and tone of thought may not have been modified by the study of the productions of those extraordinary intellects. It is true, that, not the spirit of their genius, but the forms in which it has manifested itself, are due less to the peculiarities of their own minds than to the peculiarity of the moral and intellectual condition of the minds among which they have been produced. Thus a number of writers possess the form, whilst they want the spirit of those whom, it is alleged, they imitate; because the former is the endowment of the age in which they live, and the latter must be the uncommunicated lightning of their own mind.

The peculiar style of intense and comprehensive imagery which distinguishes the modern literature of England has not been, as a general power, the product of the imitation of any particular writer. The mass of capabilities remains at every period materially the same; the circumstances which awaken it to action perpetually change. If England were divided into forty republics, each equal in population and extent to Athens, there is no reason to suppose but that, under institutions not more perfect than those of Athens, each would produce philosophers and poets equal to those who (if we except Shakespeare) have never been surpassed. We owe the great writers of the golden age of our literature to that fervid awakening of the public mind which shook to dust the oldest and most oppressive form of the Christian religion. We owe Milton to the progress and development of the same spirit: the sacred Milton was, let it ever be remembered, a republican, and a bold inquirer into morals and religion. The great writers of our own age are, we have reason to suppose, the companions and forerunners of some unimagined change in our social condition or the opinions which cement it. The cloud of mind is discharging its collected lightning, and the equilibrium between institutions and opinions is now restoring, or is about to be restored.

As to imitation, poetry is a mimetic art. It creates, but it creates by combination and representation. Poetical abstractions are beautiful and new, not because the portions of which they are composed had no previous existence in the mind of man or in nature, but because the whole produced by their combination has some intelligible and beautiful analogy with those sources of emotion and thought, and with the contemporary condition of them: one great poet is a masterpiece of nature which another not only ought to study but must study. He might as wisely and as easily determine that his mind should no longer be the mirror of all that is lovely in the visible universe as exclude from his contemplation the beautiful which exists in the writings of a great contemporary. The pretence of doing it would be a presumption in any but the greatest; the effect, even in him, would be strained, unnatural and ineffectual. A poet is the combined product of such internal powers as modify the nature of others; and of such external influences as excite and sustain these powers; he is not one, but both. Every man's mind is, in this respect, modified by all the objects of nature and art; by every word and every suggestion which he ever admitted to act upon his consciousness; it is the mirror upon which all forms are reflected, and in which they compose one form. Poets, not otherwise than philosophers, painters, sculptors and musicians, are, in one sense, the creators, and, in another, the creations, of their age. From this subjection the loftiest do not escape. There is a similarity between Homer and Hesiod, between Aeschylus and Euripides, between Virgil and Horace, between Dante and Petrarch, between Shakespeare and Fletcher, between Dryden and Pope; each has a generic resemblance under which their specific distinctions are arranged. If this similarity be the result of imitation, I am willing to confess that I have imitated.

Let this opportunity be conceded to me of acknowledging that I have, what a Scotch philosopher characteristically terms, 'a passion for reforming the world:' what passion incited him to write and publish his book, he omits to explain. For my part I had rather be damned with Plato and Lord Bacon, than go to Heaven with Paley and Malthus. But it is a mistake to suppose that I dedicate my poetical compositions solely to the direct enforcement of reform, or that I consider them in any degree as containing a reasoned system on the theory of human life. Didactic poetry is my abhorrence; nothing can be equally well expressed in prose that is not tedious and supererogatory in verse. My purpose has hitherto been simply to familiarise the highly refined imagination of the more select classes of poetical readers with beautiful idealisms of moral excellence; aware that until the mind can love, and admire, and trust, and hope, and endure, reasoned principles of moral conduct are seeds cast upon the highway of life which the unconscious passenger tramples into dust, although they would bear the harvest of his happiness. Should I live to accomplish what I purpose, that is, produce a systematical history of what appear to me to be the genuine elements of human society, let not the advocates of injustice and superstition flatter themselves that I should take Aeschylus rather than Plato as my model.

The having spoken of myself with unaffected freedom will need little apology with the candid; and let the uncandid consider that they injure me less than their own hearts and minds by misrepresentation. Whatever talents a person may possess to amuse and instruct others, be they ever so inconsiderable, he is yet bound to exert them: if his attempt be ineffectual, let the punishment of an unaccomplished purpose have been sufficient; let none trouble themselves to heap the dust of oblivion upon his efforts; the pile they raise will betray his grave which might otherwise have been unknown.

Dramatis Personae

Prometheus
Demogorgon
Jupiter
The Earth
Ocean
Apollo
Mercury
Oceanides: Asia, Panthea, Ione
Hercules
The Phantasm of Jupiter
The Spirit of The Earth
The Spirit of The Moon
Spirits of The Hours
Spirits. Echoes. Fauns. Furies

Act 1

Scene:
A *Ravine of Icy Rocks in the Indian Caucasus.*
Prometheus *is discovered bound to the Precipice.*
Pantea *and* Ione *are seated at his feet.*
Time, Night.
During, The scene morning slowly breaks.

Prometheus: Monarch of Gods and Daemons, and all Spirits
But One, who throng those bright and rolling worlds
Which Thou and I alone of living things
Behold with sleepless eyes! regard this Earth
Made multitudinous with thy slaves, whom thou
Requitest for knee-worship, prayer, and praise,
And toil, and hecatombs of broken hearts,
With fear and self-contempt and barren hope.
Whilst me, who am thy foe, eyeless in hate,
Hast thou made reign and triumph, to thy scorn,
O'er mine own misery and thy vain revenge.
Three thousand years of sleep-unsheltered hours,
And moments aye divided by keen pangs
Till they seemed years, torture and solitude,
Scorn and despair,—these are mine empire:—
More glorious far than that which thou surveyest
From thine unenvied throne, O Mighty God!
Almighty, had I deigned to share the shame
Of thine ill tyranny, and hung not here
Nailed to this wall of eagle-baffling mountain,
Black, wintry, dead, unmeasured; without herb,
Insect, or beast, or shape or sound of life.
Ah me! alas, pain, pain ever, for ever!

No change, no pause, no hope! Yet I endure.
I ask the Earth, have not the mountains felt?
I ask yon Heaven, the all-beholding Sun,
Has it not seen? The Sea, in storm or calm,
Heaven's ever-changing Shadow, spread below,

Have its deaf waves not heard my agony?
Ah me! alas, pain, pain ever, for ever!

The crawling glaciers pierce me with the spears
Of their moon-freezing crystals; the bright chains
Eat with their burning cold into my bones.
Heaven's winged hound, polluting from thy lips
His beak in poison not his own, tears up
My heart; and shapeless sights come wandering by,
The ghastly people of the realm of dream,
Mocking me: and the Earthquake-fiends are charged
To wrench the rivets from my quivering wounds
When the rocks split and close again behind:
While from their loud abysses howling throng
The genii of the storm, urging the rage
Of whirlwind, and afflict me with keen hail.
And yet to me welcome is day and night,
Whether one breaks the hoar-frost of the morn,
Or starry, dim, and slow, the other climbs
The leaden-coloured east; for then they lead
The wingless, crawling hours, one among whom
—As some dark Priest hales the reluctant victim—
Shall drag thee, cruel King, to kiss the blood
From these pale feet, which then might trample thee
If they disdained not such a prostrate slave.
Disdain! Ah, no! I pity thee. What ruin
Will hunt thee undefended through wide Heaven!
How will thy soul, cloven to its depth with terror,
Gape like a hell within! I speak in grief,
Not exultation, for I hate no more,
As then ere misery made me wise. The curse
Once breathed on thee I would recall. Ye Mountains,
Whose many-voiced Echoes, through the mist
Of cataracts, flung the thunder of that spell!
Ye icy Springs, stagnant with wrinkling frost,
Which vibrated to hear me, and then crept
Shuddering through India! Thou serenest Air,
Through which the Sun walks burning without beams!
And ye swift Whirlwinds, who on poised wings

       Hung mute and moveless o'er yon hushed abyss,
       As thunder, louder than your own, made rock
       The orbed world! If then my words had power,
       Though I am changed so that aught evil wish
       Is dead within; although no memory be
       Of what is hate, let them not lose it now!
       What was that curse? for ye all heard me speak.
FIRST VOICE (*from the mountains*): Thrice three hundred thousand years
    O'er the Earthquake's couch we stood:
    Oft, as men convulsed with fears,
    We trembled in our multitude.
SECOND VOICE (*from the springs*): Thunderbolts had parched our water,
    We had been stained with bitter blood,
    And had run mute, 'mid shrieks of slaughter,
    Thro' a city and a solitude.
THIRD VOICE (*from the air*): I had clothed, since Earth uprose,
    Its wastes in colours not their own,
    And oft had my serene repose
    Been cloven by many a rending groan.
FOURTH VOICE (*from the whirlwinds*): We had soared beneath these mountains
    Unresting ages; nor had thunder,
    Nor yon volcano's flaming fountains,
    Nor any power above or under
    Ever made us mute with wonder.
FIRST VOICE: But never bowed our snowy crest
    As at the voice of thine unrest.
SECOND VOICE: Never such a sound before
    To the Indian waves we bore.
    A pilot asleep on the howling sea
    Leaped up from the deck in agony,
    And heard, and cried, 'Ah, woe is me!'
    And died as mad as the wild waves be.
THIRD VOICE: By such dread words from Earth to Heaven
    My still realm was never riven:
    When its wound was closed, there stood
    Darkness o'er the day like blood.

FOURTH VOICE: And we shrank back: for dreams of ruin
    To frozen caves our flight pursuing
    Made us keep silence—thus—and thus—
    Though silence is a hell to us.
THE EARTH: The tongueless caverns of the craggy hills
    Cried, 'Misery!' then; the hollow Heaven replied,
    'Misery!' And the Ocean's purple waves,
    Climbing the land, howled to the lashing winds,
    And the pale nations heard it, 'Misery!'
PROMETHEUS: I hear a sound of voices: not the voice
    Which I gave forth. Mother, thy sons and thou
    Scorn him, without whose all-enduring will
    Beneath the fierce omnipotence of Jove,
    Both they and thou had vanished, like thin mist
    Unrolled on the morning wind. Know ye not me,
    The Titan? He who made his agony
    The barrier to your else all-conquering foe?
    Oh, rock-embosomed lawns, and snow-fed streams,
    Now seen athwart frore vapours, deep below,
    Through whose o'ershadowing woods I wandered once
    With Asia, drinking life from her loved eyes;
    Why scorns the spirit which informs ye, now
    To commune with me? me alone, who checked,
    As one who checks a fiend-drawn charioteer,
    The falsehood and the force of him who reigns
    Supreme, and with the groans of pining slaves
    Fills your dim glens and liquid wildernesses:
    Why answer ye not, still? Brethren!
THE EARTH: They dare not.
PROMETHEUS: Who dares? for I would hear that curse again.
    Ha, what an awful whisper rises up!
    'Tis scarce like sound: it tingles through the frame
    As lightning tingles, hovering ere it strike.
    Speak, Spirit! from thine inorganic voice
    I only know that thou art moving near
    And love. How cursed I him?
THE EARTH: How canst thou hear
    Who knowest not the language of the dead?
PROMETHEUS: Thou art a living spirit; speak as they.

THE EARTH: I dare not speak like life, lest Heaven's fell King
    Should hear, and link me to some wheel of pain
    More torturing than the one whereon I roll.
    Subtle thou art and good; and though the Gods
    Hear not this voice, yet thou art more than God,
    Being wise and kind: earnestly hearken now.
PROMETHEUS: Obscurely through my brain, like shadows dim,
    Sweep awful thoughts, rapid and thick. I feel
    Faint, like one mingled in entwining love;
    Yet 'tis not pleasure.
THE EARTH: No, thou canst not hear:
    Thou art immortal, and this tongue is known
    Only to those who die.
PROMETHEUS: And what art thou,
    O, melancholy Voice?
THE EARTH: I am the Earth,
    Thy mother; she within whose stony veins,
    To the last fibre of the loftiest tree
    Whose thin leaves trembled in the frozen air,
    Joy ran, as blood within a living frame,
    When thou didst from her bosom, like a cloud
    Of glory, arise, a spirit of keen joy!
    And at thy voice her pining sons uplifted
    Their prostrate brows from the polluting dust,
    And our almighty Tyrant with fierce dread
    Grew pale, until his thunder chained thee here.
    Then, see those million worlds which burn and roll
    Around us: their inhabitants beheld
    My sphered light wane in wide Heaven; the sea
    Was lifted by strange tempest, and new fire
    From earthquake-rifted mountains of bright snow
    Shook its portentous hair beneath Heaven's frown;
    Lightning and Inundation vexed the plains;
    Blue thistles bloomed in cities; foodless toads
    Within voluptuous chambers panting crawled:
    When Plague had fallen on man, and beast, and worm,
    And Famine; and black blight on herb and tree;
    And in the corn, and vines, and meadow-grass,
    Teemed ineradicable poisonous weeds

    Draining their growth, for my wan breast was dry
    With grief; and the thin air, my breath, was stained
    With the contagion of a mother's hate
    Breathed on her child's destroyer; ay, I heard
    Thy curse, the which, if thou rememberest not,
    Yet my innumerable seas and streams,
    Mountains, and caves, and winds, and yon wide air,
    And the inarticulate people of the dead,
    Preserve, a treasured spell. We meditate
    In secret joy and hope those dreadful words,
    But dare not speak them.
PROMETHEUS: Venerable mother!
    All else who live and suffer take from thee
    Some comfort; flowers, and fruits, and happy sounds,
    And love, though fleeting; these may not be mine.
    But mine own words, I pray, deny me not.
THE EARTH: They shall be told. Ere Babylon was dust,
    The Magus Zoroaster, my dead child,
    Met his own image walking in the garden.
    That apparition, sole of men, he saw.
    For know there are two worlds of life and death:
    One that which thou beholdest; but the other
    Is underneath the grave, where do inhabit
    The shadows of all forms that think and live
    Till death unite them and they part no more;
    Dreams and the light imaginings of men,
    And all that faith creates or love desires,
    Terrible, strange, sublime and beauteous shapes.
    There thou art, and dost hang, a writhing shade,
    'Mid whirlwind-peopled mountains; all the gods
    Are there, and all the powers of nameless worlds,
    Vast, sceptred phantoms; heroes, men, and beasts;
    And Demogorgon, a tremendous gloom;
    And he, the supreme Tyrant, on his throne
    Of burning gold. Son, one of these shall utter
    The curse which all remember. Call at will
    Thine own ghost, or the ghost of Jupiter,
    Hades or Typhon, or what mightier Gods
    From all-prolific Evil, since thy ruin,

Have sprung, and trampled on my prostrate sons.
Ask, and they must reply: so the revenge
Of the Supreme may sweep through vacant shades,
As rainy wind through the abandoned gate
Of a fallen palace.

PROMETHEUS: Mother, let not aught
Of that which may be evil, pass again
My lips, or those of aught resembling me.
Phantasm of Jupiter, arise, appear!

IONE: My wings are folded o'er mine ears:
My wings are crossed o'er mine eyes:
Yet through their silver shade appears,
And through their lulling plumes arise,
A Shape, a throng of sounds;
May it be no ill to thee
O thou of many wounds!
Near whom, for our sweet sister's sake,
Ever thus we watch and wake.

PANTHEA: The sound is of whirlwind underground,
Earthquake, and fire, and mountains cloven;
The shape is awful like the sound,
Clothed in dark purple, star-inwoven.
A sceptre of pale gold
To stay steps proud, o'er the slow cloud
His veined hand doth hold.
Cruel he looks, but calm and strong,
Like one who does, not suffers wrong.

PHANTASM OF JUPITER: Why have the secret powers of this strange world
Driven me, a frail and empty phantom, hither
On direst storms? What unaccustomed sounds
Are hovering on my lips, unlike the voice
With which our pallid race hold ghastly talk
In darkness? And, proud sufferer, who art thou?

PROMETHEUS: Tremendous Image, as thou art must be
He whom thou shadowest forth. I am his foe,
The Titan. Speak the words which I would hear,
Although no thought inform thine empty voice.

THE EARTH: Listen! And though your echoes must be mute,

  Grey mountains, and old woods, and haunted springs,
  Prophetic caves, and isle-surrounding streams,
  Rejoice to hear what yet ye cannot speak.
PHANTASM: A spirit seizes me and speaks within:
  It tears me as fire tears a thunder-cloud.
PANTHEA: See, how he lifts his mighty looks, the Heaven
  Darkens above.
IONE: He speaks! O shelter me!
PROMETHEUS: I see the curse on gestures proud and cold,
  And looks of firm defiance, and calm hate,
  And such despair as mocks itself with smiles,
  Written as on a scroll: yet speak! Oh, speak!
PHANTASM: Fiend, I defy thee! with a calm, fixed mind,
  All that thou canst inflict I bid thee do;
  Foul Tyrant both of Gods and Humankind,
  One only being shalt thou not subdue.
  Rain then thy plagues upon me here,
  Ghastly disease, and frenzying fear;
  And let alternate frost and fire
  Eat into me, and be thine ire
  Lightning, and cutting hail, and legioned forms
  Of furies, driving by upon the wounding storms.

  Ay, do thy worst. Thou art omnipotent.
  O'er all things but thyself I gave thee power,
  And my own will. Be thy swift mischiefs sent
  To blast mankind, from yon ethereal tower.
  Let thy malignant spirit move
  In darkness over those I love:
  On me and mine I imprecate
  The utmost torture of thy hate;
  And thus devote to sleepless agony,
  This undeclining head while thou must reign on high.

  But thou, who art the God and Lord: O, thou,
  Who fillest with thy soul this world of woe,
  To whom all things of Earth and Heaven do bow
  In fear and worship: all-prevailing foe!
  I curse thee! let a sufferer's curse

Clasp thee, his torturer, like remorse;
Till thine Infinity shall be
A robe of envenomed agony;
And thine Omnipotence a crown of pain,
To cling like burning gold round thy dissolving brain.

Heap on thy soul, by virtue of this Curse,
Ill deeds, then be thou damned, beholding good;
Both infinite as is the universe,
And thou, and thy self-torturing solitude.
An awful image of calm power
Though now thou sittest, let the hour
Come, when thou must appear to be
That which thou art internally;
And after many a false and fruitless crime
Scorn track thy lagging fall through boundless space and time.

PROMETHEUS: Were these my words, O Parent?
THE EARTH: They were thine.
PROMETHEUS: It doth repent me: words are quick and vain;
    Grief for awhile is blind, and so was mine.
    I wish no living thing to suffer pain.
THE EARTH: Misery, Oh misery to me,
    That Jove at length should vanquish thee.
    Wail, howl aloud, Land and Sea,
    The Earth's rent heart shall answer ye.
    Howl, Spirits of the living and the dead,
    Your refuge, your defence, lies fallen and vanquished.
FIRST ECHO: Lies fallen and vanquished!
SECOND ECHO: Fallen and vanquished!
IONE: Fear not: 'tis but some passing spasm,
    The Titan is unvanquished still.
    But see, where through the azure chasm
    Of yon forked and snowy hill
    Trampling the slant winds on high
    With golden-sandalled feet, that glow
    Under plumes of purple dye,
    Like rose-ensanguined ivory,
    A Shape comes now,
    Stretching on high from his right hand

A serpent-cinctured wand.
PANTHEA: 'Tis Jove's world-wandering herald, Mercury.
IONE: And who are those with hydra tresses
    And iron wings that climb the wind,
    Whom the frowning God represses
    Like vapours steaming up behind,
    Clanging loud, an endless crowd—
PANTHEA: These are Jove's tempest-walking hounds,
    Whom he gluts with groans and blood,
    When charioted on sulphurous cloud
    He bursts Heaven's bounds.
IONE: Are they now led, from the thin dead
    On new pangs to be fed?
PANTHEA: The Titan looks as ever, firm, not proud.
FIRST FURY: Ha! I scent life!
SECOND FURY: Let me but look into his eyes!
THIRD FURY: The hope of torturing him smells like a heap
    Of corpses, to a death-bird after battle.
FIRST FURY: Darest thou delay, O Herald! take cheer, Hounds
    Of Hell: what if the Son of Maia soon
    Should make us food and sport—who can please long
    The Omnipotent?
MERCURY: Back to your towers of iron,
    And gnash, beside the streams of fire and wail,
    Your foodless teeth. Geryon, arise! and Gorgon,
    Chimaera, and thou Sphinx, subtlest of fiends
    Who ministered to Thebes Heaven's poisoned wine,
    Unnatural love, and more unnatural hate:
    These shall perform your task.
FIRST FURY: Oh, mercy! mercy!
    We die with our desire: drive us not back!
MERCURY: Crouch then in silence.
    Awful Sufferer!
    To thee unwilling, most unwillingly
    I come, by the great Father's will driven down,
    To execute a doom of new revenge.
    Alas! I pity thee, and hate myself
    That I can do no more: aye from thy sight
    Returning, for a season, Heaven seems Hell,

So thy worn form pursues me night and day,
Smiling reproach. Wise art thou, firm and good,
But vainly wouldst stand forth alone in strife
Against the Omnipotent; as yon clear lamps
That measure and divide the weary years
From which there is no refuge, long have taught
And long must teach. Even now thy Torturer arms
With the strange might of unimagined pains
The powers who scheme slow agonies in Hell,
And my commission is to lead them here,
Or what more subtle, foul, or savage fiends
People the abyss, and leave them to their task.
Be it not so! there is a secret known
To thee, and to none else of living things,
Which may transfer the sceptre of wide Heaven,
The fear of which perplexes the Supreme:
Clothe it in words, and bid it clasp his throne
In intercession; bend thy soul in prayer,
And like a suppliant in some gorgeous fane,
Let the will kneel within thy haughty heart:
For benefits and meek submission tame
The fiercest and the mightiest.

PROMETHEUS: Evil minds
Change good to their own nature. I gave all
He has; and in return he chains me here
Years, ages, night and day: whether the Sun
Split my parched skin, or in the moony night
The crystal-winged snow cling round my hair:
Whilst my beloved race is trampled down
By his thought-executing ministers.
Such is the tyrant's recompense: 'tis just:
He who is evil can receive no good;
And for a world bestowed, or a friend lost,
He can feel hate, fear, shame; not gratitude:
He but requites me for his own misdeed.
Kindness to such is keen reproach, which breaks
With bitter stings the light sleep of Revenge.
Submission, thou dost know I cannot try:
For what submission but that fatal word,

> The death-seal of mankind's captivity,
> Like the Sicilian's hair-suspended sword,
> Which trembles o'er his crown, would he accept,
> Or could I yield? Which yet I will not yield.
> Let others flatter Crime, where it sits throned
> In brief Omnipotence: secure are they:
> For Justice, when triumphant, will weep down
> Pity, not punishment, on her own wrongs,
> Too much avenged by those who err. I wait,
> Enduring thus, the retributive hour
> Which since we spake is even nearer now.
> But hark, the hell-hounds clamour: fear delay:
> Behold! Heaven lowers under thy Father's frown.

MERCURY: Oh, that we might be spared; I to inflict
    And thou to suffer! Once more answer me:
    Thou knowest not the period of Jove's power?

PROMETHEUS: I know but this, that it must come.

MERCURY: Alas!
    Thou canst not count thy years to come of pain?

PROMETHEUS: They last while Jove must reign: nor more, nor less
    Do I desire or fear.

MERCURY: Yet pause, and plunge
    Into Eternity, where recorded time,
    Even all that we imagine, age on age,
    Seems but a point, and the reluctant mind
    Flags wearily in its unending flight,
    Till it sink, dizzy, blind, lost, shelterless;
    Perchance it has not numbered the slow years
    Which thou must spend in torture, unreprieved?

PROMETHEUS: Perchance no thought can count them, yet they pass.

MERCURY: If thou might'st dwell among the Gods the while
    Lapped in voluptuous joy?

PROMETHEUS: I would not quit
    This bleak ravine, these unrepentant pains.

MERCURY: Alas! I wonder at, yet pity thee.

PROMETHEUS: Pity the self-despising slaves of Heaven,
    Not me, within whose mind sits peace serene.
    As light in the sun, throned: how vain is talk!
    Call up the fiends.

IONE: O, sister, look! White fire
    Has cloven to the roots yon huge snow-loaded cedar;
    How fearfully God's thunder howls behind!
MERCURY: I must obey his words and thine: alas!
    Most heavily remorse hangs at my heart!
PANTHEA: See where the child of Heaven, with winged feet,
    Runs down the slanted sunlight of the dawn.
IONE: Dear sister, close thy plumes over thine eyes
    Lest thou behold and die: they come: they come
    Blackening the birth of day with countless wings,
    And hollow underneath, like death.
FIRST FURY: Prometheus!
SECOND FURY: Immortal Titan!
THIRD FURY: Champion of Heaven's slaves!
PROMETHEUS: He whom some dreadful voice invokes is here,
    Prometheus, the chained Titan. Horrible forms,
    What and who are ye? Never yet there came
    Phantasms so foul through monster-teeming Hell
    From the all-miscreative brain of Jove;
    Whilst I behold such execrable shapes,
    Methinks I grow like what I contemplate,
    And laugh and stare in loathsome sympathy.
FIRST FURY: We are the ministers of pain, and fear,
    And disappointment, and mistrust, and hate,
    And clinging crime; and as lean dogs pursue
    Through wood and lake some struck and sobbing fawn,
    We track all things that weep, and bleed, and live,
    When the great King betrays them to our will.
PROMETHEUS: Oh! many fearful natures in one name,
    I know ye; and these lakes and echoes know
    The darkness and the clangour of your wings.
    But why more hideous than your loathed selves
    Gather ye up in legions from the deep?
SECOND FURY: We knew not that: Sisters, rejoice, rejoice!
PROMETHEUS: Can aught exult in its deformity?
SECOND FURY: The beauty of delight makes lovers glad,
    Gazing on one another: so are we.
    As from the rose which the pale priestess kneels
    To gather for her festal crown of flowers

The aereal crimson falls, flushing her cheek,
So from our victim's destined agony
The shade which is our form invests us round,
Else we are shapeless as our mother Night.

PROMETHEUS: I laugh your power, and his who sent you here,
To lowest scorn. Pour forth the cup of pain.

FIRST FURY: Thou thinkest we will rend thee bone from bone,
And nerve from nerve, working like fire within?

PROMETHEUS: Pain is my element, as hate is thine;
Ye rend me now; I care not.

SECOND FURY: Dost imagine
We will but laugh into thy lidless eyes?

PROMETHEUS: I weigh not what ye do, but what ye suffer,
Being evil. Cruel was the power which called
You, or aught else so wretched, into light.

THIRD FURY: Thou think'st we will live through thee, one by one,
Like animal life, and though we can obscure not
The soul which burns within, that we will dwell
Beside it, like a vain loud multitude
Vexing the self-content of wisest men:
That we will be dread thought beneath thy brain,
And foul desire round thine astonished heart,
And blood within thy labyrinthine veins
Crawling like agony?

PROMETHEUS: Why, ye are thus now;
Yet am I king over myself, and rule
The torturing and conflicting throngs within,
As Jove rules you when Hell grows mutinous.

CHORUS OF FURIES: From the ends of the earth, from the ends
of the earth,
Where the night has its grave and the morning its birth,
Come, come, come!
Oh, ye who shake hills with the scream of your mirth,
When cities sink howling in ruin; and ye
Who with wingless footsteps trample the sea,
And close upon Shipwreck and Famine's track,
Sit chattering with joy on the foodless wreck;
Come, come, come!
Leave the bed, low, cold, and red,

    Strewed beneath a nation dead;
    Leave the hatred, as in ashes
    Fire is left for future burning:
    It will burst in bloodier flashes
    When ye stir it, soon returning:
    Leave the self-contempt implanted
    In young spirits, sense-enchanted,
    Misery's yet unkindled fuel:
    Leave Hell's secrets half unchanted
    To the maniac dreamer; cruel
    More than ye can be with hate
    Is he with fear.
    Come, come, come!
    We are steaming up from Hell's wide gate
    And we burthen the blast of the atmosphere,
    But vainly we toil till ye come here.
IONE: Sister, I hear the thunder of new wings.
PANTHEA: These solid mountains quiver with the sound
    Even as the tremulous air: their shadows make
    The space within my plumes more black than night.
FIRST FURY: Your call was as a winged car,
    Driven on whirlwinds fast and far;
    It rapped us from red gulfs of war.
SECOND FURY: From wide cities, famine-wasted;
THIRD FURY: Groans half heard, and blood untasted;
FOURTH FURY: Kingly conclaves stern and cold,
    Where blood with gold is bought and sold;
FIFTH FURY: From the furnace, white and hot,
    In which—
A FURY: Speak not: whisper not:
    I know all that ye would tell,
    But to speak might break the spell
    Which must bend the Invincible,
    The stern of thought;
    He yet defies the deepest power of Hell.
FURY: Tear the veil!
ANOTHER FURY: It is torn.
CHORUS: The pale stars of the morn
    Shine on a misery, dire to be borne.

Dost thou faint, mighty Titan? We laugh thee to scorn.
Dost thou boast the clear knowledge thou waken'dst for man?
Then was kindled within him a thirst which outran
Those perishing waters; a thirst of fierce fever,
Hope, love, doubt, desire, which consume him for ever.
One came forth of gentle worth
Smiling on the sanguine earth;
His words outlived him, like swift poison
Withering up truth, peace, and pity.
Look! where round the wide horizon
Many a million-peopled city
Vomits smoke in the bright air.
Mark that outcry of despair!
'Tis his mild and gentle ghost
Wailing for the faith he kindled:
Look again, the flames almost
To a glow-worm's lamp have dwindled:
The survivors round the embers
Gather in dread.
Joy, joy, joy!
Past ages crowd on thee, but each one remembers,
And the future is dark, and the present is spread
Like a pillow of thorns for thy slumberless head.

SEMICHORUS 1: Drops of bloody agony flow
From his white and quivering brow.
Grant a little respite now:
See a disenchanted nation
Springs like day from desolation;
To Truth its state is dedicate,
And Freedom leads it forth, her mate;
A legioned band of linked brothers
Whom Love calls children—

SEMICHORUS 2: 'Tis another's:
See how kindred murder kin:
'Tis the vintage-time for death and sin:
Blood, like new wine, bubbles within:
Till Despair smothers
The struggling world, which slaves and tyrants win.

(*All the furies vanish, except one*)

IONE: Hark, sister! what a low yet dreadful groan
    Quite unsuppressed is tearing up the heart
    Of the good Titan, as storms tear the deep,
    And beasts hear the sea moan in inland caves.
    Darest thou observe how the fiends torture him?
PANTHEA: Alas! I looked forth twice, but will no more.
IONE: What didst thou see?
PANTHEA: A woful sight: a youth
    With patient looks nailed to a crucifix.
IONE: What next?
PANTHEA: The heaven around, the earth below
    Was peopled with thick shapes of human death,
    All horrible, and wrought by human hands,
    And some appeared the work of human hearts,
    For men were slowly killed by frowns and smiles:
    And other sights too foul to speak and live
    Were wandering by. Let us not tempt worse fear
    By looking forth: those groans are grief enough.
FURY: Behold an emblem: those who do endure
    Deep wrongs for man, and scorn, and chains, but heap
    Thousand-fold torment on themselves and him.
PROMETHEUS: Remit the anguish of that lighted stare;
    Close those wan lips; let that thorn-wounded brow
    Stream not with blood; it mingles with thy tears!
    Fix, fix those tortured orbs in peace and death,
    So thy sick throes shake not that crucifix,
    So those pale fingers play not with thy gore.
    O, horrible! Thy name I will not speak,
    It hath become a curse. I see, I see
    The wise, the mild, the lofty, and the just,
    Whom thy slaves hate for being like to thee,
    Some hunted by foul lies from their heart's home,
    An early-chosen, late-lamented home;
    As hooded ounces cling to the driven hind;
    Some linked to corpses in unwholesome cells:
    Some—Hear I not the multitude laugh loud?—
    Impaled in lingering fire: and mighty realms
    Float by my feet, like sea-uprooted isles,
    Whose sons are kneaded down in common blood

    By the red light of their own burning homes.
FURY: Blood thou canst see, and fire; and canst hear groans;
    Worse things unheard, unseen, remain behind.
PROMETHEUS: Worse?
FURY: In each human heart terror survives
    The ravin it has gorged: the loftiest fear
    All that they would disdain to think were true:
    Hypocrisy and custom make their minds
    The fanes of many a worship, now outworn.
    They dare not devise good for man's estate,
    And yet they know not that they do not dare.
    The good want power, but to weep barren tears.
    The powerful goodness want: worse need for them.
    The wise want love; and those who love want wisdom;
    And all best things are thus confused to ill.
    Many are strong and rich, and would be just,
    But live among their suffering fellow-men
    As if none felt: they know not what they do.
PROMETHEUS: Thy words are like a cloud of winged snakes;
    And yet I pity those they torture not.
FURY: Thou pitiest them? I speak no more!
(*Vanishes*)
PROMETHEUS: Ah woe!
    Ah woe! Alas! pain, pain ever, for ever!
    I close my tearless eyes, but see more clear
    Thy works within my woe-illumed mind,
    Thou subtle tyrant! Peace is in the grave.
    The grave hides all things beautiful and good:
    I am a God and cannot find it there,
    Nor would I seek it: for, though dread revenge,
    This is defeat, fierce king, not victory.
    The sights with which thou torturest gird my soul
    With new endurance, till the hour arrives
    When they shall be no types of things which are.
PANTHEA: Alas! what sawest thou more?
PROMETHEUS: There are two woes:
    To speak, and to behold; thou spare me one.
    Names are there, Nature's sacred watchwords, they
    Were borne aloft in bright emblazonry;

    The nations thronged around, and cried aloud,
    As with one voice, Truth, liberty, and love!
    Suddenly fierce confusion fell from heaven
    Among them: there was strife, deceit, and fear:
    Tyrants rushed in, and did divide the spoil.
    This was the shadow of the truth I saw.
THE EARTH: I felt thy torture, son; with such mixed joy
    As pain and virtue give. To cheer thy state
    I bid ascend those subtle and fair spirits,
    Whose homes are the dim caves of human thought,
    And who inhabit, as birds wing the wind,
    Its world-surrounding aether: they behold
    Beyond that twilight realm, as in a glass,
    The future: may they speak comfort to thee!
PANTHEA: Look, sister, where a troop of spirits gather,
    Like flocks of clouds in spring's delightful weather,
    Thronging in the blue air!
IONE: And see! more come,
    Like fountain-vapours when the winds are dumb,
    That climb up the ravine in scattered lines.
    And, hark! is it the music of the pines?
    Is it the lake? Is it the waterfall?
PANTHEA: 'Tis something sadder, sweeter far than all.
CHORUS OF SPIRITS: From unremembered ages we
    Gentle guides and guardians be
    Of heaven-oppressed mortality;
    And we breathe, and sicken not,
    The atmosphere of human thought:
    Be it dim, and dank, and gray,
    Like a storm-extinguished day,
    Travelled o'er by dying gleams;
    Be it bright as all between
    Cloudless skies and windless streams,
    Silent, liquid, and serene;
    As the birds within the wind,
    As the fish within the wave,
    As the thoughts of man's own mind
    Float through all above the grave;
    We make there our liquid lair,

> Voyaging cloudlike and unpent
> Through the boundless element:
> Thence we bear the prophecy
> Which begins and ends in thee!

IONE: More yet come, one by one: the air around them
> Looks radiant as the air around a star.

FIRST SPIRIT: On a battle-trumpet's blast
> I fled hither, fast, fast, fast,
> 'Mid the darkness upward cast.
> From the dust of creeds outworn,
> From the tyrant's banner torn,
> Gathering 'round me, onward borne,
> There was mingled many a cry—
> Freedom! Hope! Death! Victory!
> Till they faded through the sky;
> And one sound, above, around,
> One sound beneath, around, above,
> Was moving; 'twas the soul of Love;
> 'Twas the hope, the prophecy,
> Which begins and ends in thee.

SECOND SPIRIT: A rainbow's arch stood on the sea,
> Which rocked beneath, immovably;
> And the triumphant storm did flee,
> Like a conqueror, swift and proud,
> Between, with many a captive cloud,
> A shapeless, dark and rapid crowd,
> Each by lightning riven in half:
> I heard the thunder hoarsely laugh:
> Mighty fleets were strewn like chaff
> And spread beneath a hell of death
> O'er the white waters. I alit
> On a great ship lightning-split,
> And speeded hither on the sigh
> Of one who gave an enemy
> His plank, then plunged aside to die.

THIRD SPIRIT: I sate beside a sage's bed,
> And the lamp was burning red
> Near the book where he had fed,
> When a Dream with plumes of flame,

    To his pillow hovering came,
    And I knew it was the same
    Which had kindled long ago
    Pity, eloquence, and woe;
    And the world awhile below
    Wore the shade, its lustre made.
    It has borne me here as fleet
    As Desire's lightning feet:
    I must ride it back ere morrow,
    Or the sage will wake in sorrow.
FOURTH SPIRIT: On a poet's lips I slept
    Dreaming like a love-adept
    In the sound his breathing kept;
    Nor seeks nor finds he mortal blisses,
    But feeds on the aereal kisses
    Of shapes that haunt thought's wildernesses.
    He will watch from dawn to gloom
    The lake-reflected sun illume
    The yellow bees in the ivy-bloom,
    Nor heed nor see, what things they be;
    But from these create he can
    Forms more real than living man,
    Nurslings of immortality!
    One of these awakened me,
    And I sped to succour thee.
IONE: Behold'st thou not two shapes from the east and west
    Come, as two doves to one beloved nest,
    Twin nurslings of the all-sustaining air
    On swift still wings glide down the atmosphere?
    And, hark! their sweet sad voices! 'tis despair
    Mingled with love and then dissolved in sound.
PANTHEA: Canst thou speak, sister? all my words are drowned.
IONE: Their beauty gives me voice. See how they float
    On their sustaining wings of skiey grain,
    Orange and azure deepening into gold:
    Their soft smiles light the air like a star's fire.
CHORUS OF SPIRITS: Hast thou beheld the form of Love?
FIFTH SPIRIT: As over wide dominions
    I sped, like some swift cloud that wings the wide air's wildernesses,

That planet-crested shape swept by on lightning-braided pinions,
Scattering the liquid joy of life from his ambrosial tresses:
His footsteps paved the world with light; but as I passed
   'twas fading,
And hollow Ruin yawned behind: great sages bound in madness,
And headless patriots, and pale youths who perished,
   unupbraiding,
Gleamed in the night. I wandered o'er, till thou, O King of sadness,
Turned by thy smile the worst I saw to recollected gladness.

SIXTH SPIRIT: Ah, sister! Desolation is a delicate thing:
   It walks not on the earth, it floats not on the air,
   But treads with lulling footstep, and fans with silent wing
   The tender hopes which in their hearts the best and gentlest bear;
   Who, soothed to false repose by the fanning plumes above
   And the music-stirring motion of its soft and busy feet,
   Dream visions of aereal joy, and call the monster, Love,
   And wake, and find the shadow Pain, as he whom now we greet.

CHORUS: Though Ruin now Love's shadow be,
   Following him, destroyingly,
   On Death's white and winged steed,
   Which the fleetest cannot flee,
   Trampling down both flower and weed,
   Man and beast, and foul and fair,
   Like a tempest through the air;
   Thou shalt quell this horseman grim,
   Woundless though in heart or limb.

PROMETHEUS: Spirits! how know ye this shall be?

CHORUS: In the atmosphere we breathe,
   As buds grow red when the snow-storms flee,
   From Spring gathering up beneath,
   Whose mild winds shake the elder-brake,
   And the wandering herdsmen know
   That the white-thorn soon will blow:
   Wisdom, Justice, Love, and Peace,
   When they struggle to increase,
   Are to us as soft winds be
   To shepherd boys, the prophecy
   Which begins and ends in thee.

IONE: Where are the Spirits fled?

PANTHEA: Only a sense
>Remains of them, like the omnipotence
>Of music, when the inspired voice and lute
>Languish, ere yet the responses are mute,
>Which through the deep and labyrinthine soul,
>Like echoes through long caverns, wind and roll.

PROMETHEUS: How fair these airborn shapes! and yet I feel
>Most vain all hope but love; and thou art far,
>Asia! who, when my being overflowed,
>Wert like a golden chalice to bright wine
>Which else had sunk into the thirsty dust.
>All things are still: alas! how heavily
>This quiet morning weighs upon my heart;
>Though I should dream I could even sleep with grief
>If slumber were denied not. I would fain
>Be what it is my destiny to be,
>The saviour and the strength of suffering man,
>Or sink into the original gulf of things:
>There is no agony, and no solace left;
>Earth can console, Heaven can torment no more.

PANTHEA: Hast thou forgotten one who watches thee
>The cold dark night, and never sleeps but when
>The shadow of thy spirit falls on her?

PROMETHEUS: I said all hope was vain but love: thou lovest.

PANTHEA: Deeply in truth; but the eastern star looks white,
>And Asia waits in that far Indian vale,
>The scene of her sad exile; rugged once
>And desolate and frozen, like this ravine;
>But now invested with fair flowers and herbs,
>And haunted by sweet airs and sounds, which flow
>Among the woods and waters, from the aether
>Of her transforming presence, which would fade
>If it were mingled not with thine. Farewell!

END OF ACT 1

Act 2

Scene 2.1:
Morning.
A Lovely Vale in the Indian Caucasus.
Asia, *Alone.*
Asia: From all the blasts of heaven thou hast descended:
   Yes, like a spirit, like a thought, which makes
   Unwonted tears throng to the horny eyes,
   And beatings haunt the desolated heart,
   Which should have learnt repose: thou hast descended
   Cradled in tempests; thou dost wake, O Spring!
   O child of many winds! As suddenly
   Thou comest as the memory of a dream,
   Which now is sad because it hath been sweet;
   Like genius, or like joy which riseth up
   As from the earth, clothing with golden clouds
   The desert of our life.
   This is the season, this the day, the hour;
   At sunrise thou shouldst come, sweet sister mine,
   Too long desired, too long delaying, come!
   How like death-worms the wingless moments crawl!
   The point of one white star is quivering still
   Deep in the orange light of widening morn
   Beyond the purple mountains: through a chasm
   Of wind-divided mist the darker lake
   Reflects it: now it wanes: it gleams again
   As the waves fade, and as the burning threads
   Of woven cloud unravel in pale air:
   'Tis lost! and through yon peaks of cloud-like snow
   The roseate sunlight quivers: hear I not
   The Aeolian music of her sea-green plumes
   Winnowing the crimson dawn?
Panthea (*Enters*): I feel, I see
   Those eyes which burn through smiles that fade in tears,
   Like stars half quenched in mists of silver dew.
   Beloved and most beautiful, who wearest
   The shadow of that soul by which I live,

>How late thou art! the sphered sun had climbed
>The sea; my heart was sick with hope, before
>The printless air felt thy belated plumes.
>
>PANTHEA: Pardon, great Sister! but my wings were faint
>>With the delight of a remembered dream,
>>As are the noontide plumes of summer winds
>>Satiate with sweet flowers. I was wont to sleep
>>Peacefully, and awake refreshed and calm
>>Before the sacred Titan's fall, and thy
>>Unhappy love, had made, through use and pity,
>>Both love and woe familiar to my heart
>>As they had grown to thine: erewhile I slept
>>Under the glaucous caverns of old Ocean
>>Within dim bowers of green and purple moss,
>>Our young Ione's soft and milky arms
>>Locked then, as now, behind my dark, moist hair,
>>While my shut eyes and cheek were pressed within
>>The folded depth of her life-breathing bosom:
>>But not as now, since I am made the wind
>>Which fails beneath the music that I bear
>>Of thy most wordless converse; since dissolved
>>Into the sense with which love talks, my rest
>>Was troubled and yet sweet; my waking hours
>>Too full of care and pain.
>
>ASIA: Lift up thine eyes,
>>And let me read thy dream.
>
>PANTHEA: As I have said
>>With our sea-sister at his feet I slept.
>>The mountain mists, condensing at our voice
>>Under the moon, had spread their snowy flakes,
>>From the keen ice shielding our linked sleep.
>>Then two dreams came. One, I remember not.
>>But in the other his pale wound-worn limbs
>>Fell from Prometheus, and the azure night
>>Grew radiant with the glory of that form
>>Which lives unchanged within, and his voice fell
>>Like music which makes giddy the dim brain,
>>Faint with intoxication of keen joy:
>>'Sister of her whose footsteps pave the world

With loveliness—more fair than aught but her,
Whose shadow thou art—lift thine eyes on me.'
I lifted them: the overpowering light
Of that immortal shape was shadowed o'er
By love; which, from his soft and flowing limbs,
And passion-parted lips, and keen, faint eyes,
Steamed forth like vaporous fire; an atmosphere
Which wrapped me in its all-dissolving power,
As the warm ether of the morning sun
Wraps ere it drinks some cloud of wandering dew.
I saw not, heard not, moved not, only felt
His presence flow and mingle through my blood
Till it became his life, and his grew mine,
And I was thus absorbed, until it passed,
And like the vapours when the sun sinks down,
Gathering again in drops upon the pines,
And tremulous as they, in the deep night
My being was condensed; and as the rays
Of thought were slowly gathered, I could hear
His voice, whose accents lingered ere they died
Like footsteps of weak melody: thy name
Among the many sounds alone I heard
Of what might be articulate; though still
I listened through the night when sound was none.
Ione wakened then, and said to me:
'Canst thou divine what troubles me to-night?
I always knew, what I desired before,
Nor ever found delight to wish in vain.
But now I cannot tell thee what I seek;
I know not; something sweet, since it is sweet
Even to desire; it is thy sport, false sister;
Thou hast discovered some enchantment old,
Whose spells have stolen my spirit as I slept
And mingled it with thine: for when just now
We kissed, I felt within thy parted lips
The sweet air that sustained me, and the warmth
Of the life-blood, for loss of which I faint,
Quivered between our intertwining arms.'
I answered not, for the Eastern star grew pale,

    But fled to thee.
Asia: Thou speakest, but thy words
    Are as the air: I feel them not: Oh, lift
    Thine eyes, that I may read his written soul!
Panthea: I lift them though they droop beneath the load
    Of that they would express: what canst thou see
    But thine own fairest shadow imaged there?
Asia: Thine eyes are like the deep, blue, boundless heaven
    Contracted to two circles underneath
    Their long, fine lashes; dark, far, measureless,
    Orb within orb, and line through line inwoven.
Panthea: Why lookest thou as if a spirit passed?
Asia: There is a change: beyond their inmost depth
    I see a shade, a shape: 'tis He, arrayed
    In the soft light of his own smiles, which spread
    Like radiance from the cloud-surrounded moon.
    Prometheus, it is thine! depart not yet!
    Say not those smiles that we shall meet again
    Within that bright pavilion which their beams
    Shall build o'er the waste world? The dream is told.
    What shape is that between us? Its rude hair
    Roughens the wind that lifts it, its regard
    Is wild and quick, yet 'tis a thing of air,
    For through its gray robe gleams the golden dew
    Whose stars the noon has quenched not.
Dream: Follow! Follow!
Panthea: It is mine other dream.
Asia: It disappears.
Panthea: It passes now into my mind. Methought
    As we sate here, the flower-infolding buds
    Burst on yon lightning-blasted almond tree,
    When swift from the white Scythian wilderness
    A wind swept forth wrinkling the Earth with frost:
    I looked, and all the blossoms were blown down;
    But on each leaf was stamped, as the blue bells
    Of Hyacinth tell Apollo's written grief,
    O, Follow, Follow!
Asia: As you speak, your words
    Fill, pause by pause, my own forgotten sleep

With shapes. Methought among these lawns together
We wandered, underneath the young gray dawn,
And multitudes of dense white fleecy clouds
Were wandering in thick flocks along the mountains
Shepherded by the slow, unwilling wind;
And the white dew on the new-bladed grass,
Just piercing the dark earth, hung silently;
And there was more which I remember not:
But on the shadows of the morning clouds,
Athwart the purple mountain slope, was written
Follow, O, Follow! as they vanished by;
And on each herb, from which Heaven's dew had fallen,
The like was stamped, as with a withering fire;
A wind arose among the pines; it shook
The clinging music from their boughs, and then
Low, sweet, faint sounds, like the farewell of ghosts,
Were heard: O, Follow, Follow, Follow Me!
And then I said, 'Panthea, look on me.'
But in the depth of those beloved eyes
Still I saw, Follow, Follow!
Echo: Follow, follow!
Panthea: The crags, this clear spring morning, mock our voices
  As they were spirit-tongued.
Asia: It is some being
  Around the crags. What fine clear sounds! O, list!
Echoes, Unseen: Echoes we: listen!
  We cannot stay:
  As dew-stars glisten
  Then fade away—
  Child of Ocean!
Asia: Hark! Spirits speak. The liquid responses
  Of their aereal tongues yet sound.
Panthea: I hear.
Echoes: Oh, follow, follow,
  As our voice recedeth
  Through the caverns hollow,
  Where the forest spreadeth;
(*More distant*)
  Oh, follow, follow!

> Through the caverns hollow,
> As the song floats thou pursue,
> Where the wild bee never flew,
> Through the noontide darkness deep,
> By the odour-breathing sleep
> Of faint night-flowers, and the waves
> At the fountain-lighted caves,
> While our music, wild and sweet,
> Mocks thy gently falling feet,
> Child of Ocean!

Asia: Shall we pursue the sound? It grows more faint
  And distant.
Panthea: List! the strain floats nearer now.
Echoes: In the world unknown
  Sleeps a voice unspoken;
  By thy step alone
  Can its rest be broken;
  Child of Ocean!
Asia: How the notes sink upon the ebbing wind!
Echoes: Oh, follow, follow!
  Through the caverns hollow,
  As the song floats thou pursue,
  By the woodland noontide dew;
  By the forests, lakes, and fountains,
  Through the many-folded mountains;
  To the rents, and gulfs, and chasms,
  Where the Earth reposed from spasms,
  On the day when He and thou
  Parted, to commingle now;
  Child of Ocean!
Asia: Come, sweet Panthea, link thy hand in mine,
  And follow, ere the voices fade away.

Scene 2.2:
A Forest, intermingled with rocks and caverns.
Asia *and* Panthea *pass into it.*
Two young fauns are sitting on a rock listening.
Semichorus 1 of Spirits: The path through which that lovely twain
  Have passed, by cedar, pine, and yew,

And each dark tree that ever grew,
Is curtained out from Heaven's wide blue;
Nor sun, nor moon, nor wind, nor rain,
Can pierce its interwoven bowers,
Nor aught, save where some cloud of dew,
Drifted along the earth-creeping breeze,
Between the trunks of the hoar trees,
Hangs each a pearl in the pale flowers
Of the green laurel, blown anew,
And bends, and then fades silently,
One frail and fair anemone:
Or when some star of many a one
That climbs and wanders through steep night,
Has found the cleft through which alone
Beams fall from high those depths upon
Ere it is borne away, away,
By the swift Heavens that cannot stay,
It scatters drops of golden light,
Like lines of rain that ne'er unite:
And the gloom divine is all around,
And underneath is the mossy ground.

SEMICHORUS 2: There the voluptuous nightingales,
Are awake through all the broad noonday.
When one with bliss or sadness fails,
And through the windless ivy-boughs,
Sick with sweet love, droops dying away
On its mate's music-panting bosom;
Another from the swinging blossom,
Watching to catch the languid close
Of the last strain, then lifts on high
The wings of the weak melody,
Till some new strain of feeling bear
The song, and all the woods are mute;
When there is heard through the dim air
The rush of wings, and rising there
Like many a lake-surrounded flute,
Sounds overflow the listener's brain
So sweet, that joy is almost pain.

SEMICHORUS 1: There those enchanted eddies play

    Of echoes, music-tongued, which draw,
    By Demogorgon's mighty law,
    With melting rapture, or sweet awe,
    All spirits on that secret way;
    As inland boats are driven to Ocean
     Down streams made strong with mountain-thaw:
    And first there comes a gentle sound
    To those in talk or slumber bound,
    And wakes the destined soft emotion,—
    Attracts, impels them; those who saw
    Say from the breathing earth behind
    There steams a plume-uplifting wind
    Which drives them on their path, while they
    Believe their own swift wings and feet
    The sweet desires within obey:
    And so they float upon their way,
    Until, still sweet, but loud and strong,
    The storm of sound is driven along,
    Sucked up and hurrying: as they fleet
    Behind, its gathering billows meet
    And to the fatal mountain bear
    Like clouds amid the yielding air.

First Faun: Canst thou imagine where those spirits live
    Which make such delicate music in the woods?
    We haunt within the least frequented caves
    And closest coverts, and we know these wilds,
    Yet never meet them, though we hear them oft:
    Where may they hide themselves?

Second Faun: 'Tis hard to tell;
    I have heard those more skilled in spirits say,
    The bubbles, which the enchantment of the sun
    Sucks from the pale faint water-flowers that pave
    The oozy bottom of clear lakes and pools,
    Are the pavilions where such dwell and float
    Under the green and golden atmosphere
    Which noontide kindles through the woven leaves;
    And when these burst, and the thin fiery air,
    The which they breathed within those lucent domes,
    Ascends to flow like meteors through the night,

They ride on them, and rein their headlong speed,
And bow their burning crests, and glide in fire
Under the waters of the earth again.
FIRST FAUN: If such live thus, have others other lives,
Under pink blossoms or within the bells
Of meadow flowers, or folded violets deep,
Or on their dying odours, when they die,
Or in the sunlight of the sphered dew?
SECOND FAUN: Ay, many more which we may well divine.
But should we stay to speak, noontide would come,
And thwart Silenus find his goats undrawn,
And grudge to sing those wise and lovely songs
Of Fate, and Chance, and God, and Chaos old,
And Love, and the chained Titan's woful doom,
And how he shall be loosed, and make the earth
One brotherhood: delightful strains which cheer
Our solitary twilights, and which charm
To silence the unenvying nightingales.

SCENE 2.3:
A pinnacle of rock among mountains.
ASIA *and* PANTHEA.
PANTHEA: Hither the sound has borne us—to the realm
Of Demogorgon, and the mighty portal,
Like a volcano's meteor-breathing chasm,
Whence the oracular vapour is hurled up
Which lonely men drink wandering in their youth,
And call truth, virtue, love, genius, or joy,
That maddening wine of life, whose dregs they drain
To deep intoxication; and uplift,
Like Maenads who cry loud, Evoe! Evoe!
The voice which is contagion to the world.
ASIA: Fit throne for such a Power! Magnificent!
How glorious art thou, Earth! And if thou be
The shadow of some spirit lovelier still,
Though evil stain its work, and it should be
Like its creation, weak yet beautiful,
I could fall down and worship that and thee.
Even now my heart adoreth: Wonderful!

Look, sister, ere the vapour dim thy brain:
Beneath is a wide plain of billowy mist,
As a lake, paving in the morning sky,
With azure waves which burst in silver light,
Some Indian vale. Behold it, rolling on
Under the curdling winds, and islanding
The peak whereon we stand, midway, around,
Encinctured by the dark and blooming forests,
Dim twilight-lawns, and stream-illumined caves,
And wind-enchanted shapes of wandering mist;
And far on high the keen sky-cleaving mountains
From icy spires of sun-like radiance fling
The dawn, as lifted Ocean's dazzling spray,
From some Atlantic islet scattered up,
Spangles the wind with lamp-like water-drops.
The vale is girdled with their walls, a howl
Of cataracts from their thaw-cloven ravines,
Satiates the listening wind, continuous, vast,
Awful as silence. Hark! the rushing snow!
The sun-awakened avalanche! whose mass,
Thrice sifted by the storm, had gathered there
Flake after flake, in heaven-defying minds
As thought by thought is piled, till some great truth
Is loosened, and the nations echo round,
Shaken to their roots, as do the mountains now.

PANTHEA: Look how the gusty sea of mist is breaking
In crimson foam, even at our feet! it rises
As Ocean at the enchantment of the moon
Round foodless men wrecked on some oozy isle.

ASIA: The fragments of the cloud are scattered up;
The wind that lifts them disentwines my hair;
Its billows now sweep o'er mine eyes; my brain
Grows dizzy; see'st thou shapes within the mist?

PANTHEA: A countenance with beckoning smiles: there burns
An azure fire within its golden locks!
Another and another: hark! they speak!

SONG OF SPIRITS: To the deep, to the deep,
Down, down!
Through the shade of sleep,

Through the cloudy strife
Of Death and of Life;
Through the veil and the bar
Of things which seem and are
Even to the steps of the remotest throne,
Down, down!

While the sound whirls around,
Down, down!
As the fawn draws the hound,
As the lightning the vapour,
As a weak moth the taper;
Death, despair; love, sorrow;
Time both; to-day, to-morrow;
As steel obeys the spirit of the stone,
Down, down!

Through the gray, void abysm,
Down, down!
Where the air is no prism,
And the moon and stars are not,
And the cavern-crags wear not
The radiance of Heaven,
Nor the gloom to Earth given,
Where there is One pervading, One alone,
Down, down!

In the depth of the deep,
Down, down!
Like veiled lightning asleep,
Like the spark nursed in embers,
The last look Love remembers,
Like a diamond, which shines
On the dark wealth of mines,
A spell is treasured but for thee alone.
Down, down!

We have bound thee, we guide thee;
Down, down!

With the bright form beside thee;
Resist not the weakness,
Such strength is in meekness
That the Eternal, the Immortal,
Must unloose through life's portal
The snake-like Doom coiled underneath his throne
By that alone.

Scene 2.4:
The Cave of Demogorgon.
Asia *and* Panthea.
Panthea: What veiled form sits on that ebon throne?
Asia: The veil has fallen.
Panthea: I see a mighty darkness
    Filling the seat of power, and rays of gloom
    Dart round, as light from the meridian sun.
    —Ungazed upon and shapeless; neither limb,
    Nor form, nor outline; yet we feel it is
    A living Spirit.
Demogorgon: Ask what thou wouldst know.
Asia: What canst thou tell?
Demogorgon: All things thou dar'st demand.
Asia: Who made the living world?
Demogorgon: God.
Asia: Who made all
    That it contains? thought, passion, reason, will,
    Imagination?
Demogorgon: God: Almighty God.
Asia: Who made that sense which, when the winds of Spring
    In rarest visitation, or the voice
    Of one beloved heard in youth alone,
    Fills the faint eyes with falling tears which dim
    The radiant looks of unbewailing flowers,
    And leaves this peopled earth a solitude
    When it returns no more?
Demogorgon: Merciful God.
Asia: And who made terror, madness, crime, remorse,
    Which from the links of the great chain of things,
    To every thought within the mind of man

> Sway and drag heavily, and each one reels
> Under the load towards the pit of death;
> Abandoned hope, and love that turns to hate;
> And self-contempt, bitterer to drink than blood;
> Pain, whose unheeded and familiar speech
> Is howling, and keen shrieks, day after day;
> And Hell, or the sharp fear of Hell?

DEMOGORGON: He reigns.

ASIA: Utter his name: a world pining in pain
> Asks but his name: curses shall drag him down.

DEMOGORGON: He reigns.

ASIA: I feel, I know it: who?

DEMOGORGON: He reigns.

ASIA: Who reigns? There was the Heaven and Earth at first,
> And Light and Love; then Saturn, from whose throne
> Time fell, an envious shadow: such the state
> Of the earth's primal spirits beneath his sway,
> As the calm joy of flowers and living leaves
> Before the wind or sun has withered them
> And semivital worms; but he refused
> The birthright of their being, knowledge, power,
> The skill which wields the elements, the thought
> Which pierces this dim universe like light,
> Self-empire, and the majesty of love;
> For thirst of which they fainted. Then Prometheus
> Gave wisdom, which is strength, to Jupiter,
> And with this law alone, 'Let man be free,'
> Clothed him with the dominion of wide Heaven.
> To know nor faith, nor love, nor law; to be
> Omnipotent but friendless is to reign;
> And Jove now reigned; for on the race of man
> First famine, and then toil, and then disease,
> Strife, wounds, and ghastly death unseen before,
> Fell; and the unseasonable seasons drove
> With alternating shafts of frost and fire,
> Their shelterless, pale tribes to mountain caves:
> And in their desert hearts fierce wants he sent,
> And mad disquietudes, and shadows idle
> Of unreal good, which levied mutual war,

So ruining the lair wherein they raged.
Prometheus saw, and waked the legioned hopes
Which sleep within folded Elysian flowers,
Nepenthe, Moly, Amaranth, fadeless blooms,
That they might hide with thin and rainbow wings
The shape of Death; and Love he sent to bind
The disunited tendrils of that vine
Which bears the wine of life, the human heart;
And he tamed fire which, like some beast of prey,
Most terrible, but lovely, played beneath
The frown of man; and tortured to his will
Iron and gold, the slaves and signs of power,
And gems and poisons, and all subtlest forms
Hidden beneath the mountains and the waves.
He gave man speech, and speech created thought,
Which is the measure of the universe;
And Science struck the thrones of earth and heaven,
Which shook, but fell not; and the harmonious mind
Poured itself forth in all-prophetic song;
And music lifted up the listening spirit
Until it walked, exempt from mortal care,
Godlike, o'er the clear billows of sweet sound;
And human hands first mimicked and then mocked,
With moulded limbs more lovely than its own,
The human form, till marble grew divine;
And mothers, gazing, drank the love men see
Reflected in their race, behold, and perish.
He told the hidden power of herbs and springs,
And Disease drank and slept. Death grew like sleep.
He taught the implicated orbits woven
Of the wide-wandering stars; and how the sun
Changes his lair, and by what secret spell
The pale moon is transformed, when her broad eye
Gazes not on the interlunar sea:
He taught to rule, as life directs the limbs,
The tempest-winged chariots of the Ocean,
And the Celt knew the Indian. Cities then
Were built, and through their snow-like columns flowed
The warm winds, and the azure ether shone,

And the blue sea and shadowy hills were seen.
Such, the alleviations of his state,
Prometheus gave to man, for which he hangs
Withering in destined pain: but who rains down
Evil, the immedicable plague, which, while
Man looks on his creation like a God
And sees that it is glorious, drives him on,
The wreck of his own will, the scorn of earth,
The outcast, the abandoned, the alone?
Not Jove: while yet his frown shook Heaven ay, when
His adversary from adamantine chains
Cursed him, he trembled like a slave. Declare
Who is his master? Is he too a slave?

DEMOGORGON: All spirits are enslaved which serve things evil:
    Thou knowest if Jupiter be such or no.

ASIA: Whom calledst thou God?

DEMOGORGON: I spoke but as ye speak,
    For Jove is the supreme of living things.

ASIA: Who is the master of the slave?

DEMOGORGON: If the abysm
    Could vomit forth its secrets. . . But a voice
    Is wanting, the deep truth is imageless;
    For what would it avail to bid thee gaze
    On the revolving world? What to bid speak
    Fate, Time, Occasion, Chance and Change? To these
    All things are subject but eternal Love.

ASIA: So much I asked before, and my heart gave
    The response thou hast given; and of such truths
    Each to itself must be the oracle.
    One more demand; and do thou answer me
    As my own soul would answer, did it know
    That which I ask. Prometheus shall arise
    Henceforth the sun of this rejoicing world:
    When shall the destined hour arrive?

DEMOGORGON: Behold!

ASIA: The rocks are cloven, and through the purple night
    I see cars drawn by rainbow-winged steeds
    Which trample the dim winds: in each there stands
    A wild-eyed charioteer urging their flight.

    Some look behind, as fiends pursued them there,
    And yet I see no shapes but the keen stars:
    Others, with burning eyes, lean forth, and drink
    With eager lips the wind of their own speed,
    As if the thing they loved fled on before,
    And now, even now, they clasped it. Their bright locks
    Stream like a comet's flashing hair; they all
    Sweep onward.
DEMOGORGON: These are the immortal Hours,
    Of whom thou didst demand. One waits for thee.
ASIA: A Spirit with a dreadful countenance
    Checks its dark chariot by the craggy gulf.
    Unlike thy brethren, ghastly charioteer,
    Who art thou? Whither wouldst thou bear me? Speak!
SPIRIT: I am the shadow of a destiny
    More dread than is my aspect: ere yon planet
    Has set, the darkness which ascends with me
    Shall wrap in lasting night heaven's kingless throne.
ASIA: What meanest thou?
PANTHEA: That terrible shadow floats
    Up from its throne, as may the lurid smoke
    Of earthquake-ruined cities o'er the sea.
    Lo! it ascends the car; the coursers fly
    Terrified: watch its path among the stars
    Blackening the night!
ASIA: Thus I am answered: strange!
PANTHEA: See, near the verge, another chariot stays;
    An ivory shell inlaid with crimson fire,
    Which comes and goes within its sculptured rim
    Of delicate strange tracery; the young spirit
    That guides it has the dove-like eyes of hope;
    How its soft smiles attract the soul! as light
    Lures winged insects through the lampless air.
SPIRIT: My coursers are fed with the lightning,
    They drink of the whirlwind's stream,
    And when the red morning is bright'ning
    They bathe in the fresh sunbeam;
    They have strength for their swiftness I deem;
    Then ascend with me, daughter of Ocean.

I desire: and their speed makes night kindle;
I fear: they outstrip the Typhoon;
Ere the cloud piled on Atlas can dwindle
We encircle the earth and the moon:
We shall rest from long labours at noon:
Then ascend with me, daughter of Ocean.

Scene 2.5:
The car pauses within a cloud on the top of a snowy mountain.
Asia, Panthea, *and the spirit of the hour.*
Spirit: On the brink of the night and the morning
   My coursers are wont to respire;
   But the Earth has just whispered a warning
   That their flight must be swifter than fire:
   They shall drink the hot speed of desire!
Asia: Thou breathest on their nostrils, but my breath
   Would give them swifter speed.
Spirit: Alas! it could not.
Panthea: Oh Spirit! pause, and tell whence is the light
   Which fills this cloud? the sun is yet unrisen.
Spirit: The sun will rise not until noon. Apollo
   Is held in heaven by wonder; and the light
   Which fills this vapour, as the aereal hue
   Of fountain-gazing roses fills the water,
   Flows from thy mighty sister.
Panthea: Yes, I feel—
Asia: What is it with thee, sister? Thou art pale.
Panthea: How thou art changed! I dare not look on thee;
   I feel but see thee not. I scarce endure
   The radiance of thy beauty. Some good change
   Is working in the elements, which suffer
   Thy presence thus unveiled. The Nereids tell
   That on the day when the clear hyaline
   Was cloven at thine uprise, and thou didst stand
   Within a veined shell, which floated on
   Over the calm floor of the crystal sea,
   Among the Aegean isles, and by the shores
   Which bear thy name; love, like the atmosphere
   Of the sun's fire filling the living world,

    Burst from thee, and illumined earth and heaven
    And the deep ocean and the sunless caves
    And all that dwells within them; till grief cast
    Eclipse upon the soul from which it came:
    Such art thou now; nor is it I alone,
    Thy sister, thy companion, thine own chosen one,
    But the whole world which seeks thy sympathy.
    Hearest thou not sounds i' the air which speak the love
    Of all articulate beings? Feelest thou not
    The inanimate winds enamoured of thee? List!
(*Music*)
ASIA: Thy words are sweeter than aught else but his
    Whose echoes they are; yet all love is sweet,
    Given or returned. Common as light is love,
    And its familiar voice wearies not ever.
    Like the wide heaven, the all-sustaining air,
    It makes the reptile equal to the God:
    They who inspire it most are fortunate,
    As I am now; but those who feel it most
    Are happier still, after long sufferings,
    As I shall soon become.
PANTHEA: List! Spirits speak.
VOICE IN THE AIR, SINGING: Life of Life! thy lips enkindle
    With their love the breath between them;
    And thy smiles before they dwindle
    Make the cold air fire; then screen them
    In those looks, where whoso gazes
    Faints, entangled in their mazes.

    Child of Light! thy limbs are burning
    Through the vest which seems to hide them;
    As the radiant lines of morning
    Through the clouds ere they divide them;
    And this atmosphere divinest
    Shrouds thee wheresoe'er thou shinest.

    Fair are others; none beholds thee,
    But thy voice sounds low and tender

    Like the fairest, for it folds thee
    From the sight, that liquid splendour,
    And all feel, yet see thee never,
    As I feel now, lost for ever!

    Lamp of Earth! where'er thou movest
    Its dim shapes are clad with brightness,
    And the souls of whom thou lovest
    Walk upon the winds with lightness,
    Till they fail, as I am failing,
    Dizzy, lost, yet unbewailing!

ASIA: My soul is an enchanted boat,
    Which, like a sleeping swan, doth float
    Upon the silver waves of thy sweet singing;
    And thine doth like an angel sit
    Beside a helm conducting it,
    Whilst all the winds with melody are ringing.
    It seems to float ever, for ever,
    Upon that many-winding river,
    Between mountains, woods, abysses,
    A paradise of wildernesses!
    Till, like one in slumber bound,
    Borne to the ocean, I float down, around,
    Into a sea profound, of ever-spreading sound:

    Meanwhile thy spirit lifts its pinions
    In music's most serene dominions;
    Catching the winds that fan that happy heaven.
    And we sail on, away, afar,
    Without a course, without a star,
    But, by the instinct of sweet music driven;
    Till through Elysian garden islets
    By thee most beautiful of pilots,
    Where never mortal pinnace glided,
    The boat of my desire is guided:
    Realms where the air we breathe is love,
    Which in the winds on the waves doth move,
    Harmonizing this earth with what we feel above.

We have passed Age's icy caves,
And Manhood's dark and tossing waves,
And Youth's smooth ocean, smiling to betray:
Beyond the glassy gulfs we flee
Of shadow-peopled Infancy,
Through Death and Birth, to a diviner day;
A paradise of vaulted bowers,
Lit by downward-gazing flowers,
And watery paths that wind between
Wildernesses calm and green,
Peopled by shapes too bright to see,
And rest, having beheld; somewhat like thee;
Which walk upon the sea, and chant melodiously!

END OF ACT 2

Act 3

Scene 3.1:
Heaven.
Jupiter on his Throne; Thetis and the other deities assembled.
Jupiter: Ye congregated powers of heaven, who share
  The glory and the strength of him ye serve,
  Rejoice! henceforth I am omnipotent.
  All else had been subdued to me; alone
  The soul of man, like unextinguished fire,
  Yet burns towards heaven with fierce reproach, and doubt,
  And lamentation, and reluctant prayer,
  Hurling up insurrection, which might make
  Our antique empire insecure, though built
  On eldest faith, and hell's coeval, fear;
  And though my curses through the pendulous air,
  Like snow on herbless peaks, fall flake by flake,
  And cling to it; though under my wrath's night
  It climbs the crags of life, step after step,
  Which wound it, as ice wounds unsandalled feet,
  It yet remains supreme o'er misery,
  Aspiring, unrepressed, yet soon to fall:
  Even now have I begotten a strange wonder,
  That fatal child, the terror of the earth,
  Who waits but till the destined hour arrive,
  Bearing from Demogorgon's vacant throne
  The dreadful might of ever-living limbs
  Which clothed that awful spirit unbeheld,
  To redescend, and trample out the spark.
  Pour forth heaven's wine, Idaean Ganymede,
  And let it fill the Daedal cups like fire,
  And from the flower-inwoven soil divine
  Ye all-triumphant harmonies arise,
  As dew from earth under the twilight stars:
  Drink! be the nectar circling through your veins
  The soul of joy, ye ever-living Gods,
  Till exultation burst in one wide voice
  Like music from Elysian winds.

And thou
Ascend beside me, veiled in the light
Of the desire which makes thee one with me,
Thetis, bright image of eternity!
When thou didst cry, 'Insufferable might!
God! Spare me! I sustain not the quick flames,
The penetrating presence; all my being,
Like him whom the Numidian seps did thaw
Into a dew with poison, is dissolved,
Sinking through its foundations:' even then
Two mighty spirits, mingling, made a third
Mightier than either, which, unbodied now,
Between us floats, felt, although unbeheld,
Waiting the incarnation, which ascends,
(Hear ye the thunder of the fiery wheels
Griding the winds?) from Demogorgon's throne.
Victory! victory! Feel'st thou not, O world,
The earthquake of his chariot thundering up
Olympus?

(The car of the hour arrives. DEMOGORGON *descends, and moves towards the throne of jupiter)*

Awful shape, what art thou? Speak!
DEMOGORGON: Eternity. Demand no direr name.
Descend, and follow me down the abyss.
I am thy child, as thou wert Saturn's child;
Mightier than thee: and we must dwell together
Henceforth in darkness. Lift thy lightnings not.
The tyranny of heaven none may retain,
Or reassume, or hold, succeeding thee:
Yet if thou wilt, as 'tis the destiny
Of trodden worms to writhe till they are dead,
Put forth thy might.
JUPITER: Detested prodigy!
Even thus beneath the deep Titanian prisons
I trample thee! thou lingerest?
Mercy! mercy!
No pity, no release, no respite! Oh,
That thou wouldst make mine enemy my judge,

Even where he hangs, seared by my long revenge,
On Caucasus! he would not doom me thus.
Gentle, and just, and dreadless, is he not
The monarch of the world? What then art thou?
No refuge! no appeal!
Sink with me then,
We two will sink on the wide waves of ruin,
Even as a vulture and a snake outspent
Drop, twisted in inextricable fight,
Into a shoreless sea. Let hell unlock
Its mounded oceans of tempestuous fire,
And whelm on them into the bottomless void
This desolated world, and thee, and me,
The conqueror and the conquered, and the wreck
Of that for which they combated.
Ai, Ai!
The elements obey me not. I sink
Dizzily down, ever, for ever, down.
And, like a cloud, mine enemy above
Darkens my fall with victory! Ai, Ai!

SCENE 3.2:
The mouth of a great river in the Island Atlantis. OCEAN *is discovered reclining near the shore;* APOLLO *stands beside him.*
OCEAN: He fell, thou sayest, beneath his conqueror's frown?
APOLLO: Ay, when the strife was ended which made dim
    The orb I rule, and shook the solid stars,
    The terrors of his eye illumined heaven
    With sanguine light, through the thick ragged skirts
    Of the victorious darkness, as he fell:
    Like the last glare of day's red agony,
    Which, from a rent among the fiery clouds,
    Burns far along the tempest-wrinkled deep.
OCEAN: He sunk to the abyss? To the dark void?
APOLLO: An eagle so caught in some bursting cloud
    On Caucasus, his thunder-baffled wings
    Entangled in the whirlwind, and his eyes
    Which gazed on the undazzling sun, now blinded

  By the white lightning, while the ponderous hail
  Beats on his struggling form, which sinks at length
  Prone, and the aereal ice clings over it.
Ocean: Henceforth the fields of heaven-reflecting sea
  Which are my realm, will heave, unstained with blood,
  Beneath the uplifting winds, like plains of corn
  Swayed by the summer air; my streams will flow
  Round many-peopled continents, and round
  Fortunate isles; and from their glassy thrones
  Blue Proteus and his humid nymphs shall mark
  The shadow of fair ships, as mortals see
  The floating bark of the light-laden moon
  With that white star, its sightless pilot's crest,
  Borne down the rapid sunset's ebbing sea;
  Tracking their path no more by blood and groans,
  And desolation, and the mingled voice
  Of slavery and command; but by the light
  Of wave-reflected flowers, and floating odours,
  And music soft, and mild, free, gentle voices,
  And sweetest music, such as spirits love.
Apollo: And I shall gaze not on the deeds which make
  My mind obscure with sorrow, as eclipse
  Darkens the sphere I guide; but list, I hear
  The small, clear, silver lute of the young Spirit
  That sits i' the morning star.
Ocean: Thou must away;
  Thy steeds will pause at even, till when farewell:
  The loud deep calls me home even now to feed it
  With azure calm out of the emerald urns
  Which stand for ever full beside my throne.
  Behold the Nereids under the green sea,
  Their wavering limbs borne on the wind-like stream,
  Their white arms lifted o'er their streaming hair
  With garlands pied and starry sea-flower crowns,
  Hastening to grace their mighty sister's joy.
(*A sound of waves is heard*)
  It is the unpastured sea hungering for calm.
  Peace, monster; I come now. Farewell.
Apollo: Farewell.

Scene 3.3:

Caucasus. Prometheus, Hercules, Ione, The Earth, Spirits, Asia, *and* Panthea, *borne in the car with the* Spirit *of the hour.* Hercules *unbinds* Prometheus, *who descends.*

Hercules: Most glorious among Spirits, thus doth strength
    To wisdom, courage, and long-suffering love,
    And thee, who art the form they animate,
    Minister like a slave.

Prometheus: Thy gentle words
    Are sweeter even than freedom long desired
    And long delayed.
    Asia, thou light of life,
    Shadow of beauty unbeheld: and ye,
    Fair sister nymphs, who made long years of pain
    Sweet to remember, through your love and care:
    Henceforth we will not part. There is a cave,
    All overgrown with trailing odorous plants,
    Which curtain out the day with leaves and flowers,
    And paved with veined emerald, and a fountain
    Leaps in the midst with an awakening sound.
    From its curved roof the mountain's frozen tears
    Like snow, or silver, or long diamond spires,
    Hang downward, raining forth a doubtful light:
    And there is heard the ever-moving air,
    Whispering without from tree to tree, and birds,
    And bees; and all around are mossy seats,
    And the rough walls are clothed with long soft grass;
    A simple dwelling, which shall be our own;
    Where we will sit and talk of time and change,
    As the world ebbs and flows, ourselves unchanged.
    What can hide man from mutability?
    And if ye sigh, then I will smile; and thou,
    Ione, shalt chant fragments of sea-music,
    Until I weep, when ye shall smile away
    The tears she brought, which yet were sweet to shed.
    We will entangle buds and flowers and beams
    Which twinkle on the fountain's brim, and make
    Strange combinations out of common things,
    Like human babes in their brief innocence;

    And we will search, with looks and words of love,
    For hidden thoughts, each lovelier than the last,
    Our unexhausted spirits; and like lutes
    Touched by the skill of the enamoured wind,
    Weave harmonies divine, yet ever new,
    From difference sweet where discord cannot be;
    And hither come, sped on the charmed winds,
    Which meet from all the points of heaven, as bees
    From every flower aereal Enna feeds,
    At their known island-homes in Himera,
    The echoes of the human world, which tell
    Of the low voice of love, almost unheard,
    And dove-eyed pity's murmured pain, and music,
    Itself the echo of the heart, and all
    That tempers or improves man's life, now free;
    And lovely apparitions,—dim at first,
    Then radiant, as the mind, arising bright
    From the embrace of beauty (whence the forms
    Of which these are the phantoms) casts on them
    The gathered rays which are reality—
    Shall visit us, the progeny immortal
    Of Painting, Sculpture, and rapt Poesy,
    And arts, though unimagined, yet to be.
    The wandering voices and the shadows these
    Of all that man becomes, the mediators
    Of that best worship love, by him and us
    Given and returned; swift shapes and sounds, which grow
    More fair and soft as man grows wise and kind,
    And, veil by veil, evil and error fall:
    Such virtue has the cave and place around.
(*Turning to the* SPIRIT *of the hour*)
    For thee, fair Spirit, one toil remains. Ione,
    Give her that curved shell, which Proteus old
    Made Asia's nuptial boon, breathing within it
    A voice to be accomplished, and which thou
    Didst hide in grass under the hollow rock.
IONE: Thou most desired Hour, more loved and lovely
    Than all thy sisters, this is the mystic shell;

    See the pale azure fading into silver
    Lining it with a soft yet glowing light:
    Looks it not like lulled music sleeping there?
SPIRIT: It seems in truth the fairest shell of Ocean:
    Its sound must be at once both sweet and strange.
PROMETHEUS: Go, borne over the cities of mankind
    On whirlwind-footed coursers: once again
    Outspeed the sun around the orbed world;
    And as thy chariot cleaves the kindling air,
    Thou breathe into the many-folded shell,
    Loosening its mighty music; it shall be
    As thunder mingled with clear echoes: then
    Return; and thou shalt dwell beside our cave.
    And thou, O Mother Earth!—
THE EARTH: I hear, I feel;
    Thy lips are on me, and thy touch runs down
    Even to the adamantine central gloom
    Along these marble nerves; 'tis life, 'tis joy,
    And, through my withered, old, and icy frame
    The warmth of an immortal youth shoots down
    Circling. Henceforth the many children fair
    Folded in my sustaining arms; all plants,
    And creeping forms, and insects rainbow-winged,
    And birds, and beasts, and fish, and human shapes,
    Which drew disease and pain from my wan bosom,
    Draining the poison of despair, shall take
    And interchange sweet nutriment; to me
    Shall they become like sister-antelopes
    By one fair dam, snow-white and swift as wind,
    Nursed among lilies near a brimming stream.
    The dew-mists of my sunless sleep shall float
    Under the stars like balm: night-folded flowers
    Shall suck unwithering hues in their repose:
    And men and beasts in happy dreams shall gather
    Strength for the coming day, and all its joy:
    And death shall be the last embrace of her
    Who takes the life she gave, even as a mother,
    Folding her child, says, 'Leave me not again.'

Asia: Oh, mother! wherefore speak the name of death?
　　Cease they to love, and move, and breathe, and speak,
　　Who die?
The Earth: It would avail not to reply:
　　Thou art immortal, and this tongue is known
　　But to the uncommunicating dead.
　　Death is the veil which those who live call life:
　　They sleep, and it is lifted: and meanwhile
　　In mild variety the seasons mild
　　With rainbow-skirted showers, and odorous winds,
　　And long blue meteors cleansing the dull night,
　　And the life-kindling shafts of the keen sun's
　　All-piercing bow, and the dew-mingled rain
　　Of the calm moonbeams, a soft influence mild,
　　Shall clothe the forests and the fields, ay, even
　　The crag-built deserts of the barren deep,
　　With ever-living leaves, and fruits, and flowers.
　　And thou! There is a cavern where my spirit
　　Was panted forth in anguish whilst thy pain
　　Made my heart mad, and those who did inhale it
　　Became mad too, and built a temple there,
　　And spoke, and were oracular, and lured
　　The erring nations round to mutual war,
　　And faithless faith, such as Jove kept with thee;
　　Which breath now rises, as amongst tall weeds
　　A violet's exhalation, and it fills
　　With a serener light and crimson air
　　Intense, yet soft, the rocks and woods around;
　　It feeds the quick growth of the serpent vine,
　　And the dark linked ivy tangling wild,
　　And budding, blown, or odour-faded blooms
　　Which star the winds with points of coloured light,
　　As they rain through them, and bright golden globes
　　Of fruit, suspended in their own green heaven,
　　And through their veined leaves and amber stems
　　The flowers whose purple and translucid bowls
　　Stand ever mantling with aereal dew,
　　The drink of spirits: and it circles round,
　　Like the soft waving wings of noonday dreams,

Inspiring calm and happy thoughts, like mine,
Now thou art thus restored. This cave is thine.
Arise! Appear!
(*A* Spirit *rises in the likeness of a winged child*)
This is my torch-bearer;
Who let his lamp out in old time with gazing
On eyes from which he kindled it anew
With love, which is as fire, sweet daughter mine,
For such is that within thine own. Run, wayward,
And guide this company beyond the peak
Of Bacchic Nysa, Maenad-haunted mountain,
And beyond Indus and its tribute rivers,
Trampling the torrent streams and glassy lakes
With feet unwet, unwearied, undelaying,
And up the green ravine, across the vale,
Beside the windless and crystalline pool,
Where ever lies, on unerasing waves,
The image of a temple, built above,
Distinct with column, arch, and architrave,
And palm-like capital, and over-wrought,
And populous with most living imagery,
Praxitelean shapes, whose marble smiles
Fill the hushed air with everlasting love.
It is deserted now, but once it bore
Thy name, Prometheus; there the emulous youths
Bore to thy honour through the divine gloom
The lamp which was thine emblem; even as those
Who bear the untransmitted torch of hope
Into the grave, across the night of life,
As thou hast borne it most triumphantly
To this far goal of Time. Depart, farewell.
Beside that temple is the destined cave.

Scene 3.4:
A forest. In the background a cave.
Prometheus, Asia, Panthea, Ione, *and the* Spirit of the Earth.
Ione: Sister, it is not earthly: how it glides
   Under the leaves! how on its head there burns
   A light, like a green star, whose emerald beams

    Are twined with its fair hair! how, as it moves,
    The splendour drops in flakes upon the grass!
    Knowest thou it?
PANTHEA: It is the delicate spirit
    That guides the earth through heaven. From afar
    The populous constellations call that light
    The loveliest of the planets; and sometimes
    It floats along the spray of the salt sea,
    Or makes its chariot of a foggy cloud,
    Or walks through fields or cities while men sleep,
    Or o'er the mountain tops, or down the rivers,
    Or through the green waste wilderness, as now,
    Wondering at all it sees. Before Jove reigned
    It loved our sister Asia, and it came
    Each leisure hour to drink the liquid light
    Out of her eyes, for which it said it thirsted
    As one bit by a dipsas, and with her
    It made its childish confidence, and told her
    All it had known or seen, for it saw much,
    Yet idly reasoned what it saw; and called her—
    For whence it sprung it knew not, nor do I—
    Mother, dear mother.
THE SPIRIT OF THE EARTH (*running to* ASIA): Mother,
    dearest mother;
    May I then talk with thee as I was wont?
    May I then hide my eyes in thy soft arms,
    After thy looks have made them tired of joy?
    May I then play beside thee the long noons,
    When work is none in the bright silent air?
ASIA: I love thee, gentlest being, and henceforth
    Can cherish thee unenvied: speak, I pray:
    Thy simple talk once solaced, now delights.
SPIRIT OF THE EARTH: Mother, I am grown wiser, though a child
    Cannot be wise like thee, within this day;
    And happier too; happier and wiser both.
    Thou knowest that toads, and snakes, and loathly worms,
    And venomous and malicious beasts, and boughs
    That bore ill berries in the woods, were ever
    An hindrance to my walks o'er the green world:

And that, among the haunts of humankind,
Hard-featured men, or with proud, angry looks,
Or cold, staid gait, or false and hollow smiles,
Or the dull sneer of self-loved ignorance,
Or other such foul masks, with which ill thoughts
Hide that fair being whom we spirits call man;
And women too, ugliest of all things evil,
(Though fair, even in a world where thou art fair,
When good and kind, free and sincere like thee)
When false or frowning made me sick at heart
To pass them, though they slept, and I unseen.
Well, my path lately lay through a great city
Into the woody hills surrounding it:
A sentinel was sleeping at the gate:
When there was heard a sound, so loud, it shook
The towers amid the moonlight, yet more sweet
Than any voice but thine, sweetest of all;
A long, long sound, as it would never end:
And all the inhabitants leaped suddenly
Out of their rest, and gathered in the streets,
Looking in wonder up to Heaven, while yet
The music pealed along. I hid myself
Within a fountain in the public square,
Where I lay like the reflex of the moon
Seen in a wave under green leaves; and soon
Those ugly human shapes and visages
Of which I spoke as having wrought me pain,
Passed floating through the air, and fading still
Into the winds that scattered them; and those
From whom they passed seemed mild and lovely forms
After some foul disguise had fallen, and all
Were somewhat changed, and after brief surprise
And greetings of delighted wonder, all
Went to their sleep again: and when the dawn
Came, wouldst thou think that toads, and snakes, and efts,
Could e'er be beautiful? yet so they were,
And that with little change of shape or hue:
All things had put their evil nature off:
I cannot tell my joy, when o'er a lake,

> Upon a drooping bough with nightshade twined,
> I saw two azure halcyons clinging downward
> And thinning one bright bunch of amber berries,
> With quick long beaks, and in the deep there lay
> Those lovely forms imaged as in a sky;
> So, with my thoughts full of these happy changes,
> We meet again, the happiest change of all.
>
> Asia: And never will we part, till thy chaste sister
> Who guides the frozen and inconstant moon
> Will look on thy more warm and equal light
> Till her heart thaw like flakes of April snow
> And love thee.
>
> Spirit of the Earth: What! as Asia loves Prometheus?
>
> Asia: Peace, wanton, thou art yet not old enough.
> Think ye by gazing on each other's eyes
> To multiply your lovely selves, and fill
> With sphered fires the interlunar air?
>
> Spirit of the Earth: Nay, mother, while my sister trims her lamp
> 'Tis hard I should go darkling.
>
> Asia: Listen; look!
>
> (*The* Spirit of the Hour *enters*)
>
> Prometheus: We feel what thou hast heard and seen: yet speak.
>
> Spirit of the Hour: Soon as the sound had ceased whose thunder filled
> The abysses of the sky and the wide earth,
> There was a change: the impalpable thin air
> And the all-circling sunlight were transformed,
> As if the sense of love dissolved in them
> Had folded itself round the sphered world.
> My vision then grew clear, and I could see
> Into the mysteries of the universe:
> Dizzy as with delight I floated down,
> Winnowing the lightsome air with languid plumes,
> My coursers sought their birthplace in the sun,
> Where they henceforth will live exempt from toil,
> Pasturing flowers of vegetable fire;
> And where my moonlike car will stand within
> A temple, gazed upon by Phidian forms
> Of thee, and Asia, and the Earth, and me,

And you fair nymphs looking the love we feel,—
In memory of the tidings it has borne,—
Beneath a dome fretted with graven flowers,
Poised on twelve columns of resplendent stone,
And open to the bright and liquid sky.
Yoked to it by an amphisbaenic snake
The likeness of those winged steeds will mock
The flight from which they find repose. Alas,
Whither has wandered now my partial tongue
When all remains untold which ye would hear?
As I have said, I floated to the earth:
It was, as it is still, the pain of bliss
To move, to breathe, to be. I wandering went
Among the haunts and dwellings of mankind,
And first was disappointed not to see
Such mighty change as I had felt within
Expressed in outward things; but soon I looked,
And behold, thrones were kingless, and men walked
One with the other even as spirits do,
None fawned, none trampled; hate, disdain, or fear,
Self-love or self-contempt, on human brows
No more inscribed, as o'er the gate of hell,
'All hope abandon ye who enter here;'
None frowned, none trembled, none with eager fear
Gazed on another's eye of cold command,
Until the subject of a tyrant's will
Became, worse fate, the abject of his own,
Which spurred him, like an outspent horse, to death.
None wrought his lips in truth-entangling lines
Which smiled the lie his tongue disdained to speak;
None, with firm sneer, trod out in his own heart
The sparks of love and hope till there remained
Those bitter ashes, a soul self-consumed,
And the wretch crept a vampire among men,
Infecting all with his own hideous ill;
None talked that common, false, cold, hollow talk
Which makes the heart deny the "yes" it breathes,
Yet question that unmeant hypocrisy
With such a self-mistrust as has no name.

And women, too, frank, beautiful, and kind
As the free heaven which rains fresh light and dew
On the wide earth, past; gentle radiant forms,
From custom's evil taint exempt and pure;
Speaking the wisdom once they could not think,
Looking emotions once they feared to feel,
And changed to all which once they dared not be,
Yet being now, made earth like heaven; nor pride,
Nor jealousy, nor envy, nor ill shame,
The bitterest of those drops of treasured gall,
Spoiled the sweet taste of the nepenthe, love.

Thrones, altars, judgement-seats, and prisons; wherein,
And beside which, by wretched men were borne
Sceptres, tiaras, swords, and chains, and tomes
Of reasoned wrong, glozed on by ignorance,
Were like those monstrous and barbaric shapes,
The ghosts of a no-more-remembered fame,
Which, from their unworn obelisks, look forth
In triumph o'er the palaces and tombs
Of those who were their conquerors: mouldering round,
These imaged to the pride of kings and priests
A dark yet mighty faith, a power as wide
As is the world it wasted, and are now
But an astonishment; even so the tools
And emblems of its last captivity,
Amid the dwellings of the peopled earth,
Stand, not o'erthrown, but unregarded now.
And those foul shapes, abhorred by god and man,—
Which, under many a name and many a form
Strange, savage, ghastly, dark and execrable,
Were Jupiter, the tyrant of the world;
And which the nations, panic-stricken, served
With blood, and hearts broken by long hope, and love
Dragged to his altars soiled and garlandless,
And slain among men's unreclaiming tears,
Flattering the thing they feared, which fear was hate,—
Frown, mouldering fast, o'er their abandoned shrines:
The painted veil, by those who were, called life,

Which mimicked, as with colours idly spread,
All men believed and hoped, is torn aside;
The loathsome mask has fallen, the man remains
Sceptreless, free, uncircumscribed, but man
Equal, unclassed, tribeless, and nationless,
Exempt from awe, worship, degree, the king
Over himself; just, gentle, wise; but man
Passionless?—no, yet free from guilt or pain,
Which were, for his will made or suffered them,
Nor yet exempt, though ruling them like slaves,
From chance, and death, and mutability,
The clogs of that which else might oversoar
The loftiest star of unascended heaven,
Pinnacled dim in the intense inane.

END OF ACT 3

Act 4

Scene 4.1:
A part of the forest near the cave of Prometheus. Panthea *and* Ione *are Sleeping: They awaken gradually during the first song.*
Voice of Unseen Spirits: The pale stars are gone!
    For the sun, their swift shepherd,
    To their folds them compelling,
    In the depths of the dawn,
    Hastes, in meteor-eclipsing array, and the flee
    Beyond his blue dwelling,
    As fawns flee the leopard.
    But where are ye?
(*A train of dark forms and shadows passes by confusedly, singing*)

    Here, oh, here:
    We bear the bier
    Of the father of many a cancelled year!
    Spectres we
    Of the dead Hours be,
    We bear Time to his tomb in eternity.

    Strew, oh, strew
    Hair, not yew!
    Wet the dusty pall with tears, not dew!
    Be the faded flowers
    Of Death's bare bowers
    Spread on the corpse of the King of Hours!

    Haste, oh, haste!
    As shades are chased,
    Trembling, by day, from heaven's blue waste.
    We melt away,
    Like dissolving spray,
    From the children of a diviner day,
    With the lullaby
    Of winds that die

    On the bosom of their own harmony!
IONE: What dark forms were they?
PANTHEA: The past Hours weak and gray,
    With the spoil which their toil
    Raked together
    From the conquest but One could foil.
IONE: Have they passed?
PANTHEA: They have passed;
    They outspeeded the blast,
    While 'tis said, they are fled:
IONE: Whither, oh, whither?
PANTHEA: To the dark, to the past, to the dead.
VOICE OF UNSEEN SPIRITS: Bright clouds float in heaven,
    Dew-stars gleam on earth,
    Waves assemble on ocean,
    They are gathered and driven
    By the storm of delight, by the panic of glee!
    They shake with emotion,
    They dance in their mirth.
    But where are ye?

    The pine boughs are singing
    Old songs with new gladness,
    The billows and fountains
    Fresh music are flinging,
    Like the notes of a spirit from land and from sea;
    The storms mock the mountains
    With the thunder of gladness.
    But where are ye?
IONE: What charioteers are these?
PANTHEA: Where are their chariots?
SEMICHORUS OF HOURS: The voice of the Spirits of Air and
    of Earth
    Has drawn back the figured curtain of sleep
    Which covered our being and darkened our birth
    In the deep.
A VOICE: In the deep?
SEMICHORUS 2: Oh, below the deep.

Semichorus 1: An hundred ages we had been kept
   Cradled in visions of hate and care,
   And each one who waked as his brother slept,
   Found the truth—
Semichorus 2: Worse than his visions were!
Semichorus 1: We have heard the lute of Hope in sleep;
   We have known the voice of Love in dreams;
   We have felt the wand of Power, and leap—
Semichorus 2: As the billows leap in the morning beams!
Chorus: Weave the dance on the floor of the breeze,
   Pierce with song heaven's silent light,
   Enchant the day that too swiftly flees,
   To check its flight ere the cave of Night.

   Once the hungry Hours were hounds
   Which chased the day like a bleeding deer,
   And it limped and stumbled with many wounds
   Through the nightly dells of the desert year.

   But now, oh weave the mystic measure
   Of music, and dance, and shapes of light,
   Let the Hours, and the spirits of might and pleasure,
   Like the clouds and sunbeams, unite—
A Voice: Unite!
Panthea: See, where the Spirits of the human mind
   Wrapped in sweet sounds, as in bright veils, approach.
Chorus of Spirits: We join the throng
   Of the dance and the song,
   By the whirlwind of gladness borne along;
   As the flying-fish leap
   From the Indian deep,
   And mix with the sea-birds, half-asleep.
Chorus of Hours: Whence come ye, so wild and so fleet,
   For sandals of lightning are on your feet,
   And your wings are soft and swift as thought,
   And your eyes are as love which is veiled not?
Chorus of Spirits: We come from the mind
   Of human kind
   Which was late so dusk, and obscene, and blind,

Now 'tis an ocean
Of clear emotion,
A heaven of serene and mighty motion.

From that deep abyss
Of wonder and bliss,
Whose caverns are crystal palaces;
From those skiey towers
Where Thought's crowned powers
Sit watching your dance, ye happy Hours!

From the dim recesses
Of woven caresses,
Where lovers catch ye by your loose tresses;
From the azure isles,
Where sweet Wisdom smiles,
Delaying your ships with her siren wiles.

From the temples high
Of Man's ear and eye,
Roofed over Sculpture and Poesy;
From the murmurings
Of the unsealed springs
Where Science bedews her Daedal wings.

Years after years,
Through blood, and tears,
And a thick hell of hatreds, and hopes, and fears;
We waded and flew,
And the islets were few
Where the bud-blighted flowers of happiness grew.

Our feet now, every palm,
Are sandalled with calm,
And the dew of our wings is a rain of balm;
And, beyond our eyes,
The human love lies
Which makes all it gazes on Paradise.

CHORUS OF SPIRITS AND HOURS: Then weave the web of the
  mystic measure;
  From the depths of the sky and the ends of the earth,
  Come, swift Spirits of might and of pleasure,
  Fill the dance and the music of mirth,
  As the waves of a thousand streams rush by
  To an ocean of splendour and harmony!
CHORUS OF SPIRITS: Our spoil is won,
  Our task is done,
  We are free to dive, or soar, or run;
  Beyond and around,
  Or within the bound
  Which clips the world with darkness round.

  We'll pass the eyes
  Of the starry skies
  Into the hoar deep to colonize;
  Death, Chaos, and Night,
  From the sound of our flight,
  Shall flee, like mist from a tempest's might.

  And Earth, Air, and Light,
  And the Spirit of Might,
  Which drives round the stars in their fiery flight;
  And Love, Thought, and Breath,
  The powers that quell Death,
  Wherever we soar shall assemble beneath.

  And our singing shall build
  In the void's loose field
  A world for the Spirit of Wisdom to wield;
  We will take our plan
  From the new world of man,
  And our work shall be called the Promethean.
CHORUS OF HOURS: Break the dance, and scatter the song;
  Let some depart, and some remain;
SEMICHORUS 1: We, beyond heaven, are driven along:
SEMICHORUS 2: Us the enchantments of earth retain:

SEMICHORUS 1: Ceaseless, and rapid, and fierce, and free,
    With the Spirits which build a new earth and sea,
    And a heaven where yet heaven could never be;
SEMICHORUS 2: Solemn, and slow, and serene, and bright,
    Leading the Day and outspeeding the Night,
    With the powers of a world of perfect light;
SEMICHORUS 1: We whirl, singing loud, round the gathering sphere,
    Till the trees, and the beasts, and the clouds appear
    From its chaos made calm by love, not fear.
SEMICHORUS 2: We encircle the ocean and mountains of earth,
    And the happy forms of its death and birth
    Change to the music of our sweet mirth.
CHORUS OF HOURS AND SPIRITS: Break the dance, and scatter
    the song;
    Let some depart, and some remain,
    Wherever we fly we lead along
    In leashes, like starbeams, soft yet strong,
    The clouds that are heavy with love's sweet rain.
PANTHEA: Ha! they are gone!
IONE: Yet feel you no delight
    From the past sweetness?
PANTHEA: As the bare green hill
    When some soft cloud vanishes into rain,
    Laughs with a thousand drops of sunny water
    To the unpavilioned sky!
IONE: Even whilst we speak
    New notes arise. What is that awful sound?
PANTHEA: 'Tis the deep music of the rolling world
    Kindling within the strings of the waved air
    Aeolian modulations.
IONE: Listen too,
    How every pause is filled with under-notes,
    Clear, silver, icy, keen awakening tones,
    Which pierce the sense, and live within the soul,
    As the sharp stars pierce winter's crystal air
    And gaze upon themselves within the sea.
PANTHEA: But see where through two openings in the forest
    Which hanging branches overcanopy,
    And where two runnels of a rivulet,

Between the close moss violet-inwoven,
Have made their path of melody, like sisters
Who part with sighs that they may meet in smiles,
Turning their dear disunion to an isle
Of lovely grief, a wood of sweet sad thoughts;
Two visions of strange radiance float upon
The ocean-like enchantment of strong sound,
Which flows intenser, keener, deeper yet
Under the ground and through the windless air.

IONE: I see a chariot like that thinnest boat,
In which the Mother of the Months is borne
By ebbing light into her western cave,
When she upsprings from interlunar dreams;
O'er which is curved an orblike canopy
Of gentle darkness, and the hills and woods,
Distinctly seen through that dusk aery veil,
Regard like shapes in an enchanter's glass;
Its wheels are solid clouds, azure and gold,
Such as the genii of the thunderstorm
Pile on the floor of the illumined sea
When the sun rushes under it; they roll
And move and grow as with an inward wind;
Within it sits a winged infant, white
Its countenance, like the whiteness of bright snow,
Its plumes are as feathers of sunny frost,
Its limbs gleam white, through the wind-flowing folds
Of its white robe, woof of ethereal pearl.
Its hair is white, the brightness of white light
Scattered in strings; yet its two eyes are heavens
Of liquid darkness, which the Deity
Within seems pouring, as a storm is poured
From jagged clouds, out of their arrowy lashes,
Tempering the cold and radiant air around,
With fire that is not brightness; in its hand
It sways a quivering moonbeam, from whose point
A guiding power directs the chariot's prow
Over its wheeled clouds, which as they roll
Over the grass, and flowers, and waves, wake sounds,
Sweet as a singing rain of silver dew.

PANTHEA: And from the other opening in the wood
    Rushes, with loud and whirlwind harmony,
    A sphere, which is as many thousand spheres,
    Solid as crystal, yet through all its mass
    Flow, as through empty space, music and light:
    Ten thousand orbs involving and involved,
    Purple and azure, white, and green, and golden,
    Sphere within sphere; and every space between
    Peopled with unimaginable shapes,
    Such as ghosts dream dwell in the lampless deep,
    Yet each inter-transpicuous, and they whirl
    Over each other with a thousand motions,
    Upon a thousand sightless axles spinning,
    And with the force of self-destroying swiftness,
    Intensely, slowly, solemnly, roll on,
    Kindling with mingled sounds, and many tones,
    Intelligible words and music wild.
    With mighty whirl the multitudinous orb
    Grinds the bright brook into an azure mist
    Of elemental subtlety, like light;
    And the wild odour of the forest flowers,
    The music of the living grass and air,
    The emerald light of leaf-entangled beams
    Round its intense yet self-conflicting speed,
    Seem kneaded into one aereal mass
    Which drowns the sense. Within the orb itself,
    Pillowed upon its alabaster arms,
    Like to a child o'erwearied with sweet toil,
    On its own folded wings, and wavy hair,
    The Spirit of the Earth is laid asleep,
    And you can see its little lips are moving,
    Amid the changing light of their own smiles,
    Like one who talks of what he loves in dream.
IONE: 'Tis only mocking the orb's harmony.
PANTHEA: And from a star upon its forehead, shoot,
    Like swords of azure fire, or golden spears
    With tyrant-quelling myrtle overtwined,
    Embleming heaven and earth united now,
    Vast beams like spokes of some invisible wheel

Which whirl as the orb whirls, swifter than thought,
Filling the abyss with sun-like lightenings,
And perpendicular now, and now transverse,
Pierce the dark soil, and as they pierce and pass,
Make bare the secrets of the earth's deep heart;
Infinite mine of adamant and gold,
Valueless stones, and unimagined gems,
And caverns on crystalline columns poised
With vegetable silver overspread;
Wells of unfathomed fire, and water springs
Whence the great sea, even as a child is fed,
Whose vapours clothe earth's monarch mountain-tops
With kingly, ermine snow. The beams flash on
And make appear the melancholy ruins
Of cancelled cycles; anchors, beaks of ships;
Planks turned to marble; quivers, helms, and spears,
And gorgon-headed targes, and the wheels
Of scythed chariots, and the emblazonry
Of trophies, standards, and armorial beasts,
Round which death laughed, sepulchred emblems
Of dead destruction, ruin within ruin!
The wrecks beside of many a city vast,
Whose population which the earth grew over
Was mortal, but not human; see, they lie,
Their monstrous works, and uncouth skeletons,
Their statues, homes and fanes; prodigious shapes
Huddled in gray annihilation, split,
Jammed in the hard, black deep; and over these,
The anatomies of unknown winged things,
And fishes which were isles of living scale,
And serpents, bony chains, twisted around
The iron crags, or within heaps of dust
To which the tortuous strength of their last pangs
Had crushed the iron crags; and over these
The jagged alligator, and the might
Of earth-convulsing behemoth, which once
Were monarch beasts, and on the slimy shores,
And weed-overgrown continents of earth,
Increased and multiplied like summer worms

On an abandoned corpse, till the blue globe
Wrapped deluge round it like a cloak, and they
Yelled, gasped, and were abolished; or some God
Whose throne was in a comet, passed, and cried,
'Be not!' And like my words they were no more.

THE EARTH: The joy, the triumph, the delight, the madness!
The boundless, overflowing, bursting gladness,
The vaporous exultation not to be confined!
Ha! ha! the animation of delight
Which wraps me, like an atmosphere of light,
And bears me as a cloud is borne by its own wind.

THE MOON: Brother mine, calm wanderer,
Happy globe of land and air,
Some Spirit is darted like a beam from thee,
Which penetrates my frozen frame,
And passes with the warmth of flame,
With love, and odour, and deep melody
Through me, through me!

THE EARTH: Ha! ha! the caverns of my hollow mountains,
My cloven fire-crags, sound-exulting fountains
Laugh with a vast and inextinguishable laughter.
The oceans, and the deserts, and the abysses,
And the deep air's unmeasured wildernesses,
Answer from all their clouds and billows, echoing after.

They cry aloud as I do. Sceptred curse,
Who all our green and azure universe
Threatenedst to muffle round with black destruction, sending
A solid cloud to rain hot thunderstones,
And splinter and knead down my children's bones,
All I bring forth, to one void mass battering and blending,—

Until each crag-like tower, and storied column,
Palace, and obelisk, and temple solemn,
My imperial mountains crowned with cloud, and snow, and fire,
My sea-like forests, every blade and blossom
Which finds a grave or cradle in my bosom,
Were stamped by thy strong hate into a lifeless mire:

How art thou sunk, withdrawn, covered, drunk up
By thirsty nothing, as the brackish cup
Drained by a desert-troop, a little drop for all;
And from beneath, around, within, above,
Filling thy void annihilation, love
Bursts in like light on caves cloven by the thunder-ball.

THE MOON: The snow upon my lifeless mountains
Is loosened into living fountains,
My solid oceans flow, and sing and shine:
A spirit from my heart bursts forth,
It clothes with unexpected birth
My cold bare bosom: Oh! it must be thine
On mine, on mine!

Gazing on thee I feel, I know
Green stalks burst forth, and bright flowers grow,
And living shapes upon my bosom move:
Music is in the sea and air,
Winged clouds soar here and there,
Dark with the rain new buds are dreaming of:
'Tis love, all love!

THE EARTH: It interpenetrates my granite mass,
Through tangled roots and trodden clay doth pass
Into the utmost leaves and delicatest flowers;
Upon the winds, among the clouds 'tis spread,
It wakes a life in the forgotten dead,
They breathe a spirit up from their obscurest bowers.

And like a storm bursting its cloudy prison
With thunder, and with whirlwind, has arisen
Out of the lampless caves of unimagined being:
With earthquake shock and swiftness making shiver
Thought's stagnant chaos, unremoved for ever,
Till hate, and fear, and pain, light-vanquished shadows, fleeing,

Leave Man, who was a many-sided mirror,
Which could distort to many a shape of error,
This true fair world of things, a sea reflecting love;
Which over all his kind, as the sun's heaven

Gliding o'er ocean, smooth, serene, and even,
Darting from starry depths radiance and life, doth move:

Leave Man, even as a leprous child is left,
Who follows a sick beast to some warm cleft
Of rocks, through which the might of healing springs is poured;
Then when it wanders home with rosy smile,
Unconscious, and its mother fears awhile
It is a spirit, then, weeps on her child restored.

Man, oh, not men! a chain of linked thought,
Of love and might to be divided not,
Compelling the elements with adamantine stress;
As the sun rules, even with a tyrant's gaze,
The unquiet republic of the maze
Of planets, struggling fierce towards heaven's free wilderness.

Man, one harmonious soul of many a soul,
Whose nature is its own divine control,
Where all things flow to all, as rivers to the sea;
Familiar acts are beautiful through love;
Labour, and pain, and grief, in life's green grove
Sport like tame beasts, none knew how gentle they could be!

His will, with all mean passions, bad delights,
And selfish cares, its trembling satellites,
A spirit ill to guide, but mighty to obey,
Is as a tempest-winged ship, whose helm
Love rules, through waves which dare not overwhelm,
Forcing life's wildest shores to own its sovereign sway.

All things confess his strength. Through the cold mass
Of marble and of colour his dreams pass;
Bright threads whence mothers weave the robes their
    children wear;
Language is a perpetual Orphic song,
Which rules with Daedal harmony a throng
Of thoughts and forms, which else senseless and shapeless were.

The lightning is his slave; heaven's utmost deep
Gives up her stars, and like a flock of sheep
They pass before his eye, are numbered, and roll on!
The tempest is his steed, he strides the air;
And the abyss shouts from her depth laid bare,
Heaven, hast thou secrets? Man unveils me; I have none.

THE MOON: The shadow of white death has passed
  From my path in heaven at last,
  A clinging shroud of solid frost and sleep;
  And through my newly-woven bowers,
  Wander happy paramours,
  Less mighty, but as mild as those who keep
  Thy vales more deep.

THE EARTH: As the dissolving warmth of dawn may fold
  A half unfrozen dew-globe, green, and gold,
  And crystalline, till it becomes a winged mist,
  And wanders up the vault of the blue day,
  Outlives the noon, and on the sun's last ray
  Hangs o'er the sea, a fleece of fire and amethyst.

THE MOON: Thou art folded, thou art lying
  In the light which is undying
  Of thine own joy, and heaven's smile divine;
  All suns and constellations shower
  On thee a light, a life, a power
  Which doth array thy sphere; thou pourest thine
  On mine, on mine!

THE EARTH: I spin beneath my pyramid of night,
  Which points into the heavens dreaming delight,
  Murmuring victorious joy in my enchanted sleep;
  As a youth lulled in love-dreams faintly sighing,
  Under the shadow of his beauty lying,
  Which round his rest a watch of light and warmth doth keep.

THE MOON: As in the soft and sweet eclipse,
  When soul meets soul on lovers' lips,
  High hearts are calm, and brightest eyes are dull;
  So when thy shadow falls on me,
  Then am I mute and still, by thee
  Covered; of thy love, Orb most beautiful,
  Full, oh, too full!

Thou art speeding round the sun
Brightest world of many a one;
Green and azure sphere which shinest
With a light which is divinest
Among all the lamps of Heaven
To whom life and light is given;
I, thy crystal paramour
Borne beside thee by a power
Like the polar Paradise,
Magnet-like of lovers' eyes;
I, a most enamoured maiden
Whose weak brain is overladen
With the pleasure of her love,
Maniac-like around thee move
Gazing, an insatiate bride,
On thy form from every side
Like a Maenad, round the cup
Which Agave lifted up
In the weird Cadmaean forest.
Brother, wheresoe'er thou soarest
I must hurry, whirl and follow
Through the heavens wide and hollow,
Sheltered by the warm embrace
Of thy soul from hungry space,
Drinking from thy sense and sight
Beauty, majesty, and might,
As a lover or a chameleon
Grows like what it looks upon,
As a violet's gentle eye
Gazes on the azure sky
Until its hue grows like what it beholds,
As a gray and watery mist
Glows like solid amethyst
Athwart the western mountain it enfolds,
When the sunset sleeps
Upon its snow—

THE EARTH: And the weak day weeps
That it should be so.
Oh, gentle Moon, the voice of thy delight

    Falls on me like thy clear and tender light
    Soothing the seaman, borne the summer night,
    Through isles for ever calm;
    Oh, gentle Moon, thy crystal accents pierce
    The caverns of my pride's deep universe,
    Charming the tiger joy, whose tramplings fierce
    Made wounds which need thy balm.
PANTHEA: I rise as from a bath of sparkling water,
    A bath of azure light, among dark rocks,
    Out of the stream of sound.
IONE: Ah me! sweet sister,
    The stream of sound has ebbed away from us,
    And you pretend to rise out of its wave,
    Because your words fall like the clear, soft dew
    Shaken from a bathing wood-nymph's limbs and hair.
PANTHEA: Peace! peace! a mighty Power, which is as darkness,
    Is rising out of Earth, and from the sky
    Is showered like night, and from within the air
    Bursts, like eclipse which had been gathered up
    Into the pores of sunlight: the bright visions,
    Wherein the singing spirits rode and shone,
    Gleam like pale meteors through a watery night.
IONE: There is a sense of words upon mine ear.
PANTHEA: An universal sound like words: Oh, list!
DEMOGORGON: Thou, Earth, calm empire of a happy soul,
    Sphere of divinest shapes and harmonies,
    Beautiful orb! gathering as thou dost roll
    The love which paves thy path along the skies:
THE EARTH: I hear: I am as a drop of dew that dies.
DEMOGORGON: Thou, Moon, which gazest on the nightly Earth
    With wonder, as it gazes upon thee;
    Whilst each to men, and beasts, and the swift birth
    Of birds, is beauty, love, calm, harmony:
THE MOON: I hear: I am a leaf shaken by thee!
DEMOGORGON: Ye Kings of suns and stars, Daemons and Gods,
    Ethereal Dominations, who possess
    Elysian, windless, fortunate abodes
    Beyond Heaven's constellated wilderness:
A VOICE FROM ABOVE: Our great Republic hears: we are blest, and bless.

DEMOGORGON: Ye happy Dead, whom beams of brightest verse
   Are clouds to hide, not colours to portray,
   Whether your nature is that universe
   Which once ye saw and suffered—
A VOICE: FROM BENEATH: Or as they
   Whom we have left, we change and pass away.
DEMOGORGON: Ye elemental Genii, who have homes
   From man's high mind even to the central stone
   Of sullen lead; from heaven's star-fretted domes
   To the dull weed some sea-worm battens on:
A CONFUSED VOICE: We hear: thy words waken Oblivion.
DEMOGORGON: Spirits, whose homes are flesh; ye beasts and birds,
   Ye worms and fish; ye living leaves and buds;
   Lightning and wind; and ye untameable herds,
   Meteors and mists, which throng air's solitudes:—
A VOICE: Thy voice to us is wind among still woods.
DEMOGORGON: Man, who wert once a despot and a slave;
   A dupe and a deceiver; a decay;
   A traveller from the cradle to the grave
   Through the dim night of this immortal day:
ALL: Speak: thy strong words may never pass away.
DEMOGORGON: This is the day, which down the void abysm
   At the Earth-born's spell yawns for Heaven's despotism,
   And Conquest is dragged captive through the deep:
   Love, from its awful throne of patient power
   In the wise heart, from the last giddy hour
   Of dread endurance, from the slippery, steep,
   And narrow verge of crag-like agony, springs
   And folds over the world its healing wings.

   Gentleness, Virtue, Wisdom, and Endurance,
   These are the seals of that most firm assurance
   Which bars the pit over Destruction's strength;
   And if, with infirm hand, Eternity,
   Mother of many acts and hours, should free
   The serpent that would clasp her with his length;
   These are the spells by which to reassume
   An empire o'er the disentangled doom.

To suffer woes which Hope thinks infinite;
To forgive wrongs darker than death or night;
To defy Power, which seems omnipotent;
To love, and bear; to hope till Hope creates
From its own wreck the thing it contemplates;
Neither to change, nor falter, nor repent;
This, like thy glory, Titan, is to be
Good, great and joyous, beautiful and free;
This is alone Life, Joy, Empire, and Victory!

Cancelled Fragments of "Prometheus Unbound"

(First printed by Mr. C.D. Locock, "Examination of the Shelley Manuscripts at the Bodleian Library", 1903, pages 33–7.)

(following 1._37.)
 When thou descendst each night with open eyes
 In torture, for a tyrant seldom sleeps,
 Thou never; . . .
 . . .

(following 1._195.)
 Which thou henceforth art doomed to interweave
 . . .

(following the first two words of 1._342.)
 (*Of Hell:*) I placed it in his choice to be
 The crown, or trampled refuse of the world
 With but one law itself a glorious boon—
 I gave—
 . . .

(following 1._707.)
SECOND SPIRIT: I leaped on the wings of the Earth-star damp
 As it rose on the steam of a slaughtered camp—
 The sleeping newt heard not our tramp
 As swift as the wings of fire may pass—
 We threaded the points of long thick grass
 Which hide the green pools of the morass

But shook a water-serpent's couch
In a cleft skull, of many such
The widest; at the meteor's touch
The snake did seem to see in dream
Thrones and dungeons overthrown
Visions how unlike his own. . .
'Twas the hope the prophecy
Which begins and ends in thee
. . .

(following 2.1._110.)
Lift up thine eyes Panthea—they pierce they burn

PANTHEA: Alas! I am consumed—I melt away
   The fire is in my heart—
ASIA: Thine eyes burn burn!—
   Hide them within thine hair—
PANTHEA: O quench thy lips
   I sink I perish
ASIA: Shelter me now—they burn
   It is his spirit in their orbs. . . my life
   Is ebbing fast—I cannot speak—
PANTHEA: Rest, rest!
   Sleep death annihilation pain! aught else
   . . .

(following 2.4._27.)
   Or looks which tell that while the lips are calm
   And the eyes cold, the spirit weeps within
   Tears like the sanguine sweat of agony;
   . . .

Uncancelled Passage

(following 2.5._71.)

ASIA: You said that spirits spoke, but it was thee
   Sweet sister, for even now thy curved lips

>   Tremble as if the sound were dying there
>   Not dead
> PANTHEA: Alas it was Prometheus spoke
>   Within me, and I know it must be so
>   I mixed my own weak nature with his love
>   . . . And my thoughts
>   Are like the many forests of a vale
>   Through which the might of whirlwind and of rain
>   Had passed—they rest rest through the evening light
>   As mine do now in thy beloved smile.

Cancelled Stage Directions

(following 1._221.)
(*The sound beneath as of earthquake and the driving of whirlwinds—the ravine is split, and the phantasm of* JUPITER *rises, surrounded by heavy clouds which dart forth lightning*)

(following 1._520.)
(*Enter rushing by groups of horrible forms; they speak as they pass in chorus*)

(following 1._552.)
(*A shadow passes over the scene, and a piercing shriek is heard*)

Note on "Prometheus Unbound",
by Mrs. Shelley

On the 12th of March, 1818, Shelley quitted England, never to return. His principal motive was the hope that his health would be improved by a milder climate; he suffered very much during the winter previous to his emigration, and this decided his vacillating purpose. In December, 1817, he had written from Marlow to a friend, saying:

'My health has been materially worse. My feelings at intervals are of a deadly and torpid kind, or awakened to such a state of unnatural and keen excitement that, only to instance the organ of sight, I find the very blades of grass and the boughs of distant trees present themselves to me with microscopic distinctness. Towards evening I sink into a state of lethargy and inanimation, and often remain for hours on the sofa between sleep and waking, a prey to the most painful irritability of thought. Such, with little intermission, is my condition. The hours devoted to study are selected with vigilant caution from among these periods of endurance. It is not for this that I think of travelling to Italy, even if I knew that Italy would relieve me. But I have experienced a decisive pulmonary attack; and although at present it has passed away without any considerable vestige of its existence, yet this symptom sufficiently shows the true nature of my disease to be consumptive. It is to my advantage that this malady is in its nature slow, and, if one is sufficiently alive to its advances, is susceptible of cure from a warm climate. In the event of its assuming any decided shape, IT WOULD BE MY DUTY to go to Italy without delay. It is not mere health, but life, that I should seek, and that not for my own sake—I feel I am capable of trampling on all such weakness; but for the sake of those to whom my life may be a source of happiness, utility, security, and honour, and to some of whom my death might be all that is the reverse.'

In almost every respect his journey to Italy was advantageous. He left behind friends to whom he was attached; but cares of a thousand kinds, many springing from his lavish generosity, crowded round him in his native country, and, except the society of one or two friends, he had no compensation. The climate caused him to consume half his existence in helpless suffering. His dearest pleasure, the free enjoyment of the scenes of Nature, was marred by the same circumstance.

He went direct to Italy, avoiding even Paris, and did not make any pause till he arrived at Milan. The first aspect of Italy enchanted Shelley; it seemed a garden of delight placed beneath a clearer and brighter heaven than any he had lived under before. He wrote long descriptive letters during the first year of his residence in Italy, which, as compositions, are the most beautiful in the world, and show how truly he appreciated and studied the wonders of Nature and Art in that divine land.

The poetical spirit within him speedily revived with all the power and with more than all the beauty of his first attempts. He meditated three subjects as the groundwork for lyrical dramas. One was the story of Tasso; of this a slight fragment of a song of Tasso remains. The other was one founded on the Book of Job, which he never abandoned in idea, but of which no trace remains among his papers. The third was the "Prometheus Unbound". The Greek tragedians were now his most familiar companions in his wanderings, and the sublime majesty of Aeschylus filled him with wonder and delight. The father of Greek tragedy does not possess the pathos of Sophocles, nor the variety and tenderness of Euripides; the interest on which he founds his dramas is often elevated above human vicissitudes into the mighty passions and throes of gods and demi-gods: such fascinated the abstract imagination of Shelley.

We spent a month at Milan, visiting the Lake of Como during that interval. Thence we passed in succession to Pisa, Leghorn, the Baths of Lucca, Venice, Este, Rome, Naples, and back again to Rome, whither we returned early in March, 1819. During all this time Shelley meditated the subject of his drama, and wrote portions of it. Other poems were composed during this interval, and while at the Bagni di Lucca he translated Plato's "Symposium". But, though he diversified his studies, his thoughts centred in the Prometheus. At last, when at Rome, during a bright and beautiful Spring, he gave up his whole time to the composition. The spot selected for his study was, as he mentions in his preface, the mountainous ruins of the Baths of Caracalla. These are little known to the ordinary visitor at Rome. He describes them in a letter, with that poetry and delicacy and truth of description which render his narrated impressions of scenery of unequalled beauty and interest.

At first he completed the drama in three acts. It was not till several months after, when at Florence, that he conceived that a fourth act, a sort of hymn of rejoicing in the fulfilment of the prophecies with regard to Prometheus, ought to be added to complete the composition.

The prominent feature of Shelley's theory of the destiny of the human species was that evil is not inherent in the system of the creation, but an accident that might be expelled. This also forms a portion of Christianity: God made earth and man perfect, till he, by his fall,

'Brought death into the world and all our woe.'

Shelley believed that mankind had only to will that there should be no evil, and there would be none. It is not my part in these Notes to notice the arguments that have been urged against this opinion, but to mention the fact that he entertained it, and was indeed attached to it with fervent enthusiasm. That man could be so perfectionized as to be able to expel evil from his own nature, and from the greater part of the creation, was the cardinal point of his system. And the subject he loved best to dwell on was the image of One warring with the Evil Principle, oppressed not only by it, but by all—even the good, who were deluded into considering evil a necessary portion of humanity; a victim full of fortitude and hope and the spirit of triumph emanating from a reliance in the ultimate omnipotence of Good. Such he had depicted in his last poem, when he made Laon the enemy and the victim of tyrants. He now took a more idealized image of the same subject. He followed certain classical authorities in figuring Saturn as the good principle, Jupiter the usurping evil one, and Prometheus as the regenerator, who, unable to bring mankind back to primitive innocence, used knowledge as a weapon to defeat evil, by leading mankind, beyond the state wherein they are sinless through ignorance, to that in which they are virtuous through wisdom. Jupiter punished the temerity of the Titan by chaining him to a rock of Caucasus, and causing a vulture to devour his still-renewed heart. There was a prophecy afloat in heaven portending the fall of Jove, the secret of averting which was known only to Prometheus; and the god offered freedom from torture on condition of its being communicated to him. According to the mythological story, this referred to the offspring of Thetis, who was destined to be greater than his father. Prometheus at last bought pardon for his crime of enriching mankind with his gifts, by revealing the prophecy. Hercules killed the vulture, and set him free; and Thetis was married to Peleus, the father of Achilles.

Shelley adapted the catastrophe of this story to his peculiar views. The son greater than his father, born of the nuptials of Jupiter and

Thetis, was to dethrone Evil, and bring back a happier reign than that of Saturn. Prometheus defies the power of his enemy, and endures centuries of torture; till the hour arrives when Jove, blind to the real event, but darkly guessing that some great good to himself will flow, espouses Thetis. At the moment, the Primal Power of the world drives him from his usurped throne, and Strength, in the person of Hercules, liberates Humanity, typified in Prometheus, from the tortures generated by evil done or suffered. Asia, one of the Oceanides, is the wife of Prometheus—she was, according to other mythological interpretations, the same as Venus and Nature. When the benefactor of mankind is liberated, Nature resumes the beauty of her prime, and is united to her husband, the emblem of the human race, in perfect and happy union. In the Fourth Act, the Poet gives further scope to his imagination, and idealizes the forms of creation—such as we know them, instead of such as they appeared to the Greeks. Maternal Earth, the mighty parent, is superseded by the Spirit of the Earth, the guide of our planet through the realms of sky; while his fair and weaker companion and attendant, the Spirit of the Moon, receives bliss from the annihilation of Evil in the superior sphere.

Shelley develops, more particularly in the lyrics of this drama, his abstruse and imaginative theories with regard to the Creation. It requires a mind as subtle and penetrating as his own to understand the mystic meanings scattered throughout the poem. They elude the ordinary reader by their abstraction and delicacy of distinction, but they are far from vague. It was his design to write prose metaphysical essays on the nature of Man, which would have served to explain much of what is obscure in his poetry; a few scattered fragments of observations and remarks alone remain. He considered these philosophical views of Mind and Nature to be instinct with the intensest spirit of poetry.

More popular poets clothe the ideal with familiar and sensible imagery. Shelley loved to idealize the real—to gift the mechanism of the material universe with a soul and a voice, and to bestow such also on the most delicate and abstract emotions and thoughts of the mind. Sophocles was his great master in this species of imagery.

I find in one of his manuscript books some remarks on a line in the "Oedipus Tyrannus", which show at once the critical subtlety of Shelley's mind, and explain his apprehension of those 'minute and remote distinctions of feeling, whether relative to external nature or the living beings which surround us,' which he pronounces, in the letter quoted in the note to the "Revolt of Islam", to comprehend all that is sublime in man.

'In the Greek Shakespeare, Sophocles, we find the image,

Pollas d' odous elthonta phrontidos planois:

a line of almost unfathomable depth of poetry; yet how simple are the images in which it is arrayed!

"Coming to many ways in the wanderings of careful thought."

If the words odous and planois had not been used, the line might have been explained in a metaphorical instead of an absolute sense, as we say "WAYS and means," and "wanderings" for error and confusion. But they meant literally paths or roads, such as we tread with our feet; and wanderings, such as a man makes when he loses himself in a desert, or roams from city to city—as Oedipus, the speaker of this verse, was destined to wander, blind and asking charity. What a picture does this line suggest of the mind as a wilderness of intricate paths, wide as the universe, which is here made its symbol; a world within a world which he who seeks some knowledge with respect to what he ought to do searches throughout, as he would search the external universe for some valued thing which was hidden from him upon its surface.'

In reading Shelley's poetry, we often find similar verses, resembling, but not imitating the Greek in this species of imagery; for, though he adopted the style, he gifted it with that originality of form and colouring which sprung from his own genius.

In the "Prometheus Unbound", Shelley fulfils the promise quoted from a letter in the Note on the "Revolt of Islam". (While correcting the proof-sheets of that poem, it struck me that the poet had indulged in an exaggerated view of the evils of restored despotism; which, however injurious and degrading, were less openly sanguinary than the triumph of anarchy, such as it appeared in France at the close of the last century. But at this time a book, "Scenes of Spanish Life", translated by Lieutenant Crawford from the German of Dr. Huber, of Rostock, fell into my hands. The account of the triumph of the priests and the serviles, after the French invasion of Spain in 1823, bears a strong and frightful resemblance to some of the descriptions of the massacre of the patriots in the "Revolt of Islam".) The tone of the composition is calmer and more majestic, the poetry more perfect as a whole, and the imagination displayed at once more pleasingly beautiful and more varied and daring. The description of the Hours, as they are seen in the cave of Demogorgon, is an instance of this—it fills the mind as the most charming picture—we long to see an artist at work to bring to our view the

> *'cars drawn by rainbow-winged steeds*
> *Which trample the dim winds: in each there stands*
> *A wild-eyed charioteer urging their flight.*
> *Some look behind, as fiends pursued them there,*
> *And yet I see no shapes but the keen stars:*
> *Others, with burning eyes, lean forth, and drink*
> *With eager lips the wind of their own speed,*
> *As if the thing they loved fled on before,*
> *And now, even now, they clasped it. Their bright locks*
> *Stream like a comet's flashing hair: they all*
> *Sweep onward.'*

Through the whole poem there reigns a sort of calm and holy spirit of love; it soothes the tortured, and is hope to the expectant, till the prophecy is fulfilled, and Love, untainted by any evil, becomes the law of the world.

England had been rendered a painful residence to Shelley, as much by the sort of persecution with which in those days all men of liberal opinions were visited, and by the injustice he had lately endured in the Court of Chancery, as by the symptoms of disease which made him regard a visit to Italy as necessary to prolong his life. An exile, and strongly impressed with the feeling that the majority of his countrymen regarded him with sentiments of aversion such as his own heart could experience towards none, he sheltered himself from such disgusting and painful thoughts in the calm retreats of poetry, and built up a world of his own—with the more pleasure, since he hoped to induce some one or two to believe that the earth might become such, did mankind themselves consent. The charm of the Roman climate helped to clothe his thoughts in greater beauty than they had ever worn before. And, as he wandered among the ruins made one with Nature in their decay, or gazed on the Praxitelean shapes that throng the Vatican, the Capitol, and the palaces of Rome, his soul imbibed forms of loveliness which became a portion of itself. There are many passages in the "Prometheus" which show the intense delight he received from such studies, and give back the impression with a beauty of poetical description peculiarly his own. He felt this, as a poet must feel when he satisfies himself by the result of his labours; and he wrote from Rome, 'My "Prometheus Unbound" is just finished, and in a month or two I shall send it. It is a drama, with characters and mechanism of a kind yet unattempted; and I think the execution is better than any of my former attempts.'

I may mention, for the information of the more critical reader, that the verbal alterations in this edition of "Prometheus" are made from a list of errata written by Shelley himself.

THE CENCI

A Tragedy in Five Acts

(Composed at Rome and near Leghorn (Villa Valsovano), May-August 5, 1819; published 1820 (spring) by C. & J. Ollier, London. This edition of two hundred and fifty copies was printed in Italy 'because,' writes Shelley to Peacock, September 21, 1819, 'it costs, with all duties and freightage, about half what it would cost in London.' A Table of Errata in Mrs. Shelley's handwriting is printed by Forman in "The Shelley Library", page 91. A second edition, published by Ollier in 1821 (C.H. Reynell, printer), embodies the corrections indicated in this Table. No manuscript of "The Cenci" is known to exist. Our text follows that of the second edition (1821); variations of the first (Italian) edition, the title-page of which bears date 1819, are given in the footnotes. The text of the "Poetical Works", 1839, 1st and 2nd editions (Mrs. Shelley), follows for the most part that of the editio princeps of 1819.)

Dedication, to Leigh Hunt, Esq.

My dear friend

I inscribe with your name, from a distant country, and after an absence whose months have seemed years, this the latest of my literary efforts.

Those writings which I have hitherto published, have been little else than visions which impersonate my own apprehensions of the beautiful and the just. I can also perceive in them the literary defects incidental to youth and impatience; they are dreams of what ought to be, or may be. The drama which I now present to you is a sad reality. I lay aside the presumptuous attitude of an instructor, and am content to paint, with such colours as my own heart furnishes, that which has been.

Had I known a person more highly endowed than yourself with all that it becomes a man to possess, I had solicited for this work the ornament of his name. One more gentle, honourable, innocent and brave; one of more exalted toleration for all who do and think evil, and yet himself more free from evil; one who knows better how to receive, and how to confer a benefit, though he must ever confer far more than he can receive; one of simpler, and, in the highest sense of the word, of purer life and manners I never knew: and I had already been fortunate in friendships when your name was added to the list.

In that patient and irreconcilable enmity with domestic and political tyranny and imposture which the tenor of your life has illustrated, and which, had I health and talents, should illustrate mine, let us, comforting each other in our task, live and die.

All happiness attend you! Your affectionate friend,

Percy B. Shelley
Rome, May 29, 1819

The Cenci: Preface

A manuscript was communicated to me during my travels in Italy, which was copied from the archives of the Cenci Palace at Rome, and contains a detailed account of the horrors which ended in the extinction of one of the noblest and richest families of that city during the Pontificate of Clement VIII, in the year 1599. The story is, that an old man having spent his life in debauchery and wickedness, conceived at length an implacable hatred towards his children; which showed itself towards one daughter under the form of an incestuous passion, aggravated by every circumstance of cruelty and violence. This daughter, after long and vain attempts to escape from what she considered a perpetual contamination both of body and mind, at length plotted with her mother-in-law and brother to murder their common tyrant. The young maiden, who was urged to this tremendous deed by an impulse which overpowered its horror, was evidently a most gentle and amiable being, a creature formed to adorn and be admired, and thus violently thwarted from her nature by the necessity of circumstance and opinion. The deed was quickly discovered, and, in spite of the most earnest prayers made to the Pope by the highest persons in Rome, the criminals were put to death. The old man had during his life repeatedly bought his pardon from the Pope for capital crimes of the most enormous and unspeakable kind, at the price of a hundred thousand crowns; the death therefore of his victims can scarcely be accounted for by the love of justice. The Pope, among other motives for severity, probably felt that whoever killed the Count Cenci deprived his treasury of a certain and copious source of revenue. (The Papal Government formerly took the most extraordinary precautions against the publicity of facts which offer so tragical a demonstration of its own wickedness and weakness; so that the communication of the manuscript had become, until very lately, a matter of some difficulty.) Such a story, if told so as to present to the reader all the feelings of those who once acted it, their hopes and fears, their confidences and misgivings, their various interests, passions, and opinions, acting upon and with each other, yet all conspiring to one tremendous end, would be as a light to make apparent some of the most dark and secret caverns of the human heart.

On my arrival at Rome I found that the story of the Cenci was a subject not to be mentioned in Italian society without awakening a deep and breathless interest; and that the feelings of the company never failed to incline to a romantic pity for the wrongs, and a passionate exculpation of the horrible deed to which they urged her, who has been mingled two centuries with the common dust. All ranks of people knew the outlines of this history, and participated in the overwhelming interest which it seems to have the magic of exciting in the human heart. I had a copy of Guido's picture of Beatrice which is preserved in the Colonna Palace, and my servant instantly recognized it as the portrait of La Cenci.

This national and universal interest which the story produces and has produced for two centuries and among all ranks of people in a great City, where the imagination is kept for ever active and awake, first suggested to me the conception of its fitness for a dramatic purpose. In fact it is a tragedy which has already received, from its capacity of awakening and sustaining the sympathy of men, approbation and success. Nothing remained as I imagined, but to clothe it to the apprehensions of my countrymen in such language and action as would bring it home to their hearts. The deepest and the sublimest tragic compositions, King Lear and the two plays in which the tale of Oedipus is told, were stories which already existed in tradition, as matters of popular belief and interest, before Shakspeare and Sophocles made them familiar to the sympathy of all succeeding generations of mankind.

This story of the Cenci is indeed eminently fearful and monstrous: anything like a dry exhibition of it on the stage would be insupportable. The person who would treat such a subject must increase the ideal, and diminish the actual horror of the events, so that the pleasure which arises from the poetry which exists in these tempestuous sufferings and crimes may mitigate the pain of the contemplation of the moral deformity from which they spring. There must also be nothing attempted to make the exhibition subservient to what is vulgarly termed a moral purpose. The highest moral purpose aimed at in the highest species of the drama, is the teaching the human heart, through its sympathies and antipathies, the knowledge of itself; in proportion to the possession of which knowledge, every human being is wise, just, sincere, tolerant and kind. If dogmas can do more, it is well: but a drama is no fit place for the enforcement of them. Undoubtedly, no person can be truly dishonoured by the act of another; and the fit return to make to the most enormous injuries is kindness and forbearance, and a resolution to convert the injurer from his dark passions by peace and love. Revenge, retaliation, atonement, are pernicious mistakes. If Beatrice had thought in this manner she would have been wiser and better; but she would never have been a tragic character: the few whom such an exhibition would have interested, could never have been sufficiently interested for a dramatic purpose, from the want of finding sympathy in their interest among the mass who surround them. It is in the restless and anatomizing casuistry with which men seek the justification of Beatrice, yet feel that she has done what needs justification; it is in the superstitious horror with which they contemplate alike her wrongs and their revenge, that the dramatic character of what she did and suffered, consists.

I have endeavoured as nearly as possible to represent the characters as they probably were, and have sought to avoid the error of making them actuated by my own conceptions of right or wrong, false or true: thus under a thin veil converting names and actions of the sixteenth century into cold impersonations of my own mind. They are represented as Catholics, and as Catholics deeply tinged with religion. To a Protestant apprehension there will appear something unnatural in the earnest and perpetual sentiment of the relations between God and men which pervade the tragedy of the Cenci. It will especially be startled at the combination of an undoubting persuasion of the truth of the popular religion with a cool and determined perseverance in enormous guilt. But religion in Italy is not, as in Protestant countries, a cloak to be worn on particular days; or a passport which those who do not wish to be railed at carry with them to exhibit; or a gloomy passion for penetrating the impenetrable mysteries of our being, which terrifies its possessor at the darkness of the abyss to the brink of which it has conducted him. Religion coexists, as it were, in the mind of an Italian Catholic, with a faith in that of which all men have the most certain knowledge. It is interwoven with the whole fabric of life. It is adoration, faith, submission, penitence, blind admiration; not a rule for moral conduct. It has no necessary connection with any one virtue. The most atrocious villain may be rigidly devout, and without any shock to established faith, confess himself to be so. Religion pervades intensely the whole frame of society, and is according to the temper of the mind which it inhabits, a passion, a persuasion, an excuse, a refuge; never a check. Cenci himself built a chapel in the court of his Palace, and dedicated it to St. Thomas the Apostle, and established masses for the peace of his soul. Thus in the first scene of the fourth act Lucretia's design in exposing herself to the consequences of an expostulation with Cenci after having administered the opiate, was to induce him by a feigned tale to confess himself before death; this being esteemed by Catholics as essential to salvation; and she only relinquishes her purpose when she perceives that her perseverance would expose Beatrice to new outrages.

I have avoided with great care in writing this play the introduction of what is commonly called mere poetry, and I imagine there will scarcely be found a detached simile or a single isolated description, unless Beatrice's description of the chasm appointed for her father's murder should be judged to be of that nature. (An idea in this speech was suggested by a most sublime passage in "El Purgaterio de San Patricio" of Calderon; the only plagiarism which I have intentionally committed in the whole piece.)

In a dramatic composition the imagery and the passion should interpenetrate one another, the former being reserved simply for the full development and illustration of the latter. Imagination is as the immortal God which should assume flesh for the redemption of mortal passion. It is thus that the most remote and the most familiar imagery may alike be fit for dramatic purposes when employed in the illustration of strong feeling, which raises what is low, and levels to the apprehension that which is lofty, casting over all the shadow of its own greatness. In other respects, I have written more carelessly; that is, without an over-fastidious and learned choice of words. In this respect I entirely agree with those modern critics who assert that in order to move men to true sympathy we must use the familiar language of men, and that our great ancestors the ancient English poets are the writers, a study of whom might incite us to do that for our own age which they have done for theirs. But it must be the real language of men in general and not that of any particular class to whose society the writer happens to belong. So much for what I have attempted; I need not be assured that success is a very different matter; particularly for one whose attention has but newly been awakened to the study of dramatic literature.

I endeavoured whilst at Rome to observe such monuments of this story as might be accessible to a stranger. The portrait of Beatrice at the Colonna Palace is admirable as a work of art: it was taken by Guido during her confinement in prison. But it is most interesting as a just representation of one of the loveliest specimens of the workmanship of Nature. There is a fixed and pale composure upon the features: she seems sad and stricken down in spirit, yet the despair thus expressed is lightened by the patience of gentleness. Her head is bound with folds of white drapery from which the yellow strings of her golden hair escape, and fall about her neck. The moulding of her face is exquisitely delicate; the eyebrows are distinct and arched: the lips have that permanent meaning of imagination and sensibility which suffering has not repressed and which it seems as if death scarcely could extinguish. Her forehead is large and clear; her eyes, which we are told were remarkable for their vivacity, are swollen with weeping and lustreless, but beautifully tender and serene. In the whole mien there is a simplicity and dignity which, united with her exquisite loveliness and deep sorrow, are inexpressibly pathetic. Beatrice Cenci appears to have been one of those rare persons in whom energy and gentleness dwell together without destroying one another: her nature was simple and profound. The crimes and miseries in which she was an actor and a sufferer are as the mask and the mantle in which circumstances clothed her for her impersonation on the scene of the world.

The Cenci Palace is of great extent; and though in part modernized, there yet remains a vast and gloomy pile of feudal architecture in the same state as during the dreadful scenes which are the subject of this tragedy. The Palace is situated in an obscure corner of Rome, near the quarter of the Jews, and from the upper windows you see the immense ruins of Mount Palatine half hidden under their profuse overgrowth of trees. There is a court in one part of the Palace (perhaps that in which Cenci built the Chapel to St. Thomas), supported by granite columns and adorned with antique friezes of fine workmanship, and built up, according to the ancient Italian fashion, with balcony over balcony of open-work. One of the gates of the Palace formed of immense stones and leading through a passage, dark and lofty and opening into gloomy subterranean chambers, struck me particularly.

Of the Castle of Petrella, I could obtain no further information than that which is to be found in the manuscript.

The Cenci: A Tragedy in Five Acts

Dramatis Personae

Count Francesco Cenci
Giacomo, Bernardo, His Sons
Cardinal Camillo
Prince Colonna
Orsino, A Prelate
Savella, The Pope's Legate
Olimpio, Marzio, Assassins
Andrea, Servant to Cenci
Nobles. Judges. Guards, Servants
Lucretia, Wife of Cenci and Step-Mother of His Children
Beatrice, His Daughter

The scene lies principally in rome, but changes during the fourth act to Petrella, *A castle among the Apulian Apennines.*

Time. During the pontificate of Clement VIII.

Act 1

Scene 1.1:
An Apartment in the Cenci Palace.
Enter Count Cenci *and Cardinal* Camillo.

Camillo: That matter of the murder is hushed up
    If you consent to yield his Holiness
    Your fief that lies beyond the Pincian gate.—
    It needed all my interest in the conclave
    To bend him to this point; he said that you
    Bought perilous impunity with your gold;
    That crimes like yours if once or twice compounded
    Enriched the Church, and respited from hell
    An erring soul which might repent and live: —
    But that the glory and the interest
    Of the high throne he fills, little consist
    With making it a daily mart of guilt
    As manifold and hideous as the deeds
    Which you scarce hide from men's revolted eyes.
Cenci: The third of my possessions—let it go!
    Ay, I once heard the nephew of the Pope
    Had sent his architect to view the ground,
    Meaning to build a villa on my vines
    The next time I compounded with his uncle:
    I little thought he should outwit me so!
    Henceforth no witness—not the lamp—shall see
    That which the vassal threatened to divulge
    Whose throat is choked with dust for his reward.
    The deed he saw could not have rated higher
    Than his most worthless life:—it angers me!
    Respited me from Hell! So may the Devil
    Respite their souls from Heaven! No doubt Pope Clement,
    And his most charitable nephews, pray
    That the Apostle Peter and the Saints
    Will grant for their sake that I long enjoy
    Strength, wealth, and pride, and lust, and length of days
    Wherein to act the deeds which are the stewards
    Of their revenue.—But much yet remains

   To which they show no title.
CAMILLO: Oh, Count Cenci!
   So much that thou mightst honourably live
   And reconcile thyself with thine own heart
   And with thy God, and with the offended world.
   How hideously look deeds of lust and blood
   Through those snow white and venerable hairs!—
   Your children should be sitting round you now,
   But that you fear to read upon their looks
   The shame and misery you have written there.
   Where is your wife? Where is your gentle daughter?
   Methinks her sweet looks, which make all things else
   Beauteous and glad, might kill the fiend within you.
   Why is she barred from all society
   But her own strange and uncomplaining wrongs?
   Talk with me, Count,—you know I mean you well.
   I stood beside your dark and fiery youth
   Watching its bold and bad career, as men
   Watch meteors, but it vanished not—I marked
   Your desperate and remorseless manhood; now
   Do I behold you in dishonoured age
   Charged with a thousand unrepented crimes.
   Yet I have ever hoped you would amend,
   And in that hope have saved your life three times.
CENCI: For which Aldobrandino owes you now
   My fief beyond the Pincian.—Cardinal,
   One thing, I pray you, recollect henceforth,
   And so we shall converse with less restraint.
   A man you knew spoke of my wife and daughter—
   He was accustomed to frequent my house;
   So the next day HIS wife and daughter came
   And asked if I had seen him; and I smiled:
   I think they never saw him any more.
CAMILLO: Thou execrable man, beware!—
CENCI: Of thee?
   Nay, this is idle: —We should know each other.
   As to my character for what men call crime
   Seeing I please my senses as I list,
   And vindicate that right with force or guile,

It is a public matter, and I care not
If I discuss it with you. I may speak
Alike to you and my own conscious heart—
For you give out that you have half reformed me,
Therefore strong vanity will keep you silent
If fear should not; both will, I do not doubt.
All men delight in sensual luxury,
All men enjoy revenge; and most exult
Over the tortures they can never feel—
Flattering their secret peace with others' pain.
But I delight in nothing else. I love
The sight of agony, and the sense of joy,
When this shall be another's, and that mine.
And I have no remorse and little fear,
Which are, I think, the checks of other men.
This mood has grown upon me, until now
Any design my captious fancy makes
The picture of its wish, and it forms none
But such as men like you would start to know,
Is as my natural food and rest debarred
Until it be accomplished.

CAMILLO: Art thou not
  Most miserable?

CENCI: Why miserable?—
  No.—I am what your theologians call
  Hardened;—which they must be in impudence,
  So to revile a man's peculiar taste.
  True, I was happier than I am, while yet
  Manhood remained to act the thing I thought;
  While lust was sweeter than revenge; and now
  Invention palls:—Ay, we must all grow old—
  And but that there remains a deed to act
  Whose horror might make sharp an appetite
  Duller than mine—I'd do,—I know not what.
  When I was young I thought of nothing else
  But pleasure; and I fed on honey sweets:
  Men, by St. Thomas! cannot live like bees,
  And I grew tired:—yet, till I killed a foe,
  And heard his groans, and heard his children's groans,

    Knew I not what delight was else on earth,
    Which now delights me little. I the rather
    Look on such pangs as terror ill conceals,
    The dry fixed eyeball; the pale, quivering lip,
    Which tell me that the spirit weeps within
    Tears bitterer than the bloody sweat of Christ.
    I rarely kill the body, which preserves,
    Like a strong prison, the soul within my power,
    Wherein I feed it with the breath of fear
    For hourly pain.
CAMILLO: Hell's most abandoned fiend
    Did never, in the drunkenness of guilt,
    Speak to his heart as now you speak to me;
    I thank my God that I believe you not.
(*Enter* ANDREA)
ANDREA: My Lord, a gentleman from Salamanca
    Would speak with you.
CENCI: Bid him attend me
    In the grand saloon.
(*Exit* ANDREA)
CAMILLO: Farewell; and I will pray
    Almighty God that thy false, impious words
    Tempt not his spirit to abandon thee.
(*Exit* CAMILLO)
CENCI: The third of my possessions! I must use
    Close husbandry, or gold, the old man's sword,
    Falls from my withered hand. But yesterday
    There came an order from the Pope to make
    Fourfold provision for my cursed sons;
    Whom I had sent from Rome to Salamanca,
    Hoping some accident might cut them off;
    And meaning if I could to starve them there.
    I pray thee, God, send some quick death upon them!
    Bernardo and my wife could not be worse
    If dead and damned:—then, as to Beatrice—
(*Looking Around Him Suspiciously*)
    I think they cannot hear me at that door;
    What if they should? And yet I need not speak
    Though the heart triumphs with itself in words.

O, thou most silent air, that shalt not hear
What now I think! Thou, pavement, which I tread
Towards her chamber,—let your echoes talk
Of my imperious step scorning surprise,
But not of my intent!—Andrea!
(*Enter* ANDREA)
ANDREA: My lord?
CENCI: Bid Beatrice attend me in her chamber
   This evening:—no, at midnight and alone.
(*Exeunt*)

SCENE 1.2:
A Garden of the Cenci Palace.
Enter BEATRICE *and* ORSINO, *as in conversation.*
BEATRICE: Pervert not truth,
   Orsino. You remember where we held
   That conversation;—nay, we see the spot
   Even from this cypress;—two long years are past
   Since, on an April midnight, underneath
   The moonlight ruins of Mount Palatine,
   I did confess to you my secret mind.
ORSINO: You said you loved me then.
BEATRICE: You are a Priest.
   Speak to me not of love.
ORSINO: I may obtain
   The dispensation of the Pope to marry.
   Because I am a Priest do you believe
   Your image, as the hunter some struck deer,
   Follows me not whether I wake or sleep?
BEATRICE: As I have said, speak to me not of love;
   Had you a dispensation I have not;
   Nor will I leave this home of misery
   Whilst my poor Bernard, and that gentle lady
   To whom I owe life, and these virtuous thoughts,
   Must suffer what I still have strength to share.
   Alas, Orsino! All the love that once
   I felt for you, is turned to bitter pain.
   Ours was a youthful contract, which you first

    Broke, by assuming vows no Pope will loose.
    And thus I love you still, but holily,
    Even as a sister or a spirit might;
    And so I swear a cold fidelity.
    And it is well perhaps we shall not marry.
    You have a sly, equivocating vein
    That suits me not.—Ah, wretched that I am!
    Where shall I turn? Even now you look on me
    As you were not my friend, and as if you
    Discovered that I thought so, with false smiles
    Making my true suspicion seem your wrong.
    Ah, no! forgive me; sorrow makes me seem
    Sterner than else my nature might have been;
    I have a weight of melancholy thoughts,
    And they forebode,—but what can they forebode
    Worse than I now endure?
ORSINO: All will be well.
    Is the petition yet prepared? You know
    My zeal for all you wish, sweet Beatrice;
    Doubt not but I will use my utmost skill
    So that the Pope attend to your complaint.
BEATRICE: Your zeal for all I wish;—Ah me, you are cold!
    Your utmost skill. . . speak but one word. . .
(*Aside*)
    Alas!
    Weak and deserted creature that I am,
    Here I stand bickering with my only friend!
(*To* ORSINO)
    This night my father gives a sumptuous feast,
    Orsino; he has heard some happy news
    From Salamanca, from my brothers there,
    And with this outward show of love he mocks
    His inward hate. 'Tis bold hypocrisy,
    For he would gladlier celebrate their deaths,
    Which I have heard him pray for on his knees:
    Great God! that such a father should be mine!
    But there is mighty preparation made,
    And all our kin, the Cenci, will be there,

>   And all the chief nobility of Rome.
>   And he has bidden me and my pale Mother
>   Attire ourselves in festival array.
>   Poor lady! She expects some happy change
>   In his dark spirit from this act; I none.
>   At supper I will give you the petition:
>   Till when—farewell.
> ORSINO: Farewell.
> (*Exit* BEATRICE)
>   I know the Pope
>   Will ne'er absolve me from my priestly vow
>   But by absolving me from the revenue
>   Of many a wealthy see; and, Beatrice,
>   I think to win thee at an easier rate.
>   Nor shall he read her eloquent petition:
>   He might bestow her on some poor relation
>   Of his sixth cousin, as he did her sister,
>   And I should be debarred from all access.
>   Then as to what she suffers from her father,
>   In all this there is much exaggeration:—
>   Old men are testy and will have their way;
>   A man may stab his enemy, or his vassal,
>   And live a free life as to wine or women,
>   And with a peevish temper may return
>   To a dull home, and rate his wife and children;
>   Daughters and wives call this foul tyranny.
>   I shall be well content if on my conscience
>   There rest no heavier sin than what they suffer
>   From the devices of my love—a net
>   From which he shall escape not. Yet I fear
>   Her subtle mind, her awe-inspiring gaze,
>   Whose beams anatomize me nerve by nerve
>   And lay me bare, and make me blush to see
>   My hidden thoughts.—Ah, no! A friendless girl
>   Who clings to me, as to her only hope:—
>   I were a fool, not less than if a panther
>   Were panic-stricken by the antelope's eye,
>   If she escape me.
> (*Exit*)

SCENE 1.3:
A magnificent hall in the Cenci Palace.
A Banquet.
Enter CENCI, LUCRETIA, BEATRICE, ORSINO, CAMILLO, NOBLES.
CENCI: Welcome, my friends and kinsmen; welcome ye,
   Princes and Cardinals, pillars of the church,
   Whose presence honours our festivity.
   I have too long lived like an anchorite,
   And in my absence from your merry meetings
   An evil word is gone abroad of me;
   But I do hope that you, my noble friends,
   When you have shared the entertainment here,
   And heard the pious cause for which 'tis given,
   And we have pledged a health or two together,
   Will think me flesh and blood as well as you;
   Sinful indeed, for Adam made all so,
   But tender-hearted, meek and pitiful.
FIRST GUEST: In truth, my Lord, you seem too light of heart,
   Too sprightly and companionable a man,
   To act the deeds that rumour pins on you.
(*To his companion*)
   I never saw such blithe and open cheer
   In any eye!
SECOND GUEST: Some most desired event,
   In which we all demand a common joy,
   Has brought us hither; let us hear it, Count.
CENCI: It is indeed a most desired event.
   If when a parent from a parent's heart
   Lifts from this earth to the great Father of all
   A prayer, both when he lays him down to sleep,
   And when he rises up from dreaming it;
   One supplication, one desire, one hope,
   That he would grant a wish for his two sons,
   Even all that he demands in their regard—
   And suddenly beyond his dearest hope
   It is accomplished, he should then rejoice,
   And call his friends and kinsmen to a feast,
   And task their love to grace his merriment,—
   Then honour me thus far—for I am he.

BEATRICE (*to* LUCRETIA): Great God! How horrible! some dreadful ill
  Must have befallen my brothers.
LUCRETIA: Fear not, child,
  He speaks too frankly.
BEATRICE: Ah! My blood runs cold.
  I fear that wicked laughter round his eye,
  Which wrinkles up the skin even to the hair.
CENCI: Here are the letters brought from Salamanca;
  Beatrice, read them to your mother. God!
  I thank thee! In one night didst thou perform,
  By ways inscrutable, the thing I sought.
  My disobedient and rebellious sons
  Are dead!—Why, dead!—What means this change of cheer?
  You hear me not, I tell you they are dead;
  And they will need no food or raiment more:
  The tapers that did light them the dark way
  Are their last cost. The Pope, I think, will not
  Expect I should maintain them in their coffins.
  Rejoice with me—my heart is wondrous glad.
(LUCRETIA *sinks, half fainting;* BEATRICE *supports her*)
BEATRICE: It is not true!—Dear Lady, pray look up.
  Had it been true, there is a God in Heaven,
  He would not live to boast of such a boon.
  Unnatural man, thou knowest that it is false.
CENCI: Ay, as the word of God; whom here I call
  To witness that I speak the sober truth;—
  And whose most favouring Providence was shown
  Even in the manner of their deaths. For Rocco
  Was kneeling at the mass, with sixteen others,
  When the church fell and crushed him to a mummy,
  The rest escaped unhurt. Cristofano
  Was stabbed in error by a jealous man,
  Whilst she he loved was sleeping with his rival;
  All in the self-same hour of the same night;
  Which shows that Heaven has special care of me.
  I beg those friends who love me, that they mark
  The day a feast upon their calendars.
  It was the twenty-seventh of December:

Ay, read the letters if you doubt my oath.
(*The assembly appears confused; several of the guests rise*)
FIRST GUEST: Oh, horrible! I will depart—
SECOND GUEST: And I.—
THIRD GUEST: No, stay!
I do believe it is some jest; though faith!
'Tis mocking us somewhat too solemnly.
I think his son has married the Infanta,
Or found a mine of gold in El Dorado.
'Tis but to season some such news; stay, stay!
I see 'tis only raillery by his smile.
CENCI (*filling a bowl of wine, and lifting it up*): Oh, thou bright wine
whose purple splendour leaps
And bubbles gaily in this golden bowl
Under the lamplight, as my spirits do,
To hear the death of my accursed sons!
Could I believe thou wert their mingled blood,
Then would I taste thee like a sacrament,
And pledge with thee the mighty Devil in Hell,
Who, if a father's curses, as men say,
Climb with swift wings after their children's souls,
And drag them from the very throne of Heaven,
Now triumphs in my triumph!—But thou art
Superfluous; I have drunken deep of joy,
And I will taste no other wine to-night.
Here, Andrea! Bear the bowl around.
A GUEST (*rising*): Thou wretch!
Will none among this noble company
Check the abandoned villain?
CAMILLO: For God's sake,
Let me dismiss the guests! You are insane,
Some ill will come of this.
SECOND GUEST: Seize, silence him!
FIRST GUEST: I will!
THIRD GUEST: And I!
CENCI (*addressing those who rise with a threatening gesture*): Who
moves? Who speaks?
(*Turning to the company*)
'tis nothing,

Enjoy yourselves.—Beware! For my revenge
Is as the sealed commission of a king
That kills, and none dare name the murderer.
(The banquet is broken up; several of the guests are departing)
BEATRICE: I do entreat you, go not, noble guests;
What, although tyranny and impious hate
Stand sheltered by a father's hoary hair?
What if 'tis he who clothed us in these limbs
Who tortures them, and triumphs? What, if we,
The desolate and the dead, were his own flesh,
His children and his wife, whom he is bound
To love and shelter? Shall we therefore find
No refuge in this merciless wide world?
O think what deep wrongs must have blotted out
First love, then reverence in a child's prone mind,
Till it thus vanquish shame and fear! O think!
I have borne much, and kissed the sacred hand
Which crushed us to the earth, and thought its stroke
Was perhaps some paternal chastisement!
Have excused much, doubted; and when no doubt
Remained, have sought by patience, love, and tears
To soften him, and when this could not be
I have knelt down through the long sleepless nights
And lifted up to God, the Father of all,
Passionate prayers: and when these were not heard
I have still borne,—until I meet you here,
Princes and kinsmen, at this hideous feast
Given at my brothers' deaths. Two yet remain,
His wife remains and I, whom if ye save not,
Ye may soon share such merriment again
As fathers make over their children's graves.
O Prince Colonna, thou art our near kinsman,
Cardinal, thou art the Pope's chamberlain,
Camillo, thou art chief justiciary,
Take us away!
CENCI (*He has been conversing with* CAMILLO *during the first part of*
BEATRICE's *speech; he hears the conclusion, and now advances*): I hope
my good friends here
Will think of their own daughters—or perhaps

    Of their own throats—before they lend an ear
    To this wild girl.
BEATRICE (*not noticing the words of* CENCI): Dare no one look on me?
    None answer? Can one tyrant overbear
    The sense of many best and wisest men?
    Or is it that I sue not in some form
    Of scrupulous law, that ye deny my suit?
    O God! That I were buried with my brothers!
    And that the flowers of this departed spring
    Were fading on my grave! And that my father
    Were celebrating now one feast for all!
CAMILLO: A bitter wish for one so young and gentle.
    Can we do nothing?
COLONNA: Nothing that I see.
    Count Cenci were a dangerous enemy:
    Yet I would second any one.
A CARDINAL: And I.
CENCI: Retire to your chamber, insolent girl!
BEATRICE: Retire thou, impious man! Ay, hide thyself
    Where never eye can look upon thee more!
    Wouldst thou have honour and obedience
    Who art a torturer? Father, never dream,
    Though thou mayst overbear this company,
    But ill must come of ill.—Frown not on me!
    Haste, hide thyself, lest with avenging looks
    My brothers' ghosts should hunt thee from thy seat!
    Cover thy face from every living eye,
    And start if thou but hear a human step:
    Seek out some dark and silent corner, there,
    Bow thy white head before offended God,
    And we will kneel around, and fervently
    Pray that he pity both ourselves and thee.
CENCI: My friends, I do lament this insane girl
    Has spoilt the mirth of our festivity.
    Good night, farewell; I will not make you longer
    Spectators of our dull domestic quarrels.
    Another time.—
(*Exeunt all but* CENCI *and* BEATRICE)
    My brain is swimming round;

Give me a bowl of wine!
(To BEATRICE)
Thou painted viper!
Beast that thou art! Fair and yet terrible!
I know a charm shall make thee meek and tame,
Now get thee from my sight!
(Exit BEATRICE)
Here, Andrea,
Fill up this goblet with Greek wine. I said
I would not drink this evening; but I must;
For, strange to say, I feel my spirits fail
With thinking what I have decreed to do.—
(Drinking the wine)
Be thou the resolution of quick youth
Within my veins, and manhood's purpose stern,
And age's firm, cold, subtle villainy;
As if thou wert indeed my children's blood
Which I did thirst to drink! The charm works well;
It must be done; it shall be done, I swear!
(Exit)

END OF ACT 1

Act 2

Scene 2.1:
An apartment in the Cenci Palace.
Enter Lucretia *and* Bernardo.
Lucretia: Weep not, my gentle boy; he struck but me
    Who have borne deeper wrongs. In truth, if he
    Had killed me, he had done a kinder deed.
    O God Almighty, do Thou look upon us,
    We have no other friend but only Thee!
    Yet weep not; though I love you as my own,
    I am not your true mother.
Bernardo: Oh, more, more,
    Than ever mother was to any child,
    That have you been to me! Had he not been
    My father, do you think that I should weep!
Lucretia: Alas! Poor boy, what else couldst thou have done?
(*Enter* Beatrice)
Beatrice (*in a hurried voice*): Did he pass this way? Have you seen
    him, brother?
    Ah, no! that is his step upon the stairs;
    'Tis nearer now; his hand is on the door;
    Mother, if I to thee have ever been
    A duteous child, now save me! Thou, great God,
    Whose image upon earth a father is,
    Dost thou indeed abandon me? He comes;
    The door is opening now; I see his face;
    He frowns on others, but he smiles on me,
    Even as he did after the feast last night.
(*Enter a servant*)
    Almighty God, how merciful Thou art!
    'Tis but Orsino's servant.—Well, what news?
Servant: My master bids me say, the Holy Father
    Has sent back your petition thus unopened.
(*Giving a paper*)
    And he demands at what hour 'twere secure
    To visit you again?
Lucretia: At the Ave Mary.

(*Exit servant*)
    So, daughter, our last hope has failed. Ah me!
    How pale you look; you tremble, and you stand
    Wrapped in some fixed and fearful meditation,
    As if one thought were over strong for you:
    Your eyes have a chill glare; O, dearest child!
    Are you gone mad? If not, pray speak to me.
BEATRICE: You see I am not mad: I speak to you.
LUCRETIA: You talked of something that your father did
    After that dreadful feast? Could it be worse
    Than when he smiled, and cried, 'My sons are dead!'
    And every one looked in his neighbour's face
    To see if others were as white as he?
    At the first word he spoke I felt the blood
    Rush to my heart, and fell into a trance;
    And when it passed I sat all weak and wild;
    Whilst you alone stood up, and with strong words
    Checked his unnatural pride; and I could see
    The devil was rebuked that lives in him.
    Until this hour thus you have ever stood
    Between us and your father's moody wrath
    Like a protecting presence; your firm mind
    Has been our only refuge and defence:
    What can have thus subdued it? What can now
    Have given you that cold melancholy look,
    Succeeding to your unaccustomed fear?
BEATRICE: What is it that you say? I was just thinking
    'Twere better not to struggle any more.
    Men, like my father, have been dark and bloody,
    Yet never—Oh! Before worse comes of it
    'Twere wise to die: it ends in that at last.
LUCRETIA: Oh, talk not so, dear child! Tell me at once
    What did your father do or say to you?
    He stayed not after that accursed feast
    One moment in your chamber.—Speak to me.
BERNARDO: Oh, sister, sister, prithee, speak to us!
BEATRICE (*Speaking very slowly, with a forced calmness*): It was one
    word, Mother, one little word;
    One look, one smile.

(*Wildly*)
>Oh! He has trampled me
>Under his feet, and made the blood stream down
>My pallid cheeks. And he has given us all
>Ditch-water, and the fever-stricken flesh
>Of buffaloes, and bade us eat or starve,
>And we have eaten.—He has made me look
>On my beloved Bernardo, when the rust
>Of heavy chains has gangrened his sweet limbs,
>And I have never yet despaired—but now!
>What could I say?

(*Recovering herself*)
>Ah, no! 'tis nothing new.
>The sufferings we all share have made me wild:
>He only struck and cursed me as he passed;
>He said, he looked, he did;—nothing at all
>Beyond his wont, yet it disordered me.
>Alas! I am forgetful of my duty,
>I should preserve my senses for your sake.

LUCRETIA: Nay, Beatrice; have courage, my sweet girl.
>If any one despairs it should be I
>Who loved him once, and now must live with him
>Till God in pity call for him or me.
>For you may, like your sister, find some husband,
>And smile, years hence, with children round your knees;
>Whilst I, then dead, and all this hideous coil
>Shall be remembered only as a dream.

BEATRICE: Talk not to me, dear lady, of a husband.
>Did you not nurse me when my mother died?
>Did you not shield me and that dearest boy?
>And had we any other friend but you
>In infancy, with gentle words and looks,
>To win our father not to murder us?
>And shall I now desert you? May the ghost
>Of my dead Mother plead against my soul
>If I abandon her who filled the place
>She left, with more, even, than a mother's love!

BERNARDO: And I am of my sister's mind. Indeed
>I would not leave you in this wretchedness,

>   Even though the Pope should make me free to live
>   In some blithe place, like others of my age,
>   With sports, and delicate food, and the fresh air.
>   Oh, never think that I will leave you, Mother!
> LUCRETIA: My dear, dear children!
> (*Enter* CENCI, *suddenly*)
> CENCI: What! Beatrice here!
>   Come hither!
> (*She shrinks back, and covers her face*)
>   Nay, hide not your face, 'tis fair;
>   Look up! Why, yesternight you dared to look
>   With disobedient insolence upon me,
>   Bending a stern and an inquiring brow
>   On what I meant; whilst I then sought to hide
>   That which I came to tell you—but in vain.
> BEATRICE (*wildly staggering towards the door*): Oh, that the earth
>   would gape! Hide me, O God!
> CENCI: Then it was I whose inarticulate words
>   Fell from my lips, and who with tottering steps
>   Fled from your presence, as you now from mine.
>   Stay, I command you—from this day and hour
>   Never again, I think, with fearless eye,
>   And brow superior, and unaltered cheek,
>   And that lip made for tenderness or scorn,
>   Shalt thou strike dumb the meanest of mankind;
>   Me least of all. Now get thee to thy chamber!
>   Thou too, loathed image of thy cursed mother,
> (*To* BERNARDO)
>   Thy milky, meek face makes me sick with hate!
> (*Exeunt* BEATRICE *and* BERNARDO)
> (*Aside*)
>   So much has passed between us as must make
>   Me bold, her fearful.—'Tis an awful thing
>   To touch such mischief as I now conceive:
>   So men sit shivering on the dewy bank,
>   And try the chill stream with their feet; once in. . .
>   How the delighted spirit pants for joy!
> LUCRETIA (*advancing timidly towards him*): O husband! Pray forgive
>   poor Beatrice.

    She meant not any ill.
CENCI: Nor you perhaps?
    Nor that young imp, whom you have taught by rote
    Parricide with his alphabet? Nor Giacomo?
    Nor those two most unnatural sons, who stirred
    Enmity up against me with the Pope?
    Whom in one night merciful God cut off:
    Innocent lambs! They thought not any ill.
    You were not here conspiring? You said nothing
    Of how I might be dungeoned as a madman;
    Or be condemned to death for some offence,
    And you would be the witnesses?—This failing,
    How just it were to hire assassins, or
    Put sudden poison in my evening drink?
    Or smother me when overcome by wine?
    Seeing we had no other judge but God,
    And He had sentenced me, and there were none
    But you to be the executioners
    Of His decree enregistered in heaven?
    Oh, no! You said not this?
LUCRETIA: So help me God,
    I never thought the things you charge me with!
CENCI: If you dare to speak that wicked lie again
    I'll kill you. What! It was not by your counsel
    That Beatrice disturbed the feast last night?
    You did not hope to stir some enemies
    Against me, and escape, and laugh to scorn
    What every nerve of you now trembles at?
    You judged that men were bolder than they are;
    Few dare to stand between their grave and me.
LUCRETIA: Look not so dreadfully! By my salvation
    I knew not aught that Beatrice designed;
    Nor do I think she designed any thing
    Until she heard you talk of her dead brothers.
CENCI: Blaspheming liar! You are damned for this!
    But I will take you where you may persuade
    The stones you tread on to deliver you:
    For men shall there be none but those who dare
    All things—not question that which I command.

On Wednesday next I shall set out: you know
That savage rock, the Castle of Petrella:
'Tis safely walled, and moated round about:
Its dungeons underground, and its thick towers
Never told tales; though they have heard and seen
What might make dumb things speak.—Why do you linger?
Make speediest preparation for the journey!
(*Exit* LUCRETIA)
The all-beholding sun yet shines; I hear
A busy stir of men about the streets;
I see the bright sky through the window panes:
It is a garish, broad, and peering day;
Loud, light, suspicious, full of eyes and ears,
And every little corner, nook, and hole
Is penetrated with the insolent light.
Come darkness! Yet, what is the day to me?
And wherefore should I wish for night, who do
A deed which shall confound both night and day?
'Tis she shall grope through a bewildering mist
Of horror: if there be a sun in heaven
She shall not dare to look upon its beams;
Nor feel its warmth. Let her then wish for night;
The act I think shall soon extinguish all
For me: I bear a darker deadlier gloom
Than the earth's shade, or interlunar air,
Or constellations quenched in murkiest cloud,
In which I walk secure and unbeheld
Towards my purpose.—Would that it were done!
(*Exit*)

SCENE 2.2:
A chamber in the Vatican.
Enter CAMILLO *and* GIACOMO, *in conversation.*
CAMILLO: There is an obsolete and doubtful law
By which you might obtain a bare provision
Of food and clothing—
GIACOMO: Nothing more? Alas!
Bare must be the provision which strict law
Awards, and aged, sullen avarice pays.

Why did my father not apprentice me
To some mechanic trade? I should have then
Been trained in no highborn necessities
Which I could meet not by my daily toil.
The eldest son of a rich nobleman
Is heir to all his incapacities;
He has wide wants, and narrow powers. If you,
Cardinal Camillo, were reduced at once
From thrice-driven beds of down, and delicate food,
An hundred servants, and six palaces,
To that which nature doth indeed require?—
CAMILLO: Nay, there is reason in your plea; 'twere hard.
GIACOMO: 'Tis hard for a firm man to bear: but I
Have a dear wife, a lady of high birth,
Whose dowry in ill hour I lent my father
Without a bond or witness to the deed:
And children, who inherit her fine senses,
The fairest creatures in this breathing world;
And she and they reproach me not. Cardinal,
Do you not think the Pope would interpose
And stretch authority beyond the law?
CAMILLO: Though your peculiar case is hard, I know
The Pope will not divert the course of law.
After that impious feast the other night
I spoke with him, and urged him then to check
Your father's cruel hand; he frowned and said,
'Children are disobedient, and they sting
Their fathers' hearts to madness and despair,
Requiting years of care with contumely.
I pity the Count Cenci from my heart;
His outraged love perhaps awakened hate,
And thus he is exasperated to ill.
In the great war between the old and young
I, who have white hairs and a tottering body,
Will keep at least blameless neutrality.'
(*Enter* ORSINO)
You, my good Lord Orsino, heard those words.
ORSINO: What words?
GIACOMO: Alas, repeat them not again!

There then is no redress for me, at least
None but that which I may achieve myself,
Since I am driven to the brink.—But, say,
My innocent sister and my only brother
Are dying underneath my father's eye.
The memorable torturers of this land,
Galeaz Visconti, Borgia, Ezzelin,
Never inflicted on their meanest slave
What these endure; shall they have no protection?
CAMILLO: Why, if they would petition to the Pope
I see not how he could refuse it—yet
He holds it of most dangerous example
In aught to weaken the paternal power,
Being, as 'twere, the shadow of his own.
I pray you now excuse me. I have business
That will not bear delay.
(*Exit* CAMILLO)
GIACOMO: But you, Orsino,
Have the petition: wherefore not present it?
ORSINO: I have presented it, and backed it with
My earnest prayers, and urgent interest;
It was returned unanswered. I doubt not
But that the strange and execrable deeds
Alleged in it—in truth they might well baffle
Any belief—have turned the Pope's displeasure
Upon the accusers from the criminal:
So I should guess from what Camillo said.
GIACOMO: My friend, that palace-walking devil Gold
Has whispered silence to his Holiness:
And we are left, as scorpions ringed with fire.
What should we do but strike ourselves to death?
For he who is our murderous persecutor
Is shielded by a father's holy name,
Or I would—
(*Stops abruptly*)
ORSINO: What? Fear not to speak your thought.
Words are but holy as the deeds they cover:
A priest who has forsworn the God he serves;
A judge who makes Truth weep at his decree;

    A friend who should weave counsel, as I now,
    But as the mantle of some selfish guile;
    A father who is all a tyrant seems,
    Were the profaner for his sacred name.
GIACOMO: Ask me not what I think; the unwilling brain
    Feigns often what it would not; and we trust
    Imagination with such fantasies
    As the tongue dares not fashion into words,
    Which have no words, their horror makes them dim
    To the mind's eye.—My heart denies itself
    To think what you demand.
ORSINO: But a friend's bosom
    Is as the inmost cave of our own mind
    Where we sit shut from the wide gaze of day,
    And from the all-communicating air.
    You look what I suspected—
GIACOMO: Spare me now!
    I am as one lost in a midnight wood,
    Who dares not ask some harmless passenger
    The path across the wilderness, lest he,
    As my thoughts are, should be—a murderer.
    I know you are my friend, and all I dare
    Speak to my soul that will I trust with thee.
    But now my heart is heavy, and would take
    Lone counsel from a night of sleepless care.
    Pardon me, that I say farewell—farewell!
    I would that to my own suspected self
    I could address a word so full of peace.
ORSINO: Farewell!—Be your thoughts better or more bold.
(*Exit* GIACOMO)
    I had disposed the Cardinal Camillo
    To feed his hope with cold encouragement:
    It fortunately serves my close designs
    That 'tis a trick of this same family
    To analyse their own and other minds.
    Such self-anatomy shall teach the will
    Dangerous secrets: for it tempts our powers,
    Knowing what must be thought, and may be done.
    Into the depth of darkest purposes:

So Cenci fell into the pit; even I,
Since Beatrice unveiled me to myself,
And made me shrink from what I cannot shun,
Show a poor figure to my own esteem,
To which I grow half reconciled. I'll do
As little mischief as I can; that thought
Shall fee the accuser conscience.

(*After a pause*)

Now what harm
If Cenci should be murdered?—Yet, if murdered,
Wherefore by me? And what if I could take
The profit, yet omit the sin and peril
In such an action? Of all earthly things
I fear a man whose blows outspeed his words
And such is Cenci: and while Cenci lives
His daughter's dowry were a secret grave
If a priest wins her.—Oh, fair Beatrice!
Would that I loved thee not, or loving thee,
Could but despise danger and gold and all
That frowns between my wish and its effect.
Or smiles beyond it! There is no escape. . .
Her bright form kneels beside me at the altar,
And follows me to the resort of men,
And fills my slumber with tumultuous dreams,
So when I wake my blood seems liquid fire;
And if I strike my damp and dizzy head
My hot palm scorches it: her very name,
But spoken by a stranger, makes my heart
Sicken and pant; and thus unprofitably
I clasp the phantom of unfelt delights
Till weak imagination half possesses
The self-created shadow. Yet much longer
Will I not nurse this life of feverous hours:
From the unravelled hopes of Giacomo
I must work out my own dear purposes.
I see, as from a tower, the end of all:
Her father dead; her brother bound to me
By a dark secret, surer than the grave;
Her mother scared and unexpostulating

From the dread manner of her wish achieved;
And she!—Once more take courage, my faint heart;
What dares a friendless maiden matched with thee?
I have such foresight as assures success:
Some unbeheld divinity doth ever,
When dread events are near, stir up men's minds
To black suggestions; and he prospers best,
Not who becomes the instrument of ill,
But who can flatter the dark spirit, that makes
Its empire and its prey of other hearts
Till it become his slave... as I will do.
(*Exit*)

END OF ACT 2

Act 3

Scene 3.1:
An apartment in the Cenci Palace.
Lucretia, *to her enter* Beatrice.
Beatrice (*she enters staggering and speaks wildly*): Reach me that
    handkerchief!—My brain is hurt;
    My eyes are full of blood; just wipe them for me. . .
    I see but indistinctly. . .
Lucretia: My sweet child,
    You have no wound; 'tis only a cold dew
    That starts from your dear brow.—Alas! Alas!
    What has befallen?
Beatrice: How comes this hair undone?
    Its wandering strings must be what blind me so,
    And yet I tied it fast.—Oh, horrible!
    The pavement sinks under my feet! The walls
    Spin round! I see a woman weeping there,
    And standing calm and motionless, whilst I
    Slide giddily as the world reels. . . My God!
    The beautiful blue heaven is flecked with blood!
    The sunshine on the floor is black! The air
    Is changed to vapours such as the dead breathe
    In charnel pits! Pah! I am choked! There creeps
    A clinging, black, contaminating mist
    About me. . .'tis substantial, heavy, thick,
    I cannot pluck it from me, for it glues
    My fingers and my limbs to one another,
    And eats into my sinews, and dissolves
    My flesh to a pollution, poisoning
    The subtle, pure, and inmost spirit of life!
    My God! I never knew what the mad felt
    Before; for I am mad beyond all doubt!
(*More wildly*)
    No, I am dead! These putrefying limbs
    Shut round and sepulchre the panting soul
    Which would burst forth into the wandering air!
(*A pause*)

What hideous thought was that I had even now?
'Tis gone; and yet its burthen remains here
O'er these dull eyes. . . upon this weary heart!
O, world! O, life! O, day! O, misery!
LUCRETIA: What ails thee, my poor child? She answers not:
Her spirit apprehends the sense of pain,
But not its cause; suffering has dried away
The source from which it sprung. . .
BEATRICE (*franticly*): Like Parricide. . .
Misery has killed its father: yet its father
Never like mine. . . O, God! What thing am I?
LUCRETIA: My dearest child, what has your father done?
BEATRICE (*doubtfully*): Who art thou, questioner? I have no father.
(*Aside*)
She is the madhouse nurse who tends on me,
It is a piteous office.
(*To* LUCRETIA, *in a slow, subdued voice*)
Do you know
I thought I was that wretched Beatrice
Men speak of, whom her father sometimes hales
From hall to hall by the entangled hair;
At others, pens up naked in damp cells
Where scaly reptiles crawl, and starves her there,
Till she will eat strange flesh. This woful story
So did I overact in my sick dreams,
That I imagined. . . no, it cannot be!
Horrible things have been in this wide world,
Prodigious mixtures, and confusions strange
Of good and ill; and worse have been conceived
Than ever there was found a heart to do.
But never fancy imaged such a deed
As. . .
(*Pauses, suddenly recollecting herself*)
Who art thou? Swear to me, ere I die
With fearful expectation, that indeed
Thou art not what thou seemest. . . Mother!
LUCRETIA: Oh!
My sweet child, know you. . .
BEATRICE: Yet speak it not:

For then if this be truth, that other too
Must be a truth, a firm enduring truth,
Linked with each lasting circumstance of life,
Never to change, never to pass away.
Why so it is. This is the Cenci Palace;
Thou art Lucretia; I am Beatrice.
I have talked some wild words, but will no more.
Mother, come near me: from this point of time,
I am...

(*Her voice dies away faintly*)

LUCRETIA: Alas! What has befallen thee, child?
   What has thy father done?

BEATRICE: What have I done?
   Am I not innocent? Is it my crime
   That one with white hair, and imperious brow,
   Who tortured me from my forgotten years,
   As parents only dare, should call himself
   My father, yet should be!—Oh, what am I?
   What name, what place, what memory shall be mine?
   What retrospects, outliving even despair?

LUCRETIA: He is a violent tyrant, surely, child:
   We know that death alone can make us free;
   His death or ours. But what can he have done
   Of deadlier outrage or worse injury?
   Thou art unlike thyself; thine eyes shoot forth
   A wandering and strange spirit. Speak to me,
   Unlock those pallid hands whose fingers twine
   With one another.

BEATRICE: 'Tis the restless life
   Tortured within them. If I try to speak,
   I shall go mad. Ay, something must be done;
   What, yet I know not... something which shall make
   The thing that I have suffered but a shadow
   In the dread lightning which avenges it;
   Brief, rapid, irreversible, destroying
   The consequence of what it cannot cure.
   Some such thing is to be endured or done:
   When I know what, I shall be still and calm,
   And never anything will move me more.

But now!—O blood, which art my father's blood,
Circling through these contaminated veins,
If thou, poured forth on the polluted earth,
Could wash away the crime, and punishment
By which I suffer... no, that cannot be!
Many might doubt there were a God above
Who sees and permits evil, and so die:
That faith no agony shall obscure in me.
LUCRETIA: It must indeed have been some bitter wrong;
Yet what, I dare not guess. Oh, my lost child,
Hide not in proud impenetrable grief
Thy sufferings from my fear.
BEATRICE: I hide them not.
What are the words which yon would have me speak?
I, who can feign no image in my mind
Of that which has transformed me: I, whose thought
Is like a ghost shrouded and folded up
In its own formless horror: of all words,
That minister to mortal intercourse,
Which wouldst thou hear? For there is none to tell
My misery: if another ever knew
Aught like to it, she died as I will die,
And left it, as I must, without a name.
Death, Death! Our law and our religion call thee
A punishment and a reward... Oh, which
Have I deserved?
LUCRETIA: The peace of innocence;
Till in your season you be called to heaven.
Whate'er you may have suffered, you have done
No evil. Death must be the punishment
Of crime, or the reward of trampling down
The thorns which God has strewed upon the path
Which leads to immortality.
BEATRICE: Ay, death...
The punishment of crime. I pray thee, God,
Let me not be bewildered while I judge.
If I must live day after day, and keep
These limbs, the unworthy temple of Thy spirit,
As a foul den from which what Thou abhorrest

May mock Thee, unavenged... it shall not be!
Self-murder... no, that might be no escape,
For Thy decree yawns like a Hell between
Our will and it:—O! In this mortal world
There is no vindication and no law
Which can adjudge and execute the doom
Of that through which I suffer.

(*Enter* ORSINO)
(*She approaches him solemnly*)

Welcome, Friend!
I have to tell you that, since last we met,
I have endured a wrong so great and strange,
That neither life nor death can give me rest.
Ask me not what it is, for there are deeds
Which have no form, sufferings which have no tongue.

ORSINO: And what is he who has thus injured you?
BEATRICE: The man they call my father: a dread name.
ORSINO: It cannot be...
BEATRICE: What it can be, or not,
Forbear to think. It is, and it has been;
Advise me how it shall not be again.
I thought to die; but a religious awe
Restrains me, and the dread lest death itself
Might be no refuge from the consciousness
Of what is yet unexpiated. Oh, speak!
ORSINO: Accuse him of the deed, and let the law
Avenge thee.
BEATRICE: Oh, ice-hearted counsellor!
If I could find a word that might make known
The crime of my destroyer; and that done,
My tongue should like a knife tear out the secret
Which cankers my heart's core; ay, lay all bare,
So that my unpolluted fame should be
With vilest gossips a stale mouthed story;
A mock, a byword, an astonishment:—
If this were done, which never shall be done,
Think of the offender's gold, his dreaded hate,
And the strange horror of the accuser's tale,
Baffling belief, and overpowering speech;

Scarce whispered, unimaginable, wrapped
In hideous hints... Oh, most assured redress!
ORSINO: You will endure it then?
BEATRICE: Endure!—Orsino,
It seems your counsel is small profit.
(*Turns from him, and speaks half to herself*)
Ay,
All must be suddenly resolved and done.
What is this undistinguishable mist
Of thoughts, which rise, like shadow after shadow,
Darkening each other?
ORSINO: Should the offender live?
Triumph in his misdeed? and make, by use,
His crime, whate'er it is, dreadful no doubt,
Thine element; until thou mayest become
Utterly lost; subdued even to the hue
Of that which thou permittest?
BEATRICE (*to herself*): Mighty death!
Thou double-visaged shadow! Only judge!
Rightfullest arbiter!
(*She retires, absorbed in thought*)
LUCRETIA: If the lightning
Of God has e'er descended to avenge...
ORSINO: Blaspheme not! His high Providence commits
Its glory on this earth, and their own wrongs
Into the hands of men; if they neglect
To punish crime...
LUCRETIA: But if one, like this wretch,
Should mock, with gold, opinion, law, and power?
If there be no appeal to that which makes
The guiltiest tremble? If because our wrongs,
For that they are unnatural, strange and monstrous,
Exceed all measure of belief? O God!
If, for the very reasons which should make
Redress most swift and sure, our injurer triumphs?
And we, the victims, bear worse punishment
Than that appointed for their torturer?
ORSINO: Think not
But that there is redress where there is wrong,

    So we be bold enough to seize it.
LUCRETIA: How?
    If there were any way to make all sure,
    I know not. . . but I think it might be good
    To. . .
ORSINO: Why, his late outrage to Beatrice;
    For it is such, as I but faintly guess,
    As makes remorse dishonour, and leaves her
    Only one duty, how she may avenge:
    You, but one refuge from ills ill endured;
    Me, but one counsel. . .
LUCRETIA: For we cannot hope
    That aid, or retribution, or resource
    Will arise thence, where every other one
    Might find them with less need.
(BEATRICE *advances*)
ORSINO: Then. . .
BEATRICE: Peace, Orsino!
    And, honoured Lady, while I speak, I pray,
    That you put off, as garments overworn,
    Forbearance and respect, remorse and fear,
    And all the fit restraints of daily life,
    Which have been borne from childhood, but which now
    Would be a mockery to my holier plea.
    As I have said, I have endured a wrong,
    Which, though it be expressionless, is such
    As asks atonement; both for what is past,
    And lest I be reserved, day after day,
    To load with crimes an overburthened soul,
    And be. . . what ye can dream not. I have prayed
    To God, and I have talked with my own heart,
    And have unravelled my entangled will,
    And have at length determined what is right.
    Art thou my friend, Orsino? False or true?
    Pledge thy salvation ere I speak.
ORSINO: I swear
    To dedicate my cunning, and my strength,
    My silence, and whatever else is mine,
    To thy commands.

LUCRETIA: You think we should devise
   His death?
BEATRICE: And execute what is devised,
   And suddenly. We must be brief and bold.
ORSINO: And yet most cautious.
LUCRETIA: For the jealous laws
   Would punish us with death and infamy
   For that which it became themselves to do.
BEATRICE: Be cautious as ye may, but prompt. Orsino,
   What are the means?
ORSINO: I know two dull, fierce outlaws,
   Who think man's spirit as a worm's, and they
   Would trample out, for any slight caprice,
   The meanest or the noblest life. This mood
   Is marketable here in Rome. They sell
   What we now want.
LUCRETIA: To-morrow before dawn,
   Cenci will take us to that lonely rock,
   Petrella, in the Apulian Apennines.
   If he arrive there. . .
BEATRICE: He must not arrive.
ORSINO: Will it be dark before you reach the tower?
LUCRETIA: The sun will scarce be set.
BEATRICE: But I remember
   Two miles on this side of the fort, the road
   Crosses a deep ravine; 'tis rough and narrow,
   And winds with short turns down the precipice;
   And in its depth there is a mighty rock,
   Which has, from unimaginable years,
   Sustained itself with terror and with toil
   Over a gulf, and with the agony
   With which it clings seems slowly coming down;
   Even as a wretched soul hour after hour,
   Clings to the mass of life; yet, clinging, leans;
   And leaning, makes more dark the dread abyss
   In which it fears to fall: beneath this crag
   Huge as despair, as if in weariness,
   The melancholy mountain yawns. . . below,
   You hear but see not an impetuous torrent

　　　　Raging among the caverns, and a bridge
　　　　Crosses the chasm; and high above there grow,
　　　　With intersecting trunks, from crag to crag,
　　　　Cedars, and yews, and pines; whose tangled hair
　　　　Is matted in one solid roof of shade
　　　　By the dark ivy's twine. At noonday here
　　　　'Tis twilight, and at sunset blackest night.
ORSINO: Before you reach that bridge make some excuse
　　　　For spurring on your mules, or loitering
　　　　Until...
BEATRICE: What sound is that?
LUCRETIA: Hark! No, it cannot be a servant's step
　　　　It must be Cenci, unexpectedly
　　　　Returned... Make some excuse for being here.
BEATRICE (*to* ORSINO *as she goes out*): That step we hear approach must never pass
　　　　The bridge of which we spoke.
(*Exeunt* LUCRETIA *and* BEATRICE)
ORSINO: What shall I do?
　　　　Cenci must find me here, and I must bear
　　　　The imperious inquisition of his looks
　　　　As to what brought me hither: let me mask
　　　　Mine own in some inane and vacant smile.
(*Enter* GIACOMO, *in a hurried manner*)
　　　　How! Have you ventured hither? Know you then
　　　　That Cenci is from home?
GIACOMO: I sought him here;
　　　　And now must wait till he returns.
ORSINO: Great God!
　　　　Weigh you the danger of this rashness?
GIACOMO: Ay!
　　　　Does my destroyer know his danger? We
　　　　Are now no more, as once, parent and child,
　　　　But man to man; the oppressor to the oppressed;
　　　　The slanderer to the slandered; foe to foe:
　　　　He has cast Nature off, which was his shield,
　　　　And Nature casts him off, who is her shame;
　　　　And I spurn both. Is it a father's throat
　　　　Which I will shake, and say, I ask not gold;

I ask not happy years; nor memories
Of tranquil childhood; nor home-sheltered love;
Though all these hast thou torn from me, and more;
But only my fair fame; only one hoard
Of peace, which I thought hidden from thy hate,
Under the penury heaped on me by thee,
Or I will... God can understand and pardon,
Why should I speak with man?

ORSINO: Be calm, dear friend.

GIACOMO: Well, I will calmly tell you what he did.
This old Francesco Cenci, as you know,
Borrowed the dowry of my wife from me,
And then denied the loan; and left me so
In poverty, the which I sought to mend
By holding a poor office in the state.
It had been promised to me, and already
I bought new clothing for my ragged babes,
And my wife smiled; and my heart knew repose.
When Cenci's intercession, as I found,
Conferred this office on a wretch, whom thus
He paid for vilest service. I returned
With this ill news, and we sate sad together
Solacing our despondency with tears
Of such affection and unbroken faith
As temper life's worst bitterness; when he,
As he is wont, came to upbraid and curse,
Mocking our poverty, and telling us
Such was God's scourge for disobedient sons.
And then, that I might strike him dumb with shame,
I spoke of my wife's dowry; but he coined
A brief yet specious tale, how I had wasted
The sum in secret riot; and he saw
My wife was touched, and he went smiling forth.
And when I knew the impression he had made,
And felt my wife insult with silent scorn
My ardent truth, and look averse and cold,
I went forth too: but soon returned again;
Yet not so soon but that my wife had taught
My children her harsh thoughts, and they all cried,

'Give us clothes, father! Give us better food!
What you in one night squander were enough
For months!' I looked, and saw that home was hell.
And to that hell will I return no more
Until mine enemy has rendered up
Atonement, or, as he gave life to me
I will, reversing Nature's law. . .
ORSINO: Trust me,
   The compensation which thou seekest here
   Will be denied.
GIACOMO: Then. . . Are you not my friend?
   Did you not hint at the alternative,
   Upon the brink of which you see I stand,
   The other day when we conversed together?
   My wrongs were then less. That word parricide,
   Although I am resolved, haunts me like fear.
ORSINO: It must be fear itself, for the bare word
   Is hollow mockery. Mark, how wisest God
   Draws to one point the threads of a just doom,
   So sanctifying it: what you devise
   Is, as it were, accomplished.
GIACOMO: Is he dead?
ORSINO: His grave is ready. Know that since we met
   Cenci has done an outrage to his daughter.
GIACOMO: What outrage?
ORSINO: That she speaks not, but you may
   Conceive such half conjectures as I do,
   From her fixed paleness, and the lofty grief
   Of her stern brow bent on the idle air,
   And her severe unmodulated voice,
   Drowning both tenderness and dread; and last
   From this; that whilst her step-mother and I,
   Bewildered in our horror, talked together
   With obscure hints; both self-misunderstood
   And darkly guessing, stumbling, in our talk,
   Over the truth, and yet to its revenge,
   She interrupted us, and with a look
   Which told, before she spoke it, he must die: . . .
GIACOMO: It is enough. My doubts are well appeased;

>   There is a higher reason for the act
>   Than mine; there is a holier judge than me,
>   A more unblamed avenger. Beatrice,
>   Who in the gentleness of thy sweet youth
>   Hast never trodden on a worm, or bruised
>   A living flower, but thou hast pitied it
>   With needless tears! Fair sister, thou in whom
>   Men wondered how such loveliness and wisdom
>   Did not destroy each other! Is there made
>   Ravage of thee? O, heart, I ask no more
>   Justification! Shall I wait, Orsino,
>   Till he return, and stab him at the door?
> ORSINO: Not so; some accident might interpose
>   To rescue him from what is now most sure;
>   And you are unprovided where to fly,
>   How to excuse or to conceal. Nay, listen:
>   All is contrived; success is so assured
>   That...
>
> (*Enter* BEATRICE)
>
> BEATRICE: 'Tis my brother's voice! You know me not?
> GIACOMO: My sister, my lost sister!
> BEATRICE: Lost indeed!
>   I see Orsino has talked with you, and
>   That you conjecture things too horrible
>   To speak, yet far less than the truth. Now, stay not,
>   He might return: yet kiss me; I shall know
>   That then thou hast consented to his death.
>   Farewell, farewell! Let piety to God,
>   Brotherly love, justice and clemency,
>   And all things that make tender hardest hearts
>   Make thine hard, brother. Answer not... farewell.
>
> (*Exeunt severally*)

SCENE 3.2:
A mean apartment in GIACOMO'*s house.*
GIACOMO *alone.*
GIACOMO: 'Tis midnight, and Orsino comes not yet.
(*Thunder, and the sound of a storm*)
>   What! can the everlasting elements

    Feel with a worm like man? If so, the shaft
    Of mercy-winged lightning would not fall
    On stones and trees. My wife and children sleep:
    They are now living in unmeaning dreams:
    But I must wake, still doubting if that deed
    Be just which is most necessary. O,
    Thou unreplenished lamp! whose narrow fire
    Is shaken by the wind, and on whose edge
    Devouring darkness hovers! Thou small flame,
    Which, as a dying pulse rises and falls,
    Still flickerest up and down, how very soon,
    Did I not feed thee, wouldst thou fail and be
    As thou hadst never been! So wastes and sinks
    Even now, perhaps, the life that kindled mine:
    But that no power can fill with vital oil
    That broken lamp of flesh. Ha! 'tis the blood
    Which fed these veins that ebbs till all is cold:
    It is the form that moulded mine that sinks
    Into the white and yellow spasms of death:
    It is the soul by which mine was arrayed
    In God's immortal likeness which now stands
    Naked before Heaven's judgement seat!
(*A bell strikes*)
    One! Two!
    The hours crawl on; and, when my hairs are white,
    My son will then perhaps be waiting thus,
    Tortured between just hate and vain remorse;
    Chiding the tardy messenger of news
    Like those which I expect. I almost wish
    He be not dead, although my wrongs are great;
    Yet. . .'tis Orsino's step. . .
(*Enter* Orsino)
    Speak!
Orsino: I am come
    To say he has escaped.
Giacomo: Escaped!
Orsino: And safe
    Within Petrella. He passed by the spot
    Appointed for the deed an hour too soon.

GIACOMO: Are we the fools of such contingencies?
    And do we waste in blind misgivings thus
    The hours when we should act? Then wind and thunder,
    Which seemed to howl his knell, is the loud laughter
    With which Heaven mocks our weakness! I henceforth
    Will ne'er repent of aught designed or done
    But my repentance.
ORSINO: See, the lamp is out.
GIACOMO: If no remorse is ours when the dim air
    Has drank this innocent flame, why should we quail
    When Cenci's life, that light by which ill spirits
    See the worst deeds they prompt, shall sink for ever?
    No, I am hardened.
ORSINO: Why, what need of this?
    Who feared the pale intrusion of remorse
    In a just deed? Although our first plan failed,
    Doubt not but he will soon be laid to rest.
    But light the lamp; let us not talk i' the dark.
GIACOMO (*lighting the lamp*): And yet once quenched I cannot thus relume
    My father's life: do you not think his ghost
    Might plead that argument with God?
ORSINO: Once gone
    You cannot now recall your sister's peace;
    Your own extinguished years of youth and hope;
    Nor your wife's bitter words; nor all the taunts
    Which, from the prosperous, weak misfortune takes;
    Nor your dead mother; nor. . .
GIACOMO: O, speak no more!
    I am resolved, although this very hand
    Must quench the life that animated it.
ORSINO: There is no need of that. Listen: you know
    Olimpio, the castellan of Petrella
    In old Colonna's time; him whom your father
    Degraded from his post? And Marzio,
    That desperate wretch, whom he deprived last year
    Of a reward of blood, well earned and due?
GIACOMO: I knew Olimpio; and they say he hated
    Old Cenci so, that in his silent rage

>   His lips grew white only to see him pass.
>   Of Marzio I know nothing.
>
> ORSINO: Marzio's hate
>   Matches Olimpio's. I have sent these men,
>   But in your name, and as at your request,
>   To talk with Beatrice and Lucretia.
>
> GIACOMO: Only to talk?
>
> ORSINO: The moments which even now
>   Pass onward to to-morrow's midnight hour
>   May memorize their flight with death: ere then
>   They must have talked, and may perhaps have done,
>   And made an end. . .
>
> GIACOMO: Listen! What sound is that?
>
> ORSINO: The house-dog moans, and the beams crack: nought else.
>
> GIACOMO: It is my wife complaining in her sleep:
>   I doubt not she is saying bitter things
>   Of me; and all my children round her dreaming
>   That I deny them sustenance.
>
> ORSINO: Whilst he
>   Who truly took it from them, and who fills
>   Their hungry rest with bitterness, now sleeps
>   Lapped in bad pleasures, and triumphantly
>   Mocks thee in visions of successful hate
>   Too like the truth of day.
>
> GIACOMO: If e'er he wakes
>   Again, I will not trust to hireling hands. . .
>
> ORSINO: Why, that were well. I must be gone; good-night.
>   When next we meet—may all be done!
>
> GIACOMO: And all
>   Forgotten: Oh, that I had never been!
>
> (*Exeunt*)
>
>   END OF ACT 3

Act 4

Scene 4.1:
An apartment in the Castle of Petrella.
Enter CENCI.
CENCI: She comes not; yet I left her even now
　　Vanquished and faint. She knows the penalty
　　Of her delay: yet what if threats are vain?
　　Am I not now within Petrella's moat?
　　Or fear I still the eyes and ears of Rome?
　　Might I not drag her by the golden hair?
　　Stamp on her? keep her sleepless till her brain
　　Be overworn? Tame her with chains and famine?
　　Less would suffice. Yet so to leave undone
　　What I most seek! No, 'tis her stubborn will
　　Which by its own consent shall stoop as low
　　As that which drags it down.
(*Enter* LUCRETIA)
　　Thou loathed wretch!
　　Hide thee from my abhorrence: fly, begone!
　　Yet stay! Bid Beatrice come hither.
LUCRETIA: Oh,
　　Husband! I pray, for thine own wretched sake
　　Heed what thou dost. A man who walks like thee
　　Through crimes, and through the danger of his crimes,
　　Each hour may stumble o'er a sudden grave.
　　And thou art old; thy hairs are hoary gray;
　　As thou wouldst save thyself from death and hell,
　　Pity thy daughter; give her to some friend
　　In marriage: so that she may tempt thee not
　　To hatred, or worse thoughts, if worse there be.
CENCI: What! like her sister who has found a home
　　To mock my hate from with prosperity?
　　Strange ruin shall destroy both her and thee
　　And all that yet remain. My death may be
　　Rapid, her destiny outspeeds it. Go,
　　Bid her come hither, and before my mood
　　Be changed, lest I should drag her by the hair.

LUCRETIA: She sent me to thee, husband. At thy presence
    She fell, as thou dost know, into a trance;
    And in that trance she heard a voice which said,
    'Cenci must die! Let him confess himself!
    Even now the accusing Angel waits to hear
    If God, to punish his enormous crimes,
    Harden his dying heart!'
CENCI: Why—such things are. . .
    No doubt divine revealings may be made.
    'Tis plain I have been favoured from above,
    For when I cursed my sons they died.—Ay. . . so. . .
    As to the right or wrong, that's talk. . . repentance. . .
    Repentance is an easy moment's work
    And more depends on God than me. Well. . . well. . .
    I must give up the greater point, which was
    To poison and corrupt her soul.
(*A pause,* LUCRETIA *approaches anxiously, and then shrinks back as he speaks*)
    One, two;
    Ay. . . Rocco and Cristofano my curse
    Strangled: and Giacomo, I think, will find
    Life a worse Hell than that beyond the grave:
    Beatrice shall, if there be skill in hate,
    Die in despair, blaspheming: to Bernardo,
    He is so innocent, I will bequeath
    The memory of these deeds, and make his youth
    The sepulchre of hope, where evil thoughts
    Shall grow like weeds on a neglected tomb.
    When all is done, out in the wide Campagna,
    I will pile up my silver and my gold;
    My costly robes, paintings, and tapestries;
    My parchments and all records of my wealth,
    And make a bonfire in my joy, and leave
    Of my possessions nothing but my name;
    Which shall be an inheritance to strip
    Its wearer bare as infamy. That done,
    My soul, which is a scourge, will I resign
    Into the hands of him who wielded it;
    Be it for its own punishment or theirs,

He will not ask it of me till the lash
Be broken in its last and deepest wound;
Until its hate be all inflicted. Yet,
Lest death outspeed my purpose, let me make
Short work and sure...

(*Going*)

LUCRETIA (*stops him*): Oh, stay! It was a feint:
She had no vision, and she heard no voice.
I said it but to awe thee.

CENCI: That is well.
Vile palterer with the sacred truth of God,
Be thy soul choked with that blaspheming lie!
For Beatrice worse terrors are in store
To bend her to my will.

LUCRETIA: Oh! to what will?
What cruel sufferings more than she has known
Canst thou inflict?

CENCI: Andrea! Go call my daughter,
And if she comes not tell her that I come.
What sufferings? I will drag her, step by step,
Through infamies unheard of among men:
She shall stand shelterless in the broad noon
Of public scorn, for acts blazoned abroad,
One among which shall be... What? Canst thou guess?
She shall become (for what she most abhors
Shall have a fascination to entrap
Her loathing will) to her own conscious self
All she appears to others; and when dead,
As she shall die unshrived and unforgiven,
A rebel to her father and her God,
Her corpse shall be abandoned to the hounds;
Her name shall be the terror of the earth;
Her spirit shall approach the throne of God
Plague-spotted with my curses. I will make
Body and soul a monstrous lump of ruin.

(*Enter* ANDREA)

ANDREA: The Lady Beatrice...

CENCI: Speak, pale slave! What
Said she?

ANDREA: My Lord, 'twas what she looked; she said:
  'Go tell my father that I see the gulf
  Of Hell between us two, which he may pass,
  I will not.'
(*Exit* ANDREA)
CENCI: Go thou quick, Lucretia,
  Tell her to come; yet let her understand
  Her coming is consent: and say, moreover,
  That if she come not I will curse her.
(*Exit* LUCRETIA)
  Ha!
  With what but with a father's curse doth God
  Panic-strike armed victory, and make pale
  Cities in their prosperity? The world's Father
  Must grant a parent's prayer against his child,
  Be he who asks even what men call me.
  Will not the deaths of her rebellious brothers
  Awe her before I speak? For I on them
  Did imprecate quick ruin, and it came.
(*Enter* LUCRETIA)
  Well; what? Speak, wretch!
LUCRETIA: She said, 'I cannot come;
  Go tell my father that I see a torrent
  Of his own blood raging between us.'
CENCI (*kneeling*): God,
  Hear me! If this most specious mass of flesh,
  Which Thou hast made my daughter; this my blood,
  This particle of my divided being;
  Or rather, this my bane and my disease,
  Whose sight infects and poisons me; this devil
  Which sprung from me as from a hell, was meant
  To aught good use; if her bright loveliness
  Was kindled to illumine this dark world;
  If nursed by Thy selectest dew of love
  Such virtues blossom in her as should make
  The peace of life, I pray Thee for my sake,
  As Thou the common God and Father art
  Of her, and me, and all; reverse that doom!
  Earth, in the name of God, let her food be

    Poison, until she be encrusted round
    With leprous stains! Heaven, rain upon her head
    The blistering drops of the Maremma's dew,
    Till she be speckled like a toad; parch up
    Those love-enkindled lips, warp those fine limbs
    To loathed lameness! All-beholding sun,
    Strike in thine envy those life-darting eyes
    With thine own blinding beams!
LUCRETIA: Peace! Peace!
    For thine own sake unsay those dreadful words.
    When high God grants He punishes such prayers.
CENCI (*leaping up, and throwing his right hand towards heaven*): He
    does his will, I mine! This in addition,
    That if she have a child...
LUCRETIA: Horrible thought!
CENCI: That if she ever have a child; and thou,
    Quick Nature! I adjure thee by thy God,
    That thou be fruitful in her, and increase
    And multiply, fulfilling his command,
    And my deep imprecation! May it be
    A hideous likeness of herself, that as
    From a distorting mirror, she may see
    Her image mixed with what she most abhors,
    Smiling upon her from her nursing breast.
    And that the child may from its infancy
    Grow, day by day, more wicked and deformed,
    Turning her mother's love to misery:
    And that both she and it may live until
    It shall repay her care and pain with hate,
    Or what may else be more unnatural.
    So he may hunt her through the clamorous scoffs
    Of the loud world to a dishonoured grave.
    Shall I revoke this curse? Go, bid her come,
    Before my words are chronicled in Heaven.
(*Exit* LUCRETIA)
    I do not feel as if I were a man,
    But like a fiend appointed to chastise
    The offences of some unremembered world.
    My blood is running up and down my veins;

A fearful pleasure makes it prick and tingle:
I feel a giddy sickness of strange awe;
My heart is beating with an expectation
Of horrid joy.

(*Enter* LUCRETIA)

What? Speak!

LUCRETIA: She bids thee curse;
And if thy curses, as they cannot do,
Could kill her soul...

CENCI: She would not come. 'Tis well,
I can do both; first take what I demand,
And then extort concession. To thy chamber!
Fly ere I spurn thee; and beware this night
That thou cross not my footsteps. It were safer
To come between the tiger and his prey.

(*Exit* LUCRETIA)

It must be late; mine eyes grow weary dim
With unaccustomed heaviness of sleep.
Conscience! Oh, thou most insolent of lies!
They say that sleep, that healing dew of Heaven,
Steeps not in balm the foldings of the brain
Which thinks thee an impostor. I will go
First to belie thee with an hour of rest,
Which will be deep and calm, I feel: and then...
O, multitudinous Hell, the fiends will shake
Thine arches with the laughter of their joy!
There shall be lamentation heard in Heaven
As o'er an angel fallen; and upon Earth
All good shall droop and sicken, and ill things
Shall with a spirit of unnatural life,
Stir and be quickened... even as I am now.

(*Exit*)

SCENE 4.2:
Before the Castle of Petrella.
Enter BEATRICE *and* LUCRETIA *above on the ramparts.*
BEATRICE: They come not yet.
LUCRETIA: 'Tis scarce midnight.
BEATRICE: How slow

Behind the course of thought, even sick with speed,
   Lags leaden-footed time!
LUCRETIA: The minutes pass...
   If he should wake before the deed is done?
BEATRICE: O, mother! He must never wake again.
   What thou hast said persuades me that our act
   Will but dislodge a spirit of deep hell
   Out of a human form.
LUCRETIA: 'Tis true he spoke
   Of death and judgement with strange confidence
   For one so wicked; as a man believing
   In God, yet recking not of good or ill.
   And yet to die without confession!...
BEATRICE: Oh!
   Believe that Heaven is merciful and just,
   And will not add our dread necessity
   To the amount of his offences.
(*Enter* OLIMPIO *and* MARZIO *below*)
LUCRETIA: See,
   They come.
BEATRICE: All mortal things must hasten thus
   To their dark end. Let us go down.
(*Exeunt* LUCRETIA *and* BEATRICE *from above*)
OLIMPIO: How feel you to this work?
MARZIO: As one who thinks
   A thousand crowns excellent market price
   For an old murderer's life. Your cheeks are pale.
OLIMPIO: It is the white reflection of your own,
   Which you call pale.
MARZIO: Is that their natural hue?
OLIMPIO: Or 'tis my hate and the deferred desire
   To wreak it, which extinguishes their blood.
MARZIO: You are inclined then to this business?
OLIMPIO: Ay,
   If one should bribe me with a thousand crowns
   To kill a serpent which had stung my child,
   I could not be more willing.
(*Enter* BEATRICE *and* LUCRETIA *below*)
   Noble ladies!

BEATRICE: Are ye resolved?
OLIMPIO: Is he asleep?
MARZIO: Is all
    Quiet?
LUCRETIA: I mixed an opiate with his drink:
    He sleeps so soundly...
BEATRICE: That his death will be
    But as a change of sin-chastising dreams,
    A dark continuance of the Hell within him,
    Which God extinguish! But ye are resolved?
    Ye know it is a high and holy deed?
OLIMPIO: We are resolved.
MARZIO: As to the how this act
    Be warranted, it rests with you.
BEATRICE: Well, follow!
OLIMPIO: Hush! Hark! What noise is that?
MARZIO: Ha! some one comes!
BEATRICE: Ye conscience-stricken cravens, rock to rest
    Your baby hearts. It is the iron gate,
    Which ye left open, swinging to the wind,
    That enters whistling as in scorn. Come, follow!
    And be your steps like mine, light, quick and bold.
(*Exeunt*)

SCENE 4.3:
An apartment in the Castle.
Enter BEATRICE *and* LUCRETIA.
LUCRETIA: They are about it now.
BEATRICE: Nay, it is done.
LUCRETIA: I have not heard him groan.
BEATRICE: He will not groan.
LUCRETIA: What sound is that?
BEATRICE: List! 'tis the tread of feet
    About his bed.
LUCRETIA: My God!
    If he be now a cold, stiff corpse...
BEATRICE: O, fear not
    What may be done, but what is left undone:
    The act seals all.

(*Enter* OLIMPIO *and* MARZIO)
    Is it accomplished?
MARZIO: What?
OLIMPIO: Did you not call?
BEATRICE: When?
OLIMPIO: Now.
BEATRICE: I ask if all is over?
OLIMPIO: We dare not kill an old and sleeping man;
    His thin gray hair, his stern and reverend brow,
    His veined hands crossed on his heaving breast,
    And the calm innocent sleep in which he lay,
    Quelled me. Indeed, indeed, I cannot do it.
MARZIO: But I was bolder; for I chid Olimpio,
    And bade him bear his wrongs to his own grave
    And leave me the reward. And now my knife
    Touched the loose wrinkled throat, when the old man
    Stirred in his sleep, and said, 'God! hear, O, hear,
    A father's curse! What, art Thou not our Father?'
    And then he laughed. I knew it was the ghost
    Of my dead father speaking through his lips,
    And could not kill him.
BEATRICE: Miserable slaves!
    Where, if ye dare not kill a sleeping man,
    Found ye the boldness to return to me
    With such a deed undone? Base palterers!
    Cowards and traitors! Why, the very conscience
    Which ye would sell for gold and for revenge
    Is an equivocation: it sleeps over
    A thousand daily acts disgracing men;
    And when a deed where mercy insults Heaven...
    Why do I talk?
(*Snatching a dagger from one of them, and raising it*)
    Hadst thou a tongue to say,
    'She murdered her own father!'—I must do it!
    But never dream ye shall outlive him long!
OLIMPIO: Stop, for God's sake!
MARZIO: I will go back and kill him.
OLIMPIO: Give me the weapon, we must do thy will.
BEATRICE: Take it! Depart! Return!

(*Exeunt* OLIMPIO *and* MARZIO)
    How pale thou art!
    We do but that which 'twere a deadly crime
    To leave undone.
LUCRETIA: Would it were done!
BEATRICE: Even whilst
    That doubt is passing through your mind, the world
    Is conscious of a change. Darkness and Hell
    Have swallowed up the vapour they sent forth
    To blacken the sweet light of life. My breath
    Comes, methinks, lighter, and the jellied blood
    Runs freely through my veins. Hark!
(*Enter* OLIMPIO *and* MARZIO)
    He is...
OLIMPIO: Dead!
MARZIO: We strangled him that there might be no blood;
    And then we threw his heavy corpse i' the garden
    Under the balcony; 'twill seem it fell.
BEATRICE (*giving them a bag of coin*): Here, take this gold, and hasten
    to your homes.
    And, Marzio, because thou wast only awed
    By that which made me tremble, wear thou this!
(*Clothes him in a rich mantle*)
    It was the mantle which my grandfather
    Wore in his high prosperity, and men
    Envied his state: so may they envy thine.
    Thou wert a weapon in the hand of God
    To a just use. Live long and thrive! And, mark,
    If thou hast crimes, repent: this deed is none.
(*A horn is sounded*)
LUCRETIA: Hark, 'tis the castle horn: my God! it sounds
    Like the last trump.
BEATRICE: Some tedious guest is coming.
LUCRETIA: The drawbridge is let down; there is a tramp
    Of horses in the court; fly, hide yourselves!
(*Exeunt* OLIMPIO *and* MARZIO)
BEATRICE: Let us retire to counterfeit deep rest;
    I scarcely need to counterfeit it now:
    The spirit which doth reign within these limbs

    Seems strangely undisturbed. I could even sleep
    Fearless and calm: all ill is surely past.
(*Exeunt*)

Scene 4.4:
Another apartment in the Castle.
Enter on one side the legate savella, introduced by a servant, and on the other
Lucretia *and* Bernardo.
Savella: Lady, my duty to his Holiness
    Be my excuse that thus unseasonably
    I break upon your rest. I must speak with
    Count Cenci; doth he sleep?
Lucretia (*in a hurried and confused manner*): I think he
    sleeps;
    Yet, wake him not, I pray, spare me awhile,
    He is a wicked and a wrathful man;
    Should he be roused out of his sleep to-night,
    Which is, I know, a hell of angry dreams,
    It were not well; indeed it were not well.
    Wait till day break. . .
(*Aside*)
    Oh, I am deadly sick!
Savella: I grieve thus to distress you, but the Count
    Must answer charges of the gravest import,
    And suddenly; such my commission is.
Lucretia (*with increased agitation*): I dare not rouse him: I know
    none who dare. . .
    'Twere perilous; . . . you might as safely waken
    A serpent; or a corpse in which some fiend
    Were laid to sleep.
Savella: Lady, my moments here
    Are counted. I must rouse him from his sleep,
    Since none else dare.
Lucretia (*aside*): O, terror! O, despair!
(*To* Bernardo)
    Bernardo, conduct you the Lord Legate to
    Your father's chamber.
(*Exeunt* Savella *and* Bernardo)
(*Enter* Beatrice)

BEATRICE: 'Tis a messenger
    Come to arrest the culprit who now stands
    Before the throne of unappealable God.
    Both Earth and Heaven, consenting arbiters,
    Acquit our deed.
LUCRETIA: Oh, agony of fear!
    Would that he yet might live! Even now I heard
    The Legate's followers whisper as they passed
    They had a warrant for his instant death.
    All was prepared by unforbidden means
    Which we must pay so dearly, having done.
    Even now they search the tower, and find the body;
    Now they suspect the truth; now they consult
    Before they come to tax us with the fact;
    O, horrible, 'tis all discovered!
BEATRICE: Mother,
    What is done wisely, is done well. Be bold
    As thou art just. 'Tis like a truant child
    To fear that others know what thou hast done,
    Even from thine own strong consciousness, and thus
    Write on unsteady eyes and altered cheeks
    All thou wouldst hide. Be faithful to thyself,
    And fear no other witness but thy fear.
    For if, as cannot be, some circumstance
    Should rise in accusation, we can blind
    Suspicion with such cheap astonishment,
    Or overbear it with such guiltless pride,
    As murderers cannot feign. The deed is done,
    And what may follow now regards not me.
    I am as universal as the light;
    Free as the earth-surrounding air; as firm
    As the world's centre. Consequence, to me,
    Is as the wind which strikes the solid rock,
    But shakes it not.
(*A cry within and tumult*)
VOICES: Murder! Murder! Murder!
(*Enter* BERNARDO *and* SAVELLA)
SAVELLA (*to his followers*): Go search the castle round; sound the alarm;
    Look to the gates, that none escape!

BEATRICE: What now?
BERNARDO: I know not what to say... my father's dead.
BEATRICE: How; dead! he only sleeps; you mistake, brother.
   His sleep is very calm, very like death;
   'Tis wonderful how well a tyrant sleeps.
   He is not dead?
BERNARDO: Dead; murdered.
LUCRETIA (*with extreme agitation*): Oh no, no!
   He is not murdered though he may be dead;
   I have alone the keys of those apartments.
SAVELLA: Ha! Is it so?
BEATRICE: My Lord, I pray excuse us;
   We will retire; my mother is not well:
   She seems quite overcome with this strange horror.
(*Exeunt* LUCRETIA *and* BEATRICE)
SAVELLA: Can you suspect who may have murdered him?
BERNARDO: I know not what to think.
SAVELLA: Can you name any
   Who had an interest in his death?
BERNARDO: Alas!
   I can name none who had not, and those most
   Who most lament that such a deed is done;
   My mother, and my sister, and myself.
SAVELLA: 'Tis strange! There were clear marks of violence.
   I found the old man's body in the moonlight
   Hanging beneath the window of his chamber,
   Among the branches of a pine: he could not
   Have fallen there, for all his limbs lay heaped
   And effortless; 'tis true there was no blood...
   Favour me, Sir; it much imports your house
   That all should be made clear; to tell the ladies
   That I request their presence.
(*Exit* BERNARDO)
(*Enter guards, bringing in* MARZIO)
GUARD: We have one.
OFFICER: My Lord, we found this ruffian and another
   Lurking among the rocks; there is no doubt
   But that they are the murderers of Count Cenci:
   Each had a bag of coin; this fellow wore

> A gold-inwoven robe, which, shining bright
> Under the dark rocks to the glimmering moon
> Betrayed them to our notice: the other fell
> Desperately fighting.

SAVELLA: What does he confess?

OFFICER: He keeps firm silence; but these lines found on him
> May speak.

SAVELLA: Their language is at least sincere.
(*Reads*)
> 'To the Lady Beatrice.
> That the atonement of what my nature sickens to conjecture may soon arrive, I send thee, at thy brother's desire, those who will speak and do more than I dare write. . .
> 'Thy devoted servant, Orsino.'

(*Enter* LUCRETIA, BEATRICE, *and* BERNARDO)
> Knowest thou this writing, Lady?

BEATRICE: No.

SAVELLA: Nor thou?

LUCRETIA (*her conduct throughout the scene is marked by extreme agitation*): Where was it found? What is it? It should be
> Orsino's hand! It speaks of that strange horror
> Which never yet found utterance, but which made
> Between that hapless child and her dead father
> A gulf of obscure hatred.

SAVELLA: Is it so?
> Is it true, Lady, that thy father did
> Such outrages as to awaken in thee
> Unfilial hate?

BEATRICE: Not hate, 'twas more than hate:
> This is most true, yet wherefore question me?

SAVELLA: There is a deed demanding question done;
> Thou hast a secret which will answer not.

BEATRICE: What sayest? My Lord, your words are bold and rash.

SAVELLA: I do arrest all present in the name
> Of the Pope's Holiness. You must to Rome.

LUCRETIA: O, not to Rome! Indeed we are not guilty.

BEATRICE: Guilty! Who dares talk of guilt? My Lord,
> I am more innocent of parricide

Than is a child born fatherless... Dear mother,
Your gentleness and patience are no shield
For this keen-judging world, this two-edged lie,
Which seems, but is not. What! will human laws,
Rather will ye who are their ministers,
Bar all access to retribution first,
And then, when Heaven doth interpose to do
What ye neglect, arming familiar things
To the redress of an unwonted crime,
Make ye the victims who demanded it
Culprits? 'Tis ye are culprits! That poor wretch
Who stands so pale, and trembling, and amazed,
If it be true he murdered Cenci, was
A sword in the right hand of justest God.
Wherefore should I have wielded it? Unless
The crimes which mortal tongue dare never name
God therefore scruples to avenge.

SAVELLA: You own
    That you desired his death?

BEATRICE: It would have been
    A crime no less than his, if for one moment
    That fierce desire had faded in my heart.
    'Tis true I did believe, and hope, and pray,
    Ay, I even knew... for God is wise and just,
    That some strange sudden death hung over him.
    'Tis true that this did happen, and most true
    There was no other rest for me on earth,
    No other hope in Heaven... now what of this?

SAVELLA: Strange thoughts beget strange deeds; and here are both:
    I judge thee not.

BEATRICE: And yet, if you arrest me,
    You are the judge and executioner
    Of that which is the life of life: the breath
    Of accusation kills an innocent name,
    And leaves for lame acquittal the poor life
    Which is a mask without it. 'Tis most false
    That I am guilty of foul parricide;
    Although I must rejoice, for justest cause,

That other hands have sent my father's soul
To ask the mercy he denied to me.
Now leave us free; stain not a noble house
With vague surmises of rejected crime;
Add to our sufferings and your own neglect
No heavier sum: let them have been enough:
Leave us the wreck we have.

SAVELLA: I dare not, Lady.
I pray that you prepare yourselves for Rome:
There the Pope's further pleasure will be known.

LUCRETIA: O, not to Rome! O, take us not to Rome!

BEATRICE: Why not to Rome, dear mother? There as here
Our innocence is as an armed heel
To trample accusation. God is there
As here, and with His shadow ever clothes
The innocent, the injured and the weak;
And such are we. Cheer up, dear Lady, lean
On me; collect your wandering thoughts. My Lord,
As soon as you have taken some refreshment,
And had all such examinations made
Upon the spot, as may be necessary
To the full understanding of this matter,
We shall be ready. Mother; will you come?

LUCRETIA: Ha! they will bind us to the rack, and wrest
Self-accusation from our agony!
Will Giacomo be there? Orsino? Marzio?
All present; all confronted; all demanding
Each from the other's countenance the thing
Which is in every heart! O, misery!

(*She faints, and is borne out*)

SAVELLA: She faints: an ill appearance this.

BEATRICE: My Lord,
She knows not yet the uses of the world.
She fears that power is as a beast which grasps
And loosens not: a snake whose look transmutes
All things to guilt which is its nutriment.
She cannot know how well the supine slaves
Of blind authority read the truth of things
When written on a brow of guilelessness:

    She sees not yet triumphant Innocence
    Stand at the judgement-seat of mortal man,
    A judge and an accuser of the wrong
    Which drags it there. Prepare yourself, my Lord;
    Our suite will join yours in the court below.
(*Exeunt*)

END OF ACT 4

Act 5

Scene 5.1:
An apartment in Orsino's *Palace.*
Enter Orsino *and* Giacomo.

Giacomo: Do evil deeds thus quickly come to end?
    O, that the vain remorse which must chastise
    Crimes done, had but as loud a voice to warn
    As its keen sting is mortal to avenge!
    O, that the hour when present had cast off
    The mantle of its mystery, and shown
    The ghastly form with which it now returns
    When its scared game is roused, cheering the hounds
    Of conscience to their prey! Alas! Alas!
    It was a wicked thought, a piteous deed,
    To kill an old and hoary-headed father.
Orsino: It has turned out unluckily, in truth.
Giacomo: To violate the sacred doors of sleep;
    To cheat kind Nature of the placid death
    Which she prepares for overwearied age;
    To drag from Heaven an unrepentant soul
    Which might have quenched in reconciling prayers
    A life of burning crimes...
Orsino: You cannot say
    I urged you to the deed.
Giacomo: O, had I never
    Found in thy smooth and ready countenance
    The mirror of my darkest thoughts; hadst thou
    Never with hints and questions made me look
    Upon the monster of my thought, until
    It grew familiar to desire...
Orsino: 'Tis thus
    Men cast the blame of their unprosperous acts
    Upon the abettors of their own resolve;
    Or anything but their weak, guilty selves.
    And yet, confess the truth, it is the peril
    In which you stand that gives you this pale sickness
    Of penitence; confess 'tis fear disguised

    From its own shame that takes the mantle now
    Of thin remorse. What if we yet were safe?
GIACOMO: How can that be? Already Beatrice,
    Lucretia and the murderer are in prison.
    I doubt not officers are, whilst we speak,
    Sent to arrest us.
ORSINO: I have all prepared
    For instant flight. We can escape even now,
    So we take fleet occasion by the hair.
GIACOMO: Rather expire in tortures, as I may.
    What! will you cast by self-accusing flight
    Assured conviction upon Beatrice?
    She, who alone in this unnatural work,
    Stands like God's angel ministered upon
    By fiends; avenging such a nameless wrong
    As turns black parricide to piety;
    Whilst we for basest ends... I fear, Orsino,
    While I consider all your words and looks,
    Comparing them with your proposal now,
    That you must be a villain. For what end
    Could you engage in such a perilous crime,
    Training me on with hints, and signs, and smiles,
    Even to this gulf? Thou art no liar? No,
    Thou art a lie! Traitor and murderer!
    Coward and slave! But no, defend thyself;
(*Drawing*)
    Let the sword speak what the indignant tongue
    Disdains to brand thee with.
ORSINO: Put up your weapon.
    Is it the desperation of your fear
    Makes you thus rash and sudden with a friend,
    Now ruined for your sake? If honest anger
    Have moved you, know, that what I just proposed
    Was but to try you. As for me, I think,
    Thankless affection led me to this point,
    From which, if my firm temper could repent,
    I cannot now recede. Even whilst we speak
    The ministers of justice wait below:
    They grant me these brief moments. Now if you

>   Have any word of melancholy comfort
>   To speak to your pale wife, 'twere best to pass
>   Out at the postern, and avoid them so.
> GIACOMO: O, generous friend! How canst thou pardon me?
>   Would that my life could purchase thine!
> ORSINO: That wish
>   Now comes a day too late. Haste; fare thee well!
>   Hear'st thou not steps along the corridor?
> (*Exit* GIACOMO)
>   I'm sorry for it; but the guards are waiting
>   At his own gate, and such was my contrivance
>   That I might rid me both of him and them.
>   I thought to act a solemn comedy
>   Upon the painted scene of this new world,
>   And to attain my own peculiar ends
>   By some such plot of mingled good and ill
>   As others weave; but there arose a Power
>   Which grasped and snapped the threads of my device
>   And turned it to a net of ruin... Ha!
> (*A shout is heard*)
>   Is that my name I hear proclaimed abroad?
>   But I will pass, wrapped in a vile disguise;
>   Rags on my back, and a false innocence
>   Upon my face, through the misdeeming crowd
>   Which judges by what seems. 'Tis easy then
>   For a new name and for a country new,
>   And a new life, fashioned on old desires,
>   To change the honours of abandoned Rome.
>   And these must be the masks of that within,
>   Which must remain unaltered... Oh, I fear
>   That what is past will never let me rest!
>   Why, when none else is conscious, but myself,
>   Of my misdeeds, should my own heart's contempt
>   Trouble me? Have I not the power to fly
>   My own reproaches? Shall I be the slave
>   Of... what? A word? which those of this false world
>   Employ against each other, not themselves;
>   As men wear daggers not for self-offence.
>   But if I am mistaken, where shall I

Find the disguise to hide me from myself,
As now I skulk from every other eye?
(*Exit*)

SCENE 5.2:
A Hall of Justice.
CAMILLO, *Judges, etc., are discovered seated;*
MARZIO *is led in.*
FIRST JUDGE: Accused, do you persist in your denial?
I ask you, are you innocent, or guilty?
I demand who were the participators
In your offence? Speak truth, and the whole truth.
MARZIO: My God! I did not kill him; I know nothing;
Olimpio sold the robe to me from which
You would infer my guilt.
SECOND JUDGE: Away with him!
FIRST JUDGE: Dare you, with lips yet white from the rack's kiss
Speak false? Is it so soft a questioner,
That you would bandy lover's talk with it
Till it wind out your life and soul? Away!
MARZIO: Spare me! O, spare! I will confess.
FIRST JUDGE: Then speak.
MARZIO: I strangled him in his sleep.
FIRST JUDGE: Who urged you to it?
MARZIO: His own son Giacomo, and the young prelate
Orsino sent me to Petrella; there
The ladies Beatrice and Lucretia
Tempted me with a thousand crowns, and I
And my companion forthwith murdered him.
Now let me die.
FIRST JUDGE: This sounds as bad as truth. Guards, there,
Lead forth the prisoner!
(*Enter* LUCRETIA, BEATRICE *and* GIACOMO, *guarded*)
Look upon this man;
When did you see him last?
BEATRICE: We never saw him.
MARZIO: You know me too well, Lady Beatrice.
BEATRICE: I know thee! How? where? when?
MARZIO: You know 'twas I

    Whom you did urge with menaces and bribes
    To kill your father. When the thing was done
    You clothed me in a robe of woven gold
    And bade me thrive: how I have thriven, you see.
    You, my Lord Giacomo, Lady Lucretia,
    You know that what I speak is true.
(BEATRICE *advances towards him; he covers his face, and shrinks back*)
    Oh, dart
    The terrible resentment of those eyes
    On the dead earth! Turn them away from me!
    They wound: 'twas torture forced the truth. My Lords,
    Having said this let me be led to death.
BEATRICE: Poor wretch, I pity thee: yet stay awhile.
CAMILLO: Guards, lead him not away.
BEATRICE: Cardinal Camillo,
    You have a good repute for gentleness
    And wisdom: can it be that you sit here
    To countenance a wicked farce like this?
    When some obscure and trembling slave is dragged
    From sufferings which might shake the sternest heart
    And bade to answer, not as he believes,
    But as those may suspect or do desire
    Whose questions thence suggest their own reply:
    And that in peril of such hideous torments
    As merciful God spares even the damned. Speak now
    The thing you surely know, which is that you,
    If your fine frame were stretched upon that wheel,
    And you were told: 'Confess that you did poison
    Your little nephew; that fair blue-eyed child
    Who was the lodestar of your life:'—and though
    All see, since his most swift and piteous death,
    That day and night, and heaven and earth, and time,
    And all the things hoped for or done therein
    Are changed to you, through your exceeding grief,
    Yet you would say, 'I confess anything:'
    And beg from your tormentors, like that slave,
    The refuge of dishonourable death.
    I pray thee, Cardinal, that thou assert
    My innocence.

CAMILLO (*much moved*): What shall we think, my Lords?
    Shame on these tears! I thought the heart was frozen
    Which is their fountain. I would pledge my soul
    That she is guiltless.
JUDGE: Yet she must be tortured.
CAMILLO: I would as soon have tortured mine own nephew
    (If he now lived he would be just her age;
    His hair, too, was her colour, and his eyes
    Like hers in shape, but blue and not so deep)
    As that most perfect image of God's love
    That ever came sorrowing upon the earth.
    She is as pure as speechless infancy!
JUDGE: Well, be her purity on your head, my Lord,
    If you forbid the rack. His Holiness
    Enjoined us to pursue this monstrous crime
    By the severest forms of law; nay even
    To stretch a point against the criminals.
    The prisoners stand accused of parricide
    Upon such evidence as justifies
    Torture.
BEATRICE: What evidence? This man's?
JUDGE: Even so.
BEATRICE (*to* MARZIO): Come near. And who art thou thus chosen forth
    Out of the multitude of living men
    To kill the innocent?
MARZIO: I am Marzio,
    Thy father's vassal.
BEATRICE: Fix thine eyes on mine;
    Answer to what I ask.
(*Turning to the Judges*)
    I prithee mark
    His countenance: unlike bold calumny
    Which sometimes dares not speak the thing it looks,
    He dares not look the thing he speaks, but bends
    His gaze on the blind earth.
(*To* MARZIO)
    What! wilt thou say
    That I did murder my own father?

Marzio: Oh!
    Spare me! My brain swims round. . . I cannot speak. . .
    It was that horrid torture forced the truth.
    Take me away! Let her not look on me!
    I am a guilty miserable wretch;
    I have said all I know; now, let me die!
Beatrice: My Lords, if by my nature I had been
    So stern, as to have planned the crime alleged,
    Which your suspicions dictate to this slave,
    And the rack makes him utter, do you think
    I should have left this two-edged instrument
    Of my misdeed; this man, this bloody knife
    With my own name engraven on the heft,
    Lying unsheathed amid a world of foes,
    For my own death? That with such horrible need
    For deepest silence, I should have neglected
    So trivial a precaution, as the making
    His tomb the keeper of a secret written
    On a thief's memory? What is his poor life?
    What are a thousand lives? A parricide
    Had trampled them like dust; and, see, he lives!
(*Turning to* Marzio)
    And thou. . .
Marzio: Oh, spare me! Speak to me no more!
    That stern yet piteous look, those solemn tones,
    Wound worse than torture.
(*To the Judges*)
    I have told it all;
    For pity's sake lead me away to death.
Camillo: Guards, lead him nearer the Lady Beatrice;
    He shrinks from her regard like autumn's leaf
    From the keen breath of the serenest north.
Beatrice: O thou who tremblest on the giddy verge
    Of life and death, pause ere thou answerest me;
    So mayst thou answer God with less dismay:
    What evil have we done thee? I, alas!
    Have lived but on this earth a few sad years,
    And so my lot was ordered, that a father
    First turned the moments of awakening life

To drops, each poisoning youth's sweet hope; and then
Stabbed with one blow my everlasting soul;
And my untainted fame; and even that peace
Which sleeps within the core of the heart's heart;
But the wound was not mortal; so my hate
Became the only worship I could lift
To our great father, who in pity and love,
Armed thee, as thou dost say, to cut him off;
And thus his wrong becomes my accusation;
And art thou the accuser? If thou hopest
Mercy in heaven, show justice upon earth:
Worse than a bloody hand is a hard heart.
If thou hast done murders, made thy life's path
Over the trampled laws of God and man,
Rush not before thy Judge, and say: 'My maker,
I have done this and more; for there was one
Who was most pure and innocent on earth;
And because she endured what never any
Guilty or innocent endured before:
Because her wrongs could not be told, not thought;
Because thy hand at length did rescue her;
I with my words killed her and all her kin.'
Think, I adjure you, what it is to slay
The reverence living in the minds of men
Towards our ancient house, and stainless fame!
Think what it is to strangle infant pity,
Cradled in the belief of guileless looks,
Till it become a crime to suffer. Think
What 'tis to blot with infamy and blood
All that which shows like innocence, and is,
Hear me, great God! I swear, most innocent,
So that the world lose all discrimination
Between the sly, fierce, wild regard of guilt,
And that which now compels thee to reply
To what I ask: Am I, or am I not
A parricide?

MARZIO: Thou art not!

JUDGE: What is this?

MARZIO: I here declare those whom I did accuse

      Are innocent. 'Tis I alone am guilty.
JUDGE: Drag him away to torments; let them be
    Subtle and long drawn out, to tear the folds
    Of the heart's inmost cell. Unbind him not
    Till he confess.
MARZIO: Torture me as ye will:
    A keener pang has wrung a higher truth
    From my last breath. She is most innocent!
    Bloodhounds, not men, glut yourselves well with me;
    I will not give you that fine piece of nature
    To rend and ruin.
(*Exit* MARZIO, *guarded*)
CAMILLO: What say ye now, my Lords?
JUDGE: Let tortures strain the truth till it be white
    As snow thrice sifted by the frozen wind.
CAMILLO: Yet stained with blood.
JUDGE (*to* BEATRICE): Know you this paper, Lady?
BEATRICE: Entrap me not with questions. Who stands here
    As my accuser? Ha! wilt thou be he,
    Who art my judge? Accuser, witness, judge,
    What, all in one? Here is Orsino's name;
    Where is Orsino? Let his eye meet mine.
    What means this scrawl? Alas! ye know not what,
    And therefore on the chance that it may be
    Some evil, will ye kill us?
(*Enter an officer*)
OFFICER: Marzio's dead.
JUDGE: What did he say?
OFFICER: Nothing. As soon as we
    Had bound him on the wheel, he smiled on us,
    As one who baffles a deep adversary;
    And holding his breath, died.
JUDGE: There remains nothing
    But to apply the question to those prisoners,
    Who yet remain stubborn.
CAMILLO: I overrule
    Further proceedings, and in the behalf
    Of these most innocent and noble persons
    Will use my interest with the Holy Father.

JUDGE: Let the Pope's pleasure then be done. Meanwhile
    Conduct these culprits each to separate cells;
    And be the engines ready; for this night
    If the Pope's resolution be as grave,
    Pious, and just as once, I'll wring the truth
    Out of those nerves and sinews, groan by groan.
(*Exeunt*)

SCENE 5.3:
The cell of a prison.
BEATRICE *is discovered asleep on a couch.*
Enter BERNARDO.
BERNARDO: How gently slumber rests upon her face,
    Like the last thoughts of some day sweetly spent
    Closing in night and dreams, and so prolonged.
    After such torments as she bore last night,
    How light and soft her breathing comes. Ay me!
    Methinks that I shall never sleep again.
    But I must shake the heavenly dew of rest
    From this sweet folded flower, thus... wake, awake!
    What, sister, canst thou sleep?
BEATRICE (*awaking*): I was just dreaming
    That we were all in Paradise. Thou knowest
    This cell seems like a kind of Paradise
    After our father's presence.
BERNARDO: Dear, dear sister,
    Would that thy dream were not a dream! O God!
    How shall I tell?
BEATRICE: What wouldst thou tell, sweet brother?
BERNARDO: Look not so calm and happy, or even whilst
    I stand considering what I have to say
    My heart will break.
BEATRICE: See now, thou mak'st me weep:
    How very friendless thou wouldst be, dear child,
    If I were dead. Say what thou hast to say.
BERNARDO: They have confessed; they could endure no more
    The tortures...
BEATRICE: Ha! What was there to confess?
    They must have told some weak and wicked lie

    To flatter their tormentors. Have they said
    That they were guilty? O white innocence,
    That thou shouldst wear the mask of guilt to hide
    Thine awful and serenest countenance
    From those who know thee not!
(*Enter Judge with* LUCRETIA *and* GIACOMO, *guarded*)
    Ignoble hearts!
    For some brief spasms of pain, which are at least
    As mortal as the limbs through which they pass,
    Are centuries of high splendour laid in dust?
    And that eternal honour which should live
    Sunlike, above the reek of mortal fame,
    Changed to a mockery and a byword? What!
    Will you give up these bodies to be dragged
    At horses' heels, so that our hair should sweep
    The footsteps of the vain and senseless crowd,
    Who, that they may make our calamity
    Their worship and their spectacle, will leave
    The churches and the theatres as void
    As their own hearts? Shall the light multitude
    Fling, at their choice, curses or faded pity,
    Sad funeral flowers to deck a living corpse,
    Upon us as we pass to pass away,
    And leave... what memory of our having been?
    Infamy, blood, terror, despair? O thou,
    Who wert a mother to the parentless,
    Kill not thy child! Let not her wrongs kill thee!
    Brother, lie down with me upon the rack,
    And let us each be silent as a corpse;
    It soon will be as soft as any grave.
    'Tis but the falsehood it can wring from fear
    Makes the rack cruel.
GIACOMO: They will tear the truth
    Even from thee at last, those cruel pains:
    For pity's sake say thou art guilty now.
LUCRETIA: Oh, speak the truth! Let us all quickly die;
    And after death, God is our judge, not they;
    He will have mercy on us.
BERNARDO: If indeed

It can be true, say so, dear sister mine;
And then the Pope will surely pardon you,
And all be well.
JUDGE: Confess, or I will warp
Your limbs with such keen tortures. . .
BEATRICE: Tortures! Turn
The rack henceforth into a spinning-wheel!
Torture your dog, that he may tell when last
He lapped the blood his master shed. . . not me!
My pangs are of the mind, and of the heart,
And of the soul; ay, of the inmost soul,
Which weeps within tears as of burning gall
To see, in this ill world where none are true,
My kindred false to their deserted selves.
And with considering all the wretched life
Which I have lived, and its now wretched end,
And the small justice shown by Heaven and Earth
To me or mine; and what a tyrant thou art,
And what slaves these; and what a world we make,
The oppressor and the oppressed. . . such pangs compel
My answer. What is it thou wouldst with me?
JUDGE: Art thou not guilty of thy father's death?
BEATRICE: Or wilt thou rather tax high-judging God
That He permitted such an act as that
Which I have suffered, and which He beheld;
Made it unutterable, and took from it
All refuge, all revenge, all consequence,
But that which thou hast called my father's death?
Which is or is not what men call a crime,
Which either I have done, or have not done;
Say what ye will. I shall deny no more.
If ye desire it thus, thus let it be,
And so an end of all. Now do your will;
No other pains shall force another word.
JUDGE: She is convicted, but has not confessed.
Be it enough. Until their final sentence
Let none have converse with them. You, young Lord,
Linger not here!
BEATRICE: Oh, tear him not away!

JUDGE: Guards! do your duty.
BERNARDO (*embracing* BEATRICE): Oh! would ye divide
    Body from soul?
OFFICER: That is the headsman's business.
(*Exeunt all but* LUCRETIA, BEATRICE, *and* GIACOMO)
GIACOMO: Have I confessed? Is it all over now?
    No hope! No refuge! O weak, wicked tongue
    Which hast destroyed me, would that thou hadst been
    Cut out and thrown to dogs first! To have killed
    My father first, and then betrayed my sister;
    Ay, thee! the one thing innocent and pure
    In this black, guilty world, to that which I
    So well deserve! My wife! my little ones!
    Destitute, helpless, and I. . . Father! God!
    Canst Thou forgive even the unforgiving,
    When their full hearts break thus, thus! . . .
(*Covers his face and weeps*)
LUCRETIA: O my child!
    To what a dreadful end are we all come!
    Why did I yield? Why did I not sustain
    Those torments? Oh, that I were all dissolved
    Into these fast and unavailing tears,
    Which flow and feel not!
BEATRICE: What 'twas weak to do,
    'Tis weaker to lament, once being done;
    Take cheer! The God who knew my wrong, and made
    Our speedy act the angel of His wrath,
    Seems, and but seems, to have abandoned us.
    Let us not think that we shall die for this.
    Brother, sit near me; give me your firm hand,
    You had a manly heart. Bear up! Bear up!
    O dearest Lady, put your gentle head
    Upon my lap, and try to sleep awhile:
    Your eyes look pale, hollow, and overworn,
    With heaviness of watching and slow grief.
    Come, I will sing you some low, sleepy tune,
    Not cheerful, nor yet sad; some dull old thing,
    Some outworn and unused monotony,
    Such as our country gossips sing and spin,

    Till they almost forget they live: lie down!
    So, that will do. Have I forgot the words?
    Faith! They are sadder than I thought they were.
SONG: False friend, wilt thou smile or weep
    When my life is laid asleep?
    Little cares for a smile or a tear,
    The clay-cold corpse upon the bier!
    Farewell! Heighho!
    What is this whispers low?
    There is a snake in thy smile, my dear;
    And bitter poison within thy tear.

    Sweet sleep, were death like to thee,
    Or if thou couldst mortal be,
    I would close these eyes of pain;
    When to wake? Never again.
    O World! Farewell!
    Listen to the passing bell!
    It says, thou and I must part,
    With a light and a heavy heart.
(*The scene closes*)

SCENE 5.4:
A hall of the prison.
Enter CAMILLO *and* BERNARDO.
CAMILLO: The Pope is stern; not to be moved or bent.
    He looked as calm and keen as is the engine
    Which tortures and which kills, exempt itself
    From aught that it inflicts; a marble form,
    A rite, a law, a custom: not a man.
    He frowned, as if to frown had been the trick
    Of his machinery, on the advocates
    Presenting the defences, which he tore
    And threw behind, muttering with hoarse, harsh voice:
    'Which among ye defended their old father
    Killed in his sleep?' Then to another: 'Thou
    Dost this in virtue of thy place; 'tis well.'
    He turned to me then, looking deprecation,
    And said these three words, coldly: 'They must die.'

BERNARDO: And yet you left him not?
CAMILLO: I urged him still;
    Pleading, as I could guess, the devilish wrong
    Which prompted your unnatural parent's death.
    And he replied: 'Paolo Santa Croce
    Murdered his mother yester evening,
    And he is fled. Parricide grows so rife
    That soon, for some just cause no doubt, the young
    Will strangle us all, dozing in our chairs.
    Authority, and power, and hoary hair
    Are grown crimes capital. You are my nephew,
    You come to ask their pardon; stay a moment;
    Here is their sentence; never see me more
    Till, to the letter, it be all fulfilled.'
BERNARDO: O God, not so! I did believe indeed
    That all you said was but sad preparation
    For happy news. Oh, there are words and looks
    To bend the sternest purpose! Once I knew them,
    Now I forget them at my dearest need.
    What think you if I seek him out, and bathe
    His feet and robe with hot and bitter tears?
    Importune him with prayers, vexing his brain
    With my perpetual cries, until in rage
    He strike me with his pastoral cross, and trample
    Upon my prostrate head, so that my blood
    May stain the senseless dust on which he treads,
    And remorse waken mercy? I will do it!
    Oh, wait till I return!
(*Rushes out*)
CAMILLO: Alas, poor boy!
    A wreck-devoted seaman thus might pray
    To the deaf sea.
(*Enter* LUCRETIA, BEATRICE, *and* GIACOMO, *guarded*)
BEATRICE: I hardly dare to fear
    That thou bring'st other news than a just pardon.
CAMILLO: May God in heaven be less inexorable
    To the Pope's prayers than he has been to mine.
    Here is the sentence and the warrant.
BEATRICE (*wildly*): O

My God! Can it be possible I have
To die so suddenly? So young to go
Under the obscure, cold, rotting, wormy ground!
To be nailed down into a narrow place;
To see no more sweet sunshine; hear no more
Blithe voice of living thing; muse not again
Upon familiar thoughts, sad, yet thus lost—
How fearful! to be nothing! Or to be. . .
What? Oh, where am I? Let me not go mad!
Sweet Heaven, forgive weak thoughts! If there should be
No God, no Heaven, no Earth in the void world;
The wide, gray, lampless, deep, unpeopled world!
If all things then should be. . . my father's spirit,
His eye, his voice, his touch surrounding me;
The atmosphere and breath of my dead life!
If sometimes, as a shape more like himself,
Even the form which tortured me on earth,
Masked in gray hairs and wrinkles, he should come
And wind me in his hellish arms, and fix
His eyes on mine, and drag me down, down, down!
For was he not alone omnipotent
On Earth, and ever present? Even though dead,
Does not his spirit live in all that breathe,
And work for me and mine still the same ruin,
Scorn, pain, despair? Who ever yet returned
To teach the laws of Death's untrodden realm?
Unjust perhaps as those which drive us now,
Oh, whither, whither?

LUCRETIA: Trust in God's sweet love,
The tender promises of Christ: ere night,
Think, we shall be in Paradise.

BEATRICE: 'Tis past!
Whatever comes, my heart shall sink no more.
And yet, I know not why, your words strike chill:
How tedious, false, and cold seem all things. I
Have met with much injustice in this world;
No difference has been made by God or man,
Or any power moulding my wretched lot,
'Twixt good or evil, as regarded me.

    I am cut off from the only world I know,
    From light, and life, and love, in youth's sweet prime.
    You do well telling me to trust in God;
    I hope I do trust in him. In whom else
    Can any trust? And yet my heart is cold.

(*During the latter speeches* GIACOMO *has retired conversing with* CAMILLO, *who now goes out*; GIACOMO *advances*)

GIACOMO: Know you not, Mother... Sister, know you not?
    Bernardo even now is gone to implore
    The Pope to grant our pardon.

LUCRETIA: Child, perhaps
    It will be granted. We may all then live
    To make these woes a tale for distant years:
    Oh, what a thought! It gushes to my heart
    Like the warm blood.

BEATRICE: Yet both will soon be cold.
    Oh, trample out that thought! Worse than despair,
    Worse than the bitterness of death, is hope:
    It is the only ill which can find place
    Upon the giddy, sharp, and narrow hour
    Tottering beneath us. Plead with the swift frost
    That it should spare the eldest flower of spring:
    Plead with awakening earthquake, o'er whose couch
    Even now a city stands, strong, fair, and free;
    Now stench and blackness yawn, like death. Oh, plead
    With famine, or wind-walking Pestilence,
    Blind lightning, or the deaf sea, not with man!
    Cruel, cold, formal man; righteous in words,
    In deeds a Cain. No, Mother, we must die:
    Since such is the reward of innocent lives;
    Such the alleviation of worst wrongs.
    And whilst our murderers live, and hard, cold men,
    Smiling and slow, walk through a world of tears
    To death as to life's sleep; 'twere just the grave
    Were some strange joy for us. Come, obscure Death,
    And wind me in thine all-embracing arms!
    Like a fond mother hide me in thy bosom,
    And rock me to the sleep from which none wake.
    Live ye, who live, subject to one another

As we were once, who now...
(BERNARDO *rushes in*)
BERNARDO: Oh, horrible!
   That tears, that looks, that hope poured forth in prayer,
   Even till the heart is vacant and despairs,
   Should all be vain! The ministers of death
   Are waiting round the doors. I thought I saw
   Blood on the face of one... What if 'twere fancy?
   Soon the heart's blood of all I love on earth
   Will sprinkle him, and he will wipe it off
   As if 'twere only rain. O life! O world!
   Cover me! let me be no more! To see
   That perfect mirror of pure innocence
   Wherein I gazed, and grew happy and good,
   Shivered to dust! To see thee, Beatrice,
   Who made all lovely thou didst look upon...
   Thee, light of life... dead, dark! while I say, sister,
   To hear I have no sister; and thou, Mother,
   Whose love was as a bond to all our loves...
   Dead! The sweet bond broken!
(*Enter* CAMILLO *and guards*)
   They come! Let me
   Kiss those warm lips before their crimson leaves
   Are blighted... white... cold. Say farewell, before
   Death chokes that gentle voice! Oh, let me hear
   You speak!
BEATRICE: Farewell, my tender brother. Think
   Of our sad fate with gentleness, as now:
   And let mild, pitying thoughts lighten for thee
   Thy sorrow's load. Err not in harsh despair,
   But tears and patience. One thing more, my child:
   For thine own sake be constant to the love
   Thou bearest us; and to the faith that I,
   Though wrapped in a strange cloud of crime and shame,
   Lived ever holy and unstained. And though
   Ill tongues shall wound me, and our common name
   Be as a mark stamped on thine innocent brow
   For men to point at as they pass, do thou
   Forbear, and never think a thought unkind

> Of those, who perhaps love thee in their graves.
> So mayest thou die as I do; fear and pain
> Being subdued. Farewell! Farewell! Farewell!

BERNARDO: I cannot say, farewell!

CAMILLO: Oh, Lady Beatrice!

BEATRICE: Give yourself no unnecessary pain,
> My dear Lord Cardinal. Here, Mother, tie
> My girdle for me, and bind up this hair
> In any simple knot; ay, that does well.
> And yours I see is coming down. How often
> Have we done this for one another; now
> We shall not do it any more. My Lord,
> We are quite ready. Well, 'tis very well.

THE END

Note on The Cenci, by Mrs. Shelley

The sort of mistake that Shelley made as to the extent of his own genius and powers, which led him deviously at first, but lastly into the direct track that enabled him fully to develop them, is a curious instance of his modesty of feeling, and of the methods which the human mind uses at once to deceive itself, and yet, in its very delusion, to make its way out of error into the path which Nature has marked out as its right one. He often incited me to attempt the writing a tragedy: he conceived that I possessed some dramatic talent, and he was always most earnest and energetic in his exhortations that I should cultivate any talent I possessed, to the utmost. I entertained a truer estimate of my powers; and above all (though at that time not exactly aware of the fact) I was far too young to have any chance of succeeding, even moderately, in a species of composition that requires a greater scope of experience in, and sympathy with, human passion than could then have fallen to my lot,—or than any perhaps, except Shelley, ever possessed, even at the age of twenty-six, at which he wrote The Cenci.

On the other hand, Shelley most erroneously conceived himself to be destitute of this talent. He believed that one of the first requisites was the capacity of forming and following-up a story or plot. He fancied himself to he defective in this portion of imagination: it was that which gave him least pleasure in the writings of others, though he laid great store by it as the proper framework to support the sublimest efforts of poetry. He asserted that he was too metaphysical and abstract, too fond of the theoretical and the ideal, to succeed as a tragedian. It perhaps is not strange that I shared this opinion with himself; for he had hitherto shown no inclination for, nor given any specimen of his powers in framing and supporting the interest of a story, either in prose or verse. Once or twice, when he attempted such, he had speedily thrown it aside, as being even disagreeable to him as an occupation.

The subject he had suggested for a tragedy was Charles I: and he had written to me: 'Remember, remember Charles I. I have been already imagining how you would conduct some scenes. The second volume of "St. Leon" begins with this proud and true sentiment: "There is nothing which the human mind can conceive which it may not execute." Shakespeare was only a human being.' These words were written in 1818, while we were in Lombardy, when he little thought how soon a work of his own would prove a proud comment on the passage he quoted. When in Rome, in 1819, a friend put into our hands the old manuscript account of the story of the Cenci. We visited the Colonna and Doria palaces, where the portraits of Beatrice were to be found; and her beauty cast the reflection of its own grace over her appalling story. Shelley's imagination became strongly excited, and he urged the subject to me as one fitted for a tragedy. More than ever I felt my incompetence; but I entreated him to write it instead; and he began, and proceeded swiftly, urged on by intense sympathy with the sufferings of the human beings whose passions, so long cold in the tomb, he revived, and gifted with poetic language. This tragedy is the only one of his works that he communicated to me during its progress. We talked over the arrangement of the scenes together. I speedily saw the great mistake we had made, and triumphed in the discovery of the new talent brought to light from that mine of wealth (never, alas, through his untimely death, worked to its depths)—his richly gifted mind.

We suffered a severe affliction in Rome by the loss of our eldest child, who was of such beauty and promise as to cause him deservedly to be the idol of our hearts. We left the capital of the world, anxious for a time to escape a spot associated too intimately with his presence and loss. (Such feelings haunted him when, in "The Cenci", he makes Beatrice speak to Cardinal Camillo of

> *'that fair blue-eyed child*
> *Who was the lodestar of your life.'—and say—*
> *All see, since his most swift and piteous death,*
> *That day and night, and heaven and earth, and time,*
> *And all the things hoped for or done therein*
> *Are changed to you, through your exceeding grief.')*

Some friends of ours were residing in the neighbourhood of Leghorn, and we took a small house, Villa Valsovano, about half-way between the town and Monte Nero, where we remained during the summer. Our villa was situated in the midst of a podere; the peasants sang as they worked beneath our windows, during the heats of a very hot season, and in the evening the water-wheel creaked as the process of irrigation went on, and the fireflies flashed from among the myrtle hedges: Nature was bright, sunshiny, and cheerful, or diversified by storms of a majestic terror, such as we had never before witnessed.

At the top of the house there was a sort of terrace. There is often such in Italy, generally roofed: this one was very small, yet not only roofed but glazed. This Shelley made his study; it looked out on a wide prospect of fertile country, and commanded a view of the near sea. The storms that sometimes varied our day showed themselves most picturesquely as they were driven across the ocean; sometimes the dark lurid clouds dipped towards the waves, and became water-spouts that churned up the waters beneath, as they were chased onward and scattered by the tempest. At other times the dazzling sunlight and heat made it almost intolerable to every other; but Shelley basked in both, and his health and spirits revived under their influence. In this airy cell he wrote the principal part of "The Cenci". He was making a study of Calderon at the time, reading his best tragedies with an accomplished lady living near us, to whom his letter from Leghorn was addressed during the following year. He admired Calderon, both for his poetry and his dramatic genius; but it shows his judgement and originality that, though greatly struck by his first acquaintance with the Spanish poet, none of his peculiarities crept into the composition of "The Cenci"; and there is no trace of his new studies, except in that passage to which he himself alludes as suggested by one in "El Purgatorio de San Patricio".

Shelley wished "The Cenci" to be acted. He was not a playgoer, being of such fastidious taste that he was easily disgusted by the bad filling-up of the inferior parts. While preparing for our departure from England, however, he saw Miss O'Neil several times. She was then in the zenith of her glory; and Shelley was deeply moved by her impersonation of several parts, and by the graceful sweetness, the intense pathos, the sublime vehemence of passion she displayed. She was often in his thoughts as he wrote: and, when he had finished, he became anxious that his tragedy should be acted, and receive the advantage of having this accomplished actress to fill the part of the heroine. With this view he wrote the following letter to a friend in London:

'The object of the present letter us to ask a favour of you. I have written a tragedy on a story well known in Italy, and, in my conception, eminently dramatic. I have taken some pains to make my play fit for representation, and those who have already seen it judge favourably. It is written without any of the peculiar feelings and opinions which characterize my other compositions; I have attended simply to the impartial development of such characters as it is probable the persons represented really were, together with the greatest degree of popular effect to be produced by such a development. I send you a translation of the Italian manuscript on which my play is founded; the chief circumstance of which I have touched very delicately; for my principal doubt as to whether it would succeed as an acting play hangs entirely on the question as to whether any such a thing as incest in this shape, however treated, would be admitted on the stage. I think, however, it will form no objection; considering, first, that the facts are matter of history, and, secondly, the peculiar delicacy with which I have treated it. (In speaking of his mode of treating this main incident, Shelley said that it might be remarked that, in the course of the play, he had never mentioned expressly Cenci's worst crime. Every one knew what it must be, but it was never imaged in words—the nearest allusion to it being that portion of Cenci's curse beginning—

"That, if she have a child," etc.)

'I am exceedingly interested in the question of whether this attempt of mine will succeed or not. I am strongly inclined to the affirmative at present; founding my hopes on this—that, as a composition, it is certainly not inferior to any of the modern plays that have been acted, with the exception of "Remorse"; that the interest of the plot is incredibly greater and more real; and that there is nothing beyond what the multitude are contented to believe that they can understand, either in imagery, opinion, or sentiment. I wish to preserve a complete incognito, and can trust to you that, whatever else you do, you will at least favour me on this point. Indeed, this is essential, deeply essential, to its success. After it had been acted, and successfully (could I hope for such a thing), I would own it if I pleased, and use the celebrity it might acquire to my own purposes.

'What I want you to do is to procure for me its presentation at Covent Garden. The principal character, Beatrice, is precisely fitted for Miss O'Neil, and it might even seem to have been written for her (God forbid that I should see her play it—it would tear my nerves to pieces); and in all respects it is fitted only for Covent Garden. The chief male character I confess I should be very unwilling that any one but Kean should play. That is impossible, and I must be contented with an inferior actor.'

The play was accordingly sent to Mr. Harris. He pronounced the subject to be so objectionable that he could not even submit the part to Miss O'Neil for perusal, but expressed his desire that the author would write a tragedy on some other subject, which he would gladly accept.

Shelley printed a small edition at Leghorn, to ensure its correctness; as he was much annoyed by the many mistakes that crept into his text when distance prevented him from correcting the press.

Universal approbation soon stamped "The Cenci" as the best tragedy of modern times. Writing concerning it, Shelley said: 'I have been cautious to avoid the introducing faults of youthful composition; diffuseness, a profusion of inapplicable imagery, vagueness, generality, and, as Hamlet says, "words, words".' There is nothing that is not purely dramatic throughout; and the character of Beatrice, proceeding, from vehement struggle, to horror, to deadly resolution, and lastly to the elevated dignity of calm suffering, joined to passionate tenderness and pathos, is touched with hues so vivid and so beautiful that the poet seems to have read intimately the secrets of the noble heart imaged in the lovely countenance of the unfortunate girl. The Fifth Act is a masterpiece. It is the finest thing he ever wrote, and may claim proud comparison not only with any contemporary, but preceding, poet. The varying feelings of Beatrice are expressed with passionate, heart-reaching eloquence. Every character has a voice that echoes truth in its tones. It is curious, to one acquainted with the written story, to mark the success with which the poet has inwoven the real incidents of the tragedy into his scenes, and yet, through the power of poetry, has obliterated all that would otherwise have shown too harsh or too hideous in the picture. His success was a double triumph; and often after he was earnestly entreated to write again in a style that commanded popular favour, while it was not less instinct with truth and genius. But the bent of his mind went the other way; and, even when employed on subjects whose interest depended on character and incident, he would start off in another direction, and leave the delineations of human passion, which he could depict in so able a manner, for fantastic creations of his fancy, or the expression of those opinions and sentiments, with regard to human nature and its destiny, a desire to diffuse which was the master passion of his soul.

THE MASK OF ANARCHY

WRITTEN ON THE OCCASION OF THE MASSACRE AT MANCHESTER

(Composed at the Villa Valsovano near Leghorn—or possibly later, during Shelley's sojourn at Florence—in the autumn of 1819, shortly after the Peterloo riot at Manchester, August 16; edited with Preface by Leigh Hunt, and published under the poet's name by Edward Moxon, 1832 (Bradbury & Evans, printers). Two manuscripts are extant: a transcript by Mrs. Shelley with Shelley's autograph corrections, known as the 'Hunt manuscript'; and an earlier draft, not quite complete, in the poet's handwriting, presented by Mrs. Shelley to (Sir) John Bowring in 1826, and now in the possession of Mr. Thomas J. Wise (the 'Wise manuscript'). Mrs. Shelley's copy was sent to Leigh Hunt in 1819 with view to its publication in "The Examiner"; hence the name 'Hunt manuscript.' A facsimile of the Wise manuscript was published by the Shelley Society in 1887. Sources of the text are (1) the Hunt manuscript; (2) the Wise manuscript; (3) the editio princeps, editor Leigh Hunt, 1832; (4) Mrs. Shelley's two editions ("Poetical Works") of 1839. Of the two manuscripts Mrs. Shelley's transcript is the later and more authoritative.)

1

As I lay asleep in Italy
There came a voice from over the Sea,
And with great power it forth led me
To walk in the visions of Poesy.

2

I met Murder on the way—
He had a mask like Castlereagh—
Very smooth he looked, yet grim;
Seven blood-hounds followed him:

3

All were fat; and well they might
Be in admirable plight,
For one by one, and two by two,
He tossed them human hearts to chew
Which from his wide cloak he drew.

4

Next came Fraud, and he had on,
Like Eldon, an ermined gown;
His big tears, for he wept well,
Turned to mill-stones as they fell.

5

And the little children, who
Round his feet played to and fro,
Thinking every tear a gem,
Had their brains knocked out by them.

6

Clothed with the Bible, as with light,
And the shadows of the night,
Like Sidmouth, next, Hypocrisy
On a crocodile rode by.

7

And many more Destructions played
In this ghastly masquerade,
All disguised, even to the eyes,
Like Bishops, lawyers, peers, or spies.

8

Last came Anarchy: he rode
On a white horse, splashed with blood;
He was pale even to the lips,
Like Death in the Apocalypse.

9

And he wore a kingly crown;
And in his grasp a sceptre shone;
On his brow this mark I saw—
'I AM GOD, AND KING, AND LAW!'

10

With a pace stately and fast,
Over English land he passed,
Trampling to a mire of blood
The adoring multitude.

11

And a mighty troop around,
With their trampling shook the ground,

Waving each a bloody sword,
For the service of their Lord.

12

And with glorious triumph, they
Rode through England proud and gay,
Drunk as with intoxication
Of the wine of desolation.

13

O'er fields and towns, from sea to sea,
Passed the Pageant swift and free,
Tearing up, and trampling down;
Till they came to London town.

14

And each dweller, panic-stricken,
Felt his heart with terror sicken
Hearing the tempestuous cry
Of the triumph of Anarchy.

15

For with pomp to meet him came,
Clothed in arms like blood and flame,
The hired murderers, who did sing
'Thou art God, and Law, and King.

16

'We have waited, weak and lone
For thy coming, Mighty One!
Our purses are empty, our swords are cold,
Give us glory, and blood, and gold.'

17

Lawyers and priests, a motley crowd,
To the earth their pale brows bowed;
Like a bad prayer not over loud,
Whispering—'Thou art Law and God.'—

18

Then all cried with one accord,
'Thou art King, and God, and Lord;
Anarchy, to thee we bow,
Be thy name made holy now!'

19

And Anarchy, the Skeleton,
Bowed and grinned to every one,
As well as if his education
Had cost ten millions to the nation.

20

For he knew the Palaces
Of our Kings were rightly his;
His the sceptre, crown, and globe,
And the gold-inwoven robe.

21

So he sent his slaves before
To seize upon the Bank and Tower,
And was proceeding with intent
To meet his pensioned Parliament

22

When one fled past, a maniac maid,
And her name was Hope, she said:

But she looked more like Despair,
And she cried out in the air:

23

'My father Time is weak and gray
With waiting for a better day;
See how idiot-like he stands,
Fumbling with his palsied hands!

24

'He has had child after child,
And the dust of death is piled
Over every one but me—
Misery, oh, Misery!'

25

Then she lay down in the street,
Right before the horses' feet,
Expecting, with a patient eye,
Murder, Fraud, and Anarchy.

26

When between her and her foes
A mist, a light, an image rose,
Small at first, and weak, and frail
Like the vapour of a vale:

27

Till as clouds grow on the blast,
Like tower-crowned giants striding fast,
And glare with lightnings as they fly,
And speak in thunder to the sky,

28

It grew—a Shape arrayed in mail
Brighter than the viper's scale,
And upborne on wings whose grain
Was as the light of sunny rain.

29

On its helm, seen far away,
A planet, like the Morning's, lay;
And those plumes its light rained through
Like a shower of crimson dew.

30

With step as soft as wind it passed
O'er the heads of men—so fast
That they knew the presence there,
And looked,—but all was empty air.

31

As flowers beneath May's footstep waken,
As stars from Night's loose hair are shaken,
As waves arise when loud winds call,
Thoughts sprung where'er that step did fall.

32

And the prostrate multitude
Looked—and ankle-deep in blood,
Hope, that maiden most serene,
Was walking with a quiet mien:

33

And Anarchy, the ghastly birth,
Lay dead earth upon the earth;

The Horse of Death tameless as wind
Fled, and with his hoofs did grind
To dust the murderers thronged behind.

34

A rushing light of clouds and splendour,
A sense awakening and yet tender
Was heard and felt—and at its close
These words of joy and fear arose

35

As if their own indignant Earth
Which gave the sons of England birth
Had felt their blood upon her brow,
And shuddering with a mother's throe

36

Had turned every drop of blood
By which her face had been bedewed
To an accent unwithstood,—
As if her heart had cried aloud:

37

'Men of England, heirs of Glory,
Heroes of unwritten story,
Nurslings of one mighty Mother,
Hopes of her, and one another;

38

'Rise like Lions after slumber
In unvanquishable number,
Shake your chains to earth like dew
Which in sleep had fallen on you—
Ye are many—they are few.

39

'What is Freedom?—ye can tell
That which slavery is, too well—
For its very name has grown
To an echo of your own.

40

''Tis to work and have such pay
As just keeps life from day to day
In your limbs, as in a cell
For the tyrants' use to dwell,

41

'So that ye for them are made
Loom, and plough, and sword, and spade,
With or without your own will bent
To their defence and nourishment.

42

''Tis to see your children weak
With their mothers pine and peak,
When the winter winds are bleak,—
They are dying whilst I speak.

43

''Tis to hunger for such diet
As the rich man in his riot
Casts to the fat dogs that lie
Surfeiting beneath his eye;

44

''Tis to let the Ghost of Gold
Take from Toil a thousandfold

More than e'er its substance could
In the tyrannies of old.

45

'Paper coin—that forgery
Of the title-deeds, which ye
Hold to something of the worth
Of the inheritance of Earth.

46

''Tis to be a slave in soul
And to hold no strong control
Over your own wills, but be
All that others make of ye.

47

'And at length when ye complain
With a murmur weak and vain
'Tis to see the Tyrant's crew
Ride over your wives and you
Blood is on the grass like dew.

48

'Then it is to feel revenge
Fiercely thirsting to exchange
Blood for blood—and wrong for wrong—
Do not thus when ye are strong.

49

'Birds find rest, in narrow nest
When weary of their winged quest;
Beasts find fare, in woody lair
When storm and snow are in the air.

50

'Asses, swine, have litter spread
And with fitting food are fed;
All things have a home but one—
Thou, Oh, Englishman, hast none!

51

'This is Slavery—savage men,
Or wild beasts within a den
Would endure not as ye do—
But such ills they never knew.

52

'What art thou Freedom? O! could slaves
Answer from their living graves
This demand—tyrants would flee
Like a dream's dim imagery:

53

'Thou art not, as impostors say,
A shadow soon to pass away,
A superstition, and a name
Echoing from the cave of Fame.

54

'For the labourer thou art bread,
And a comely table spread
From his daily labour come
In a neat and happy home.

55

Thou art clothes, and fire, and food
For the trampled multitude—

No—in countries that are free
Such starvation cannot be
As in England now we see.

56

'To the rich thou art a check,
When his foot is on the neck
Of his victim, thou dost make
That he treads upon a snake.

57

Thou art Justice—ne'er for gold
May thy righteous laws be sold
As laws are in England—thou
Shield'st alike the high and low.

58

'Thou art Wisdom—Freemen never
Dream that God will damn for ever
All who think those things untrue
Of which Priests make such ado.

59

'Thou art Peace—never by thee
Would blood and treasure wasted be
As tyrants wasted them, when all
Leagued to quench thy flame in Gaul.

60

'What if English toil and blood
Was poured forth, even as a flood?
It availed, Oh, Liberty,
To dim, but not extinguish thee.

61

'Thou art Love—the rich have kissed
Thy feet, and like him following Christ,
Give their substance to the free
And through the rough world follow thee,

62

'Or turn their wealth to arms, and make
War for thy beloved sake
On wealth, and war, and fraud—whence they
Drew the power which is their prey.

63

'Science, Poetry, and Thought
Are thy lamps; they make the lot
Of the dwellers in a cot
So serene, they curse it not.

64

'Spirit, Patience, Gentleness,
All that can adorn and bless
Art thou—let deeds, not words, express
Thine exceeding loveliness.

65

'Let a great Assembly be
Of the fearless and the free
On some spot of English ground
Where the plains stretch wide around.

66

'Let the blue sky overhead,
The green earth on which ye tread,

All that must eternal be
Witness the solemnity.

67

'From the corners uttermost
Of the bounds of English coast;
From every hut, village, and town
Where those who live and suffer moan
For others' misery or their own,

68

'From the workhouse and the prison
Where pale as corpses newly risen,
Women, children, young and old
Groan for pain, and weep for cold—

69

'From the haunts of daily life
Where is waged the daily strife
With common wants and common cares
Which sows the human heart with tares—

70

'Lastly from the palaces
Where the murmur of distress
Echoes, like the distant sound
Of a wind alive around

71

'Those prison halls of wealth and fashion,
Where some few feel such compassion
For those who groan, and toil, and wail
As must make their brethren pale—

72

'Ye who suffer woes untold,
Or to feel, or to behold
Your lost country bought and sold
With a price of blood and gold—

73

'Let a vast assembly be,
And with great solemnity
Declare with measured words that ye
Are, as God has made ye, free—

74

'Be your strong and simple words
Keen to wound as sharpened swords,
And wide as targes let them be,
With their shade to cover ye.

75

'Let the tyrants pour around
With a quick and startling sound,
Like the loosening of a sea,
Troops of armed emblazonry.

76

'Let the charged artillery drive
Till the dead air seems alive
With the clash of clanging wheels,
And the tramp of horses' heels.

77

'Let the fixed bayonet
Gleam with sharp desire to wet

Its bright point in English blood
Looking keen as one for food.

78

Let the horsemen's scimitars
Wheel and flash, like sphereless stars
Thirsting to eclipse their burning
In a sea of death and mourning.

79

'Stand ye calm and resolute,
Like a forest close and mute,
With folded arms and looks which are
Weapons of unvanquished war,

80

'And let Panic, who outspeeds
The career of armed steeds
Pass, a disregarded shade
Through your phalanx undismayed.

81

'Let the laws of your own land,
Good or ill, between ye stand
Hand to hand, and foot to foot,
Arbiters of the dispute,

82

'The old laws of England—they
Whose reverend heads with age are gray,
Children of a wiser day;
And whose solemn voice must be
Thine own echo—Liberty!

83

'On those who first should violate
Such sacred heralds in their state
Rest the blood that must ensue,
And it will not rest on you.

84

'And if then the tyrants dare
Let them ride among you there,
Slash, and stab, and maim, and hew,—
What they like, that let them do.

85

'With folded arms and steady eyes,
And little fear, and less surprise,
Look upon them as they slay
Till their rage has died away.

86

Then they will return with shame
To the place from which they came,
And the blood thus shed will speak
In hot blushes on their cheek.

87

'Every woman in the land
Will point at them as they stand—
They will hardly dare to greet
Their acquaintance in the street.

88

'And the bold, true warriors
Who have hugged Danger in wars

Will turn to those who would be free,
Ashamed of such base company.

89

'And that slaughter to the Nation
Shall steam up like inspiration,
Eloquent, oracular;
A volcano heard afar.

90

'And these words shall then become
Like Oppression's thundered doom
Ringing through each heart and brain,
Heard again—again—again—

91

'Rise like Lions after slumber
In unvanquishable number—
Shake your chains to earth like dew
Which in sleep had fallen on you—
Ye are many—they are few.'

Note on the Mask of Anarchy, by Mrs. Shelley

Though Shelley's first eager desire to excite his countrymen to resist openly the oppressions existent during 'the good old times' had faded with early youth, still his warmest sympathies were for the people. He was a republican, and loved a democracy. He looked on all human beings as inheriting an equal right to possess the dearest privileges of our nature; the necessaries of life when fairly earned by labour, and intellectual instruction. His hatred of any despotism that looked upon the people as not to be consulted, or protected from want and ignorance, was intense. He was residing near Leghorn, at Villa Valsovano, writing "The Cenci", when the news of the Manchester Massacre reached us; it roused in him violent emotions of indignation and compassion. The great truth that the many, if accordant and resolute, could control the few, as was shown some years after, made him long to teach his injured countrymen how to resist. Inspired by these feelings, he wrote the "Mask of Anarchy", which he sent to his friend Leigh Hunt, to be inserted in the Examiner, of which he was then the Editor.

'I did not insert it,' Leigh Hunt writes in his valuable and interesting preface to this poem, when he printed it in 1832, 'because I thought that the public at large had not become sufficiently discerning to do justice to the sincerity and kind-heartedness of the spirit that walked in this flaming robe of verse.' Days of outrage have passed away, and with them the exasperation that would cause such an appeal to the many to be injurious. Without being aware of them, they at one time acted on his suggestions, and gained the day. But they rose when human life was respected by the Minister in power; such was not the case during the Administration which excited Shelley's abhorrence.

The poem was written for the people, and is therefore in a more popular tone than usual: portions strike as abrupt and unpolished, but many stanzas are all his own. I heard him repeat, and admired, those beginning

'My Father Time is old and gray,'

before I knew to what poem they were to belong. But the most touching passage is that which describes the blessed effects of liberty; it might make a patriot of any man whose heart was not wholly closed against his humbler fellow-creatures.

PETER BELL THE THIRD

By Miching Mallecho, Esq.

Is it a party in a parlour,
Crammed just as they on earth were crammed,
Some sipping punch—some sipping tea;
But, as you by their faces see,
All silent, and all—damned!

—"Peter Bell", by W. WORDSWORTH.

OPHELIA:—What means this, my lord?
HAMLET:—Marry, this is Miching Mallecho; it means mischief.

—SHAKESPEARE

(Composed at Florence, October, 1819, and forwarded to Hunt (November 2) to be published by C. & J. Ollier without the author's name; ultimately printed by Mrs. Shelley in the second edition of the "Poetical Works", 1839. A skit by John Hamilton Reynolds, "Peter Bell, a Lyrical Ballad", had already appeared (April, 1819), a few days before the publication of Wordsworth's "Peter Bell, a Tale". These productions were reviewed in Leigh Hunt's "Examiner" (April 26, May 3, 1819); and to the entertainment derived from his perusal of Hunt's criticisms the composition of Shelley's "Peter Bell the Third" is chiefly owing.)

Dedication

To Thomas Brown, Esq., The Younger, H.F.

Dear Tom,

Allow me to request you to introduce Mr. Peter Bell to the respectable family of the Fudges. Although he may fall short of those very considerable personages in the more active properties which characterize the Rat and the Apostate, I suspect that even you, their historian, will confess that he surpasses them in the more peculiarly legitimate qualification of intolerable dulness.

You know Mr. Examiner Hunt; well—it was he who presented me to two of the Mr. Bells. My intimacy with the younger Mr. Bell naturally sprung from this introduction to his brothers. And in presenting him to you, I have the satisfaction of being able to assure you that he is considerably the dullest of the three.

There is this particular advantage in an acquaintance with any one of the Peter Bells, that if you know one Peter Bell, you know three Peter Bells; they are not one, but three; not three, but one. An awful mystery, which, after having caused torrents of blood, and having been hymned by groans enough to deafen the music of the spheres, is at length illustrated to the satisfaction of all parties in the theological world, by the nature of Mr. Peter Bell.

Peter is a polyhedric Peter, or a Peter with many sides. He changes colours like a chameleon, and his coat like a snake. He is a Proteus of a Peter. He was at first sublime, pathetic, impressive, profound; then dull; then prosy and dull; and now dull—oh so very dull! it is an ultra-legitimate dulness.

You will perceive that it is not necessary to consider Hell and the Devil as supernatural machinery. The whole scene of my epic is in 'this world which is'—so Peter informed us before his conversion to "White Obi"—

'The world of all of us, And Where
We Find Our Happiness, Or Not At All.'

Let me observe that I have spent six or seven days in composing this sublime piece; the orb of my moonlike genius has made the fourth part of its revolution round the dull earth which you inhabit, driving you mad, while it has retained its calmness and its splendour, and I have been fitting this its last phase 'to occupy a permanent station in the literature of my country.'

Your works, indeed, dear Tom, sell better; but mine are far superior. The public is no judge; posterity sets all to rights.

Allow me to observe that so much has been written of Peter Bell, that the present history can be considered only, like the Iliad, as a continuation of that series of cyclic poems, which have already been candidates for bestowing immortality upon, at the same time that they receive it from, his character and adventures. In this point of view I have violated no rule of syntax in beginning my composition with a conjunction; the full stop which closes the poem continued by me being, like the full stops at the end of the Iliad and Odyssey, a full stop of a very qualified import.

Hoping that the immortality which you have given to the Fudges, you will receive from them; and in the firm expectation, that when London shall be an habitation of bitterns; when St. Paul's and Westminster Abbey shall stand, shapeless and nameless ruins, in the midst of an unpeopled marsh; when the piers of Waterloo Bridge shall become the nuclei of islets of reeds and osiers, and cast the jagged shadows of their broken arches on the solitary stream, some transatlantic commentator will be weighing in the scales of some new and now unimagined system of criticism, the respective merits of the Bells and the Fudges, and their historians. I remain, dear Tom, yours sincerely,

MICHING MALLECHO
December 1, 1819

P.S.—Pray excuse the date of place; so soon as the profits of the publication come in, I mean to hire lodgings in a more respectable street.

Prologue

Peter Bells, one, two and three,
O'er the wide world wandering be.—
First, the antenatal Peter,
Wrapped in weeds of the same metre,
The so-long-predestined raiment
Clothed in which to walk his way meant
The second Peter; whose ambition
Is to link the proposition,
As the mean of two extremes—
(This was learned from Aldric's themes)
Shielding from the guilt of schism
The orthodoxal syllogism;
The First Peter—he who was
Like the shadow in the glass
Of the second, yet unripe,
His substantial antitype.—

Then came Peter Bell the Second,
Who henceforward must be reckoned
The body of a double soul,
And that portion of the whole
Without which the rest would seem
Ends of a disjointed dream.—
And the Third is he who has
O'er the grave been forced to pass
To the other side, which is,—
Go and try else,—just like this.

Peter Bell the First was Peter
Smugger, milder, softer, neater,
Like the soul before it is
Born from THAT world into THIS.
The next Peter Bell was he,
Predevote, like you and me,
To good or evil as may come;
His was the severer doom,—

For he was an evil Cotter,
And a polygamic Potter.
And the last is Peter Bell,
Damned since our first parents fell,
Damned eternally to Hell—
Surely he deserves it well!

Part 1

Death

1

And Peter Bell, when he had been
With fresh-imported Hell-fire warmed,
Grew serious—from his dress and mien
'Twas very plainly to be seen
Peter was quite reformed.

2

His eyes turned up, his mouth turned down;
His accent caught a nasal twang;
He oiled his hair; there might be heard
The grace of God in every word
Which Peter said or sang.

3

But Peter now grew old, and had
An ill no doctor could unravel:
His torments almost drove him mad;—
Some said it was a fever bad—
Some swore it was the gravel.

4

His holy friends then came about,
And with long preaching and persuasion
Convinced the patient that, without
The smallest shadow of a doubt,
He was predestined to damnation.

5

They said—'Thy name is Peter Bell;
Thy skin is of a brimstone hue;
Alive or dead—ay, sick or well—
The one God made to rhyme with hell;
The other, I think, rhymes with you.

6

Then Peter set up such a yell!—
The nurse, who with some water gruel
Was climbing up the stairs, as well
As her old legs could climb them—fell,
And broke them both—the fall was cruel.

7

The Parson from the casement lept
Into the lake of Windermere—
And many an eel—though no adept
In God's right reason for it—kept
Gnawing his kidneys half a year.

8

And all the rest rushed through the door
And tumbled over one another,
And broke their skulls.—Upon the floor
Meanwhile sat Peter Bell, and swore,
And cursed his father and his mother;

9

And raved of God, and sin, and death,
Blaspheming like an infidel;
And said, that with his clenched teeth
He'd seize the earth from underneath,
And drag it with him down to hell.

10

As he was speaking came a spasm,
And wrenched his gnashing teeth asunder;
Like one who sees a strange phantasm
He lay,—there was a silent chasm
Between his upper jaw and under.

11

And yellow death lay on his face;
And a fixed smile that was not human
Told, as I understand the case,
That he was gone to the wrong place:—
I heard all this from the old woman.

12

Then there came down from Langdale Pike
A cloud, with lightning, wind and hail;
It swept over the mountains like
An ocean,—and I heard it strike
The woods and crags of Grasmere vale.

13

And I saw the black storm come
Nearer, minute after minute;
Its thunder made the cataracts dumb;
With hiss, and clash, and hollow hum,
It neared as if the Devil was in it.

14

The Devil WAS in it:—he had bought
Peter for half-a-crown; and when
The storm which bore him vanished, nought
That in the house that storm had caught
Was ever seen again.

15

The gaping neighbours came next day—
They found all vanished from the shore:
The Bible, whence he used to pray,
Half scorched under a hen-coop lay;
Smashed glass—and nothing more!

Part 2

The Devil

1

The Devil, I safely can aver,
Has neither hoof, nor tail, nor sting;
Nor is he, as some sages swear,
A spirit, neither here nor there,
In nothing—yet in everything.

2

He is—what we are; for sometimes
The Devil is a gentleman;
At others a bard bartering rhymes
For sack; a statesman spinning crimes;
A swindler, living as he can;

3

A thief, who cometh in the night,
With whole boots and net pantaloons,
Like some one whom it were not right
To mention;—or the luckless wight
From whom he steals nine silver spoons.

4

But in this case he did appear
Like a slop-merchant from Wapping,
And with smug face, and eye severe,
On every side did perk and peer
Till he saw Peter dead or napping.

5

He had on an upper Benjamin
(For he was of the driving schism)
In the which he wrapped his skin
From the storm he travelled in,
For fear of rheumatism.

6

He called the ghost out of the corse;—
It was exceedingly like Peter,—
Only its voice was hollow and hoarse—
It had a queerish look of course—
Its dress too was a little neater.

7

The Devil knew not his name and lot;
Peter knew not that he was Bell:
Each had an upper stream of thought,
Which made all seem as it was not;
Fitting itself to all things well.

8

Peter thought he had parents dear,
Brothers, sisters, cousins, cronies,
In the fens of Lincolnshire;
He perhaps had found them there
Had he gone and boldly shown his

9

Solemn phiz in his own village;
Where he thought oft when a boy
He'd clomb the orchard walls to pillage
The produce of his neighbour's tillage,
With marvellous pride and joy.

10

And the Devil thought he had,
'Mid the misery and confusion
Of an unjust war, just made
A fortune by the gainful trade
Of giving soldiers rations bad—
The world is full of strange delusion—

11

That he had a mansion planned
In a square like Grosvenor Square,
That he was aping fashion, and
That he now came to Westmoreland
To see what was romantic there.

12

And all this, though quite ideal,—
Ready at a breath to vanish,—
Was a state not more unreal
Than the peace he could not feel,
Or the care he could not banish.

13

After a little conversation,
The Devil told Peter, if he chose,
He'd bring him to the world of fashion
By giving him a situation
In his own service—and new clothes.

14

And Peter bowed, quite pleased and proud,
And after waiting some few days
For a new livery—dirty yellow
Turned up with black—the wretched fellow
Was bowled to Hell in the Devil's chaise.

Part 3

Hell

1

Hell is a city much like London—
A populous and a smoky city;
There are all sorts of people undone,
And there is little or no fun done;
Small justice shown, and still less pity.

2

There is a Castles, and a Canning,
A Cobbett, and a Castlereagh;
All sorts of caitiff corpses planning
All sorts of cozening for trepanning
Corpses less corrupt than they.

3

There is a ***, who has lost
His wits, or sold them, none knows which;
He walks about a double ghost,
And though as thin as Fraud almost—
Ever grows more grim and rich.

4

There is a Chancery Court; a King;
A manufacturing mob; a set
Of thieves who by themselves are sent
Similar thieves to represent;
An army; and a public debt.

5

Which last is a scheme of paper money,
And means—being interpreted—
'Bees, keep your wax—give us the honey,
And we will plant, while skies are sunny,
Flowers, which in winter serve instead.'

6

There is a great talk of revolution—
And a great chance of despotism—
German soldiers—camps—confusion—
Tumults—lotteries—rage—delusion—
Gin—suicide—and methodism;

7

Taxes too, on wine and bread,
And meat, and beer, and tea, and cheese,
From which those patriots pure are fed,
Who gorge before they reel to bed
The tenfold essence of all these.

8

There are mincing women, mewing,
(Like cats, who amant misere,)
Of their own virtue, and pursuing
Their gentler sisters to that ruin,
Without which—what were chastity?

9

Lawyers—judges—old hobnobbers
Are there—bailiffs—chancellors—
Bishops—great and little robbers—
Rhymesters—pamphleteers—stock-jobbers—
Men of glory in the wars,—

10

Things whose trade is, over ladies
To lean, and flirt, and stare, and simper,
Till all that is divine in woman
Grows cruel, courteous, smooth, inhuman,
Crucified 'twixt a smile and whimper.

11

Thrusting, toiling, wailing, moiling,
Frowning, preaching—such a riot!
Each with never-ceasing labour,
Whilst he thinks he cheats his neighbour,
Cheating his own heart of quiet.

12

And all these meet at levees;—
Dinners convivial and political;—
Suppers of epic poets;—teas,
Where small talk dies in agonies;—
Breakfasts professional and critical;

13

Lunches and snacks so aldermanic
That one would furnish forth ten dinners,
Where reigns a Cretan-tongued panic,
Lest news Russ, Dutch, or Alemannic
Should make some losers, and some winners—

14

At conversazioni—balls—
Conventicles—and drawing-rooms—
Courts of law—committees—calls
Of a morning—clubs—book-stalls—
Churches—masquerades—and tombs.

15

And this is Hell—and in this smother
All are damnable and damned;
Each one damning, damns the other;
They are damned by one another,
By none other are they damned.

16

'Tis a lie to say, 'God damns'!
Where was Heaven's Attorney General
When they first gave out such flams?
Let there be an end of shams,
They are mines of poisonous mineral.

17

Statesmen damn themselves to be
Cursed; and lawyers damn their souls
To the auction of a fee;
Churchmen damn themselves to see
God's sweet love in burning coals.

18

The rich are damned, beyond all cure,
To taunt, and starve, and trample on
The weak and wretched; and the poor
Damn their broken hearts to endure
Stripe on stripe, with groan on groan.

19

Sometimes the poor are damned indeed
To take,—not means for being blessed,—
But Cobbett's snuff, revenge; that weed
From which the worms that it doth feed
Squeeze less than they before possessed.

20

And some few, like we know who,
Damned—but God alone knows why—
To believe their minds are given
To make this ugly Hell a Heaven;
In which faith they live and die.

21

Thus, as in a town, plague-stricken,
Each man be he sound or no
Must indifferently sicken;
As when day begins to thicken,
None knows a pigeon from a crow,—

22

So good and bad, sane and mad,
The oppressor and the oppressed;
Those who weep to see what others
Smile to inflict upon their brothers;
Lovers, haters, worst and best;

23

All are damned—they breathe an air,
Thick, infected, joy-dispelling:
Each pursues what seems most fair,
Mining like moles, through mind, and there
Scoop palace-caverns vast, where Care
In throned state is ever dwelling.

Part 4

Sin

1

Lo. Peter in Hell's Grosvenor Square,
A footman in the Devil's service!
And the misjudging world would swear
That every man in service there
To virtue would prefer vice.

2

But Peter, though now damned, was not
What Peter was before damnation.
Men oftentimes prepare a lot
Which ere it finds them, is not what
Suits with their genuine station.

3

All things that Peter saw and felt
Had a peculiar aspect to him;
And when they came within the belt
Of his own nature, seemed to melt,
Like cloud to cloud, into him.

4

And so the outward world uniting
To that within him, he became
Considerably uninviting
To those who, meditation slighting,
Were moulded in a different frame.

5

And he scorned them, and they scorned him;
And he scorned all they did; and they
Did all that men of their own trim
Are wont to do to please their whim,
Drinking, lying, swearing, play.

6

Such were his fellow-servants; thus
His virtue, like our own, was built
Too much on that indignant fuss
Hypocrite Pride stirs up in us
To bully one another's guilt.

7

He had a mind which was somehow
At once circumference and centre
Of all he might or feel or know;
Nothing went ever out, although
Something did ever enter.

8

He had as much imagination
As a pint-pot;—he never could
Fancy another situation,
From which to dart his contemplation,
Than that wherein he stood.

9

Yet his was individual mind,
And new created all he saw
In a new manner, and refined
Those new creations, and combined
Them, by a master-spirit's law.

10

Thus—though unimaginative—
An apprehension clear, intense,
Of his mind's work, had made alive
The things it wrought on; I believe
Wakening a sort of thought in sense.

11

But from the first 'twas Peter's drift
To be a kind of moral eunuch,
He touched the hem of Nature's shift,
Felt faint—and never dared uplift
The closest, all-concealing tunic.

12

She laughed the while, with an arch smile,
And kissed him with a sister's kiss,
And said—My best Diogenes,
I love you well—but, if you please,
Tempt not again my deepest bliss.

13

''Tis you are cold—for I, not coy,
Yield love for love, frank, warm, and true;
And Burns, a Scottish peasant boy—
His errors prove it—knew my joy
More, learned friend, than you.

14

'Boeca bacciata non perde ventura,
Anzi rinnuova come fa la luna:—
So thought Boccaccio, whose sweet words might cure a
Male prude, like you, from what you now endure, a
Low-tide in soul, like a stagnant laguna.

15

Then Peter rubbed his eyes severe.
And smoothed his spacious forehead down
With his broad palm;—'twixt love and fear,
He looked, as he no doubt felt, queer,
And in his dream sate down.

16

The Devil was no uncommon creature;
A leaden-witted thief—just huddled
Out of the dross and scum of nature;
A toad-like lump of limb and feature,
With mind, and heart, and fancy muddled.

17

He was that heavy, dull, cold thing,
The spirit of evil well may be:
A drone too base to have a sting;
Who gluts, and grimes his lazy wing,
And calls lust, luxury.

18

Now he was quite the kind of wight
Round whom collect, at a fixed aera,
Venison, turtle, hock, and claret,—
Good cheer—and those who come to share it—
And best East Indian madeira!

19

It was his fancy to invite
Men of science, wit, and learning,
Who came to lend each other light;
He proudly thought that his gold's might
Had set those spirits burning.

20

And men of learning, science, wit,
Considered him as you and I
Think of some rotten tree, and sit
Lounging and dining under it,
Exposed to the wide sky.

21

And all the while with loose fat smile,
The willing wretch sat winking there,
Believing 'twas his power that made
That jovial scene—and that all paid
Homage to his unnoticed chair.

22

Though to be sure this place was Hell;
He was the Devil—and all they—
What though the claret circled well,
And wit, like ocean, rose and fell?—
Were damned eternally.

Part 5

Grace

1

Among the guests who often stayed
Till the Devil's petits-soupers,
A man there came, fair as a maid,
And Peter noted what he said,
Standing behind his master's chair.

2

He was a mighty poet—and
A subtle-souled psychologist;
All things he seemed to understand,
Of old or new—of sea or land—
But his own mind—which was a mist.

3

This was a man who might have turned
Hell into Heaven—and so in gladness
A Heaven unto himself have earned;
But he in shadows undiscerned
Trusted,—and damned himself to madness.

4

He spoke of poetry, and how
'Divine it was—a light—a love—
A spirit which like wind doth blow
As it listeth, to and fro;
A dew rained down from God above;

5

'A power which comes and goes like dream,
And which none can ever trace—
Heaven's light on earth—Truth's brightest beam.'
And when he ceased there lay the gleam
Of those words upon his face.

6

Now Peter, when he heard such talk,
Would, heedless of a broken pate,
Stand like a man asleep, or balk
Some wishing guest of knife or fork,
Or drop and break his master's plate.

7

At night he oft would start and wake
Like a lover, and began
In a wild measure songs to make
On moor, and glen, and rocky lake,
And on the heart of man—

8

And on the universal sky—
And the wide earth's bosom green,—
And the sweet, strange mystery
Of what beyond these things may lie,
And yet remain unseen.

9

For in his thought he visited
The spots in which, ere dead and damned,
He his wayward life had led;
Yet knew not whence the thoughts were fed
Which thus his fancy crammed.

10

And these obscure remembrances
Stirred such harmony in Peter,
That, whensoever he should please,
He could speak of rocks and trees
In poetic metre.

11

For though it was without a sense
Of memory, yet he remembered well
Many a ditch and quick-set fence;
Of lakes he had intelligence,
He knew something of heath and fell.

12

He had also dim recollections
Of pedlars tramping on their rounds;
Milk-pans and pails; and odd collections
Of saws, and proverbs; and reflections
Old parsons make in burying-grounds.

13

But Peter's verse was clear, and came
Announcing from the frozen hearth
Of a cold age, that none might tame
The soul of that diviner flame
It augured to the Earth:

14

Like gentle rains, on the dry plains,
Making that green which late was gray,
Or like the sudden moon, that stains
Some gloomy chamber's window-panes
With a broad light like day.

15

For language was in Peter's hand
Like clay while he was yet a potter;
And he made songs for all the land,
Sweet both to feel and understand,
As pipkins late to mountain Cotter.

16

And Mr. —, the bookseller,
Gave twenty pounds for some;—then scorning
A footman's yellow coat to wear,
Peter, too proud of heart, I fear,
Instantly gave the Devil warning.

17

Whereat the Devil took offence,
And swore in his soul a great oath then,
'That for his damned impertinence
He'd bring him to a proper sense
Of what was due to gentlemen!'

Part 6

Damnation

1

'O that mine enemy had written
A book!'—cried Job:—a fearful curse,
If to the Arab, as the Briton,
'Twas galling to be critic-bitten:—
The Devil to Peter wished no worse.

2

When Peter's next new book found vent,
The Devil to all the first Reviews
A copy of it slyly sent,
With five-pound note as compliment,
And this short notice—'Pray abuse.'

3

Then seriatim, month and quarter,
Appeared such mad tirades.—One said—
'Peter seduced Mrs. Foy's daughter,
Then drowned the mother in Ullswater,
The last thing as he went to bed.'

4

Another—'Let him shave his head!
Where's Dr. Willis?—Or is he joking?
What does the rascal mean or hope,
No longer imitating Pope,
In that barbarian Shakespeare poking?'

5

One more, 'Is incest not enough?
And must there be adultery too?
Grace after meat? Miscreant and Liar!
Thief! Blackguard! Scoundrel! Fool! hell-fire
Is twenty times too good for you.

6

'By that last book of yours WE think
You've double damned yourself to scorn;
We warned you whilst yet on the brink
You stood. From your black name will shrink
The babe that is unborn.'

7

All these Reviews the Devil made
Up in a parcel, which he had
Safely to Peter's house conveyed.
For carriage, tenpence Peter paid—
Untied them—read them—went half mad.

8

'What!' cried he, 'this is my reward
For nights of thought, and days, of toil?
Do poets, but to be abhorred
By men of whom they never heard,
Consume their spirits' oil?

9

'What have I done to them?—and who
Is Mrs. Foy? 'Tis very cruel
To speak of me and Betty so!
Adultery! God defend me! Oh!
I've half a mind to fight a duel.

10

'Or,' cried he, a grave look collecting,
'Is it my genius, like the moon,
Sets those who stand her face inspecting,
That face within their brain reflecting,
Like a crazed bell-chime, out of tune?'

11

For Peter did not know the town,
But thought, as country readers do,
For half a guinea or a crown,
He bought oblivion or renown
From God's own voice in a review.

12

All Peter did on this occasion
Was, writing some sad stuff in prose.
It is a dangerous invasion
When poets criticize; their station
Is to delight, not pose.

13

The Devil then sent to Leipsic fair
For Born's translation of Kant's book;
A world of words, tail foremost, where
Right—wrong—false—true—and foul—and fair
As in a lottery-wheel are shook.

14

Five thousand crammed octavo pages
Of German psychologics,—he
Who his furor verborum assuages
Thereon, deserves just seven months' wages
More than will e'er be due to me.

15

I looked on them nine several days,
And then I saw that they were bad;
A friend, too, spoke in their dispraise,—
He never read them;—with amaze
I found Sir William Drummond had.

16

When the book came, the Devil sent
It to P. Verbovale, Esquire,
With a brief note of compliment,
By that night's Carlisle mail. It went,
And set his soul on fire.

17

Fire, which ex luce praebens fumum,
Made him beyond the bottom see
Of truth's clear well—when I and you, Ma'am,
Go, as we shall do, subter humum,
We may know more than he.

18

Now Peter ran to seed in soul
Into a walking paradox;
For he was neither part nor whole,
Nor good, nor bad—nor knave nor fool;
—Among the woods and rocks.

19

Furious he rode, where late he ran,
Lashing and spurring his tame hobby;
Turned to a formal puritan,
A solemn and unsexual man,—
He half believed "White Obi".

20

This steed in vision he would ride,
High trotting over nine-inch bridges,
With Flibbertigibbet, imp of pride,
Mocking and mowing by his side—
A mad-brained goblin for a guide—
Over corn-fields, gates, and hedges.

21

After these ghastly rides, he came
Home to his heart, and found from thence
Much stolen of its accustomed flame;
His thoughts grew weak, drowsy, and lame
Of their intelligence.

22

To Peter's view, all seemed one hue;
He was no Whig, he was no Tory;
No Deist and no Christian he;—
He got so subtle, that to be
Nothing, was all his glory.

23

One single point in his belief
From his organization sprung,
The heart-enrooted faith, the chief
Ear in his doctrines' blighted sheaf,
That 'Happiness is wrong';

24

So thought Calvin and Dominic;
So think their fierce successors, who
Even now would neither stint nor stick

Our flesh from off our bones to pick,
If they might 'do their do.'

25

His morals thus were undermined:—
The old Peter—the hard, old Potter—
Was born anew within his mind;
He grew dull, harsh, sly, unrefined,
As when he tramped beside the Otter.

26

In the death hues of agony
Lambently flashing from a fish,
Now Peter felt amused to see
Shades like a rainbow's rise and flee,
Mixed with a certain hungry wish.

27

So in his Country's dying face
He looked—and, lovely as she lay,
Seeking in vain his last embrace,
Wailing her own abandoned case,
With hardened sneer he turned away:

28

And coolly to his own soul said;—
'Do you not think that we might make
A poem on her when she's dead:—
Or, no—a thought is in my head—
Her shroud for a new sheet I'll take:

29

'My wife wants one.—Let who will bury
This mangled corpse! And I and you,

My dearest Soul, will then make merry,
As the Prince Regent did with Sherry,—'
'Ay—and at last desert me too.'

30

And so his Soul would not be gay,
But moaned within him; like a fawn
Moaning within a cave, it lay
Wounded and wasting, day by day,
Till all its life of life was gone.

31

As troubled skies stain waters clear,
The storm in Peter's heart and mind
Now made his verses dark and queer:
They were the ghosts of what they were,
Shaking dim grave-clothes in the wind.

32

For he now raved enormous folly,
Of Baptisms, Sunday-schools, and Graves,
'Twould make George Colman melancholy
To have heard him, like a male Molly,
Chanting those stupid staves.

33

Yet the Reviews, who heaped abuse
On Peter while he wrote for freedom,
So soon as in his song they spy
The folly which soothes tyranny,
Praise him, for those who feed 'em.

34

'He was a man, too great to scan;—
A planet lost in truth's keen rays:—
His virtue, awful and prodigious;—
He was the most sublime, religious,
Pure-minded Poet of these days.'

35

As soon as he read that, cried Peter,
'Eureka! I have found the way
To make a better thing of metre
Than e'er was made by living creature
Up to this blessed day.'

36

Then Peter wrote odes to the Devil;—
In one of which he meekly said:
'May Carnage and Slaughter,
Thy niece and thy daughter,
May Rapine and Famine,
Thy gorge ever cramming,
Glut thee with living and dead!

37

'May Death and Damnation,
And Consternation,
Flit up from Hell with pure intent!
Slash them at Manchester,
Glasgow, Leeds, and Chester;
Drench all with blood from Avon to Trent.

38

'Let thy body-guard yeomen
Hew down babes and women,

And laugh with bold triumph till Heaven be rent!
When Moloch in Jewry
Munched children with fury,
It was thou, Devil, dining with pure intent.

Part 7

Double Damnation

1

The Devil now knew his proper cue.—
Soon as he read the ode, he drove
To his friend Lord MacMurderchouse's,
A man of interest in both houses,
And said:—'For money or for love,

2

'Pray find some cure or sinecure;
To feed from the superfluous taxes
A friend of ours—a poet—fewer
Have fluttered tamer to the lure
Than he.' His lordship stands and racks his

3

Stupid brains, while one might count
As many beads as he had boroughs,—
At length replies; from his mean front,
Like one who rubs out an account,
Smoothing away the unmeaning furrows:

4

'It happens fortunately, dear Sir,
I can. I hope I need require
No pledge from you, that he will stir
In our affairs;—like Oliver.
That he'll be worthy of his hire.'

5

These words exchanged, the news sent off
To Peter, home the Devil hied,—
Took to his bed; he had no cough,
No doctor,—meat and drink enough.—
Yet that same night he died.

6

The Devil's corpse was leaded down;
His decent heirs enjoyed his pelf,
Mourning-coaches, many a one,
Followed his hearse along the town:—
Where was the Devil himself?

7

When Peter heard of his promotion,
His eyes grew like two stars for bliss:
There was a bow of sleek devotion
Engendering in his back; each motion
Seemed a Lord's shoe to kiss.

8

He hired a house, bought plate, and made
A genteel drive up to his door,
With sifted gravel neatly laid,—
As if defying all who said,
Peter was ever poor.

9

But a disease soon struck into
The very life and soul of Peter—
He walked about—slept—had the hue
Of health upon his cheeks—and few
Dug better—none a heartier eater.

10

And yet a strange and horrid curse
Clung upon Peter, night and day;
Month after month the thing grew worse,
And deadlier than in this my verse
I can find strength to say.

11

Peter was dull—he was at first
Dull—oh, so dull—so very dull!
Whether he talked, wrote, or rehearsed—
Still with this dulness was he cursed—
Dull—beyond all conception—dull.

12

No one could read his books—no mortal,
But a few natural friends, would hear him;
The parson came not near his portal;
His state was like that of the immortal
Described by Swift—no man could bear him.

13

His sister, wife, and children yawned,
With a long, slow, and drear ennui,
All human patience far beyond;
Their hopes of Heaven each would have pawned,
Anywhere else to be.

14

But in his verse, and in his prose,
The essence of his dulness was
Concentred and compressed so close,
'Twould have made Guatimozin doze
On his red gridiron of brass.

15

A printer's boy, folding those pages,
Fell slumbrously upon one side;
Like those famed Seven who slept three ages.
To wakeful frenzy's vigil—rages,
As opiates, were the same applied.

16

Even the Reviewers who were hired
To do the work of his reviewing,
With adamantine nerves, grew tired;—
Gaping and torpid they retired,
To dream of what they should be doing.

17

And worse and worse, the drowsy curse
Yawned in him, till it grew a pest—
A wide contagious atmosphere,
Creeping like cold through all things near;
A power to infect and to infest.

18

His servant-maids and dogs grew dull;
His kitten, late a sportive elf;
The woods and lakes, so beautiful,
Of dim stupidity were full.
All grew dull as Peter's self.

19

The earth under his feet—the springs,
Which lived within it a quick life,
The air, the winds of many wings,
That fan it with new murmurings,
Were dead to their harmonious strife.

20

The birds and beasts within the wood,
The insects, and each creeping thing,
Were now a silent multitude;
Love's work was left unwrought—no brood
Near Peter's house took wing.

21

And every neighbouring cottager
Stupidly yawned upon the other:
No jackass brayed; no little cur
Cocked up his ears;—no man would stir
To save a dying mother.

22

Yet all from that charmed district went
But some half-idiot and half-knave,
Who rather than pay any rent,
Would live with marvellous content,
Over his father's grave.

23

No bailiff dared within that space,
For fear of the dull charm, to enter;
A man would bear upon his face,
For fifteen months in any case,
The yawn of such a venture.

24

Seven miles above—below—around—
This pest of dulness holds its sway;
A ghastly life without a sound;
To Peter's soul the spell is bound—
How should it ever pass away?

Note on Peter Bell the Third,
by Mrs. Shelley

In this new edition I have added "Peter Bell the Third". A critique on Wordsworth's "Peter Bell" reached us at Leghorn, which amused Shelley exceedingly, and suggested this poem.

I need scarcely observe that nothing personal to the author of "Peter Bell" is intended in this poem. No man ever admired Wordsworth's poetry more;—he read it perpetually, and taught others to appreciate its beauties. This poem is, like all others written by Shelley, ideal. He conceived the idealism of a poet—a man of lofty and creative genius— quitting the glorious calling of discovering and announcing the beautiful and good, to support and propagate ignorant prejudices and pernicious errors; imparting to the unenlightened, not that ardour for truth and spirit of toleration which Shelley looked on as the sources of the moral improvement and happiness of mankind, but false and injurious opinions, that evil was good, and that ignorance and force were the best allies of purity and virtue. His idea was that a man gifted, even as transcendently as the author of "Peter Bell", with the highest qualities of genius, must, if he fostered such errors, be infected with dulness. This poem was written as a warning—not as a narration of the reality. He was unacquainted personally with Wordsworth, or with Coleridge (to whom he alludes in the fifth part of the poem), and therefore, I repeat, his poem is purely ideal;—it contains something of criticism on the compositions of those great poets, but nothing injurious to the men themselves.

No poem contains more of Shelley's peculiar views with regard to the errors into which many of the wisest have fallen, and the pernicious effects of certain opinions on society. Much of it is beautifully written: and, though, like the burlesque drama of "Swellfoot", it must be looked on as a plaything, it has so much merit and poetry—so much of HIMSELF in it—that it cannot fail to interest greatly, and by right belongs to the world for whose instruction and benefit it was written.

LETTER TO MARIA GISBORNE

(Composed during Shelley's occupation of the Gisbornes' house at Leghorn, July, 1820; published in "Posthumous Poems", 1824. Sources of the text are (1) a draft in Shelley's hand, 'partly illegible' (Forman), amongst the Boscombe manuscripts; (2) a transcript by Mrs. Shelley; (3) the editio princeps, 1824; the text in "Poetical Works", 1839, 1st and 2nd editions. Our text is that of Mrs. Shelley's transcript, modified by the Boscombe manuscript. Here, as elsewhere in this edition, the readings of the editio princeps are preserved in the footnotes.)

Leghorn, July 1, 1820

The spider spreads her webs, whether she be
In poet's tower, cellar, or barn, or tree;
The silk-worm in the dark green mulberry leaves
His winding sheet and cradle ever weaves;
So I, a thing whom moralists call worm,
Sit spinning still round this decaying form,
From the fine threads of rare and subtle thought—
No net of words in garish colours wrought
To catch the idle buzzers of the day—
But a soft cell, where when that fades away,
Memory may clothe in wings my living name
And feed it with the asphodels of fame,
Which in those hearts which must remember me
Grow, making love an immortality.

Whoever should behold me now, I wist,
Would think I were a mighty mechanist,
Bent with sublime Archimedean art
To breathe a soul into the iron heart
Of some machine portentous, or strange gin,
Which by the force of figured spells might win
Its way over the sea, and sport therein;
For round the walls are hung dread engines, such
As Vulcan never wrought for Jove to clutch
Ixion or the Titan:—or the quick
Wit of that man of God, St. Dominic,
To convince Atheist, Turk, or Heretic,
Or those in philanthropic council met,
Who thought to pay some interest for the debt
They owed to Jesus Christ for their salvation,
By giving a faint foretaste of damnation
To Shakespeare, Sidney, Spenser, and the rest
Who made our land an island of the blest,
When lamp-like Spain, who now relumes her fire
On Freedom's hearth, grew dim with Empire:—
With thumbscrews, wheels, with tooth and spike and jag,

Which fishers found under the utmost crag
Of Cornwall and the storm-encompassed isles,
Where to the sky the rude sea rarely smiles
Unless in treacherous wrath, as on the morn
When the exulting elements in scorn,
Satiated with destroyed destruction, lay
Sleeping in beauty on their mangled prey,
As panthers sleep;—and other strange and dread
Magical forms the brick floor overspread,—
Proteus transformed to metal did not make
More figures, or more strange; nor did he take
Such shapes of unintelligible brass,
Or heap himself in such a horrid mass
Of tin and iron not to be understood;
And forms of unimaginable wood,
To puzzle Tubal Cain and all his brood:
Great screws, and cones, and wheels, and grooved blocks,
The elements of what will stand the shocks
Of wave and wind and time.—Upon the table
More knacks and quips there be than I am able
To catalogize in this verse of mine:—
A pretty bowl of wood—not full of wine,
But quicksilver; that dew which the gnomes drink
When at their subterranean toil they swink,
Pledging the demons of the earthquake, who
Reply to them in lava—cry halloo!
And call out to the cities o'er their head,—
Roofs, towers, and shrines, the dying and the dead,
Crash through the chinks of earth—and then all quaff
Another rouse, and hold their sides and laugh.
This quicksilver no gnome has drunk—within
The walnut bowl it lies, veined and thin,
In colour like the wake of light that stains
The Tuscan deep, when from the moist moon rains
The inmost shower of its white fire—the breeze
Is still—blue Heaven smiles over the pale seas.
And in this bowl of quicksilver—for I
Yield to the impulse of an infancy
Outlasting manhood—I have made to float

A rude idealism of a paper boat:—
A hollow screw with cogs—Henry will know
The thing I mean and laugh at me,—if so
He fears not I should do more mischief.—Next
Lie bills and calculations much perplexed,
With steam-boats, frigates, and machinery quaint
Traced over them in blue and yellow paint.
Then comes a range of mathematical
Instruments, for plans nautical and statical,
A heap of rosin, a queer broken glass
With ink in it;—a china cup that was
What it will never be again, I think,—
A thing from which sweet lips were wont to drink
The liquor doctors rail at—and which I
Will quaff in spite of them—and when we die
We'll toss up who died first of drinking tea,
And cry out,—'Heads or tails?' where'er we be.
Near that a dusty paint-box, some odd hooks,
A half-burnt match, an ivory block, three books,
Where conic sections, spherics, logarithms,
To great Laplace, from Saunderson and Sims,
Lie heaped in their harmonious disarray
Of figures,—disentangle them who may.
Baron de Tott's Memoirs beside them lie,
And some odd volumes of old chemistry.
Near those a most inexplicable thing,
With lead in the middle—I'm conjecturing
How to make Henry understand; but no—
I'll leave, as Spenser says, with many mo,
This secret in the pregnant womb of time,
Too vast a matter for so weak a rhyme.

And here like some weird Archimage sit I,
Plotting dark spells, and devilish enginery,
The self-impelling steam-wheels of the mind
Which pump up oaths from clergymen, and grind
The gentle spirit of our meek reviews
Into a powdery foam of salt abuse,
Ruffling the ocean of their self-content;—

I sit—and smile or sigh as is my bent,
But not for them—Libeccio rushes round
With an inconstant and an idle sound,
I heed him more than them—the thunder-smoke
Is gathering on the mountains, like a cloak
Folded athwart their shoulders broad and bare;
The ripe corn under the undulating air
Undulates like an ocean;—and the vines
Are trembling wide in all their trellised lines—
The murmur of the awakening sea doth fill
The empty pauses of the blast;—the hill
Looks hoary through the white electric rain,
And from the glens beyond, in sullen strain,
The interrupted thunder howls; above
One chasm of Heaven smiles, like the eye of Love
On the unquiet world;—while such things are,
How could one worth your friendship heed the war
Of worms? the shriek of the world's carrion jays,
Their censure, or their wonder, or their praise?

You are not here! the quaint witch Memory sees,
In vacant chairs, your absent images,
And points where once you sat, and now should be
But are not.—I demand if ever we
Shall meet as then we met;—and she replies.
Veiling in awe her second-sighted eyes;
'I know the past alone—but summon home
My sister Hope,—she speaks of all to come.'
But I, an old diviner, who knew well
Every false verse of that sweet oracle,
Turned to the sad enchantress once again,
And sought a respite from my gentle pain,
In citing every passage o'er and o'er
Of our communion—how on the sea-shore
We watched the ocean and the sky together,
Under the roof of blue Italian weather;
How I ran home through last year's thunder-storm,
And felt the transverse lightning linger warm
Upon my cheek—and how we often made

Feasts for each other, where good will outweighed
The frugal luxury of our country cheer,
As well it might, were it less firm and clear
Than ours must ever be;—and how we spun
A shroud of talk to hide us from the sun
Of this familiar life, which seems to be
But is not:—or is but quaint mockery
Of all we would believe, and sadly blame
The jarring and inexplicable frame
Of this wrong world:—and then anatomize
The purposes and thoughts of men whose eyes
Were closed in distant years;—or widely guess
The issue of the earth's great business,
When we shall be as we no longer are—
Like babbling gossips safe, who hear the war
Of winds, and sigh, but tremble not;—or how
You listened to some interrupted flow
Of visionary rhyme,—in joy and pain
Struck from the inmost fountains of my brain,
With little skill perhaps;—or how we sought
Those deepest wells of passion or of thought
Wrought by wise poets in the waste of years,
Staining their sacred waters with our tears;
Quenching a thirst ever to be renewed!
Or how I, wisest lady! then endued
The language of a land which now is free,
And, winged with thoughts of truth and majesty,
Flits round the tyrant's sceptre like a cloud,
And bursts the peopled prisons, and cries aloud,
'My name is Legion!'—that majestic tongue
Which Calderon over the desert flung
Of ages and of nations; and which found
An echo in our hearts, and with the sound
Startled oblivion;—thou wert then to me
As is a nurse—when inarticulately
A child would talk as its grown parents do.
If living winds the rapid clouds pursue,
If hawks chase doves through the aethereal way,
Huntsmen the innocent deer, and beasts their prey,

Why should not we rouse with the spirit's blast
Out of the forest of the pathless past
These recollected pleasures?
You are now
In London, that great sea, whose ebb and flow
At once is deaf and loud, and on the shore
Vomits its wrecks, and still howls on for more.
Yet in its depth what treasures! You will see
That which was Godwin,—greater none than he
Though fallen—and fallen on evil times—to stand
Among the spirits of our age and land,
Before the dread tribunal of "to come"
The foremost,—while Rebuke cowers pale and dumb.
You will see Coleridge—he who sits obscure
In the exceeding lustre and the pure
Intense irradiation of a mind,
Which, with its own internal lightning blind,
Flags wearily through darkness and despair—
A cloud-encircled meteor of the air,
A hooded eagle among blinking owls.—
You will see Hunt—one of those happy souls
Which are the salt of the earth, and without whom
This world would smell like what it is—a tomb;
Who is, what others seem; his room no doubt
Is still adorned with many a cast from Shout,
With graceful flowers tastefully placed about;
And coronals of bay from ribbons hung,
And brighter wreaths in neat disorder flung;
The gifts of the most learned among some dozens
Of female friends, sisters-in-law, and cousins.
And there is he with his eternal puns,
Which beat the dullest brain for smiles, like duns
Thundering for money at a poet's door;
Alas! it is no use to say, 'I'm poor!'
Or oft in graver mood, when he will look
Things wiser than were ever read in book,
Except in Shakespeare's wisest tenderness.—
You will see Hogg,—and I cannot express
His virtues,—though I know that they are great,

Because he locks, then barricades the gate
Within which they inhabit;—of his wit
And wisdom, you'll cry out when you are bit.
He is a pearl within an oyster shell.
One of the richest of the deep;—and there
Is English Peacock, with his mountain Fair,
Turned into a Flamingo;—that shy bird
That gleams i' the Indian air—have you not heard
When a man marries, dies, or turns Hindoo,
His best friends hear no more of him?—but you
Will see him, and will like him too, I hope,
With the milk-white Snowdonian Antelope
Matched with this cameleopard—his fine wit
Makes such a wound, the knife is lost in it;
A strain too learned for a shallow age,
Too wise for selfish bigots; let his page,
Which charms the chosen spirits of the time,
Fold itself up for the serener clime
Of years to come, and find its recompense
In that just expectation.—Wit and sense,
Virtue and human knowledge; all that might
Make this dull world a business of delight,
Are all combined in Horace Smith.—And these.
With some exceptions, which I need not tease
Your patience by descanting on,—are all
You and I know in London.
I recall
My thoughts, and bid you look upon the night.
As water does a sponge, so the moonlight
Fills the void, hollow, universal air—
What see you?—unpavilioned Heaven is fair,
Whether the moon, into her chamber gone,
Leaves midnight to the golden stars, or wan
Climbs with diminished beams the azure steep;
Or whether clouds sail o'er the inverse deep,
Piloted by the many-wandering blast,
And the rare stars rush through them dim and fast:—
All this is beautiful in every land.—
But what see you beside?—a shabby stand

Of Hackney coaches—a brick house or wall
Fencing some lonely court, white with the scrawl
Of our unhappy politics;—or worse—
A wretched woman reeling by, whose curse
Mixed with the watchman's, partner of her trade,
You must accept in place of serenade—
Or yellow-haired Pollonia murmuring
To Henry, some unutterable thing.
I see a chaos of green leaves and fruit
Built round dark caverns, even to the root
Of the living stems that feed them—in whose bowers
There sleep in their dark dew the folded flowers;
Beyond, the surface of the unsickled corn
Trembles not in the slumbering air, and borne
In circles quaint, and ever-changing dance,
Like winged stars the fire-flies flash and glance,
Pale in the open moonshine, but each one
Under the dark trees seems a little sun,
A meteor tamed; a fixed star gone astray
From the silver regions of the milky way;—
Afar the Contadino's song is heard,
Rude, but made sweet by distance—and a bird
Which cannot be the Nightingale, and yet
I know none else that sings so sweet as it
At this late hour;—and then all is still—
Now—Italy or London, which you will!

Next winter you must pass with me; I'll have
My house by that time turned into a grave
Of dead despondence and low-thoughted care,
And all the dreams which our tormentors are;
Oh! that Hunt, Hogg, Peacock, and Smith were there,
With everything belonging to them fair!—
We will have books, Spanish, Italian, Greek;
And ask one week to make another week
As like his father, as I'm unlike mine,
Which is not his fault, as you may divine.
Though we eat little flesh and drink no wine,
Yet let's be merry: we'll have tea and toast;

Custards for supper, and an endless host
Of syllabubs and jellies and mince-pies,
And other such lady-like luxuries,—
Feasting on which we will philosophize!
And we'll have fires out of the Grand Duke's wood,
To thaw the six weeks' winter in our blood.
And then we'll talk;—what shall we talk about?
Oh! there are themes enough for many a bout
Of thought-entangled descant;—as to nerves—
With cones and parallelograms and curves
I've sworn to strangle them if once they dare
To bother me—when you are with me there.
And they shall never more sip laudanum,
From Helicon or Himeros;—well, come,
And in despite of God and of the devil,
We'll make our friendly philosophic revel
Outlast the leafless time; till buds and flowers
Warn the obscure inevitable hours,
Sweet meeting by sad parting to renew;—
'To-morrow to fresh woods and pastures new.'

THE WITCH OF ATLAS

(Composed at the Baths of San Giuliano, near Pisa, August 14–16, 1820; published in Posthumous Poems, edition Mrs. Shelley, 1824. The dedication To Mas-y first appeared in the Poetical Works, 1839, 1st edition Sources of the text are (1) the editio princeps, 1824; (2) editions 1839 (which agree, and, save in two instances, follow edition 1824); (3) an early and incomplete manuscript in Shelley's handwriting (now at the Bodleian, here, as throughout, cited as B.), carefully collated by Mr. C.D. Locock, who printed the results in his Examination of the Shelley manuscripts, etc., Oxford, Clarendon Press, 1903; (4) a later, yet intermediate, transcript by Mrs. Shelley, the variations of which are noted by Mr. H. Buxton Forman. The original text is modified in many places by variants from the manuscripts, but the readings of edition 1824 are, in every instance, given in the footnotes.)

To Mary

(On her Objecting to the Following Poem, upon the Score of its Containing no Human Interest)

1

How, my dear Mary,—are you critic-bitten
(For vipers kill, though dead) by some review,
That you condemn these verses I have written,
Because they tell no story, false or true?
What, though no mice are caught by a young kitten,
May it not leap and play as grown cats do,
Till its claws come? Prithee, for this one time,
Content thee with a visionary rhyme.

2

What hand would crush the silken-winged fly,
The youngest of inconstant April's minions,
Because it cannot climb the purest sky,
Where the swan sings, amid the sun's dominions?
Not thine. Thou knowest 'tis its doom to die,
When Day shall hide within her twilight pinions
The lucent eyes, and the eternal smile,
Serene as thine, which lent it life awhile.

3

To thy fair feet a winged Vision came,
Whose date should have been longer than a day,
And o'er thy head did beat its wings for fame,
And in thy sight its fading plumes display;
The watery bow burned in the evening flame.
But the shower fell, the swift Sun went his way—
And that is dead.—O, let me not believe
That anything of mine is fit to live!

4

Wordsworth informs us he was nineteen years
Considering and retouching Peter Bell;
Watering his laurels with the killing tears
Of slow, dull care, so that their roots to Hell
Might pierce, and their wide branches blot the spheres
Of Heaven, with dewy leaves and flowers; this well
May be, for Heaven and Earth conspire to foil
The over-busy gardener's blundering toil.

5

My Witch indeed is not so sweet a creature
As Ruth or Lucy, whom his graceful praise
Clothes for our grandsons—but she matches Peter,
Though he took nineteen years, and she three days
In dressing. Light the vest of flowing metre
She wears; he, proud as dandy with his stays,
Has hung upon his wiry limbs a dress
Like King Lear's 'looped and windowed raggedness.'

6

If you strip Peter, you will see a fellow
Scorched by Hell's hyperequatorial climate
Into a kind of a sulphureous yellow:
A lean mark, hardly fit to fling a rhyme at;
In shape a Scaramouch, in hue Othello.
If you unveil my Witch, no priest nor primate
Can shrive you of that sin,—if sin there be
In love, when it becomes idolatry.

The Witch of Atlas

1

Before those cruel Twins, whom at one birth
Incestuous Change bore to her father Time,
Error and Truth, had hunted from the Earth
All those bright natures which adorned its prime,
And left us nothing to believe in, worth
The pains of putting into learned rhyme,
A lady-witch there lived on Atlas' mountain
Within a cavern, by a secret fountain.

2

Her mother was one of the Atlantides:
The all-beholding Sun had ne'er beholden
In his wide voyage o'er continents and seas
So fair a creature, as she lay enfolden
In the warm shadow of her loveliness;—
He kissed her with his beams, and made all golden
The chamber of gray rock in which she lay—
She, in that dream of joy, dissolved away.

3

'Tis said, she first was changed into a vapour,
And then into a cloud, such clouds as flit,
Like splendour-winged moths about a taper,
Round the red west when the sun dies in it:
And then into a meteor, such as caper
On hill-tops when the moon is in a fit:
Then, into one of those mysterious stars
Which hide themselves between the Earth and Mars.

4

Ten times the Mother of the Months had bent
Her bow beside the folding-star, and bidden
With that bright sign the billows to indent
The sea-deserted sand—like children chidden,
At her command they ever came and went—
Since in that cave a dewy splendour hidden
Took shape and motion: with the living form
Of this embodied Power, the cave grew warm.

5

A lovely lady garmented in light
From her own beauty—deep her eyes, as are
Two openings of unfathomable night
Seen through a Temple's cloven roof—her hair
Dark—the dim brain whirls dizzy with delight.
Picturing her form; her soft smiles shone afar,
And her low voice was heard like love, and drew
All living things towards this wonder new.

6

And first the spotted cameleopard came,
And then the wise and fearless elephant;
Then the sly serpent, in the golden flame
Of his own volumes intervolved;—all gaunt
And sanguine beasts her gentle looks made tame.
They drank before her at her sacred fount;
And every beast of beating heart grew bold,
Such gentleness and power even to behold.

7

The brinded lioness led forth her young,
That she might teach them how they should forego
Their inborn thirst of death; the pard unstrung
His sinews at her feet, and sought to know

With looks whose motions spoke without a tongue
How he might be as gentle as the doe.
The magic circle of her voice and eyes
All savage natures did imparadise.

8

And old Silenus, shaking a green stick
Of lilies, and the wood-gods in a crew
Came, blithe, as in the olive copses thick
Cicadae are, drunk with the noonday dew:
And Dryope and Faunus followed quick,
Teasing the God to sing them something new;
Till in this cave they found the lady lone,
Sitting upon a seat of emerald stone.

9

And universal Pan, 'tis said, was there,
And though none saw him,—through the adamant
Of the deep mountains, through the trackless air,
And through those living spirits, like a want,
He passed out of his everlasting lair
Where the quick heart of the great world doth pant,
And felt that wondrous lady all alone,—
And she felt him, upon her emerald throne.

10

And every nymph of stream and spreading tree,
And every shepherdess of Ocean's flocks,
Who drives her white waves over the green sea,
And Ocean with the brine on his gray locks,
And quaint Priapus with his company,
All came, much wondering how the enwombed rocks
Could have brought forth so beautiful a birth;—
Her love subdued their wonder and their mirth.

11

The herdsmen and the mountain maidens came,
And the rude kings of pastoral Garamant—
Their spirits shook within them, as a flame
Stirred by the air under a cavern gaunt:
Pigmies, and Polyphemes, by many a name,
Centaurs, and Satyrs, and such shapes as haunt
Wet clefts,—and lumps neither alive nor dead,
Dog-headed, bosom-eyed, and bird-footed.

12

For she was beautiful—her beauty made
The bright world dim, and everything beside
Seemed like the fleeting image of a shade:
No thought of living spirit could abide,
Which to her looks had ever been betrayed,
On any object in the world so wide,
On any hope within the circling skies,
But on her form, and in her inmost eyes.

13

Which when the lady knew, she took her spindle
And twined three threads of fleecy mist, and three
Long lines of light, such as the dawn may kindle
The clouds and waves and mountains with; and she
As many star-beams, ere their lamps could dwindle
In the belated moon, wound skilfully;
And with these threads a subtle veil she wove—
A shadow for the splendour of her love.

14

The deep recesses of her odorous dwelling
Were stored with magic treasures—sounds of air,
Which had the power all spirits of compelling,
Folded in cells of crystal silence there;

Such as we hear in youth, and think the feeling
Will never die—yet ere we are aware,
The feeling and the sound are fled and gone,
And the regret they leave remains alone.

15

And there lay Visions swift, and sweet, and quaint,
Each in its thin sheath, like a chrysalis,
Some eager to burst forth, some weak and faint
With the soft burthen of intensest bliss.
It was its work to bear to many a saint
Whose heart adores the shrine which holiest is,
Even Love's:—and others white, green, gray, and black,
And of all shapes—and each was at her beck.

16

And odours in a kind of aviary
Of ever-blooming Eden-trees she kept,
Clipped in a floating net, a love-sick Fairy
Had woven from dew-beams while the moon yet slept;
As bats at the wired window of a dairy,
They beat their vans; and each was an adept,
When loosed and missioned, making wings of winds,
To stir sweet thoughts or sad, in destined minds.

17

And liquors clear and sweet, whose healthful might
Could medicine the sick soul to happy sleep,
And change eternal death into a night
Of glorious dreams—or if eyes needs must weep,
Could make their tears all wonder and delight,
She in her crystal vials did closely keep:
If men could drink of those clear vials, 'tis said
The living were not envied of the dead.

18

Her cave was stored with scrolls of strange device,
The works of some Saturnian Archimage,
Which taught the expiations at whose price
Men from the Gods might win that happy age
Too lightly lost, redeeming native vice;
And which might quench the Earth-consuming rage
Of gold and blood—till men should live and move
Harmonious as the sacred stars above;

19

And how all things that seem untameable,
Not to be checked and not to be confined,
Obey the spells of Wisdom's wizard skill;
Time, earth, and fire—the ocean and the wind,
And all their shapes—and man's imperial will;
And other scrolls whose writings did unbind
The inmost lore of Love—let the profane
Tremble to ask what secrets they contain.

20

And wondrous works of substances unknown,
To which the enchantment of her father's power
Had changed those ragged blocks of savage stone,
Were heaped in the recesses of her bower;
Carved lamps and chalices, and vials which shone
In their own golden beams—each like a flower,
Out of whose depth a fire-fly shakes his light
Under a cypress in a starless night.

21

At first she lived alone in this wild home,
And her own thoughts were each a minister,
Clothing themselves, or with the ocean foam,
Or with the wind, or with the speed of fire,

To work whatever purposes might come
Into her mind; such power her mighty Sire
Had girt them with, whether to fly or run,
Through all the regions which he shines upon.

22

The Ocean-nymphs and Hamadryades,
Oreads and Naiads, with long weedy locks,
Offered to do her bidding through the seas,
Under the earth, and in the hollow rocks,
And far beneath the matted roots of trees,
And in the gnarled heart of stubborn oaks,
So they might live for ever in the light
Of her sweet presence—each a satellite.

23

'This may not be,' the wizard maid replied;
'The fountains where the Naiades bedew
Their shining hair, at length are drained and dried;
The solid oaks forget their strength, and strew
Their latest leaf upon the mountains wide;
The boundless ocean like a drop of dew
Will be consumed—the stubborn centre must
Be scattered, like a cloud of summer dust.

24

'And ye with them will perish, one by one;—
If I must sigh to think that this shall be,
If I must weep when the surviving Sun
Shall smile on your decay—oh, ask not me
To love you till your little race is run;
I cannot die as ye must—over me
Your leaves shall glance—the streams in which ye dwell
Shall be my paths henceforth, and so—farewell!'—

25

She spoke and wept:—the dark and azure well
Sparkled beneath the shower of her bright tears,
And every little circlet where they fell
Flung to the cavern-roof inconstant spheres
And intertangled lines of light:—a knell
Of sobbing voices came upon her ears
From those departing Forms, o'er the serene
Of the white streams and of the forest green.

26

All day the wizard lady sate aloof,
Spelling out scrolls of dread antiquity,
Under the cavern's fountain-lighted roof;
Or broidering the pictured poesy
Of some high tale upon her growing woof,
Which the sweet splendour of her smiles could dye
In hues outshining heaven—and ever she
Added some grace to the wrought poesy.

27

While on her hearth lay blazing many a piece
Of sandal wood, rare gums, and cinnamon;
Men scarcely know how beautiful fire is—
Each flame of it is as a precious stone
Dissolved in ever-moving light, and this
Belongs to each and all who gaze upon.
The Witch beheld it not, for in her hand
She held a woof that dimmed the burning brand.

28

This lady never slept, but lay in trance
All night within the fountain—as in sleep.
Its emerald crags glowed in her beauty's glance;
Through the green splendour of the water deep

She saw the constellations reel and dance
Like fire-flies—and withal did ever keep
The tenour of her contemplations calm,
With open eyes, closed feet, and folded palm.

29

And when the whirlwinds and the clouds descended
From the white pinnacles of that cold hill,
She passed at dewfall to a space extended,
Where in a lawn of flowering asphodel
Amid a wood of pines and cedars blended,
There yawned an inextinguishable well
Of crimson fire—full even to the brim,
And overflowing all the margin trim.

30

Within the which she lay when the fierce war
Of wintry winds shook that innocuous liquor
In many a mimic moon and bearded star
O'er woods and lawns;—the serpent heard it flicker
In sleep, and dreaming still, he crept afar—
And when the windless snow descended thicker
Than autumn leaves, she watched it as it came
Melt on the surface of the level flame.

31

She had a boat, which some say Vulcan wrought
For Venus, as the chariot of her star;
But it was found too feeble to be fraught
With all the ardours in that sphere which are,
And so she sold it, and Apollo bought
And gave it to this daughter: from a car
Changed to the fairest and the lightest boat
Which ever upon mortal stream did float.

32

And others say, that, when but three hours old,
The first-born Love out of his cradle lept,
And clove dun Chaos with his wings of gold,
And like a horticultural adept,
Stole a strange seed, and wrapped it up in mould,
And sowed it in his mother's star, and kept
Watering it all the summer with sweet dew,
And with his wings fanning it as it grew.

33

The plant grew strong and green, the snowy flower
Fell, and the long and gourd-like fruit began
To turn the light and dew by inward power
To its own substance; woven tracery ran
Of light firm texture, ribbed and branching, o'er
The solid rind, like a leaf's veined fan—
Of which Love scooped this boat—and with soft motion
Piloted it round the circumfluous ocean.

34

This boat she moored upon her fount, and lit
A living spirit within all its frame,
Breathing the soul of swiftness into it.
Couched on the fountain like a panther tame,
One of the twain at Evan's feet that sit—
Or as on Vesta's sceptre a swift flame—
Or on blind Homer's heart a winged thought,—
In joyous expectation lay the boat.

35

Then by strange art she kneaded fire and snow
Together, tempering the repugnant mass
With liquid love—all things together grow
Through which the harmony of love can pass;

And a fair Shape out of her hands did flow—
A living Image, which did far surpass
In beauty that bright shape of vital stone
Which drew the heart out of Pygmalion.

36

A sexless thing it was, and in its growth
It seemed to have developed no defect
Of either sex, yet all the grace of both,—
In gentleness and strength its limbs were decked;
The bosom swelled lightly with its full youth,
The countenance was such as might select
Some artist that his skill should never die,
Imaging forth such perfect purity.

37

From its smooth shoulders hung two rapid wings,
Fit to have borne it to the seventh sphere,
Tipped with the speed of liquid lightenings,
Dyed in the ardours of the atmosphere:
She led her creature to the boiling springs
Where the light boat was moored, and said: 'Sit here!'
And pointed to the prow, and took her seat
Beside the rudder, with opposing feet.

38

And down the streams which clove those mountains vast,
Around their inland islets, and amid
The panther-peopled forests whose shade cast
Darkness and odours, and a pleasure hid
In melancholy gloom, the pinnace passed;
By many a star-surrounded pyramid
Of icy crag cleaving the purple sky,
And caverns yawning round unfathomably.

39

The silver noon into that winding dell,
With slanted gleam athwart the forest tops,
Tempered like golden evening, feebly fell;
A green and glowing light, like that which drops
From folded lilies in which glow-worms dwell,
When Earth over her face Night's mantle wraps;
Between the severed mountains lay on high,
Over the stream, a narrow rift of sky.

40

And ever as she went, the Image lay
With folded wings and unawakened eyes;
And o'er its gentle countenance did play
The busy dreams, as thick as summer flies,
Chasing the rapid smiles that would not stay,
And drinking the warm tears, and the sweet sighs
Inhaling, which, with busy murmur vain,
They had aroused from that full heart and brain.

41

And ever down the prone vale, like a cloud
Upon a stream of wind, the pinnace went:
Now lingering on the pools, in which abode
The calm and darkness of the deep content
In which they paused; now o'er the shallow road
Of white and dancing waters, all besprent
With sand and polished pebbles:—mortal boat
In such a shallow rapid could not float.

42

And down the earthquaking cataracts which shiver
Their snow-like waters into golden air,
Or under chasms unfathomable ever
Sepulchre them, till in their rage they tear

A subterranean portal for the river,
It fled—the circling sunbows did upbear
Its fall down the hoar precipice of spray,
Lighting it far upon its lampless way.

43

And when the wizard lady would ascend
The labyrinths of some many-winding vale,
Which to the inmost mountain upward tend—
She called 'Hermaphroditus!'—and the pale
And heavy hue which slumber could extend
Over its lips and eyes, as on the gale
A rapid shadow from a slope of grass,
Into the darkness of the stream did pass.

44

And it unfurled its heaven-coloured pinions,
With stars of fire spotting the stream below;
And from above into the Sun's dominions
Flinging a glory, like the golden glow
In which Spring clothes her emerald-winged minions,
All interwoven with fine feathery snow
And moonlight splendour of intensest rime,
With which frost paints the pines in winter time.

45

And then it winnowed the Elysian air
Which ever hung about that lady bright,
With its aethereal vans—and speeding there,
Like a star up the torrent of the night,
Or a swift eagle in the morning glare
Breasting the whirlwind with impetuous flight,
The pinnace, oared by those enchanted wings,
Clove the fierce streams towards their upper springs.

46

The water flashed, like sunlight by the prow
Of a noon-wandering meteor flung to Heaven;
The still air seemed as if its waves did flow
In tempest down the mountains; loosely driven
The lady's radiant hair streamed to and fro:
Beneath, the billows having vainly striven
Indignant and impetuous, roared to feel
The swift and steady motion of the keel.

47

Or, when the weary moon was in the wane,
Or in the noon of interlunar night,
The lady-witch in visions could not chain
Her spirit; but sailed forth under the light
Of shooting stars, and bade extend amain
Its storm-outspeeding wings, the Hermaphrodite;
She to the Austral waters took her way,
Beyond the fabulous Thamondocana,—

48

Where, like a meadow which no scythe has shaven,
Which rain could never bend, or whirl-blast shake,
With the Antarctic constellations paven,
Canopus and his crew, lay the Austral lake—
There she would build herself a windless haven
Out of the clouds whose moving turrets make
The bastions of the storm, when through the sky
The spirits of the tempest thundered by:

49

A haven beneath whose translucent floor
The tremulous stars sparkled unfathomably,
And around which the solid vapours hoar,
Based on the level waters, to the sky

Lifted their dreadful crags, and like a shore
Of wintry mountains, inaccessibly
Hemmed in with rifts and precipices gray,
And hanging crags, many a cove and bay.

50

And whilst the outer lake beneath the lash
Of the wind's scourge, foamed like a wounded thing,
And the incessant hail with stony clash
Ploughed up the waters, and the flagging wing
Of the roused cormorant in the lightning flash
Looked like the wreck of some wind-wandering
Fragment of inky thunder-smoke—this haven
Was as a gem to copy Heaven engraven,—

51

On which that lady played her many pranks,
Circling the image of a shooting star,
Even as a tiger on Hydaspes' banks
Outspeeds the antelopes which speediest are,
In her light boat; and many quips and cranks
She played upon the water, till the car
Of the late moon, like a sick matron wan,
To journey from the misty east began.

52

And then she called out of the hollow turrets
Of those high clouds, white, golden and vermilion,
The armies of her ministering spirits—
In mighty legions, million after million,
They came, each troop emblazoning its merits
On meteor flags; and many a proud pavilion
Of the intertexture of the atmosphere
They pitched upon the plain of the calm mere.

53

They framed the imperial tent of their great Queen
Of woven exhalations, underlaid
With lambent lightning-fire, as may be seen
A dome of thin and open ivory inlaid
With crimson silk—cressets from the serene
Hung there, and on the water for her tread
A tapestry of fleece-like mist was strewn,
Dyed in the beams of the ascending moon.

54

And on a throne o'erlaid with starlight, caught
Upon those wandering isles of aery dew,
Which highest shoals of mountain shipwreck not,
She sate, and heard all that had happened new
Between the earth and moon, since they had brought
The last intelligence—and now she grew
Pale as that moon, lost in the watery night—
And now she wept, and now she laughed outright.

55

These were tame pleasures; she would often climb
The steepest ladder of the crudded rack
Up to some beaked cape of cloud sublime,
And like Arion on the dolphin's back
Ride singing through the shoreless air;—oft-time
Following the serpent lightning's winding track,
She ran upon the platforms of the wind,
And laughed to bear the fire-balls roar behind.

56

And sometimes to those streams of upper air
Which whirl the earth in its diurnal round,
She would ascend, and win the spirits there
To let her join their chorus. Mortals found

That on those days the sky was calm and fair,
And mystic snatches of harmonious sound
Wandered upon the earth where'er she passed,
And happy thoughts of hope, too sweet to last.

57

But her choice sport was, in the hours of sleep,
To glide adown old Nilus, where he threads
Egypt and Aethiopia, from the steep
Of utmost Axume, until he spreads,
Like a calm flock of silver-fleeced sheep,
His waters on the plain: and crested heads
Of cities and proud temples gleam amid,
And many a vapour-belted pyramid.

58

By Moeris and the Mareotid lakes,
Strewn with faint blooms like bridal chamber floors,
Where naked boys bridling tame water-snakes,
Or charioteering ghastly alligators,
Had left on the sweet waters mighty wakes
Of those huge forms—within the brazen doors
Of the great Labyrinth slept both boy and beast,
Tired with the pomp of their Osirian feast.

59

And where within the surface of the river
The shadows of the massy temples lie,
And never are erased—but tremble ever
Like things which every cloud can doom to die,
Through lotus-paven canals, and wheresoever
The works of man pierced that serenest sky
With tombs, and towers, and fanes, 'twas her delight
To wander in the shadow of the night.

60

With motion like the spirit of that wind
Whose soft step deepens slumber, her light feet
Passed through the peopled haunts of humankind.
Scattering sweet visions from her presence sweet,
Through fane, and palace-court, and labyrinth mined
With many a dark and subterranean street
Under the Nile, through chambers high and deep
She passed, observing mortals in their sleep.

61

A pleasure sweet doubtless it was to see
Mortals subdued in all the shapes of sleep.
Here lay two sister twins in infancy;
There, a lone youth who in his dreams did weep;
Within, two lovers linked innocently
In their loose locks which over both did creep
Like ivy from one stem;—and there lay calm
Old age with snow-bright hair and folded palm.

62

But other troubled forms of sleep she saw,
Not to be mirrored in a holy song—
Distortions foul of supernatural awe,
And pale imaginings of visioned wrong;
And all the code of Custom's lawless law
Written upon the brows of old and young:
'This,' said the wizard maiden, 'is the strife
Which stirs the liquid surface of man's life.'

63

And little did the sight disturb her soul.—
We, the weak mariners of that wide lake
Where'er its shores extend or billows roll,
Our course unpiloted and starless make

O'er its wild surface to an unknown goal:—
But she in the calm depths her way could take,
Where in bright bowers immortal forms abide
Beneath the weltering of the restless tide.

64

And she saw princes couched under the glow
Of sunlike gems; and round each temple-court
In dormitories ranged, row after row,
She saw the priests asleep—all of one sort—
For all were educated to be so.—
The peasants in their huts, and in the port
The sailors she saw cradled on the waves,
And the dead lulled within their dreamless graves.

65

And all the forms in which those spirits lay
Were to her sight like the diaphanous
Veils, in which those sweet ladies oft array
Their delicate limbs, who would conceal from us
Only their scorn of all concealment: they
Move in the light of their own beauty thus.
But these and all now lay with sleep upon them,
And little thought a Witch was looking on them.

66

She, all those human figures breathing there,
Beheld as living spirits—to her eyes
The naked beauty of the soul lay bare,
And often through a rude and worn disguise
She saw the inner form most bright and fair—
And then she had a charm of strange device,
Which, murmured on mute lips with tender tone,
Could make that spirit mingle with her own.

67

Alas! Aurora, what wouldst thou have given
For such a charm when Tithon became gray?
Or how much, Venus, of thy silver heaven
Wouldst thou have yielded, ere Proserpina
Had half (oh! why not all?) the debt forgiven
Which dear Adonis had been doomed to pay,
To any witch who would have taught you it?
The Heliad doth not know its value yet.

68

'Tis said in after times her spirit free
Knew what love was, and felt itself alone—
But holy Dian could not chaster be
Before she stooped to kiss Endymion,
Than now this lady—like a sexless bee
Tasting all blossoms, and confined to none,
Among those mortal forms, the wizard-maiden
Passed with an eye serene and heart unladen.

69

To those she saw most beautiful, she gave
Strange panacea in a crystal bowl:—
They drank in their deep sleep of that sweet wave,
And lived thenceforward as if some control,
Mightier than life, were in them; and the grave
Of such, when death oppressed the weary soul,
Was as a green and overarching bower
Lit by the gems of many a starry flower.

70

For on the night when they were buried, she
Restored the embalmers' ruining, and shook
The light out of the funeral lamps, to be
A mimic day within that deathy nook;

And she unwound the woven imagery
Of second childhood's swaddling bands, and took
The coffin, its last cradle, from its niche,
And threw it with contempt into a ditch.

71

And there the body lay, age after age.
Mute, breathing, beating, warm, and undecaying,
Like one asleep in a green hermitage,
With gentle smiles about its eyelids playing,
And living in its dreams beyond the rage
Of death or life; while they were still arraying
In liveries ever new, the rapid, blind
And fleeting generations of mankind.

72

And she would write strange dreams upon the brain
Of those who were less beautiful, and make
All harsh and crooked purposes more vain
Than in the desert is the serpent's wake
Which the sand covers—all his evil gain
The miser in such dreams would rise and shake
Into a beggar's lap;—the lying scribe
Would his own lies betray without a bribe.

73

The priests would write an explanation full,
Translating hieroglyphics into Greek,
How the God Apis really was a bull,
And nothing more; and bid the herald stick
The same against the temple doors, and pull
The old cant down; they licensed all to speak
Whate'er they thought of hawks, and cats, and geese,
By pastoral letters to each diocese.

74

The king would dress an ape up in his crown
And robes, and seat him on his glorious seat,
And on the right hand of the sunlike throne
Would place a gaudy mock-bird to repeat
The chatterings of the monkey.—Every one
Of the prone courtiers crawled to kiss the feet
Of their great Emperor, when the morning came,
And kissed—alas, how many kiss the same!

75

The soldiers dreamed that they were blacksmiths, and
Walked out of quarters in somnambulism;
Round the red anvils you might see them stand
Like Cyclopses in Vulcan's sooty abysm,
Beating their swords to ploughshares;—in a band
The gaolers sent those of the liberal schism
Free through the streets of Memphis, much, I wis,
To the annoyance of king Amasis.

76

And timid lovers who had been so coy,
They hardly knew whether they loved or not,
Would rise out of their rest, and take sweet joy,
To the fulfilment of their inmost thought;
And when next day the maiden and the boy
Met one another, both, like sinners caught,
Blushed at the thing which each believed was done
Only in fancy—till the tenth moon shone;

77

And then the Witch would let them take no ill:
Of many thousand schemes which lovers find,
The Witch found one,—and so they took their fill
Of happiness in marriage warm and kind.

Friends who, by practice of some envious skill,
Were torn apart—a wide wound, mind from mind!—
She did unite again with visions clear
Of deep affection and of truth sincere.

78

These were the pranks she played among the cities
Of mortal men, and what she did to Sprites
And Gods, entangling them in her sweet ditties
To do her will, and show their subtle sleights,
I will declare another time; for it is
A tale more fit for the weird winter nights
Than for these garish summer days, when we
Scarcely believe much more than we can see.

Note on the Witch of Atlas, by Mrs. Shelley

We spent the summer of 1820 at the Baths of San Giuliano, four miles from Pisa. These baths were of great use to Shelley in soothing his nervous irritability. We made several excursions in the neighbourhood. The country around is fertile, and diversified and rendered picturesque by ranges of near hills and more distant mountains. The peasantry are a handsome intelligent race; and there was a gladsome sunny heaven spread over us, that rendered home and every scene we visited cheerful and bright. During some of the hottest days of August, Shelley made a solitary journey on foot to the summit of Monte San Pellegrino—a mountain of some height, on the top of which there is a chapel, the object, during certain days of the year, of many pilgrimages. The excursion delighted him while it lasted; though he exerted himself too much, and the effect was considerable lassitude and weakness on his return. During the expedition he conceived the idea, and wrote, in the three days immediately succeeding to his return, the "Witch of Atlas". This poem is peculiarly characteristic of his tastes—wildly fanciful, full of brilliant imagery, and discarding human interest and passion, to revel in the fantastic ideas that his imagination suggested.

The surpassing excellence of "The Cenci" had made me greatly desire that Shelley should increase his popularity by adopting subjects that would more suit the popular taste than a poem conceived in the abstract and dreamy spirit of the "Witch of Atlas". It was not only that I wished him to acquire popularity as redounding to his fame; but I believed that he would obtain a greater mastery over his own powers, and greater happiness in his mind, if public applause crowned his endeavours. The few stanzas that precede the poem were addressed to me on my representing these ideas to him. Even now I believe that I was in the right. Shelley did not expect sympathy and approbation from the public; but the want of it took away a portion of the ardour that ought to have sustained him while writing. He was thrown on his own resources, and on the inspiration of his own soul; and wrote because his mind overflowed, without the hope of being appreciated. I had not the most distant wish that he should truckle in opinion, or submit his lofty aspirations for the human race to the low ambition and pride of the many; but I felt sure that, if his poems were more addressed to the common feelings of men, his proper rank among the writers of the day would be acknowledged, and that popularity as a poet would enable his countrymen to do justice to his character and virtues, which in those days it was the mode to attack with the most flagitious calumnies and insulting abuse. That he felt these things deeply cannot be doubted, though he armed himself with the consciousness of acting from a lofty and heroic sense of right. The truth burst from his heart sometimes in solitude, and he would writes few unfinished verses that showed that he felt the sting; among such I find the following:—

> *'Alas! this is not what I thought Life was.*
> *I knew that there were crimes and evil men,*
> *Misery and hate; nor did I hope to pass*
> *Untouched by suffering through the rugged glen.*
> *In mine own heart I saw as in a glass*
> *The hearts of others. . . And, when*
> *I went among my kind, with triple brass*
> *Of calm endurance my weak breast I armed,*
> *To bear scorn, fear, and hate—a woful mass!'*

I believed that all this morbid feeling would vanish if the chord of sympathy between him and his countrymen were touched. But my persuasions were vain, the mind could not be bent from its natural inclination. Shelley shrunk instinctively from portraying human passion, with its mixture of good and evil, of disappointment and disquiet. Such opened again the wounds of his own heart; and he loved to shelter himself rather in the airiest flights of fancy, forgetting love and hate, and regret and lost hope, in such imaginations as borrowed their hues from sunrise or sunset, from the yellow moonshine or paly twilight, from the aspect of the far ocean or the shadows of the woods,—which celebrated the singing of the winds among the pines, the flow of a murmuring stream, and the thousand harmonious sounds which Nature creates in her solitudes. These are the materials which form the "Witch of Atlas": it is a brilliant congregation of ideas such as his senses gathered, and his fancy coloured, during his rambles in the sunny land he so much loved.

OEDIPUS TYRANNUS

OR

SWELLFOOT THE TYRANT

A TRAGEDY IN TWO ACTS
TRANSLATED FROM THE ORIGINAL DORIC

'Choose Reform or Civil War,
When through thy streets, instead of hare with dogs,
A CONSORT-QUEEN shall hunt a king with hogs,
Riding on the IONIAN MINOTAUR.'

(Begun at the Baths of San Giuliano, near Pisa, August 24, 1819; published anonymously by J. Johnston, Cheapside (imprint C.F. Seyfang), 1820. On a threat of prosecution the publisher surrendered the whole impression, seven copies—the total number sold—excepted. "Oedipus" does not appear in the first edition of the "Poetical Works", 1839, but it was included by Mrs. Shelley in the second edition of that year. Our text is that of the editio princeps, 1820, save in three places, where the reading of edition 1820 will be found in the notes.)

Advertisement

This Tragedy is one of a triad, or system of three Plays (an arrangement according to which the Greeks were accustomed to connect their dramatic representations), elucidating the wonderful and appalling fortunes of the SWELLFOOT dynasty. It was evidently written by some LEARNED THEBAN, and, from its characteristic dulness, apparently before the duties on the importation of ATTIC SALT had been repealed by the Boeotarchs. The tenderness with which he treats the PIGS proves him to have been a sus Boeotiae; possibly Epicuri de grege porcus; for, as the poet observes,

'A fellow feeling makes us wondrous kind.'

No liberty has been taken with the translation of this remarkable piece of antiquity, except the suppressing a seditious and blasphemous Chorus of the Pigs and Bulls at the last Act. The work Hoydipouse (or more properly Oedipus) has been rendered literally SWELLFOOT, without its having been conceived necessary to determine whether a swelling of the hind or the fore feet of the Swinish Monarch is particularly indicated.

Should the remaining portions of this Tragedy be found, entitled, "Swellfoot in Angaria", and "Charite", the Translator might be tempted to give them to the reading Public.

Dramatis Personae

Tyrant Swellfoot, King of Thebes
Iona Taurina, His Queen
Mammon, Arch-Priest of Famine
Purganax, Dakry, Laoctonos—Wizards, Ministers of Swellfoot
The Gadfly
The Leech
The Rat
Moses, The Sow-Gelder
Solomon, The Porkman
Zephaniah, Pig-Butcher
The Minotaur
Chorus of The Swinish Multitude
Guards, Attendants, Priests, Etc., Etc.

Scene.—*Thebes.*

Act 1

Scene 1.1.—*A magnificent temple, built of thigh-bones and death's-heads, and tiled with scalps. Over the altar the statue of famine, veiled; a number of boars, sows, and sucking-pigs, crowned with thistle, shamrock, and oak, sitting on the steps, and clinging round the altar of the temple.*

Enter Swellfoot, *in his royal robes, without perceiving the pigs.*

Swellfoot: Thou supreme Goddess! by whose power divine
 These graceful limbs are clothed in proud array
(*He contemplates himself with satisfaction*)
 Of gold and purple, and this kingly paunch
 Swells like a sail before a favouring breeze,
 And these most sacred nether promontories
 Lie satisfied with layers of fat; and these
 Boeotian cheeks, like Egypt's pyramid,
 (*Nor with less toil were their foundations laid*),
 Sustain the cone of my untroubled brain,
 That point, the emblem of a pointless nothing!
 Thou to whom Kings and laurelled Emperors,
 Radical-butchers, Paper-money-millers,
 Bishops and Deacons, and the entire army
 Of those fat martyrs to the persecution
 Of stifling turtle-soup, and brandy-devils,
 Offer their secret vows! Thou plenteous Ceres
 Of their Eleusis, hail!
Swine: Eigh! eigh! eigh! eigh!
Swellfoot: Ha! what are ye,
 Who, crowned with leaves devoted to the Furies,
 Cling round this sacred shrine?
Swine: Aigh! aigh! aigh!
Swellfoot: What! ye that are
 The very beasts that, offered at her altar
 With blood and groans, salt-cake, and fat, and inwards,
 Ever propitiate her reluctant will
 When taxes are withheld?
Swine: Ugh! ugh! ugh!
Swellfoot: What! ye who grub
 With filthy snouts my red potatoes up

   In Allan's rushy bog? Who eat the oats
   Up, from my cavalry in the Hebrides?
   Who swill the hog-wash soup my cooks digest
   From bones, and rags, and scraps of shoe-leather,
   Which should be given to cleaner Pigs than you?
SWINE—SEMICHORUS 1: The same, alas! the same;
  Though only now the name
  Of Pig remains to me.
SEMICHORUS 2: If 'twere your kingly will
  Us wretched Swine to kill,
  What should we yield to thee?
SWELLFOOT: Why, skin and bones, and some few hairs for mortar.
CHORUS OF SWINE: I have heard your Laureate sing,
  That pity was a royal thing;
  Under your mighty ancestors, we Pigs
  Were bless'd as nightingales on myrtle sprigs,
  Or grasshoppers that live on noonday dew,
  And sung, old annals tell, as sweetly too;
  But now our sties are fallen in, we catch
  The murrain and the mange, the scab and itch;
  Sometimes your royal dogs tear down our thatch,
  And then we seek the shelter of a ditch;
  Hog-wash or grains, or ruta-baga, none
  Has yet been ours since your reign begun.
FIRST SOW: My Pigs, 'tis in vain to tug.
SECOND SOW: I could almost eat my litter.
FIRST PIG: I suck, but no milk will come from the dug.
SECOND PIG: Our skin and our bones would be bitter.
THE BOARS: We fight for this rag of greasy rug,
  Though a trough of wash would be fitter.
SEMICHORUS: Happier Swine were they than we,
  Drowned in the Gadarean sea—
  I wish that pity would drive out the devils,
  Which in your royal bosom hold their revels,
  And sink us in the waves of thy compassion!
  Alas! the Pigs are an unhappy nation!
  Now if your Majesty would have our bristles
  To bind your mortar with, or fill our colons
  With rich blood, or make brawn out of our gristles,

  In policy—ask else your royal Solons—
  You ought to give us hog-wash and clean straw,
  And sties well thatched; besides it is the law!
SWELLFOOT: This is sedition, and rank blasphemy!
  Ho! there, my guards!
(*Enter a guard*)
GUARD: Your sacred Majesty.
SWELLFOOT: Call in the Jews, Solomon the court porkman,
  Moses the sow-gelder, and Zephaniah
  The hog-butcher.
GUARD: They are in waiting, Sire.
(*Enter* SOLOMON, MOSES, *and* ZEPHANIAH)
SWELLFOOT: Out with your knife, old Moses, and spay those Sows
(*The pigs run about in consternation*)
  That load the earth with Pigs; cut close and deep.
  Moral restraint I see has no effect,
  Nor prostitution, nor our own example,
  Starvation, typhus-fever, war, nor prison—
  This was the art which the arch-priest of Famine
  Hinted at in his charge to the Theban clergy—
  Cut close and deep, good Moses.
MOSES: Let your Majesty
  Keep the Boars quiet, else—
SWELLFOOT: Zephaniah, cut
  That fat Hog's throat, the brute seems overfed;
  Seditious hunks! to whine for want of grains.
ZEPHANIAH: Your sacred Majesty, he has the dropsy;—
  We shall find pints of hydatids in 's liver,
  He has not half an inch of wholesome fat
  Upon his carious ribs—
SWELLFOOT: 'Tis all the same,
  He'll serve instead of riot money, when
  Our murmuring troops bivouac in Thebes' streets
  And January winds, after a day
  Of butchering, will make them relish carrion.
  Now, Solomon, I'll sell you in a lump
  The whole kit of them.
SOLOMON: Why, your Majesty,
  I could not give—

SWELLFOOT: Kill them out of the way,
    That shall be price enough, and let me hear
    Their everlasting grunts and whines no more!
(*Exeunt, driving in the swine.*
Enter MAMMON, *the arch-priest, and* PURGANAX, *Chief of the Council of wizards*)
PURGANAX: The future looks as black as death, a cloud,
    Dark as the frown of Hell, hangs over it—
    The troops grow mutinous—the revenue fails—
    There's something rotten in us—for the level
    Of the State slopes, its very bases topple,
    The boldest turn their backs upon themselves!
MAMMON: Why what's the matter, my dear fellow, now?
    Do the troops mutiny?—decimate some regiments;
    Does money fail?—come to my mint—coin paper,
    Till gold be at a discount, and ashamed
    To show his bilious face, go purge himself,
    In emulation of her vestal whiteness.
PURGANAX: Oh, would that this were all! The oracle!!
MAMMON: Why it was I who spoke that oracle,
    And whether I was dead drunk or inspired,
    I cannot well remember; nor, in truth,
    The oracle itself!
PURGANAX: The words went thus:—
    'Boeotia, choose reform or civil war!
    When through the streets, instead of hare with dogs,
    A Consort Queen shall hunt a King with Hogs,
    Riding on the Ionian Minotaur.'
MAMMON: Now if the oracle had ne'er foretold
    This sad alternative, it must arrive,
    Or not, and so it must now that it has;
    And whether I was urged by grace divine
    Or Lesbian liquor to declare these words,
    Which must, as all words must, he false or true,
    It matters not: for the same Power made all,
    Oracle, wine, and me and you—or none—
    'Tis the same thing. If you knew as much
    Of oracles as I do—

PURGANAX: You arch-priests
    Believe in nothing; if you were to dream
    Of a particular number in the Lottery,
    You would not buy the ticket?
MAMMON: Yet our tickets
    Are seldom blanks. But what steps have you taken?
    For prophecies, when once they get abroad,
    Like liars who tell the truth to serve their ends,
    Or hypocrites who, from assuming virtue,
    Do the same actions that the virtuous do,
    Contrive their own fulfilment. This Iona—
    Well—you know what the chaste Pasiphae did,
    Wife to that most religious King of Crete,
    And still how popular the tale is here;
    And these dull Swine of Thebes boast their descent
    From the free Minotaur. You know they still
    Call themselves Bulls, though thus degenerate,
    And everything relating to a Bull
    Is popular and respectable in Thebes.
    Their arms are seven Bulls in a field gules;
    They think their strength consists in eating beef,—
    Now there were danger in the precedent
    If Queen Iona—
PURGANAX: I have taken good care
    That shall not be. I struck the crust o' the earth
    With this enchanted rod, and Hell lay bare!
    And from a cavern full of ugly shapes
    I chose a LEECH, a GADFLY, and a RAT.
    The Gadfly was the same which Juno sent
    To agitate Io, and which Ezekiel mentions
    That the Lord whistled for out of the mountains
    Of utmost Aethiopia, to torment
    Mesopotamian Babylon. The beast
    Has a loud trumpet like the scarabee,
    His crooked tail is barbed with many stings,
    Each able to make a thousand wounds, and each
    Immedicable; from his convex eyes
    He sees fair things in many hideous shapes,

And trumpets all his falsehood to the world.
Like other beetles he is fed on dung—
He has eleven feet with which he crawls,
Trailing a blistering slime, and this foul beast
Has tracked Iona from the Theban limits,
From isle to isle, from city unto city,
Urging her flight from the far Chersonese
To fabulous Solyma, and the Aetnean Isle,
Ortygia, Melite, and Calypso's Rock,
And the swart tribes of Garamant and Fez,
Aeolia and Elysium, and thy shores,
Parthenope, which now, alas! are free!
And through the fortunate Saturnian land,
Into the darkness of the West.

MAMMON: But if
    This Gadfly should drive Iona hither?

PURGANAX: Gods! what an IF! but there is my gray RAT:
    So thin with want, he can crawl in and out
    Of any narrow chink and filthy hole,
    And he shall creep into her dressing-room,
    And—

MAMMON: My dear friend, where are your wits? as if
    She does not always toast a piece of cheese
    And bait the trap? and rats, when lean enough
    To crawl through SUCH chinks—

PURGANAX: But my LEECH—a leech
    Fit to suck blood, with lubricous round rings,
    Capaciously expatiative, which make
    His little body like a red balloon,
    As full of blood as that of hydrogen,
    Sucked from men's hearts; insatiably he sucks
    And clings and pulls—a horse-leech, whose deep maw
    The plethoric King Swellfoot could not fill,
    And who, till full, will cling for ever.

MAMMON: This
    For Queen Jona would suffice, and less;
    But 'tis the Swinish multitude I fear,
    And in that fear I have—

PURGANAX: Done what?

MAMMON: Disinherited
My eldest son Chrysaor, because he
Attended public meetings, and would always
Stand prating there of commerce, public faith,
Economy, and unadulterate coin,
And other topics, ultra-radical;
And have entailed my estate, called the Fool's Paradise,
And funds in fairy-money, bonds, and bills,
Upon my accomplished daughter Banknotina,
And married her to the gallows.
PURGANAX: A good match!
MAMMON: A high connexion, Purganax. The bridegroom
Is of a very ancient family,
Of Hounslow Heath, Tyburn, and the New Drop,
And has great influence in both Houses;—oh!
He makes the fondest husband; nay, Too fond,—
New-married people should not kiss in public;
But the poor souls love one another so!
And then my little grandchildren, the gibbets,
Promising children as you ever saw,—
The young playing at hanging, the elder learning
How to hold radicals. They are well taught too,
For every gibbet says its catechism
And reads a select chapter in the Bible
Before it goes to play.
(*A most tremendous humming is heard*)
PURGANAX: Ha! what do I hear?
(*Enter the* GADFLY)
MAMMON: Your Gadfly, as it seems, is tired of gadding.
GADFLY: Hum! hum! hum!
From the lakes of the Alps, and the cold gray scalps
Of the mountains, I come!
Hum! hum! hum!
From Morocco and Fez, and the high palaces
Of golden Byzantium;
From the temples divine of old Palestine,
From Athens and Rome,
With a ha! and a hum!
I come! I come!

All inn-doors and windows
Were open to me:
I saw all that sin does,
Which lamps hardly see
That burn in the night by the curtained bed,—
The impudent lamps! for they blushed not red,
Dinging and singing,
From slumber I rung her,
Loud as the clank of an ironmonger;
Hum! hum! hum!

Far, far, far!
With the trump of my lips, and the sting at my hips,
I drove her—afar!
Far, far, far!
From city to city, abandoned of pity,
A ship without needle or star;—
Homeless she passed, like a cloud on the blast,
Seeking peace, finding war;—
She is here in her car,
From afar, and afar;—
Hum! hum!

I have stung her and wrung her,
The venom is working;—
And if you had hung her
With canting and quirking,
She could not be deader than she will be soon;—
I have driven her close to you, under the moon,
Night and day, hum! hum! ha!
I have hummed her and drummed her
From place to place, till at last I have dumbed her,
Hum! hum! hum!
(*Enter the* LEECH *and the* RAT)
LEECH: I will suck
   Blood or muck!
   The disease of the state is a plethory,
   Who so fit to reduce it as I?
RAT: I'll slily seize and

Let blood from her weasand,—
　　Creeping through crevice, and chink, and cranny,
　　With my snaky tail, and my sides so scranny.
PURGANAX: Aroint ye! thou unprofitable worm!
(*To the* LEECH)
　　And thou, dull beetle, get thee back to hell!
(*To the* GADFLY)
　　To sting the ghosts of Babylonian kings,
　　And the ox-headed Io—
SWINE (*within*): Ugh, ugh, ugh!
　　Hail! Iona the divine,
　　We will be no longer Swine,
　　But Bulls with horns and dewlaps.
RAT: For,
　　You know, my lord, the Minotaur—
PURGANAX (*fiercely*): Be silent! get to hell! or I will call
　　The cat out of the kitchen. Well, Lord Mammon,
　　This is a pretty business.
(*Exit the* RAT)
MAMMON: I will go
　　And spell some scheme to make it ugly then.—
(*Exit*)
(*Enter* SWELLFOOT)
SWELLFOOT: She is returned! Taurina is in Thebes,
　　When Swellfoot wishes that she were in hell!
　　Oh, Hymen, clothed in yellow jealousy,
　　And waving o'er the couch of wedded kings
　　The torch of Discord with its fiery hair;
　　This is thy work, thou patron saint of queens!
　　Swellfoot is wived! though parted by the sea,
　　The very name of wife had conjugal rights;
　　Her cursed image ate, drank, slept with me,
　　And in the arms of Adiposa oft 290
　　Her memory has received a husband's—
(*A loud tumult, and cries of* 'IONA *for ever—no* SWELLFOOT!')
　　Hark!
　　How the Swine cry Iona Taurina;
　　I suffer the real presence; Purganax,
　　Off with her head!

PURGANAX: But I must first impanel
    A jury of the Pigs.
SWELLFOOT: Pack them then.
PURGANAX: Or fattening some few in two separate sties.
    And giving them clean straw, tying some bits
    Of ribbon round their legs—giving their Sows
    Some tawdry lace, and bits of lustre glass,
    And their young Boars white and red rags, and tails
    Of cows, and jay feathers, and sticking cauliflowers
    Between the ears of the old ones; and when
    They are persuaded, that by the inherent virtue
    Of these things, they are all imperial Pigs,
    Good Lord! they'd rip each other's bellies up,
    Not to say, help us in destroying her.
SWELLFOOT: This plan might be tried too;—where's General Laoctonos?
(*Enter* LAOCTONOS *and* DAKRY)
    It is my royal pleasure
    That you, Lord General, bring the head and body,
    If separate it would please me better, hither
    Of Queen Iona.
LAOCTONOS: That pleasure I well knew,
    And made a charge with those battalions bold,
    Called, from their dress and grin, the royal apes,
    Upon the Swine, who in a hollow square
    Enclosed her, and received the first attack
    Like so many rhinoceroses, and then
    Retreating in good order, with bare tusks
    And wrinkled snouts presented to the foe,
    Bore her in triumph to the public sty.
    What is still worse, some Sows upon the ground
    Have given the ape-guards apples, nuts, and gin,
    And they all whisk their tails aloft, and cry,
    'Long live Iona! down with Swellfoot!'
PURGANAX: Hark!
THE SWINE (*without*): Long live Iona! down with Swellfoot!
DAKRY: I
    Went to the garret of the swineherd's tower,
    Which overlooks the sty, and made a long

Harangue (all words) to the assembled Swine,
Of delicacy mercy, judgement, law,
Morals, and precedents, and purity,
Adultery, destitution, and divorce,
Piety, faith, and state necessity,
And how I loved the Queen!—and then I wept
With the pathos of my own eloquence,
And every tear turned to a mill-stone, which
Brained many a gaping Pig, and there was made
A slough of blood and brains upon the place,
Greased with the pounded bacon; round and round
The mill-stones rolled, ploughing the pavement up,
And hurling Sucking-Pigs into the air,
With dust and stones.—

(*Enter* MAMMON)

MAMMON: I wonder that gray wizards
    Like you should be so beardless in their schemes;
    It had been but a point of policy
    To keep Iona and the Swine apart.
    Divide and rule! but ye have made a junction
    Between two parties who will govern you
    But for my art.—Behold this BAG! it is
    The poison BAG of that Green Spider huge,
    On which our spies skulked in ovation through
    The streets of Thebes, when they were paved with dead:
    A bane so much the deadlier fills it now
    As calumny is worse than death,—for here
    The Gadfly's venom, fifty times distilled,
    Is mingled with the vomit of the Leech,
    In due proportion, and black ratsbane, which
    That very Rat, who, like the Pontic tyrant,
    Nurtures himself on poison, dare not touch;—
    All is sealed up with the broad seal of Fraud,
    Who is the Devil's Lord High Chancellor,
    And over it the Primate of all Hell
    Murmured this pious baptism:—'Be thou called
    The GREEN BAG; and this power and grace be thine:
    That thy contents, on whomsoever poured,
    Turn innocence to guilt, and gentlest looks

To savage, foul, and fierce deformity.
Let all baptized by thy infernal dew
Be called adulterer, drunkard, liar, wretch!
No name left out which orthodoxy loves,
Court Journal or legitimate Review!—
Be they called tyrant, beast, fool, glutton, lover
Of other wives and husbands than their own—
The heaviest sin on this side of the Alps!
Wither they to a ghastly caricature
Of what was human!—let not man or beast
Behold their face with unaverted eyes!
Or hear their names with ears that tingle not
With blood of indignation, rage, and shame!'—
This is a perilous liquor;—good my Lords.—
(SWELLFOOT *approaches to touch the green bag*)
    Beware! for God's sake, beware!-if you should break
    The seal, and touch the fatal liquor—
PURGANAX: There,
    Give it to me. I have been used to handle
    All sorts of poisons. His dread Majesty
    Only desires to see the colour of it.
MAMMON: Now, with a little common sense, my Lords,
    Only undoing all that has been done
    (Yet so as it may seem we but confirm it),
    Our victory is assured. We must entice
    Her Majesty from the sty, and make the Pigs
    Believe that the contents of the GREEN BAG
    Are the true test of guilt or innocence.
    And that, if she be guilty, 'twill transform her
    To manifest deformity like guilt.
    If innocent, she will become transfigured
    Into an angel, such as they say she is;
    And they will see her flying through the air,
    So bright that she will dim the noonday sun;
    Showering down blessings in the shape of comfits.
    This, trust a priest, is just the sort of thing
    Swine will believe. I'll wager you will see them
    Climbing upon the thatch of their low sties,
    With pieces of smoked glass, to watch her sail

Among the clouds, and some will hold the flaps
Of one another's ears between their teeth,
To catch the coming hail of comfits in.
You, Purganax, who have the gift o' the gab,
Make them a solemn speech to this effect:
I go to put in readiness the feast
Kept to the honour of our goddess Famine,
Where, for more glory, let the ceremony
Take place of the uglification of the Queen.

DAKRY (*to* SWELLFOOT): I, as the keeper of your sacred conscience,
Humbly remind your Majesty that the care
Of your high office, as Man-milliner
To red Bellona, should not be deferred.

PURGANAX: All part, in happier plight to meet again.
(*Exeunt*)

END OF THE ACT 1

Act 2

Scene 1.2:
The Public Sty.
The boars in full assembly.
Enter Pueganax.
Purganax: Grant me your patience, Gentlemen and Boars,
    Ye, by whose patience under public burthens
    The glorious constitution of these sties
    Subsists, and shall subsist. The Lean-Pig rates
    Grow with the growing populace of Swine,
    The taxes, that true source of Piggishness
    (How can I find a more appropriate term
    To include religion, morals, peace, and plenty,
    And all that fit Boeotia as a nation
    To teach the other nations how to live?),
    Increase with Piggishness itself; and still
    Does the revenue, that great spring of all
    The patronage, and pensions, and by-payments,
    Which free-born Pigs regard with jealous eyes,
    Diminish, till at length, by glorious steps,
    All the land's produce will be merged in taxes,
    And the revenue will amount to—nothing!
    The failure of a foreign market for
    Sausages, bristles, and blood-puddings,
    And such home manufactures, is but partial;
    And, that the population of the Pigs,
    Instead of hog-wash, has been fed on straw
    And water, is a fact which is—you know—
    That is—it is a state-necessity—
    Temporary, of course. Those impious Pigs,
    Who, by frequent squeaks, have dared impugn
    The settled Swellfoot system, or to make
    Irreverent mockery of the genuflexions
    Inculcated by the arch-priest, have been whipped
    Into a loyal and an orthodox whine.
    Things being in this happy state, the Queen
    Iona—

A Loud Cry from the Pigs: She is innocent! most innocent!
Purganax: That is the very thing that I was saying,
    Gentlemen Swine; the Queen Iona being
    Most innocent, no doubt, returns to Thebes,
    And the lean Sows and Bears collect about her,
    Wishing to make her think that We believe
    (I mean those more substantial Pigs, who swill
    Rich hog-wash, while the others mouth damp straw)
    That she is guilty; thus, the Lean-Pig faction
    Seeks to obtain that hog-wash, which has been
    Your immemorial right, and which I will
    Maintain you in to the last drop of—
A Boar (*interrupting him*): What
    Does any one accuse her of?
Purganax: Why, no one
    Makes Any positive accusation;—but
    There were hints dropped, and so the privy wizards
    Conceived that it became them to advise
    His Majesty to investigate their truth;—
    Not for his own sake; he could be content
    To let his wife play any pranks she pleased,
    If, by that sufferance, He could please the Pigs;
    But then he fears the morals of the Swine,
    The Sows especially, and what effect
    It might produce upon the purity and
    Religion of the rising generation
    Of Sucking-Pigs, if it could be suspected
    That Queen Iona—
(*A pause*)
First boar: Well, go on; we long
    To hear what she can possibly have done.
Purganax: Why, it is hinted, that a certain Bull—
    Thus much is Known:—the milk-white Bulls that feed
    Beside Clitumnus and the crystal lakes
    Of the Cisalpine mountains, in fresh dews
    Of lotus-grass and blossoming asphodel
    Sleeking their silken hair, and with sweet breath
    Loading the morning winds until they faint
    With living fragrance, are so beautiful!—

>   Well, *I* say nothing;—but Europa rode
>   On such a one from Asia into Crete,
>   And the enamoured sea grew calm beneath
>   His gliding beauty. And Pasiphae,
>   Iona's grandmother,—but She is innocent!
>   And that both you and I, and all assert.
> First Boar: Most innocent!
> Purganax: Behold this Bag; a bag—
> Second Boar: Oh! no Green Bags!! Jealousy's eyes are green,
>   Scorpions are green, and water-snakes, and efts,
>   And verdigris, and—
> Purganax: Honourable Swine,
>   In Piggish souls can prepossessions reign?
>   Allow me to remind you, grass is green—
>   All flesh is grass;—no bacon but is flesh—
>   Ye are but bacon. This divining Bag
>   (Which is not green, but only bacon colour)
>   Is filled with liquor, which if sprinkled o'er
>   A woman guilty of—we all know what—
>   Makes her so hideous, till she finds one blind
>   She never can commit the like again.
>   If innocent, she will turn into an angel,
>   And rain down blessings in the shape of comfits
>   As she flies up to heaven. Now, my proposal
>   Is to convert her sacred Majesty
>   Into an angel (as I am sure we shall do),
>   By pouring on her head this mystic water.
> (*Showing the bag*)
>   I know that she is innocent; I wish
>   Only to prove her so to all the world.
> First Boar: Excellent, just, and noble Purganax.
> Second Boar: How glorious it will be to see her Majesty
>   Flying above our heads, her petticoats
>   Streaming like—like—like—
> Third Boar: Anything.
> Purganax: Oh no!
>   But like a standard of an admiral's ship,
>   Or like the banner of a conquering host,
>   Or like a cloud dyed in the dying day,

    Unravelled on the blast from a white mountain;
    Or like a meteor, or a war-steed's mane,
    Or waterfall from a dizzy precipice
    Scattered upon the wind.

FIRST BOAR: Or a cow's tail.

SECOND BOAR: Or ANYTHING, as the learned Boar observed.

PURGANAX: Gentlemen Boars, I move a resolution,
    That her most sacred Majesty should be
    Invited to attend the feast of Famine,
    And to receive upon her chaste white body
    Dews of Apotheosis from this BAG.

(*A great confusion is heard of the pigs out of doors, which communicates itself to those within. During the first strophe, the doors of the sty are staved in, and a number of exceedingly lean pigs and sows and boars rush in*)

SEMICHORUS 1: No! Yes!

SEMICHORUS 2: Yes! No!

SEMICHORUS 1: A law!

SEMICHORUS 2: A flaw!

SEMICHORUS 1: Porkers, we shall lose our wash,
    Or must share it with the Lean-Pigs!

FIRST BOAR: Order! order! be not rash!
    Was there ever such a scene, Pigs!

AN OLD SOW (*rushing in*): I never saw so fine a dash
    Since I first began to wean Pigs.

SECOND BOAR (*solemnly*): The Queen will be an angel time enough.
    I vote, in form of an amendment, that
    Purganax rub a little of that stuff
    Upon his face.

PURGANAX (*his heart is seen to beat through his waistcoat*): Gods! What would ye be at?

SEMICHORUS 1: Purganax has plainly shown a
    Cloven foot and jackdaw feather.

SEMICHORUS 2: I vote Swellfoot and Iona
    Try the magic test together;
    Whenever royal spouses bicker,
    Both should try the magic liquor.

AN OLD BOAR (*aside*): A miserable state is that of Pigs,
    For if their drivers would tear caps and wigs,
    The Swine must bite each other's ear therefore.

AN OLD SOW (*aside*): A wretched lot Jove has assigned to Swine,
    Squabbling makes Pig-herds hungry, and they dine
    On bacon, and whip Sucking-Pigs the more.
CHORUS: Hog-wash has been ta'en away:
    If the Bull-Queen is divested,
    We shall be in every way
    Hunted, stripped, exposed, molested;
    Let us do whate'er we may,
    That she shall not be arrested.
    QUEEN, we entrench you with walls of brawn,
    And palisades of tusks, sharp as a bayonet:
    Place your most sacred person here. We pawn
    Our lives that none a finger dare to lay on it.
    Those who wrong you, wrong us;
    Those who hate you, hate us;
    Those who sting you, sting us;
    Those who bait you, bait us;
    The ORACLE is now about to be
    Fulfilled by circumvolving destiny;
    Which says: 'Thebes, choose REFORM or CIVIL WAR,
    When through your streets, instead of hare with dogs,
    A CONSORT QUEEN shall hunt a KING with Hogs,
    Riding upon the IONIAN MINOTAUR.'
(*Enter* IONA TAURINA)
IONA TAURINA (*coming forward*): Gentlemen Swine, and gentle Lady-Pigs,
    The tender heart of every Boar acquits
    Their QUEEN, of any act incongruous
    With native Piggishness, and she, reposing
    With confidence upon the grunting nation,
    Has thrown herself, her cause, her life, her all,
    Her innocence, into their Hoggish arms;
    Nor has the expectation been deceived
    Of finding shelter there. Yet know, great Boars,
    (For such whoever lives among you finds you,
    And so do I), the innocent are proud!
    I have accepted your protection only
    In compliment of your kind love and care,
    Not for necessity. The innocent

Are safest there where trials and dangers wait;
Innocent Queens o'er white-hot ploughshares tread
Unsinged, and ladies, Erin's laureate sings it,
Decked with rare gems, and beauty rarer still,
Walked from Killarney to the Giant's Causeway,
Through rebels, smugglers, troops of yeomanry,
White-boys and Orange-boys, and constables,
Tithe-proctors, and excise people, uninjured!
Thus I!—
Lord Purganax, I do commit myself
Into your custody, and am prepared
To stand the test, whatever it may be!
PURGANAX: This magnanimity in your sacred Majesty
   Must please the Pigs. You cannot fail of being
   A heavenly angel. Smoke your bits of glass,
   Ye loyal Swine, or her transfiguration
   Will blind your wondering eyes.
AN OLD BOAR (*aside*): Take care, my Lord,
   They do not smoke you first.
PURGANAX: At the approaching feast
   Of Famine, let the expiation be.
SWINE: Content! content!
IONA TAURINA (*aside*): I, most content of all,
   Know that my foes even thus prepare their fall!
(*Exeunt omnes*)

SCENE 2.2:
The interior of the temple of famine. The statue of the goddess, a skeleton clothed in parti-coloured rags, seated upon a heap of skulls and loaves intermingled. A number of exceedingly fat priests in black garments arrayed on each side, with marrow-bones and cleavers in their hands. (SOLOMON, *the court porkman*) *a flourish of trumpets.*

Enter MAMMON *as arch-priest*, SWELLFOOT, DAKRY, PURGANAX, LAOCTONOS, *followed by* IONA TAURINA *guarded. On the other side enter the swine.*

CHORUS OF PRIESTS, ACCOMPANIED BY THE COURT PORKMAN ON
   MARROW-BONES AND CLEAVERS: GODDESS bare, and gaunt, and pale,
   Empress of the world, all hail!

What though Cretans old called thee
City-crested Cybele?
We call thee FAMINE!
Goddess of fasts and feasts, starving and cramming!
Through thee, for emperors, kings, and priests and lords,
Who rule by viziers, sceptres, bank-notes, words,
The earth pours forth its plenteous fruits,
Corn, wool, linen, flesh, and roots—
Those who consume these fruits through thee grow fat,
Those who produce these fruits through thee grow lean,
Whatever change takes place, oh, stick to that!
And let things be as they have ever been;
At least while we remain thy priests,
And proclaim thy fasts and feasts.
Through thee the sacred SWELLFOOT dynasty
Is based upon a rock amid that sea
Whose waves are Swine—so let it ever be!

(SWELLFOOT, *etc.*, *seat themselves at a table magnificently covered at the upper end of the temple.*
Attendants pass over the stage with hog-wash in pails.
A number of pigs, exceedingly lean, follow them licking up the wash)

MAMMON: I fear your sacred Majesty has lost
    The appetite which you were used to have.
    Allow me now to recommend this dish—
    A simple kickshaw by your Persian cook,
    Such as is served at the great King's second table.
    The price and pains which its ingredients cost
    Might have maintained some dozen families
    A winter or two—not more—so plain a dish
    Could scarcely disagree.—

SWELLFOOT: After the trial,
    And these fastidious Pigs are gone, perhaps
    I may recover my lost appetite,—
    I feel the gout flying about my stomach—
    Give me a glass of Maraschino punch.

PURGANAX (*filling his glass, and standing up*): The glorious
    Constitution of the Pigs!

ALL: A toast! a toast! stand up, and three times three!

DAKRY: No heel-taps—darken daylights!—

LAOCTONOS: Claret, somehow,
    Puts me in mind of blood, and blood of claret!
SWELLFOOT: Laoctonos is fishing for a compliment,
    But 'tis his due. Yes, you have drunk more wine,
    And shed more blood, than any man in Thebes.
(*To* PURGANAX)
    For God's sake stop the grunting of those Pigs!
PURGANAX: We dare not, Sire, 'tis Famine's privilege.
CHORUS OF SWINE: Hail to thee, hail to thee, Famine!
    Thy throne is on blood, and thy robe is of rags;
    Thou devil which livest on damning;
    Saint of new churches, and cant, and GREEN BAGS,
    Till in pity and terror thou risest,
    Confounding the schemes of the wisest;
    When thou liftest thy skeleton form,
    When the loaves and the skulls roll about,
    We will greet thee-the voice of a storm
    Would be lost in our terrible shout!

    Then hail to thee, hail to thee, Famine!
    Hail to thee, Empress of Earth!
    When thou risest, dividing possessions;
    When thou risest, uprooting oppressions,
    In the pride of thy ghastly mirth;
    Over palaces, temples, and graves,
    We will rush as thy minister-slaves,
    Trampling behind in thy train,
    Till all be made level again!
MAMMON: I hear a crackling of the giant bones
    Of the dread image, and in the black pits
    Which once were eyes, I see two livid flames.
    These prodigies are oracular, and show
    The presence of the unseen Deity.
    Mighty events are hastening to their doom!
SWELLFOOT: I only hear the lean and mutinous Swine
    Grunting about the temple.
DAKRY: In a crisis
    Of such exceeding delicacy, I think
    We ought to put her Majesty, the QUEEN,

    Upon her trial without delay.
MAMMON: THE BAG
    Is here.
PURGANAX: I have rehearsed the entire scene
    With an ox-bladder and some ditchwater,
    On Lady P—; it cannot fail.
(*Taking up the bag*)
    Your Majesty
(*To* SWELLFOOT)
    In such a filthy business had better
    Stand on one side, lest it should sprinkle you.
    A spot or two on me would do no harm,
    Nay, it might hide the blood, which the sad Genius
    Of the Green Isle has fixed, as by a spell,
    Upon my brow—which would stain all its seas,
    But which those seas could never wash away!
IONA TAURINA: My Lord, I am ready—nay, I am impatient
    To undergo the test.

(*A graceful figure in a semi-transparent veil passes unnoticed through the temple; the word "liberty" is seen through the veil, as if it were written in fire upon its forehead. its words are almost drowned in the furious grunting of the pigs, and the business of the trial. she kneels on the steps of the altar, and speaks in tones at first faint and low, but which ever become louder and louder*)

    Mighty Empress! Death's white wife!
    Ghastly mother-in-law of Life!
    By the God who made thee such,
    By the magic of thy touch,
    By the starving and the cramming
    Of fasts and feasts! by thy dread self, O Famine!
    I charge thee! when thou wake the multitude,
    Thou lead them not upon the paths of blood.
    The earth did never mean her foison
    For those who crown life's cup with poison
    Of fanatic rage and meaningless revenge—
    But for those radiant spirits, who are still
    The standard-bearers in the van of Change.
    Be they th' appointed stewards, to fill
    The lap of Pain, and Toil, and Age!—

Remit, O Queen! thy accustomed rage!
Be what thou art not! In voice faint and low
FREEDOM calls "Famine",—her eternal foe,
To brief alliance, hollow truce.—Rise now!
(*Whilst the veiled figure has been chanting this* STROPHE, MAMMON, DAKRY,
LAOCTONOS, *and* SWELLFOOT, *have surrounded* IONA TAURINA, *who, with
her hands folded on her breast, and her eyes lifted to heaven, stands, as with
saint-like resignation, to wait the issue of the business, in perfect confidence of
her innocence*)
(PURGANAX, *after unsealing the green bag, is gravely about to pour the
liquor upon her head, when suddenly the whole expression of her figure
and countenance changes; she snatches it from his hand with a loud laugh
of triumph, and empties it over* SWELLFOOT *and his whole court, who are
instantly changed into a number of filthy and ugly animals, and rush out
of the temple. The image of famine then arises with a tremendous sound,
the pigs begin scrambling for the loaves, and are trjpped up by the skulls;
all those who eat the loaves are turned into bulls, and arrange themselves
quietly behind the altar. The image of famine sinks through a chasm in the
earth, and a minotaur rises*)
MINOTAUR: I am the Ionian Minotaur, the mightiest
    Of all Europa's taurine progeny—
    I am the old traditional Man-Bull;
    And from my ancestors having been Ionian,
    I am called Ion, which, by interpretation,
    Is JOHN; in plain Theban, that is to say,
    My name's JOHN BULL; I am a famous hunter,
    And can leaf any gate in all Boeotia,
    Even the palings of the royal park,
    Or double ditch about the new enclosures;
    And if your Majesty will deign to mount me,
    At least till you have hunted down your game,
    I will not throw you.
IONA TAURINA (*during this speech she has been putting on boots and spurs,
    and a hunting-cap, buckishly cocked on one side, and tucking up her
    hair, she leaps nimbly on his back*): Hoa! hoa! tallyho! tallyho! ho! ho!
    Come, let us hunt these ugly badgers down,
    These stinking foxes, these devouring otters,
    These hares, these wolves, these anything but men.
    Hey, for a whipper-in! my loyal Pigs

Now let your noses be as keen as beagles',
Your steps as swift as greyhounds', and your cries
More dulcet and symphonious than the bells
Of village-towers, on sunshine holiday;
Wake all the dewy woods with jangling music.
Give them no law (are they not beasts of blood?)
But such as they gave you. Tallyho! ho!
Through forest, furze, and bog, and den, and desert,
Pursue the ugly beasts! tallyho! ho!

FULL CHORUS OF IONA AND THE SWINE: Tallyho! tallyho!
Through rain, hail, and snow,
Through brake, gorse, and briar,
Through fen, flood, and mire,
We go! we go!

Tallyho! tallyho!
Through pond, ditch, and slough,
Wind them, and find them,
Like the Devil behind them,
Tallyho! tallyho!
(*Exeunt, in full cry,*
IONA *driving on the swine, with the empty geeen bag*)

THE END

Note on Oedipus Tyrannus,
by Mrs. Shelley

In the brief journal I kept in those days, I find recorded, in August, 1820, Shelley 'begins "Swellfoot the Tyrant", suggested by the pigs at the fair of San Giuliano.' This was the period of Queen Caroline's landing in England, and the struggles made by George IV to get rid of her claims; which failing, Lord Castlereagh placed the "Green Bag" on the table of the House of Commons, demanding in the King's name that an enquiry should be instituted into his wife's conduct. These circumstances were the theme of all conversation among the English. We were then at the Baths of San Giuliano. A friend came to visit us on the day when a fair was held in the square, beneath our windows: Shelley read to us his "Ode to Liberty"; and was riotously accompanied by the grunting of a quantity of pigs brought for sale to the fair. He compared it to the 'chorus of frogs' in the satiric drama of Aristophanes; and, it being an hour of merriment, and one ludicrous association suggesting another, he imagined a political-satirical drama on the circumstances of the day, to which the pigs would serve as chorus—and "Swellfoot" was begun. When finished, it was transmitted to England, printed, and published anonymously; but stifled at the very dawn of its existence by the Society for the Suppression of Vice, who threatened to prosecute it, if not immediately withdrawn. The friend who had taken the trouble of bringing it out, of course did not think it worth the annoyance and expense of a contest, and it was laid aside.

Hesitation of whether it would do honour to Shelley prevented my publishing it at first. But I cannot bring myself to keep back anything he ever wrote; for each word is fraught with the peculiar views and sentiments which he believed to be beneficial to the human race, and the bright light of poetry irradiates every thought. The world has a right to the entire compositions of such a man; for it does not live and thrive by the outworn lesson of the dullard or the hypocrite, but by the original free thoughts of men of genius, who aspire to pluck bright truth

'from the pale-faced moon;
Or dive into the bottom of the deep
Where fathom-line would never touch the ground,
And pluck up drowned'

truth. Even those who may dissent from his opinions will consider that he was a man of genius, and that the world will take more interest in his slightest word than in the waters of Lethe which are so eagerly prescribed as medicinal for all its wrongs and woe. This drama, however, must not be judged for more than was meant. It is a mere plaything of the imagination; which even may not excite smiles among many, who will not see wit in those combinations of thought which were full of the ridiculous to the author. But, like everything he wrote, it breathes that deep sympathy for the sorrows of humanity, and indignation against its oppressors, which make it worthy of his name.

EPIPSYCHIDION

VERSES ADDRESSED TO THE NOBLE AND UNFORTUNATE LADY,
EMILIA V—,
NOW IMPRISONED IN THE CONVENT OF —.

*L'anima amante si slancia fuori del creato, e si crea nell' infinito
un Mondo tutto per essa, diverso assai da questo oscuro e pauroso
baratro.* HER OWN WORDS.

("Epipsychidion" was composed at Pisa, January, February, 1821, and published without the author's name, in the following summer, by C. & J. Ollier, London. The poem was included by Mrs. Shelley in the "Poetical Works", 1839, both editions. Amongst the Shelley manuscripts in the Bodleian is a first draft of "Epipsychidion", 'consisting of three versions, more or less complete, of the "Preface (Advertisement)", a version in ink and pencil, much cancelled, of the last eighty lines of the poem, and some additional lines which did not appear in print' ("Examination of the Shelley manuscripts in the Bodleian Library, by C.D. Locock".

Oxford, Clarendon Press, 1903, page 3). This draft, the writing of which is 'extraordinarily confused and illegible,' has been carefully deciphered and printed by Mr. Locock in the volume named above. Our text follows that of the editio princeps, 1821.)

Advertisement

The Writer of the following lines died at Florence, as he was preparing for a voyage to one of the wildest of the Sporades, which he had bought, and where he had fitted up the ruins of an old building, and where it was his hope to have realised a scheme of life, suited perhaps to that happier and better world of which he is now an inhabitant, but hardly practicable in this. His life was singular; less on account of the romantic vicissitudes which diversified it, than the ideal tinge which it received from his own character and feelings. The present Poem, like the "Vita Nuova" of Dante, is sufficiently intelligible to a certain class of readers without a matter-of-fact history of the circumstances to which it relates and to a certain other class it must ever remain incomprehensible, from a defect of a common organ of perception for the ideas of which it treats. Not but that gran vergogna sarebbe a colui, che rimasse cosa sotto veste di figura, o di colore rettorico: e domandato non sapesse denudare le sue parole da cotal veste, in guisa che avessero verace intendimento.

The present poem appears to have been intended by the Writer as the dedication to some longer one. The stanza on the opposite page* is almost a literal translation from Dante's famous Canzone

Voi, ch' intendendo, il terzo ciel movete, etc.

The presumptuous application of the concluding lines to his own composition will raise a smile at the expense of my unfortunate friend: be it a smile not of contempt, but pity. S.

My Song, I fear that thou wilt find but few
Who fitly shalt conceive thy reasoning,
Of such hard matter dost thou entertain;
Whence, if by misadventure, chance should bring
Thee to base company (as chance may do),
Quite unaware of what thou dost contain,
I prithee, comfort thy sweet self again,
My last delight! tell them that they are dull,
And bid them own that thou art beautiful.

---

* i.e. the nine lines which follow, beginning, 'My Song, I fear,' etc.—Ed.

Epipsychidion

Sweet Spirit! Sister of that orphan one,
Whose empire is the name thou weepest on,
In my heart's temple I suspend to thee
These votive wreaths of withered memory.

Poor captive bird! who, from thy narrow cage,
Pourest such music, that it might assuage
The rugged hearts of those who prisoned thee,
Were they not deaf to all sweet melody;
This song shall be thy rose: its petals pale
Are dead, indeed, my adored Nightingale!
But soft and fragrant is the faded blossom,
And it has no thorn left to wound thy bosom.

High, spirit-winged Heart! who dost for ever
Beat thine unfeeling bars with vain endeavour,
Till those bright plumes of thought, in which arrayed
It over-soared this low and worldly shade,
Lie shattered; and thy panting, wounded breast
Stains with dear blood its unmaternal nest!
I weep vain tears: blood would less bitter be,
Yet poured forth gladlier, could it profit thee.

Seraph of Heaven! too gentle to be human,
Veiling beneath that radiant form of Woman
All that is insupportable in thee
Of light, and love, and immortality!
Sweet Benediction in the eternal Curse!
Veiled Glory of this lampless Universe!
Thou Moon beyond the clouds! Thou living Form
Among the Dead! Thou Star above the Storm!
Thou Wonder, and thou Beauty, and thou Terror!
Thou Harmony of Nature's art! Thou Mirror
In whom, as in the splendour of the Sun,
All shapes look glorious which thou gazest on!
Ay, even the dim words which obscure thee now

Flash, lightning-like, with unaccustomed glow;
I pray thee that thou blot from this sad song
All of its much mortality and wrong,
With those clear drops, which start like sacred dew
From the twin lights thy sweet soul darkens through,
Weeping, till sorrow becomes ecstasy:
Then smile on it, so that it may not die.

I never thought before my death to see
Youth's vision thus made perfect. Emily,
I love thee; though the world by no thin name
Will hide that love from its unvalued shame.
Would we two had been twins of the same mother!
Or, that the name my heart lent to another
Could be a sister's bond for her and thee,
Blending two beams of one eternity!
Yet were one lawful and the other true,
These names, though dear, could paint not, as is due.
How beyond refuge I am thine. Ah me!
I am not thine: I am a part of THEE.

Sweet Lamp! my moth-like Muse has burned its wings
Or, like a dying swan who soars and sings,
Young Love should teach Time, in his own gray style,
All that thou art. Art thou not void of guile,
A lovely soul formed to be blessed and bless?
A well of sealed and secret happiness,
Whose waters like blithe light and music are,
Vanquishing dissonance and gloom? A Star
Which moves not in the moving heavens, alone?
A Smile amid dark frowns? a gentle tone
Amid rude voices? a beloved light?
A Solitude, a Refuge, a Delight?
A Lute, which those whom Love has taught to play
Make music on, to soothe the roughest day
And lull fond Grief asleep? a buried treasure?
A cradle of young thoughts of wingless pleasure?
A violet-shrouded grave of Woe?—I measure

The world of fancies, seeking one like thee,
And find—alas! mine own infirmity.

She met me, Stranger, upon life's rough way,
And lured me towards sweet Death; as Night by Day,
Winter by Spring, or Sorrow by swift Hope,
Led into light, life, peace. An antelope,
In the suspended impulse of its lightness,
Were less aethereally light: the brightness
Of her divinest presence trembles through
Her limbs, as underneath a cloud of dew
Embodied in the windless heaven of June
Amid the splendour-winged stars, the Moon
Burns, inextinguishably beautiful:
And from her lips, as from a hyacinth full
Of honey-dew, a liquid murmur drops,
Killing the sense with passion; sweet as stops
Of planetary music heard in trance.
In her mild lights the starry spirits dance,
The sunbeams of those wells which ever leap
Under the lightnings of the soul—too deep
For the brief fathom-line of thought or sense.
The glory of her being, issuing thence,
Stains the dead, blank, cold air with a warm shade
Of unentangled intermixture, made
By Love, of light and motion: one intense
Diffusion, one serene Omnipresence,
Whose flowing outlines mingle in their flowing,
Around her cheeks and utmost fingers glowing
With the unintermitted blood, which there
Quivers, (as in a fleece of snow-like air
The crimson pulse of living morning quiver,)
Continuously prolonged, and ending never,
Till they are lost, and in that Beauty furled
Which penetrates and clasps and fills the world;
Scarce visible from extreme loveliness.
Warm fragrance seems to fall from her light dress
And her loose hair; and where some heavy tress
The air of her own speed has disentwined,

The sweetness seems to satiate the faint wind;
And in the soul a wild odour is felt
Beyond the sense, like fiery dews that melt
Into the bosom of a frozen bud.—
See where she stands! a mortal shape indued
With love and life and light and deity,
And motion which may change but cannot die;
An image of some bright Eternity;
A shadow of some golden dream; a Splendour
Leaving the third sphere pilotless; a tender
Reflection of the eternal Moon of Love
Under whose motions life's dull billows move;
A Metaphor of Spring and Youth and Morning;
A Vision like incarnate April, warning,
With smiles and tears, Frost the Anatomy
Into his summer grave.
Ah, woe is me!
What have I dared? where am I lifted? how
Shall I descend, and perish not? I know
That Love makes all things equal: I have heard
By mine own heart this joyous truth averred:
The spirit of the worm beneath the sod
In love and worship, blends itself with God.

Spouse! Sister! Angel! Pilot of the Fate
Whose course has been so starless! O too late
Beloved! O too soon adored, by me!
For in the fields of Immortality
My spirit should at first have worshipped thine,
A divine presence in a place divine;
Or should have moved beside it on this earth,
A shadow of that substance, from its birth;
But not as now:—I love thee; yes, I feel
That on the fountain of my heart a seal
Is set, to keep its waters pure and bright
For thee, since in those TEARS thou hast delight.
We—are we not formed, as notes of music are,
For one another, though dissimilar;
Such difference without discord, as can make

Those sweetest sounds, in which all spirits shake
As trembling leaves in a continuous air?

Thy wisdom speaks in me, and bids me dare
Beacon the rocks on which high hearts are wrecked.
I never was attached to that great sect,
Whose doctrine is, that each one should select
Out of the crowd a mistress or a friend,
And all the rest, though fair and wise, commend
To cold oblivion, though it is in the code
Of modern morals, and the beaten road
Which those poor slaves with weary footsteps tread,
Who travel to their home among the dead
By the broad highway of the world, and so
With one chained friend, perhaps a jealous foe,
The dreariest and the longest journey go.

True Love in this differs from gold and clay,
That to divide is not to take away.
Love is like understanding, that grows bright,
Gazing on many truths; 'tis like thy light,
Imagination! which from earth and sky,
And from the depths of human fantasy,
As from a thousand prisms and mirrors, fills
The Universe with glorious beams, and kills
Error, the worm, with many a sun-like arrow
Of its reverberated lightning. Narrow
The heart that loves, the brain that contemplates,
The life that wears, the spirit that creates
One object, and one form, and builds thereby
A sepulchre for its eternity.

Mind from its object differs most in this:
Evil from good; misery from happiness;
The baser from the nobler; the impure
And frail, from what is clear and must endure.
If you divide suffering and dross, you may
Diminish till it is consumed away;
If you divide pleasure and love and thought,

Each part exceeds the whole; and we know not
How much, while any yet remains unshared,
Of pleasure may be gained, of sorrow spared:
This truth is that deep well, whence sages draw
The unenvied light of hope; the eternal law
By which those live, to whom this world of life
Is as a garden ravaged, and whose strife
Tills for the promise of a later birth
The wilderness of this Elysian earth.

There was a Being whom my spirit oft
Met on its visioned wanderings, far aloft,
In the clear golden prime of my youth's dawn,
Upon the fairy isles of sunny lawn,
Amid the enchanted mountains, and the caves
Of divine sleep, and on the air-like waves
Of wonder-level dream, whose tremulous floor
Paved her light steps;—on an imagined shore,
Under the gray beak of some promontory
She met me, robed in such exceeding glory,
That I beheld her not. In solitudes
Her voice came to me through the whispering woods,
And from the fountains, and the odours deep
Of flowers, which, like lips murmuring in their sleep
Of the sweet kisses which had lulled them there,
Breathed but of HER to the enamoured air;
And from the breezes whether low or loud,
And from the rain of every passing cloud,
And from the singing of the summer-birds,
And from all sounds, all silence. In the words
Of antique verse and high romance,—in form,
Sound, colour—in whatever checks that Storm
Which with the shattered present chokes the past;
And in that best philosophy, whose taste
Makes this cold common hell, our life, a doom
As glorious as a fiery martyrdom;
Her Spirit was the harmony of truth.—

Then, from the caverns of my dreamy youth
I sprang, as one sandalled with plumes of fire,
And towards the lodestar of my one desire,
I flitted, like a dizzy moth, whose flight
Is as a dead leaf's in the owlet light,
When it would seek in Hesper's setting sphere
A radiant death, a fiery sepulchre,
As if it were a lamp of earthly flame.—
But She, whom prayers or tears then could not tame,
Passed, like a God throned on a winged planet,
Whose burning plumes to tenfold swiftness fan it,
Into the dreary cone of our life's shade;
And as a man with mighty loss dismayed,
I would have followed, though the grave between
Yawned like a gulf whose spectres are unseen:
When a voice said:—'O thou of hearts the weakest,
The phantom is beside thee whom thou seekest.'
Then I—'Where?'—the world's echo answered 'where?'
And in that silence, and in my despair,
I questioned every tongueless wind that flew
Over my tower of mourning, if it knew
Whither 'twas fled, this soul out of my soul;
And murmured names and spells which have control
Over the sightless tyrants of our fate;
But neither prayer nor verse could dissipate
The night which closed on her; nor uncreate
That world within this Chaos, mine and me,
Of which she was the veiled Divinity,
The world I say of thoughts that worshipped her:
And therefore I went forth, with hope and fear
And every gentle passion sick to death,
Feeding my course with expectation's breath,
Into the wintry forest of our life;
And struggling through its error with vain strife,
And stumbling in my weakness and my haste,
And half bewildered by new forms, I passed,
Seeking among those untaught foresters
If I could find one form resembling hers,
In which she might have masked herself from me.

There,—One, whose voice was venomed melody
Sate by a well, under blue nightshade bowers:
The breath of her false mouth was like faint flowers,
Her touch was as electric poison,—flame
Out of her looks into my vitals came,
And from her living cheeks and bosom flew
A killing air, which pierced like honey-dew
Into the core of my green heart, and lay
Upon its leaves; until, as hair grown gray
O'er a young brow, they hid its unblown prime
With ruins of unseasonable time.

In many mortal forms I rashly sought
The shadow of that idol of my thought.
And some were fair—but beauty dies away:
Others were wise—but honeyed words betray:
And One was true—oh! why not true to me?
Then, as a hunted deer that could not flee,
I turned upon my thoughts, and stood at bay,
Wounded and weak and panting; the cold day
Trembled, for pity of my strife and pain.
When, like a noonday dawn, there shone again
Deliverance. One stood on my path who seemed
As like the glorious shape which I had d reamed
As is the Moon, whose changes ever run
Into themselves, to the eternal Sun;
The cold chaste Moon, the Queen of Heaven's bright isles,
Who makes all beautiful on which she smiles,
That wandering shrine of soft yet icy flame
Which ever is transformed, yet still the same,
And warms not but illumines. Young and fair
As the descended Spirit of that sphere,
She hid me, as the Moon may hide the night
From its own darkness, until all was bright
Between the Heaven and Earth of my calm mind,
And, as a cloud charioted by the wind,
She led me to a cave in that wild place,
And sate beside me, with her downward face
Illumining my slumbers, like the Moon

Waxing and waning o'er Endymion.
And I was laid asleep, spirit and limb,
And all my being became bright or dim
As the Moon's image in a summer sea,
According as she smiled or frowned on me;
And there I lay, within a chaste cold bed:
Alas, I then was nor alive nor dead:—
For at her silver voice came Death and Life,
Unmindful each of their accustomed strife,
Masked like twin babes, a sister and a brother,
The wandering hopes of one abandoned mother,
And through the cavern without wings they flew,
And cried 'Away, he is not of our crew.'
I wept, and though it be a dream, I weep.

What storms then shook the ocean of my sleep,
Blotting that Moon, whose pale and waning lips
Then shrank as in the sickness of eclipse;—
And how my soul was as a lampless sea,
And who was then its Tempest; and when She,
The Planet of that hour, was quenched, what frost
Crept o'er those waters, till from coast to coast
The moving billows of my being fell
Into a death of ice, immovable;—
And then—what earthquakes made it gape and split,
The white Moon smiling all the while on it,
These words conceal:—If not, each word would be
The key of staunchless tears. Weep not for me!

At length, into the obscure Forest came
The Vision I had sought through grief and shame.
Athwart that wintry wilderness of thorns
Flashed from her motion splendour like the Morn's,
And from her presence life was radiated
Through the gray earth and branches bare and dead;
So that her way was paved, and roofed above
With flowers as soft as thoughts of budding love;
And music from her respiration spread
Like light,—all other sounds were penetrated

By the small, still, sweet spirit of that sound,
So that the savage winds hung mute around;
And odours warm and fresh fell from her hair
Dissolving the dull cold in the frore air:
Soft as an Incarnation of the Sun,
When light is changed to love, this glorious One
Floated into the cavern where I lay,
And called my Spirit, and the dreaming clay
Was lifted by the thing that dreamed below
As smoke by fire, and in her beauty's glow
I stood, and felt the dawn of my long night
Was penetrating me with living light:
I knew it was the Vision veiled from me
So many years—that it was Emily.

Twin Spheres of light who rule this passive Earth,
This world of loves, this ME; and into birth
Awaken all its fruits and flowers, and dart
Magnetic might into its central heart;
And lift its billows and its mists, and guide
By everlasting laws, each wind and tide
To its fit cloud, and its appointed cave;
And lull its storms, each in the craggy grave
Which was its cradle, luring to faint bowers
The armies of the rainbow-winged showers;
And, as those married lights, which from the towers
Of Heaven look forth and fold the wandering globe
In liquid sleep and splendour, as a robe;
And all their many-mingled influence blend,
If equal, yet unlike, to one sweet end;—
So ye, bright regents, with alternate sway
Govern my sphere of being, night and day!
Thou, not disdaining even a borrowed might;
Thou, not eclipsing a remoter light;
And, through the shadow of the seasons three,
From Spring to Autumn's sere maturity,
Light it into the Winter of the tomb,
Where it may ripen to a brighter bloom.
Thou too, O Comet beautiful and fierce,

Who drew the heart of this frail Universe
Towards thine own; till, wrecked in that convulsion,
Alternating attraction and repulsion,
Thine went astray and that was rent in twain;
Oh, float into our azure heaven again!
Be there Love's folding-star at thy return;
The living Sun will feed thee from its urn
Of golden fire; the Moon will veil her horn
In thy last smiles; adoring Even and Morn
Will worship thee with incense of calm breath
And lights and shadows; as the star of Death
And Birth is worshipped by those sisters wild
Called Hope and Fear—upon the heart are piled
Their offerings,—of this sacrifice divine
A World shall be the altar.
Lady mine,
Scorn not these flowers of thought, the fading birth
Which from its heart of hearts that plant puts forth
Whose fruit, made perfect by thy sunny eyes,
Will be as of the trees of Paradise.

The day is come, and thou wilt fly with me.
To whatsoe'er of dull mortality
Is mine, remain a vestal sister still;
To the intense, the deep, the imperishable,
Not mine but me, henceforth be thou united
Even as a bride, delighting and delighted.
The hour is come:—the destined Star has risen
Which shall descend upon a vacant prison.
The walls are high, the gates are strong, thick set
The sentinels—but true Love never yet
Was thus constrained: it overleaps all fence:
Like lightning, with invisible violence
Piercing its continents; like Heaven's free breath,
Which he who grasps can hold not; liker Death,
Who rides upon a thought, and makes his way
Through temple, tower, and palace, and the array
Of arms: more strength has Love than he or they;
For it can burst his charnel, and make free

The limbs in chains, the heart in agony,
The soul in dust and chaos.
Emily,
A ship is floating in the harbour now,
A wind is hovering o'er the mountain's brow;
There is a path on the sea's azure floor,
No keel has ever ploughed that path before;
The halcyons brood around the foamless isles;
The treacherous Ocean has forsworn its wiles;
The merry mariners are bold and free:
Say, my heart's sister, wilt thou sail with me?
Our bark is as an albatross, whose nest
Is a far Eden of the purple East;
And we between her wings will sit, while Night,
And Day, and Storm, and Calm, pursue their flight,
Our ministers, along the boundless Sea,
Treading each other's heels, unheededly.
It is an isle under Ionian skies,
Beautiful as a wreck of Paradise,
And, for the harbours are not safe and good,
This land would have remained a solitude
But for some pastoral people native there,
Who from the Elysian, clear, and golden air
Draw the last spirit of the age of gold,
Simple and spirited; innocent and bold.
The blue Aegean girds this chosen home,
With ever-changing sound and light and foam,
Kissing the sifted sands, and caverns hoar;
And all the winds wandering along the shore
Undulate with the undulating tide:
There are thick woods where sylvan forms abide;
And many a fountain, rivulet, and pond,
As clear as elemental diamond,
Or serene morning air; and far beyond,
The mossy tracks made by the goats and deer
(Which the rough shepherd treads but once a year)
Pierce into glades, caverns, and bowers, and halls
Built round with ivy, which the waterfalls
Illumining, with sound that never fails

Accompany the noonday nightingales;
And all the place is peopled with sweet airs;
The light clear element which the isle wears
Is heavy with the scent of lemon-flowers,
Which floats like mist laden with unseen showers.
And falls upon the eyelids like faint sleep;
And from the moss violets and jonquils peep,
And dart their arrowy odour through the brain
Till you might faint with that delicious pain.
And every motion, odour, beam and tone,
With that deep music is in unison:
Which is a soul within the soul—they seem
Like echoes of an antenatal dream.—
It is an isle 'twixt Heaven, Air, Earth, and Sea,
Cradled, and hung in clear tranquillity;
Bright as that wandering Eden Lucifer,
Washed by the soft blue Oceans of young air.
It is a favoured place. Famine or Blight,
Pestilence, War and Earthquake, never light
Upon its mountain-peaks; blind vultures, they
Sail onward far upon their fatal way:
The winged storms, chanting their thunder-psalm
To other lands, leave azure chasms of calm
Over this isle, or weep themselves in dew,
From which its fields and woods ever renew
Their green and golden immortality.
And from the sea there rise, and from the sky
There fall, clear exhalations, soft and bright.
Veil after veil, each hiding some delight,
Which Sun or Moon or zephyr draw aside,
Till the isle's beauty, like a naked bride
Glowing at once with love and loveliness,
Blushes and trembles at its own excess:
Yet, like a buried lamp, a Soul no less
Burns in the heart of this delicious isle,
An atom of th' Eternal, whose own smile
Unfolds itself, and may be felt, not seen
O'er the gray rocks, blue waves, and forests green,
Filling their bare and void interstices.—

But the chief marvel of the wilderness
Is a lone dwelling, built by whom or how
None of the rustic island-people know:
'Tis not a tower of strength, though with its height
It overtops the woods; but, for delight,
Some wise and tender Ocean-King, ere crime
Had been invented, in the world's young prime,
Reared it, a wonder of that simple time,
An envy of the isles, a pleasure-house
Made sacred to his sister and his spouse.
It scarce seems now a wreck of human art,
But, as it were Titanic; in the heart
Of Earth having assumed its form, then grown
Out of the mountains, from the living stone,
Lifting itself in caverns light and high:
For all the antique and learned imagery
Has been erased, and in the place of it
The ivy and the wild-vine interknit
The volumes of their many-twining stems;
Parasite flowers illume with dewy gems
The lampless halls, and when they fade, the sky
Peeps through their winter-woof of tracery
With moonlight patches, or star atoms keen,
Or fragments of the day's intense serene;—
Working mosaic on their Parian floors.
And, day and night, aloof, from the high towers
And terraces, the Earth and Ocean seem
To sleep in one another's arms, and dream
Of waves, flowers, clouds, woods, rocks, and all that we
Read in their smiles, and call reality.

This isle and house are mine, and I have vowed
Thee to be lady of the solitude.—
And I have fitted up some chambers there
Looking towards the golden Eastern air,
And level with the living winds, which flow
Like waves above the living waves below.—
I have sent books and music there, and all
Those instruments with which high Spirits call

The future from its cradle, and the past
Out of its grave, and make the present last
In thoughts and joys which sleep, but cannot die,
Folded within their own eternity.
Our simple life wants little, and true taste
Hires not the pale drudge Luxury, to waste
The scene it would adorn, and therefore still,
Nature with all her children haunts the hill.
The ring-dove, in the embowering ivy, yet
Keeps up her love-lament, and the owls flit
Round the evening tower, and the young stars glance
Between the quick bats in their twilight dance;
The spotted deer bask in the fresh moonlight
Before our gate, and the slow, silent night
Is measured by the pants of their calm sleep.
Be this our home in life, and when years heap
Their withered hours, like leaves, on our decay,
Let us become the overhanging day,
The living soul of this Elysian isle,
Conscious, inseparable, one. Meanwhile
We two will rise, and sit, and walk together,
Under the roof of blue Ionian weather,
And wander in the meadows, or ascend
The mossy mountains, where the blue heavens bend
With lightest winds, to touch their paramour;
Or linger, where the pebble-paven shore,
Under the quick, faint kisses of the sea
Trembles and sparkles as with ecstasy,—
Possessing and possessed by all that is
Within that calm circumference of bliss,
And by each other, till to love and live
Be one:—or, at the noontide hour, arrive
Where some old cavern hoar seems yet to keep
The moonlight of the expired night asleep,
Through which the awakened day can never peep;
A veil for our seclusion, close as night's,
Where secure sleep may kill thine innocent lights:
Sleep, the fresh dew of languid love, the rain
Whose drops quench kisses till they burn again.

And we will talk, until thought's melody
Become too sweet for utterance, and it die
In words, to live again in looks, which dart
With thrilling tone into the voiceless heart,
Harmonizing silence without a sound.
Our breath shall intermix, our bosoms bound,
And our veins beat together; and our lips
With other eloquence than words, eclipse
The soul that burns between them, and the wells
Which boil under our being's inmost cells,
The fountains of our deepest life, shall be
Confused in Passion's golden purity,
As mountain-springs under the morning sun.
We shall become the same, we shall be one
Spirit within two frames, oh! wherefore two?
One passion in twin-hearts, which grows and grew,
Till like two meteors of expanding flame,
Those spheres instinct with it become the same,
Touch, mingle, are transfigured; ever still
Burning, yet ever inconsumable:
In one another's substance finding food,
Like flames too pure and light and unimbued
To nourish their bright lives with baser prey,
Which point to Heaven and cannot pass away:
One hope within two wills, one will beneath
Two overshadowing minds, one life, one death,
One Heaven, one Hell, one immortality,
And one annihilation. Woe is me!
The winged words on which my soul would pierce
Into the height of Love's rare Universe,
Are chains of lead around its flight of fire—
I pant, I sink, I tremble, I expire!

. . .

Weak Verses, go, kneel at your Sovereign's feet,
And say:—'We are the masters of thy slave;
What wouldest thou with us and ours and thine?'
Then call your sisters from Oblivion's cave,
All singing loud: 'Love's very pain is sweet,
But its reward is in the world divine

Which, if not here, it builds beyond the grave.'
So shall ye live when I am there. Then haste
Over the hearts of men, until ye meet
Marina, Vanna, Primus, and the rest,
And bid them love each other and be blessed:
And leave the troop which errs, and which reproves,
And come and be my guest,—for I am Love's.

Fragments Connected with Epipsychidion

(Of the fragments of verse that follow, lines 1–37, 62–92 were printed by Mrs. Shelley in "Posthumous Works", 1839, 2nd edition; lines 1–174 were printed or reprinted by Dr. Garnett in "Relics of Shelley", 1862; and lines 175–186 were printed by Mr. C.D. Locock from the first draft of "Epipsychidion" amongst the Shelley manuscripts in the Bodleian Library. See "Examination, etc.", 1903, pages 12, 13. The three early drafts of the "Preface (Advertisement)" were printed by Mr. Locock in the same volume, pages 4, 5.)

Three Early Drafts of the Preface

(Advertisement)

Preface 1

THE FOLLOWING POEM WAS FOUND amongst other papers in the Portfolio of a young Englishman with whom the Editor had contracted an intimacy at Florence, brief indeed, but sufficiently long to render the Catastrophe by which it terminated one of the most painful events of his life.—

The literary merit of the Poem in question may not be considerable; but worse verses are printed every day.

He was an accomplished & amiable person but his error was, thuntos on un thunta phronein,—his fate is an additional proof that 'The tree of Knowledge is not that of Life.'—He had framed to himself certain opinions, founded no doubt upon the truth of things, but built up to a Babel height; they fell by their own weight, & the thoughts that were his architects, became unintelligible one to the other, as men upon whom confusion of tongues has fallen.

(These) verses seem to have been written as a sort of dedication of some work to have been presented to the person whom they address: but his papers afford no trace of such a work—The circumstances to which (they) the poem allude, may easily be understood by those to whom (the) spirit of the poem itself is (un)intelligible: a detail of facts, sufficiently romantic in (themselves but) their combinations.

The melancholy (task) charge of consigning the body of my poor friend to the grave, was committed to me by his desolated family. I caused him to be buried in a spot selected by himself.

Preface 2

(Epips) T. E. V. Epipsych
Lines addressed to
the Noble Lady
(Emilia) (E. V.)
Emilia

(The following Poem was found in the PF. of a young Englishman, who died on his passage from Leghorn to the Levant. He had bought one of the Sporades) He was accompanied by a lady (who might have been) supposed to be his wife, & an effeminate looking youth, to whom he shewed an (attachment) so (singular) excessive an attachment as to give rise to the suspicion, that she was a woman—At his death this suspicion was confirmed; . . . object speedily found a refuge both from the taunts of the brute multitude, and from the. . . of her grief in the same grave that contained her lover.—He had bought one of the Sporades, & fitted up a Saracenic castle which accident had preserved in some repair with simple elegance, & it was his intention to dedicate the remainder of his life to undisturbed intercourse with his companions

These verses apparently were intended as a dedication of a longer poem or series of poems

Preface 3

THE WRITER OF THESE LINES died at Florence in (January 1820) while he was preparing * * for one wildest of the of the Sporades, where he bought & fitted up the ruins of some old building—His life was singular, less on account of the romantic vicissitudes which diversified it, than the ideal tinge which they received from his own character & feelings—

The verses were apparently intended by the writer to accompany some longer poem or collection of poems, of which there* (are no remnants in his) * * * remains (in his) portfolio.—

The editor is induced to

The present poem, like the vita Nova of Dante, is sufficiently intelligible to a certain class of readers without a matter of fact history of the circumstances to which it relate, & to a certain other class, it must & ought ever to remain incomprehensible—It was evidently intended to be prefixed to a longer poem or series of poems—but among his papers there are no traces of such a collection.

Passages of the Poem, or Connected Therewith

Here, my dear friend, is a new book for you;
I have already dedicated two
To other friends, one female and one male,—
What you are, is a thing that I must veil;
What can this be to those who praise or rail?
I never was attached to that great sect
Whose doctrine is that each one should select
Out of the world a mistress or a friend,
And all the rest, though fair and wise, commend
To cold oblivion—though 'tis in the code
Of modern morals, and the beaten road
Which those poor slaves with weary footsteps tread
Who travel to their home among the dead
By the broad highway of the world—and so
With one sad friend, and many a jealous foe,
The dreariest and the longest journey go.

Free love has this, different from gold and clay,
That to divide is not to take away.
Like ocean, which the general north wind breaks
Into ten thousand waves, and each one makes
A mirror of the moon—like some great glass,
Which did distort whatever form might pass,
Dashed into fragments by a playful child,
Which then reflects its eyes and forehead mild;
Giving for one, which it could ne'er express,
A thousand images of loveliness.

If I were one whom the loud world held wise,
I should disdain to quote authorities

In commendation of this kind of love:—
Why there is first the God in heaven above,
Who wrote a book called Nature, 'tis to be
Reviewed, I hear, in the next Quarterly;
And Socrates, the Jesus Christ of Greece,
And Jesus Christ Himself, did never cease
To urge all living things to love each other,
And to forgive their mutual faults, and smother
The Devil of disunion in their souls.

. . .

I love you!—Listen, O embodied Ray
Of the great Brightness; I must pass away
While you remain, and these light words must be
Tokens by which you may remember me.
Start not—the thing you are is unbetrayed,
If you are human, and if but the shade
Of some sublimer spirit. . .

. . .

And as to friend or mistress, 'tis a form;
Perhaps I wish you were one. Some declare
You a familiar spirit, as you are;
Others with a. . . more inhuman
Hint that, though not my wife, you are a woman;
What is the colour of your eyes and hair?
Why, if you were a lady, it were fair
The world should know—but, as I am afraid,
The Quarterly would bait you if betrayed;
And if, as it will be sport to see them stumble
Over all sorts of scandals. hear them mumble
Their litany of curses—some guess right,
And others swear you're a Hermaphrodite;
Like that sweet marble monster of both sexes,
Which looks so sweet and gentle that it vexes
The very soul that the soul is gone
Which lifted from her limbs the veil of stone.

. . .

It is a sweet thing, friendship, a dear balm,
A happy and auspicious bird of calm,
Which rides o'er life's ever tumultuous Ocean;

A God that broods o'er chaos in commotion;
A flower which fresh as Lapland roses are,
Lifts its bold head into the world's frore air,
And blooms most radiantly when others die,
Health, hope, and youth, and brief prosperity;
And with the light and odour of its bloom,
Shining within the dun eon and the tomb;
Whose coming is as light and music are
'Mid dissonance and gloom—a star
Which moves not 'mid the moving heavens alone—
A smile among dark frowns—a gentle tone
Among rude voices, a beloved light,
A solitude, a refuge, a delight.
If I had but a friend! Why, I have three
Even by my own confession; there may be
Some more, for what I know, for 'tis my mind
To call my friends all who are wise and kind,-
And these, Heaven knows, at best are very few;
But none can ever be more dear than you.
Why should they be? My muse has lost her wings,
Or like a dying swan who soars and sings,
I should describe you in heroic style,
But as it is, are you not void of guile?
A lovely soul, formed to be blessed and bless:
A well of sealed and secret happiness;
A lute which those whom Love has taught to play
Make music on to cheer the roughest day,
And enchant sadness till it sleeps? . . .

. . .
To the oblivion whither I and thou,
All loving and all lovely, hasten now
With steps, ah, too unequal! may we meet
In one Elysium or one winding-sheet!

If any should be curious to discover
Whether to you I am a friend or lover,
Let them read Shakespeare's sonnets, taking thence
A whetstone for their dull intelligence
That tears and will not cut, or let them guess

How Diotima, the wise prophetess,
Instructed the instructor, and why he
Rebuked the infant spirit of melody
On Agathon's sweet lips, which as he spoke
Was as the lovely star when morn has broke
The roof of darkness, in the golden dawn,
Half-hidden, and yet beautiful.
I'll pawn
My hopes of Heaven-you know what they are worth—
That the presumptuous pedagogues of Earth,
If they could tell the riddle offered here
Would scorn to be, or being to appear
What now they seem and are—but let them chide,
They have few pleasures in the world beside;
Perhaps we should be dull were we not chidden,
Paradise fruits are sweetest when forbidden.
Folly can season Wisdom, Hatred Love.

. . .

Farewell, if it can be to say farewell
To those who

. . .

I will not, as most dedicators do,
Assure myself and all the world and you,
That you are faultless—would to God they were
Who taunt me with your love! I then should wear
These heavy chains of life with a light spirit,
And would to God I were, or even as near it
As you, dear heart. Alas! what are we? Clouds
Driven by the wind in warring multitudes,
Which rain into the bosom of the earth,
And rise again, and in our death and birth,
And through our restless life, take as from heaven
Hues which are not our own, but which are given,
And then withdrawn, and with inconstant glance
Flash from the spirit to the countenance.
There is a Power, a Love, a Joy, a God
Which makes in mortal hearts its brief abode,
A Pythian exhalation, which inspires
Love, only love—a wind which o'er the wires

Of the soul's giant harp
There is a mood which language faints beneath;
You feel it striding, as Almighty Death
His bloodless steed. . .

. . .

And what is that most brief and bright delight
Which rushes through the touch and through the sight,
And stands before the spirit's inmost throne,
A naked Seraph? None hath ever known.
Its birth is darkness, and its growth desire;
Untameable and fleet and fierce as fire,
Not to be touched but to be felt alone,
It fills the world with glory–and is gone.

. . .

It floats with rainbow pinions o'er the stream
Of life, which flows, like a. . . dream
Into the light of morning, to the grave
As to an ocean. . .

. . .

What is that joy which serene infancy
Perceives not, as the hours content them by,
Each in a chain of blossoms, yet enjoys
The shapes of this new world, in giant toys
Wrought by the busy. . . ever new?
Remembrance borrows Fancy's glass, to show
These forms more. . . sincere
Than now they are, than then, perhaps, they were.
When everything familiar seemed to be
Wonderful, and the immortality
Of this great world, which all things must inherit,
Was felt as one with the awakening spirit,
Unconscious of itself, and of the strange
Distinctions which in its proceeding change
It feels and knows, and mourns as if each were
A desolation. . .

. . .

Were it not a sweet refuge, Emily,
For all those exiles from the dull insane
Who vex this pleasant world with pride and pain,

For all that band of sister-spirits known
To one another by a voiceless tone?

. . .

If day should part us night will mend division
And if sleep parts us—we will meet in vision
And if life parts us—we will mix in death
Yielding our mite (?) of unreluctant breath
Death cannot part us—we must meet again
In all in nothing in delight in pain:
How, why or when or where—it matters not
So that we share an undivided lot. . .

. . .

And we will move possessing and possessed
Wherever beauty on the earth's bare (?) breast
Lies like the shadow of thy soul—till we
Become one being with the world we see. . .

ADONAIS

An Elegy on the Death of John Keats, Author of Endymion, Hyperion, Etc.

*Aster prin men elampes eni zooisin Eoos
nun de thanon lampeis Esperos en phthimenois.*

—Plato

("Adonais" was composed at Pisa during the early days of June, 1821, and printed, with the author's name, at Pisa, 'with the types of Didot,' by July 13, 1821. Part of the impression was sent to the brothers Ollier for sale in London. An exact reprint of this Pisa edition (a few typographical errors only being corrected) was issued in 1829 by Gee & Bridges, Cambridge, at the instance of Arthur Hallam and Richard Monckton Milnes (Lord Houghton). The poem was included in Galignani's edition of "Coleridge, Shelley and Keats", Paris, 1829, and by Mrs. Shelley in the "Poetical Works" of 1839. Mrs. Shelley's text presents three important variations from that of the editio princeps. In 1876 an edition of the "Adonais", with Introduction and Notes, was printed for private circulation by Mr. H. Buxton Forman, C.B. Ten years later a reprint 'in exact facsimile' of the Pisa edition was edited with a Bibliographical Introduction by Mr. T.J. Wise ("Shelley Society Publications", 2nd Series, No. 1, Reeves & Turner, London, 1886). Our text is that of the editio princeps, Pisa, 1821, modified by Mrs. Shelley's text of 1839. The readings of the editio princeps, wherever superseded, are recorded in the footnotes. The Editor's Notes at the end of the Volume 3 should be consulted.)

Preface

Pharmakon elthe, Bion, poti son stoma, pharmakon eides.
pos ten tois cheilessi potesrame, kouk eglukanthe;
tis de Brotos tossouton anameros, e kerasai toi,
e dounai laleonti to pharmakon; ekphugen odan.

—Moschus, Epitaph. Bion

It is my intention to subjoin to the London edition of this poem a criticism upon the claims of its lamented object to be classed among the writers of the highest genius who have adorned our age. My known repugnance to the narrow principles of taste on which several of his earlier compositions were modelled prove at least that I am an impartial judge. I consider the fragment of "Hyperion" as second to nothing that was ever produced by a writer of the same years.

John Keats died at Rome of a consumption, in his twenty-fourth year, on the — of — 1821; and was buried in the romantic and lonely cemetery of the Protestants in that city, under the pyramid which is the tomb of Cestius, and the massy walls and towers, now mouldering and desolate, which formed the circuit of ancient Rome. The cemetery is an open space among the ruins, covered in winter with violets and daisies. It might make one in love with death, to think that one should be buried in so sweet a place.

The genius of the lamented person to whose memory I have dedicated these unworthy verses was not less delicate and fragile than it was beautiful; and where cankerworms abound, what wonder if its young flower was blighted in the bud? The savage criticism on his "Endymion", which appeared in the "Quarterly Review", produced the most violent effect on his susceptible mind; the agitation thus originated ended in the rupture of a blood-vessel in the lungs; a rapid consumption ensued, and the succeeding acknowledgements from more candid critics of the true greatness of his powers were ineffectual to heal the wound thus wantonly inflicted.

It may be well said that these wretched men know not what they do. They scatter their insults and their slanders without heed as to whether the poisoned shaft lights on a heart made callous by many blows or one like Keats's composed of more penetrable stuff. One of their associates is, to my knowledge, a most base and unprincipled calumniator. As to "Endymion", was it a poem, whatever might be its defects, to be treated contemptuously by those who had celebrated, with various degrees of complacency and panegyric, "Paris", and "Woman", and a "Syrian Tale", and Mrs. Lefanu, and Mr. Barrett, and Mr. Howard Payne, and a long list of the illustrious obscure? Are these the men who in their venal good nature presumed to draw a parallel between the Reverend Mr. Milman and Lord Byron? What gnat did they strain at here, after having swallowed all those camels? Against what woman taken in adultery dares the foremost of these literary prostitutes to cast his opprobrious stone? Miserable man! you, one of the meanest, have wantonly defaced one of the noblest specimens of the workmanship of God. Nor shall it be your excuse, that, murderer as you are, you have spoken daggers, but used none.

The circumstances of the closing scene of poor Keats's life were not made known to me until the "Elegy" was ready for the press. I am given to understand that the wound which his sensitive spirit had received from the criticism of "Endymion" was exasperated by the bitter sense of unrequited benefits; the poor fellow seems to have been hooted from the stage of life, no less by those on whom he had wasted the promise of his genius, than those on whom he had lavished his fortune and his care. He was accompanied to Rome, and attended in his last illness by Mr. Severn, a young artist of the highest promise, who, I have been informed, 'almost risked his own life, and sacrificed every prospect to unwearied attendance upon his dying friend.' Had I known these circumstances before the completion of my poem, I should have been tempted to add my feeble tribute of applause to the more solid recompense which the virtuous man finds in the recollection of his own motives. Mr. Severn can dispense with a reward from 'such stuff as dreams are made of.' His conduct is a golden augury of the success of his future career—may the unextinguished Spirit of his illustrious friend animate the creations of his pencil, and plead against Oblivion for his name!

Adonais

I weep for Adonais—he is dead!
O, weep for Adonais! though our tears
Thaw not the frost which binds so dear a head!
And thou, sad Hour, selected from all years
To mourn our loss, rouse thy obscure compeers,
And teach them thine own sorrow, say: "With me
Died Adonais; till the Future dares
Forget the Past, his fate and fame shall be
An echo and a light unto eternity!"

2

Where wert thou, mighty Mother, when he lay,
When thy Son lay, pierced by the shaft which flies
In darkness? where was lorn Urania
When Adonais died? With veiled eyes,
'Mid listening Echoes, in her Paradise
She sate, while one, with soft enamoured breath,
Rekindled all the fading melodies,
With which, like flowers that mock the corse beneath,
He had adorned and hid the coming bulk of Death.

3

Oh, weep for Adonais—he is dead!
Wake, melancholy Mother, wake and weep!
Yet wherefore? Quench within their burning bed
Thy fiery tears, and let thy loud heart keep
Like his, a mute and uncomplaining sleep;
For he is gone, where all things wise and fair
Descend;—oh, dream not that the amorous Deep
Will yet restore him to the vital air;
Death feeds on his mute voice, and laughs at our despair.

4

Most musical of mourners, weep again!
Lament anew, Urania!—He died,
Who was the Sire of an immortal strain,
Blind, old and lonely, when his country's pride,
The priest, the slave, and the liberticide,
Trampled and mocked with many a loathed rite
Of lust and blood; he went, unterrified,
Into the gulf of death; but his clear Sprite
Yet reigns o'er earth; the third among the sons of light.

5

Most musical of mourners, weep anew!
Not all to that bright station dared to climb;
And happier they their happiness who knew,
Whose tapers yet burn through that night of time
In which suns perished; others more sublime,
Struck by the envious wrath of man or god,
Have sunk, extinct in their refulgent prime;
And some yet live, treading the thorny road,
Which leads, through toil and hate, to Fame's serene abode.

6

But now, thy youngest, dearest one, has perished—
The nursling of thy widowhood, who grew,
Like a pale flower by some sad maiden cherished,
And fed with true-love tears, instead of dew;
Most musical of mourners, weep anew!
Thy extreme hope, the loveliest and the last,
The bloom, whose petals nipped before they blew
Died on the promise of the fruit, is waste;
The broken lily lies—the storm is overpast.

7

To that high Capital, where kingly Death
Keeps his pale court in beauty and decay,
He came; and bought, with price of purest breath,
A grave among the eternal.—Come away!
Haste, while the vault of blue Italian day
Is yet his fitting charnel-roof! while still
He lies, as if in dewy sleep he lay;
Awake him not! surely he takes his fill
Of deep and liquid rest, forgetful of all ill.

8

He will awake no more, oh, never more!—
Within the twilight chamber spreads apace
The shadow of white Death, and at the door
Invisible Corruption waits to trace
His extreme way to her dim dwelling-place;
The eternal Hunger sits, but pity and awe
Soothe her pale rage, nor dares she to deface
So fair a prey, till darkness and the law
Of change, shall o'er his sleep the mortal curtain draw.

9

Oh, weep for Adonais!—The quick Dreams,
The passion-winged Ministers of thought,
Who were his flocks, whom near the living streams
Of his young spirit he fed, and whom he taught
The love which was its music, wander not,—
Wander no more, from kindling brain to brain,
But droop there, whence they sprung; and mourn their lot
Round the cold heart, where, after their sweet pain,
They ne'er will gather strength, or find a home again.

10

And one with trembling hands clasps his cold head,
And fans him with her moonlight wings, and cries;
'Our love, our hope, our sorrow, is not dead;
See, on the silken fringe of his faint eyes,
Like dew upon a sleeping flower, there lies
A tear some Dream has loosened from his brain.'
Lost Angel of a ruined Paradise!
She knew not 'twas her own; as with no stain
She faded, like a cloud which had outwept its rain.

11

One from a lucid urn of starry dew
Washed his light limbs as if embalming them;
Another clipped her profuse locks, and threw
The wreath upon him, like an anadem,
Which frozen tears instead of pearls begem;
Another in her wilful grief would break
Her bow and winged reeds, as if to stem
A greater loss with one which was more weak;
And dull the barbed fire against his frozen cheek.

12

Another Splendour on his mouth alit,
That mouth, whence it was wont to draw the breath
Which gave it strength to pierce the guarded wit,
And pass into the panting heart beneath
With lightning and with music: the damp death
Quenched its caress upon his icy lips;
And, as a dying meteor stains a wreath
Of moonlight vapour, which the cold night clips,
It flushed through his pale limbs, and passed to its eclipse.

13

And others came... Desires and Adorations,
Winged Persuasions and veiled Destinies,
Splendours, and Glooms, and glimmering Incarnations
Of hopes and fears, and twilight Phantasies;
And Sorrow, with her family of Sighs,
And Pleasure, blind with tears, led by the gleam
Of her own dying smile instead of eyes,
Came in slow pomp;—the moving pomp might seem
Like pageantry of mist on an autumnal stream.

14

All he had loved, and moulded into thought,
From shape, and hue, and odour, and sweet sound,
Lamented Adonais. Morning sought
Her eastern watch-tower, and her hair unbound,
Wet with the tears which should adorn the ground,
Dimmed the aereal eyes that kindle day;
Afar the melancholy thunder moaned,
Pale Ocean in unquiet slumber lay,
And the wild Winds flew round, sobbing in their dismay.

15

Lost Echo sits amid the voiceless mountains,
And feeds her grief with his remembered lay,
And will no more reply to winds or fountains,
Or amorous birds perched on the young green spray,
Or herdsman's horn, or bell at closing day;
Since she can mimic not his lips, more dear
Than those for whose disdain she pined away
Into a shadow of all sounds:—a drear
Murmur, between their songs, is all the woodmen hear.

16

Grief made the young Spring wild, and she threw down
Her kindling buds, as if she Autumn were,
Or they dead leaves; since her delight is flown,
For whom should she have waked the sullen year?
To Phoebus was not Hyacinth so dear
Nor to himself Narcissus, as to both
Thou, Adonais: wan they stand and sere
Amid the faint companions of their youth,
With dew all turned to tears; odour, to sighing ruth.

17

Thy spirit's sister, the lorn nightingale
Mourns not her mate with such melodious pain;
Not so the eagle, who like thee could scale
Heaven, and could nourish in the sun's domain
Her mighty youth with morning, doth complain,
Soaring and screaming round her empty nest,
As Albion wails for thee: the curse of Cain
Light on his head who pierced thy innocent breast,
And scared the angel soul that was its earthly guest!

18

Ah, woe is me! Winter is come and gone,
But grief returns with the revolving year;
The airs and streams renew their joyous tone;
The ants, the bees, the swallows reappear;
Fresh leaves and flowers deck the dead Seasons' bier;
The amorous birds now pair in every brake,
And build their mossy homes in field and brere;
And the green lizard, and the golden snake,
Like unimprisoned flames, out of their trance awake.

19

Through wood and stream and field and hill and Ocean
A quickening life from the Earth's heart has burst
As it has ever done, with change and motion,
From the great morning of the world when first
God dawned on Chaos; in its stream immersed,
The lamps of Heaven flash with a softer light;
All baser things pant with life's sacred thirst;
Diffuse themselves; and spend in love's delight,
The beauty and the joy of their renewed might.

20

The leprous corpse, touched by this spirit tender,
Exhales itself in flowers of gentle breath;
Like incarnations of the stars, when splendour
Is changed to fragrance, they illumine death
And mock the merry worm that wakes beneath;
Nought we know, dies. Shall that alone which knows
Be as a sword consumed before the sheath
By sightless lightning?—the intense atom glows
A moment, then is quenched in a most cold repose.

21

Alas! that all we loved of him should be,
But for our grief, as if it had not been,
And grief itself be mortal! Woe is me!
Whence are we, and why are we? of what scene
The actors or spectators? Great and mean
Meet massed in death, who lends what life must borrow.
As long as skies are blue, and fields are green,
Evening must usher night, night urge the morrow,
Month follow month with woe, and year wake year to sorrow.

22

He will awake no more, oh, never more!
'Wake thou,' cried Misery, 'childless Mother, rise
Out of thy sleep, and slake, in thy heart's core,
A wound more fierce than his, with tears and sighs.'
And all the Dreams that watched Urania's eyes,
And all the Echoes whom their sister's song
Had held in holy silence, cried: 'Arise!'
Swift as a Thought by the snake Memory stung,
From her ambrosial rest the fading Splendour sprung.

23

She rose like an autumnal Night, that springs
Out of the East, and follows wild and drear
The golden Day, which, on eternal wings,
Even as a ghost abandoning a bier,
Had left the Earth a corpse. Sorrow and fear
So struck, so roused, so rapped Urania;
So saddened round her like an atmosphere
Of stormy mist; so swept her on her way
Even to the mournful place where Adonais lay.

24

Out of her secret Paradise she sped,
Through camps and cities rough with stone, and steel,
And human hearts, which to her aery tread
Yielding not, wounded the invisible
Palms of her tender feet where'er they fell:
And barbed tongues, and thoughts more sharp than they,
Rent the soft Form they never could repel,
Whose sacred blood, like the young tears of May,
Paved with eternal flowers that undeserving way.

25

In the death-chamber for a moment Death,
Shamed by the presence of that living Might,
Blushed to annihilation, and the breath
Revisited those lips, and Life's pale light
Flashed through those limbs, so late her dear delight.
'Leave me not wild and drear and comfortless,
As silent lightning leaves the starless night!
Leave me not!' cried Urania: her distress
Roused Death: Death rose and smiled, and met her vain caress.

26

'Stay yet awhile! speak to me once again;
Kiss me, so long but as a kiss may live;
And in my heartless breast and burning brain
That word, that kiss, shall all thoughts else survive,
With food of saddest memory kept alive,
Now thou art dead, as if it were a part
Of thee, my Adonais! I would give
All that I am to be as thou now art!
But I am chained to Time, and cannot thence depart!

27

'O gentle child, beautiful as thou wert,
Why didst thou leave the trodden paths of men
Too soon, and with weak hands though mighty heart
Dare the unpastured dragon in his den?
Defenceless as thou wert, oh, where was then
Wisdom the mirrored shield, or scorn the spear?
Or hadst thou waited the full cycle, when
Thy spirit should have filled its crescent sphere,
The monsters of life's waste had fled from thee like deer.

28

'The herded wolves, bold only to pursue;
The obscene ravens, clamorous o'er the dead;
The vultures to the conqueror's banner true
Who feed where Desolation first has fed,
And whose wings rain contagion;—how they fled,
When, like Apollo, from his golden bow
The Pythian of the age one arrow sped
And smiled!—The spoilers tempt no second blow,
They fawn on the proud feet that spurn them lying low.

29

'The sun comes forth, and many reptiles spawn;
He sets, and each ephemeral insect then
Is gathered into death without a dawn,
And the immortal stars awake again;
So is it in the world of living men:
A godlike mind soars forth, in its delight
Making earth bare and veiling heaven, and when
It sinks, the swarms that dimmed or shared its light
Leave to its kindred lamps the spirit's awful night.'

30

Thus ceased she: and the mountain shepherds came,
Their garlands sere, their magic mantles rent;
The Pilgrim of Eternity, whose fame
Over his living head like Heaven is bent,
An early but enduring monument,
Came, veiling all the lightnings of his song
In sorrow; from her wilds Ierne sent
The sweetest lyrist of her saddest wrong,
And Love taught Grief to fall like music from his tongue.

31

Midst others of less note, came one frail Form,
A phantom among men; companionless
As the last cloud of an expiring storm
Whose thunder is its knell; he, as I guess,
Had gazed on Nature's naked loveliness,
Actaeon-like, and now he fled astray
With feeble steps o'er the world's wilderness,
And his own thoughts, along that rugged way,
Pursued, like raging hounds, their father and their prey.

32

A pardlike Spirit beautiful and swift—
A Love in desolation masked;—a Power
Girt round with weakness;—it can scarce uplift
The weight of the superincumbent hour;
It is a dying lamp, a falling shower,
A breaking billow;—even whilst we speak
Is it not broken? On the withering flower
The killing sun smiles brightly: on a cheek
The life can burn in blood, even while the heart may break.

33

His head was bound with pansies overblown,
And faded violets, white, and pied, and blue;
And a light spear topped with a cypress cone,
Round whose rude shaft dark ivy-tresses grew
Yet dripping with the forest's noonday dew,
Vibrated, as the ever-beating heart
Shook the weak hand that grasped it; of that crew
He came the last, neglected and apart;
A herd-abandoned deer struck by the hunter's dart.

34

All stood aloof, and at his partial moan
Smiled through their tears; well knew that gentle band
Who in another's fate now wept his own,
As in the accents of an unknown land
He sung new sorrow; sad Urania scanned
The Stranger's mien, and murmured: 'Who art thou?'
He answered not, but with a sudden hand
Made bare his branded and ensanguined brow,
Which was like Cain's or Christ's—oh! that it should be so!

35

What softer voice is hushed over the dead?
Athwart what brow is that dark mantle thrown?
What form leans sadly o'er the white death-bed,
In mockery of monumental stone,
The heavy heart heaving without a moan?
If it be He, who, gentlest of the wise,
Taught, soothed, loved, honoured the departed one,
Let me not vex, with inharmonious sighs,
The silence of that heart's accepted sacrifice.

36

Our Adonais has drunk poison—oh!
What deaf and viperous murderer could crown
Life's early cup with such a draught of woe?
The nameless worm would now itself disown:
It felt, yet could escape, the magic tone
Whose prelude held all envy, hate and wrong,
But what was howling in one breast alone,
Silent with expectation of the song,
Whose master's hand is cold, whose silver lyre unstrung.

37

Live thou, whose infamy is not thy fame!
Live! fear no heavier chastisement from me,
Thou noteless blot on a remembered name!
But be thyself, and know thyself to be!
And ever at thy season be thou free
To spill the venom when thy fangs o'erflow;
Remorse and Self-contempt shall cling to thee;
Hot Shame shall burn upon thy secret brow,
And like a beaten hound tremble thou shalt—as now.

38

Nor let us weep that our delight is fled
Far from these carrion kites that scream below;
He wakes or sleeps with the enduring dead;
Thou canst not soar where he is sitting now—
Dust to the dust! but the pure spirit shall flow
Back to the burning fountain whence it came,
A portion of the Eternal, which must glow
Through time and change, unquenchably the same,
Whilst thy cold embers choke the sordid hearth of shame.

39

Peace, peace! he is not dead, he doth not sleep—
He hath awakened from the dream of life—
'Tis we, who lost in stormy visions, keep
With phantoms an unprofitable strife,
And in mad trance, strike with our spirit's knife
Invulnerable nothings.—WE decay
Like corpses in a charnel; fear and grief
Convulse us and consume us day by day,
And cold hopes swarm like worms within our living clay.

40

He has outsoared the shadow of our night;
Envy and calumny and hate and pain,
And that unrest which men miscall delight,
Can touch him not and torture not again;
From the contagion of the world's slow stain
He is secure, and now can never mourn
A heart grown cold, a head grown gray in vain;
Nor, when the spirit's self has ceased to burn,
With sparkless ashes load an unlamented urn.

41

He lives, he wakes—'tis Death is dead, not he;
Mourn not for Adonais.—Thou young Dawn,
Turn all thy dew to splendour, for from thee
The spirit thou lamentest is not gone;
Ye caverns and ye forests, cease to moan!
Cease, ye faint flowers and fountains, and thou Air,
Which like a mourning veil thy scarf hadst thrown
O'er the abandoned Earth, now leave it bare
Even to the joyous stars which smile on its despair!

42

He is made one with Nature: there is heard
His voice in all her music, from the moan
Of thunder, to the song of night's sweet bird;
He is a presence to be felt and known
In darkness and in light, from herb and stone,
Spreading itself where'er that Power may move
Which has withdrawn his being to its own;
Which wields the world with never-wearied love,
Sustains it from beneath, and kindles it above.

43

He is a portion of the loveliness
Which once he made more lovely: he doth bear
His part, while the one Spirit's plastic stress
Sweeps through the dull dense world, compelling there
All new successions to the forms they wear;
Torturing th' unwilling dross that checks its flight
To its own likeness, as each mass may bear;
And bursting in its beauty and its might
From trees and beasts and men into the Heaven's light.

44

The splendours of the firmament of time
May be eclipsed, but are extinguished not;
Like stars to their appointed height they climb,
And death is a low mist which cannot blot
The brightness it may veil. When lofty thought
Lifts a young heart above its mortal lair,
And love and life contend in it, for what
Shall be its earthly doom, the dead live there
And move like winds of light on dark and stormy air.

45

The inheritors of unfulfilled renown
Rose from their thrones, built beyond mortal thought,
Far in the Unapparent. Chatterton
Rose pale,—his solemn agony had not
Yet faded from him; Sidney, as he fought
And as he fell and as he lived and loved
Sublimely mild, a Spirit without spot,
Arose; and Lucan, by his death approved:
Oblivion as they rose shrank like a thing reproved.

46

And many more, whose names on Earth are dark,
But whose transmitted effluence cannot die
So long as fire outlives the parent spark,
Rose, robed in dazzling immortality.
'Thou art become as one of us,' they cry,
'It was for thee yon kingless sphere has long
Swung blind in unascended majesty,
Silent alone amid a Heaven of Song.
Assume thy winged throne, thou Vesper of our throng!'

47

Who mourns for Adonais? Oh, come forth,
Fond wretch! and know thyself and him aright.
Clasp with thy panting soul the pendulous Earth;
As from a centre, dart thy spirit's light
Beyond all worlds, until its spacious might
Satiate the void circumference: then shrink
Even to a point within our day and night;
And keep thy heart light lest it make thee sink
When hope has kindled hope, and lured thee to the brink.

48

Or go to Rome, which is the sepulchre,
Oh, not of him, but of our joy: 'tis nought
That ages, empires and religions there
Lie buried in the ravage they have wrought;
For such as he can lend,—they borrow not
Glory from those who made the world their prey;
And he is gathered to the kings of thought
Who waged contention with their time's decay,
And of the past are all that cannot pass away.

49

Go thou to Rome,—at once the Paradise,
The grave, the city, and the wilderness;
And where its wrecks like shattered mountains rise,
And flowering weeds, and fragrant copses dress
The bones of Desolation's nakedness
Pass, till the spirit of the spot shall lead
Thy footsteps to a slope of green access
Where, like an infant's smile, over the dead
A light of laughing flowers along the grass is spread;

50

And gray walls moulder round, on which dull Time
Feeds, like slow fire upon a hoary brand;
And one keen pyramid with wedge sublime,
Pavilioning the dust of him who planned
This refuge for his memory, doth stand
Like flame transformed to marble; and beneath,
A field is spread, on which a newer band
Have pitched in Heaven's smile their camp of death,
Welcoming him we lose with scarce extinguished breath.

51

Here pause: these graves are all too young as yet
To have outgrown the sorrow which consigned
Its charge to each; and if the seal is set,
Here, on one fountain of a mourning mind,
Break it not thou! too surely shalt thou find
Thine own well full, if thou returnest home,
Of tears and gall. From the world's bitter wind
Seek shelter in the shadow of the tomb.
What Adonais is, why fear we to become?

52

The One remains, the many change and pass;
Heaven's light forever shines, Earth's shadows fly;
Life, like a dome of many-coloured glass,
Stains the white radiance of Eternity,
Until Death tramples it to fragments.—Die,
If thou wouldst be with that which thou dost seek!
Follow where all is fled!—Rome's azure sky,
Flowers, ruins, statues, music, words, are weak
The glory they transfuse with fitting truth to speak.

53

Why linger, why turn back, why shrink, my Heart?
Thy hopes are gone before: from all things here
They have departed; thou shouldst now depart!
A light is passed from the revolving year,
And man, and woman; and what still is dear
Attracts to crush, repels to make thee wither.
The soft sky smiles,—the low wind whispers near:
'Tis Adonais calls! oh, hasten thither,
No more let Life divide what Death can join together.

54

That Light whose smile kindles the Universe,
That Beauty in which all things work and move,
That Benediction which the eclipsing Curse
Of birth can quench not, that sustaining Love
Which through the web of being blindly wove
By man and beast and earth and air and sea,
Burns bright or dim, as each are mirrors of
The fire for which all thirst; now beams on me,
Consuming the last clouds of cold mortality.

55

The breath whose might I have invoked in song
Descends on me; my spirit's bark is driven,
Far from the shore, far from the trembling throng
Whose sails were never to the tempest given;
The massy earth and sphered skies are riven!
I am borne darkly, fearfully, afar;
Whilst, burning through the inmost veil of Heaven,
The soul of Adonais, like a star,
Beacons from the abode where the Eternal are.

Cancelled Passages of Adonais

(Published by Dr. Garnett, "Relics of Shelley", 1862.)

Passages of the Preface

. . . the expression of my indignation and sympathy. I will allow myself a first and last word on the subject of calumny as it relates to me. As an author I have dared and invited censure. If I understand myself, I have written neither for profit nor for fame. I have employed my poetical compositions and publications simply as the instruments of that sympathy between myself and others which the ardent and unbounded love I cherished for my kind incited me to acquire. I expected all sorts of stupidity and insolent contempt from those. . .

. . . These compositions (excepting the tragedy of "The Cenci", which was written rather to try my powers than to unburthen my full heart) are insufficiently. . . commendation than perhaps they deserve, even from their bitterest enemies; but they have not attained any corresponding popularity. As a man, I shrink from notice and regard; the ebb and flow of the world vexes me; I desire to be left in peace. Persecution, contumely, and calumny have been heaped upon me in profuse measure; and domestic conspiracy and legal oppression have violated in my person the most sacred rights of nature and humanity. The bigot will say it was the recompense of my errors; the man of the world will call it the result of my imprudence; but never upon one head. . .

. . . Reviewers, with some rare exceptions, are a most stupid and malignant race. As a bankrupt thief turns thieftaker in despair, so an unsuccessful author turns critic. But a young spirit panting for fame, doubtful of its powers, and certain only of its aspirations, is ill qualified to assign its true value to the sneer of this world. He knows not that such stuff as this is of the abortive and monstrous births which time consumes as fast as it produces. He sees the truth and falsehood, the merits and demerits, of his case inextricably entangled. . . No personal offence should have drawn from me this public comment upon such stuff. . .

. . . The offence of this poor victim seems to have consisted solely in his intimacy with Leigh Hunt, Mr. Hazlitt, and some other enemies of despotism and superstition. My friend Hunt has a very hard skull to crack, and will take a deal of killing. I do not know much of Mr. Hazlitt, but. . .

. . . I knew personally but little of Keats; but on the news of his situation I wrote to him, suggesting the propriety of trying the Italian climate, and inviting him to join me. Unfortunately he did not allow me. . .

Passages of the Poem

And ever as he went he swept a lyre
Of unaccustomed shape, and. . . strings
Now like the. . . of impetuous fire,
Which shakes the forest with its murmurings,
Now like the rush of the aereal wings
Of the enamoured wind among the treen,
Whispering unimaginable things,
And dying on the streams of dew serene,
Which feed the unmown meads with ever-during green.
. . .
And the green Paradise which western waves
Embosom in their ever-wailing sweep,
Talking of freedom to their tongueless caves,
Or to the spirits which within them keep
A record of the wrongs which, though they sleep,
Die not, but dream of retribution, heard
His hymns, and echoing them from steep to steep,
Kept—
. . .
And then came one of sweet and earnest looks,
Whose soft smiles to his dark and night-like eyes
Were as the clear and ever-living brooks
Are to the obscure fountains whence they rise,
Showing how pure they are: a Paradise
Of happy truth upon his forehead low
Lay, making wisdom lovely, in the guise

Of earth-awakening morn upon the brow
Of star-deserted heaven, while ocean gleams below.

His song, though very sweet, was low and faint,
A simple strain—
. . .
A mighty Phantasm, half concealed
In darkness of his own exceeding light,
Which clothed his awful presence unrevealed,
Charioted on the. . . night
Of thunder-smoke, whose skirts were chrysolite.

And like a sudden meteor, which outstrips
The splendour-winged chariot of the sun,
. . . eclipse
The armies of the golden stars, each one
Pavilioned in its tent of light—all strewn
Over the chasms of blue night—

HELLAS

A Lyrical Drama

Mantis Eim Ezthlon Agonun.
—Oedip. Colon.

("Hellas" was composed at Pisa in the autumn of 1821, and dispatched to London, November 11. It was published, with the author's name, by C. & J. Ollier in the spring of 1822. A transcript of the poem by Edward Williams is in the Rowfant Library. Ollier availed himself of Shelley's permission to cancel certain passages in the notes; he also struck out certain lines of the text. These omissions were, some of them, restored in Galignani's one-volume edition of "Coleridge, Shelley and Keats", Paris, 1829, and also by Mrs. Shelley in the "Poetical Works", 1839. A passage in the "Preface", suppressed by Ollier, was restored by Mr. Buxton Forman (1892) from a proof copy of "Hellas" in his possession. The "Prologue to Hellas" was edited by Dr. Garnett in 1862 ("Relics of Shelley") from the manuscripts at Boscombe Manor.

Our text is that of the editio princeps, 1822, corrected by a list of "Errata" sent by Shelley to Ollier, April 11, 1822. The Editor's Notes at the end of Volume 3 should be consulted.)

To his Excellency

PRINCE ALEXANDER MAVROCORDATO
LATE SECRETARY FOR FOREIGN AFFAIRS TO THE HOSPODAR
OF WALLACHIA
THE DRAMA OF HELLAS IS INSCRIBED AS AN
IMPERFECT TOKEN OF THE ADMIRATION,
SYMPATHY, AND FRIENDSHIP OF
THE AUTHOR.
Pisa, November 1, 1821.

Preface

The poem of "Hellas", written at the suggestion of the events of the moment, is a mere improvise, and derives its interest (should it be found to possess any) solely from the intense sympathy which the Author feels with the cause he would celebrate.

The subject, in its present state, is insusceptible of being treated otherwise than lyrically, and if I have called this poem a drama from the circumstance of its being composed in dialogue, the licence is not greater than that which has been assumed by other poets who have called their productions epics, only because they have been divided into twelve or twenty-four books.

The "Persae" of Aeschylus afforded me the first model of my conception, although the decision of the glorious contest now waging in Greece being yet suspended forbids a catastrophe parallel to the return of Xerxes and the desolation of the Persians. I have, therefore, contented myself with exhibiting a series of lyric pictures, and with having wrought upon the curtain of futurity, which falls upon the unfinished scene, such figures of indistinct and visionary delineation as suggest the final triumph of the Greek cause as a portion of the cause of civilisation and social improvement.

The drama (if drama it must be called) is, however, so inartificial that I doubt whether, if recited on the Thespian waggon to an Athenian village at the Dionysiaca, it would have obtained the prize of the goat. I shall bear with equanimity any punishment, greater than the loss of such a reward, which the Aristarchi of the hour may think fit to inflict.

The only "goat-song" which I have yet attempted has, I confess, in spite of the unfavourable nature of the subject, received a greater and a more valuable portion of applause than I expected or than it deserved.

Common fame is the only authority which I can allege for the details which form the basis of the poem, and I must trespass upon the forgiveness of my readers for the display of newspaper erudition to which I have been reduced. Undoubtedly, until the conclusion of the war, it will be impossible to obtain an account of it sufficiently authentic for historical materials; but poets have their privilege, and it is unquestionable that actions of the most exalted courage have been performed by the Greeks—that they have gained more than one naval victory, and that their defeat in Wallachia was signalized by circumstances of heroism more glorious even than victory.

The apathy of the rulers of the civilised world to the astonishing circumstance of the descendants of that nation to which they owe their civilisation, rising as it were from the ashes of their ruin, is something perfectly inexplicable to a mere spectator of the shows of this mortal scene. We are all Greeks. Our laws, our literature, our religion, our arts have their root in Greece. But for Greece—Rome, the instructor, the conqueror, or the metropolis of our ancestors, would have spread no illumination with her arms, and we might still have been savages and idolaters; or, what is worse, might have arrived at such a stagnant and miserable state of social institution as China and Japan possess.

The human form and the human mind attained to a perfection in Greece which has impressed its image on those faultless productions, whose very fragments are the despair of modern art, and has propagated impulses which cannot cease, through a thousand channels of manifest or imperceptible operation, to ennoble and delight mankind until the extinction of the race.

The modern Greek is the descendant of those glorious beings whom the imagination almost refuses to figure to itself as belonging to our kind, and he inherits much of their sensibility, their rapidity of conception, their enthusiasm, and their courage. If in many instances he is degraded by moral and political slavery to the practice of the basest vices it engenders—and that below the level of ordinary degradation—let us reflect that the corruption of the best produces the worst, and that habits which subsist only in relation to a peculiar state of social institution may be expected to cease as soon as that relation is dissolved. In fact, the Greeks, since the admirable novel of Anastasius could have been a faithful picture of their manners, have undergone most important changes; the flower of their youth, returning to their country from the universities of Italy, Germany, and France, have communicated to their fellow-citizens the latest results of that social perfection of which their ancestors were the original source. The University of Chios contained before the breaking out of the revolution eight hundred students, and among them several Germans and Americans. The munificence and energy of many of the Greek princes and merchants, directed to the renovation of their country with a spirit and a wisdom which has few examples, is above all praise.

The English permit their own oppressors to act according to their natural sympathy with the Turkish tyrant, and to brand upon their name the indelible blot of an alliance with the enemies of domestic happiness, of Christianity and civilisation.

Russia desires to possess, not to liberate Greece; and is contented to see the Turks, its natural enemies, and the Greeks, its intended slaves, enfeeble each other until one or both fall into its net. The wise and generous policy of England would have consisted in establishing the independence of Greece, and in maintaining it both against Russia and the Turk;—but when was the oppressor generous or just?

(Should the English people ever become free, they will reflect upon the part which those who presume to represent their will have played in the great drama of the revival of liberty, with feelings which it would become them to anticipate. This is the age of the war of the oppressed against the oppressors, and every one of those ringleaders of the privileged gangs of murderers and swindlers, called Sovereigns, look to each other for aid against the common enemy, and suspend their mutual jealousies in the presence of a mightier fear. Of this holy alliance all the despots of the earth are virtual members. But a new race has arisen throughout Europe, nursed in the abhorrence of the opinions which are its chains, and she will continue to produce fresh generations to accomplish that destiny which tyrants foresee and dread. (This paragraph, suppressed in 1822 by Charles Ollier, was first restored in 1892 by Mr. Buxton Forman ("Poetical Works of P. B. S.", volume 4 pages 40–41) from a proof copy of Hellas in his possession.)

The Spanish Peninsula is already free. France is tranquil in the enjoyment of a partial exemption from the abuses which its unnatural and feeble government are vainly attempting to revive. The seed of blood and misery has been sown in Italy, and a more vigorous race is arising to go forth to the harvest. The world waits only the news of a revolution of Germany to see the tyrants who have pinnacled themselves on its supineness precipitated into the ruin from which they shall never arise. Well do these destroyers of mankind know their enemy, when they impute the insurrection in Greece to the same spirit before which they tremble throughout the rest of Europe, and that enemy well knows the power and the cunning of its opponents, and watches the moment of their approaching weakness and inevitable division to wrest the bloody sceptres from their grasp.

Prologue to Hellas

HERALD OF ETERNITY: It is the day when all the sons of God
   Wait in the roofless senate-house, whose floor
   Is Chaos, and the immovable abyss
   Frozen by His steadfast word to hyaline
. . .
   The shadow of God, and delegate
   Of that before whose breath the universe
   Is as a print of dew.
   Hierarchs and kings
   Who from your thrones pinnacled on the past
   Sway the reluctant present, ye who sit
   Pavilioned on the radiance or the gloom
   Of mortal thought, which like an exhalation
   Steaming from earth, conceals the. . . of heaven
   Which gave it birth. . . assemble here
   Before your Father's throne; the swift decree
   Yet hovers, and the fiery incarnation
   Is yet withheld, clothed in which it shall
   annul
   The fairest of those wandering isles that gem
   The sapphire space of interstellar air,
   That green and azure sphere, that earth enwrapped
   Less in the beauty of its tender light
   Than in an atmosphere of living spirit
   Which interpenetrating all the. . .
   it rolls from realm to realm
   And age to age, and in its ebb and flow
   Impels the generations
   To their appointed place,
   Whilst the high Arbiter
   Beholds the strife, and at the appointed time
   Sends His decrees veiled in eternal. . .

   Within the circuit of this pendent orb
   There lies an antique region, on which fell
   The dews of thought in the world's golden dawn

    Earliest and most benign, and from it sprung
    Temples and cities and immortal forms
    And harmonies of wisdom and of song,
    And thoughts, and deeds worthy of thoughts so fair.
    And when the sun of its dominion failed,
    And when the winter of its glory came,
    The winds that stripped it bare blew on and swept
    That dew into the utmost wildernesses
    In wandering clouds of sunny rain that thawed
    The unmaternal bosom of the North.
    Haste, sons of God, . . . for ye beheld,
    Reluctant, or consenting, or astonished,
    The stern decrees go forth, which heaped on Greece
    Ruin and degradation and despair.
    A fourth now waits: assemble, sons of God,
    To speed or to prevent or to suspend,
    If, as ye dream, such power be not withheld,
    The unaccomplished destiny.
  . . .

CHORUS: The curtain of the Universe
  Is rent and shattered,
  The splendour-winged worlds disperse
  Like wild doves scattered.

  Space is roofless and bare,
  And in the midst a cloudy shrine,
  Dark amid thrones of light.
  In the blue glow of hyaline
  Golden worlds revolve and shine.
  In. . . flight
  From every point of the Infinite,
  Like a thousand dawns on a single night
  The splendours rise and spread;
  And through thunder and darkness dread
  Light and music are radiated,
  And in their pavilioned chariots led
  By living wings high overhead
  The giant Powers move,
  Gloomy or bright as the thrones they fill.

. . .
    A chaos of light and motion
    Upon that glassy ocean.
. . .
    The senate of the Gods is met,
    Each in his rank and station set;
    There is silence in the spaces—
    Lo! Satan, Christ, and Mahomet
    Start from their places!
CHRIST: Almighty Father!
    Low-kneeling at the feet of Destiny
. . .
    There are two fountains in which spirits weep
    When mortals err, Discord and Slavery named,
    And with their bitter dew two Destinies
    Filled each their irrevocable urns; the third
    Fiercest and mightiest, mingled both, and added
    Chaos and Death, and slow Oblivion's lymph,
    And hate and terror, and the poisoned rain
. . .
    The Aurora of the nations. By this brow
    Whose pores wept tears of blood, by these wide wounds,
    By this imperial crown of agony,
    By infamy and solitude and death,
    For this I underwent, and by the pain
    Of pity for those who would. . . for me
    The unremembered joy of a revenge,
    For this I felt—by Plato's sacred light,
    Of which my spirit was a burning morrow—
    By Greece and all she cannot cease to be.
    Her quenchless words, sparks of immortal truth,
    Stars of all night—her harmonies and forms,
    Echoes and shadows of what Love adores
    In thee, I do compel thee, send forth Fate,
    Thy irrevocable child: let her descend,
    A seraph-winged Victory (*arrayed*)
    In tempest of the omnipotence of God
    Which sweeps through all things.

From hollow leagues, from Tyranny which arms
Adverse miscreeds and emulous anarchies
To stamp, as on a winged serpent's seed,
Upon the name of Freedom; from the storm
Of faction, which like earthquake shakes and sickens
The solid heart of enterprise; from all
By which the holiest dreams of highest spirits
Are stars beneath the dawn. . .
She shall arise
Victorious as the world arose from Chaos!
And as the Heavens and the Earth arrayed
Their presence in the beauty and the light
Of Thy first smile, O Father,—as they gather
The spirit of Thy love which paves for them
Their path o'er the abyss, till every sphere
Shall be one living Spirit,—so shall Greece—

SATAN: Be as all things beneath the empyrean,
Mine! Art thou eyeless like old Destiny,
Thou mockery-king, crowned with a wreath of thorns?
Whose sceptre is a reed, the broken reed
Which pierces thee! whose throne a chair of scorn;
For seest thou not beneath this crystal floor
The innumerable worlds of golden light
Which are my empire, and the least of them
which thou wouldst redeem from me?
Know'st thou not them my portion?
Or wouldst rekindle the. . . strife
Which our great Father then did arbitrate
Which he assigned to his competing sons
Each his apportioned realm?
Thou Destiny,
Thou who art mailed in the omnipotence
Of Him who tends thee forth, whate'er thy task,
Speed, spare not to accomplish, and be mine
Thy trophies, whether Greece again become
The fountain in the desert whence the earth
Shall drink of freedom, which shall give it strength
To suffer, or a gulf of hollow death
To swallow all delight, all life, all hope.

Go, thou Vicegerent of my will, no less
Than of the Father's; but lest thou shouldst faint,
The winged hounds, Famine and Pestilence,
Shall wait on thee, the hundred-forked snake
Insatiate Superstition still shall. . .
The earth behind thy steps, and War shall hover
Above, and Fraud shall gape below, and Change
Shall flit before thee on her dragon wings,
Convulsing and consuming, and I add
Three vials of the tears which daemons weep
When virtuous spirits through the gate of Death
Pass triumphing over the thorns of life,
Sceptres and crowns, mitres and swords and snares,
Trampling in scorn, like Him and Socrates.
The first is Anarchy; when Power and Pleasure,
Glory and science and security,
On Freedom hang like fruit on the green tree,
Then pour it forth, and men shall gather ashes.
The second Tyranny—

CHRIST: Obdurate spirit!
Thou seest but the Past in the To-come.
Pride is thy error and thy punishment.
Boast not thine empire, dream not that thy worlds
Are more than furnace-sparks or rainbow-drops
Before the Power that wields and kindles them.
True greatness asks not space, true excellence
Lives in the Spirit of all things that live,
Which lends it to the worlds thou callest thine.
. . .

MAHOMET: . . . Haste thou and fill the waning crescent
With beams as keen as those which pierced the shadow
Of Christian night rolled back upon the West,
When the orient moon of Islam rode in triumph
From Tmolus to the Acroceraunian snow.
. . .
Wake, thou Word
Of God, and from the throne of Destiny
Even to the utmost limit of thy way

May Triumph

. . .

Be thou a curse on them whose creed
Divides and multiplies the most high God.

Hellas

Dramatis Personae:

Mahmud
Hassan
Daood
Ahasuerus, A Jew
Chorus Of Greek Captive Women
(The Phantom Of Mahomet II. (Omitted, Edition 1822.))
Messengers, Slaves, And Attendants

Scene:
Constantinople.

Time: Sunset.

Scene:
A terrace on the seraglio.
mahmud sleeping,
An indian slave sitting beside his couch.
Chorus of Greek Captive Women: We strew these opiate
  flowers
  On thy restless pillow,—
  They were stripped from Orient bowers,
  By the Indian billow.
  Be thy sleep
  Calm and deep,
  Like theirs who fell—not ours who weep!
Indian: Away, unlovely dreams!
  Away, false shapes of sleep
  Be his, as Heaven seems,
  Clear, and bright, and deep!
  Soft as love, and calm as death,
  Sweet as a summer night without a breath.
Chorus: Sleep, sleep! our song is laden
  With the soul of slumber;
  It was sung by a Samian maiden,
  Whose lover was of the number

    Who now keep
    That calm sleep
    Whence none may wake, where none shall weep.
INDIAN: I touch thy temples pale!
    I breathe my soul on thee!
    And could my prayers avail,
    All my joy should be
    Dead, and I would live to weep,
    So thou mightst win one hour of quiet sleep.
CHORUS: Breathe low, low
    The spell of the mighty mistress now!
    When Conscience lulls her sated snake,
    And Tyrants sleep, let Freedom wake.
    Breathe low—low
    The words which, like secret fire, shall flow
    Through the veins of the frozen earth—low, low!
SEMICHORUS 1: Life may change, but it may fly not;
    Hope may vanish, but can die not;
    Truth be veiled, but still it burneth;
    Love repulsed,—but it returneth!
SEMICHORUS 2: Yet were life a charnel where
    Hope lay coffined with Despair;
    Yet were truth a sacred lie,
    Love were lust—
SEMICHORUS 1: If Liberty
    Lent not life its soul of light,
    Hope its iris of delight,
    Truth its prophet's robe to wear,
    Love its power to give and bear.
CHORUS: In the great morning of the world,
    The Spirit of God with might unfurled
    The flag of Freedom over Chaos,
    And all its banded anarchs fled,
    Like vultures frighted from Imaus,
    Before an earthquake's tread.—
    So from Time's tempestuous dawn
    Freedom's splendour burst and shone:—
    Thermopylae and Marathon
    Caught like mountains beacon-lighted,

The springing Fire.—The winged glory
On Philippi half-alighted,
Like an eagle on a promontory.
Its unwearied wings could fan
The quenchless ashes of Milan.
From age to age, from man to man,
It lived; and lit from land to land
Florence, Albion, Switzerland.

Then night fell; and, as from night,
Reassuming fiery flight,
From the West swift Freedom came,
Against the course of Heaven and doom.
A second sun arrayed in flame,
To burn, to kindle, to illume.
From far Atlantis its young beams
Chased the shadows and the dreams.
France, with all her sanguine steams,
Hid, but quenched it not; again
Through clouds its shafts of glory rain
From utmost Germany to Spain.
As an eagle fed with morning
Scorns the embattled tempest's warning,
When she seeks her aerie hanging
In the mountain-cedar's hair,
And her brood expect the clanging
Of her wings through the wild air,
Sick with famine:—Freedom, so
To what of Greece remaineth now
Returns; her hoary ruins glow
Like Orient mountains lost in day;
Beneath the safety of her wings
Her renovated nurslings prey,
And in the naked lightenings
Of truth they purge their dazzled eyes.
Let Freedom leave—where'er she flies,
A Desert, or a Paradise:
Let the beautiful and the brave
Share her glory, or a grave.

SEMICHORUS 1: With the gifts of gladness
    Greece did thy cradle strew;
SEMICHORUS 2: With the tears of sadness
    Greece did thy shroud bedew!
SEMICHORUS 1: With an orphan's affection
    She followed thy bier through Time;
SEMICHORUS 2: And at thy resurrection
    Reappeareth, like thou, sublime!
SEMICHORUS 1: If Heaven should resume thee,
    To Heaven shall her spirit ascend;
SEMICHORUS 2: If Hell should entomb thee,
    To Hell shall her high hearts bend.
SEMICHORUS 1: If Annihilation—
SEMICHORUS 2: Dust let her glories be!
    And a name and a nation
    Be forgotten, Freedom, with thee!
INDIAN: His brow grows darker—breathe not—move not!
    He starts—he shudders—ye that love not,
    With your panting loud and fast,
    Have awakened him at last.
MAHMUD (*starting from his sleep*): Man the Seraglio-guard! make fast the gate!
    What! from a cannonade of three short hours?
    'Tis false! that breach towards the Bosphorus
    Cannot be practicable yet—who stirs?
    Stand to the match; that when the foe prevails
    One spark may mix in reconciling ruin
    The conqueror and the conquered! Heave the tower
    Into the gap—wrench off the roof!
(*Enter* HASSAN)
    Ha! what!
    The truth of day lightens upon my dream
    And I am Mahmud still.
HASSAN: Your Sublime Highness
    Is strangely moved.
MAHMUD: The times do cast strange shadows
    On those who watch and who must rule their course,
    Lest they, being first in peril as in glory,
    Be whelmed in the fierce ebb:—and these are of them.

Thrice has a gloomy vision hunted me
As thus from sleep into the troubled day;
It shakes me as the tempest shakes the sea,
Leaving no figure upon memory's glass.
Would that—no matter. Thou didst say thou knewest
A Jew, whose spirit is a chronicle
Of strange and secret and forgotten things.
I bade thee summon him:—'tis said his tribe
Dream, and are wise interpreters of dreams.

HASSAN: The Jew of whom I spake is old,—so old
  He seems to have outlived a world's decay;
  The hoary mountains and the wrinkled ocean
  Seem younger still than he;—his hair and beard
  Are whiter than the tempest-sifted snow;
  His cold pale limbs and pulseless arteries
  Are like the fibres of a cloud instinct
  With light, and to the soul that quickens them
  Are as the atoms of the mountain-drift
  To the winter wind:—but from his eye looks forth
  A life of unconsumed thought which pierces
  The Present, and the Past, and the To-come.
  Some say that this is he whom the great prophet
  Jesus, the son of Joseph, for his mockery,
  Mocked with the curse of immortality.
  Some feign that he is Enoch: others dream
  He was pre-adamite and has survived
  Cycles of generation and of ruin.
  The sage, in truth, by dreadful abstinence
  And conquering penance of the mutinous flesh,
  Deep contemplation, and unwearied study,
  In years outstretched beyond the date of man,
  May have attained to sovereignty and science
  Over those strong and secret things and thoughts
  Which others fear and know not.

MAHMUD: I would talk
  With this old Jew.

HASSAN: Thy will is even now
  Made known to him, where he dwells in a sea-cavern
  'Mid the Demonesi, less accessible

Than thou or God! He who would question him
Must sail alone at sunset, where the stream
Of Ocean sleeps around those foamless isles,
When the young moon is westering as now,
And evening airs wander upon the wave;
And when the pines of that bee-pasturing isle,
Green Erebinthus, quench the fiery shadow
Of his gilt prow within the sapphire water,
Then must the lonely helmsman cry aloud
'Ahasuerus!' and the caverns round
Will answer 'Ahasuerus!' If his prayer
Be granted, a faint meteor will arise
Lighting him over Marmora, and a wind
Will rush out of the sighing pine-forest,
And with the wind a storm of harmony
Unutterably sweet, and pilot him
Through the soft twilight to the Bosphorus:
Thence at the hour and place and circumstance
Fit for the matter of their conference
The Jew appears. Few dare, and few who dare
Win the desired communion—but that shout
Bodes—

(*A shout within*)

MAHMUD: Evil, doubtless; Like all human sounds.
   Let me converse with spirits.
HASSAN: That shout again.
MAHMUD: This Jew whom thou hast summoned—
HASSAN: Will be here—
MAHMUD: When the omnipotent hour to which are yoked
   He, I, and all things shall compel—enough!
   Silence those mutineers—that drunken crew,
   That crowd about the pilot in the storm.
   Ay! strike the foremost shorter by a head!
   They weary me, and I have need of rest.
   Kinks are like stars—they rise and set, they have
   The worship of the world, but no repose.

(*Exeunt severally*)

CHORUS: Worlds on worlds are rolling ever
   From creation to decay,

Like the bubbles on a river
Sparkling, bursting, borne away.
But they are still immortal
Who, through birth's orient portal
And death's dark chasm hurrying to and fro,
Clothe their unceasing flight
In the brief dust and light
Gathered around their chariots as they go;
New shapes they still may weave,
New gods, new laws receive,
Bright or dim are they as the robes they last
On Death's bare ribs had cast.

A power from the unknown God,
A Promethean conqueror, came;
Like a triumphal path he trod
The thorns of death and shame.
A mortal shape to him
Was like the vapour dim
Which the orient planet animates with light;
Hell, Sin, and Slavery came,
Like bloodhounds mild and tame,
Nor preyed, until their Lord had taken flight;
The moon of Mahomet
Arose, and it shall set:
While blazoned as on Heaven's immortal noon
The cross leads generations on.

Swift as the radiant shapes of sleep
From one whose dreams are Paradise
Fly, when the fond wretch wakes to weep,
And Day peers forth with her blank eyes;
So fleet, so faint, so fair,
The Powers of earth and air
Fled from the folding-star of Bethlehem:
Apollo, Pan, and Love,
And even Olympian Jove
Grew weak, for killing Truth had glared on them;
Our hills and seas and streams,

    Dispeopled of their dreams,
    Their waters turned to blood, their dew to tears,
    Wailed for the golden years.
(*Enter* MAHMUD, HASSAN, DAOOD, *and others*)
MAHMUD: More gold? our ancestors bought gold with victory,
    And shall I sell it for defeat?
DAOOD: The Janizars
    Clamour for pay.
MAHMUD: Go! bid them pay themselves
    With Christian blood! Are there no Grecian virgins
    Whose shrieks and spasms and tears they may enjoy?
    No infidel children to impale on spears?
    No hoary priests after that Patriarch
    Who bent the curse against his country's heart,
    Which clove his own at last? Go! bid them kill,
    Blood is the seed of gold.
DAOOD: It has been sown,
    And yet the harvest to the sicklemen
    Is as a grain to each.
MAHMUD: Then, take this signet,
    Unlock the seventh chamber in which lie
    The treasures of victorious Solyman,—
    An empire's spoil stored for a day of ruin.
    O spirit of my sires! is it not come?
    The prey-birds and the wolves are gorged and sleep;
    But these, who spread their feast on the red earth,
    Hunger for gold, which fills not.—See them fed;
    Then, lead them to the rivers of fresh death.
(*Exit* DAOOD)
    O miserable dawn, after a night
    More glorious than the day which it usurped!
    O faith in God! O power on earth! O word
    Of the great prophet, whose o'ershadowing wings
    Darkened the thrones and idols of the West,
    Now bright!—For thy sake cursed be the hour,
    Even as a father by an evil child,
    When the orient moon of Islam rolled in triumph
    From Caucasus to White Ceraunia!
    Ruin above, and anarchy below;

    Terror without, and treachery within;
    The Chalice of destruction full, and all
    Thirsting to drink; and who among us dares
    To dash it from his lips? and where is Hope?
HASSAN: The lamp of our dominion still rides high;
    One God is God—Mahomet is His prophet.
    Four hundred thousand Moslems, from the limits
    Of utmost Asia, irresistibly
    Throng, like full clouds at the Sirocco's cry;
    But not like them to weep their strength in tears:
    They bear destroying lightning, and their step
    Wakes earthquake to consume and overwhelm,
    And reign in ruin. Phrygian Olympus,
    Tmolus, and Latmos, and Mycale, roughen
    With horrent arms; and lofty ships even now,
    Like vapours anchored to a mountain's edge,
    Freighted with fire and whirlwind, wait at Scala
    The convoy of the ever-veering wind.
    Samos is drunk with blood;—the Greek has paid
    Brief victory with swift loss and long despair.
    The false Moldavian serfs fled fast and far
    When the fierce shout of 'Allah-illa-Allah!'
    Rose like the war-cry of the northern wind
    Which kills the sluggish clouds, and leaves a flock
    Of wild swans struggling with the naked storm.
    So were the lost Greeks on the Danube's day!
    If night is mute, yet the returning sun
    Kindles the voices of the morning birds;
    Nor at thy bidding less exultingly
    Than birds rejoicing in the golden day,
    The Anarchies of Africa unleash
    Their tempest-winged cities of the sea,
    To speak in thunder to the rebel world.
    Like sulphurous clouds, half-shattered by the storm,
    They sweep the pale Aegean, while the Queen
    Of Ocean, bound upon her island-throne,
    Far in the West, sits mourning that her sons
    Who frown on Freedom spare a smile for thee:
    Russia still hovers, as an eagle might

Within a cloud, near which a kite and crane
Hang tangled in inextricable fight,
To stoop upon the victor;—for she fears
The name of Freedom, even as she hates thine.
But recreant Austria loves thee as the Grave
Loves Pestilence, and her slow dogs of war
Fleshed with the chase, come up from Italy,
And howl upon their limits; for they see
The panther, Freedom, fled to her old cover,
Amid seas and mountains, and a mightier brood
Crouch round. What Anarch wears a crown or mitre,
Or bears the sword, or grasps the key of gold,
Whose friends are not thy friends, whose foes thy foes?
Our arsenals and our armouries are full;
Our forts defy assault; ten thousand cannon
Lie ranged upon the beach, and hour by hour
Their earth-convulsing wheels affright the city;
The galloping of fiery steeds makes pale
The Christian merchant; and the yellow Jew
Hides his hoard deeper in the faithless earth.
Like clouds, and like the shadows of the clouds,
Over the hills of Anatolia,
Swift in wide troops the Tartar chivalry
Sweep;—the far flashing of their starry lances
Reverberates the dying light of day.
We have one God, one King, one Hope, one Law;
But many-headed Insurrection stands
Divided in itself, and soon must fall.
MAHMUD: Proud words, when deeds come short, are seasonable:
Look, Hassan, on yon crescent moon, emblazoned
Upon that shattered flag of fiery cloud
Which leads the rear of the departing day;
Wan emblem of an empire fading now!
See how it trembles in the blood-red air,
And like a mighty lamp whose oil is spent
Shrinks on the horizon's edge, while, from above,
One star with insolent and victorious light
Hovers above its fall, and with keen beams,
Like arrows through a fainting antelope,

Strikes its weak form to death.
HASSAN: Even as that moon
Renews itself—
MAHMUD: Shall we be not renewed!
Far other bark than ours were needed now
To stem the torrent of descending time:
The Spirit that lifts the slave before his lord
Stalks through the capitals of armed kings,
And spreads his ensign in the wilderness:
Exults in chains; and, when the rebel falls,
Cries like the blood of Abel from the dust;
And the inheritors of the earth, like beasts
When earthquake is unleashed, with idiot fear
Cower in their kingly dens—as I do now.
What were Defeat when Victory must appal?
Or Danger, when Security looks pale?—
How said the messenger—who, from the fort
Islanded in the Danube, saw the battle
Of Bucharest?—that—
HASSAN: Ibrahim's scimitar
Drew with its gleam swift victory from Heaven,
To burn before him in the night of battle—
A light and a destruction.
MAHMUD: Ay! the day
Was ours: but how?—
HASSAN: The light Wallachians,
The Arnaut, Servian, and Albanian allies
Fled from the glance of our artillery
Almost before the thunderstone alit.
One half the Grecian army made a bridge
Of safe and slow retreat, with Moslem dead;
The other—
MAHMUD: Speak—tremble not.—
HASSAN: Islanded
By victor myriads, formed in hollow square
With rough and steadfast front, and thrice flung back
The deluge of our foaming cavalry;
Thrice their keen wedge of battle pierced our lines.
Our baffled army trembled like one man

Before a host, and gave them space; but soon,
From the surrounding hills, the batteries blazed,
Kneading them down with fire and iron rain:
Yet none approached; till, like a field of corn
Under the hook of the swart sickleman,
The band, intrenched in mounds of Turkish dead,
Grew weak and few.—Then said the Pacha, 'Slaves,
Render yourselves—they have abandoned you—
What hope of refuge, or retreat, or aid?
We grant your lives.' 'Grant that which is thine own!'
Cried one, and fell upon his sword and died!
Another—'God, and man, and hope abandon me;
But I to them, and to myself, remain
Constant:'—he bowed his head, and his heart burst.
A third exclaimed, 'There is a refuge, tyrant,
Where thou darest not pursue, and canst not harm
Shouldst thou pursue; there we shall meet again.'
Then held his breath, and, after a brief spasm,
The indignant spirit cast its mortal garment
Among the slain—dead earth upon the earth!
So these survivors, each by different ways,
Some strange, all sudden, none dishonourable,
Met in triumphant death; and when our army
Closed in, while yet wonder, and awe, and shame
Held back the base hyaenas of the battle
That feed upon the dead and fly the living,
One rose out of the chaos of the slain:
And if it were a corpse which some dread spirit
Of the old saviours of the land we rule
Had lifted in its anger, wandering by;—
Or if there burned within the dying man
Unquenchable disdain of death, and faith
Creating what it feigned;—I cannot tell—
But he cried, 'Phantoms of the free, we come!
Armies of the Eternal, ye who strike
To dust the citadels of sanguine kings,
And shake the souls throned on their stony hearts,
And thaw their frostwork diadems like dew;—
O ye who float around this clime, and weave

The garment of the glory which it wears,
Whose fame, though earth betray the dust it clasped,
Lies sepulchred in monumental thought;—
Progenitors of all that yet is great,
Ascribe to your bright senate, O accept
In your high ministrations, us, your sons—
Us first, and the more glorious yet to come!
And ye, weak conquerors! giants who look pale
When the crushed worm rebels beneath your tread,
The vultures and the dogs, your pensioners tame,
Are overgorged; but, like oppressors, still
They crave the relic of Destruction's feast.
The exhalations and the thirsty winds
Are sick with blood; the dew is foul with death;
Heaven's light is quenched in slaughter: thus, where'er
Upon your camps, cities, or towers, or fleets,
The obscene birds the reeking remnants cast
Of these dead limbs,—upon your streams and mountains,
Upon your fields, your gardens, and your housetops,
Where'er the winds shall creep, or the clouds fly,
Or the dews fall, or the angry sun look down
With poisoned light—Famine, and Pestilence,
And Panic, shall wage war upon our side!
Nature from all her boundaries is moved
Against ye: Time has found ye light as foam.
The Earth rebels; and Good and Evil stake
Their empire o'er the unborn world of men
On this one cast;—but ere the die be thrown,
The renovated genius of our race,
Proud umpire of the impious game, descends,
A seraph-winged Victory, bestriding
The tempest of the Omnipotence of God,
Which sweeps all things to their appointed doom,
And you to oblivion!'—More he would have said,
But—

MAHMUD: Died—as thou shouldst ore thy lips had painted
Their ruin in the hues of our success.
A rebel's crime, gilt with a rebel's tongue!
Your heart is Greek, Hassan.

HASSAN: It may be so:
>   A spirit not my own wrenched me within,
>   And I have spoken words I fear and hate;
>   Yet would I die for—

MAHMUD: Live! oh live! outlive
>   Me and this sinking empire. But the fleet—

HASSAN: Alas!—

MAHMUD: The fleet which, like a flock of clouds
>   Chased by the wind, flies the insurgent banner!
>   Our winged castles from their merchant ships!
>   Our myriads before their weak pirate bands!
>   Our arms before their chains! our years of empire
>   Before their centuries of servile fear!
>   Death is awake! Repulse is on the waters!
>   They own no more the thunder-bearing banner
>   Of Mahmud; but, like hounds of a base breed,
>   Gorge from a stranger's hand, and rend their master.

HASSAN: Latmos, and Ampelos, and Phanae saw
>   The wreck—

MAHMUD: The caves of the Icarian isles
>   Told each to the other in loud mockery,
>   And with the tongue as of a thousand echoes,
>   First of the sea-convulsing fight—and, then,—
>   Thou darest to speak—senseless are the mountains:
>   Interpret thou their voice!

HASSAN: My presence bore
>   A part in that day's shame. The Grecian fleet
>   Bore down at daybreak from the North, and hung
>   As multitudinous on the ocean line,
>   As cranes upon the cloudless Thracian wind.
>   Our squadron, convoying ten thousand men,
>   Was stretching towards Nauplia when the battle
>   Was kindled.—
>   First through the hail of our artillery
>   The agile Hydriote barks with press of sail
>   Dashed:—ship to ship, cannon to cannon, man
>   To man were grappled in the embrace of war,
>   Inextricable but by death or victory.
>   The tempest of the raging fight convulsed

    To its crystalline depths that stainless sea,
    And shook Heaven's roof of golden morning clouds,
    Poised on an hundred azure mountain-isles.
    In the brief trances of the artillery
    One cry from the destroyed and the destroyer
    Rose, and a cloud of desolation wrapped
    The unforeseen event, till the north wind
    Sprung from the sea, lifting the heavy veil
    Of battle-smoke—then victory—victory!
    For, as we thought, three frigates from Algiers
    Bore down from Naxos to our aid, but soon
    The abhorred cross glimmered behind, before,
    Among, around us; and that fatal sign
    Dried with its beams the strength in Moslem hearts,
    As the sun drinks the dew.—What more? We fled!—
    Our noonday path over the sanguine foam
    Was beaconed,—and the glare struck the sun pale,—
    By our consuming transports: the fierce light
    Made all the shadows of our sails blood-red,
    And every countenance blank. Some ships lay feeding
    The ravening fire, even to the water's level;
    Some were blown up; some, settling heavily,
    Sunk; and the shrieks of our companions died
    Upon the wind, that bore us fast and far,
    Even after they were dead. Nine thousand perished!
    We met the vultures legioned in the air
    Stemming the torrent of the tainted wind;
    They, screaming from their cloudy mountain-peaks,
    Stooped through the sulphurous battle-smoke and perched
    Each on the weltering carcase that we loved,
    Like its ill angel or its damned soul,
    Riding upon the bosom of the sea.
    We saw the dog-fish hastening to their feast.
    Joy waked the voiceless people of the sea,
    And ravening Famine left his ocean cave
    To dwell with War, with us, and with Despair.
    We met night three hours to the west of Patmos,
        And with night, tempest—
MAHMUD: Cease!

(*Enter a messenger*)
MESSENGER: Your Sublime Highness,
　That Christian hound, the Muscovite Ambassador,
　Has left the city.—If the rebel fleet
　Had anchored in the port, had victory
　Crowned the Greek legions in the Hippodrome,
　Panic were tamer.—Obedience and Mutiny,
　Like giants in contention planet-struck,
　Stand gazing on each other.—There is peace
　In Stamboul.—
MAHMUD: Is the grave not calmer still?
　Its ruins shall be mine.
HASSAN: Fear not the Russian:
　The tiger leagues not with the stag at bay
　Against the hunter.—Cunning, base, and cruel,
　He crouches, watching till the spoil be won,
　And must be paid for his reserve in blood.
　After the war is fought, yield the sleek Russian
　That which thou canst not keep, his deserved portion
　Of blood, which shall not flow through streets and fields,
　Rivers and seas, like that which we may win,
　But stagnate in the veins of Christian slaves!
(*Enter second messenger*)
SECOND MESSENGER: Nauplia, Tripolizza, Mothon, Athens,
　Navarin, Artas, Monembasia,
　Corinth, and Thebes are carried by assault,
　And every Islamite who made his dogs
　Fat with the flesh of Galilean slaves
　Passed at the edge of the sword: the lust of blood,
　Which made our warriors drunk, is quenched in death;
　But like a fiery plague breaks out anew
　In deeds which make the Christian cause look pale
　In its own light. The garrison of Patras
　Has store but for ten days, nor is there hope
　But from the Briton: at once slave and tyrant,
　His wishes still are weaker than his fears,
　Or he would sell what faith may yet remain
　From the oaths broke in Genoa and in Norway;
　And if you buy him not, your treasury

Is empty even of promises—his own coin.
The freedman of a western poet-chief
Holds Attica with seven thousand rebels,
And has beat back the Pacha of Negropont:
The aged Ali sits in Yanina
A crownless metaphor of empire:
His name, that shadow of his withered might,
Holds our besieging army like a spell
In prey to famine, pest, and mutiny;
He, bastioned in his citadel, looks forth
Joyless upon the sapphire lake that mirrors
The ruins of the city where he reigned
Childless and sceptreless. The Greek has reaped
The costly harvest his own blood matured,
Not the sower, Ali—who has bought a truce
From Ypsilanti with ten camel-loads
Of Indian gold.

(*Enter a third messenger*)

MAHMUD: What more?

THIRD MESSENGER: The Christian tribes
Of Lebanon and the Syrian wilderness
Are in revolt;—Damascus, Hems, Aleppo
Tremble;—the Arab menaces Medina,
The Aethiop has intrenched himself in Sennaar,
And keeps the Egyptian rebel well employed,
Who denies homage, claims investiture
As price of tardy aid. Persia demands
The cities on the Tigris, and the Georgians
Refuse their living tribute. Crete and Cyprus,
Like mountain-twins that from each other's veins
Catch the volcano-fire and earthquake-spasm,
Shake in the general fever. Through the city,
Like birds before a storm, the Santons shriek,
And prophesyings horrible and new
Are heard among the crowd: that sea of men
Sleeps on the wrecks it made, breathless and still.
A Dervise, learned in the Koran, preaches
That it is written how the sins of Islam
Must raise up a destroyer even now.

The Greeks expect a Saviour from the West,
Who shall not come, men say, in clouds and glory,
But in the omnipresence of that Spirit
In which all live and are. Ominous signs
Are blazoned broadly on the noonday sky:
One saw a red cross stamped upon the sun;
It has rained blood; and monstrous births declare
The secret wrath of Nature and her Lord.
The army encamped upon the Cydaris
Was roused last night by the alarm of battle,
And saw two hosts conflicting in the air,
The shadows doubtless of the unborn time
Cast on the mirror of the night. While yet
The fight hung balanced, there arose a storm
Which swept the phantoms from among the stars.
At the third watch the Spirit of the Plague
Was heard abroad flapping among the tents;
Those who relieved watch found the sentinels dead.
The last news from the camp is, that a thousand
Have sickened, and—

(*Enter a fourth messenger*)

MAHMUD: And thou, pale ghost, dim shadow
   Of some untimely rumour, speak!
FOURTH MESSENGER: One comes
   Fainting with toil, covered with foam and blood:
   He stood, he says, on Chelonites'
   Promontory, which o'erlooks the isles that groan
   Under the Briton's frown, and all their waters
   Then trembling in the splendour of the moon,
   When as the wandering clouds unveiled or hid
   Her boundless light, he saw two adverse fleets
   Stalk through the night in the horizon's glimmer,
   Mingling fierce thunders and sulphureous gleams,
   And smoke which strangled every infant wind
   That soothed the silver clouds through the deep air.
   At length the battle slept, but the Sirocco
   Awoke, and drove his flock of thunder-clouds
   Over the sea-horizon, blotting out
   All objects—save that in the faint moon-glimpse

He saw, or dreamed he saw, the Turkish admiral
And two the loftiest of our ships of war,
With the bright image of that Queen of Heaven,
Who hid, perhaps, her face for grief, reversed;
And the abhorred cross—

(*Enter an attendant*)

ATTENDANT: Your Sublime Highness,
    The Jew, who—
MAHMUD: Could not come more seasonably:
    Bid him attend. I'll hear no more! too long
    We gaze on danger through the mist of fear,
    And multiply upon our shattered hopes
    The images of ruin. Come what will!
    To-morrow and to-morrow are as lamps
    Set in our path to light us to the edge
    Through rough and smooth, nor can we suffer aught
    Which He inflicts not in whose hand we are.

(*Exeunt*)

SEMICHORUS 1: Would I were the winged cloud
    Of a tempest swift and loud!
    I would scorn
    The smile of morn
    And the wave where the moonrise is born!
    I would leave
    The spirits of eve
    A shroud for the corpse of the day to weave
    From other threads than mine!
    Bask in the deep blue noon divine.
    Who would? Not I.
SEMICHORUS 2: Whither to fly?
SEMICHORUS 1: Where the rocks that gird th' Aegean
    Echo to the battle paean
    Of the free—
    I would flee
    A tempestuous herald of victory!
    My golden rain
    For the Grecian slain
    Should mingle in tears with the bloody main,
    And my solemn thunder-knell

    Should ring to the world the passing-bell
    Of Tyranny!
SEMICHORUS 2: Ah king! wilt thou chain
    The rack and the rain?
    Wilt thou fetter the lightning and hurricane?
    The storms are free,
    But we—
CHORUS: O Slavery! thou frost of the world's prime,
    Killing its flowers and leaving its thorns bare!
    Thy touch has stamped these limbs with crime,
    These brows thy branding garland bear,
    But the free heart, the impassive soul
    Scorn thy control!
SEMICHORUS 1: Let there be light! said Liberty,
    And like sunrise from the sea,
    Athens arose!—Around her born,
    Shone like mountains in the morn
    Glorious states;—and are they now
    Ashes, wrecks, oblivion?
SEMICHORUS 2: Go,
    Where Thermae and Asopus swallowed
    Persia, as the sand does foam:
    Deluge upon deluge followed,
    Discord, Macedon, and Rome:
    And lastly thou!
SEMICHORUS 1: Temples and towers,
    Citadels and marts, and they
    Who live and die there, have been ours,
    And may be thine, and must decay;
    But Greece and her foundations are
    Built below the tide of war,
    Based on the crystalline sea
    Of thought and its eternity;
    Her citizens, imperial spirits,
    Rule the present from the past,
    On all this world of men inherits
    Their seal is set.
SEMICHORUS 2: Hear ye the blast,
    Whose Orphic thunder thrilling calls

From ruin her Titanian walls?
Whose spirit shakes the sapless bones
Of Slavery? Argos, Corinth, Crete
Hear, and from their mountain thrones
The daemons and the nymphs repeat
The harmony.

SEMICHORUS 1: I hear! I hear!

SEMICHORUS 2: The world's eyeless charioteer,
Destiny, is hurrying by!
What faith is crushed, what empire bleeds
Beneath her earthquake-footed steeds?
What eagle-winged victory sits
At her right hand? what shadow flits
Before? what splendour rolls behind?
Ruin and renovation cry
'Who but We?'

SEMICHORUS 1: I hear! I hear!
The hiss as of a rushing wind,
The roar as of an ocean foaming,
The thunder as of earthquake coming.
I hear! I hear!
The crash as of an empire falling,
The shrieks as of a people calling
'Mercy! mercy!'—How they thrill!
Then a shout of 'kill! kill! kill!'
And then a small still voice, thus—

SEMICHORUS 2: For
Revenge and Wrong bring forth their kind,
The foul cubs like their parents are,
Their den is in the guilty mind,
And Conscience feeds them with despair.

SEMICHORUS 1: In sacred Athens, near the fane
Of Wisdom, Pity's altar stood:
Serve not the unknown God in vain.
But pay that broken shrine again,
Love for hate and tears for blood.

(*Enter* MAHMUD *and* AHASUERUS)

MAHMUD: Thou art a man, thou sayest, even as we.

AHASUERUS: No more!

MAHMUD: But raised above thy fellow-men
    By thought, as I by power.
AHASUERUS: Thou sayest so.
MAHMUD: Thou art an adept in the difficult lore
    Of Greek and Frank philosophy; thou numberest
    The flowers, and thou measurest the stars;
    Thou severest element from element;
    Thy spirit is present in the Past, and sees
    The birth of this old world through all its cycles
    Of desolation and of loveliness,
    And when man was not, and how man became
    The monarch and the slave of this low sphere,
    And all its narrow circles—it is much—
    I honour thee, and would be what thou art
    Were I not what I am; but the unborn hour,
    Cradled in fear and hope, conflicting storms,
    Who shall unveil? Nor thou, nor I, nor any
    Mighty or wise. I apprehended not
    What thou hast taught me, but I now perceive
    That thou art no interpreter of dreams;
    Thou dost not own that art, device, or God,
    Can make the Future present—let it come!
    Moreover thou disdainest us and ours;
    Thou art as God, whom thou contemplatest.
AHASUERUS: Disdain thee?—not the worm beneath thy feet!
    The Fathomless has care for meaner things
    Than thou canst dream, and has made pride for those
    Who would be what they may not, or would seem
    That which they are not. Sultan! talk no more
    Of thee and me, the Future and the Past;
    But look on that which cannot change—the One,
    The unborn and the undying. Earth and ocean,
    Space, and the isles of life or light that gem
    The sapphire floods of interstellar air,
    This firmament pavilioned upon chaos,
    With all its cressets of immortal fire,
    Whose outwall, bastioned impregnably
    Against the escape of boldest thoughts, repels them
    As Calpe the Atlantic clouds—this Whole

Of suns, and worlds, and men, and beasts, and flowers,
With all the silent or tempestuous workings
By which they have been, are, or cease to be,
Is but a vision;—all that it inherits
Are motes of a sick eye, bubbles and dreams;
Thought is its cradle and its grave, nor less
The Future and the Past are idle shadows
Of thought's eternal flight—they have no being:
Nought is but that which feels itself to be.

MAHMUD: What meanest thou? Thy words stream like a tempest
 Of dazzling mist within my brain—they shake
 The earth on which I stand, and hang like night
 On Heaven above me. What can they avail?
 They cast on all things surest, brightest, best,
 Doubt, insecurity, astonishment.

AHASUERUS: Mistake me not! All is contained in each.
 Dodona's forest to an acorn's cup
 Is that which has been, or will be, to that
 Which is—the absent to the present. Thought
 Alone, and its quick elements, Will, Passion,
 Reason, Imagination, cannot die;
 They are, what that which they regard appears,
 The stuff whence mutability can weave
 All that it hath dominion o'er, worlds, worms,
 Empires, and superstitions. What has thought
 To do with time, or place, or circumstance?
 Wouldst thou behold the Future?—ask and have!
 Knock and it shall be opened—look, and lo!
 The coming age is shadowed on the Past
 As on a glass.

MAHMUD: Wild, wilder thoughts convulse
 My spirit—Did not Mahomet the Second
 Win Stamboul?

AHASUERUS: Thou wouldst ask that giant spirit
 The written fortunes of thy house and faith.
 Thou wouldst cite one out of the grave to tell
 How what was born in blood must die.

MAHMUD: Thy words
 Have power on me! I see—

AHASUERUS: What hearest thou?
MAHMUD: A far whisper—
  Terrible silence.
AHASUERUS: What succeeds?
MAHMUD: The sound
  As of the assault of an imperial city,
  The hiss of inextinguishable fire,
  The roar of giant cannon; the earthquaking
  Fall of vast bastions and precipitous towers,
  The shock of crags shot from strange enginery,
  The clash of wheels, and clang of armed hoofs,
  And crash of brazen mail as of the wreck
  Of adamantine mountains—the mad blast
  Of trumpets, and the neigh of raging steeds,
  The shrieks of women whose thrill jars the blood,
  And one sweet laugh, most horrible to hear,
  As of a joyous infant waked and playing
  With its dead mother's breast, and now more loud
  The mingled battle-cry,—ha! hear I not
  'En touto nike!' 'Allah-illa-Allah!'?
AHASUERUS: The sulphurous mist is raised—thou seest—
MAHMUD: A chasm,
  As of two mountains in the wall of Stamboul;
  And in that ghastly breach the Islamites,
  Like giants on the ruins of a world,
  Stand in the light of sunrise. In the dust
  Glimmers a kingless diadem, and one
  Of regal port has cast himself beneath
  The stream of war. Another proudly clad
  In golden arms spurs a Tartarian barb
  Into the gap, and with his iron mace
  Directs the torrent of that tide of men,
  And seems—he is—Mahomet!
AHASUERUS: What thou seest
  Is but the ghost of thy forgotten dream.
  A dream itself, yet less, perhaps, than that
  Thou call'st reality. Thou mayst behold
  How cities, on which Empire sleeps enthroned,
  Bow their towered crests to mutability.

    Poised by the flood, e'en on the height thou holdest,
    Thou mayst now learn how the full tide of power
    Ebbs to its depths.—Inheritor of glory,
    Conceived in darkness, born in blood, and nourished
    With tears and toil, thou seest the mortal throes
    Of that whose birth was but the same. The Past
    Now stands before thee like an Incarnation
    Of the To-come; yet wouldst thou commune with
    That portion of thyself which was ere thou
    Didst start for this brief race whose crown is death,
    Dissolve with that strong faith and fervent passion
    Which called it from the uncreated deep,
    Yon cloud of war, with its tempestuous phantoms
    Of raging death; and draw with mighty will
    The imperial shade hither.
(*Exit* AHASUERUS)
(*The Phantom of mahomet the second appears*)
MAHMUD: Approach!
PHANTOM: I come
    Thence whither thou must go! The grave is fitter
    To take the living than give up the dead;
    Yet has thy faith prevailed, and I am here.
    The heavy fragments of the power which fell
    When I arose, like shapeless crags and clouds,
    Hang round my throne on the abyss, and voices
    Of strange lament soothe my supreme repose,
    Wailing for glory never to return.—
    A later Empire nods in its decay:
    The autumn of a greener faith is come,
    And wolfish change, like winter, howls to strip
    The foliage in which Fame, the eagle, built
    Her aerie, while Dominion whelped below.
    The storm is in its branches, and the frost
    Is on its leaves, and the blank deep expects
    Oblivion on oblivion, spoil on spoil,
    Ruin on ruin:—Thou art slow, my son;
    The Anarchs of the world of darkness keep
    A throne for thee, round which thine empire lies
    Boundless and mute; and for thy subjects thou,

    Like us, shalt rule the ghosts of murdered life,
    The phantoms of the powers who rule thee now—
    Mutinous passions, and conflicting fears,
    And hopes that sate themselves on dust, and die!—
    Stripped of their mortal strength, as thou of thine.
    Islam must fall, but we will reign together
    Over its ruins in the world of death:—
    And if the trunk be dry, yet shall the seed
    Unfold itself even in the shape of that
    Which gathers birth in its decay. Woe! woe!
    To the weak people tangled in the grasp
    Of its last spasms.
MAHMUD: Spirit, woe to all!
    Woe to the wronged and the avenger! Woe
    To the destroyer, woe to the destroyed!
    Woe to the dupe, and woe to the deceiver!
    Woe to the oppressed, and woe to the oppressor!
    Woe both to those that suffer and inflict;
    Those who are born and those who die! but say,
    Imperial shadow of the thing I am,
    When, how, by whom, Destruction must accomplish
    Her consummation!
PHANTOM: Ask the cold pale Hour,
    Rich in reversion of impending death,
    When HE shall fall upon whose ripe gray hairs
    Sit Care, and Sorrow, and Infirmity—
    The weight which Crime, whose wings are plumed with years,
    Leaves in his flight from ravaged heart to heart
    Over the heads of men, under which burthen
    They bow themselves unto the grave: fond wretch!
    He leans upon his crutch, and talks of years
    To come, and how in hours of youth renewed
    He will renew lost joys, and—
VOICE WITHOUT: Victory! Victory!
(*The* PHANTOM *vanishes*)
MAHMUD: What sound of the importunate earth has broken
    My mighty trance?
VOICE WITHOUT: Victory! Victory!
MAHMUD: Weak lightning before darkness! poor faint smile

Of dying Islam! Voice which art the response
Of hollow weakness! Do I wake and live?
Were there such things, or may the unquiet brain,
Vexed by the wise mad talk of the old Jew,
Have shaped itself these shadows of its fear?
It matters not!—for nought we see or dream,
Possess, or lose, or grasp at, can be worth
More than it gives or teaches. Come what may,
The Future must become the Past, and I
As they were to whom once this present hour,
This gloomy crag of time to which I cling,
Seemed an Elysian isle of peace and joy
Never to be attained.—I must rebuke
This drunkenness of triumph ere it die,
And dying, bring despair. Victory! poor slaves!
(*Exit* MAHMUD)
VOICE WITHOUT: Shout in the jubilee of death! The Greeks
   Are as a brood of lions in the net
   Round which the kingly hunters of the earth
   Stand smiling. Anarchs, ye whose daily food
   Are curses, groans, and gold, the fruit of death,
   From Thule to the girdle of the world,
   Come, feast! the board groans with the flesh of men;
   The cup is foaming with a nation's blood,
   Famine and Thirst await! eat, drink, and die!
SEMICHORUS 1: Victorious Wrong, with vulture scream,
   Salutes the rising sun, pursues the flying day!
   I saw her, ghastly as a tyrant's dream,
   Perch on the trembling pyramid of night,
   Beneath which earth and all her realms pavilioned lay
   In visions of the dawning undelight.
   Who shall impede her flight?
   Who rob her of her prey?
VOICE WITHOUT: Victory! Victory! Russia's famished eagles
   Dare not to prey beneath the crescent's light.
   Impale the remnant of the Greeks! despoil!
   Violate! make their flesh cheaper than dust!
SEMICHORUS 2: Thou voice which art
   The herald of the ill in splendour hid!

    Thou echo of the hollow heart
    Of monarchy, bear me to thine abode
    When desolation flashes o'er a world destroyed:
    Oh, bear me to those isles of jagged cloud
    Which float like mountains on the earthquake, mid
    The momentary oceans of the lightning,
    Or to some toppling promontory proud
    Of solid tempest whose black pyramid,
    Riven, overhangs the founts intensely bright'ning
    Of those dawn-tinted deluges of fire
    Before their waves expire,
    When heaven and earth are light, and only light
    In the thunder-night!
VOICE WITHOUT: Victory! Victory! Austria, Russia, England,
    And that tame serpent, that poor shadow, France,
    Cry peace, and that means death when monarchs speak.
    Ho, there! bring torches, sharpen those red stakes,
    These chains are light, fitter for slaves and poisoners
    Than Greeks. Kill! plunder! burn! let none remain.
SEMICHORUS 1: Alas! for Liberty!
    If numbers, wealth, or unfulfilling years,
    Or fate, can quell the free!
    Alas! for Virtue, when
    Torments, or contumely, or the sneers
    Of erring judging men
    Can break the heart where it abides.
    Alas! if Love, whose smile makes this obscure world splendid,
    Can change with its false times and tides,
    Like hope and terror,—
    Alas for Love!
    And Truth, who wanderest lone and unbefriended,
    If thou canst veil thy lie-consuming mirror
    Before the dazzled eyes of Error,
    Alas for thee! Image of the Above.
SEMICHORUS 2: Repulse, with plumes from conquest torn,
    Led the ten thousand from the limits of the morn
    Through many an hostile Anarchy!
    At length they wept aloud, and cried, 'The Sea! the Sea!'
    Through exile, persecution, and despair,

Rome was, and young Atlantis shall become
The wonder, or the terror, or the tomb
Of all whose step wakes Power lulled in her savage lair:
But Greece was as a hermit-child,
Whose fairest thoughts and limbs were built
To woman's growth, by dreams so mild,
She knew not pain or guilt;
And now, O Victory, blush! and Empire, tremble
When ye desert the free—
If Greece must be
A wreck, yet shall its fragments reassemble,
And build themselves again impregnably
In a diviner clime,
To Amphionic music on some Cape sublime,
Which frowns above the idle foam of Time.

SEMICHORUS 1: Let the tyrants rule the desert they have made;
Let the free possess the Paradise they claim;
Be the fortune of our fierce oppressors weighed
With our ruin, our resistance, and our name!

SEMICHORUS 2: Our dead shall be the seed of their decay,
Our survivors be the shadow of their pride,
Our adversity a dream to pass away—
Their dishonour a remembrance to abide!

VOICE WITHOUT: Victory! Victory! The bought Briton sends
The keys of ocean to the Islamite.—
Now shall the blazon of the cross be veiled,
And British skill directing Othman might,
Thunder-strike rebel victory. Oh, keep holy
This jubilee of unrevenged blood!
Kill! crush! despoil! Let not a Greek escape!

SEMICHORUS 1: Darkness has dawned in the East
On the noon of time:
The death-birds descend to their feast
From the hungry clime.
Let Freedom and Peace flee far
To a sunnier strand,
And follow Love's folding-star
To the Evening land!

SEMICHORUS 2: The young moon has fed

    Her exhausted horn
    With the sunset's fire:
    The weak day is dead,
    But the night is not born;
    And, like loveliness panting with wild desire
    While it trembles with fear and delight,
    Hesperus flies from awakening night,
    And pants in its beauty and speed with light
    Fast-flashing, soft, and bright.
    Thou beacon of love! thou lamp of the free!
    Guide us far, far away,
    To climes where now veiled by the ardour of day
    Thou art hidden
    From waves on which weary Noon
    Faints in her summer swoon,
    Between kingless continents sinless as Eden,
    Around mountains and islands inviolably
    Pranked on the sapphire sea.

SEMICHORUS 1: Through the sunset of hope,
    Like the shapes of a dream.
    What Paradise islands of glory gleam!
    Beneath Heaven's cope,
    Their shadows more clear float by—
    The sound of their oceans, the light of their sky,
    The music and fragrance their solitudes breathe
    Burst, like morning on dream, or like Heaven on death,
    Through the walls of our prison;
    And Greece, which was dead, is arisen!

CHORUS: The world's great age begins anew,
    The golden years return,
    The earth doth like a snake renew
    Her winter weeds outworn:
    Heaven smiles, and faiths and empires gleam,
    Like wrecks of a dissolving dream.

    A brighter Hellas rears its mountains
    From waves serener far;
    A new Peneus rolls his fountains
    Against the morning star.

Where fairer Tempes bloom, there sleep
Young Cyclads on a sunnier deep.

A loftier argo cleaves the main,
Fraught with a later prize;
Another Orpheus sings again,
And loves, and weeps, and dies.
A new Ulysses leaves once more
Calypso for his native shore.

Oh, write no more the tale of Troy,
If earth Death's scroll must be!
Nor mix with Laian rage the joy
Which dawns upon the free:
Although a subtler Sphinx renew
Riddles of death Thebes never knew.

Another Athens shall arise,
And to remoter time
Bequeath, like sunset to the skies,
The splendour of its prime;
And leave, if nought so bright may live,
All earth can take or Heaven can give.

Saturn and Love their long repose
Shall burst, more bright and good
Than all who fell, than One who rose,
Than many unsubdued:
Not gold, not blood, their altar dowers,
But votive tears and symbol flowers.

Oh, cease! must hate and death return?
Cease! must men kill and die?
Cease! drain not to its dregs the urn
Of bitter prophecy.
The world is weary of the past,
Oh, might it die or rest at last!

Notes

(1) The Quenchless Ashes of Milan.

Milan was the centre of the resistance of the Lombard league against the Austrian tyrant. Frederic Barbarossa burnt the city to the ground, but liberty lived in its ashes, and it rose like an exhalation from its ruin. See Sismondi's "Histoire des Republiques Italiennes", a book which has done much towards awakening the Italians to an imitation of their great ancestors.

(2) The Chorus.

The popular notions of Christianity are represented in this chorus as true in their relation to the worship they superseded, and that which in all probability they will supersede, without considering their merits in a relation more universal. The first stanza contrasts the immortality of the living and thinking beings which inhabit the planets, and to use a common and inadequate phrase, "clothe themselves in matter", with the transience of the noblest manifestations of the external world.

The concluding verses indicate a progressive state of more or loss exalted existence, according to the degree of perfection which every distinct intelligence may have attained. Let it not be supposed that I mean to dogmatise upon a subject, concerning which all men are equally ignorant, or that I think the Gordian knot of the origin of evil can be disentangled by that or any similar assertions. The received hypothesis of a Being resembling men in the moral attributes of His nature, having called us out of non-existence, and after inflicting on us the misery of the commission of error, should superadd that of the punishment and the privations consequent upon it, still would remain inexplicable and incredible. That there is a true solution of the riddle, and that in our present state that solution is unattainable by us, are propositions which may be regarded as equally certain: meanwhile, as it is the province of the poet to attach himself to those ideas which exalt and ennoble humanity, let him be permitted to have conjectured the condition of that futurity towards which we are all impelled by an inextinguishable thirst for immortality. Until better arguments can be produced than sophisms which disgrace the cause, this desire itself must remain the strongest and the only presumption that eternity is the inheritance of every thinking being.

(3) No Hoary Priests After That Patriarch.

The Greek Patriarch, after having been compelled to fulminate an anathema against the insurgents, was put to death by the Turks.

Fortunately the Greeks have been taught that they cannot buy security by degradation, and the Turks, though equally cruel, are less cunning than the smooth-faced tyrants of Europe. As to the anathema, his Holiness might as well have thrown his mitre at Mount Athos for any effect that it produced. The chiefs of the Greeks are almost all men of comprehension and enlightened views on religion and politics.

(4) The Freedman of a Western Poet-Chief.

A Greek who had been Lord Byron's servant commands the insurgents in Attica. This Greek, Lord Byron informs me, though a poet and an enthusiastic patriot, gave him rather the idea of a timid and unenterprising person. It appears that circumstances make men what they are, and that we all contain the germ of a degree of degradation or of greatness whose connection with our character is determined by events.

(5) The Greeks Expect a Saviour from the West.

It is reported that this Messiah had arrived at a seaport near Lacedaemon in an American brig. The association of names and ideas is irresistibly ludicrous, but the prevalence of such a rumour strongly marks the state of popular enthusiasm in Greece.

(6) The Sound as of the Assault of an Imperial City.

For the vision of Mahmud of the taking of Constantinople in 1453, see Gibbon's "Decline and Fall of the Roman Empire", volume 12 page 223.

The manner of the invocation of the spirit of Mahomet the Second will be censured as over subtle. I could easily have made the Jew a regular conjuror, and the Phantom an ordinary ghost. I have preferred to represent the Jew as disclaiming all pretension, or even belief, in supernatural agency, and as tempting Mahmud to that state of mind in which ideas may be supposed to assume the force of sensations through the confusion of thought with the objects of thought, and the excess of passion animating the creations of imagination.

It is a sort of natural magic, susceptible of being exercised in a degree by any one who should have made himself master of the secret associations of another's thoughts.

(7) THE CHORUS.

The final chorus is indistinct and obscure, as the event of the living drama whose arrival it foretells. Prophecies of wars, and rumours of wars, etc., may safely be made by poet or prophet in any age, but to anticipate however darkly a period of regeneration and happiness is a more hazardous exercise of the faculty which bards possess or feign. It will remind the reader 'magno NEC proximus intervallo' of Isaiah and Virgil, whose ardent spirits overleaping the actual reign of evil which we endure and bewail, already saw the possible and perhaps approaching state of society in which the 'lion shall lie down with the lamb,' and 'omnis feret omnia tellus.' Let these great names be my authority and my excuse.

(8) SATURN AND LOVE THEIR LONG REPOSE SHALL BURST.

Saturn and Love were among the deities of a real or imaginary state of innocence and happiness. ALL those WHO FELL, or the Gods of Greece, Asia, and Egypt; the ONE WHO ROSE, or Jesus Christ, at whose appearance the idols of the Pagan World wore amerced of their worship; and the MANY UNSUBDUED, or the monstrous objects of the idolatry of China, India, the Antarctic islands, and the native tribes of America, certainly have reigned over the understandings of men in conjunction or in succession, during periods in which all we know of evil has been in a state of portentous, and, until the revival of learning and the arts, perpetually increasing, activity. The Grecian gods seem indeed to have been personally more innocent, although it cannot be said, that as far as temperance and chastity are concerned, they gave so edifying an example as their successor. The sublime human character of Jesus Christ was deformed by an imputed identification with a Power, who tempted, betrayed, and punished the innocent beings who were called into existence by His sole will; and for the period of a thousand years, the spirit of this most just, wise, and benevolent of men has been propitiated with myriads of hecatombs of those who approached the nearest to His innocence and wisdom, sacrificed under every aggravation of atrocity and variety of torture. The horrors of the Mexican, the Peruvian, and the Indian superstitions are well known.

Note on Hellas, by Mrs. Shelley

The South of Europe was in a state of great political excitement at the beginning of the year 1821. The Spanish Revolution had been a signal to Italy; secrete societies were formed; and, when Naples rose to declare the Constitution, the call was responded to from Brundusium to the foot of the Alps. To crush these attempts to obtain liberty, early in 1821 the Austrians poured their armies into the Peninsula: at first their coming rather seemed to add energy and resolution to a people long enslaved. The Piedmontese asserted their freedom; Genoa threw off the yoke of the King of Sardinia; and, as if in playful imitation, the people of the little state of Massa and Carrara gave the conge to their sovereign, and set up a republic.

Tuscany alone was perfectly tranquil. It was said that the Austrian minister presented a list of sixty Carbonari to the Grand Duke, urging their imprisonment; and the Grand Duke replied, 'I do not know whether these sixty men are Carbonari, but I know, if I imprison them, I shall directly have sixty thousand start up.' But, though the Tuscans had no desire to disturb the paternal government beneath whose shelter they slumbered, they regarded the progress of the various Italian revolutions with intense interest, and hatred for the Austrian was warm in every bosom. But they had slender hopes; they knew that the Neapolitans would offer no fit resistance to the regular German troops, and that the overthrow of the constitution in Naples would act as a decisive blow against all struggles for liberty in Italy.

We have seen the rise and progress of reform. But the Holy Alliance was alive and active in those days, and few could dream of the peaceful triumph of liberty. It seemed then that the armed assertion of freedom in the South of Europe was the only hope of the liberals, as, if it prevailed, the nations of the north would imitate the example. Happily the reverse has proved the fact. The countries accustomed to the exercise of the privileges of freemen, to a limited extent, have extended, and are extending, these limits. Freedom and knowledge have now a chance of proceeding hand in hand; and, if it continue thus, we may hope for the durability of both. Then, as I have said—in 1821—Shelley, as well as every other lover of liberty, looked upon the struggles in Spain and Italy as decisive of the destinies of the world, probably for centuries to come. The interest he took in the progress of affairs was intense. When

Genoa declared itself free, his hopes were at their highest. Day after day he read the bulletins of the Austrian army, and sought eagerly to gather tokens of its defeat. He heard of the revolt of Genoa with emotions of transport. His whole heart and soul were in the triumph of the cause. We were living at Pisa at that time; and several well-informed Italians, at the head of whom we may place the celebrated Vacca, were accustomed to seek for sympathy in their hopes from Shelley: they did not find such for the despair they too generally experienced, founded on contempt for their southern countrymen.

While the fate of the progress of the Austrian armies then invading Naples was yet in suspense, the news of another revolution filled him with exultation. We had formed the acquaintance at Pisa of several Constantinopolitan Greeks, of the family of Prince Caradja, formerly Hospodar of Wallachia; who, hearing that the bowstring, the accustomed finale of his viceroyalty, was on the road to him, escaped with his treasures, and took up his abode in Tuscany. Among these was the gentleman to whom the drama of "Hellas" is dedicated. Prince Mavrocordato was warmed by those aspirations for the independence of his country which filled the hearts of many of his countrymen. He often intimated the possibility of an insurrection in Greece; but we had no idea of its being so near at hand, when, on the 1st of April 1821, he called on Shelley, bringing the proclamation of his cousin, Prince Ypsilanti, and, radiant with exultation and delight, declared that henceforth Greece would be free.

Shelley had hymned the dawn of liberty in Spain and Naples, in two odes dictated by the warmest enthusiasm; he felt himself naturally impelled to decorate with poetry the uprise of the descendants of that people whose works he regarded with deep admiration, and to adopt the vaticinatory character in prophesying their success. "Hellas" was written in a moment of enthusiasm. It is curious to remark how well he overcomes the difficulty of forming a drama out of such scant materials. His prophecies, indeed, came true in their general, not their particular, purport. He did not foresee the death of Lord Londonderry, which was to be the epoch of a change in English politics, particularly as regarded foreign affairs; nor that the navy of his country would fight for instead of against the Greeks, and by the battle of Navarino secure their enfranchisement from the Turks. Almost against reason, as it appeared to him, he resolved to believe that Greece would prove triumphant; and in this spirit, auguring ultimate good, yet grieving over the vicissitudes to be endured in the interval, he composed his drama.

"Hellas" was among the last of his compositions, and is among the most beautiful. The choruses are singularly imaginative, and melodious in their versification. There are some stanzas that beautifully exemplify Shelley's peculiar style; as, for instance, the assertion of the intellectual empire which must be for ever the inheritance of the country of Homer, Sophocles, and Plato:—

> *'But Greece and her foundations are*
> *Built below the tide of war,*
> *Based on the crystalline sea*
> *Of thought and its eternity.'*

And again, that philosophical truth felicitously imaged forth—

> *'Revenge and Wrong bring forth their kind,*
> *The foul cubs like their parents are,*
> *Their den is in the guilty mind,*
> *And Conscience feeds them with despair.'*

The conclusion of the last chorus is among the most beautiful of his lyrics. The imagery is distinct and majestic; the prophecy, such as poets love to dwell upon, the Regeneration of Mankind—and that regeneration reflecting back splendour on the foregone time, from which it inherits so much of intellectual wealth, and memory of past virtuous deeds, as must render the possession of happiness and peace of tenfold value.

Fragments of an Unfinished Drama

(Published in part (lines 1–69, 100–120) by Mrs. Shelley, "Posthumous Poems", 1824; and again, with the notes, in "Poetical Works", 1839. Lines 127–238 were printed by Dr. Garnett under the title of "The Magic Plant" in his "Relics of Shelley", 1862. The whole was edited in its present form from the Boscombe manuscript by Mr. W.M. Rossetti in 1870 ("Complete Poetical Works of P. B. S.", Moxon, 2 volumes.). 'Written at Pisa during the late winter or early spring of 1822' (Garnett).)

The following fragments are part of a Drama undertaken for the amusement of the individuals who composed our intimate society, but left unfinished. I have preserved a sketch of the story as far as it had been shadowed in the poet's mind.

An Enchantress, living in one of the islands of the Indian Archipelago, saves the life of a Pirate, a man of savage but noble nature. She becomes enamoured of him; and he, inconstant to his mortal love, for a while returns her passion; but at length, recalling the memory of her whom he left, and who laments his loss, he escapes from the Enchanted Island, and returns to his lady. His mode of life makes him again go to sea, and the Enchantress seizes the opportunity to bring him, by a spirit-brewed tempest, back to her Island.—(Mrs. Shelley's Note, 1839.)

Scene.—Before the Cavern of the Indian Enchantress.

The enchantress comes forth.
Enchantress: He came like a dream in the dawn of life,
    He fled like a shadow before its noon;
    He is gone, and my peace is turned to strife,
    And I wander and wane like the weary moon.
    O, sweet Echo, wake,
    And for my sake
    Make answer the while my heart shall break!

    But my heart has a music which Echo's lips,
    Though tender and true, yet can answer not,
    And the shadow that moves in the soul's eclipse
    Can return not the kiss by his now forgot;
    Sweet lips! he who hath

On my desolate path
Cast the darkness of absence, worse than death!
(*The enchantress makes her spell: she is answered by a spirit*)
SPIRIT: Within the silent centre of the earth
    My mansion is; where I have lived insphered
    From the beginning, and around my sleep
    Have woven all the wondrous imagery
    Of this dim spot, which mortals call the world;
    Infinite depths of unknown elements
    Massed into one impenetrable mask;
    Sheets of immeasurable fire, and veins
    Of gold and stone, and adamantine iron.
    And as a veil in which I walk through Heaven
    I have wrought mountains, seas, and waves, and clouds,
    And lastly light, whose interfusion dawns
    In the dark space of interstellar air.

ANOTHER SCENE.

INDIAN YOUTH AND LADY.
INDIAN: And, if my grief should still be dearer to me
    Than all the pleasures in the world beside,
    Why would you lighten it?—
LADY: I offer only
    That which I seek, some human sympathy
    In this mysterious island.
INDIAN: Oh! my friend,
    My sister, my beloved!—What do I say?
    My brain is dizzy, and I scarce know whether
    I speak to thee or her.
LADY: Peace, perturbed heart!
    I am to thee only as thou to mine,
    The passing wind which heals the brow at noon,
    And may strike cold into the breast at night,
    Yet cannot linger where it soothes the most,
    Or long soothe could it linger.
INDIAN: But you said
    You also loved?
LADY: Loved! Oh, I love. Methinks

This word of love is fit for all the world,
And that for gentle hearts another name
Would speak of gentler thoughts than the world owns.
I have loved.
INDIAN: And thou lovest not? if so,
Young as thou art thou canst afford to weep.
LADY: Oh! would that I could claim exemption
From all the bitterness of that sweet name.
I loved, I love, and when I love no more
Let joys and grief perish, and leave despair
To ring the knell of youth. He stood beside me,
The embodied vision of the brightest dream,
Which like a dawn heralds the day of life;
The shadow of his presence made my world
A Paradise. All familiar things he touched,
All common words he spoke, became to me
Like forms and sounds of a diviner world.
He was as is the sun in his fierce youth,
As terrible and lovely as a tempest;
He came, and went, and left me what I am.
Alas! Why must I think how oft we two
Have sate together near the river springs,
Under the green pavilion which the willow
Spreads on the floor of the unbroken fountain,
Strewn, by the nurslings that linger there,
Over that islet paved with flowers and moss,
While the musk-rose leaves, like flakes of crimson snow,
Showered on us, and the dove mourned in the pine,
Sad prophetess of sorrows not her own?
The crane returned to her unfrozen haunt,
And the false cuckoo bade the spray good morn;
And on a wintry bough the widowed bird,
Hid in the deepest night of ivy-leaves,
Renewed the vigils of a sleepless sorrow.
I, left like her, and leaving one like her,
Alike abandoned and abandoning
(Oh! unlike her in this!) the gentlest youth,
Whose love had made my sorrows dear to him,
Even as my sorrow made his love to me!

INDIAN: One curse of Nature stamps in the same mould
    The features of the wretched; and they are
    As like as violet to violet,
    When memory, the ghost, their odours keeps
    Mid the cold relics of abandoned joy.—
    Proceed.
LADY: He was a simple innocent boy.
    I loved him well, but not as he desired;
    Yet even thus he was content to be:—
    A short content, for I was—
INDIAN (*aside*): God of Heaven!
    From such an islet, such a river-spring—!
    I dare not ask her if there stood upon it
    A pleasure-dome surmounted by a crescent,
    With steps to the blue water.
(*Aloud*)
    It may be
    That Nature masks in life several copies
    Of the same lot, so that the sufferers
    May feel another's sorrow as their own,
    And find in friendship what they lost in love.
    That cannot be: yet it is strange that we,
    From the same scene, by the same path to this
    Realm of abandonment— But speak! your breath—
    Your breath is like soft music, your words are
    The echoes of a voice which on my heart
    Sleeps like a melody of early days.
    But as you said—
LADY: He was so awful, yet
    So beautiful in mystery and terror,
    Calming me as the loveliness of heaven
    Soothes the unquiet sea:—and yet not so,
    For he seemed stormy, and would often seem
    A quenchless sun masked in portentous clouds;
    For such his thoughts, and even his actions were;
    But he was not of them, nor they of him,
    But as they hid his splendour from the earth.
    Some said he was a man of blood and peril,
    And steeped in bitter infamy to the lips.

        More need was there I should be innocent,
        More need that I should be most true and kind,
        And much more need that there should be found one
        To share remorse and scorn and solitude,
        And all the ills that wait on those who do
        The tasks of ruin in the world of life.
        He fled, and I have followed him.
INDIAN: Such a one
    Is he who was the winter of my peace.
    But, fairest stranger, when didst thou depart
    From the far hills where rise the springs of India?
    How didst thou pass the intervening sea?
LADY: If I be sure I am not dreaming now,
    I should not doubt to say it was a dream.
    Methought a star came down from heaven,
    And rested mid the plants of India,
    Which I had given a shelter from the frost
    Within my chamber. There the meteor lay,
    Panting forth light among the leaves and flowers,
    As if it lived, and was outworn with speed;
    Or that it loved, and passion made the pulse
    Of its bright life throb like an anxious heart,
    Till it diffused itself; and all the chamber
    And walls seemed melted into emerald fire
    That burned not; in the midst of which appeared
    A spirit like a child, and laughed aloud
    A thrilling peal of such sweet merriment
    As made the blood tingle in my warm feet:
    Then bent over a vase, and murmuring
    Low, unintelligible melodies,
    Placed something in the mould like melon-seeds,
    And slowly faded, and in place of it
    A soft hand issued from the veil of fire,
    Holding a cup like a magnolia flower,
    And poured upon the earth within the vase
    The element with which it overflowed,
    Brighter than morning light, and purer than
    The water of the springs of Himalah.
INDIAN: You waked not?

LADY: Not until my dream became
  Like a child's legend on the tideless sand.
  Which the first foam erases half, and half
  Leaves legible. At length I rose, and went,
  Visiting my flowers from pot to pot, and thought
  To set new cuttings in the empty urns,
  And when I came to that beside the lattice,
  I saw two little dark-green leaves
  Lifting the light mould at their birth, and then
  I half-remembered my forgotten dream.
  And day by day, green as a gourd in June,
  The plant grew fresh and thick, yet no one knew
  What plant it was; its stem and tendrils seemed
  Like emerald snakes, mottled and diamonded
  With azure mail and streaks of woven silver;
  And all the sheaths that folded the dark buds
  Rose like the crest of cobra-di-capel,
  Until the golden eye of the bright flower,
  Through the dark lashes of those veined lids,
  ... disencumbered of their silent sleep,
  Gazed like a star into the morning light.
  Its leaves were delicate, you almost saw
  The pulses
  With which the purple velvet flower was fed
  To overflow, and like a poet's heart
  Changing bright fancy to sweet sentiment,
  Changed half the light to fragrance. It soon fell,
  And to a green and dewy embryo-fruit
  Left all its treasured beauty. Day by day
  I nursed the plant, and on the double flute
  Played to it on the sunny winter days
  Soft melodies, as sweet as April rain
  On silent leaves, and sang those words in which
  Passion makes Echo taunt the sleeping strings;
  And I would send tales of forgotten love
  Late into the lone night, and sing wild songs
  Of maids deserted in the olden time,
  And weep like a soft cloud in April's bosom
  Upon the sleeping eyelids of the plant,

So that perhaps it dreamed that Spring was come,
And crept abroad into the moonlight air,
And loosened all its limbs, as, noon by noon,
The sun averted less his oblique beam.

INDIAN: And the plant died not in the frost?

LADY: It grew;
And went out of the lattice which I left
Half open for it, trailing its quaint spires
Along the garden and across the lawn,
And down the slope of moss and through the tufts
Of wild-flower roots, and stumps of trees o'ergrown
With simple lichens, and old hoary stones,
On to the margin of the glassy pool,
Even to a nook of unblown violets
And lilies-of-the-valley yet unborn,
Under a pine with ivy overgrown.
And theme its fruit lay like a sleeping lizard
Under the shadows; but when Spring indeed
Came to unswathe her infants, and the lilies
Peeped from their bright green masks to wonder at
This shape of autumn couched in their recess,
Then it dilated, and it grew until
One half lay floating on the fountain wave,
Whose pulse, elapsed in unlike sympathies,
Kept time
Among the snowy water-lily buds.
Its shape was such as summer melody
Of the south wind in spicy vales might give
To some light cloud bound from the golden dawn
To fairy isles of evening, and it seemed
In hue and form that it had been a mirror
Of all the hues and forms around it and
Upon it pictured by the sunny beams
Which, from the bright vibrations of the pool,
Were thrown upon the rafters and the roof
Of boughs and leaves, and on the pillared stems
Of the dark sylvan temple, and reflections
Of every infant flower and star of moss
And veined leaf in the azure odorous air.

And thus it lay in the Elysian calm
Of its own beauty, floating on the line
Which, like a film in purest space, divided
The heaven beneath the water from the heaven
Above the clouds; and every day I went
Watching its growth and wondering;
And as the day grew hot, methought I saw
A glassy vapour dancing on the pool,
And on it little quaint and filmy shapes.
With dizzy motion, wheel and rise and fall,
Like clouds of gnats with perfect lineaments.
. . .
O friend, sleep was a veil uplift from Heaven—
As if Heaven dawned upon the world of dream—
When darkness rose on the extinguished day
Out of the eastern wilderness.

INDIAN: I too
Have found a moment's paradise in sleep
Half compensate a hell of waking sorrow.

Charles the First

("Charles the First" was designed in 1818, begun towards the close of 1819 (Medwin, "Life", 2 page 62), resumed in January, and finally laid aside by June, 1822. It was published in part in the "Posthumous Poems", 1824, and printed, in its present form (with the addition of some 530 lines), by Mr. W.M. Rossetti, 1870. Further particulars are given in the Editor's Notes at the end of Volume 3.)

Dramatis Personae

King Charles I
Queen Henrietta
Laud, Archbishop Of Canterbury
Wentworth, Earl Of Strafford
Lord Cottington
Lord Weston
Lord Coventry
Williams, Bishop Of Lincoln
Secretary Lyttelton
Juxon
St. John
Archy, The Court Fool
Hampden
Pym
Cromwell
Cromwell's Daughter
Sir Harry Vane The Younger
Leighton
Bastwick
Prynne
Gentlemen of the Inns of Court, Citizens, Pursuivants, Marshalsmen, Law Students, Judges, Clerk.

Scene 1:
The masque of the inns of court.
A Pursuivant: Place, for the Marshal of the Masque!
First Citizen: What thinkest thou of this quaint masque which turns,

  Like morning from the shadow of the night,
  The night to day, and London to a place
  Of peace and joy?
SECOND CITIZEN: And Hell to Heaven.
  Eight years are gone,
  And they seem hours, since in this populous street
  I trod on grass made green by summer's rain,
  For the red plague kept state within that palace
  Where now that vanity reigns. In nine years more
  The roots will be refreshed with civil blood;
  And thank the mercy of insulted Heaven
  That sin and wrongs wound, as an orphan's cry,
  The patience of the great Avenger's ear.
A YOUTH: Yet, father, 'tis a happy sight to see,
  Beautiful, innocent, and unforbidden
  By God or man;—'tis like the bright procession
  Of skiey visions in a solemn dream
  From which men wake as from a Paradise,
  And draw new strength to tread the thorns of life.
  If God be good, wherefore should this be evil?
  And if this be not evil, dost thou not draw
  Unseasonable poison from the flowers
  Which bloom so rarely in this barren world?
  Oh, kill these bitter thoughts which make the present
  Dark as the future!—

. . .

  When Avarice and Tyranny, vigilant Fear,
  And open-eyed Conspiracy lie sleeping
  As on Hell's threshold; and all gentle thoughts
  Waken to worship Him who giveth joys
  With His own gift.
SECOND CITIZEN: How young art thou in this old age of time!
  How green in this gray world? Canst thou discern
  The signs of seasons, yet perceive no hint
  Of change in that stage-scene in which thou art
  Not a spectator but an actor? or
  Art thou a puppet moved by (enginery)?
  The day that dawns in fire will die in storms,
  Even though the noon be calm. My travel's done,—

Before the whirlwind wakes I shall have found
My inn of lasting rest; but thou must still
Be journeying on in this inclement air.
Wrap thy old cloak about thy back;
Nor leave the broad and plain and beaten road,
Although no flowers smile on the trodden dust,
For the violet paths of pleasure. This Charles the First
Rose like the equinoctial sun, . . .
By vapours, through whose threatening ominous veil
Darting his altered influence he has gained
This height of noon—from which he must decline
Amid the darkness of conflicting storms,
To dank extinction and to latest night. . .
There goes
The apostate Strafford; he whose titles
whispered aphorisms
From Machiavel and Bacon: and, if Judas
Had been as brazen and as bold as he—

First Citizen: That
   Is the Archbishop.
Second Citizen: Rather say the Pope:
   London will be soon his Rome: he walks
   As if he trod upon the heads of men:
   He looks elate, drunken with blood and gold;—
   Beside him moves the Babylonian woman
   Invisibly, and with her as with his shadow,
   Mitred adulterer! he is joined in sin,
   Which turns Heaven's milk of mercy to revenge.
Third Citizen (*lifting up his eyes*): Good Lord! rain it down upon him! . . .
   Amid her ladies walks the papist queen,
   As if her nice feet scorned our English earth.
   The Canaanitish Jezebel! I would be
   A dog if I might tear her with my teeth!
   There's old Sir Henry Vane, the Earl of Pembroke,
   Lord Essex, and Lord Keeper Coventry,
   And others who make base their English breed
   By vile participation of their honours
   With papists, atheists, tyrants, and apostates.

When lawyers masque 'tis time for honest men
To strip the vizor from their purposes.
A seasonable time for masquers this!
When Englishmen and Protestants should sit
dust on their dishonoured heads
To avert the wrath of Him whose scourge is felt
For the great sins which have drawn down from Heaven
and foreign overthrow.
The remnant of the martyred saints in Rochefort
Have been abandoned by their faithless allies
To that idolatrous and adulterous torturer
Lewis of France,—the Palatinate is lost—
(*Enter* LEIGHTON (*who has been branded in the face*) *and* BASTWICK)
Canst thou be—art thou?
LEIGHTON: I WAS Leighton: what
I AM thou seest. And yet turn thine eyes,
And with thy memory look on thy friend's mind,
Which is unchanged, and where is written deep
The sentence of my judge.
THIRD CITIZEN: Are these the marks with which
Laud thinks to improve the image of his Maker
Stamped on the face of man? Curses upon him,
The impious tyrant!
SECOND CITIZEN: It is said besides
That lewd and papist drunkards may profane
The Sabbath with their
And has permitted that most heathenish custom
Of dancing round a pole dressed up with wreaths
On May-day.
A man who thus twice crucifies his God
May well. . . his brother.—In my mind, friend,
The root of all this ill is prelacy.
I would cut up the root.
THIRD CITIZEN: And by what means?
SECOND CITIZEN: Smiting each Bishop under the fifth rib.
THIRD CITIZEN: You seem to know the vulnerable place
Of these same crocodiles.
SECOND CITIZEN: I learnt it in
Egyptian bondage, sir. Your worm of Nile

        Betrays not with its flattering tears like they;
        For, when they cannot kill, they whine and weep.
        Nor is it half so greedy of men's bodies
        As they of soul and all; nor does it wallow
        In slime as they in simony and lies
        And close lusts of the flesh.
A Marshalsman: Give place, give place!
    You torch-bearers, advance to the great gate,
    And then attend the Marshal of the Masque
    Into the Royal presence.
A Law Student: What thinkest thou
    Of this quaint show of ours, my aged friend?
    Even now we see the redness of the torches
    Inflame the night to the eastward, and the clarions
    (Gasp?) to us on the wind's wave. It comes!
    And their sounds, floating hither round the pageant,
    Rouse up the astonished air.
First Citizen: I will not think but that our country's wounds
    May yet be healed. The king is just and gracious,
    Though wicked counsels now pervert his will:
    These once cast off—
Second Citizen: As adders cast their skins
    And keep their venom, so kings often change;
    Councils and counsellors hang on one another,
    Hiding the loathsome
    Like the base patchwork of a leper's rags.
The Youth: Oh, still those dissonant thoughts!—List how the music
    Grows on the enchanted air! And see, the torches
    Restlessly flashing, and the crowd divided
    Like waves before an admiral's prow!
A Marshalsman: Give place
    To the Marshal of the Masque!
A Pursuivant: Room for the King!
The Youth: How glorious! See those thronging chariots
    Rolling, like painted clouds before the wind,
    Behind their solemn steeds: how some are shaped
    Like curved sea-shells dyed by the azure depths
    Of Indian seas; some like the new-born moon;
    And some like cars in which the Romans climbed

(Canopied by Victory's eagle-wings outspread)
The Capitolian—See how gloriously
The mettled horses in the torchlight stir
Their gallant riders, while they check their pride,
Like shapes of some diviner element
Than English air, and beings nobler than
The envious and admiring multitude.

SECOND CITIZEN: Ay, there they are—
Nobles, and sons of nobles, patentees,
Monopolists, and stewards of this poor farm,
On whose lean sheep sit the prophetic crows,
Here is the pomp that strips the houseless orphan,
Here is the pride that breaks the desolate heart.
These are the lilies glorious as Solomon,
Who toil not, neither do they spin,—unless
It be the webs they catch poor rogues withal.
Here is the surfeit which to them who earn
The niggard wages of the earth, scarce leaves
The tithe that will support them till they crawl
Back to her cold hard bosom. Here is health
Followed by grim disease, glory by shame,
Waste by lame famine, wealth by squalid want,
And England's sin by England's punishment.
And, as the effect pursues the cause foregone,
Lo, giving substance to my words, behold
At once the sign and the thing signified—
A troop of cripples, beggars, and lean outcasts,
Horsed upon stumbling jades, carted with dung,
Dragged for a day from cellars and low cabins
And rotten hiding-holes, to point the moral
Of this presentment, and bring up the rear
Of painted pomp with misery!

THE YOUTH: 'Tis but
The anti-masque, and serves as discords do
In sweetest music. Who would love May flowers
If they succeeded not to Winter's flaw;
Or day unchanged by night; or joy itself
Without the touch of sorrow?

SECOND CITIZEN: I and thou-

A MARSHALSMAN: Place, give place!

Scene 2:
A chamber in Whitehall.
Enter The King, Queen, Laud, *Lord* Straftord,
Lord Cottington, *and other Lords;* Archy;
Also St. John, *with some Gentlemen of the Inns of Court.*

King: Thanks, gentlemen. I heartily accept
    This token of your service: your gay masque
    Was performed gallantly. And it shows well
    When subjects twine such flowers of (observance?)
    With the sharp thorns that deck the English crown.
    A gentle heart enjoys what it confers,
    Even as it suffers that which it inflicts,
    Though Justice guides the stroke.
    Accept my hearty thanks.
Queen: And gentlemen,
    Call your poor Queen your debtor. Your quaint pageant
    Rose on me like the figures of past years,
    Treading their still path back to infancy,
    More beautiful and mild as they draw nearer
    The quiet cradle. I could have almost wept
    To think I was in Paris, where these shows
    Are well devised—such as I was ere yet
    My young heart shared a portion of the burthen,
    The careful weight, of this great monarchy.
    There, gentlemen, between the sovereign's pleasure
    And that which it regards, no clamour lifts
    Its proud interposition.
    In Paris ribald censurers dare not move
    Their poisonous tongues against these sinless sports;
    And His smile
    Warms those who bask in it, as ours would do
    If... Take my heart's thanks: add them, gentlemen,
    To those good words which, were he King of France,
    My royal lord would turn to golden deeds.
St. John: Madam, the love of Englishmen can make
    The lightest favour of their lawful king
    Outweigh a despot's.—We humbly take our leaves,
    Enriched by smiles which France can never buy.
(*Exeunt* St. John *and the Gentlemen of the Inns of Court*)

KING: My Lord Archbishop,
   Mark you what spirit sits in St. John's eyes?
   Methinks it is too saucy for this presence.
ARCHY: Yes, pray your Grace look: for, like an unsophisticated (eye) sees everything upside down, you who are wise will discern the shadow of an idiot in lawn sleeves and a rochet setting springes to catch woodcocks in haymaking time. Poor Archy, whose owl-eyes are tempered to the error of his age, and because he is a fool, and by special ordinance of God forbidden ever to see himself as he is, sees now in that deep eye a blindfold devil sitting on the ball, and weighing words out between king and subjects. One scale is full of promises, and the other full of protestations: and then another devil creeps behind the first out of the dark windings (of a) pregnant lawyer's brain, and takes the bandage from the other's eyes, and throws a sword into the left-hand scale, for all the world like my Lord Essex's there.
STRAFFORD: A rod in pickle for the Fool's back!
ARCHY: Ay, and some are now smiling whose tears will make the brine; for the Fool sees—
STRAFFORD: Insolent! You shall have your coat turned and be whipped out of the palace for this.
ARCHY: When all the fools are whipped, and all the Protestant writers, while the knaves are whipping the fools ever since a thief was set to catch a thief. If all turncoats were whipped out of palaces, poor Archy would be disgraced in good company. Let the knaves whip the fools, and all the fools laugh at it. (Let the) wise and godly slit each other's noses and ears (having no need of any sense of discernment in their craft); and the knaves, to marshal them, join in a procession to Bedlam, to entreat the madmen to omit their sublime Platonic contemplations, and manage the state of England. Let all the honest men who lie (pinched?) up at the prisons or the pillories, in custody of the pursuivants of the High-Commission Court, marshal them.

(*Enter Secretary Lyttelton, with papers*)

KING (*looking over the papers*): These stiff Scots
   His Grace of Canterbury must take order
   To force under the Church's yoke.—You, Wentworth,
   Shall be myself in Ireland, and shall add
   Your wisdom, gentleness, and energy,

    To what in me were wanting.—My Lord Weston,
    Look that those merchants draw not without loss
    Their bullion from the Tower; and, on the payment
    Of shipmoney, take fullest compensation
    For violation of our royal forests,
    Whose limits, from neglect, have been o'ergrown
    With cottages and cornfields. The uttermost
    Farthing exact from those who claim exemption
    From knighthood: that which once was a reward
    Shall thus be made a punishment, that subjects
    May know how majesty can wear at will
    The rugged mood.—My Lord of Coventry,
    Lay my command upon the Courts below
    That bail be not accepted for the prisoners
    Under the warrant of the Star Chamber.
    The people shall not find the stubbornness
    Of Parliament a cheap or easy method
    Of dealing with their rightful sovereign:
    And doubt not this, my Lord of Coventry,
    We will find time and place for fit rebuke.—
    My Lord of Canterbury.
ARCHY: The fool is here.
LAUD: I crave permission of your Majesty
    To order that this insolent fellow be
    Chastised: he mocks the sacred character,
    Scoffs at the state, and—
KING: What, my Archy?
    He mocks and mimics all he sees and hears,
    Yet with a quaint and graceful licence—Prithee
    For this once do not as Prynne would, were he
    Primate of England. With your Grace's leave,
    He lives in his own world; and, like a parrot
    Hung in his gilded prison from the window
    Of a queen's bower over the public way,
    Blasphemes with a bird's mind:—his words, like arrows
    Which know no aim beyond the archer's wit,
    Strike sometimes what eludes philosophy.—
(*To* ARCHY)
    Go, sirrah, and repent of your offence

Ten minutes in the rain; be it your penance
To bring news how the world goes there.
(*Exit* ARCHY)
Poor Archy!
He weaves about himself a world of mirth
Out of the wreck of ours.
LAUD: I take with patience, as my Master did,
All scoffs permitted from above.
KING: My lord,
Pray overlook these papers. Archy's words
Had wings, but these have talons.
QUEEN: And the lion
That wears them must be tamed. My dearest lord,
I see the new-born courage in your eye
Armed to strike dead the Spirit of the Time,
Which spurs to rage the many-headed beast.
Do thou persist: for, faint but in resolve,
And it were better thou hadst still remained
The slave of thine own slaves, who tear like curs
The fugitive, and flee from the pursuer;
And Opportunity, that empty wolf,
Flies at his throat who falls. Subdue thy actions
Even to the disposition of thy purpose,
And be that tempered as the Ebro's steel;
And banish weak-eyed Mercy to the weak,
Whence she will greet thee with a gift of peace
And not betray thee with a traitor's kiss,
As when she keeps the company of rebels,
Who think that she is Fear. This do, lest we
Should fall as from a glorious pinnacle
In a bright dream, and wake as from a dream
Out of our worshipped state.
KING: Beloved friend,
God is my witness that this weight of power,
Which He sets me my earthly task to wield
Under His law, is my delight and pride
Only because thou lovest that and me.
For a king bears the office of a God
To all the under world; and to his God

Alone he must deliver up his trust,
Unshorn of its permitted attributes.
(It seems) now as the baser elements
Had mutinied against the golden sun
That kindles them to harmony, and quells
Their self-destroying rapine. The wild million
Strike at the eye that guides them; like as humours
Of the distempered body that conspire
Against the spirit of life throned in the heart,—
And thus become the prey of one another,
And last of death—

STRAFFORD: That which would be ambition in a subject
Is duty in a sovereign; for on him,
As on a keystone, hangs the arch of life,
Whose safety is its strength. Degree and form,
And all that makes the age of reasoning man
More memorable than a beast's, depend on this—
That Right should fence itself inviolably
With Power; in which respect the state of England
From usurpation by the insolent commons
Cries for reform.
Get treason, and spare treasure. Fee with coin
The loudest murmurers; feed with jealousies
Opposing factions,—be thyself of none;
And borrow gold of many, for those who lend
Will serve thee till thou payest them; and thus
Keep the fierce spirit of the hour at bay,
Till time, and its coming generations
Of nights and days unborn, bring some one chance,

. . .

Or war or pestilence or Nature's self,—
By some distemperature or terrible sign,
Be as an arbiter betwixt themselves.
Nor let your Majesty
Doubt here the peril of the unseen event.
How did your brother Kings, coheritors
In your high interest in the subject earth,
Rise past such troubles to that height of power
Where now they sit, and awfully serene

    Smile on the trembling world? Such popular storms
    Philip the Second of Spain, this Lewis of France,
    And late the German head of many bodies,
    And every petty lord of Italy,
    Quelled or by arts or arms. Is England poorer
    Or feebler? or art thou who wield'st her power
    Tamer than they? or shall this island be—
    (Girdled) by its inviolable waters—
    To the world present and the world to come
    Sole pattern of extinguished monarchy?
    Not if thou dost as I would have thee do.
KING: Your words shall be my deeds:
    You speak the image of my thought. My friend
    (If Kings can have a friend, I call thee so),
    Beyond the large commission which (belongs)
    Under the great seal of the realm, take this:
    And, for some obvious reasons, let there be
    No seal on it, except my kingly word
    And honour as I am a gentleman.
    Be—as thou art within my heart and mind—
    Another self, here and in Ireland:
    Do what thou judgest well, take amplest licence,
    And stick not even at questionable means.
    Hear me, Wentworth. My word is as a wall
    Between thee and this world thine enemy—
    That hates thee, for thou lovest me.
STRAFFORD: I own
    No friend but thee, no enemies but thine:
    Thy lightest thought is my eternal law.
    How weak, how short, is life to pay—
KING: Peace, peace.
    Thou ow'st me nothing yet.
(*To* LAUD)
    My lord, what say
    Those papers?
LAUD: Your Majesty has ever interposed,
    In lenity towards your native soil,
    Between the heavy vengeance of the Church
    And Scotland. Mark the consequence of warming

This brood of northern vipers in your bosom.
The rabble, instructed no doubt
By London, Lindsay, Hume, and false Argyll
(For the waves never menace heaven until
Scourged by the wind's invisible tyranny),
Have in the very temple of the Lord
Done outrage to His chosen ministers.
They scorn the liturgy of the Holy Church,
Refuse to obey her canons, and deny
The apostolic power with which the Spirit
Has filled its elect vessels, even from him
Who held the keys with power to loose and bind,
To him who now pleads in this royal presence.—
Let ample powers and new instructions be
Sent to the High Commissioners in Scotland.
To death, imprisonment, and confiscation,
Add torture, add the ruin of the kindred
Of the offender, add the brand of infamy,
Add mutilation: and if this suffice not,
Unleash the sword and fire, that in their thirst
They may lick up that scum of schismatics.
I laugh at those weak rebels who, desiring
What we possess, still prate of Christian peace,
As if those dreadful arbitrating messengers
Which play the part of God 'twixt right and wrong,
Should be let loose against the innocent sleep
Of templed cities and the smiling fields,
For some poor argument of policy
Which touches our own profit or our pride
(Where it indeed were Christian charity
To turn the cheek even to the smiter's hand):
And, when our great Redeemer, when our God,
When He who gave, accepted, and retained
Himself in propitiation of our sins,
Is scorned in His immediate ministry,
With hazard of the inestimable loss
Of all the truth and discipline which is
Salvation to the extremest generation
Of men innumerable, they talk of peace!

Such peace as Canaan found, let Scotland now:
For, by that Christ who came to bring a sword,
Not peace, upon the earth, and gave command
To His disciples at the Passover
That each should sell his robe and buy a sword,-
Once strip that minister of naked wrath,
And it shall never sleep in peace again
Till Scotland bend or break.

KING: My Lord Archbishop,
Do what thou wilt and what thou canst in this.
Thy earthly even as thy heavenly King
Gives thee large power in his unquiet realm.
But we want money, and my mind misgives me
That for so great an enterprise, as yet,
We are unfurnished.

STRAFFORD: Yet it may not long
Rest on our wills.

COTTINGTON: The expenses
Of gathering shipmoney, and of distraining
For every petty rate (for we encounter
A desperate opposition inch by inch
In every warehouse and on every farm),
Have swallowed up the gross sum of the imposts;
So that, though felt as a most grievous scourge
Upon the land, they stand us in small stead
As touches the receipt.

STRAFFORD: 'Tis a conclusion
Most arithmetical: and thence you infer
Perhaps the assembling of a parliament.
Now, if a man should call his dearest enemies
T0 sit in licensed judgement on his life,
His Majesty might wisely take that course.

(*Aside to* COTTINGTON)
It is enough to expect from these lean imposts
That they perform the office of a scourge,
Without more profit.

(*Aloud*)
Fines and confiscations,
And a forced loan from the refractory city,

     Will fill our coffers: and the golden love
     Of loyal gentlemen and noble friends
     For the worshipped father of our common country,
     With contributions from the catholics,
     Will make Rebellion pale in our excess.
     Be these the expedients until time and wisdom
     Shall frame a settled state of government.
Laud: And weak expedients they! Have we not drained
     All, till the. . . which seemed
     A mine exhaustless?
Strafford: And the love which Is,
     If loyal hearts could turn their blood to gold.
Laud: Both now grow barren: and I speak it not
     As loving parliaments, which, as they have been
     In the right hand of bold bad mighty kings
     The scourges of the bleeding Church, I hate.
     Methinks they scarcely can deserve our fear.
Strafford: Oh! my dear liege, take back the wealth thou
     gavest:
     With that, take all I held, but as in trust
     For thee, of mine inheritance: leave me but
     This unprovided body for thy service,
     And a mind dedicated to no care
     Except thy safety:—but assemble not
     A parliament. Hundreds will bring, like me,
     Their fortunes, as they would their blood, before—
King: No! thou who judgest them art but one. Alas!
     We should be too much out of love with Heaven,
     Did this vile world show many such as thee,
     Thou perfect, just, and honourable man!
     Never shall it be said that Charles of England
     Stripped those he loved for fear of those he scorns;
     Nor will he so much misbecome his throne
     As to impoverish those who most adorn
     And best defend it. That you urge, dear Strafford,
     Inclines me rather—
Queen: To a parliament?
     Is this thy firmness? and thou wilt preside
     Over a knot of. . . censurers,

To the unswearing of thy best resolves,
And choose the worst, when the worst comes too soon?
Plight not the worst before the worst must come.
Oh, wilt thou smile whilst our ribald foes,
Dressed in their own usurped authority,
Sharpen their tongues on Henrietta's fame?
It is enough! Thou lovest me no more!
(*Weeps*)
KING: Oh, Henrietta!
(*They talk apart*)
COTTINGTON (*to* LAUD): Money we have none:
  And all the expedients of my Lord of Strafford
  Will scarcely meet the arrears.
LAUD: Without delay
  An army must be sent into the north;
  Followed by a Commission of the Church,
  With amplest power to quench in fire and blood,
  And tears and terror, and the pity of hell,
  The intenser wrath of Heresy. God will give
  Victory; and victory over Scotland give
  The lion England tamed into our hands.
  That will lend power, and power bring gold.
COTTINGTON: Meanwhile
  We must begin first where your Grace leaves off.
  Gold must give power, or—
LAUD: I am not averse
  From the assembling of a parliament.
  Strong actions and smooth words might teach them soon
  The lesson to obey. And are they not
  A bubble fashioned by the monarch's mouth,
  The birth of one light breath? If they serve no purpose,
  A word dissolves them.
STRAFFORD: The engine of parliaments
  Might be deferred until I can bring over
  The Irish regiments: they will serve to assure
  The issue of the war against the Scots.
  And, this game won—which if lost, all is lost—
  Gather these chosen leaders of the rebels,
  And call them, if you will, a parliament.

KING: Oh, be our feet still tardy to shed blood.
    Guilty though it may be! I would still spare
    The stubborn country of my birth, and ward
    From countenances which I loved in youth
    The wrathful Church's lacerating hand.
(*To* LAUD)
    Have you o'erlooked the other articles?
(*Enter* ARCHY)
LAUD: Hazlerig, Hampden, Pym, young Harry Vane,
    Cromwell, and other rebels of less note,
    Intend to sail with the next favouring wind
    For the Plantations.
ARCHY: Where they think to found
    A commonwealth like Gonzalo's in the play,
    Gynaecocoenic and pantisocratic.
KING: What's that, sirrah?
ARCHY: New devil's politics.
    Hell is the pattern of all commonwealths:
    Lucifer was the first republican.
    Will you hear Merlin's prophecy, how three (posts?)
    'In one brainless skull, when the whitethorn is full,
    Shall sail round the world, and come back again:
    Shall sail round the world in a brainless skull,
    And come back again when the moon is at full:'—
    When, in spite of the Church,
    They will hear homilies of whatever length
    Or form they please.
(COTTINGTON?): So please your Majesty to sign this order
    For their detention.
ARCHY: If your Majesty were tormented night and day by fever, gout, rheumatism, and stone, and asthma, etc., and you found these diseases had secretly entered into a conspiracy to abandon you, should you think it necessary to lay an embargo on the port by which they meant to dispeople your unquiet kingdom of man?
KING: If fear were made for kings, the Fool mocks wisely;
    But in this case—(*writing*). Here, my lord, take the warrant,
    And see it duly executed forthwith.—
    That imp of malice and mockery shall be punished.

(*Exeunt all but* KING, QUEEN, *and* ARCHY)

ARCHY: Ay, I am the physician of whom Plato prophesied, who was to be accused by the confectioner before a jury of children, who found him guilty without waiting for the summing-up, and hanged him without benefit of clergy. Thus Baby Charles, and the Twelfth-night Queen of Hearts, and the overgrown schoolboy Cottington, and that little urchin Laud—who would reduce a verdict of 'guilty, death,' by famine, if it were impregnable by composition—all impannelled against poor Archy for presenting them bitter physic the last day of the holidays.

QUEEN: Is the rain over, sirrah?

KING: When it rains
And the sun shines, 'twill rain again to-morrow:
And therefore never smile till you've done crying.

ARCHY: But 'tis all over now: like the April anger of woman, the gentle sky has wept itself serene.

QUEEN: What news abroad? how looks the world this morning?

ARCHY: Gloriously as a grave covered with virgin flowers. There's a rainbow in the sky. Let your Majesty look at it, for

'A rainbow in the morning
Is the shepherd's warning;'

and the flocks of which you are the pastor are scattered among the mountain-tops, where every drop of water is a flake of snow, and the breath of May pierces like a January blast.

KING: The sheep have mistaken the wolf for their shepherd, my poor boy; and the shepherd, the wolves for their watchdogs.

QUEEN: But the rainbow was a good sign, Archy: it says that the waters of the deluge are gone, and can return no more.

ARCHY: Ay, the salt-water one: but that of tears and blood must yet come down, and that of fire follow, if there be any truth in lies.— The rainbow hung over the city with all its shops, . . . and churches, from north to south, like a bridge of congregated lightning pieced by the masonry of heaven—like a balance in which the angel that distributes the coming hour was weighing that heavy one whose poise is now felt in the lightest hearts, before it bows the proudest heads under the meanest feet.

QUEEN: Who taught you this trash, sirrah?

ARCHY: A torn leaf out of an old book trampled in the dirt.—But for
the rainbow. It moved as the sun moved, and. . . until the top of
the Tower. . . of a cloud through its left-hand tip, and Lambeth
Palace look as dark as a rock before the other. Methought I saw a
crown figured upon one tip, and a mitre on the other. So, as I had
heard treasures were found where the rainbow quenches its points
upon the earth, I set off, and at the Tower— But I shall not tell
your Majesty what I found close to the closet-window on which
the rainbow had glimmered.

KING: Speak: I will make my Fool my conscience.

ARCHY: Then conscience is a fool.—I saw there a cat caught in a rat-
trap. I heard the rats squeak behind the wainscots: it seemed to me
that the very mice were consulting on the manner of her death.

QUEEN: Archy is shrewd and bitter.

ARCHY: Like the season,
So blow the winds.—But at the other end of the rainbow, where
the gray rain was tempered along the grass and leaves by a
tender interfusion of violet and gold in the meadows beyond
Lambeth, what think you that I found instead of a mitre?

KING: Vane's wits perhaps.

ARCHY: Something as vain. I saw a gross vapour hovering in a stinking
ditch over the carcass of a dead ass, some rotten rags, and broken
dishes—the wrecks of what once administered to the stuffing-out
and the ornament of a worm of worms. His Grace of Canterbury
expects to enter the New Jerusalem some Palm Sunday in triumph
on the ghost of this ass.

QUEEN: Enough, enough! Go desire Lady Jane
She place my lute, together with the music
Mari received last week from Italy,
In my boudoir, and—

(*Exit* ARCHY)

KING: I'll go in.

QUEEN: My beloved lord,
Have you not noted that the Fool of late
Has lost his careless mirth, and that his words
Sound like the echoes of our saddest fears?
What can it mean? I should be loth to think
Some factious slave had tutored him.

KING: Oh, no!

He is but Occasion's pupil. Partly 'tis
That our minds piece the vacant intervals
Of his wild words with their own fashioning,—
As in the imagery of summer clouds,
Or coals of the winter fire, idlers find
The perfect shadows of their teeming thoughts:
And partly, that the terrors of the time
Are sown by wandering Rumour in all spirits;
And in the lightest and the least, may best
Be seen the current of the coming wind.

QUEEN: Your brain is overwrought with these deep thoughts.
Come, I will sing to you; let us go try
These airs from Italy; and, as we pass
The gallery, we'll decide where that Correggio
Shall hang—the Virgin Mother
With her child, born the King of heaven and earth,
Whose reign is men's salvation. And you shall see
A cradled miniature of yourself asleep,
Stamped on the heart by never-erring love;
Liker than any Vandyke ever made,
A pattern to the unborn age of thee,
Over whose sweet beauty I have wept for joy
A thousand times, and now should weep for sorrow,
Did I not think that after we were dead
Our fortunes would spring high in him, and that
The cares we waste upon our heavy crown
Would make it light and glorious as a wreath
Of Heaven's beams for his dear innocent brow.

KING: Dear Henrietta!

SCENE 3:
The Star Chamber.
LAUD, JUXON, STRAFFORD, *and others, as Judges.*
Prynne as a prisoner, and then BASTWICK.

LAUD: Bring forth the prisoner Bastwick: let the clerk
Recite his sentence.

CLERK: 'That he pay five thousand
Pounds to the king, lose both his ears, be branded
With red-hot iron on the cheek and forehead,

    And be imprisoned within Lancaster Castle
    During the pleasure of the Court.'
LAUD: Prisoner,
    If you have aught to say wherefore this sentence
    Should not be put into effect, now speak.
JUXON: If you have aught to plead in mitigation,
    Speak.
BASTWICK: Thus, my lords. If, like the prelates, I
    Were an invader of the royal power
    A public scorner of the word of God,
    Profane, idolatrous, popish, superstitious,
    Impious in heart and in tyrannic act,
    Void of wit, honesty, and temperance;
    If Satan were my lord, as theirs,—our God
    Pattern of all I should avoid to do;
    Were I an enemy of my God and King
    And of good men, as ye are;—I should merit
    Your fearful state and gilt prosperity,
    Which, when ye wake from the last sleep, shall turn
    To cowls and robes of everlasting fire.
    But, as I am, I bid ye grudge me not
    The only earthly favour ye can yield,
    Or I think worth acceptance at your hands,—
    Scorn, mutilation, and imprisonment.
    even as my Master did,
    Until Heaven's kingdom shall descend on earth,
    Or earth be like a shadow in the light
    Of Heaven absorbed—some few tumultuous years
    Will pass, and leave no wreck of what opposes
    His will whose will is power.
LAUD: Officer, take the prisoner from the bar,
    And be his tongue slit for his insolence.
BASTWICK: While this hand holds a pen—
LAUD: Be his hands—
JUXON: Stop!
    Forbear, my lord! The tongue, which now can speak
    No terror, would interpret, being dumb,
    Heaven's thunder to our harm; . . .
    And hands, which now write only their own shame,

With bleeding stumps might sign our blood away.
LAUD: Much more such 'mercy' among men would be,
    Did all the ministers of Heaven's revenge
    Flinch thus from earthly retribution. I
    Could suffer what I would inflict.
(*Exit* BASTWICK *guarded*)
    Bring up
    The Lord Bishop of Lincoln.—
(*To* STRATFORD)
    Know you not
    That, in distraining for ten thousand pounds
    Upon his books and furniture at Lincoln,
    Were found these scandalous and seditious letters
    Sent from one Osbaldistone, who is fled?
    I speak it not as touching this poor person;
    But of the office which should make it holy,
    Were it as vile as it was ever spotless.
    Mark too, my lord, that this expression strikes
    His Majesty, if I misinterpret not.
(*Enter Bishop* WILLIAMS *guarded*)
STRAFFORD: 'Twere politic and just that Williams taste
    The bitter fruit of his connection with
    The schismatics. But you, my Lord Archbishop,
    Who owed your first promotion to his favour,
    Who grew beneath his smile—
LAUD: Would therefore beg
    The office of his judge from this High Court,—
    That it shall seem, even as it is, that I,
    In my assumption of this sacred robe,
    Have put aside all worldly preference,
    All sense of all distinction of all persons,
    All thoughts but of the service of the Church.—
    Bishop of Lincoln!
WILLIAMS: Peace, proud hierarch!
    I know my sentence, and I own it just.
    Thou wilt repay me less than I deserve,
    In stretching to the utmost
    . . .

SCENE 4:
HAMPDEN, PYM, CROMWELL, *His Daughter, and young Sir* HARRY VANE.
HAMPDEN: England, farewell! thou, who hast been my cradle,
    Shalt never be my dungeon or my grave!
    I held what I inherited in thee
    As pawn for that inheritance of freedom
    Which thou hast sold for thy despoiler's smile:
    How can I call thee England, or my country?—
    Does the wind hold?
VANE: The vanes sit steady
    Upon the Abbey towers. The silver lightnings
    Of the evening star, spite of the city's smoke,
    Tell that the north wind reigns in the upper air.
    Mark too that flock of fleecy-winged clouds
    Sailing athwart St. Margaret's.
HAMPDEN: Hail, fleet herald
    Of tempest! that rude pilot who shall guide
    Hearts free as his, to realms as pure as thee,
    Beyond the shot of tyranny,
    Beyond the webs of that swoln spider. . .
    Beyond the curses, calumnies, and (lies?)
    Of atheist priests! . . . And thou
    Fair star, whose beam lies on the wide Atlantic,
    Athwart its zones of tempest and of calm,
    Bright as the path to a beloved home
    Oh, light us to the isles of the evening land!
    Like floating Edens cradled in the glimmer
    Of sunset, through the distant mist of years
    Touched by departing hope, they gleam! lone regions,
    Where Power's poor dupes and victims yet have never
    Propitiated the savage fear of kings
    With purest blood of noblest hearts; whose dew
    Is yet unstained with tears of those who wake
    To weep each day the wrongs on which it dawns;
    Whose sacred silent air owns yet no echo
    Of formal blasphemies; nor impious rites
    Wrest man's free worship, from the God who loves,
    To the poor worm who envies us His love!
    Receive, thou young. . . of Paradise.

These exiles from the old and sinful world!
. . .
This glorious clime, this firmament, whose lights
Dart mitigated influence through their veil
Of pale blue atmosphere; whose tears keep green
The pavement of this moist all-feeding earth;
This vaporous horizon, whose dim round
Is bastioned by the circumfluous sea,
Repelling invasion from the sacred towers,
Presses upon me like a dungeon's grate,
A low dark roof, a damp and narrow wall.
The boundless universe
Becomes a cell too narrow for the soul
That owns no master; while the loathliest ward
Of this wide prison, England, is a nest
Of cradling peace built on the mountain tops,—
To which the eagle spirits of the free,
Which range through heaven and earth, and scorn the storm
Of time, and gaze upon the light of truth,
Return to brood on thoughts that cannot die
And cannot be repelled.
Like eaglets floating in the heaven of time,
They soar above their quarry, and shall stoop
Through palaces and temples thunderproof.

Scene 5:
Archy: I'll go live under the ivy that overgrows the terrace, and count the tears shed on its old (roots?) as the (wind?) plays the song of

 'A widow bird sate mourning
 Upon a wintry bough.'
(*Sings*)
 Heigho! the lark and the owl!
 One flies the morning, and one lulls the night:—
 Only the nightingale, poor fond soul,
 Sings like the fool through darkness and light.

 'A widow bird sate mourning for her love
 Upon a wintry bough;

The frozen wind crept on above,
The freezing stream below.

There was no leaf upon the forest bare.
No flower upon the ground,
And little motion in the air
Except the mill-wheel's sound.'

The Triumph of Life

(Composed at Lerici on the Gulf of Spezzia in the spring and early summer of 1822—the poem on which Shelley was engaged at the time of his death. Published by Mrs. Shelley in the "Posthumous Poems" of 1824, pages 73–95. Several emendations, the result of Dr. Garnett's examination of the Boscombe manuscript, were given to the world by Miss Mathilde Blind, "Westminster Review", July, 1870. The poem was, of course, included in the "Poetical Works", 1839, both editions. See Editor's Notes.)

Swift as a spirit hastening to his task
Of glory and of good, the Sun sprang forth
Rejoicing in his splendour, and the mask

Of darkness fell from the awakened Earth—
The smokeless altars of the mountain snows
Flamed above crimson clouds, and at the birth

Of light, the Ocean's orison arose,
To which the birds tempered their matin lay.
All flowers in field or forest which unclose

Their trembling eyelids to the kiss of day,
Swinging their censers in the element,
With orient incense lit by the new ray

Burned slow and inconsumably, and sent
Their odorous sighs up to the smiling air;
And, in succession due, did continent,

Isle, ocean, and all things that in them wear
The form and character of mortal mould,
Rise as the Sun their father rose, to bear

Their portion of the toil, which he of old
Took as his own, and then imposed on them:
But I, whom thoughts which must remain untold

Had kept as wakeful as the stars that gem
The cone of night, now they were laid asleep
Stretched my faint limbs beneath the hoary stem

Which an old chestnut flung athwart the steep
Of a green Apennine: before me fled
The night; behind me rose the day; the deep

Was at my feet, and Heaven above my head,—
When a strange trance over my fancy grew
Which was not slumber, for the shade it spread

Was so transparent, that the scene came through
As clear as when a veil of light is drawn
O'er evening hills they glimmer; and I knew

That I had felt the freshness of that dawn
Bathe in the same cold dew my brow and hair,
And sate as thus upon that slope of lawn

Under the self-same bough, and heard as there
The birds, the fountains and the ocean hold
Sweet talk in music through the enamoured air,
And then a vision on my train was rolled.

. . .

As in that trance of wondrous thought I lay,
This was the tenour of my waking dream:—
Methought I sate beside a public way

Thick strewn with summer dust, and a great stream
Of people there was hurrying to and fro,
Numerous as gnats upon the evening gleam,

All hastening onward, yet none seemed to know
Whither he went, or whence he came, or why
He made one of the multitude, and so

Was borne amid the crowd, as through the sky
One of the million leaves of summer's bier;
Old age and youth, manhood and infancy,

Mixed in one mighty torrent did appear,
Some flying from the thing they feared, and some
Seeking the object of another's fear;

And others, as with steps towards the tomb,
Pored on the trodden worms that crawled beneath,
And others mournfully within the gloom

Of their own shadow walked, and called it death;
And some fled from it as it were a ghost,
Half fainting in the affliction of vain breath:

But more, with motions which each other crossed,
Pursued or shunned the shadows the clouds threw,
Or birds within the noonday aether lost,

Upon that path where flowers never grew,—
And, weary with vain toil and faint for thirst,
Heard not the fountains, whose melodious dew

Out of their mossy cells forever burst;
Nor felt the breeze which from the forest told
Of grassy paths and wood-lawns interspersed

With overarching elms and caverns cold,
And violet banks where sweet dreams brood, but they
Pursued their serious folly as of old.

And as I gazed, methought that in the way
The throng grew wilder, as the woods of June
When the south wind shakes the extinguished day,

And a cold glare, intenser than the noon,
But icy cold, obscured with blinding light
The sun, as he the stars. Like the young moon—

When on the sunlit limits of the night
Her white shell trembles amid crimson air,
And whilst the sleeping tempest gathers might—

Doth, as the herald of its coming, bear
The ghost of its dead mother, whose dim form
Bends in dark aether from her infant's chair,—

So came a chariot on the silent storm
Of its own rushing splendour, and a Shape
So sate within, as one whom years deform,

Beneath a dusky hood and double cape,
Crouching within the shadow of a tomb;
And o'er what seemed the head a cloud-like crape

Was bent, a dun and faint aethereal gloom
Tempering the light. Upon the chariot-beam
A Janus-visaged Shadow did assume

The guidance of that wonder-winged team;
The shapes which drew it in thick lightenings
Were lost:—I heard alone on the air's soft stream

The music of their ever-moving wings.
All the four faces of that Charioteer
Had their eyes banded; little profit brings

Speed in the van and blindness in the rear,
Nor then avail the beams that quench the sun,—
Or that with banded eyes could pierce the sphere

Of all that is, has been or will be done;
So ill was the car guided—but it passed
With solemn speed majestically on.

The crowd gave way, and I arose aghast,
Or seemed to rise, so mighty was the trance,
And saw, like clouds upon the thunder-blast,

The million with fierce song and maniac dance
Raging around—such seemed the jubilee
As when to greet some conqueror's advance

Imperial Rome poured forth her living sea
From senate-house, and forum, and theatre,
When. . . upon the free

Had bound a yoke, which soon they stooped to bear.
Nor wanted here the just similitude
Of a triumphal pageant, for where'er

The chariot rolled, a captive multitude
Was driven;—all those who had grown old in power
Or misery,—all who had their age subdued

By action or by suffering, and whose hour
Was drained to its last sand in weal or woe,
So that the trunk survived both fruit and flower;—

All those whose fame or infamy must grow
Till the great winter lay the form and name
Of this green earth with them for ever low;—

All but the sacred few who could not tame
Their spirits to the conquerors—but as soon
As they had touched the world with living flame,

Fled back like eagles to their native noon,
Or those who put aside the diadem
Of earthly thrones or gems. . .

Were there, of Athens or Jerusalem.
Were neither mid the mighty captives seen,
Nor mid the ribald crowd that followed them,

Nor those who went before fierce and obscene.
The wild dance maddens in the van, and those
Who lead it—fleet as shadows on the green,

Outspeed the chariot, and without repose
Mix with each other in tempestuous measure
To savage music, wilder as it grows,

They, tortured by their agonizing pleasure,
Convulsed and on the rapid whirlwinds spun
Of that fierce Spirit, whose unholy leisure

Was soothed by mischief since the world begun,
Throw back their heads and loose their streaming hair;
And in their dance round her who dims the sun,

Maidens and youths fling their wild arms in air
As their feet twinkle; they recede, and now
Bending within each other's atmosphere,

Kindle invisibly—and as they glow,
Like moths by light attracted and repelled,
Oft to their bright destruction come and go,

Till like two clouds into one vale impelled,
That shake the mountains when their lightnings mingle
And die in rain—the fiery band which held

Their natures, snaps—while the shock still may tingle
One falls and then another in the path
Senseless—nor is the desolation single,

Yet ere I can say WHERE—the chariot hath
Passed over them—nor other trace I find
But as of foam after the ocean's wrath

Is spent upon the desert shore;—behind,
Old men and women foully disarrayed,
Shake their gray hairs in the insulting wind,

And follow in the dance, with limbs decayed,
Seeking to reach the light which leaves them still
Farther behind and deeper in the shade.

But not the less with impotence of will
They wheel, though ghastly shadows interpose
Round them and round each other, and fulfil

Their work, and in the dust from whence they rose
Sink, and corruption veils them as they lie,
And past in these performs what... in those.

Struck to the heart by this sad pageantry,
Half to myself I said—'And what is this?
Whose shape is that within the car? And why—'

I would have added—'is all here amiss?—'
But a voice answered—'Life!'—I turned, and knew
(O Heaven, have mercy on such wretchedness!)

That what I thought was an old root which grew
To strange distortion out of the hill side,
Was indeed one of those deluded crew,

And that the grass, which methought hung so wide
And white, was but his thin discoloured hair,
And that the holes he vainly sought to hide,

Were or had been eyes:—'If thou canst forbear
To join the dance, which I had well forborne,'
Said the grim Feature, of my thought aware,

'I will unfold that which to this deep scorn
Led me and my companions, and relate
The progress of the pageant since the morn;

'If thirst of knowledge shall not then abate,
Follow it thou even to the night, but I
Am weary.'—Then like one who with the weight

Of his own words is staggered, wearily
He paused; and ere he could resume, I cried:
'First, who art thou?'—'Before thy memory,

'I feared, loved, hated, suffered, did and died,
And if the spark with which Heaven lit my spirit
Had been with purer nutriment supplied,

'Corruption would not now thus much inherit
Of what was once Rousseau,—nor this disguise
Stain that which ought to have disdained to wear it;

'If I have been extinguished, yet there rise
A thousand beacons from the spark I bore'—
'And who are those chained to the car?'—'The wise,

'The great, the unforgotten,—they who wore
Mitres and helms and crowns, or wreaths of light,
Signs of thought's empire over thought—their lore

'Taught them not this, to know themselves; their might
Could not repress the mystery within,
And for the morn of truth they feigned, deep night

'Caught them ere evening.'—'Who is he with chin
Upon his breast, and hands crossed on his chain?'—
'The child of a fierce hour; he sought to win

'The world, and lost all that it did contain
Of greatness, in its hope destroyed; and more
Of fame and peace than virtue's self can gain

'Without the opportunity which bore
Him on its eagle pinions to the peak
From which a thousand climbers have before

'Fallen, as Napoleon fell.'—I felt my cheek
Alter, to see the shadow pass away,
Whose grasp had left the giant world so weak

That every pigmy kicked it as it lay;
And much I grieved to think how power and will
In opposition rule our mortal day,

And why God made irreconcilable
Good and the means of good; and for despair
I half disdained mine eyes' desire to fill

With the spent vision of the times that were
And scarce have ceased to be.—'Dost thou behold,'
Said my guide, 'those spoilers spoiled, Voltaire,

'Frederick, and Paul, Catherine, and Leopold,
And hoary anarchs, demagogues, and sage—
names which the world thinks always old,

'For in the battle Life and they did wage,
She remained conqueror. I was overcome
By my own heart alone, which neither age,

'Nor tears, nor infamy, nor now the tomb
Could temper to its object.'—'Let them pass,'
I cried, 'the world and its mysterious doom

'Is not so much more glorious than it was,
That I desire to worship those who drew
New figures on its false and fragile glass

'As the old faded.'—'Figures ever new
Rise on the bubble, paint them as you may;
We have but thrown, as those before us threw,

'Our shadows on it as it passed away.
But mark how chained to the triumphal chair
The mighty phantoms of an elder day;

'All that is mortal of great Plato there
Expiates the joy and woe his master knew not;
The star that ruled his doom was far too fair.

'And life, where long that flower of Heaven grew not,
Conquered that heart by love, which gold, or pain,
Or age, or sloth, or slavery could subdue not.

'And near him walk the... twain,
The tutor and his pupil, whom Dominion
Followed as tame as vulture in a chain.

'The world was darkened beneath either pinion
Of him whom from the flock of conquerors
Fame singled out for her thunder-bearing minion;

'The other long outlived both woes and wars,
Throned in the thoughts of men, and still had kept
The jealous key of Truth's eternal doors,

'If Bacon's eagle spirit had not lept
Like lightning out of darkness—he compelled
The Proteus shape of Nature, as it slept

'To wake, and lead him to the caves that held
The treasure of the secrets of its reign.
See the great bards of elder time, who quelled

'The passions which they sung, as by their strain
May well be known: their living melody
Tempers its own contagion to the vein

'Of those who are infected with it—I
Have suffered what I wrote, or viler pain!
And so my words have seeds of misery—

'Even as the deeds of others, not as theirs.'
And then he pointed to a company,

'Midst whom I quickly recognized the heirs
Of Caesar's crime, from him to Constantine;
The anarch chiefs, whose force and murderous snares

Had founded many a sceptre-bearing line,
And spread the plague of gold and blood abroad:
And Gregory and John, and men divine,

Who rose like shadows between man and God;
Till that eclipse, still hanging over heaven,
Was worshipped by the world o'er which they strode,

For the true sun it quenched—'Their power was given
But to destroy,' replied the leader:—'I
Am one of those who have created, even

'If it be but a world of agony.'—
'Whence camest thou? and whither goest thou?
How did thy course begin?' I said, 'and why?

'Mine eyes are sick of this perpetual flow
Of people, and my heart sick of one sad thought—
Speak!'—'Whence I am, I partly seem to know,

'And how and by what paths I have been brought
To this dread pass, methinks even thou mayst guess;—
Why this should be, my mind can compass not;

'Whither the conqueror hurries me, still less;—
But follow thou, and from spectator turn
Actor or victim in this wretchedness,

'And what thou wouldst be taught I then may learn
From thee. Now listen:—In the April prime,
When all the forest-tips began to burn

'With kindling green, touched by the azure clime
Of the young season, I was laid asleep
Under a mountain, which from unknown time

'Had yawned into a cavern, high and deep;
And from it came a gentle rivulet,
Whose water, like clear air, in its calm sweep

'Bent the soft grass, and kept for ever wet
The stems of the sweet flowers, and filled the grove
With sounds, which whoso hears must needs forget

'All pleasure and all pain, all hate and love,
Which they had known before that hour of rest;
A sleeping mother then would dream not of

'Her only child who died upon the breast
At eventide—a king would mourn no more
The crown of which his brows were dispossessed

'When the sun lingered o'er his ocean floor
To gild his rival's new prosperity.
'Thou wouldst forget thus vainly to deplore

'Ills, which if ills can find no cure from thee,
The thought of which no other sleep will quell,
Nor other music blot from memory,

'So sweet and deep is the oblivious spell;
And whether life had been before that sleep
The Heaven which I imagine, or a Hell

'Like this harsh world in which I woke to weep,
I know not. I arose, and for a space
The scene of woods and waters seemed to keep,

Though it was now broad day, a gentle trace
Of light diviner than the common sun
Sheds on the common earth, and all the place

'Was filled with magic sounds woven into one
Oblivious melody, confusing sense
Amid the gliding waves and shadows dun;

'And, as I looked, the bright omnipresence
Of morning through the orient cavern flowed,
And the sun's image radiantly intense

'Burned on the waters of the well that glowed
Like gold, and threaded all the forest's maze
With winding paths of emerald fire; there stood

'Amid the sun, as he amid the blaze
Of his own glory, on the vibrating
Floor of the fountain, paved with flashing rays,

'A Shape all light, which with one hand did fling
Dew on the earth, as if she were the dawn,
And the invisible rain did ever sing

'A silver music on the mossy lawn;
And still before me on the dusky grass,
Iris her many-coloured scarf had drawn:

'In her right hand she bore a crystal glass,
Mantling with bright Nepenthe; the fierce splendour
Fell from her as she moved under the mass

'Of the deep cavern, and with palms so tender,
Their tread broke not the mirror of its billow,
Glided along the river, and did bend her

'Head under the dark boughs, till like a willow
Her fair hair swept the bosom of the stream
That whispered with delight to be its pillow.

'As one enamoured is upborne in dream
O'er lily-paven lakes, mid silver mist
To wondrous music, so this shape might seem

'Partly to tread the waves with feet which kissed
The dancing foam; partly to glide along
The air which roughened the moist amethyst,

'Or the faint morning beams that fell among
The trees, or the soft shadows of the trees;
And her feet, ever to the ceaseless song

'Of leaves, and winds, and waves, and birds, and bees,
And falling drops, moved in a measure new
Yet sweet, as on the summer evening breeze,

'Up from the lake a shape of golden dew
 Between two rocks, athwart the rising moon,
 Dances i' the wind, where never eagle flew;

'And still her feet, no less than the sweet tune
 To which they moved, seemed as they moved to blot
 The thoughts of him who gazed on them; and soon

'All that was, seemed as if it had been not;
 And all the gazer's mind was strewn beneath
 Her feet like embers; and she, thought by thought,

'Trampled its sparks into the dust of death
 As day upon the threshold of the east
 Treads out the lamps of night, until the breath

'Of darkness re-illumine even the least
 Of heaven's living eyes—like day she came,
 Making the night a dream; and ere she ceased

'To move, as one between desire and shame
 Suspended, I said—If, as it doth seem,
 Thou comest from the realm without a name

'Into this valley of perpetual dream,
 Show whence I came, and where I am, and why—
 Pass not away upon the passing stream.

'Arise and quench thy thirst, was her reply.
 And as a shut lily stricken by the wand
 Of dewy morning's vital alchemy,

'I rose; and, bending at her sweet command,
 Touched with faint lips the cup she raised,
 And suddenly my brain became as sand

'Where the first wave had more than half erased
 The track of deer on desert Labrador;
 Whilst the wolf, from which they fled amazed,

'Leaves his stamp visibly upon the shore,
Until the second bursts;—so on my sight
Burst a new vision, never seen before,

'And the fair shape waned in the coming light,
As veil by veil the silent splendour drops
From Lucifer, amid the chrysolite

'Of sunrise, ere it tinge the mountain-tops;
And as the presence of that fairest planet,
Although unseen, is felt by one who hopes

'That his day's path may end as he began it,
In that star's smile, whose light is like the scent
Of a jonquil when evening breezes fan it,

'Or the soft note in which his dear lament
The Brescian shepherd breathes, or the caress
That turned his weary slumber to content;

'So knew I in that light's severe excess
The presence of that Shape which on the stream
Moved, as I moved along the wilderness,

'More dimly than a day-appearing dream,
The host of a forgotten form of sleep;
A light of heaven, whose half-extinguished beam

'Through the sick day in which we wake to weep
Glimmers, for ever sought, for ever lost;
So did that shape its obscure tenour keep

'Beside my path, as silent as a ghost;
But the new Vision, and the cold bright car,
With solemn speed and stunning music, crossed

'The forest, and as if from some dread war
Triumphantly returning, the loud million
Fiercely extolled the fortune of her star.

'A moving arch of victory, the vermilion
And green and azure plumes of Iris had
Built high over her wind-winged pavilion,

'And underneath aethereal glory clad
The wilderness, and far before her flew
The tempest of the splendour, which forbade

'Shadow to fall from leaf and stone; the crew
Seemed in that light, like atomies to dance
Within a sunbeam;—some upon the new

'Embroidery of flowers, that did enhance
The grassy vesture of the desert, played,
Forgetful of the chariot's swift advance;

'Others stood gazing, till within the shade
Of the great mountain its light left them dim;
Others outspeeded it; and others made

'Circles around it, like the clouds that swim
Round the high moon in a bright sea of air;
And more did follow, with exulting hymn,

'The chariot and the captives fettered there:—
But all like bubbles on an eddying flood
Fell into the same track at last, and were

'Borne onward.—I among the multitude
Was swept—me, sweetest flowers delayed not long;
Me, not the shadow nor the solitude;

'Me, not that falling stream's Lethean song;
Me, not the phantom of that early Form
Which moved upon its motion—but among

'The thickest billows of that living storm
I plunged, and bared my bosom to the clime
Of that cold light, whose airs too soon deform.

'Before the chariot had begun to climb
The opposing steep of that mysterious dell,
Behold a wonder worthy of the rhyme

'Of him who from the lowest depths of hell,
Through every paradise and through all glory,
Love led serene, and who returned to tell

'The words of hate and awe; the wondrous story
How all things are transfigured except Love;
For deaf as is a sea, which wrath makes hoary,

'The world can hear not the sweet notes that move
The sphere whose light is melody to lovers—
A wonder worthy of his rhyme.—The grove

'Grew dense with shadows to its inmost covers,
The earth was gray with phantoms, and the air
Was peopled with dim forms, as when there hovers

'A flock of vampire-bats before the glare
Of the tropic sun, bringing, ere evening,
Strange night upon some Indian isle;—thus were

'Phantoms diffused around; and some did fling
Shadows of shadows, yet unlike themselves,
Behind them; some like eaglets on the wing

'Were lost in the white day; others like elves
Danced in a thousand unimagined shapes
Upon the sunny streams and grassy shelves;

'And others sate chattering like restless apes
On vulgar hands, . . .
Some made a cradle of the ermined capes

'Of kingly mantles; some across the tiar
Of pontiffs sate like vultures; others played
Under the crown which girt with empire

'A baby's or an idiot's brow, and made
Their nests in it. The old anatomies
Sate hatching their bare broods under the shade

'Of daemon wings, and laughed from their dead eyes
To reassume the delegated power,
Arrayed in which those worms did monarchize,

'Who made this earth their charnel. Others more
Humble, like falcons, sate upon the fist
Of common men, and round their heads did soar;

Or like small gnats and flies, as thick as mist
On evening marshes, thronged about the brow
Of lawyers, statesmen, priest and theorist;—

'And others, like discoloured flakes of snow
On fairest bosoms and the sunniest hair,
Fell, and were melted by the youthful glow

'Which they extinguished; and, like tears, they were
A veil to those from whose faint lids they rained
In drops of sorrow. I became aware

'Of whence those forms proceeded which thus stained
The track in which we moved. After brief space,
From every form the beauty slowly waned;

'From every firmest limb and fairest face
The strength and freshness fell like dust, and left
The action and the shape without the grace

'Of life. The marble brow of youth was cleft
With care; and in those eyes where once hope shone,
Desire, like a lioness bereft

'Of her last cub, glared ere it died; each one
Of that great crowd sent forth incessantly
These shadows, numerous as the dead leaves blown

'In autumn evening from a poplar tree.
Each like himself and like each other were
At first; but some distorted seemed to be

'Obscure clouds, moulded by the casual air;
And of this stuff the car's creative ray
Wrought all the busy phantoms that were there,

'As the sun shapes the clouds; thus on the way
Mask after mask fell from the countenance
And form of all; and long before the day

'Was old, the joy which waked like heaven's glance
The sleepers in the oblivious valley, died;
And some grew weary of the ghastly dance,

'And fell, as I have fallen, by the wayside;—
Those soonest from whose forms most shadows passed,
And least of strength and beauty did abide.

'Then, what is life? I cried.'—

        Cancelled Opening of the Triumph of Life

(Published by Miss M. Blind, "Westminster Review", July, 1870.)

> *Out of the eastern shadow of the Earth,*
> *Amid the clouds upon its margin gray*
> *Scattered by Night to swathe in its bright birth*
>
> *In gold and fleecy snow the infant Day,*
> *The glorious Sun arose: beneath his light,*
> *The earth and all. . .*

A Note About the Author

Percy Bysshe Shelley (1792–1822) was an English Romantic poet. Born into a prominent political family, Shelley enjoyed a quiet and happy childhood in West Sussex, developing a passion for nature and literature at a young age. He struggled in school, however, and was known by his colleagues at Eton College and University College, Oxford as an outsider and eccentric who spent more time acquainting himself with radical politics and the occult than with the requirements of academia. During his time at Oxford, he began his literary career in earnest, publishing *Original Poetry by Victor and Cazire* (1810) and *St. Irvine; or, The Rosicrucian: A Romance* (1811). In 1811, he married Harriet Westbrook, with whom he lived an itinerant lifestyle while pursuing affairs with other women. Through the poet Robert Southey, he fell under the influence of political philosopher William Godwin, whose daughter Mary soon fell in love with the precocious young poet. In the summer of 1814, Shelley eloped to France with Mary and her stepsister Claire Claremont, travelling to Holland, Germany, and Switzerland before returning to England in the fall. Desperately broke, Shelley struggled to provide for Mary through several pregnancies while balancing his financial obligations to Godwin, Harriet, and his own father. In 1816, Percy and Mary accepted an invitation to join Claremont and Lord Byron in Europe, spending a summer in Switzerland at a house on Lake Geneva. In 1818, following several years of unhappy life in England, the Shelleys—now married—moved to Italy, where Percy worked on *The Masque of Anarchy* (1819), *Prometheus Unbound* (1820), and *Adonais* (1821), now considered some of his most important works. In July of 1822, Shelley set sail on the *Don Juan* and was lost in a storm only hours later. His death at the age of 29 was met with despair and contempt throughout England and Europe, and he is now considered a leading poet and radical thinker of the Romantic era.

A Note from the Publisher

Spanning many genres, from non-fiction essays to literature classics to children's books and lyric poetry, Mint Edition books showcase the master works of our time in a modern new package. The text is freshly typeset, is clean and easy to read, and features a new note about the author in each volume. Many books also include exclusive new introductory material. Every book boasts a striking new cover, which makes it as appropriate for collecting as it is for gift giving. Mint Edition books are only printed when a reader orders them, so natural resources are not wasted. We're proud that our books are never manufactured in excess and exist only in the exact quantity they need to be read and enjoyed.

Discover more of your favorite classics with Bookfinity™.

- Track your reading with custom book lists.
- Get great book recommendations for your personalized Reader Type.
- Add reviews for your favorite books.
- AND MUCH MORE!

Visit **bookfinity.com** and take the fun Reader Type quiz to get started.

Enjoy our classic and modern companion pairings!

Bookfinity is a registered trademark of Ingram Book Group LLC. © 2023 Bookfinity. All rights reserved.

www.ingramcontent.com/pod-product-compliance
Lightning Source LLC
Chambersburg PA
CBHW031716230426
43669CB00007B/163